W9-CCW-452

CHILD DEVELOPMENT THROUGH LITERATURE

CHILD DEVELOPMENT THROUGH LITERATURE

Edited by
ELLIOTT D. LANDAU
University of Utah

SHERRIE LANDAU EPSTEIN
Psychological Services
Millbrae School District

ANN PLAAT STONE
Department of English
San Mateo Union High School District

Prentice-Hall, Inc., *Englewood Cliffs, New Jersey*

ISBN; P 0-13-130674-X
C 0-13-130682-O

Library of Congress Catalog Card Number: 75-179622

10 9 8 7 6 5 4 3 2 1

Printed in the United States of America

PRENTICE-HALL INTERNATIONAL, INC., London
PRENTICE-HALL OF AUSTRALIA, PTY. LTD., Sydney
PRENTICE-HALL OF CANADA, LTD., Toronto
PRENTICE-HALL OF INDIA PRIVATE LIMITED, New Delhi
PRENTICE-HALL OF JAPAN, INC., Tokyo

For our children: **Ann**
Carolyn
David
Elizabeth
Eve
Gordon
Jane
Janet
Karen
Stewart

Contents

Introduction

When George H. Frank (1965)* summarized the research on the influence of the family on human development, he concluded that nothing had been discovered about the effect of child-rearing practices on the personalities of children. In his child psychology text (1967 p. 103) Boyd McCandless contends that "on the basis of our actual contact as parents, teachers, and professional workers we 'know in our hearts' that Frank is wrong."

This volume recognizes that research data in child development are vast, often scrupulous, and too frequently contradictory.† In their preface to *Human Development* (1966) Morris and Natalie Haimowitz support this idea: "Outstanding studies sometimes contradict studies equally outstanding. Much of what we believe to be true today may be found inadequate tomorrow." Empirical research

---

* George H. Frank, "The Role of the Family in the Development of Psychopathology," *Psychological Bulletin* 65 (1965), pp. 191–205.

† A recent instance of contradictory conclusions that have been drawn from evaluations of numerous studies assessing the results of early education programs designed for children from low-income families is cited by William D. Rohwer in his article, "Prime Time for Education: Early Childhood or Adolescence," in *Harvard Educational Review,* Vol. 41, No. 3 (August 1971), pp. 316–341. He says, ". . . A case in point is supplied by the controversies surrounding the effectiveness of programs of early childhood education." In a widely-noted recent article, Jensen (1969) reviewed studies evaluating the results of early education programs . . . In summary, Jensen concluded that, "Compensatory education has been tried and it apparently has failed." It is remarkable that the opposite conclusion can be justified just as well: early childhood education programs have been tried and they apparently have succeeded. Pp. 317–318.

is indispensable to the accumulation of knowledge, but when artificial and contrived laboratory conditions prevail, the results are frequently not applicable to nonlaboratory circumstances. Yet these research results often constitute the major emphasis in child development classes.

Courses in child psychology and development that stress research data may seem removed from problems students will encounter in work situations with children. Those who are teaching future teachers, counselors, psychologists, and nurses need to "turn on" their students so that the learner wants to immerse himself in the field not only with a cognitive understanding of the field's concepts but with an affective commitment to the world of childhood.

Those who teach or counsel need to bring their own childhood experiences to the conscious level in order to function with empathy. We feel that each person can bring deepened insight to the study of child development when he encounters the emotions of childhood in the fresh light of his maturity. In a sense we are prisoners of our past until independent modes of thinking free us from the myths and biases carried unexamined into adulthood. It is particularly important that those who work with children see them in multifaceted ways and bring every human resource to bear upon the living and learning experience of childhood.

The editors of this volume asked themselves if there was another way to teach child development so that students would not only learn the facts but would also become emotionally involved in their studies. We concluded that through literature students could enter into the child's experiences and glimpse the beauty and intensity the artist conveys in the short story and the novel. Literature portrays the resources of the human spirit and allows the student to gain understanding that brings his own life experiences into focus. We decided, therefore, that we would attempt to provide the reader with literature that would catch the color of life itself.

The art of literature lies in its power to elicit emotion, and we hope that literature will add a personal, emotional dimension to the usual intellective approach to the subject. The principles of child development may be gleaned in many ways and through the many authoritative traditional texts, but to step into the moccasins of a child or of a parent requires more than the statement of a problem and the tabulation of data. Emotional involvement other than that attained through firsthand experience is possible only through the perceptions and narration of the literary artist.

The selections in this anthology are organized into categories and cross-indexed with most of the standard texts in child development and psychology (see Appendix I). Each major section is accompanied by a statement that looks broadly at the topic, and each subsection is accompanied by an essay that briefly reviews the state of knowledge about each topic. Following each fictional piece is a discussion of the psychological aspects of the story and a set of questions we have called Springboards for Inquiry.

A literary piece, like an incident from life, has many facets and may arouse a variety of emotions and involve a number of relationships. Many selections in this text thus could have been placed under several headings. For the convenience of the instructor we have provided a list of the topics covered in this volume and the literary selections we consider to be related to each topic (see Appendix). Instructors are urged to use the selections as they see fit.

We feel that the literary approach to child development theory offers a balance to the usual research-oriented methodology. We feel it would be wise to keep the door open and swinging between literature and the laboratory and let each contribute to the other to extend the knowledge of child development.

We acknowledge the critical responses to selected portions of the manuscript of Dr. Donna Gelfand, Department of Psychology; Dr. Anthony La Pray, Department of Special Education; and Dr. Howard Sloane, Bureau of Educational Research, University of Utah. The authors also wish to express appreciation to Dr. Ladd Holt, Department of Education, University of Utah, for suggestions for using this text with college students. Special mention should be made of Nancy Brockbank Livingston, graduate student in the Department of Education, University of Utah, for careful reading of the manuscript; Jodi Shreeve and Bea Landau, for patient typing and retyping; and Julius Plaat, for his assistance.

E. D. L.
S. L. E.
A. P. S.

To The Instructor

The volume in unpublished form has been used in a variety of ways in university classes in child development. Those who wish to use *Child Development through Literature* as the sole text in a course will find that the introductory essays, the ten major headings, the accompanying thirty-five subsections, and the Springboards for Inquiry will provide ample material for independent student reading and research. Supplemented by the instructor's knowledge and experience, these materials, although not intended to form a basic text, may be used as a resource for introducing the student to clinical and experimental data.

The fictional pieces in this volume have been used successfully as the basis for weekly one-hour, seminar-type discussions. Other professors have used critical incidents in the stories as the focus for role-playing activities and creative dramatics. The inner–outer group technique lends itself well to the use of the fictional material. An inner group of students discusses selected incidents and an outer group surrounds them, listens to their discussion, and at appropriate times raises questions about the relevance and interpretation of content. In this way reaction is generated from two groups of students and from two vantage points—the inner group, as it interprets the characters and events of the story, and the outer group, as it perceives the same story and the responses of peers to the story.

Another way the selections may be used is to assign roles to students who then reinterpret selected incidents in the story under discussion. A group observes B group's interpretations and makes written suggestions, B observes A and does the same, and so on for all groups. The author's point of view as expressed through his characters and their behavior is thus subject to widespread pupil analysis. The selections also lend themselves to the subdivision of classes into six–six–six groups,* with either the Springboards for Inquiry or the students' personal responses as the basis for discussion. Where panel discussion techniques have been tried, each panel addressed itself to one or two of the springboard questions, thus bringing to the class the thinking of a group of students.

Another possibility is the use of different points of view. Students can be assigned to view characters, incidents, or solutions through the eyes of a teacher, a school psychologist, a parent, a principal, a nurse, a social worker, a babysitter, or whatever view interests them. Discussions that present a variety of points of view bring out the complexity of some areas of child development. Whatever direction instructors take with this text, the authors hope that they have provided instructors and students with the proper material to facilitate learning.

---

* Six–six–six refers to six groups of six students for six minutes.

CHILD
DEVELOPMENT
THROUGH
LITERATURE

Early Development

From the moment the newborn's birth cry heralds his arrival, he enters a world that will increasingly impinge upon his being in its attempt to mold him to its expectations. In Samoa he will learn the Samoan way; in black America he will learn a different way. Each newborn possesses a dual heritage: his physical development recapitulates the evolution of homo sapiens, and his way of life—his mental, emotional, moral, and religious development—is dependent on his cultural heritage. He will grow into a cultural heritage that is the product of the accumulated experiences of his particular ethnic group. The child's maturation and development, although definitely limited by his genetic heritage, is inextricably bound to the peculiar circumstances of his culture.

If there is any immutable law of development, it is that growth is a continuous, orderly process. No child learns to walk without having learned to stand or to speak clearly without having babbled. Although development is highly individual, the facts of its sequentiality and continuity are indisputable. It has become almost a cliché to say that the child develops as a whole human being. The implications of the idea that there is an interrelationship between the components of growth are numerous. An essential implication is that exclusive consideration for one component—physical growth, for instance — over any or all of the others will inevitably lead to lopsided human development.

The infant requires not only food, warmth, and diapering, but he increasingly needs the stimulation of socializing experiences to develop the whole child. In infancy the lack of physical care may mean ill health; an absence of socializing nurturance may mean distortion of emotional development. Erik Erikson (1950, pp. 247–74) emphasizes that the period of infancy is one in which trust in others should be developed. During the first fifteen months of life, in which the infant is totally dependent on others for his sustenance, the foundations for his future personality are laid. As he develops locomotor and verbal skills he leaves the state of abject dependence and becomes a tireless explorer. How he fares during early development and how he becomes a part of the society that surrounds him have always interested the adult world.

The Infant

The student of child development may be puzzled that his study should include some understanding of infancy, since for the most part he is concerned with the child in either nursery or elementary school. Yet even those who never see the child in his earliest days need to attempt some reconstruction of a child's lifespace as they seek to understand why one child refuses to enter the classroom unless accompanied by his mother or why another child's behavior is so aggressive. In other words, the preschooler has lived before somewhere, someplace, and when you meet him he is the sum of all that he has experienced. Those first fifteen months of life called infancy may provide professionals with valid clues to an understanding of the child as he enters the child care center or elementary school. In fact, psychiatrically oriented teachers, nurses, and physicians agree with Theodore Lidz (1968, p. 118): "These (the first fifteen months) are the months when the foundations are laid, not only for future emotional stability, but also for basic though global character traits and for intellectual development. No part of his life experience will be as solidly incorporated in the individual, become so irrevocably a part of him, as his infancy."

A review of the literature about infancy shows clearly that the most significant human relationship is between mother and child (Lidz 1968; McCandless 1967; Rogers 1969; Abrahamsen 1969; Levy 1937). We would postulate the opposite, too: the most significant and devastating experience for a child is the lack of a mother–child relationship in the period of infancy. Lidz (1968, p. 119) is so emphatic here that he quotes Edna St. Vincent Millay's poem "Love is not all" and maintains that "it appears as if many infants make friends with death for lack of love alone." No other species needs so lengthy and so dependent a period of infancy.* The human infant needs almost total nurture, and he requires not only physical care but also a socializing atmosphere that contributes to his emotional and intellectual growth. Lidz (1968) and Abrahamsen (1969, p. 95) stress the importance of reducing the "tension of infancy" so that a physiochemical equilibrium or homeostasis may be maintained. Perhaps as vital are the proper social, perceptual, and sensory stimulations so necessary to heterostasis. (The heterostatic impulse refers to the normal human being's desire to grow, to learn, to satisfy curiosity.)

Unlike other species, the human infant reacts primarily to his mother. Her prenatal nutrition (Lowe 1959)† and emotional status (Ferreiras 1965), her reactions to her pregnancy (Sears, Maccoby, and Levin 1957), and her earliest handling of the infant (Cobliner 1965) are correlated with responses in the infant. Recent literature talks of a mutuality of nurture between mother and child. This infant–mother interaction (mutuality) is now seen as a crucial relationship in infancy (Yarrow 1963).

Earlier ideas saw the infant as a passive, dependent, submissive vessel, and it was assumed that the "right" set of rules would be equally effective with all infants. Today the infant is seen as an individual with differences that are clearly identifiable and unique to him. As early as the first few weeks clear personality differences are observed with regard to irritability, reactions to stimuli, and sleep patterns (Chess, Thomas, and Birch 1959). We conclude from a review of research that the mother–child relationship is vital, but not the only factor in the overall emotional development of the child.

When human development is viewed as the accomplishment of certain developmental tasks, it is necessary to shift the focus of study from the effects of diet, stimulation, and mother instincts to these tasks. Erikson (1950) believes that the essential task of infancy is the development of a basic trust in others. Since the human infant is completely dependent so long, he needs to know that he can depend on the outside world. If his basic needs are met by this world, he develops a trust in the world and thus begins to develop a nucleus of self-trust, which is indispensable to his later development.

John Bowlby (1958) suggests that one of the important developmental tasks

---

* Arthur Koestler's "Man—One of Evolution's Mistakes?" attributes man's present urge to self-destruct to five striking phenomena, one of which is his protracted period of dependence on his mother, which has allowed man to be molded into "the loyal, affectionate, and sociable creature which he is, may be partly responsible for man's ready submission to authority wielded by individuals or groups." He continues with this perceptive rationale for our willingness to go to war: "We are thus driven to the unfashionable and uncomfortable conclusion that the trouble with our species is not an overdose . . . of aggression, but an excess of self-transcending devotion" (*New York Times*, 19 October 1969, p. 112).

† Recent data collected by the Office of Economic Opportunity seem to relate pre-conception and early pregnancy protein consumption with the development of the brain in the fetus.

of infancy is attachment behavior. The smiling, cooing, sucking, touching, and crying of infants serve to strengthen a bond of attachment between mother and child. We may properly refer to mother–child mutuality and the development of trust or its absence as affective components of infancy—feelings that serve to develop the emotional life of the child.

In the cognitive domain there is considerable development too. Jean Piaget (1963) traces the development of motor skills, sensory perceptions, and cognitive abilities and indicates that there is a steplike assimilation of experiences in infancy. A significant contribution of this Swiss psychologist is his refutation of the idea that children think like adults but without the variety of experiences adults have had (for a discussion of this matter see Almy 1968). Piaget concludes that children are not miniature adults. He terms the infancy period as defined in this text as the prelanguage or sensorimotor stage. From the innate sucking and grasp reflexes and the modification of eye movements, the child progresses by the age of eight or nine months to the ability to search for an object that has been removed from his visual perception. (Until the infant is about eight months old a removed object is simply something that never existed for him.) By the fifteenth month of life the "senior" infant has become an experimenter and no longer needs only to repeat experiences. Piaget doubts that environmental manipulation can alter these stages of cognitive development, but he leaves the door open for a final analysis of cognitive development. It seems likely that infancy can be made richer through experience, and work in the Soviet Union and the United States points in this direction.*

The time of infancy is, then, a period of total dependence of the child on his entire environment. Profound physical and mental changes occur in these fifteen months. The emotional survival of the infant hinges on the quality and quantity of the interaction he experiences with every facet of his milieu. His relationship to his mother is especially important so that he learns to trust those who wait on him. His experiences in this area will eventually contribute to his self-concept, and his conception of himself will to a great extent regulate the success and vitality of the experiences of his later years. All that happens prepares him for his toddler years when he will walk, talk, explore, and hopefully gradually become an autonomous, happy, and self-actualizing human being.

---

* The work of Albert Bandura and Richard Walters, *Social Learning and Personality Development* (New York: Holt, Rinehart, and Winston, 1963), and their sociobehaviorist's approach to the development and modification of human behavior is recommended for alternative views of growth and development.

"Taken over, bag and baggage, for him," she thought. "Complex, civilized being that I am, I am turned into an hour-glass."

The Door of Life

by Enid Bagnold

The baby was four days old. Now he would come in in the dawn, regally in the midwife's arms, already expectant. He fed greedily at one breast, and as his mother passed him over her body in the darkness to the other, he snuffled in a passion of impatience, learning already that there was a second meal, seizing the nipple, choking, and sinking to hardworking silence. Sensory exploration, which in the peril of his first day on earth had centered only in his lips, now spread to his limbs; and his hand, as he worked, from lying stiff like a star, began to move, travelling over the squire's silk nightdress, scratching the silk with his nail in a flurry of his finger, trying the linen sheet, learning the textures. Flinging his hand with a sudden movement behind his head he hit the silver travelling clock. Instantly, in the half light, a look of interest broke into his eyes. Letting go, half turning his head. "What, what?" his marmoset eyes demanded. But, the moment of concentration over, he went back to his life's work. All his power was in his lips. His hands were fronds, convolvulus-tendrils, catching at surfaces, but only half informed.

Watching the squire, piercingly sleepless, he would be asleep in a moment.

When he had ridden away and been tucked down, the squire and the midwife talked about him, two women in love; but during the breast-feeds the midwife withdrew, leaving the squire alone to let down her milk.

Strange, concentrated life, that no man knows, shared with the cat in the stable and the bitch in the straw of the kennel, but lit with the questions of the marveling human brain.

The regularity of her milk, as always, astonished the squire. At six and ten and two and six and ten, to the tick, to the instant, her breasts swelled and reminded her. A moment later she heard the midwife's hand on the door. Even in the dawn she woke punctually, or her breasts woke her. "Taken over, bag and baggage, for him," she thought. "Complex, civilized being that I am, I am turned into an hour-glass." The baby too moved through his ritual, punctual as a clock. And behind both of them watched the midwife, keeping mother and child on the rails of development with fine movements, setting order into the baby's life, creating peace, keeping off the world, watching, reflecting, adjusting jockeying the untidiness of civilization into perfection, teaching even so tiny a baby manners and endurance; to cry at the proper time for exercise, to sleep at the proper hour.

Discussion

This short selection was taken from a larger work that is a gentle ode to motherhood. The story is set in a large, comfortable English home at the turn of the century, when births were attended by a midwife at home.

The mother, or squire as she is called in this selection, gives birth to her fifth child. She and the midwife are close, not only by previous association but also in their female attachment to the birth process and in their inclination to minister to the needs of the newborn. Miss Bagnold calls them "two women in love." Each adopts a different role as she cares for the infant's needs. After the midwife brings the baby to the squire for his feeding she is careful to withdraw. In her wisdom and experience as a midwife she honors the special relationship between mother and child; the communications that flow between mother and child must be permitted to flower without distraction.

The author accurately describes the many sensory experiences of the infant. With his immature nervous system the infant makes inexact hand movements that touch the sheet and the squire's nightdress. He is hungry and impatiently roots to find the nipple. Both mother and child make small adapting movements to achieve the most comfortable position so that the infant feels secure and comfortable as he relies on the reflexes of sucking and swallowing for feeding. His gaze is inconstant. He may turn to look in the direction of a noise or object but he is unable to track reliably the object in his visual field. All energy is concentrated in his mouth and lips.

Freud (1949) describes this period in infancy as the oral stage because the infant's main channel of satisfaction is concentrated in the mouth. At the conclusion of the feeding the baby's energies are sapped and he sleeps until the discomfort of hunger awakens him again. In approximately four hours the mother's milk will fill her breasts and she too will be ready to be relieved. When things go well, as they do in this selection, a beautiful natural harmony is established between mother and child.

Springboards for Inquiry

(1) Point to fundamental physical and psychological needs of the newborn that are met in this selection.

(2) Cite examples in this selection that verify Piaget's description of infancy as the sensorimotor stage.

(3) Specify some of the elements in the infant's environment that can contribute to his emotional health and intellectual development.

(4) Name some unique qualities of the individual that are evident in the first days of infancy.

(5) The ability to make births safe at home has fostered interest in natural childbirth at home. What emotional factors favor childbirth at home, from the point of view of the mother, father, and other children in the family?

The Toddler

Some years ago it was fashionable to refer to the years between infancy and preschool age as the "terrible twos." Despite the near extinction of the term, it is true that the toddler, "in his pursuit of autonomy, . . . collides with the people and things around him" (Stone and Church 1968, p. 259). Erikson (1950, pp.251–54) emphasizes that the years between two and four are for the development of the child's sense of autonomy—a basic trust in himself (presumably in infancy he has developed trust in others) and a will to explore and initiate activities.

When carefully examined, the phrase *pursuit of autonomy* epitomizes the tasks of toddlerhood. As we have already seen, up to the age of fifteen months the child is completely dependent on his mother for nurturance. Now he can walk a bit, talk quite meaningfully (Lidz 1968, pp. 169–77), at least to his mother, and instead of being the epicenter of family attention he now is becoming a member of this larger unit—his family. Furthermore, in this crucial period when he needs to gain mastery over his body and his environment, nearly everything he does conflicts with the orderliness established for him by mother and family.

Let us step into his mother's shoes for a moment. What had once been a pleasant, emotionally symbiotic relationship—a give and take between baby and mother—is now becoming a catch-me-if-you-can relationship. Whereas in infancy she set the pace and called the shots, that once compliant, gurgling, dependent thing is now exercising his newfound power. His food intake is being channeled away from physical maturation purposes and used for the intense physical activity that wears his mother out at the end of each day. Nearly everything the toddler now does is exploratory and thus subject to parental admonition (Bernard 1962, pp. 248–49). A great danger to the child during this period of development is that his intense seeking behavior will be met by a barrage of denials, thus stifling the development of his autonomy. The major tasks of motherhood during this time are to develop a sensitivity to the child's need to get into everything and not to fence him in so that he becomes a docile, obedient, and lackluster individual. Wise parents learn to revel in their toddler's forays into their home; they put away precious china, fragile furniture, and heirloom lamps until their child is older.

Lidz (1968) cites three major areas of development for the toddler: ambulation, speech, and primary socialization. Each task brings its subproblem satellites; for instance, during the time the youngster is tirelessly exploring all manner of things, both physical and social, he is also being urged to control his bowels, his eating habits, and his physical initiative. It is therefore easy to understand that conflict between the toddler's needs and parental fear and exhaustion creates these subproblems. For example, no pediatrics authority thinks that toilet training should begin before twenty-four to thirty months, since the anal sphincter control—because of cephalocaudal development (Rogers 1969)—is minimal until after twenty-four months. Yet the major battle of the toddler years is focused on bowel control (see also Freud 1908).

Ambulation can cause concern because of the dangers the toddler faces as he seeks to explore, but his attempts to speak are generally pleasurable for his mother and family. Speech is uniquely a human adaptation. The acquisition of speech requires that not only must the youngster learn a pre-existent set of sounds and meanings, but he must also assimilate his culture's system of meaning and its folkways.* Whereas we have indicated that the toddler is separating himself gradually from his mother—he is walking and beginning to seek peer association—in the area of speech development he is still greatly dependent on his mother to interpret his early attempts to vocalize. Lidz (1968, p. 171) describes how the word *mama* may mean anything from "I want more" to "pick up my bottle." The child's early use of words is thus expansive; his words include a variety of possible meanings depending on the specific context. As he grows older, however, words gradually stand for specific things. The responses he receives from his mother (or anyone who is primarily responsible for his daily welfare) extend or contract meaning. The degree to which the child's audience is willing to add words to rudimentary utterances will tremendously influence the child's speech development.† For example, if the child says, "Mama, bye-bye" and the mother responds with, "Yes, mama is going to the store," the mother has started to add to his syntactical storehouse. Preschool programs such as Project Head Start and "Sesame Street"

* Kornei Chukovsky, in his classic *From Two to Five* (Berkeley and Los Angeles: University of California Press, 1968), calls the child a linguistic genius.

† Reinforcement psychology would say that the mother's responses to the child's attempts to speak reinforce his verbal behavior and encourage its development.

contribute to the linguistic expertise of children who may not have had the opportunity to build a reservoir of meanings.

His mother's attitudes toward the toddler's total development are crucial to that development. We mentioned mothers who fear the feverish physical explorations of toddlers and pen them up. Those who cannot be bothered to fill in rudimentary sentences or to answer questions limit speech development. Mothers who think of the infant's soiling diapers as "bad" or of his crawling into unlikely places as "naughty" retard the toddler's efforts to become a social being. Mothers who are unable to cope with the toddler's ways may resort to highly aggressive behavior, thus encouraging in the child unnecessary hostility that can become a permanent part of his personality.

The toddler years, then, are far from years of separation from the mother but are rather a time when the mother either facilitates or inhibits physical and verbal development. It is not the time to "let him fly on his own" or to assume that he can safely be separated from his mother. His primary socialization has been and still is through his mother and his immediate family, and any prolonged loss of either influence may be a serious detriment to further development. Nor must the primary task of developing self-confidence and autonomy be negated by parental despair at the healthy exploratory behavior the toddler exhibits.

"You sure a damn nice Little Mouthful," Cora said.

Trio for Three Gentle Voices

by Harold Brodkey

Faith skittered out of the narrow hallway into the living room, her red telephone hanging around her neck, a toothbrush clutched in one hand. She swaggered to the desk, her telephone bumping against her chest. "Don't go in the desk drawers," Laura called warningly from the back room where she was folding diapers. "And don't you dare touch the ink." Faith opened the desk drawer and took out the ink bottle, which she placed in the crook of her arm. She closed the desk drawer, her tongue creeping out between her lips in concentration. She considered the drawer for a moment; then she pulled it out about an inch. That pleased her and she tottered into the kitchen. "What are you doing, Faith?" Laura called.

Faith, fifteen months old, didn't talk yet; or rather, she didn't say anything except words like hot dog, bye-bye, Mommee and Daddee. Now she pulled open the cabinets under the sink and took out a large aluminum pan, into which she dropped the bottle of ink. She took a paper napkin out and put it on the top of her head. It blew off. She put it on again. It blew off. Her lip quivered contemptuously and she wedged it under the ink bottle in the aluminum pan. Her mother's purse was lying on the kitchen table, its strap hanging over the edge. Faith walked over on tiptoe, gripped the edge of the table and peeked; she saw that the purse was still on the other end of the strap. She yanked the strap and the purse tumbled to the floor. Faith bent and fumbled in the purse until she found her mother's wallet. "Munn," she whispered, "munn-munn."

"Faith, come see what Mother's

From *First Love and Other Sorrows* (New York: The Dial Press, Inc., 1958). Reprinted by permission of Harold Brodkey c/o IFA.

doing," Laura called from the back room. "Come help Mummy fold diapers." Faith tucked a dollar bill into the top of her overalls and put a ten in the aluminum pan, which she picked up, grunting slightly. She had two ones and a five clutched in her hand. Fully loaded, she staggered down the hallway toward her mother, "Momm-ee, Momm-ee, I come."

Laura looked at her daughter and sighed. As far as she was concerned her daughter was a nearly flawless thing; Laura would look at her and think to herself, Isn't she rare? And she would shiver with a kind of delight. She could see her daughter at twenty, tall, slender, with curly hair and brilliant eyes—brave, honorable, dashing, appealing, intelligent. . . . The great problem with such a child was to keep the fine mechanism from being damaged; not that Faith couldn't take care of herself under most circumstances. "She copes," Laura was fond of saying, "she copes all the time." But Laura didn't want her child subjected to the more frequent childhood horrors—the maid that beat her, the cruel playmate. Laura investigated and watched Faith's playmates; the mean ones Faith was allowed to see only once or twice a month; the nice ones, the kind and jolly ones, Faith played with almost every day.

However, maids and baby sitters were a different problem. Martin, Laura's husband, insisted often on short notice that Laura get a baby sitter; and Laura would be desperate, her news-gathering and -reporting system being useless without a good deal of time. "Do you know a good-hearted, playful sort of sitter?" she'd asked her friends one by one. "The kind that doesn't curdle a child? A responsible one?" Sometimes they did; sometimes they laughed at her. Whenever a new sitter came Laura had her come either a day before to play with Faith or else early on the same day. If the sitter was difficult Laura, in tears, would refuse to go out and nothing Martin could do would move her. However, on this particular day Martin was going to a cocktail party at his biggest client's new apartment. Martin was a lawyer and he had laid down the law. Laura's usual baby sitter, Mad Margaret, a somewhat retarded but very gentle woman who lived in the neighborhood, was busy; and all of Laura's emergency girls were unavailable. Laura was going to try a girl named Cora, whom she had never met but who had been recommended by Mary Ellen Cabany, her dearest friend, from Wellesley.

Cora arrived at ten minutes after three. She was a tall, handsome colored woman, with fine eyes and a firm mouth. Cora got paid by the hour and she didn't mind being trained at all. She straightened her back, pushed her full breasts toward the door, and she looked down across this passionate topography at the earnest and ladylike Laura.

"Oh, come in, come in. You must be Cora."

"You hit it, ma'am," Cora said. "Right on your very first try."

"Well, I'm very glad to see you. My name is Laura Andrews and this is my daughter, whose name is Faith. Won't you say 'Hi' to the nice lady, dear?" Laura desperately wanted Faith to do something charming, to win over the solemn and warlike colored woman, who stood impassive and slightly mocking by the door. Faith, rosy and cheerful, refused to say anything, but her face, distended with good feeling and smiles, was fixed on Cora like an obedient searchlight.

Cora sauntered into the living room, smoothing her cherry red skirt over the tumult of her hips. "Hi, Little Mouthful," Cora said, "how ya doing?"

Faith, flushed with coquetry, hurled herself to the floor and squirmed under the couch. She stuck her head out and looked up seriously at Cora; Cora refused to look down.

Laura, distraught by Cora's coldness, said: "Cora, would you like a cup of tea? Or coffee?"

"Coffee, ma'am," Cora said casually, "good and black." From her purple bodice Cora fetched a package of cork-tipped Tareytons. She reached into the pocket of her skirt and pulled out a wooden match, which she lit with her thumbnail. She blew a prodigious cloud of smoke.

"O do [hot dog]," said Faith. "O do, o do."

"You like that, do you, Little Mouthful?" Cora blew a smoke ring.

Faith watched for a minute and then turned to her mother. "Mommee—ooop." That meant pick me up.

Laura swooped down, relieved to be able to hold her daughter, and hauled her out from underneath the couch. Faith looked at the last smoke ring and let out a squeal of uncontrollable pleasure.

"Has a good time, don't she?" Cora said.

Faith, still smiling in her mother's arms, leaned over and swatted Cora on the side of her head.

Cora remained impassive.

"You mustn't do that," Laura said desperately to her daughter. She felt perspiration bead her upper lip. Faith held out her hand for her mother to slap.

"Don't hit her," Cora said suddenly. "Let me hold her. Y'all treat your baby rough?"

Laura closed her eyes and held out her child. It was Martin's fault: where there was no trust, no love existed, and she had to love this sitter before five o'clock.

Cora ruffled Faith's curls. "Y'all kinda pretty," she said dispassionately. She threw Faith into the air; Faith giggled. Cora looked at the baby, squinting slightly. Then she threw her again; Faith laughed. Cora put her cigarette in the corner of her mouth and threw Faith again. "O do!" Faith said breathlessly. Cora sighed and lay down on the floor, placing Faith on the firm knoll of her stomach. Cora began to bump up and down on the floor. Laura looked at Cora in her red skirt and purple blouse on the yellow rug. That rug's a mistake in the city, Laura thought. She poured the coffee.

Faith gripped Cora's purple blouse; she rolled and tumbled on Cora's grinding stomach. Her laughter broke off into nearly soundless gasps. Cora sat up. Faith's arms encircled Cora's neck and hugged it. "You sure a damn nice Little Mouthful," Cora said.

Cora and Laura sat down with their cups of coffee. Laura asked, "How many sugars?" "Four or five," Cora said. "I don't pay no mind to getting fat the way some women do." Laura asked Cora to tell her a little about herself. Cora said she was from Baltimore, her husband was no good and she had left him. "Your husband any good, ma'am?" "Oh, yes," Laura said, conscious of Faith being in the room. "Very good," she added piously. Faith was down on her stomach hiding spoons under the rug. "Is he good-looking?" Cora asked. "I can't abide men who aren't good-looking." "He has a very Italian quality in dim light," Laura said absently. "Faith, not with Mamma's sterling. You can play with the plate, not the sterling." Laura reached on the coffee table for a cigarette and placed it unlit in her mouth. Once, in college, she had learned to strike wooden matches with her thumbnail, and now she looked Cora in the eye and asked for a match. Cora handed her one impassively. Laura, anxious to love, to be loved, to show her friendliness, hoped her thumbnail wouldn't break. The match lit on her first try and Laura held it to her cigarette. But Cora didn't smile. Laura wondered if Cora disliked her. She wondered how she would ever get such a fierce woman to like her.

Faith lifted the rug and swept out the five spoons she had hidden. She sat up, her back straight, her small neck holding the rosy weight of her head; her mouth was open, the upper lip curling like a bud. She could get two spoons in each hand and a fifth in her mouth. She stood up and walked away. Then guilt seized her. "No, no, no," she muttered and dropped the spoons. She toppled to the floor and lay on her back; idly she kicked her heels." "Otsee wah-wah," she said. "Otsee poosfah." She sat up and put two spoons down the front of her overalls. She took two more spoons in her left hand and the last one in her right hand. She rolled over until she was on all fours; it was the only way she could rise. Then she stood up. She glided toward the kitchen, leaning slightly to one side, perhaps because the spoons inside her overalls tickled. Then she stumbled and looked down and saw that a spoon had fallen down her pants leg. "Oh," she breathed, "oh." She bent, straight from the rump, and tried to push the spoon back up her pants leg. "Mamma," she said angrily. The spoon slipped down again. "Mamma." Faith lifted her head and gazed at the ceiling, then swooped and shoved at the spoon again; she was chortling as she fell forward; her head bumped on the floor and Faith collapsed. "Mamma!" Faith cried, "Maa-maa!" Laura came running and started to pick her up. "Aagh," said Faith and took a swipe at her mother's nose. "Oh, you want me to take out the spoon," Laura said and removed it. Faith burst into screams of rage. Laura looked blank.

"She wants you to shove it up her pants leg," Cora said calmly. "Don't you, Little Mouthful?"

At quarter of four Cora began to dress Faith in her snowsuit. Laura thought it was time for her to take her shower and begin to get ready. She was planning to wear the black dress that made her look indecent and with that dress she felt she had to be perfectly groomed. Cora sat Faith on the bureau and began to work the baby's legs into the snowsuit pants. Faith laughed and swung her legs around. "Put your legs in before I pound you," Cora snarled. Faith stunned, looked up and then slipped her legs into the snowsuit. Cora looked grim.

"O do?" Faith tried, experimentally.

"Hot dog yourself," Cora said, forcing Faith's strangely limp arms into the sleeves of the jacket.

Faith laughed happily. "O do," she caroled. "O do do," she went on. Then she played dead. She rolled backward with her mouth open and her entire body limp.

"Where's your ear," said Cora. "I'm roaring hungry." Faith sat up and tugged at her ear and looked at Cora. Cora said, "I'm gonna chew the damn thing off," and with a deft motion slipped Faith's cap on and fastened the strap.

Faith, encased in her snowsuit, waddled toward the front door. Laura stuck her head out of the bathroom and said to Cora: "Don't worry about whether she's warm enough. She's very warm in that suit. It's made of the same cloth Admiral Byrd wore when he flew over the South Pole."

Cora nodded sagely and followed Faith out the front door. A minute later the doorbell rang. Laura slipped to the peephole and looked out and saw Cora. "What's the matter?" Laura asked.

"She's walking funny," Cora said.

"She always walks funny," Laura said. "She's built like me."

"Open the door," Cora said wearily. "I got to give your child a medical examination."

Laura swung the door open. Faith waddled into the house. With every third step she listed noticeably to port.

"Well, that's new," Laura said.

"It hasn't got much chance of getting popular," Cora snapped.

Faith seemed undisturbed. She waddled on into the living room, lurching regularly but seemingly paying no attention to it. She circled the coffee table once.

"Maybe her shoes are too tight," Laura said thoughtfully.

"Well, go and look at them," Cora said.

Laura knelt by her child. "You sound just like my husband," she muttered under her breath. "Everybody's smarter than I am."

Faith leaned forward, holding out her arms toward her mother; then she gave a cry of pain and clutched her side. "Mamma!" she said rebukingly.

"Don't panic," Cora cried and came running.

Laura said, half-laughing with relief that Cora cared: "Oh, Cora, I don't know what I'd do without you."

"I'm here, I'm here," Cora said, squatting down beside mother and daughter. Laura poked at her daughter for a moment and then unzipped her jacket. She reached a maternal hand down the front of Faith's overalls and pulled out a spoon that had stuck in the diaper.

It was time for Laura to leave. She leaned out the window and called Cora. At the sound of her mother's voice Faith came running up the sidewalk. She was pulling a small yellow Holgate toy that had three pegs sitting in three holes in it; one peg was yellow, one blue, one red. Faith yelled, "Toot-toot-toot–" The toy hit a crack in the sidewalk and the pegs spilled out. "Oh," said Faith, stopping. "O dee, o dee [oh dear]." She bent and carefully replaced the pegs one by one. As she lifted the red one, she murmured—affectionately—"Dadd-ee, Dadd-ee." She pounded the peg on the sidewalk for a moment. Then she worked it into its hole.

"Are you going now?" Cora asked Laura.

"Yes, bring her in and I'll kiss her good-by."

"You'll do nothing of the sort. Get the Little Mouthful all upset . . . no, indeedy. You just sneak out when she's not looking. That's what you do. I'll call you at your party when she goes to sleep."

Laura protested.

"Don't try to think, you'll just get yourself all upset," Cora said, "and you'll give the Little Mouthful distresses."

Faith ran down the street, her feet flying in odd rhythms, her arms outspread, her toy slamming along behind her. "Toot," came from the distance, "Toot-toot, toot-toot."

Discussion

Little Faith is an example of a textbook toddler. She is well nourished both physically and emotionally, and her behavior in the areas of motor, language, and social skills are well within the parameters of normalcy for her age. At fifteen months she is no longer confined to the playpen and moves freely about the house. The control of large motor actions is still undergoing development and Faith's walk is aptly described as a swagger. Exacting small motor movements, such as closing a desk drawer require Faith's utmost concentration to coordinate balance, arm movements, and fingers. Faith thrusts out her tongue to help her achieve this complex task. Her course through the house is completely experimental—she tugs at this and pulls at that as household bric-a-brac catches her interest. For parents like Laura and Martin, who have some valuable possessions, there is good cause for concern when Faith is out of parental earshot and vision.

The toddler's image of himself is imprecise. He isn't aware of how far he can reach, how close he is to the ground, nor just where up, down, right, and left are. Even pain and discomfort are not readily localized, as demonstrated by Faith's discomfort with a spoon jammed in her diaper. She is in need of assistance both to locate the problem and to extricate the spoon. We expect Faith still to be in diapers at fifteen months, although Laura may be making some efforts toward toilet training. Laura's educational background suggests that she is aware of Freud and the anal stage of psychosexual development, which he postulates for this period in early childhood, and she is undoubtedly aware of the adverse future effects predicted by Freud of being unduly severe or insistent about toilet training. Judging from Laura's overconcern for Faith's emotional health, we would probably be right in guessing that this is another area in which she would be careful not to "damage the fine mechanism."

Faith has passed the babbling stage, and her language now consists of one and two-word sentences and word fusions such as "Mommee—ooop." Faith comprehends more than she can say, and her frustration when she is verbally unable to communicate her wishes is expressed in screams of rage. Faith displays an impressive amount of social development. In Erikson's terms (1950, pp. 219–222), she seems to have passed successfully through the infant stage of building trust. She now meets new situations such as the advent of a new and strange baby-sitter with confidence and good humor.

Like all children, Faith is the product of her hereditary endowment and her cultural environment. As the first child of well-educated, socially mobile parents, she can be expected to display a well-developed language pattern, respect for personal possessions, and a marked sense of right and wrong. Her behavior at fifteen months is characterized by curiosity and exploration. She seems to be achieving sufficient success and parental approval to be well on her way to meeting the criteria for the second stage in Erikson's (1950) scheme of the life cycle, autonomy versus shame and doubt.

Springboards for Inquiry

(1) How do you think Laura or Martin would describe Faith to a director of a nursery school? How would you evaluate Faith's strengths and areas of need? Describe the experiences you think parents particularly want for their children in nursery school and those they wish to avoid.

(2) Where on the scale of permissiveness–strict control do Laura's child-rearing techniques fit?

(3) What steps in language acquisition will Faith progress through from her present age until she is about four?

(4) What might be some of the behavioral consequences for Faith of being the firstborn child in this family?

(5) How will Faith's sex role affect her development in the next few years?

Early Conditioning

When the Russian physiologist Pavlov showed that he could elicit salivation in a dog in response to the ringing of a bell that had been previously paired with food, he opened the way* to intensive study in associative learning, now called conditioning. More recently B. F. Skinner of Harvard, building on the classic conditioning paradigm of Pavlov, has changed conceptions of human and animal behavior by carefully structuring the nature of the conditions that affect organismic responses.

Years before Skinner experimented with the systematic shaping of behavior, Jean Jacques Rousseau, a nineteenth century philosopher and author of the

---

* The following letter (New York Times Magazine, 9 August 1970) suggests some error in assigning the term *opened the way* to Pavlov: "Editor: The article "A Talk with Konrad Lorenz" (July 5) makes mention of Pavlov as "discoverer of the conditioned reflex." Although Pavlov is generally credited with being the innovator of this particular method of animal (and human) education, it is an interesting sidelight to recall that the conditioning technique was known and used for years, quite possibly for centuries, before Pavlov by peasants and gypsies in Central Europe, and doubtless in many other parts of the world, to train their "dancing" bears. In the past century — and who knows how long before that? — no traveling fair in the Balkans would have been complete without its performing bears, who had been taught to "dance" by hearing the same tunes played over and over while they were harnessed upright on top of a hot stove and thus induced to lift their blistering feet for momentary relief. In due course an educated bear needed only the stimulus of the same tune to activate the response of the dance . . . and a star was born" Marjorie Gerlach Duffy, clinical psychologist, Manhasset, N.Y.).

revolutionary educational novel *Emile*, proposed a method of teaching a child to withstand a specific frightening experience (reported in Skinner 1968). Rousseau proposed that the teacher wear a series of masks that ranged in quality from pleasant to grotesque. The principle is that as the child becomes accustomed to successively more frightening masks, he is not afraid when finally presented with the most grotesque mask.

In many situations crying is a nonreflex example of simple learning. A baby soon learns that his cries bring a friendly face that results in a change of diaper and warm milk. Research indicates that the termination of wetness or hunger is "rewarding," or reinforcing. The infant quickly learns* to cry if tears stop the wetness or produce food. As soon as he is dry and fed he cries no longer.

A similar type of human learning occurs when a child learns to speak. He learns to associate an object with a sound in a specific situation. For example, the word *mama* becomes associated in time with the woman who holds him, feeds him, and loves him. As he lies in his crib babbling, his speech includes many consonant and vowel sounds, and the sound *mama* occurs by accident and by shaping. His mother hears the familiar sound, immediately picks up the infant, and loves him while repeating the sound. The child soon learns to associate *mama* with the person who gives him so much pleasure.

This conditioning example suggests others, like the temper tantrum an older child may resort to in order to get what he wants. Furthermore it is entirely plausible that this early conditioning experience is responsible for the fact that females in our culture continue to use tears to bring desired responses from parents and later from husbands. Males, on the other hand, are conditioned to practice an almost unrealistic inhibition of tears: "Boys don't cry, do they?" or "Chin up, no tears—be a man."

McCandless (1967, p. 187) indicates that older children and adults who respond to vomit or excrement in unfamiliar places by gagging do so because they associate these with childhood experiences that were traumatic. To extinguish the learned response is no simple matter, but it may be achieved through "unlearning" by reinforcement techniques that gradually lessen the emotional response to vomit. Undoubtedly many children are deprived of valuable experiences with insects because their female elementary school teachers, who serve as models, were in childhood conditioned to be afraid of things with antennae, wings, and six legs.

Traditional child development texts report and extrapolate from research data that is essentially humanistic in nature. Despite the work of Pavlov (and John B. Watson) the bulk of child development data does not report on conditioning experiments. In the last few years B. F. Skinner's students and others influenced by Skinner have been fecund in their research. Sidney W. Bijou and Donald M. Baer (1967) report dozens of studies in which operant con-

---

* Since he cannot tell us what he has learned, we assume that a change in his behavior that operates on the environment indicates learning. For further explication of these terms see Evans 1968, pp. 18–19.

ditioning techniques were used in the study of infant vocalizations, autistic children, and mental retardation. Arthur Koestler (1967) and Joseph Wood Krutch (1954) argue that preplanning the contingencies of living environments is antihuman in its lack of concern for man's individuality and self-responsibility.

This we do know: conditioning is the simplest form of learning.* Behaviorists believe that early experiences of children condition later responses and that there is a remarkably similar pattern in the learning responses of children and animals. We are certain that the behavior of young children can be encouraged by things or events that reinforce that behavior.† Food, for example, can serve as a positive reinforcer; spankings and disapproval are negative reinforcers.

Skinner sees humans as complicated pigeons.‡ The study of emotions as internal states is of little concern to the operant conditioner, since such an emphasis states causal linkages in terms of feelings and emotions. Skinner, then, by his own admission is uninterested in Freudian musings about "adjustment, adaptation, homeostatic development" (Evans 1968, p. 8). He would not try to understand the behavior of children in terms of needs but rather in the analysis of the contingencies of reinforcement, stimulus situations, level of deprivation, and past learning history of the child. Perhaps Krutch's statement, quoted on the dust jacket of Evans' volume, best sums up the essence of the argument that still rages between the "superscientific" views of Skinner and the more mellow views of his opponents: "Whether or not man is to some extent a self-mover rather than merely the product of forces he cannot modify—whether he can resist conditioning as well as submit to it—these are questions as fateful as any it is possible to ask."

---

* The behaviorist maintains that learning and conditioning are synonymous.

† Two kinds of reinforcers are possible: *positive* reinforcers actively support the activity, *negative* reinforcers terminate a response.

‡ Skinner says, "Of course, pigeons aren't people, but it's only a matter of complexity, and we're learning the difference now" (quoted in Berkeley Rice, "Skinner Agrees He Is the Most Important Influence in Psychology," *New York Times*, 17 March 1968).

"And now," the Director shouted, "now we proceed to rub in the lesson with a mild electric shock."

Brave New World

by Aldous Huxley

Mr. Foster was left in the Decanting Room. The D.H.C. and his students stepped into the nearest lift and were carried up to the fifth floor.

Infant Nurseries. Neo-Pavlovian Conditioning Rooms, announced the notice board.

The Director opened a door. They were in a large bare room, very bright and sunny; for the whole of the southern wall was a single window. Half a dozen nurses, trousered and jacketed in the regulation white viscose-linen uniform, their hair aseptically hidden under white caps, were engaged in setting out bowls of roses in a long row across the floor. Big bowls, packed tight with blossom. Thousands of petals, ripe-blown and silkily smooth, like the cheeks of innumerable little cherubs, but of cherubs, in that bright light, not exclusively pink and Aryan, but also luminously Chinese, also Mexican, also apoplectic with too much blowing of celestial trumpets, also pale as death, pale with the posthumous whiteness of marble.

The nurses stiffened to attention as the D.H.C. came in.

"Set out the books," he said curtly.

In silence the nurses obeyed his command. Between the rose bowls the books were duly set out—a row of nursery quartos opened invitingly each at some gaily coloured image of beast or fish or bird.

"Now bring in the children."

They hurried out of the room and returned in a minute or two, each pushing a kind of tall dumb-waiter laden, on all its four wire-netted shelves, with eight-month-old babies, all exactly alike (a Bokanovsky Group, it was evident) and all

---

(since their caste was Delta) dressed in khaki.

"Put them down on the floor."

The infants were unloaded.

"Now turn them so that they can see the flowers and books."

Turned, the babies at once fell silent, then began to crawl towards those clusters of sleek colours, those shapes so gay and brilliant on the white pages. As they approached, the sun came out of a momentary eclipse behind a cloud. The roses flamed up as though with a sudden passion from within; a new and profound significance seemed to suffuse the shining pages of the books. From the ranks of the crawling babies came little squeals of excitement, gurgles and twitterings of pleasure.

The Director rubbed his hands. "Excellent" he said. "It might almost have been done on purpose."

The swiftest crawlers were already at their goal. Small hands reached out uncertainly, touched, grasped, unpetaling the transfigured roses, crumpling the illuminated pages of the books. The Director waited until all were happily busy. Then, "Watch carefully," he said. And, lifting his hand, he gave the signal.

The Head Nurse, who was standing by a switchboard at the other end of the room, pressed down a little lever.

There was a violent explosion. Shriller and ever shriller, a siren shrieked. Alarm bells maddeningly sounded.

The children started, screamed; their faces were distorted with terror.

"And now," the Director shouted (for the noise was deafening), "now we proceed to rub in the lesson with a mild electric shock."

He waved his hand again, and the Head Nurse pressed a second lever. The screaming of the babies suddenly changed its tone. There was something desperate, almost insane, about the sharp spasmodic yelps to which they now gave utterance. Their little bodies twitched and stiffened; their limbs moved jerkily as if to the tug of unseen wires.

"We can electrify that whole strip of floor," bawled the Director in explanation. 'But that's enough," he signalled to the nurse.

The explosions ceased, the bells stopped ringing, the shriek of the siren died down from tone to tone into silence. The stiffly twitching bodies relaxed, and what had become the sob and yelp of infant maniacs broadened out once more into a normal howl of ordinary terror.

"Offer them the flowers and the books again."

The nurses obeyed; but at the approach of the roses, at the mere sight of those gaily-coloured images of pussy and cock-a-doodle-doo and baa-baa black sheep, the infants shrank away in horror; the volume of their howling suddenly increased.

"Observe," said the Director triumphantly, "observe."

Books and loud noises, flowers and electric shocks—already in the infant mind these couples were compromisingly linked; and after two hundred repetitions of the same or a similar lesson would be wedded indissolubly. What man has joined, nature is powerless to put asunder.

"They'll grow up with what the psychologists used to call an 'instinctive' hatred of books and flowers. Reflexes unalterably conditioned. They'll be safe from books and botany all their lives." The Director turned to his nurses. "Take them away again."

Still yelling, the khaki babies were loaded on to their dumb-waiters and wheeled out, leaving behind them the smell of sour milk and a most welcome silence.

One of the students held up his hand; and though he could see quite well why you couldn't have lower-caste people wasting the Community's time over books, and that there was always the risk of their reading something which might undesirably decondition one of their reflexes, yet . . . well, he couldn't understand about the flowers. Why go to the trouble of making is psychologically impossible for Deltas to like flowers?

Patiently the D.H.C. explained. If the children were made to scream at the sight of a rose, that was on grounds of high economic policy. Not so very long ago (a century or thereabouts), Gammas, Deltas, even Epsilons, had been conditioned to like flowers—flowers in particular and wild nature in general. The idea was to make them want to be going out into the country at every available opportunity, and so compel them to consume transport.

"And didn't they consume transport?" asked the student.

"Quite a lot," the D.H.C. replied. "But nothing else."

Primroses and landscapes, he pointed out, have one grave defect: they are gratuitous. A love of nature keeps no factories busy. It was decided to abolish the love of nature, at any rate among the lower classes; to abolish the love of nature, but *not* the tendency to consume transport. For of course it was essential that they should keep on going to the country, even though they hated it. The problem was to find an economically sounder reason for consuming transport than a mere affection for primroses and landscapes. It was duly found.

"We condition the masses to hate the country," concluded the Director. "But simultaneously we condition them to love all country sports. At the same time, we see to it that all country sports shall entail the use of elaborate apparatus. So that they consume manufactured articles as well as transport. Hence those electric shocks."

"I see," said the student, and was silent, lost in admiration.

There was a silence; then clearing his throat, "Once upon a time," the Director began, "while our Ford was still on earth, there was a little boy called Reuben Rabinovitch. Reuben was the child of Polish-speaking parents." The Director interrupted himself. "You know what Polish is, I suppose?"

"A dead language."

"Like French and German," added another student, officiously showing off his learning.

"And 'parent'?" questioned the D.H.C.

There was an uneasy silence. Several of the boys blushed. They had not yet learned to draw the significant but often very fine distinction between smut and pure science. One, at last, had the courage to raise a hand.

"Human beings used to be . . ." he hesitated; the blood rushed to his cheeks. "Well, they used to be viviparous."

"Quite right." The Director nodded approvingly.

"And when the babies were decanted . . ."

" 'Born,' " came the correction.

"Well, then they were the parents —I mean, not the babies, of course; the other ones." The poor boy was overwhelmed with confusion.

"In brief," the Director summed up, "the parents were the father and the mother." The smut that was really science fell with a crash into the boys' eye-avoiding silence. "Mother," he repeated loudly rubbing in the science; and, leaning back in his chair, "These," he said gravely, "are unpleasant facts; I know it. But then most historical facts *are* unpleasant."

He returned to Little Reuben—to Little Reuben, in whose room, one evening, by an oversight, his father and mother (crash, crash!) happened to leave the radio turned on.

("For you must remember that in those days of gross viviparous reproduction, children were always brought up by their parents and not in State Conditioning Centres.")

While the child was asleep, a broadcast programme from London suddenly started to come through; and the next morning, to the astonishment of his crash and crash (the more daring of the boys ventured to grin at one another), Little Reuben woke up repeating word for word a long lecture by that curious old writer ("one of the very few whose works have been permitted to come down to us"), George Bernard Shaw, who was speaking, according to a well-authenticated tradition, about his own genius. To Little Reuben's wink and snigger, this lecture was, of course, perfectly incomprehensible and, imagining that their child had suddenly gone mad, they sent for a doctor. He, fortunately, understood English, recognized the discourse as that which Shaw had broadcasted the previous evening, realized the significance of what had happened, and sent a letter to the medical press about it.

"The principle of sleep-teaching, or hypnopædia, had been discovered." The D.H.C. made an impressive pause.

The principle had been discovered; but many, many years were to elapse before that principle was usefully applied.

"The case of Little Reuben occurred only twenty-three years after Our Ford's first T-Model was put on the market." (Here the Director made a sign of the T on his stomach and all the students reverently followed suit.) "And yet . . ."

Furiously the students scribbled. *"Hypnopædia, first used officially in A.F. 214. Why not before? Two reasons. (a) . . ."*

"These early experimenters," the D.H.C. was saying, "were on the wrong track. They thought that hypnopædia could be made an instrument of intellectual education . . ."

(A small boy asleep on his right side, the right arm stuck out, the right hand hanging limp over the edge of the bed. Through a round grating in the side of a box a voice speaks softly.

"The Nile is the longest river in Africa and the second in length of all the rivers of the globe. Although falling short of the length of the Mississippi-Missouri, the Nile is at the head of all rivers as regards the length of its basin, which extends through 35 degrees of latitude . . ."

At breakfast the next morning, "Tommy," some one says, "do you know which is the longest river in

Africa?" A shaking of the head. "But don't you remember something that begins: The Nile is the . . ."

"The - Nile - is - the - longest - river - in - Africa - and - the - second - in - length - of - all - the - rivers - of - the - globe . . ." The words come rushing out. "Although - falling - short - of . . ."

"Well now, which is the longest river in Africa?"

The eyes are blank. "I don't know."

"But the Nile, Tommy."

"The - Nile - is - the - longest - river - in Africa - and - second . . ."

"Then which river is the longest, Tommy?"

Tommy burst into tears. "I don't know," he howls.)

That howl, the Director made it plain, discouraged the earliest investigators. The experiments were abandoned. No further attempt was made to teach children the length of the Nile in their sleep. Quite rightly. You can't learn a science unless you know what it's all about.

"Whereas, if they'd only started on *moral* education," said the Director, leading the way towards the door. The students followed him, desperately scribbling as they walked and all the way up in the lift. "Moral education, which ought never, in any circumstances, to be rational."

"Silence, silence," whispered a loud speaker as they stepped out at the fourteenth floor, and "Silence, silence," the trumpet mouths indefatigably repeated at intervals down every corridor. The students and even the Director himself rose automatically to the tips of their toes. They were Alphas, of course; but even Alphas have been well conditioned. "Silence, silence." All the air of the fourteenth floor was sibilant with the categorical imperative.

Fifty yards of tiptoeing brought them to a door which the Director cautiously opened. They stepped over the threshold into the twilight of a shuttered dormitory. Eighty cots stood in a row against the wall. There was a sound of light regular breathing and a continuous murmur, as of very faint voices remotely whispering.

A nurse rose as they entered and came to attention before the Director.

"What's the lesson this afternoon?" he asked.

"We had Elementary Sex for the first forty minutes," she answered. "But now it's switched over to Elementary Class Consciousness."

The Director walked slowly down the long line of cots. Rosy and relaxed with sleep, eighty little boys and girls lay softly breathing. There was a whisper under every pillow. The D.H.C. halted and, bending over one of the little beds, listened attentively.

"Elementary Class Consciousness, did you say? Let's have it repeated a little louder by the trumpet."

At the end of the room a loud speaker projected from the wall. The Director walked up to it and pressed a switch.

". . . all wear green," said a soft but very distinct voice, beginning in the middle of a sentence, "and Delta Children wear khaki. Oh no, I don't want to play with Delta children. And Epsilons are still worse. They're too stupid to be able to read or write. Besides they wear black, which is such a beastly colour. I'm *so* glad I'm a Beta."

There was a pause; then the voice began again.

"Alpha children wear grey. They work much harder than we do, because they're so frightfully clever. I'm really awfully glad I'm a Beta, because I don't work so hard. And then we are much better than the Gammas and Deltas. Gammas are stupid. They all wear green, and Delta children wear khaki. Oh no, I *don't* want to play with Delta children. And Epsilons are still worse. They're too stupid to be able . . ."

The Director pushed back the switch. The voice was silent. Only its thin ghost continued to mutter from beneath the eighty pillows.

"They'll have that repeated forty or fifty times more before they wake; then again on Thursday, and again on Saturday. A hundred and twenty times three times a week for thirty months. After which they go on to a more advanced lesson."

Roses and electric shocks, the khaki of Deltas and a whiff of asafoetida—wedded indissolubly before the child can speak. But wordless conditioning is crude and wholesale; cannot bring home the finer distinctions, cannot inculcate the more complex courses of behaviour. For that there must be words, but words without reason. In brief, hypnopaedia.

"The greatest moralizing and socializing force of all time."

The students took it down in their little books. Straight from the horse's mouth.

Once more the Director touched the switch.

". . . so frightfully clever," the soft, insinuating, indefatigable voice was saying, "I'm really awfully glad I'm a Beta, because . . ."

Not so much like drops of water, though water, it is true, can wear holes in the hardest granite; rather, drops of liquid sealing-wax, drops that adhere, incrust, incorporate themselves with what they fall on, till finally the rock is all one scarlet blob.

"Till at last the child's mind *is* these suggestions, and the sum of the suggestions *is* the child's mind. And not the child's mind only. The adult's mind too—all his life long. The mind that judges and desires and decides—made up of these suggestions. But all these suggestions are *our* suggestions!" The Director almost shouted in his triumph. "Suggestions from the State." He banged the nearest table. "It therefore follows . . ."

A noise made him turn round.

"Oh, Ford!" he said in another tone, "I've gone and woken the children."

Discussion

In 1932, when *Brave New World* was published, Aldous Huxley considered his work a Utopia projected six hundred years into the future. He envisioned a society profoundly affected by the advanced state of scientific knowledge and technology that would have accrued by then. The world he created, in which every aspect of life was controlled and manipulated to conform to the needs of this bizarre society, was an abhorrent conception to Huxley.

He foresaw the world he created as the alternative to the tragic human consequences that resulted from the completely uncontrolled society of the early 1900s, which produced the human tragedies of World War I and the Depression. At the time of the conception of *Brave New World,* Huxley visualized neither the thought control of Hitler and Stalin nor the nuclear fission that culminated in Hiroshima. In his introduction to the second edition of *Brave New World* in 1946, Huxley expresses amazement that many of his science fiction ideas would exist or be very real possibilities not six hundred years hence but in just fifteen years.

Preceding the chapter on early conditioning in *Brave New World* we learn that birth is accomplished in a Decanting Room, where in a predetermined number of bottles biologically superior ova are fertilized by biologically superior sperm to produce superior castes of people labeled Betas, Alphas, and Alpha Pluses. Inferior groups are also decanted in order to fill the society's need for the abundance of unskilled work that must be performed. After the babies are decanted they are immediately placed in state conditioning centers where they are cared for and conditioned to like and to perform well in the life style that has been predetermined for them.

Pavlovian or classic conditioning is well illustrated in this selection. When it is decided that the enjoyment of nature and the reading of books by Deltas would be an economic disadvantage to the larger society, conditioning is initiated in infancy to ensure that both these relatively free activities will be hated and avoided by Deltas all through their lives. The conditioning consists of pairing the pleasant and attractive stimuli of flowers and books with the very unpleasant stimuli of loud noises, sirens, and electric shock (in case the alarm bells were not sufficiently aversive) to produce a reaction of horrified withdrawal. Following two hundred repetitions of the paired stimuli, the presentation of flowers and books alone, without the noise and shock, will produce the same negative withdrawal behavior. When conditioning is completed early in life and with sufficient repetitions, the effects can be lasting.

In *Brave New World* moral conditioning was also instituted in the child's early years, when attitudes and psychological set are in their formative stages. The children were taught class consciousness and attitudes toward sex through hypnopedia, that is, many repetitions of information during sleep. The Director considered Pavlovian conditioning crude as compared with the subtle and complex conditioning of attitudes that can be accomplished through repetitions of messages through the spoken word while all conflicting messages are nonexistent.

Huxley himself was appalled at how close our own society had moved toward the nightmare Utopia he envisioned in *Brave New World.* Students will also be interested in *Brave New World Revisited,* which Huxley wrote in 1958, in which he speaks eloquently of the conditioning children are subjected to by the mass media. He also discusses Soma, the *Brave New World* mythical drug that so closely approximates the mood-altering drugs that are being used today in epidemic proportions.

Since the knowledge and techniques for modifying behavior through conditioning has reached a sophisticated level, the possibilities posed by this knowledge is an important topic for students of child psychology.

Springboards for Inquiry

(1) How are we moving toward a society somewhat like the one described in *Brave New World?*

(2) Discuss the view that all learning can be classified as conditioning.

(3) How can individuals maintain freedom of choice in a society in which the mass media are controlled by biased interests?

(4) What, if any, are the desirable aspects of behavioral conditioning that may be deliberately used in the home and school?

"Put the lollipop out of sight as quickly as possible."

Walden Two

by B. F. Skinner

"Each of us," Frazier began, "is engaged in a pitched battle with the rest of mankind."

"A curious premise for a Utopia," said Castle. "Even a pessimist like myself takes a more hopeful view than that."

"You do, you do," said Frazier. "But let's be realistic. Each of us has interests which conflict with the interests of everybody else. That's our original sin, and it can't be helped. Now, 'everybody else' we call 'society.' It's a powerful opponent, and it always wins. Oh, here and there an individual prevails for a while and gets what he wants. Sometimes he storms the culture of a society and changes it slightly to his own advantage. But society wins in the long run, for it has the advantage of numbers and of age. Many prevail against one, and men against a baby. Society attacks early, when the individual is helpless. It enslaves him almost before he has tasted freedom. The 'ologies' will tell you how it's done. Theology calls it building a conscience or developing a spirit of selflessness. Psychology calls it the growth of the superego.

"Considering how long society has been at it, you'd expect a better job. But the campaigns have been badly planned and the victory has never been secure. The behavior of the individuals has been shaped according to revelations of 'good conduct,' never as the result of experimental study. But why not experiment? The questions are simple enough. What's the best behavior for the individual so far as the group is concerned? And how can the individual be induced to behave in that way? Why not explore these questions in a scientific spirit?

"We could do just that in Walden Two. We had already worked out a code of conduct—subject, of course, to experimental modification. The code would keep things running smoothly if everybody lived up to it. Our job was to see that everybody did. Now, you can't get people to follow a useful code by making them into so many jacks-in-the-box. You can't foresee all future circumstances, and you can't specify adequate future conduct. You don't know what will be required. Instead you have to set up certain behavioral processes which will lead the individual to design his own 'good' conduct when the time comes. We call that sort of thing 'self-control.' But don't be misled, the control always rests in the last analysis in the hands of society.

"One of our Planners, a young man named Simmons, worked with me. It was the first time in history that the matter was approached in an experimental way. Do you question that statement, Mr. Castle?"

"I'm not sure I know what you are talking about," said Castle.

"Then let me go on. Simmons and I began by studying the great works on morals and ethics—Plato, Aristotle, Confucius, the New Testament, the Puritan divines, Machiavelli, Chesterfield, Freud—there were scores of them. We were looking for any and every method of shaping human behavior by imparting techniques of self-control. Some techniques were obvious enough, for they had marked turning points in human history. 'Love your enemies' is an example—a psychological invention for easing the lot of an oppressed people. The severest trial of oppression is the constant rage which one suffers at the thought of the oppressor. What Jesus discovered was how to avoid these inner devastations. His technique was to *practice the opposite emotion*. If a man can succeed in 'loving his enemies' and 'taking no thought for the morrow,' he will no longer be assailed by hatred of the oppressor or rage at the loss of his freedom or possessions. He may not get his freedom or possessions back, but he's less miserable. It's a difficult lesson. It comes late in our program."

"I thought you were opposed to modifying emotions and instincts until the world was ready for it," said Castle. "According to you, the principle of 'love your enemies' should have been suicidal."

"It would have been suicidal, except for an entirely unforseen consequence. Jesus must have been quite astonished at the effect of his discovery. We are only just beginning to understand the power of love because we are just beginning to understand the weakness of force and aggression. But the science of behavior is clear about all that now. Recent discoveries in the analysis of punishment—but I am falling into one digression after another. Let me save my explanation of why the Christian virtues—and I mean merely the Christian techniques of self-control—have not disappeared from the face of the earth, with due recognition of the fact that they suffered a narrow squeak within recent memory.

"When Simmons and I had collected our techniques of control, we had to discover how to teach them. That was more difficult. Current educational practices were of little value, and religious practices scarcely any better. Promising paradise or threatening hell-fire is, we assumed, generally admitted to be unproductive. It is based upon a fundamental fraud which, when discovered, turns the individual against society and nourishes the very thing it tries to stamp out. What Jesus offered in return for loving one's enemies was heaven *on earth,* better known as peace of mind.

"We found a few suggestions worth following in the practices of the clinical psychologist. We undertook to build a tolerance for annoying experiences. The sunshine of midday is extremely painful if you come from a dark room, but take it in easy stages and you can avoid pain altogether. The analogy can be misleading, but in much the same way it's possible to build a tolerance to painful or distasteful stimuli, or to frustration, or to situations which arouse fear, anger or rage. Society and nature throw these annoyances at the individual with no regard for the development of tolerances. Some achieve tolerances, most fail. Where would the science of immunization be if it followed a schedule of accidental dosages?

"Take the principle of 'Get thee behind me, Satan,' for example," Frazier continued. "It's a special case of self-control by altering the environment. Subclass A 3, I believe. We give each child a lollipop which has been dipped in powdered sugar so that a single touch of the tongue can be detected. We tell him he may eat the lollipop later in the day, provided it hasn't already been licked. Since the child is only three or four, it is a fairly diff—"

"Three or four!" Castle exclaimed.

"All our ethical training is completed by the age of six," said Frazier quietly. "A simple principle like putting temptation out of sight would be acquired before four. But at such an early age the problem of not licking the lollipop isn't easy. Now, what would you do, Mr. Castle, in a similar situation?"

"Put the lollipop out of sight as quickly as possible."

"Exactly. I can see you've been well trained. Or perhaps you discovered the principle for yourself. We're in favor of original inquiry wherever possible, but in this case we have a more important goal and we don't hesitate to give verbal help. First of all, the children are urged to examine their own behavior while looking at the lollipops. This helps them to recognize the need for self-control. Then the lollipops are concealed, and the children are asked to notice any gain in happiness or any reduction in tension. Then a strong distraction is arranged—say, an interesting game. Later the children are reminded of the candy and encouraged to examine their reaction. The value of the distraction is generally obvious. Well, need I go on? When the experiment is repeated a day or so later, the children all run with the lollipops to their lockers and do exactly what Mr. Castle would do—a sufficient indication of the success of our training."

"I wish to report an objective observation of my reaction to your story," said Castle, controlling his voice with great precision. "I find myself revolted by this display of sadistic tyranny."

"I don't wish to deny you the exercise of an emotion which you seem to find enjoyable," said Frazier. "So let me go on. Concealing a tempting but forbidden object is a crude solution. For one thing, it's not always feasible. We want a sort of psychological concealment—covering up the candy by paying no attention. In a later experiment the children wear their lollipops like crucifies for a few hours."

" 'Instead of the cross, the lollipop,
About my neck was hung,' "

said Castle.

" I wish somebody had taught me that, though," said Rodge, with a glance at Barbara.

"Don't we all?" said Frazier. "Some of us learn control, more or less by accident. The rest of us go all our lives not even understanding how it is possible, and blaming our failure on being born the wrong way."

"How do you build up a tolerance to an annoying situation?" I said.

"Oh, for example, by having the children 'take' a more and more painful shock, or drink cocoa with less and less sugar in it until a bitter concoction can be savored without a bitter face."

"But jealousy or envy—you can't administer them in graded doses," I said.

"And why not? Remember, we control the social environment, too, at this age. That's why we get our ethical training in early. Take this case. A group of children arrive home after a long walk tired and hungry. They're expecting supper; they find, instead, that it's time for a lesson in self-control: they must stand for five minutes in front of steaming bowls of soup.

"The assignment is accepted like a problem in arithmetic. Any groaning or complaining is a wrong answer. Instead, the children begin at once to work upon themselves to avoid any unhappiness during the delay. One of them may make a joke of it. We encourage a sense of humor as a good way of not taking an annoyance seriously. The joke won't be much, according to adult standards—perhaps the child will simply pretend to empty the bowl of soup into his upturned mouth. Another may start a song with many verses. The rest join in at once, for they've learned that it's a good way to make time pass."

Frazier glanced uneasily at Castle, who was not to be appeased.

"That also strikes you as a form of torture, Mr. Castle?" he asked.

"I'd rather be put on the rack," said Castle.

"Then you have by no means had the thorough training I supposed. You can't imagine how lightly the children take such an experience. It's a rather severe biological frustration, for the children are tired and hungry and they must stand and look at food; but it's passed off as lightly as a five-minute delay at curtain time. We regard it as a fairly elementary test. Much more difficult problems follow."

"I suspected as much," muttered Castle.

"In a later stage we forbid all social devices. No songs, no jokes—merely silence. Each child is forced back upon his own resources—a very important step."

"I should think so," I said. "And how do you know it's successful? You might produce a lot of silently resentful children. It's certainly a dangerous stage."

"It is, and we follow each child carefully. If he hasn't picked up the necessary techniques, we start back a little. A still more advanced stage" —Frazier glanced again at Castle, who stirred uneasily—"brings me to my point. When it's time to sit down to the soup, the children count off—heads and tails. Then a coin is tossed and if it comes up heads, the 'heads' sit down and eat. The 'tails' remain standing for another five minutes."

Castle groaned.

"And you call that envy?" I asked.

"Perhaps not exactly," said Frazier. "At least there's seldom any aggression against the lucky ones. The emotion, if any, is directed against Lady Luck herself, against the toss of the coin. That, in itself, is a lesson worth learning, for it's the only direction in which emotion has a surviving chance to be useful. And resentment toward things in general, while perhaps just as silly as personal aggression, is more easily controlled. Its expression is not socially objectionable."

Frazier looked nervously from one of us to the other. He seemed to be trying to discover whether we shared Castle's prejudice. I began to realize, also, that he had not really wanted to tell this story. He was vulnerable. He was treading on sanctified ground, and I was pretty sure he had not established the value of most of these practices in an experimental fashion. He could scarcely have done so in the short space of ten years. He was working on faith, and it bothered him.

I tried to bolster his confidence by reminding him that he had a professional colleague among his listeners. "May you not inadvertently teach your children some of the very emotions you're trying to eliminate?" I said. "What's the effect, for example, of finding the anticipation of a warm supper suddenly thwarted? Doesn't that eventually lead to feelings of uncertainty, or even anxiety?"

"It might. We had to discover how often our lessons could be safely administered. But all our schedules are worked out experimentally. We watch for undesired consequences just as any scientist watches for disrupting factors in his experiments.

"After all, it's a simple and sensible program," he went on in a tone of appeasement. "We set up a system of gradually increasing annoyances and frustrations against a background of complete serenity. An easy environment is made more and more difficult as the children acquire the capacity to adjust."

"But *why?*" said Castle. "Why these deliberate unpleasantnesses—to put it mildly? I must say I think you and your friend Simmons are really very subtle sadists."

"You've reversed your position, Mr. Castle," said Frazier in a sudden flash of anger with which I rather sympathized. Castle was calling names, and he was also being unaccountably and perhaps intentionally obtuse. "A while ago you accused me of breeding a race of softies," Frazier continued. "Now you object to toughening them up. But what you don't understand is that these potentially unhappy situations are never very annoying. Our schedules make sure of that. You wouldn't understand, however, because you're not so far advanced as our children."

Castle grew black.

"But what do your children get out of it?" he insisted, apparently trying to press some vague advantage in Frazier's anger.

"What do they get out of it!" exclaimed Frazier, his eyes flashing with a sort of helpless contempt. His lips curled and he dropped his head to look at his fingers, which were crushing a few blades of grass.

"They must get happiness and freedom and strength," I said, putting myself in a ridiculous position in attempting to make peace.

"They don't sound happy or free to me, standing in front of bowls of Forbidden Soup," said Castle, answering me parenthetically while continuing to stare at Frazier.

"If I must spell it out," Frazier began with a deep sigh, "what they get is escape from the petty emotions which eat the heart out of the unprepared. They get the satisfaction of pleasant and profitable social relations on a scale almost undreamed of in the world at large. They get immeasurably increased efficiency, because they can stick to a job without suffering the aches and pains which soon beset most of us. They get new horizons, for they are spared the emotions characteristic of frustration and failure. They get—" His eyes searched the branches of the trees. "Is that enough?" he said at last.

"And the community must gain their loyalty," I said, "when they discover the fears and jealousies and diffidences in the world at large."

"I'm glad you put it that way," said Frazier. "You might have said that they must feel superior to the miserable products of our public schools. But we're at pains to keep any feeling of superiority or contempt under control, too. Having suffered most acutely from it myself, I put the subject first on our agenda. We carefully avoid any joy in a personal triumph which means the personal failure of somebody else. We take no pleasure in the sophistical, the disputative, the dialectical." He threw a vicious glance at Castle. "We don't use the motive of domination, because we are always thinking of the whole group. We could motivate a few geniuses that way—it was certainly my own motivation—but we'd sacrifice some of the happiness of everyone else. Triumph over nature and over oneself, yes. But over others, never."

"You've taken the mainspring out of the watch," said Castle flatly.

"That's an experimental question, Mr. Castle, and you have the wrong answer."

Frazier was making no effort to conceal his feeling. If he had been riding Castle, he was now using his spurs. Perhaps he sensed that the rest of us had come round and that he could change his tactics with a single holdout. But it was more than strategy, it was genuine feeling. Castle's undeviating skepticism was a growing frustration.

"Are your techniques really so very new?" I said hurriedly. "What about the primitive practice of submitting a boy to various tortures before granting him a place among adults? What about the disciplinary techniques of Puritanism? Or of the modern school for that matter?"

"In one sense you're right," said Frazier. "And I think you've nicely answered Mr. Castle's tender concern for our little ones. The unhappinesses we deliberately impose are far milder than the normal unhappinesses from which we offer protection. Even at the height of our ethical training, the unhappiness is ridiculously trivial—to the well-trained child.

"But there's a world of difference in the way we use these annoyances," he continued. "For one thing, we don't punish. We never administer an unpleasantness in the hope of repressing or eliminating undesirable behavior. But there's another difference. In most cultures the child meets up with annoyances and reverses of uncontrolled magnitude. Some are imposed in the name of discipline by persons in authority. Some, like hazings, are condoned though not authorized. Others are merely accidental. No one cares to, or is able to, prevent them.

"We all know what happens. A few hardy children emerge, particularly those who have got their unhappiness in doses that could be swallowed. They become brave men. Others become sadists or masochists of varying degrees of pathology. Not having conquered a painful environment, they become preoccupied with pain and make a devious art of it. Others submit—and hope to inherit the earth. The rest—the cravens, the cowards—live in fear for the rest of their lives. And that's only a single field—the reaction to pain. I could cite a dozen parallel cases. The optimist and the pessimist, the contented and the disgruntled, the loved and the unloved, the ambitious and the discouraged—these are only the extreme products of a miserable system.

"Traditional practices are admittedly better than nothing," Frazier went on. "Spartan or Puritan—no one can question the occasional happy result. But the whole system rests upon the wasteful principle of selection. The English public school of the nineteenth century produced brave men—by setting up almost insurmountable barriers and making the most of the few who came over. But selection isn't education. Its crops of brave men will always be small, and the waste enormous. Like all primitive principles, selection serves in place of education only through a profligate use of material. Multiply extravagantly and select with rigor. It's the philosophy of the 'big litter' as an alternative to good child hygiene.

"In Walden Two we have a different objective. We make every man a brave man. They all come over the barriers. Some require more preparation than others, but they all come over. The traditional use of adversity is to select the strong. We control adversity to build strength. And we do it deliberately, no matter how sadistic Mr. Castle may think us, in order to prepare for adversities which are beyond control. Our children eventually experience the 'heartache and the thousand natural shocks that flesh is heir to.' It would be the cruelest possible practice to protect them as long as possible, especially when we *could* protect them so well."

Frazier held out his hands in an exaggerated gesture of appeal.

"What alternative *had* we?" he said, as if he were in pain. "What else could we do? For four or five years we could provide a life in which no important need would go unsatisfied, a life practically free of anxiety or frustration or annoyance. What would *you* do? Would you let the child enjoy this paradise with no thought for the future—like an idolatrous and pampering mother? Or would you relax control of the environment and let the child meet accidental frustrations? *But what is the virtue of accident?* No, there was only one course open to us. We had to *design* a series of adversities, so that the child would develop the greatest possible self-control. Call it deliberate, if you like, and accuse us of sadism; there was no other course." Frazier turned to Castle, but he was scarcely challenging him. He seemed to be waiting anxiously, for his capitulation. But Castle merely shifted his ground.

"I find it difficult to classify these practices," he said. Frazier emitted a disgruntled "Ha!" and sat back. "Your system seems to have usurped the place as well as the techniques of religion."

"Of religion and family culture," said Frazier wearily. "But I don't call it usurpation. Ethical training belongs to the community. As for techniques, we took every suggestion we could find without prejudice as to the source. But not on faith. We disregarded all claims of revealed truth and put every principle to an experimental test. And by the way, I've very much misrepresented the whole system if you suppose that any of the practices I've described are fixed. We try out many different techniques. Gradually we work toward the best possible set. And we don't pay much attention to the apparent success of a principle in the course of history. History is honored in Walden Two only as entertainment. It isn't taken seriously as food for thought. Which reminds me, very rudely, of our original plan for the morning. Have you had enough of emotion? Shall we turn to intellect?"

Frazier addressed these questions to Castle in a very friendly way and I was glad to see that Castle responded in kind. It was perfectly clear, however, that neither of them had ever worn a lollipop about the neck or faced a bowl of Forbidden Soup.

Discussion

B. F. Skinner wrote *Walden Two* "because man dreams forever of the almost Perfect State" (Poore 1948, p. 6). He set about to create a world that emphasized naturalness and peaceful, healthful living in uncrowded conditions in the tradition of Thoreau's *Walden.* Unlike the cynical superstate Aldous Huxley created in *Brave New World,* Skinner intended *Walden Two* to represent his most pleasant Utopian vision of society. Skinner's Utopia provides peace of mind and security for its inhabitants. The development and maintenance of this ideal society was to be made possible through the scientific application of Skinner's theories of behavioral engineering.

Reviews of *Walden Two* at the time of its publication included descriptions such as "curiously sterile" and "fascinatingly abhorrent." Yet students and admirers of Skinner take his concepts of social organizations seriously. One of his suggested innovations in child rearing, the Aircrib, has actually been commercially manufactured. The box is made entirely of glass and is designed to maintain the warmth and humidity necessary for the healthful environment of the infant. The baby wears no clothes in this box and lies on a mattress of stretched plastic that can be wiped clean as needed.

The behavioral engineering described in this selection may seem shocking at first because we are so used to thinking in terms of coping with or adjusting to unpleasant emotions. We may decry destructive human emotions such as jealousy and rage, but we closely associate them with the inevitable condition of being human. Skinner is not content to permit negative emotions to play a significant part in our lives and is willing to define and eliminate in an individual those emotions that are unhealthy for the interests of the larger society. Having once identified these emotions, he would employ techniques of behavioral engineering to eliminate them systematically. Today's psychology employs techniques of behavior modification based on Skinner's theories of operant conditioning.*

In this selection Frazier explains how young children are trained to build tolerance to temptation through a system of rewards. The system of rewards and the time interval between presentation of the stimulus (lollipop or soup in this case) and the reward are carefully worked out experimentally and are subject to change on an individual basis if disruptive or negative side effects are noted. By the time children are six years old they have been taught to recognize even the most stressful emotions and to participate in their modification or extinction. In the case of learning to withstand temptation the children are shown that a diversion such as an enjoyable game or a funny story can help to build self-control. As controls are strengthened through graduated periods of time spent in exercising self-restraint followed by immediate reward, the children reach a point when they can wear sugarcoated lollipops around their necks for long periods of time without licking them. Punishment is not used to control behavior; rather, the desired behavior is shaped through a well-designed schedule of rewards and delayed rewards.

Skinner has frequently been asked to defend his techniques of behavioral shaping, which if misused seem similar to the brainwashing techniques the Chinese were accused of using during the Korean War. Although Skinner (Evans 1968, p. 54) agrees that advances in the science of behavior modification can be "just as dangerous as the atom bomb," he does not think that to declare a moratorium on science would solve the problem. Rather he suggests that we "devote ourselves to a better governmental design which will have some control over all destructive instruments" (Evans 1968, p. 54).

---

* Reports of the work of Neal Miller and Leo Dicara at the Rockefeller Institute indicate that trained rats can alter their heart rates by as much as 20 percent through operant conditioning techniques. Bernard I. Engel and Theodore Weiss in Baltimore are experimenting with human control of heartbeats through deliberate use of the brain (New York Times, 10 January 1971, p. 48).

Springboards for Inquiry

(1) What is your view of planned behavioral conditioning as opposed to humanistic views of self-responsibility in society?

(2) If you were to plan a *Walden Three,* which aspects of human emotion would you condition and which would you extinguish?

(3) What other aspects of the "good life" would you be sure to include in your *Walden Three?*

(4) Can we move toward a Utopian society without using conditioning techniques? If so, what would you substitute?

(5) In conditioning, both rewards (reinforcement) and punishment (aversive control) are used to shape behavior. How can one condone reinforcement without sanctioning aversive control?

References

Abrahamsen, David. *The Emotional Care of Your Child.* New York: Trident Press, 1969.

Almy, Millie. "Wishful Thinking about Children's Thinking." In *Readings in Psychological Foundations of Education,* edited by Walter H. MacGinitie and Samuel Ball. New York: McGraw-Hill Book Co., 1968.

Bernard, Harold W. *Human Development in Western Culture.* Boston: Allyn & Bacon, 1962.

Bijou, Sidney W., and Donald M. Baer. *Child Development.* New York: Appleton-Century-Crofts, 1967.

Bowlby, John. "The Nature of the Child's Tie to His Mother." *Internal. Journal of Psycho-Analysis* 39 (1958): 350–73.

Chess, Stella, Alexander Thomas, and Herbert Birch. "Characteristics of the Individual Child's Behavioral Responses to the Environment." *American Journal of Orthopsychiatry* 29 (1959): 791–802.

Cobliner, W. Godfrey. "Some Maternal Attitudes towards Conception." *Mental Hygiene* 49 (1965): 552–557.

Erikson, Erik. *Childhood and Society,* 2nd. ed. New York: W. W. Norton & Co., 1950.

Evans, Richard. *B. F. Skinner: The Man and His Ideas.* New York: E. P. Dutton & Co., 1968.

Ferreira, Antonis J. "Emotional Factors in Prenatal Environment: A Review." *Journal of Nervous and Mental Disease* 141 (1965): 108–118.

Frank, George H. "The Role of the Family in the Development of Psychopathology." *Psychology Bulletin* 65 (1965): 191–205.

Freud, Sigmund. "Character and Anal Erotism," 1908. In *The Standard Edition of the Complete Works of Sigmund Freud,* vol. II, edited by Jerome Strachey. London: Hogarth Press and Institute of Psychoanalysis, 1953.

Freud, Sigmund. *Three Essays on the Theory of Sexuality.* 1905. London: Imago Publishing Co., 1949.

Haimowitz, Morris L., and Haimowitz, Natalie R. *Human Development.* New York: Thomas Y. Crowell, 1966.

Koestler, Arthur. *The Ghost in the Machine.* London: Hutchinson Co., 1967.

Krutch, Joseph Wood. *The Measure of Man.* New York: Bobbs-Merrill Co., 1954.

Levy, S. David. "Primary Affect Hunger," *American Journal of Psychiatry.* 94 (1937): 643–652.

Lidz, Theodore. *The Person.* New York: Basic Books, 1968.

Lowe, Charles Ronald. "Effects of Mothers' Smoking Habits on Birth Weight of Their Children." *British Medical Journal* October 10, 1959: 673–676.

McCandless, Boyd R. *Children: Behavior and Development.* 2nd ed. New York: Holt, Rinehart, and Winston, 1967.

Piaget, Jean. *Origins of Intelligence in Children.* Translated by Margaret Cook. New York: International Universities Press, 1952.

Poore, Charles. "Tour of an Almost Perfect Utopia." *New York Times Book Review*, 13 June 1948.

Rogers, Dorothy. *Child Psychology.* Belmont, Calif.: Brooks/Cole Publishing Co., 1969.

Sears, Robert, Eleanor E. Maccoby, and Harry Levin. *Patterns of Child Rearing.* New York: Harper & Row, Publishers, 1957.

Skinner, B. F. *The Technology of Teaching.* New York: Appleton-Century-Crofts, 1968.

Stone, L. Joseph, and Church, Joseph. *Childhood and Adolescence.* 2nd ed. New York: Random House, 1968.

Yarrow, Leon J. "Research in Dimensions of Early Maternal Care." *Merrill-Palmer Quarterly of Behavior and Development* 9 (1963): 101–114.

Personality Development

When personality is defined as all that one is, the student is faced with an encompassing term that nearly defies explication. Gordon Allport (1937, p. 48) calls personality the "dynamic organization within the individual or those psychosocial systems that determine his unique adjustment to his environment." The sum total of a person's ways of behavior is what we mean by personality. A further and perhaps more relevant emphasis that must be considered is that what a person is depends on that which is outwardly evident—his measurable characteristics, physique, talents, abilities, and qualities—and what is concealed or related to his "inner dimensions" (Jersild 1960)—his drives, emotional tendencies, impulses, feelings, and unconscious motivations. Baller and Charles (1968, p. 397) say, "He is that unique combination of all the characteristics that are outwardly evident, and he *is* at the same all that is concealed in his inner and relatively private experience."

Although there is considerable evidence (Knop 1946; Birns 1965) that many characteristics of adult personality are present in infancy, much data suggests that the interrelationships between the individual and his environment are also important in forming these characteristics. And yet it would be difficult to turn away from some of the biological facts about differences in infants.* One early life task is to assume

---

* The data presented by R. J. Williams to the 1960 Berkeley (California) Conference on Personality Development in Childhood indicates that in every system of the body — skeletal, digestive, muscular, circulatory, respiratory, endocrine, and nervous — there are wide variations between people and that every person is endowed with a distinctive set of systems. Baller and Charles (1968, p. 401) quote from his address: "Can it be that this fact is inconsequential in relation to the problem of personality differences?"

a "proper" sex role. For example, girls are expected to be petite and dainty; therefore, a girl whose body type and demeanor are not typically female might find herself uncomfortable in assuming the typical role. A boy who has grown into his preadolescent years as mild and diligent with an endomorphic body type may have difficulties in assuming the role that is expected of him as a junior high school student—a bouncing, jaunty, tussling boy.

It seems clear that the parent–child relationship plays a significant part in the overall personality development of the child. Such trait patterns of personality as dominance–submissiveness, sociability–isolation, aggression–passiveness, anxiety–complacence, and dependence–independence have received much attention. The seriousness (at least in Western culture) of overdependency on parents beyond the early childhood years has resulted in a plethora of research data. In general, as the child matures, his affection–seeking behavior shifts to approval–seeking behavior; his dependence shifts from his parents (mother, generally) to his peers. This shift to independence so highly valued in Western society does not happen by chance but through the patterns of interaction between mother, family, and child.

Finally, we need to note the inner aspect of personality. The child's view of his self is mirrored by all that he experiences. In his early years the child processes what goes on within him and around him, and his interpretation constitutes his emerging life style. Erich Fromm (1947, p. 237) organizes the relationship between a person's self-perceptions, reflected by the forces that surround him, and his developmental tasks in maturing: "Man's main task in life is to give birth to himself, to become what he potentially is."

Sex-Role Development*

The interest in the psychosexual development of human beings has intrigued mankind since time began. Freud once said (1933, p. 113), "When you meet a human being, the first distinction you make is 'male or female?' and you are accustomed to make the distinction with unhesitating certainty." Even though in many ways the distinctions between the sexes are becoming blurred, we still tend to believe that "boys will be boys." One sociologist (Sexton 1969) has published an entire volume devoted to what she calls the boy-school syndrome; and often a school teacher totals the number of girls and boys in class, and should the girls prevail he breathes a sigh of relief and knows that a modicum of peace and gentility will prevail.

According to Dorothy Rogers (1969, pp. 230–31) there is no primary "genetic or other innate mechanism which preordains a psychosexual differentiation." On the other hand, Erikson (1959) and other neo-Freudians† emphatically state that the sexual organs of males and females contribute to their psychosexual development. Margaret Mead (1949), however, describing her New Guinea experiences among the Arapesh, Mundugumor, and Tchambuli tribes, comments that both Arapesh men and women are gentle, cooperative, and

---

* For a biological/physiological discussion of the sex-role development of women see Lionel Tiger, "Male Dominance? Yes, Alas. A Sexist Plot? No" (*New York Times Magazine*, 25 October 1970), p. 35.

† Lidz (1968, p. 208) refers to the child's sex as being genetically determined but "biological factors only influence the gender identity." McKeachie and Doyle, in *Psychology* (Reading, Mass.: Addison-Wesley Publishing Co., 1966), p. 24, say, "If men are inherently more aggressive, more competitive, more dominant, and less emotional than women, we should expect them to display these characteristics in all societies."

loving. They would think it odd that men and women should be expected to be different in personality. In contrast, the Mundugumor men are fierce warriors and the women are not in the least gentle and do not enjoy being mothers. If we observed them, Dr. Mead says, we would consider that both men and women were more masculine than feminine.

In this text we adopt a middle point of view, holding that there is both a strong cultural background to behavior and a definite biological background.* The cultural influences on sex-role development are more easily subject to observation; the biological influences are still in the realm of conjecture from an empirical point of view. For instance, both male and female infants "establish their initial and principal identification with the mother" (Mead 1935). We might fairly assume that in at least the first two years of a child's life in the nuclear family (mother, father, child living under one roof) the mother's attention to her child is irrespective of the baby's sex. In Western culture there is no readily observable difference in nurture owing to the sex of the infant (Lynn 1969). From the moment toilet training starts, however, there seem to be concerted efforts to foster masculinity in the boys.

In the process of growing up, males tend to identify with both their mothers and fathers, whereas females identify more closely with the mother. It is not unusual for boys of three and four years to express the wish to grow up to be a mother, because both boys and girls start life in this symbiotic relationship with their mothers. Society casts little girls into "little girl" roles and most adopt the role rather easily. David Lynn (1969, p. 97) maintains that boys have a harder time achieving identification with their fathers than girls do with their mothers, because the wish to retain the childhood pleasure of mother–son identity are not easily cast off. But the little boy sees himself like his father anatomically and otherwise, and his gender identity is consolidated; he begins to deny his dependency on his mother; he even begins to hate girls: he is well on his way toward establishing a secure gender identity.

What has just been described represents the resolution of the Oedipal attachment. Freud recognized what was evident in Sophocles' *Oedipus* and Shakespeare's *Hamlet*: in the course of the "normal" family constellation a little child develops a strong sexualized love for the parent of the opposite sex.

---

* The sex of the developing fetus depends on the presence of either the x or y chromosome in the sperm (thus, the sex of the child is in no way related to the mother). Lidz (1968, p. 210) maintains that the y chromosome ensures the secretion of androgen from the fetal testes, which influences the development of the male internal and external organs. The relationship between certain hormones and sexual circuitry seems well established. See M. Diamond, "A Critical Evaluation of the Ontogeny of Human Sexual Behavior," *Quarterly Review of Biology*, 40 (1965): 147–75 and William Young, Robert Goy, and Charles Phoenix, "Hormones and Sexual Behavior," *Science,* 143 (1964): 212–18. Injections of androgen into female monkeys produce offspring who, although they are biological females, show male behavior patterns (sexual mounting behavior).

These feelings of intense love are accompanied by jealousy, guilt, and anxiety. In order to emotionally survive this trauma, the child pushes these sexual feelings below the level of consciousness (Lidz 1968, p. 234)* and thus identifies with the parent of the same sex. A girl has to model herself after her mother, with whom she has had this early symbiotic relationship, and still transfer her love to her father. Her brother, by contrast, had the same early relationship with his mother, but he has to shift his identification to his father in his sex-role development cycle. In both cases one of the vital tasks of maturation is to become a discrete individual despite the variety of attachments that have been described.

The step toward self-realization and independence and the temporary resolution of one's erotic attachments to his parents has been called "the family romance." Whether conscious or unconscious, whether Oedipal or not, it may be a necessary trauma in the history of each human's development.

---

* This formulation is quite controversial and is rejected by Jungians, Adlerians, and more recently by ego psychologists.

"Mummy," I said that night when she was tucking me up, "do you think if I prayed hard God would send Daddy back to the war?"

My Oedipus Complex

by Frank O'Connor

Father was in the army all through the war—the first war, I mean—so, up to the age of five, I never saw much of him, and what I saw did not worry me. Sometimes I woke and there was a big figure in khaki peering down at me in the candlelight. Sometimes in the early morning I heard the slamming of the front door and the clatter of nailed boots down the cobbles of the lane. These were Father's entrances and exits. Like Santa Claus he came and went mysteriously.

In fact, I rather liked his visits, though it was an uncomfortable squeeze between Mother and him when I got into the big bed in the early morning. He smoked, which gave him a pleasant musty smell, and shaved, an operation of astounding interest. Each time he left a trail of souvenirs—model tanks and Gurkha knives with handles made of bullet cases, and German helmets and cap badges and button-sticks, and all sorts of military equipment —carefully stowed away in a long box on top of the wardrobe, in case they ever came in handy. There was a bit of the magpie about Father; he expected everything to come in handy. When his back was turned, Mother let me get a chair and rummage through his treasures. She didn't seem to think so highly of them as he did.

The war was the most peaceful period of my life. The window of my attic faced southeast. My mother had curtained it, but that had small effect. I always woke with the first light and, with all the responsibilities of the previous day melted, feeling myself rather like the sun, ready to illumine and rejoice. Life never seemed so simple and clear and full of possibilities as then. I put my feet out from under the clothes—I called them Mrs. Left and Mrs. Right—and invented dramatic situations for them in which they discussed the problems of the day. At least Mrs.

Right did; she was very demonstrative, but I hadn't the same control of Mrs. Left, so she mostly contented herself with nodding agreement.

They discussed what Mother and I should do during the day, what Santa Claus should give a fellow for Christmas, and what steps should be taken to brighten the home. There was that little matter of the baby, for instance. Mother and I could never agree about that. Ours was the only house in the terrace without a new baby, and Mother said we couldn't afford one till Father came back from the war because they cost seventeen and six. That showed how simple she was. The Geneys up the road had a baby, and everyone knew they couldn't afford seventeen and six. It was probably a cheap baby, and Mother wanted something really good, but I felt she was too exclusive. The Geneys' baby would have done us fine.

Having settled my plans for the day, I got up, put a chair under the attic window, and lifted the frame high enough to stick out my head. The window overlooked the front gardens of the terrace behind ours, and beyond these it looked over a deep valley to the tall, red-brick houses terraced up the opposite hillside, which were all still in shadow, while those at our side of the valley were all lit up, though with long strange shadows that made them seem unfamiliar; rigid and painted.

After that I went into Mother's room and climbed into the big bed. She woke and I began to tell her of my schemes. By this time, though I never seem to have noticed it, I was petrified in my nightshirt, and I thawed as I talked until, the last frost melted, I fell asleep beside her and woke again only when I heard her below in the kitchen, making the breakfast.

After breakfast we went into town; heard Mass at St. Augustine's and said a prayer for Father, and did the shopping. If the afternoon was fine we either went for a walk in the country or a visit to Mother's great friend in the convent, Mother St. Dominic. Mother had them all praying for Father, and every night, going to bed, I asked God to send him back safe from the war to us. Little, indeed, did I know what I was praying for!

One morning, I got into the big bed, and there, sure enough, was Father in his usual Santa Claus manner, but later, instead of uniform, he put on his best blue suit, and Mother was as pleased as anything. I saw nothing to be pleased about, because, out of uniform, Father was altogether less interesting, but she only beamed, and explained that our prayers had been answered and off we went to Mass to thank God for having brought Father safely home.

The irony of it! That very day when he came in to dinner he took off his boots and put on his slippers, donned the dirty old cap he wore about the house to save him from colds, crossed his legs, and began to talk gravely to Mother, who looked anxious. Naturally, I disliked her looking anxious, because it destroyed her good looks, so I interrupted him.

"Just a moment, Larry!" she said gently.

This was only what she said when we had boring visitors, so I attached no importance to it and went on talking.

"Do be quiet, Larry!" she said impatiently. "Don't you hear me talking to Daddy?"

This was the first time I had heard those ominous words, "talking to Daddy," and I couldn't help feeling that if this was how God answered prayers, he couldn't listen to them very attentively.

"Why are you talking to Daddy?" I asked with as great a show of indifference as I could muster.

"Because Daddy and I have business to discuss. Now, don't interrupt again!"

In the afternoon, at Mother's request, Father took me for a walk. This time we went into town instead of out into the country, and I thought at first, in my usual optimistic way, that it might be an improvement. It was nothing of the sort. Father and I had quite different notions of a walk in town. He had no proper interest in trams, ships, and horses, and the only thing that seemed to divert him was talking to fellows as old as himself. When I wanted to stop he simply went on, dragging me behind him by the hand; when he wanted to stop I had no alternative but to do the same. I noticed that it seemed to be a sign that he wanted to stop for a long time whenever he leaned against a wall. The second time I saw him do it I got wild. He seemed to be settling himself forever. I pulled him by the coat and trousers, but, unlike Mother who, if you were too persistent, got into a wax and said: 'Larry, if you don't behave yourself, I'll give you a good slap," Father had an extraordinary capacity for amiable inattention. I sized him up and wondered would I cry, but he seemed to be too remote to be annoyed even by that. Really, it was like going for a walk with a mountain! He either ignored the wrenching and pummeling entirely, or else glanced down with a grin of amusement from his peak. I had never met anyone so absorbed in himself as he seemed.

At teatime, "talking to Daddy" began again, complicated this time by the fact that he had an evening paper, and every few minutes he put it down and told Mother something new out of it. I felt this was foul play. Man for man, I was prepared to compete with him any time for Mother's attention, but when he had it all made up for him by other people it left me no chance. Several times I tried to change the subject without success.

"You must be quiet while Daddy is reading, Larry," Mother said impatiently.

It was clear that she either genuinely liked talking to Father better than talking to me, or else that he had some terrible hold on her which made her afraid to admit the truth.

"Mummy," I said that night when she was tucking me up, "do you think if I prayed hard God would send Daddy back to the war?"

She seemed to think about that for a moment.

"No, dear," she said with a smile, "I don't think he would."

"Why wouldn't he, Mummy?"

"Because there isn't a war any longer, dear."

"But, Mummy, couldn't God make another war, if He liked?"

"He wouldn't like to, dear. It's not God who makes wars, but bad people."

"Oh!" I said.

I was disappointed about that. I began to think that God wasn't quite what he was cracked up to be.

Next morning I woke at my usual hour, feeling like a bottle of champagne. I put out my feet and invented a long conversation in which Mrs. Right talked of the trouble she had with her own father till she put him in the Home. I didn't quite know what the Home was but it sounded the right place for Father. Then I got my chair and stuck my head out of the attic window. Dawn was just breaking, with a guilty air that made me feel I had caught it in the act. My head bursting with stories and schemes, I stumbled in next door, and in the half-darkness scrambled into the big bed. There was no room at Mother's side so I had to get between her and Father. For the time being I had forgotten about him, and for several minutes I sat bolt upright, racking my brains to know what I could do with him. He was taking up more than his fair share of the bed, and I couldn't get comfortable, so I gave him several kicks that made him grunt and stretch. He made room all right, though. Mother waked and felt for me. I settled back comfortably in the warmth of the bed with my thumb in my mouth.

"Mummy!" I hummed, loudly and contentedly.

"Ssh! dear," she whispered. "Don't wake Daddy!"

This was a new development, which threatened to be even more serious than "talking to Daddy." Life without my early-morning conferences was unthinkable.

"Why?" I asked severely.

"Because poor Daddy is tired."

This seemed to me a quite inadequate reason, and I was sickened by the sentimentality of her "poor Daddy." I never liked that sort of gush; it always struck me as insincere.

"Oh!" I said lightly. Then in my most winning tone: "Do you know where I want to go with you today, Mummy?"

"No, dear," she sighed.

"I want to go down the Glen and fish for thorny-backs with my new net, and then I want to go out to the Fox and Hounds, and—"

"Don't-wake-Daddy!" she hissed angrily, clapping her hand across my mouth.

But it was too late. He was awake, or nearly so. He grunted and reached for the matches. Then he stared incredulously at his watch.

"Like a cup of tea, dear?" asked Mother in a meek, hushed voice I had never heard her use before. It sounded almost as though she were afraid.

"Tea?" he exclaimed indignantly. "Do you know what the time is?"

"And after that I want to go up the Rathcooney Road," I said loudly, afraid I'd forget something in all those interruptions.

"Go to sleep at once, Larry!" she said sharply.

I began to snivel. I couldn't concentrate, the way that pair went on, and smothering my early-morning schemes was like burying a family from the cradle.

Father said nothing, but lit his pipe and sucked it, looking out into the shadows without minding Mother or me. I knew he was mad. Every time I made a remark Mother hushed me irritably. I was mortified. I felt it wasn't fair; there was even something sinister in it. Every time I had pointed out to her the waste of making two beds when we could both sleep in one, she had told me it was healthier like that, and now here was this man, this stranger, sleeping with her without the least regard for her health!

He got up early and made tea, but though he brought Mother a cup he brought none for me.

"Mummy," I shouted, "I want a cup of tea, too."

"Yes, dear," she said patiently. "You can drink from Mummy's saucer."

That settled it. Either Father or I would have to leave the house. I didn't want to drink from Mother's saucer; I wanted to be treated as an equal in my own home, so, just to spite her, I drank it all and left none for her. She took that quietly, too.

But that night when she was putting me to bed she said gently:

"Larry, I want you to promise me something."

"What is it?" I asked.

"Not to come in and disturb poor Daddy in the morning. Promise?"

"Poor Daddy" again! I was becoming suspicious of everything involving that quite impossible man.

"Why?" I asked.

"Because poor Daddy is worried and tired and he doesn't sleep well."

"Why doesn't he, Mummy?"

"Well, you know, don't you, that while he was at the war Mummy got the pennies from the Post Office?"

"From Miss MacCarthy?"

"That's right. But now, you see, Miss MacCarthy hasn't any more pennies, so Daddy must go out and find us some. You know what would happen if he couldn't?"

"No," I said, "tell us."

"Well, I think we might have to go out and beg for them like the poor old woman on Fridays. We wouldn't like that, would we?"

"No," I agreed. "We wouldn't."

"So you'll promise not to come in and wake him?"

"Promise."

Mind you, I meant that. I knew pennies were a serious matter, and I was all against having to go out and beg like the old woman on Fridays. Mother laid out all my toys in a complete ring round the bed so that, whatever way I got out, I was bound to fall over one of them.

When I woke I remembered my promise all right. I got up and sat on the floor and played—for hours, it seemed to me. Then I got my chair and looked out the attic window for more hours. I wished it was time for Father to wake; I wished someone would make me a cup of tea. I didn't feel in the least like the sun; instead, I was bored and so very, very cold! I simply longed for the warmth and depth of the big featherbed.

At long last I could stand it no longer. I went into the next room. As there was still no room at Mother's side I climbed over her and she woke with a start.

"Larry," she whispered, gripping my arm very tightly, "what did you promise?"

"But I did, Mummy," I wailed, caught in the very act. "I was quiet for ever so long."

"Oh, dear, and you're perished!" she said sadly, feeling me all over. "Now, if I let you stay will you promise not to talk?"

"But I want to talk, Mummy," I wailed.

"That has nothing to do with it," she said with a firmness that was new to me. "Daddy wants to sleep. Now do you understand that?"

I understood it only too well. I wanted to talk, he wanted to sleep —whose house was it, anyway?

"Mummy," I said with equal firmness, "I think it would be healthier for Daddy to sleep in his own bed."

That seemed to stagger her, because she said nothing for a while.

"Now, once for all," she went on, "you're to be perfectly quiet or go back to your own bed. Which is it to be?"

The injustice of it got me down. I had convicted her out of her own mouth of inconsistency and unreasonableness, and she hadn't even attempted to reply. Full of spite, I gave Father a kick, which she didn't notice but which made him grunt and open his eyes in alarm.

"What time is it?" he asked in a panic-stricken voice, not looking at Mother but at the door, as if he saw someone there.

"It's early yet," she replied soothingly. "It's only the child. Go to sleep again. . . . Now, Larry," she added, getting out of bed, "you've wakened Daddy and you must go back."

This time, for all her quiet air, I knew she meant it, and I knew that my principal rights and privileges were as good as lost unless I asserted them at once. As she lifted me, I gave a screech, enough to wake the dead, not to mind Father. He groaned.

"That damn child! Doesn't he ever sleep?"

"It's only a habit, dear," she said quietly, though I could see she was vexed.

"Well, it's time he got out of it," shouted Father, beginning to heave in the bed. He suddenly gathered all the bedclothes about him, turned to the wall, and then looked back over his shoulder with nothing showing only two small, spiteful, dark eyes. The man looked very wicked.

To open the bedroom door, Mother had to let me down, and I broke free and dashed for the farthest corner, screeching. Father sat bolt upright in bed.

"Shut up, you little puppy!" he said in a choking voice.

I was so astonished that I stopped screeching. Never, never had anyone spoken to me in that tone before. I looked at him incredulously and saw his face convulsed with rage. It was only then that I fully realized how God had coddled me, listening to my prayers for the safe return of this monster.

"Shut up, you!" I bawled, beside myself.

"What's that you said?" shouted Father, making a wild leap out of the bed.

"Mick, Mick!" cried Mother. "Don't you see the child isn't used to you?"

"I see he's better fed than taught," snarled Father, waving his arms wildly. "He wants his bottom smacked."

All his previous shouting was as nothing to these obscene words referring to my person. They really made my blood boil.

"Smack your own!" I screamed hysterically. "Smack your own! Shut up! Shut up!"

At this he lost his patience and let fly at me. He did it with the lack of conviction you'd expect of a man under Mother's horrified eyes, and it ended up as a mere tap, but the sheer indignity of being struck at all by a stranger, a total stranger who had cajoled his way back from the war into our big bed as a result of my innocent intercession, made me completely dotty. I shrieked and shrieked, and danced in my bare feet, and Father, looking awkward and hairy in nothing but a short grey army shirt, glared down at me like a mountain out for murder. I think it must have been then that I realized that he was jealous too. And there stood Mother in her nightdress, looking as if her heart was broken between us. I hoped she felt as she looked. It seemed to me that she deserved it all.

From that morning out my life was a hell. Father and I were enemies, open and avowed. We conducted a series of skirmishes against one another, he trying to steal my time with Mother and I his. When she was sitting on my bed, telling me a story, he took to looking for some pair of old boots which he alleged he had left behind him at the beginning of the war. While he talked to Mother I played loudly with my toys to show my total lack of concern. He created a terrible scene one evening when he came in from work and found me at his box, playing with his regimental badges, Gurkha knives and button-sticks. Mother got up and took the box from me.

"You mustn't play with Daddy's toys unless he lets you, Larry," she said severely. "Daddy doesn't play with yours."

For some reason Father looked at her as if she had struck him and then turned away with a scowl.

"Those are not toys," he growled, taking down the box again to see had I lifted anything. "Some of those curios are very rare and valuable."

But as time went on I saw more and more how he managed to alienate Mother and me. What made it worse was that I couldn't grasp his method or see what attraction he had for Mother. In every possible way he was less winning than I. He had a common accent and made noises at his tea. I thought for a while that it might be the newspapers she was interested in, so I made up bits of news of my own to read to her. Then I thought it might be the smoking, which I personally thought attractive, and took his pipes and went round the house dribbling into them till he caught me. I even made noises at my tea, but Mother only told me I was disgusting. It all seemed to hinge round that unhealthy habit of sleeping together, so I made a point of dropping into their bedroom and nosing round, talking to myself, so that they wouldn't know I was watching them, but they were never up to anything that I could see. In the end it beat me. It seemed to depend on being grown-up and giving people rings, and I realized I'd have to wait.

But at the same time I wanted him to see that I was only waiting, not giving up the fight. One evening when he was being particularly obnoxious, chattering away well above my head, I let him have it.

"Mummy," I said, "do you know what I'm going to do when I grow up?"

"No, dear," she replied. "What?"

"I'm going to marry you," I said quietly.

Father gave a great guffaw out of him, but he didn't take me in. I knew it must only be pretence. And Mother, in spite of everything, was pleased. I felt she was probably relieved to know that one day Father's hold on her would be broken.

"Won't that be nice?" she said with a smile.

"It'll be very nice," I said confidently. "Because we're going to have lots and lots of babies."

"That's right, dear," she said placidly. "I think we'll have one soon, and then you'll have plenty of company."

I was no end pleased about that because it showed that in spite of the way she gave in to Father she still considered my wishes. Besides, it would put the Geneys in their place.

It didn't turn out like that, though. To begin with, she was very preoccupied—I supposed about where she would get the seventeen and six—and though Father took to staying out late in the evenings it did me no particular good. She stopped taking me for walks, became as touchy as blazes, and smacked me for nothing at all. Sometimes I wished I'd never mentioned the confounded baby—I seemed to have a genius for bringing calamity on myself.

And calamity it was! Sonny arrived in the most appalling hullabaloo—even that much he couldn't do without a fuss—and from the first moment I disliked him. He was a difficult child—so far as I was concerned he was always difficult—and demanded far too much attention. Mother was simply silly about him, and couldn't see when he was only showing off. As company he was worse than useless. He slept all day, and I had to go round the house on tiptoe to avoid waking him. It wasn't any longer a question of not waking Father. The slogan now was "Don't-wake-Sonny!" I couldn't understand why the child wouldn't sleep at the proper time, so whenever Mother's back was turned I woke him. Sometimes to keep him awake I pinched him as well. Mother caught me at it one day and gave me a most unmerciful flaking.

One evening, when Father was coming in from work, I was playing trains in the front garden. I let on not to notice him; instead, I pretended to be talking to myself, and said in a loud voice: "If another bloody baby comes into this house, I'm going out."

Father stopped dead and looked at me over his shoulder.

"What's that you said?" he asked sternly.

"I was only talking to myself," I replied, trying to conceal my panic. "It's private."

He turned and went in without a word. Mind you, I intended it as a solemn warning, but its effect was quite different. Father started being quite nice to me. I could understand that, of course. Mother was quite sickening about Sonny. Even at mealtimes she'd get up and gawk at him in the cradle with an idiotic smile, and tell Father to do the same. He was always polite about it, but he looked so puzzled you could see he didn't know what she was talking about. He complained of the way Sonny cried at night, but she only got cross and said that Sonny never cried except when there was something up with him—which was a flaming lie, because Sonny never had anything up with him, and only cried for attention. It was really painful to see how simple-minded she was. Father wasn't attractive, but he had a fine intelligence. He saw through Sonny, and now he knew that I saw through him as well.

One night I woke with a start. There was someone beside me in the bed. For one wild moment I felt sure it must be Mother, having come to her senses and left Father for good, but then I heard Sonny in convulsions in the next room, and Mother saying: "There! There! There!" and I knew it wasn't she. It was Father. He was lying beside me, wide awake, breathing hard and apparently as mad as hell.

After a while it came to me what he was mad about. It was his turn now. After turning me out of the big bed, he had been turned out himself. Mother had no consideration now for anyone but that poisonous pup, Sonny. I couldn't help feeling sorry for Father. I had been through it all myself, and even at that age I was magnanimous. I bcgan to stroke him down and say: "There! There!" He wasn't exactly responsive.

"Aren't you asleep either?" he snarled.

"Ah, come on and put your arm around us, can't you?" I said, and he did, in a sort of way. Gingerly, I suppose, is how you'd describe it. He was very bony but better than nothing.

At Christmas he went out of his way to buy me a really nice model railway.

Discussion

Frank O'Connor, a well-known short story writer of our time, spent his youth in Ireland and set many of his stories in the Irish milieu of his youth. Writing about his own work, O'Connor says that most of his stories are written and rewritten many times over, but "My Oedipus Complex" was one of the few stories that was set down as it came to him and needed little revision.

Although the story seems to be set in Ireland after the First World War, its central theme of a small boy coming to identify and join forces with his father is universal. O'Connor appropriately named the story for Freud's theory of the family romance, the Oedipus complex, because the story is gently built on this conceptual framework. According to Freud, the first love object of both male and female children is the mother, because all little children are so dependent on the mother and are in close association with her in the first three to four years of their lives.

In this story the father is away during Larry's early years, making the relationship between mother and son more intense and exclusive than is normally the case. Larry views his father as Santa Claus-like, a pleasant but once-a-year visitor. Fortunately for Larry his father returns from the war at the psychologically appropriate time for Larry to make the transition from mother to father admiration and identification. This transition is not easy for Larry at first, because his father is not a familiar adult in his life, and Larry finds his ways strange and unpleasant. In fact, Larry considers his father to be the source of his own loss of status in his mother's eyes. In order to recoup his place in his mother's affection he attempts to model his behavior on his father's example. He borrows his father's pipe and pretends to smoke it. He mimics his style in conversation. Finally he declares that he intends to marry his mother.

As the Oedipus complex develops, the child's craving for the parent of the opposite sex brings him into conflict with the parent of the same sex. The resolution occurs when the boy is able to repress the desire to possess his mother in favor of identifying with the masculinity the male parent represents, a process that takes place over a period of time. In this story we are made aware of the long period in which Larry unhappily tries out many poses and postures to supersede his father in his mother's affection. Although written in a humorous vein, the story genuinely portrays Larry's feeling of jealousy and rage. The birth of the new baby finally creates the condition that induces Larry to form a genuine alignment with his father. In the shadow of mutual rejection by the mother, Larry and his father seek each other's company and comfort.

Springboards for Inquiry

(1) In this story Larry declares his intention of marrying his mother. Little girls, too, at this age will very commonly suggest marriage with their fathers. How, according to Freudian theory, is the girl's Oedipus (or Electra) complex resolved?

(2) How do you view the classic Freudian definition of the Oedipus complex? Neo-Freudians have challenged and discarded the Oedipus Complex as a stage in the personality development of all children. How would Erich Fromm* and Harry Stack Sullivan† view the period of childhood to which Freud assigned the Oedipal situation?

(3) Sex typing refers to the way in which sex roles are taught and learned. We know that there is often a gap between the early sex typing we perpetuate in our culture and the sex roles which adults realistically must assume in our society. If those involved in the early experiences of children reevaluated this gap what changes might they make in early expectations and experiences for girls and boys?

(4) What aspects of sex typing in the early years would you consider desirable for our culture?

---

* Fromm, Erich, "The Oedipus Complex and the Oedipus Myth." In Ruth Anshen (ed) *The Family: Its Function & Destiny*. Vol. 5, New York: Harper & Row, Publishers, Inc. 1945.

† Hall, Calvin and Gardner Lindzey, *Theories of Personality*, in the chapter "Social Psychological Theories," New York: John Wiley & Sons, Inc., 1961, and Sullivan, Harry S., *The Interpersonal Theory of Psychiatry*. New York: W. W. Norton & Co., Inc., 1953.

Growth of Independence

It is nearly axiomatic to say that the growth of independence in a child is directly related to the manner in which the parents raise the child. A number of possible variables might delineate further the phrase *manner in which,* but for the purposes of this discussion we shall examine the matter of dependence–independence. Two major sources of information are the Sears, Maccoby, and Levin study (1957) and the study by Whiting and Child (1953). We define independence as "confidence in one's ability to cope with problems without unusual help from others" (Rogers 1969, p. 324).

Our essay on the toddler indicates that in those critical years when a child is naturally exploring and developing, an all-important sense of autonomy needs to be developed. Yet it is precisely at this age, when he is acquiring new skills and needs the opportunity to practice these skills, that the child's ways come into severe conflict with the patience and love of his parents. If the child meets continual rejection (Hutt 1969) at this time in his life, the development of a sense of trust may be permanently thwarted. Let us reiterate here that since the mother is the primary socializing agent during the infancy and early childhood, much of the research* revolves about her role in the development of independence.

Jerome Kagan and Howard Moss (1962) did a longitudinal study (at the Fels Research Institute) of personality development from birth to early adulthood, and

* For some interesting questions about the validity of mothers' responses and researchers' interpretations see Marian Yarrow *et al. Child Rearing: An Inquiry into Research and Methods* (San Francisco: Jossey-Bass Inc., Publishers, 1968), pp. 140–42.

they show interesting comparisons between the effects on male and female children of maternal child-rearing practices. The authors describe four maternal attitudes, which they characterize as protection, restrictiveness, hostility, and acceleration.* Maternal protectiveness, typified by "unsolicited and unnecessary nurturance," caused male children to become passive and dependent at ages six through ten, whereas maternal protectiveness was not so predictive of passive, dependent behavior in girls. When faced with restrictiveness and punishment for deviation from the mother's standards, the male child became more dependent on others, while the female child showed "independence and reluctance to withdraw from stress." This observation should be compared with the previous discussion of sex-role development.

We now shift to the effect of the total home atmosphere. Other studies (Lewin et al. 1939; Foster 1927) have observed the behavior of children in a variety of artificially designed social climates, but the work of Marian Radke (1946), who studied parental authority and its relation to the behavior of children in preschool situations, is the most relevant to our purposes. Although the child from an autocratic home† was rated as "unpopular . . . more frequently fighting and quarreling, more inconsiderate, more emotionally unstable, . . . he is uninhibited and bold in meeting preschool situations. He does not show rivalry. . . but rather assumes his own autocratic domination and mastery over others, . . . in this way rating somewhat higher on leadership . . ." (Radke 1946, pp. 76–77). Findings show that children from democratic homes are "more popular, considerate, compliant, emotionally stable, sensitive to the opinions of others, and rivalrous and less quarrelsome with other children" (Radke 1946, p. 77).

One may conclude that there is a relationship between home atmosphere and child behavior. The terms *uninhibited, bold,* and *assumes an autocratic domination* listed for the child from an autocratic family lead to the conclusion that certain attributes of independence are nurtured by authoritarianism of a mild order. Extreme freedom and restrictive family control can produce poor degrees of independence. Parents with strong neurotic and psychotic traits seem to depress the urge for independence in children. For example, if a mother sees her child's submissive behavior as an expression of love, or if a father gains a feeling of power when his children show that they depend on him, and they thus encourage dependent behavior, dependency will follow. Similarly, parents who interpret independence or assertiveness as a threat to their authority tend to reward compliant behavior only, thus reinforcing such dependence. Finally,

---

* The student might enjoy comparing this study with the discussions Bruno Bettelheim has with mothers in *Dialogues with Mothers* (Glencoe: Free Press, 1962). While on the topic of the maternal role, it would be well to mention the intricate volumes of John Bowlby, *Attachment and Loss* (New York: Basic Books, 1969), wherein he makes careful observations of attachment and loss behavior in children.

† The autocratic home is defined as one "in which a respect for the child's rights and wishes is lacking; in which the child's needs are entirely subordinated to the power of the parent" (Radke 1946, p. 76).

when parents have deep unmet needs for dependency, they often project them onto their children, whom they can control by virtue of their parenthood.

In general, sex differences are apparent in dependency. In the work of Douvan and Adelson (1966), Kagan and Moss (1960), and Douvan (1960), all of whom consider the adolescent's behavior, there is a uniformity of opinion about the greater dependency exhibited by girls as they grow toward adulthood. Our remarks on sex-role development may clarify this statement.

The data related to the growth of independence say that rejection, inconsistency, and domination in extreme form hinder the development of independence. Similarly, license and "smother-love" inhibit the healthy growth of independence. The data show that the ideal pattern for teaching independence is balanced family interaction. Neither patriarchal aloofness nor mother-henning help children to become healthy, independent human beings.

She sensed something different in the atmosphere than she had ever known before . . . a faint notion of what mama had meant when she had said that this would not be visiting.

A Start in Life

by Ruth Suckow

The Switzers were scurrying around to get Daisy ready by the time that Elmer Kruse should get through in town. They had known all week that Elmer might be in for her any day. But they hadn't done a thing until he appeared. "Oh, it was so rainy today, the roads were so muddy, they hadn't thought he'd get in until maybe next week." It would have been the same any other day.

Mrs. Switzer was trying now at the last moment to get all of Daisy's things into the battered telescope that lay on the bed. The bed had not "got made"; and just as soon as Daisy was gone, Mrs. Switzer would have to hurry off to the Woodworths, where she was to wash today. Daisy's things were scattered over the dark brown quilt and the rumpled sheet that were dingy and clammy in this damp weather. So was the whole bedroom with its sloping ceiling, and old-fashioned square-paned windows, the commode that they used for a dresser littered with pin trays, curlers, broken combs, ribbons, smoky lamp, all mixed up together; the door of the closet open, showing the confusion of clothes and shabby shoes. . . . They all slept in this room —Mrs. Switzer and Dwight in the bed, the two girls in the cot against the wall.

"Mama, I can't find the belt to that plaid dress."

"Oh, ain't it somewheres around? Well, I guess you'll have to let it go. If I come across it I can send it out to you. Someone'll be going past there."

She had meant to get Daisy all mended and "fixed up" before she went out to the country. But somehow . . . oh, there was always so much to see to when she came home. Gone all day, washing and cleaning for other people; it didn't leave her much time for her own home.

She was late now. The Woodworths liked to have her get the washing out early so that she could do some cleaning too before she left. But she couldn't help it. She would have to get Daisy off first. She had already had on her wraps ready to go, when Elmer came—her cleaning cap, of a blue faded almost gray, and the ancient black coat with gathered sleeves that she wore over her work dress when she went out to wash.

"What's become of all your underclothes? They ain't all dirty, are they?"

"They are, too. You didn't wash for us last week, mama."

"Well, you'll just have to take along what you've got. Maybe there'll be some way of getting the rest to you."

"Elmers come in every week, don't they?" Daisy demanded.

"Yes, but maybe they won't always be bringing you in."

She jammed what she could into the telescope, thinking with her helpless, anxious fatalism that it would have to do somehow.

"Daisy, you get yourself ready now."

"I am ready, mama, I want to put on my other ribbon."

"Oh, that's 'way down in the telescope somewhere. You needn't be so anxious to fix yourself up. This ain't like going visiting."

Daisy stood at the little mirror preening herself—such a homely child, "all Switzer," skinny, with pale sharp eyes set close together and thin, stringy, reddish hair. But she had never really learned yet how homely she was. She was the oldest, and she got the pick of what clothes were given to the Switzers. Goldie and Dwight envied her. She was important in her small world. She was proud of her blue coat that had belonged to Alice Brooker, the town lawyer's daughter. It hung unevenly above her bony little knees, and the buttons came down too far. Her mother had tried to make it over for her.

Mrs. Switzer looked at her, troubled, but not knowing how she could tell her all the things she ought to be told. Daisy had never been away before except to go to her Uncle Fred's at Lehigh. She seemed to think that this would be the same. She had so many things to learn. Well, she would find them out soon enough—only too soon. Working for other people—she would learn what that meant. Elmer and Edna Kruse were nice young people. They would mean well enough by Daisy. It was a good chance for her to start in. But it wasn't the same.

Daisy was so proud. She thought it was quite a thing to be "starting in to earn." She thought she could buy herself so much with her dollar and a half a week. The other children stood back watching her, round-eyed and impressed. They wished that they were going away, like Daisy.

They heard a car come splashing through the mud on low. "There he is back! Have you got your things on? Goldie—go out and tell him she's coming."

"No, me tell him, me!" Dwight shouted jealously.

"Well—both of you tell him. Land! . . ."

She tried hastily to put on the cover of the bulging telescope and to fasten the straps. One of them broke.

"Well, you'll have to take it the way it is."

It was an old thing, hadn't been used since her husband, Mert, had "left off canvassing" before he died. And he had worn it all to pieces.

'Well, I guess you'll have to go now. He won't want to wait. I'll try and send you out what you ain't got with you." She turned to Daisy. Her face was working. There was nothing else to do, as everyone said. Daisy would have to help, and she might as well learn it now. Only, she hated to see Daisy go off, to have her starting in. She knew what it meant. "Well—you try and work good this summer, so they'll want you to stay. I hope they'll bring you in sometimes."

Daisy's homely little face grew pale with awe, suddenly, at the sight of her mother crying, at something that she dimly sensed in the pressure of her mother's thin strong arms. Her vanity in her new importance was somehow shamed and dampened.

Elmer's big new Buick, mud-splashed but imposing, stood tilted on the uneven road. Mud was thick on the wheels. It was a bad day for driving, with the roads a yellow mass, water lying in all the wheel ruts. The little road that led past these few houses on the outskirts of town, and up over the hill, had a cold, rainy loneliness. Elmer sat in the front seat of the Buick, and in the back was a big box of groceries.

"Got any room to sit in there?" he asked genially. "I didn't get out, it's so muddy here."

"No, don't get out," Mrs. Switzer said hastily. "She can put this right on the floor there in the back." She added, with a timid attempt at courtesy, "Ain't the roads pretty bad out that way?"

"Yes, but farmers get so they don't think so much about the roads."

"I s'pose that's so."

He saw the signs of tears on Mrs. Switzer's face, and they made him anxious to get away. She embraced Daisy hastily again. Daisy climbed over the grocery box and scrunched herself into the seat.

"I guess you'll bring her in with you some time when you're coming," Mrs. Switzer hinted.

"Sure. We'll bring her."

He started the engine. It roared, half died down as the wheels of the car spun in the thick wet mud.

In that moment, Daisy had a startled view of home—the small house standing on a rough rise of land, weathered to a dim color that showed dark streaks from the rain; the narrow sloping front porch whose edge had a soaked, gnawed look; the chickens, grayish-black, pecking at the wet ground; their playthings, stones, a wagon, some old pail covers littered about; a soaked, discolored piece of underwear hanging on the line in the back yard. The yard was tussocky and overhung the road with shaggy long grass where the yellow bank was caved in under it. Goldie and Dwight were gazing at her solemnly. She saw her mother's face—a thin, weak, loving face, drawn with neglected weeping, with its reddened eyes and poor teeth . . . in the old coat and heavy shoes and cleaning cap, her work-worn hand with its big knuckles clutching at her coat. She saw the playthings they had used yesterday, and the old swing that hung from one of the trees, the ropes sodden, the seat in crooked. . . .

The car went off, slipping on the wet clay. She waved frantically, suddenly understanding that she was leaving them. They waved at her.

Mrs. Switzer stood there a little while. Then came the harsh rasp of the old black iron pump that stood out under the box elder tree. She was pumping water to leave for the children before she went off to work.

Daisy held on as the car skidded going down the short clay hill. Elmer didn't bother with chains. He was too used to the roads. But her eyes brightened with scared excitement. When they were down, and Elmer slowed up going along the tracks in the deep wet grass that led to the main road, she looked back, holding on her hat with her small scrawny hand.

Just down this little hill—and home was gone. The big car, the feel of her telescope on the floor under her feet, the fact that she was going out to the country, changed the looks of everything. She saw it all now.

Dunkels' house stood on one side of the road. A closed-up white house. The windows stared blank and cold between the old shutters. There was a chair with a broken straw seat under the fruit trees. The Dunkels were old Catholic people who seldom went anywhere. In the front yard was a clump of tall pines, the rough brown trunks wet, the green branches, dark and shining, heavy with rain, the ground underneath mournfully sodden and black.

The pasture on the other side. The green grass, lush, wet and cold, and the outcroppings of limestone that held little pools of rain water in all the tiny holes. Beyond, the low hills gloomy with timber against the lowering sky.

They slid out onto the main road. They bumped over the small wooden bridge above the swollen creek that came from the pasture. Daisy looked down. She saw the little swirls of foam, the long grass that swished with the water, the old rusted tin cans lodged between the rocks.

She sat up straight and important, her thin, homely little face strained with excitement, her sharp eyes taking in everything. The watery mud holes in the road, the little thickets of plum trees, low and wet, in dark interlacings. She held on fiercely, but made no sound when the car skidded.

She felt the grandeur of having a ride. One wet Sunday, Mr. Brooker had driven them all home from church, she and Goldie and Dwight packed tightly into the back seat of the car, shut in by the side curtains, against which the rain lashed, catching the muddy scent of the roads. Sometimes they could plan to go to town just when Mr. Pattey was going to work in his Ford. Then they would run out and shout eagerly, "Mr. Pattey! Are you going through town?" Sometimes he said, with curt good nature, "Well, pile in"; and they all hopped into the truck back. "He says we can go along with him."

She looked at the black wet fields through which little leaves of bright green corn grew in rows, at showery bushes of sumac along the roadside. A gasoline engine pumping water made a loud desolate sound. There were somber-looking cattle in the wet grass, and lonely, thick-foliaged trees growing here and there in the pastures. She felt her telescope on the floor of the car, the box of groceries beside her. She eyed these with a sharp curiosity. There was a fresh pineapple—something the Switzers didn't often get at home. She wondered if Edna would have it for dinner. Maybe she could hint a little to Edna.

She was out in the country. She

could no longer see her house even if she wanted to—standing dingy, streaked with rain, in its rough grass on the little hill. A lump came into her throat. She had looked forward to playing with Edna's children. But Goldie and Dwight would play all morning without her. She was still proud of being the oldest, of going out with Elmer and Edna; but now there was a forlornness in the pride.

She wished she were in the front seat with Elmer. She didn't see why he hadn't put her there. She would have liked to know who all the people were who lived on these farms; how old Elmer's babies were; and if he and Edna always went to the movies when they went into town on Saturday nights. Elmer must have lots of money to buy a car like this. He had a new house on his farm, too, and Mrs. Metzinger had said that it had plumbing. Maybe they would take her to the movies, too. She might hint about that.

When she had to visit Uncle Fred, she had had to go on the train. She liked this better. She hoped they had a long way to go. She called out to Elmer:

"Say, how much farther is your place?"

"What's that?" He turned around. "Oh, just down the road a ways. Scared to drive in the mud?"

"No, I ain't scared. I like to drive most any way."

She looked at Elmer's back, the old felt hat crammed down carelessly on his head, the back of his neck with the golden hair on the sunburned skin above the blue of his shirt collar. Strong and easy and slouched a little over the steering wheel that he handled so masterly. Elmer and Edna were just young folks; but Mrs. Metzinger said that they had more to start with than most young farmers did, and that they were hustlers. Daisy felt that the pride of this belonged to her too, now.

"Here we are!"

"Oh, is this where you folks live?" Daisy cried eagerly.

The house stood back from the road, beyond a space of bare yard with a little scattering of grass just starting—small, modern, painted a bright new white and yellow. The barn was new, too, a big splendid barn of frescoed brick, with a silo of the same. There were no trees. A raw, desolate wind blew across the back yard as they drove up beside the back door.

Edna had come out on the step. Elmer grinned at her as he took out the box of groceries, and she slightly raised her eyebrows. She said kindly enough:

"Well, you brought Daisy. Hello, Daisy, are you going to stay with us this summer?"

"I guess so," Daisy said importantly. But she suddenly felt a little shy and forlorn as she got out of the car and stood on the bare ground in the chilly wind.

"Yes, I brought her along," Elmer said.

"Are the roads very bad?"

"Kind of bad. Why?"

"Well, I'd like to get over to mama's some time today."

"Oh, I guess they aren't too bad for that."

Daisy pricked up her sharp little ears. Another ride. That cheered her.

"Look in the door," Edna said in a low fond voice, motioning with her head.

Two little round, blond heads were pressed tightly against the screen door. There was a clamor of

"Daddy, daddy!" Elmer grinned with a bashful pride as he stood with the box of groceries, raising his eyebrows with mock surprise and demanding, "Who's this? What you shoutin' 'daddy' for? You don't think daddy's got anything for you, do you?" He and Edna were going into the kitchen together, until Edna remembered and called back hastily:

"Oh, come in, Daisy!"

Daisy stood, a little left out and solitary, there in the kitchen, as Billy, the older of the babies, climbed frantically over Elmer, demanding candy, and the little one toddled smilingly about. Her eyes took in all of it. She was impressed by the shining blue-and-white linoleum, the range with its nickel and enamel, the bright new woodwork. Edna was laughing and scolding at Elmer and the baby. Billy had made his father produce the candy. Daisy's sharp little eyes looked hungrily at the lemon drops and Edna remembered her.

"Give Daisy a piece of your candy," she said.

He would not go up to Daisy. She had to come forward and take one of the lemon drops herself. She saw where Edna put the sack, in a dish high in the cupboard. She hoped they would get some more before long.

"My telescope's out there in the car," she reminded them.

"Oh! Elmer, you go and get it and take it up for her," Edna said.

"What?"

"Her valise—or whatever it is—out in the car."

"Oh, sure," Elmer said with a cheerful grin.

"It's kind of an old telescope," Daisy said conversationally. "I guess it's been used a lot. My papa used to have it. The strap broke when mama was fastening it this morning. We ain't got any suitcase. I had to take this because it was all there was in the house, and mama didn't want to get me a new one."

Edna raised her eyebrows politely. She leaned over and pretended to spat the baby as he came toddling up to her, then rubbed her cheek against his round head with its fuzzy fuzz of hair.

Daisy watched solemnly. "I didn't know both of your children was boys. I thought one of 'em was a girl. That's what there is at home now—one boy and one girl."

"Um-hm," Edna replied absently. "You can go up with Elmer and take off your things, Daisy," she said. "You can stop and unpack your valise now, I guess, if you'd like to. Then you can come down and help me in the kitchen. You know we got you to help me," she reminded.

Daisy, subdued, followed Elmer up the bright new stairs. In the upper hall, two strips of very clean rag rug were laid over the shining yellow of the floor. Elmer had put her telescope in one of the bedrooms.

"There you are!"

She heard him go clattering down the stairs, and then a kind of murmuring and laughing in the kitchen. The back door slammed. She hurried to the window in time to see Elmer go striding off toward the barn.

She looked about her room with intense curiosity. It, too, had a bright varnished floor. She had a bed all her own—a small, old-fashioned bed, left from some old furnishings, that had been put in this room that had the pipes and the hot water tank. She had to see everything, but she had a stealthy look as she tiptoed about, started to open the drawers of the dresser, looked out of her window. She put her coat and hat on the bed. She would rather be down in the kitchen with Edna than unpack her telescope now.

She guessed she would go down where the rest of them were.

Elmer came into the house for dinner. He brought in a cold, muddy, outdoor breath with him. The range was going, but the bright little kitchen seemed chilly, with the white oilcloth on the table, the baby's varnished high chair and his little fat mottled hands.

Edna made a significant little face at Elmer. Daisy did not see. She was standing back from the stove, where Edna was at work, looking at the baby.

"He can talk pretty good, can't he? Dwight couldn't say anything but 'mama' when he was that little."

Edna's back was turned. She said meaningly:

"Now, Elmer's come in for dinner, Daisy, we'll have to hurry. You must help me get on the dinner. You can cut bread and get things on the table. You must help, you know. That's what you are supposed to do."

Daisy looked startled, a little scared and resentful. "Well, I don't know where you keep your bread."

"Don't you remember where I told you to put it this morning? Right over in the cabinet, in that big box. You must watch, Daisy, and learn where things are."

Elmer, a little embarrassed at the look that Edna gave him, whistled as he began to wash his hands at the sink.

"How's daddy's old boy?" he said loudly, giving a poke at the baby's chin.

As Edna passed him, she shook her head and her lips just formed, "Been like that all morning!"

He grinned comprehendingly. Then both their faces became expressionless.

Daisy had not exactly heard, but she looked from one to the other, silent and dimly wondering. The queer ache that had kept starting all through the morning, under her interest in Edna's things and doings, came over her again. She sensed something different in the atmosphere than she had ever known before—some queer difference between the position of herself and of the two babies, a faint notion of what mama had meant when she had said that this would not be visiting.

"I guess I'm going to have the toothache again," she said faintly.

No one seemed to hear her.

Edna whisked off the potatoes, drained the water. . . . "You might bring me a dish, Daisy." Daisy searched a long time while Edna turned impatiently and pointed. Edna put the rest of the things on the table herself. Her young, fresh, capable mouth was tightly closed, and she was making certain resolutions.

Daisy stood hesitating in the middle of the room, a scrawny, unappealing little figure. Billy—fat, blond, in funny, dark blue union-alls—was trotting busily about the kitchen. Daisy swooped down upon him and tried to bring him to the table. He set up a howl. Edna turned, looked astonished, severe.

"I was trying to make him come to the table," Daisy explained weakly.

"You scared him. He isn't used to you. He doesn't like it. Don't cry,

Billy. The girl didn't mean anything."

"Here, daddy'll put him in his place," Elmer said hastily.

Billy looked over his father's shoulder at Daisy with suffused, resentful blue eyes. She did not understand it, and felt strangely at a loss. She had been left with Goldie and Dwight so often. She had always made Dwight go to the table. She had been the boss.

Edna said in a cool, held-in voice, "Put these things on the table, Daisy."

They sat down. Daisy and the other children had always felt it a great treat to eat away from home instead of at their own scanty, hastily set table. They had hung around Mrs. Metzinger's house at noon, hoping to be asked to stay, not offended when told that "it was time for them to run off now." Her pinched little face had a hungry look as she stared at the potatoes and fried ham and pie. But they did not watch and urge her to have more, as Mrs. Metzinger did, and Mrs. Booker when she took pity on the Switzers and had them there. Daisy wanted more pie. But none of them seemed to be taking more, and so she said nothing. She remembered what her mother had said, with now a faint comprehension. "You must remember you're out working for other folks, and it won't be like it is at home."

After dinner Edna said, "Now you can wash the dishes, Daisy."

She went into the next room with the children. Daisy, as she went hesitatingly about the kitchen alone, could hear Edna's low contented humming as she sat in there rocking, the baby in her lap. The bright kitchen was empty and lonely now. Through the window, Daisy could see the great barn looming up against the rainy sky. She hoped that they would drive to Edna's mother's soon.

She finished as soon as she could and went into the dining room where Edna was sewing on the baby's rompers. Edna went on sewing. Daisy sat down disconsolately. That queer low ache went all through her. She said in a small dismal voice:

"I guess I got the toothache again."

Edna bit off a thread.

"I had it awful hard awhile ago. Mama come pretty near taking me to the dentist."

"That's too bad," Edna murmured politely. But she offered no other condolence. She gave a little secret smile at the baby asleep on a blanket and a pillow in one corner of the shiny leather davenport.

"Is Elmer going to drive into town tomorrow?"

"Tomorrow? I don't suppose so."

"Mama couldn't find the belt of my plaid dress and I thought if he was, maybe I could go along and get it. I'd like to have it."

Daisy's homely mouth drooped at the corners. Her toothache did not seem to matter to anyone. Edna did not seem to want to see that anything was wrong with her. She had expected Edna to be concerned, to mention remedies. But it wasn't toothache, that strange lonesome ache all over her. Maybe she was going to be terribly sick. Mama wouldn't come home for supper to be told about it.

She saw mama's face as in that last glimpse of it—drawn with crying, and yet trying to smile, under the old cleaning cap, her hand holding her coat together . . .

Edna glanced quickly at her. The child was so mortally unattractive, unappealing even in her forlornness. Edna frowned a little, but said kindly:

"Now you might take Billy into the kitchen out of my way, Daisy, and amuse him."

"Well, he cries when I pick him up," Daisy said faintly.

"He won't cry this time. Take him out and help him play with his blocks. You must help me with the children, you know."

"Well, if he'll go with me."

"He'll go with you, won't he, Billy boy? Won't you go with Daisy, sweetheart?"

Billy stared and then nodded. Daisy felt a thrill of comfort as Billy put his little fat hand in hers and trotted into the kitchen beside her. He had the fattest hands, she thought. Edna brought the blocks and put the box down on the floor beside Daisy.

"Now, see if you can amuse him so that I can get my sewing done."

"Shall you and me play blocks, Billy?" Daisy murmured.

He nodded. Then he got hold of the box with one hand, tipped out all the blocks on the floor with a bang and a rattle, and looked at her with a pleased proud smile.

"Oh no, Billy. You mustn't spill out the blocks. Look, you're too little to play with them. No, now—now wait! Let Daisy show you. Daisy'll build you something real nice—shall she?"

He gave a solemn nod of consent.

Daisy set out the blocks on the bright linoleum. She had never had such blocks as these to handle before. Dwight's were only a few old, unmatched, broken ones. Her spirit of leadership came back, and she firmly put away that fat hand of Billy's whenever he meddled with her building. She could make something really wonderful with these blocks.

"No, Billy, you mustn't. See, when Daisy's got it all done, then you can see what the lovely building is."

She put the blocks together with great interest. She knew what she was going to make—it was going to be a new house; no, a new church. Just as she got the walls up, in came that little hand again, and then with a delighted grunt Billy swept the blocks pellmell about the floor. At the clatter, he sat back, pursing his mouth to give an ecstatic "Ooh!"

"Oh, Billy—you mustn't, the building wasn't done! Look, you've spoiled it. Now, you've got to sit 'way off here while I try to build it over again."

Billy's look of triumph turned to surprise and then to vociferous protest as Daisy picked him up and firmly transplanted him to another corner of the room. He set up a tremendous howl. He had never been set aside like that before. Edna came hurrying out. Daisy looked at Edna for justification, but instinctively on the defensive.

"Billy knocked over the blocks. He spoiled the building."

"Wah! Wah!" Billy gave loud heartbroken sobs. The tears ran down his fat cheeks and he held out his arms piteously toward his mother.

"I didn't hurt him," Daisy said, scared.

"Never mind, lover," Edna was crooning. "Of course he can play with his blocks. They're Billy's blocks, Daisy," she said. "He doesn't like to sit and see you put up buildings. He wants to play, too. See, you've made him cry now."

"Do' wanna stay here," Billy wailed.

"Well, come in with mother then." She picked him up, wiping his tears.

"I didn't hurt him," Daisy protested.

"Well, never mind now. You can pick up the blocks and then sweep up the floor, Daisy. You didn't do that when you finished the dishes. Never mind," she was saying to Billy. "Pretty soon daddy'll come in and we'll have a nice ride."

Daisy soberly picked up the blocks and got the broom. What had she done to Billy? He had tried to spoil her building. She had always made Dwight keep back until she had finished. Of course it was Daisy, the oldest, who should lead and manage. There had been no one to hear her side. Everything was different. She winked back tears as she swept, poorly and carelessly.

Then she brightened up as Elmer came tramping up on the back porch and then through the kitchen.

"Edna!"

"She's in there," Daisy offered.

"Want to go now? What? Is the baby asleep?" he asked blankly.

Edna gave him a warning look and the door was closed.

Daisy listened hard. She swept very softly. She could catch only a little of what they said—"Kind of hate to go off . . . I know, but if we once start . . . not a thing all day . . . what we got her for . . ." She had no real comprehension of it. She hurried and put away the broom. She wanted to be sure and be ready to go.

Elmer tramped out, straight past her. She saw from the window that he was backing the car out from the shed. She could hear Edna and Billy upstairs, could hear the baby cry a little as he was wakened. Maybe she ought to go out and get her wraps, too.

Elmer honked the horn. A moment later Edna came hurrying downstairs, in her hat and coat, and Billy in a knitted cap and a red sweater crammed over his union-alls, so that he looked like a little brownie. The baby had on his little coat, too.

Edna called out, "Come in and get this boy, daddy." She did not look at Daisy, but said hurriedly, "We're going for a little ride, Daisy. Have you finished the sweeping? Well, then, you can pick up those pieces in the dining room. We won't be gone so very long. When it's a quarter past five, you start the fire, like I showed you this noon, and slice the potatoes that were left, and the meat. And set the table."

The horn was honked again.

"Yes! Well, we'll be back, Daisy. Come, lover, daddy's in a hurry."

Daisy stood looking after them. Billy clamored to sit beside his daddy. Edna took the baby from Elmer and put him beside her on the back seat. There was room—half of the big back seat. There wasn't anything, really, to be done at home. That was the worst of it. They just didn't want to take her. They all belonged together. They didn't want to take anyone else along. She was an outsider. They all—even the baby—had a freshened look of expectancy.

The engine roared—they had started; slipping on the mud of the drive, then forging straight ahead, around the turn, out of sight.

She went forlornly into the dining

room. The light from the windows was dim now in the rainy, late afternoon. The pink pieces from the baby's rompers were scattered over the gay rug. She got down on her hands and knees, slowly picking them up, sniffing a little. She heard the Big Ben clock in the kitchen ticking loudly.

That dreadful ache submerged her. No one would ask about it, no one would try to comfort her. Before, there had always been mama coming home, anxious, scolding sometimes, but worried over them if they didn't feel right, caring about them. Mama and Goldie and Dwight cared about her—but she was away out in the country, and they were at home. She didn't want to stay here, where she didn't belong. But mama had told her that she must begin helping this summer.

Her ugly little mouth contorted into a grimace of weeping. But silent weeping, without any tears; because she already had the cold knowledge that no one would notice or comfort it.

Discussion

We can predict Daisy's inadequacy as she "scrunched" herself into Elmer's car on her way to "starting to earn." Daisy is unprepared for the independence and the assumption of responsibility that is prematurely thrust on her. Would Daisy be better prepared one year or even two years hence? Probably not.

Daisy's home environment does not provide the atmosphere that fosters healthy striving for independence. We know that feelings of adequacy and willingness to assume responsibility thrive in a home environment that provides an adequate measure of nurture along with approval for independent decision making. Mrs. Switzer's style is "helpless, anxious fatalism." There are few, if any, opportunities for Daisy to assume responsibility for her younger siblings with supportive guidance from Mrs. Switzer. Daisy assumes the role of "boss" by virtue of being the eldest. Mrs. Switzer is a poor model for Daisy since her own ability to cope with her responsibilities is marginal. We may assume that Mrs. Switzer has experienced early deprivation and limited education; therefore, Mrs. Switzer is not a model of intellectual ability and emotional resourcefulness.

Daisy feels helpless and defensive when Edna is displeased with her performance. Daisy's inability to meet the complex requirements of handling the household chores and the two little boys causes Daisy physical pain. Her toothache becomes generalized and she feels a "strange lonesome ache all over her." Daisy's "ache" is her means of retreat from a painful situation. The use of hypochondriacal symptoms is not an uncommon form of retreat from life's realities.

Springboards for Inquiry

1. Comment on the likelihood of Daisy's use of physical symptoms as a response to stress if Edna and Elmer send Daisy home because of the toothache. If Edna and Elmer keep Daisy and ignore her physical complaints, do you see any possibility that Daisy will learn to be comfortably independent?

2. How does Daisy's sex, birth order, and inferred earlier child-rearing experiences relate to her present dependent personality characteristics?

3. Discuss Daisy's view of herself in relation to her mother, her siblings, and her fantasy life. How does Daisy's self-concept effect her competency?

Coping

The world in which the child lives is a hostile environment in many ways. Despite the attention he receives from his mother in his early days, he is faced with the problems of adjusting to feeding schedules and living with physiological discomfort and the problems that accompany normal growth. Discomfort initiates his only way to seek help to relieve tension—crying. As language and locomotion develop, new situations demand adequate coping* behavior. Running away sometimes helps, and attacking alters the situation. Words of anger or of persuasion help meet some situations. As the child's personality is shaped, he tries out a variety of responses to his environment. What works he will use again. If crying brings early relief, he will try it again and again until it no longer works.

Before much problem-solving behavior develops, the child's early attempts to escape from unpleasant situations are quite random. If, after withdrawing, blaming others, or daydreaming he is still unsuccessful in coping with the threat, he may learn to deal with reality in another manner (Strang 1959). Hopefully, as the child matures he learns a variety of responses to stress situations† by developing a rational method of approaching each problem so that a resort to ego-

* Coping is defined as the process of selecting from a number of alternatives those that lead to a desired goal.

† A more complete review of stress situations and responses to them may be found in Hans Selye, *The Stress of Life* (New York: McGraw-Hill Book Co., 1956).

defense mechanisms† is unnecessary. Defense mechanisms, according to Rogers (1969, p. 200), are habitual methods of coping with problems while not getting at the problem. Coming to grips with problems is often difficult, and so children (and adults who behave as children) find ways of circumventing their problems. There are three basic types of defense attitudes (Pollard and Geoghehan 1969, pp. 425–28): (a) techniques of deception, (b) mechanisms of substitution, and (c) avoidance.

Techniques of Deception

Rationalization / The process of thinking rationally is the goal in the solution of problems. The term *rationalization,* however, refers to the process of concocting plausible reasons to account for one's beliefs or actions. Thus, when a child cannot achieve in a particular manner, he may learn to live with the failure by convincing himself that he did not want to achieve anyway.

Projection / The process of ascribing to others one's own unacknowledged desires and faults is *projection,* a normal mechanism when a person assumes unconsciously that "others feel what I feel." When a person feels guilty, however, he may protect himself from a recognition of his own feelings by projecting these feelings to someone else and saying, "He accuses me" instead of "I feel guilty."

Displacement / Attaching a feeling to something other than its proper object is *displacement.* A child's anger at his father can be transferred to his father's typewriter, which he proceeds to wreck, since for a variety of reasons he may not attack his father.

Repression / Excluding facts from a person's consciousness without his own knowledge is *repression.* A child may deceive himself by refusing to acknowledge the existence of the problem. It is not uncommon for children whose parents have died to behave as if they never had parents—facing the facts is too unpleasant. When the blocking of reality is voluntary and conscious the term *suppression* is used.

Mechanisms of Substitution

Compensation / When a child is unable to perform athletically, he may make up for this lack by his scholastic attainments, an effort to exclude a painful awareness of a deficiency.

---

† See Robert Wallder, *Basic Theory of Psychoanalysis* (New York: International University Press, 1960) for a review of Freud's basic theory.

Substitution / A compromise with a problem may result when a child does not receive a toy he wants, substitutes another, and "makes do."

Reaction Formation / It is possible to cope with one's fear, by denying this fear and engaging in aggressive behavior. For example, a person with a great fear of heights can react by becoming a mountain climber.

Sublimation / An alteration that brings behavior within the bounds of conventional approval is *sublimation*. When a child's environment prohibits the smearing of food or feces, for example, the smearing may then take place on sheets of paper with paint.

Avoidance

Fantasy / A means of imagining pleasant things that are not constructive or reproductive, yet are not necessarily delusive or pathological is *fantasy.* In Maurice Sendak's *Where the Wild Things Are,** Max, just punished by his mother for his wildness, fantasizes that he has journeyed to an island where he gains control over terrible monsters. This control is very pleasant for him and it represents a temporary fulfillment of his wishes.

Negativism / When children scowl, shake their heads, and verbally refuse to do as suggested, they are resisting suggestions often for no apparent reason. Freud contends that negativism is a defense against years of submission. When it becomes a fixed attitude of opposition directed against everybody, negativism is a serious mental health problem (Eidelberg 1968, p. 265).

Identification / When a child dissolves the barriers between himself and another person to the point where he consciously or unconsciously mimics the behavior of the other person, he is said to be *identifying* with that other person. Firstborn girls tend to show the greatest mother-identification of any children in the family.

To an extent all the mechanisms described are normal reactions to the solution of human problems. Only when these methods persist and become the learned response—the only response—to problems does the coping behavior become neurotic. The responses themselves are neither bad nor good; their value depends on their use.

In general, the child who is developing a healthy personality meets the problems of life rationally. Aggression and hostility, although part of normal behavior, are like sublimation and fantasy—temporary reactions to the frustrations of specific situations. It is important for those who work with children to reinforce verbally and nonverbally any adaptive behavior that indicates rational reactions. It is interesting to note that children can be trained to meet frustration (Updegraff and Keister 1937); the educative process can help children consciously cope with situations in a problem-solving manner.

---

* New York: Harper & Row, Publishers, Inc., 1963.

Luke knew in his heart that he couldn't move his uncle. All he could do he thought, was keep the dog away from his uncle, keep him out of the house, feed him when Uncle Henry wasn't around.

Luke Baldwin's Vow

by Morley Callaghan

That summer when twelve-year-old Luke Baldwin came to live with his Uncle Henry in the house on the stream by the sawmill, he did not forget that he had promised his dying father he would try to learn things from his uncle; so he used to watch him very carefully.

Uncle Henry, who was the manager of the sawmill, was a big, burly man, weighing more than two hundred and thirty pounds, and he had a rough-skinned, brick-colored face. He looked like a powerful man, but his health was not good. He had aches and pains in his back and shoulders which puzzled the doctor. The first thing Luke learned about Uncle Henry was that everybody had great respect for him. The four men he employed in the sawmill were always polite and attentive when he spoke to them. His wife, Luke's Aunt Helen, a kindly, plump, straightforward woman, never argued with him. "You should try and be like your Uncle Henry," she would say to Luke. "He's so wonderfully practical. He takes care of everything in a sensible, easy way."

Luke used to trail around the sawmill after Uncle Henry not only because he liked the fresh clean smell of the newly cut wood and the big piles of sawdust, but because he was impressed by his uncle's precise, firm tone when he spoke to the men.

Sometimes Uncle Henry would stop and explain to Luke something about a piece of lumber. "Always try and learn the essential facts, son," he would say. "If you've got the facts, you know what's useful and what isn't useful, and no one can fool you."

He showed Luke that nothing of value was ever wasted around the

---

mill. Luke used to listen, and wonder if there was another man in the world who knew so well what was needed and what ought to be thrown away. Uncle Henry had known at once that Luke needed a bicycle to ride to his school, which was two miles away in town, and he bought him a good one. He knew that Luke needed good, serviceable clothes. He also knew exactly how much Aunt Helen needed to run the house, the price of everything, and how much a woman should be paid for doing the family washing. In the evenings Luke used to sit in the living room watching his uncle making notations in a black notebook which he always carried in his vest pocket, and he knew that he was assessing the value of the smallest transaction that had taken place during the day.

Luke promised himself that when he grew up he, too, would be admired for his good, sound judgment. But, of course, he couldn't always be watching and learning from his Uncle Henry, for too often when he watched him he thought of his own father; then he was lonely. So he began to build up another secret life for himself around the sawmill, and his companion was the eleven-year-old collie, Dan, a dog blind in one eye and with a slight limp in his left hind leg. Dan was a fat, slow-moving old dog. He was very affectionate and his eye was the color of amber. His fur was amber too. When Luke left for school in the morning, the old dog followed him for half a mile down the road, and when he returned in the afternoon, there was Dan waiting at the gate.

Sometimes they would play around the millpond or by the dam, or go down the stream to the lake. Luke was never lonely when the dog was with him. There was an old rowboat that they used as a pirate ship in the stream, and they would be pirates together, with Luke shouting instructions to Captain Dan and with the dog seeming to understand and wagging his tail enthusiastically. Its amber eye was alert, intelligent, and approving. Then they would plunge into the brush on the other side of the stream, pretending they were hunting tigers. Of course, the old dog was no longer much good for hunting; he was too slow and too lazy. Uncle Henry no longer used him for hunting rabbits or anything else.

When they came out of the brush, they would lie together on the cool, grassy bank being affectionate with each other, with Luke talking earnestly, while the collie, as Luke believed, smiled with the good eye. Lying in the grass, Luke would say things to Dan he could not say to his uncle or his aunt. Not that what he said was important; it was just stuff about himself that he might have told to his own father or mother if they had been alive. Then they would go back to the house for dinner, and after dinner Dan would follow him down the road to Mr. Kemp's house, where they would ask old Mr. Kemp if they could go with him to round up his four cows. The old man was always glad to see them. He seemed to like watching Luke and the collie running around the cows, pretending they were riding on a vast range in the foothills of the Rockies.

Uncle Henry no longer paid much attention to the collie, though once when he tripped over him on the veranda he shook his head and said thoughtfully, "Poor old fellow, he's through. Can't use him for anything. He just eats and sleeps and gets in the way."

One Sunday during Luke's summer holidays, when they had returned from church and had had their lunch, they had all moved out to the veranda where the collie was sleeping. Luke sat down on the steps, his back against the veranda post, Uncle Henry took the rocking chair, and Aunt Helen stretched herself out in the hammock, sighing contentedly. Then Luke, eyeing the collie, tapped the step with the palm of his hand, giving three little taps like a signal, and the old collie, lifting his head, got up stiffly with a slow wagging of the tail as an acknowledgment that the signal had been heard, and began to cross the veranda to Luke. But the dog was sleepy; his bad eye was turned to the rocking chair; in passing, his left front paw went under the rocker. With a frantic yelp, the dog went bounding down the steps and hobbled around the corner of the house, where he stopped, hearing Luke coming after him. All he needed was the touch of Luke's hand. Then he began to lick the hand methodically, as if apologizing.

"Luke," Uncle Henry called sharply, "bring that dog here."

When Luke led the collie back to the veranda, Uncle Henry nodded and said, "Thanks, Luke." Then he took out a cigar, lit it, put his big hands on his knees, and began to rock in the chair while he frowned and eyed the dog steadily. Obviously he was making some kind of an important decision about the collie.

"What's the matter, Uncle Henry?" Luke asked nervously.

"That dog can't see any more," Uncle Henry said.

"Oh, yes, he can," Luke said quickly. "His bad eye got turned to the chair, that's all, Uncle Henry."

"And his teeth are gone, too. Uncle Henry went on, paying no attention to what Luke had said. Turning to the hammock, he called, "Helen, sit up a minute, will you?"

When she got up and stood beside him, he went on, "I was thinking about this old dog the other day, Helen. It's not only that he's just about blind, but did you notice that when we drove up after church he didn't even bark?"

"It's a fact he didn't, Henry."

"No, not much good even as a watchdog now."

"And no good for hunting either. And he eats a lot, I suppose."

"About as much as he ever did, Henry."

"The plain fact is the old dog isn't worth his keep any more. It's time we got rid of him."

"It's always so hard to know how to get rid of a dog, Henry."

"I was thinking about it the other day. Some people think it's best to shoot a dog. I haven't had any shells for that shotgun for over a year. Poisoning is a hard death for a dog. Maybe drowning is the easiest and quickest way. Well, I'll speak to one of the mill hands and have him look after it."

Crouching on the ground, his arms around the old collie's neck, Luke cried out, "Uncle Henry, Dan's a wonderful dog! You don't know how wonderful he is!"

"He's just a very old dog, son,"

Uncle Henry said calmly. "The time comes when you have to get rid of any old dog. We've got to be practical about it. I'll get you a pup, son. A smart little dog that'll be worth its keep. A pup that will grow up with you.

"I don't want a pup!" Luke cried, turning his face away. Circling around him, the dog began to bark, then flick his long pink tongue at the back of Luke's neck.

Aunt Helen, catching her husband's eye, put her finger on her lips, warning him not to go on talking in front of the boy. "An old dog like that often wanders off into the brush and sort of picks a place to die when the time comes. Isn't that so, Henry?"

"Oh, sure," he agreed quickly. "In fact, when Dan didn't show up yesterday, I was sure that was what had happened." Then he yawned and seemed to forget about the dog.

But Luke was frightened, for he knew what his uncle was like. He knew that if his uncle had decided that the dog was useless and that it was sane and sensible to get rid of it, he would be ashamed of himself if he were diverted by any sentimental consideration. Luke knew in his heart that he couldn't move his uncle. All he could do, he thought, was keep the dog away from his uncle, keep him out of the house, feed him when Uncle Henry wasn't around.

Next day at noontime Luke saw his uncle walking from the mill toward the house with old Sam Carter, a mill hand. Sam Carter was a dull, stooped, slow-witted man of sixty with an iron-gray beard, who was wearing blue overalls and a blue shirt. He hardly ever spoke to anybody. Watching from the veranda, Luke noticed that his uncle suddenly gave Sam Carter a cigar, which Sam put in his pocket. Luke had never seen his uncle give Sam a cigar or pay much attention to him.

Then, after lunch, Uncle Henry said lazily that he would like Luke to take his bicycle and go into town and get him some cigars.

"I'll take Dan," Luke said.

"Better not, son," Uncle Henry said, "It'll take you all afternoon. I want those cigars. Get going, Luke."

His uncle's tone was so casual that Luke tried to believe they were not merely getting rid of him. Of course he had to do what he was told. He had never dared to refuse to obey an order from his uncle. But when he had taken his bicycle and had ridden down the path that followed the stream to the town road and had got about a quarter of a mile along the road, he found that all he could think of was his uncle handing old Sam Carter the cigar.

Slowing down, sick with worry now, he got off the bike and stood uncertainly on the sunlit road. Sam Carter was a gruff, aloof old man who would have no feeling for a dog. Then suddenly Luke could go no farther without getting some assurance that the collie would not be harmed while he was away. Across the fields he could see the house.

Leaving the bike in the ditch, he started to cross the field, intending to get close enough to the house so Dan could hear him if he whistled softly. He got about fifty yards away from the house and whistled and waited, but there was no sign of the dog, which might be asleep at the front of the house, he knew, or over at the sawmill. With the saws whining, the dog couldn't hear the soft whistle. For a few minutes Luke couldn't make up his mind what to do, then he decided to go back to the road, get on his bike, and go back the way he had come until he got to the place where the river path joined the road. There he could leave his bike, go up the path, then into the tall grass and get close to the front of the house and the sawmill without being seen.

He had followed the river path for about a hundred yards, and when he came to the place where the river began to bend sharply toward the house his heart fluttered and his legs felt paralyzed, for he saw the old rowboat in the one place where the river was deep, and in the rowboat was Sam Carter with the collie.

The bearded man in the blue overalls was smoking the cigar; the dog, with a rope around its neck, sat contentedly beside him, its tongue going out in a friendly lick at the hand holding the rope. It was all like a crazy dream picture to Luke; all wrong because it looked so lazy and friendly, even the curling smoke from Sam Carter's cigar. But as Luke cried out, "Dan! Dan! Come on, boy!" and the dog jumped at the water, he saw that Sam Carter's left hand was hanging deep in the water, holding a foot of rope with a heavy stone at the end. As Luke cried out wildly, "Don't. Please don't!" Carter dropped the stone, for the cry came too late; it was blurred by the screech of the big saws at the mill. But Carter was startled, and he stared stupidly at the riverbank, then he ducked his head and began to row quickly to the bank.

But Luke was watching the collie take what looked like a long, shallow dive, except that the hind legs suddenly kicked up above the surface, then shot down, and while he watched, Luke sobbed and trembled, for it was as if the happy secret part of his life around the sawmill was being torn away from him. But even while he watched, he seemed to be following a plan without knowing it, for he was already fumbling in his pocket for his jackknife, jerking the blade open, pulling off his pants, kicking his shoes off, while he muttered fiercely and prayed that Sam Carter would get out of sight.

It hardly took the mill hand a minute to reach the bank and go slinking furtively around the bend as if he felt that the boy was following him. But Luke hadn't taken his eyes off the exact spot in the water where Dan had disappeared. As soon as the mill hand was out of sight, Luke slid down the bank and took a leap at the water, the sun glistening on his slender body, his eyes wild with eagerness as he ran out to the deep place, then arched his back and dived, swimming under water, his open eyes getting used to the greenish-gray haze of the water, the sandy bottom, and the imbedded rocks.

His lungs began to ache, then he saw the shadow of the collie floating at the end of the taut rope, rock-held in the sand. He slashed at the rope with his knife. He couldn't get much strength in his arm because of the resistance of the water. He grabbed the rope with his left hand, hacking with his knife. The collie suddenly drifted up slowly, like a water-soaked log. Then his own head shot above the surface, and, while he was sucking in the air, he was drawing in the rope, pulling the collie toward him and treading water. In a few strokes he was away from the deep place and his feet touched the bottom.

Hoisting the collie out of the water, he scrambled toward the bank, lurching and stumbling in fright because the collie felt like a dead weight.

He went on up the bank and across the path to the tall grass, where he fell flat, hugging the dog and trying to warm him with his own body. But the collie didn't stir, the good amber eye remained closed. Then suddenly Luke wanted to act like a resourceful, competent man. Getting up on his knees, he stretched the dog out on its belly, drew him between his knees, felt with trembling hands for the soft places on the flanks just above the hipbones, and rocked back and forth, pressing with all his weight, then relaxing the pressure as he straightened up. He hoped that he was working the dog's lungs like a bellows. He had read that men who had been thought drowned had been saved in this way.

"Come on, Dan. Come on, old boy," he pleaded softly. As a little water came from the collie's mouth, Luke's heart jumped, and he muttered over and over, "You can't be dead, Dan! You can't, you can't! I won't let you die, Dan!" He rocked back and forth tirelessly, applying the pressure to the flanks. More water dribbled from the mouth. In the collie's body he felt a faint tremor. "Oh, gee, Dan, you're alive," he whispered. "Come on, boy. Keep it up."

With a cough the collie suddenly jerked his head back, the amber eye opened, and there they were looking at each other. Then the collie, thrusting his legs out stiffly, tried to hoist himself up, staggered, tried again, then stood there in a stupor. Then he shook himself like any other wet dog, turned his head, eyed Luke, and the red tongue came out in a weak flick at Luke's cheek.

"Lie down, Dan," Luke said. As the dog lay down beside him, Luke closed his eyes, buried his head in the wet fur, and wondered why all the muscles of his arms and legs began to jerk in a nervous reaction, now that it was all over. "Stay there, Dan," he said softly, and he went back to the path, got his clothes, and came back beside Dan and put them on. "I think we'd better get away from this spot, Dan," he said. "Keep down, boy. Come on." And he crawled on through the tall grass till they were about seventy-five yards from the place where he had undressed. There they lay down together.

In a little while he heard his aunt's voice calling, "Luke. Oh, Luke! Come here, Luke!"

"Quiet, Dan," Luke whispered. A few minutes passed, and then Uncle Henry called, "Luke, Luke!" and he began to come down the path. They could see him standing there, massive and imposing, his hands on his hips as he looked down the path; then he turned and went back to the house.

As he watched the sunlight shine on the back of his uncle's neck, the exultation Luke had felt at knowing the collie was safe beside him turned to bewildered despair, for he knew that even if he should be forgiven for saving the dog when he saw it drowning, the fact was that his uncle had been thwarted. His mind was made up to get rid of Dan, and in a few days' time, in another way, he would get rid of him, as he got rid of anything around the mill that he believed to be useless or a waste of money.

As he lay back and looked up at the hardly moving clouds, he began to grow frightened. He couldn't go back to the house, nor could he take the collie into the woods and hide him and feed him there unless he tied him up. If he didn't tie him up, Dan would wander back to the house.

"I guess there's just no place to go, Dan," he whispered sadly. "Even if we start off along the road, somebody is sure to see us."

But Dan was watching a butterfly that was circling crazily above them. Raising himself a little, Luke looked through the grass at the corner of the house, then he turned and looked the other way to the wide blue lake. With a sigh he lay down again, and for hours they lay there together, until there was no sound from the saws in the mill and the sun moved low in the western sky.

"Well, we can't stay here any longer, Dan," he said at last. "We'll just have to get as far away as we can. Keep down, old boy," and he began to crawl through the grass, going farther away from the house. When he could no longer be seen, he got up and began to trot across the field toward the gravel road leading to town.

On the road, the collie would turn from time to time as if wondering why Luke shuffled along, dragging his feet wearily, head down. "I'm stumped, that's all, Dan," Luke explained. "I can't seem to think of a place to take you."

When they were passing the Kemp place, they saw the old man sitting on the veranda, and Luke stopped. All he could think of was that Mr. Kemp had liked them both and it had been a pleasure to help him get the cows in the evening. Dan had always been with them. Staring at the figure of the old man on the veranda, he said in a worried tone, "I wish I could be sure of him, Dan. I wish he was a dumb, stupid man who wouldn't know or care whether you were worth anything. . . . Well, come on." He opened the gate bravely, but he felt shy and unimportant.

"Hello, son What's on your mind?" Mr. Kemp called from the veranda. He was a thin, wiry man in a tan-colored shirt. He had a gray, untidy mustache, his skin was wrinkled and leathery, but his eyes were always friendly and amused.

"Could I speak to you, Mr. Kemp?" Luke asked when they were close to the veranda.

"Sure. Go ahead."

"It's about Dan. He's a great dog, but I guess you know that as well as I do. I was wondering if you could keep him here for me."

"Why should I keep Dan here, son?"

"Well, it's like this," Luke said, fumbling the words awkwardly. "My uncle won't let me keep him any more . . . says he's too old." His mouth began to tremble, then he blurted out the story.

"I see, I see," Mr. Kemp said slowly, and he got up and came over to the steps and sat down and began to stroke the collie's head. "Of course, Dan's an old dog, son," he said quietly. "And sooner or later you've got to get rid of an old dog. Your uncle knows that. Maybe it's true that Dan isn't worth his keep."

"He doesn't eat much, Mr. Kemp. Just one meal a day."

"I wouldn't want you to think your uncle was cruel and unfeeling, Luke," Mr. Kemp went on. "He's a fine man . . . maybe just a little bit too practical and straightforward."

"I guess that's right," Luke agreed, but he was really waiting and trusting the expression in the old man's eyes.

"Maybe you should make him a practical proposition."

"I—I don't know what you mean."

"Well, I sort of like the way you get the cows for me in the evening," Mr. Kemp said, smiling to himself. "In fact, I don't think you need me to go along with you at all. Now, supposing I gave you seventy-five cents a week. Would you get the cows for me every night?"

"Sure I would, Mr. Kemp. I like doing it, anyway."

"All right, son. It's a deal. Now I'll tell you what to do. You go back to your uncle, and before he has a chance to open up on you you say right out that you've come to him with a business proposition. Say it like a man, just like that. Offer to pay him the seventy-five cents a week for the dog's keep."

"But my uncle doesn't need seventy-five cents, Mr. Kemp," Luke said uneasily.

"Of course not," Mr. Kemp agreed. "It's the principle of the thing. Be confident. Remember that he's got nothing against the dog. Go to it, son. Let me know how you do," he added, with an amused smile. "If I know your uncle at all, I think it'll work."

"I'll try it, Mr. Kemp," Luke said. "Thanks very much." But he didn't have any confidence, for even though he knew that Mr. Kemp was a wise old man who would not deceive him, he couldn't believe that seventy-five cents a week would stop his uncle, who was an important man. "Come on, Dan," he called, and he went slowly and apprehensively back to the house.

When they were going up the path, his aunt cried from the open window, "Henry, Henry, in heaven's name, it's Luke with the dog!"

Ten paces from the veranda, Luke stopped and waited nervously for his uncle to come out. Uncle Henry came out in a rush, but when he saw the collie and Luke standing there, he stopped stiffly, turned pale, and his mouth hung open loosely.

"Luke," he whispered, "that dog had a stone around his neck."

"I fished him out of the stream," Luke said uneasily.

"Oh, oh, I see," Uncle Henry said, and gradually the color came back to his face. "You fished him out, eh?" he asked, still looking at the dog uneasily. "Well, you shouldn't have done that. I told Sam Carter to get rid of the dog, you know."

"Just a minute, Uncle Henry," Luke said, trying not to falter. He gained confidence as Aunt Helen came out and stood beside her husband, for her eyes seemed to be gentle and he went on bravely, "I want to make you a practical proposition, Uncle Henry."

"A what?" Uncle Henry asked, still feeling insecure, and wishing the boy and the dog weren't confronting him.

"A practical proposition," Luke blurted out quickly. "I know Dan isn't worth his keep to you. I guess he isn't worth anything to anybody but me. So I'll pay you seventy-five cents a week for his keep."

"What's this?" Uncle Henry asked,

looking bewildered. "Where would you get seventy-five cents a week, Luke?"

"I'm going to get the cows every night for Mr. Kemp."

"Oh, for heaven's sake, Henry," Aunt Helen pleaded, looking distressed, "let him keep the dog!" and she fled into the house.

"None of that kind of talk!" Uncle Henry called after her. "We've got to be sensible about this!" But he was shaken himself, and overwhelmed with a distress that destroyed all his confidence. As he sat down slowly in the rocking chair and stroked the side of his big face, he wanted to say weakly, "All right, keep the dog," but he was ashamed of being so weak and sentimental. He stubbornly refused to yield to this emotion; he was trying desperately to turn his emotion into a bit of good, useful common sense, so he could justify his distress. So he rocked and pondered. At last he smiled. "You're a smart little shaver, Luke," he said slowly. "Imagine you working it out like this. I'm tempted to accept your proposition."

"Gee, thanks, Uncle Henry."

"I'm accepting it because I think you'll learn something out of this," he went on ponderously.

"Yes, Uncle Henry."

"You'll learn that useless luxuries cost the smartest men hard-earned money."

"I don't mind."

"Well, it's a thing you'll have to learn sometime. I think you'll learn, too, because you certainly seem to have a practical streak in you. It's a streak I like to see in a boy. O.K., son," he said, and he smiled with relief and went into the house.

Turning to Dan, Luke whispered softly, "Well, what do you know about that?"

As he sat down on the step with the collie beside him and listened to Uncle Henry talking to his wife, he began to glow with exultation. Then gradually his exultation began to change to a vast wonder that Mr. Kemp should have had such a perfect understanding of Uncle Henry. He began to dream of someday being as wise as old Mr. Kemp and knowing exactly how to handle people. It was possible, too, that he had already learned some of the things about his uncle that his father had wanted him to learn.

Putting his head down on the dog's neck, he vowed to himself fervently that he would always have some money on hand, no matter what became of him, so that he would be able to protect all that was truly valuable from the practical people in the world.

Discussion

Luke Baldwin has learned early in life to cope effectively with difficult situations. The story suggests that his relationship with his father was warm and satisfying, providing a good basis for using healthy coping techniques. He accepts his new life with his aunt and uncle with good grace. He is able to accept his aunt and uncle as they are, despite the fact that they do not meet his needs in many essential ways. They are a couple who are restrained and practical, without the inclination for emotional openness to which Luke is accustomed. Luke copes with his new feelings of lonesomeness through fantasy. He spends time with the old collie dog sharing confidences, affection, and games of make-believe. Luke is able to use his affection for the dog as a substitute for human closeness. We are not surprised that he will go to lengths to save the collie's life. Characteristically, Luke does not run away from problems. He is resilient and has a strong drive to find successful solutions or alternatives to problem situations. Mr. Kemp suggests to Luke that "he know his opposition," and Luke takes this advice. We can say that Luke's orientation to life is realistic and optimistic.

Springboards for Inquiry

(1) Explain how Luke uses compensation, sublimation, and fantasy in appropriate ways to solve an immediate problem.

(2) How would Luke have behaved in each situation had he used poor coping techniques such as projection, rationalization, and denial?

(3) What is the relationship between the child's coping behavior and his personality development?

(4) Give examples of how adults in the home, school, and clinic can help the child to learn to adapt realistically to conflict situations.

Self-Concept

It has been said that the child's self-concept is one of the vitamins of personality (Lane and Beauchamp, 1955, p. 132). As he develops, the child not only learns whom to love and trust and where to find nurture; he also learns something about himself. Life's persistent inner problems such as "Who am I?" and "What am I doing here?" need to be answered to the maximum satisfaction of each person for good mental health (Rogers 1969, p. 88).*

The concept of self is a construct that research labels as one of the most significant developmental tasks of childhood. Wylie (1961) cites Freud (1950), Fromm (1939), Karen Horney (1937), Maslow (1954), McClelland (1951), Carl Rogers (1951), Snygg and Combs (1949), and Harry Sullivan (1947) as important contributors to the theory. These scholars stress the role of the self-concept as a determiner of a person's behavior. There seems to be widespread agreement about the importance of the construct, but Boyd McCandless (1967, p. 260) raises interesting questions about the measurement of the concept. Despite the difficulties inherent in the validation of a theory, men of stature in the world of psychology accept the concept of self as a definable, observable entity. And so, Erikson (1963, p. 249) suggests that infancy is the time in life when the person learns basic trust in others: Lidz (1968, p. 123) maintains that "a basic trust in the self, a pervasive sense of confidence that becomes an *inherent characteristic in later life* [italic ours], rests upon trust in others during infancy" and must be developed in those early months of life.

---

* Refer also to the previous essay, "The Toddler."

"But let it be said here that the amount of trust derived from earliest infantile experience does not seem to depend on absolute quantities of food or demonstrations of love, but rather on the quality of the maternal relationship. Mothers create a sense of trust in their children. . . . This forms the basis in the child for a sense of identity which will later combine a sense of being 'all right,' of being oneself."

Dinkmeyer (1965) subtitles his text *The Emerging Self*, indicating his confidence in the construct. In the report *Negro Self-Concept* by William Kvaraceus and others (1964), an entire conference predicated its deliberations on the validity of Erikson's theory and subscribed to Arthur Jersild's dictum that if the reflected appraisals "of which the self is made up are mainly derogatory, . . . then the growing child's attitudes toward himself will be mainly derogatory" (1952, p. 13).

The parental and family role in the development of a good self-concept has been studied by Coopersmith,* who suggests that feeling good about oneself is a highly subjective experience which does not always correlate with peer and teacher judgments. His conclusions emphasize that the critical elements in the home environment which foster self-esteem are total or nearly total acceptance of the child by the parents and clearly defined and enforced limits. The role of the school in the development of the ego or in its role as an ego-supporting institution needs scrutiny. It is generally agreed that the curriculum, relationships with teachers, and the special services of the school can contribute to building self-concepts, but most school achievement is related to a preexistent concept of self (Hill and Sarason 1965). When a child enters school already convinced of his intellectual power, he tends to succeed.

Kvaraceus (1964, p. 12) shows how the school's effect on the self-image can be graded along two dimensions of a simple diagram. The first dimension is the school's goals as they are related to values that range on a continuum from conformity and standardization to self-realization and divergency. The second dimension is the school's use of materials, which is graded for emphasis on the utilitarian or the abstract. The teacher's attitudes, expectancies, and verbal responses to children affect how children view themselves. For example, Davidson and Lang (1960) found that children's perceptions of their teacher's feelings toward them correlated significantly with their self-perception. It seems clear, too, that teachers can teach ideas that affect the self-concept of minority children in their rooms (Trager 1952). The function of the teacher will be explored further in this volume under the heading "The School Influence."

In our essay on coping we discussed the wide variety of defense mechanisms people use to change the meaning of real situations. To develop adequate self-esteem is a very important life task. The fact that people project, rationalize, and compensate in order to avoid the often difficult task of building an accurate appraisal of themselves nearly always guarantees that a wide discrepancy exists between the ideal self and the perceived self. Studies of these self-

---

* See Stanley Coopersmith, *The Antecedents of Self-esteem.* San Francisco and London: W. H. Freeman & Co., 1967.

appraisals suggest that happiness is directly related to realistic perceptions of self at any stage in life.

We indicated that the concept of self develops from the early days of infancy and is nurtured by the relationship with mothers and families and the culture in which people live. Children learn about themselves through a multiplicity of interactions, including the school curriculum and staff. People use a variety of deceptive behaviors to make up for low self-esteem, and the closer the real self is to the ideal self the better adjusted a person is.

From the first year of coherent memory, George had the sense of the overpowering immanence of the golden life.

The Web and The Rock

by Thomas Wolfe

From the first years of coherent memory, George had the sense of the overpowering immanence of the golden life. It seemed to him that he was always on the verge of finding it. In his childhood it was all around him, impending numbly, softly, filling him with an intolerable exultancy of wordless joy. It wrenched his heart with its wild pain of ecstasy and tore the sinews of his life asunder, but yet it filled his soul with the triumphant sense of instant release, impending discovery—as if a great wall in the air would suddenly be revealed and sundered, as if an enormous door would open slowly, awfully, with the tremendous majesty of an utter and invisible silence. He never found a word for it, but he had a thousand spells and prayers and images that would give it coherence, shape, and meanings that no words could do.

He thought that he could twist his hand a certain way, or turn his wrist, or make a certain simple movement of rotation into space (as boys will learn the movement to unsolve a puzzle of linked chains, or as an expert in the mysteries of locks can feel the bearings faintly, softly, rolling through his finger tips, and know the instant that he finds the combination to unlock the safe—and that by making this rotation with his hand, he would find the lost dimension of that secret world, and instantly step through the door that he had opened.

And he had other chants and incantations that would make that world reveal itself to him. Thus, for a period of ten years or more, he had a spell for almost everything he did. He would hold his breath along a certain block, or take four breaths in pounding down the hill from

---

school, or touch each cement block upon a wall as he went past, and touch each of the end-blocks where the steps went up two times, and if he failed to touch them twice, go back and touch the whole wall over from the start.

And on Sunday he would always do the second thing: he would never do the first on Sunday. All through the day, from midnight Saturday until midnight Monday morning, he would always do the second thing he thought about and not the first. If he woke up on Sunday morning and swung over to the left side to get out of bed, he would swing back and get out on the right. If he started with the right sock, he would take it off and pull the left one on instead. And if he wanted first to use one tie, he would discard it and put on another.

And so it went the whole day through on Sunday. In every act and moment of his life that day he would always do the second thing he thought about instead of the first. But then when midnight came again, he would, with the same fantastic superstition, do the first thing that he thought about; and if he failed in any detail of this ritual, he would be as gloomy, restless, and full of uneasy boding doubts as if all the devils of mischance were already out in force against him, and posting on their way to do him harm.

These spells, chants, incantations, and compulsions grew, interwove, and constantly increased in the complexity and denseness of their web until at times they governed everything he did—not only the way he touched a wall, or held his breath while pounding down a hill from school, or measured out a block in punctual distances of breathing, or spanned the cement blocks of sidewalks in strides of four, but even in the way he went along a street, the side he took, the place he had to stop and look, the place he strode by sternly even when he wanted bitterly to stay and look, the trees out in his uncle's orchard that he climbed until he had to climb a certain tree four times a day and use four movements to get up the trunk.

And this tyrannic mystery of four would also get into the way he threw a ball, or chanted over Latin when preparing it, or muttered παιδεύσω four times in the Subjunctive of the First Aorist, or ἔθηκα in the Indicative Active of the First. And it was also in the way he washed his neck and ears, or sat down at a table, split up kindling (using four strokes of the axe to make a stick), or brought up coal (using four scoops of the shovel to fill the scuttle).

Then there were also days of stern compulsion when he could look at only a single feature of people's faces. On Monday he would look upon men's noses, on Tuesday he would stare into their teeth, on Wednesday he would peer into their eyes, save Thursday for their hands, and Friday for their feet, and sternly meditate the conformation of their brows on Saturday, saving Sunday always for the second feature that occurred to him—eyes when feet were thought of, teeth for eyes, and foreheads when his fine first rapture had been noses. And he would go about this duty of observing with such a stern, fanatical devotion, peering savagely at people's teeth or hands or brows, that sometimes they looked at him uneasily, resentfully, wondering what he saw amiss in their appearance, or shaking their heads and muttering angrily as they passed each other by.

At night, he said his prayers in rhymes of four—for four, eight, sixteen, thirty-two were somehow the key numbers in his arithmetic of sorcery. He would say his one set prayer in chants of four times four, until all the words and meanings of the prayer (which he had composed himself with four times four in mind) were lost, and all that he would follow would be the rhythm and the number of the chant, muttered so rapidly that the prayer was just a rapid blur—but muttered always sixteen times. And if he failed to do this, or doubted he had got the proper count, then he could not sleep or rest after he got into bed, and would get up instantly and go down upon his knees again, no matter how cold or raw the weather was, no matter how he felt, and would not pause until he did the full count to his satisfaction, with another sixteen thrown in as penalty. It was not piety he felt, it was not thought of God or reverence or religion: it was just superstitious mystery, a belief in the wizard-charm of certain numbers, and the conviction that he had to do it in this way in order to have luck.

Thus, each night he paid his punctual duty to "their" dark authorities, in order to keep himself in "their" good graces, to assure himself that "they" would not forsake him, that "they" would still be for him, not against him, that "they"—immortal, secret, "they" that will not give us rest!—would keep him, guard him, make his life prevail, frustrate his evil enemies, and guide him on to all the glory, love, and triumph, and to that great door, the huge, hinged, secret wall of life—that immanent and unutterable world of joy which was so near, so strangely, magically, and intolerably near, which he would find at any moment, and for which his life was panting.

Discussion

An ever-present seeking for the full life gives *The Web and the Rock* its epic quality. The story traces George Webber from childhood to early manhood. In the opening pages of the novel, which precede this selection, we learn that George has been brought up in the drab environment of his deceased mother's relatives. Thomas Wolfe says of George's early discontent: "He found himself longing constantly for another universe shaped in the colors of his own desire." This bitterly dissatisfied boy perhaps spends more time than usual turning inward to explore the "overpowering immanence" he feels for himself, but it is not unusual for ten-year-olds to twelve-year-olds to be interested in their own becoming. At this time they will frequently develop a number of rituals, such as counting or avoiding sidewalk cracks, as a way of testing their individual powers to order their world. In the case of George these magical rituals take on the aspect of compulsions. The rituals are not pathological in intent but rather represent efforts to gain assurance at a time when the child is feeling ambivalent about giving up the comforts of childhood in favor of establishing an independent identity.

As George moves toward self-identity, it is important for him to understand the reach or parameters of his new capacities. It is also necessary to ward off any unknown authorities that may block his entrance into the joyous future that must surely be awaiting him. Reliance on mystical incantations is satisfactory and it appeals to youthful imagination, but as the story proceeds we find that George is at odds with himself as he grows into manhood reaching for an illusory state of happiness and success that lies just ahead. There seems to be a grave disparity between George's estimate of his real self and his ideal self. This lack of congruence between the self that reflects reality and the self he would like to be saps his energy and makes him susceptible to rages of dissatisfaction with himself. We know that the individual's growth toward maturity requires a good adjustment toward oneself, an acceptance of weaknesses and limitations without feeling overwhelmingly defeated by them. Self-esteem is a continuing growth process rooted in one's early years. We cannot say that George developed positive emotional bonds in his family relationships at this critical time. Thomas Wolfe's novel is a beautiful literary example of how the early years relate to early youth and maturity which lies just ahead.

Springboards for Inquiry

(1) How do you relate George's faltering self-concept to his complex spells, chants and incantations?

(2) Growth toward self identity proceeds through several identifiable stages. Describe the development of self awareness at ages two to four, preschool to six. Include a description of activities that move the child away from the family into the world of school and peers.

(3) The school age child is turning from his family to his friends to learn more about his self identity. The childhood culture provides him with games, skills and rituals to share. What are some of the experiences during the school years which fortify a sense of self worth for boys? For girls?

(4) Recall some of the chants and rituals popular with your friends in your own middle school years.*

---

* See the descriptions of the society of children in the chapter "The Middle Years of Childhood" by L. Joseph Stone and Joseph Church, 361–392, *Childhood and Adolescence*, New York: Random House, Inc., 1968.

References

Allport, Gordon W. *Personality: A Psychological Interpretation.* New York: Holt, Rinehart and Winston, 1937, p. 48.

Baller, Warren, and Don. C. Charles. *The Psychology of Human Growth and Development.* New York: Holt, Rinehart, and Winston, 1968.

Birns, Beverly M. "Individual Differences in Human Neonates' Responses to Stimulation." *Child Development* 36 (1965): 249–56.

Davidson, Helen, and Gerhard Lang. "Children's Perceptions of Their Teacher's Feelings towards Them Related to Self Perception, School Achievement and Behavior." *Journal of Experimental Education* 29 (December 1960): 107–18.

Dinkmeyer, Don. *Child Development: The Emerging Self.* Englewood Cliffs, N. J.: Prentice-Hall, 1965.

Douvan, Elizabeth. "Sex Differences in the Adolescent Character Process." *Merrill-Palmer Quarterly of Behavior and Development* 6 (1960): 203–11.

Douvan, Elizabeth, and Joseph Adelson. *The Adolescent Experience.* New York: John Wiley and Sons, 1966.

Eidelberg, Ludwig. *Encyclopedia of Psychoanalysis.* New York: Free Press, 1968.

Erikson, Erik. *Childhood and Society.* 2nd. ed. New York: W. W. Norton & Co., 1963.

Erikson, Erik. *Growth and Crises of the "Healthy Personality."* Psychological Issues, vol. 1, no. 1, monograph 1. New York: International University Press, 1959.

Foster, Sybil. "A Study of the Personality Make-up and Social Setting of Fifty Jealous Children." *Mental Hygiene* 11 (1927): 53–77.

Freud, Sigmund. *The Ego and the Id.* London: Hogarth Press, 1950.

Freud, Sigmund. *New Introductory Lectures on Psycho-Analysis.* New York: W. W. Norton & Co., 1933.

Fromm, Erich. *Man for Himself.* New York: Holt, Rinehart, and Winston, 1947.

Fromm, Erich. "Selfishness and Self-Love." *Psychiatry* 2 (1939): 507–23.

Hill, Kennedy T., Seymour B. Sarason, and Philip G. Limbardo. "A Further Longitudinal Study of the Relation of the Test Anxiety and Defensiveness to Test and School Performance over the Elementary School Years." Chicago: University of Chicago Press, *Monographs of the Society for Research in Child Development,* No. 31 (1965), pp. 1–16.

Horney, Karen. *The Neurotic Personality of Our Times.* New York: W. W. Norton & Co., 1937.

Hutt, Max L. and Daniel R. Miller. "Value Determination and Personality Development." *Journal of Social Issues* 5, No. 4 (1949): 2–30.

Jersild, Arthur T. *Child Psychology.* 5th ed. Englewood Cliffs, N. J.: Prentice-Hall, 1960.

Jersild, Arthur T. *In Search of Self.* New York: Teachers College, Columbia University, 1952.

Kagan, Jerome M. and Howard A. Moss. *Birth to Maturity.* New York: John Wiley and Sons, 1962.

Kagan, Jerome M. and Howard A. Moss. "The Stability of Passive and Dependent Behavior from Childhood through Adulthood." *Child Development* 31 (1960): 577–91.

Knop, Catherine. "The Dynamics of Newly Born Babies." *Journal of Pediatrics* 29 (1946): 721–28.

Kvaraceus, William C. John S. Gibson, Franklin Patterson, Bradbury Seasholes, and Jean D. Grambs. *Negro Self-Concept: Implications for School and Citizenship.* Medford, Mass.: Tufts University, 1964.

Lane, Howard, and Mary Beauchamp. *Human Relations in Teaching.* Englewood Cliffs, N. J.: Prentice-Hall, Inc., 1955, p. 132.

Lewin, Kurt, Ronald Lippitt, and Ralph White. "Patterns of Aggressive Behavior in Experimentally Created 'Social Climates.'" *Journal of Social Psychology* 10 (1939): 271–299.

Lidz, Theodore. *The Person.* New York: Basic Books, 1968.

Lynn, David B. *Parental and Sex Role Identification.* Berkeley, Calif.: McCatchan Publishing Corp., 1969.

McCandless, Boyd R. *Children: Behavior and Development.* 2nd ed. New .York: Holt, Rinehart, and Winston, 1967.

McClelland, David C. *Personality.* New York: Sloane, 1951.

Maslow, Abraham H. *Motivation and Personality.* New York: Harper & Row, Publishers, Inc., 1954.

Mead, Margaret. *Sex and Temperament in Three Primitive Societies.* New York: William Morrow & Co., 1949.

Pollard, Marie B., and Barbara Geoghehan. *The Growing Child in Contemporary Society.* Milwaukee, Wis.: Bruce Publishing Co., 1969.

Radke, Marian. *The Relation of Parental Authority to Children's Behavior and Attitudes.* Minneapolis: University of Minnesota Press, 1946.

Rogers, Carl R. *Client-Centered Therapy.* Boston: Houghton Mifflin Co., 1951.

Rogers, Dorothy. *Child Psychology.* Belmont, Calif.: Brooks/Cole Publishing Co., 1969.

Sears, Robert, Eleanor E. Maccoby, and Harry Levin. *Patterns of Child Rearing.* New York: Harper & Row, Publishers, Inc., 1957.

Sexton, Patricia. *The Feminized Male: Classrooms, White Collars, and the Decline of Manliness.* New York: Random House, Inc., 1969.

Snygg, Donald, and Arthur Combs. *Individual Behavior: A New Frame of Reference for Psychology.* New York: Harper & Row, Publishers, Inc., 1949.

Strang, Ruth. *An Introduction to Child Study,* 4th ed. New York: The Macmillan Company, 1959.

Sullivan, Harry S. *Conceptions of Modern Psychiatry.* Washington, D. C.: William A. White Foundation, 1947.

Trager, Helen G. *They Learn What They Live.* New York: Harper & Row, Publishers, Inc., 1952.

Updegraff, Ruth, and Mary E. Keister. "A Study of Children's Reactions to Failure and an Experimental Approach to Modify Them." *Child Development* 8 (1937): 241–48.

Whiting, John W. M., and Irvin L. Child. *Child Training and Personality.* New Haven, Conn.: Yale University Press, 1953.

Wylie, Ruth. *The Self-Concept.* Lincoln: University of Nebraska Press, 1961.

Emotional Development

The capacity to express emotion is present in the newborn. The quickening heartbeat, the increase in muscle tension, and the release of adrenal hormone are unlearned physiological responses. In infancy the expression of emotion is limited to a simple pleasure–pain continuum, but as the child grows older his emotional responses become specific and are associated with particular people, events, and objects. Pleasure may be felt specifically as joy, love, or physical well-being; pain may be felt as anger, fear, jealousy, or shame. Therefore, although the physiological response remains identical, there is a vast difference in psychological complexity between the newborn's response to a loud noise and the five-year-old's feelings of guilt when Daddy scolds.

The expression of emotions is influenced by cultural demands and expectations as well as by parental expectation and example. In our culture girls and women may cry, but we expect little boys to give up tears rather early and they are chided to "be brave" and to "act like a man." Individual parents provide liaison between the society and their children and either support the standards of society or encourage other emotional development.

Some psychologists believe that in order to develop good mental health children should express their feelings in early years—not always by action but at least by giving verbal expression to these feelings. Feelings are facts in the life of the young child, and it is important for children to know that their feelings are accepted and understood. Children also need adults to help them cope with their feelings. Fear, anger, and concern are often too strong for the young child to manage. Instead of denying or forbidding their existence, the wise parent or teacher helps the child to recognize the emotion and then helps him to find acceptable outlets for his emotions.

The emotion of fear deserves special mention in a discussion of emotional development in children, because fear is so closely associated with childhood. Fear of real dangers may protect the child from harm, but fear may also be associated with the unknown or the imaginary. It is natural for children to experience fear because their world is constantly expanding and often they cannot assimilate new experiences by relating them to anything in their past. Although there is no predictable timetable for the appearance and working through of fears, certain fears do seem to be related to particular ages. Preschool children tend to fear animals, the dark, imaginary creatures, and separation from parents. These early childhood fears are replaced in the middle school years by fear of school, interpersonal relationships, and situations related to these central forces in their lives.

Just as the definition of personality is difficult, so is the precise meaning of the term *emotions.* Broadly conceived, "the term emotion refers to a whole system of behavior" (Alexander 1969, p. 83). Affective responses to the experiences of life may be called emotions.

Love

It has been said that a child is born long before he is conceived. Abrahamsen (1969, p. 29) maintains that the physical and emotional imprint of at least the two preceding generations determines the kind of emotional care a child will receive. It is difficult to discover research data that identify love or are able to isolate it as an independent variable, but everybody talks about love and so it appears to be a tangible construct. In the film *The Quiet One* a grandmother is shown taking care of her daughter's abandoned ten-year-old boy. The grandmother, already old and tired, speaks irascibly to the child, tosses food on the table before him, and beats him for his transgressions. The commentator, attempting to epitomize the conditions that surround these two, says, "Duty without love. . . ."*

We alluded to the studies of maternal deprivation and of loss and attachment; we discussed the significance of the quality of maternal affection and attention as it relates to the early developmental tasks of childhood. Wherever we turn in the literature of childhood, whether in research or in fiction, the nebulous term *love* appears. Operational definitions are easier than abstract ones, yet it would be safe to say that love is a feeling of interrelatedness transmitted from one person to another. Bowlby (1958) uses the term *attachment* and this is perhaps a more visual embodiment of the idea. The mere satisfaction of the physical needs of an infant are relatively useless in his total development, since

* See some of love's components are described with beauty and clarity in the script written by James Agee for the movie *The Quiet One*. McGraw-Hill Films, 1948.

nutritional deficiencies can arise among children who have eaten well but have not tasted the food of love (Levy 1937).

At this point let us explore the relationship between "self-love"* and love for a child. In the beginning of this essay it was stated that a child is born long before he is conceived. Since parents can do little about their antecedents, the only fruitful attention they can pay is to themselves, because whether one is a parent, nurse, or teacher, his reactions to children ultimately depend not only on the cumulative effect of his experiences with his own parents and their experiences with their parents, but on his understanding of himself as a loving human being. Fromm defines self-love as a form of greediness (Evans 1966; Fromm 1956). Although it is a fundamental human vice, self-love negates the definition of love described above, because greediness makes the concept of interrelatedness virtually impossible.

Fromm uses the term *love of self* to describe the productive individual (as opposed to the nonproductive one characterized by self-love). Love of self means a loving, friendly, affirmative attitude toward oneself, which results in an attitude of love that allows an authentic interrelatedness with others. As a child develops at home and at school, his own productivity is enhanced by the quality of love he grows up with. When those who are responsible for the interaction love themselves, yet are not selfish, they transmit their relatedness to the child whose modes of assimilation will be fashioned out of the "stuff" of these interactions. To display love toward others fosters this type of love in the recipients.

Some discussion in the literature about childhood divides methods of disciplining children into either power-oriented or love-oriented techniques (McCord, McCord, and Howard 1961; Eron, Walder, Toigo, and Lefhowitz 1963; Sears 1961). Power-oriented techniques use physical punishment; love-oriented methods use love, praise, and reasoning to alter or stop undesirable behavior in children. We also have clear implications of the denial of love to children for poor behavior ("Mommy is sad because you hurt your sister"): the withholding of love may have immediate effects that retard bad behavior, but it can be as detrimental to the emotional health of the child as pure physical aggression. The conception of love in this volume is one in which love is not used as a club. Love is not dependent on acceptable behavior, but it permeates any type of behavior, even physical. It is not a conditional thing that is dangled before the child as a reward for conformity; it is a mystique that allows no tantalizing, no bargaining. We should not love children so that they will love us back and further satisfy greediness.

The quality of a child's early love relationships determine his own capacity for loving. When he is deprived of unqualified love, fear and aggression develop in the child, and his chances to raise his own children lovingly are severely limited. The effects of life in an atmosphere devoid of a sense of attachment are so harsh it has been said that when a child is most in need of love, he is the most unlovely.

---

* Erich Fromm's definition will be juxtaposed with the usual definition for greater clarity.

"I feel so awful all the time," Tim said. "Inside, I feel awful."

Don't You Wish You Were Dead

by L. Woiwode

Bruce Stuttlemeyer was not well-loved in town. He had just moved from an outlying farm into Pettibone—a village in central Illinois known for its export of peat—at the beginning of winter, and he wore bib overalls, flannel shirts, and high hook-and-eye shoes. Though his dress had been acceptable enough while he lived on a farm, he was now looked upon by his seventh grade classmates as a hick. He was diminutive and thin, with an elongated face longer than most adults', large and fleshy lips, eyebrows so blond they were invisible, and a big gap between his front teeth, one of which had the end broken off. And as if all this weren't more than enough to make him an object of derision among his classmates, who were at one of the most sensitive and snobbish of ages, he was uncircumcised and poorly endowed, and had picked up the nickname of "Needledick, the canary raper." The more he heard the name, the more wild-eyed and violent he became, and he began to attack anybody he thought was using it or mocking him in any way. Parents complained to the principal that their sons were being injured at school, and shortly after Easter vacation Bruce turned on a bully from the eighth grade who had been taunting him for days, and knocked him unconscious. He was expelled from school for a week.

When Bruce's grandaunt said that she had too many cats and wondered if Bruce and some of his nice friends couldn't get rid of a few, he went to see Charles Neumiller, his only acquaintance neutral enough to be called a friend. Charles, though not an outcast, was, in his own way, nearly as friendless as Bruce, but

---

with him it appeared a deliberate choice; he was sullen and aloof, he read much of the time, and all he seemed to enjoy was acting the fool for girls or playing football—which he would play only if it was tackle instead of touch. Nobody in the village, of course, owned or wore equipment.

Bruce knocked on Neumiller's front door. After a long pause, it opened halfway and Charles appeared, shadowy and detached behind the screen door.

"Stuttlemeyer," he said.

"Chuck."

Charles was amazed to see Bruce at the door; he didn't know him that well, and Bruce had never been to the house.

Bruce couldn't wait to tell Charles about the cats.

They appraised one another with blank faces. Bruce, shifting his weight on his feet, finally spoke. "What are you doing today?"

"Working on a model airplane."

"Oh."

"Why?"

"I just wondered," Bruce said.

They continued to study one another with noncommittal expressions. Charles assumed that Bruce was looking for someone to serve as his buddy, now that school was over and the long summer lay ahead.

"Do you want to come in and see my airplane?'

"Sure."

Charles opened the screen door and Bruce followed him into a tiny bedroom just inside the entrance. Next to the bed was a rickety card table covered with balsa shavings, tissue paper, glue, straight pins, paint brushes, and the skeleton of a fuselage.

"What's that stink?" Bruce said.

"Banana dope. You paint it on the paper you've glued over the ribs—like on this wing—and it pulls the paper up tight. Then you keep putting it on and putting it on until the paper is like a drum, and then you put the plane together, put on the landing gear and things, and it's ready to fly."

"How do you fly it?"

"When it's finished, I'm going to buy a motor. Free flight. Isn't it a beauty?" Charles said, and held up a picture, an artist's rendition of the finished plane, and studied it.

"Yeah." Bruce looked around the room. The bed was unmade and dozens of snapshots, as though undergoing arrangement, were spread across it. The door of the closet was open and Bruce could see, piled along its bottom, old clothes, crushed boxes, old work shoes caked with plaster (Charles's father was in the plastering business), bent coat hangers, and a torn pillow spilling feathers. There were books and magazines scattered around, and the floor was dirty. Bruce had never seen such disorder. At his house, even when they lived in the country, everybody made their beds as soon as they rose, the floors were waxed and shining, the furniture glowed, and there was a place for everything, as his mother expressed it, and everything was in its place; one asked permission before moving a piece of furniture and there was a special hassock on which to place the evening paper. Bruce knew that Charles's mother had died several years ago—he'd signed the sympathy card to Charles along with the rest of the class—and he imagined her death helped explain this mess. "Is this where you sleep?"

"Not in summer. It's too hot. Sometimes in winter I do. It's my Dad's room. He never uses it."

"Do you know my aunt, old Emma Dawson, on the other side of town?"

"Sure. What about her?"

"She wants to clean out the cats in that old barn behind her house."

"What do you mean?"

"She wants me to kill them."

"Kill them?"

"Any way I want to do it, she said. Do you want to help?"

Charles tried to suppress a surge of exhilaration that made his ribs ache. "I'm supposed to stay here and watch my sisters."

"Where are they?"

"Over on the other side of the house, I guess." It was a task he resented and felt was unnecessary; they were six and four, self-sufficient. "Maybe my brother can watch them," Charles said. He went to the doorway and called in a loud voice, "Tim! Hey, *Tim!*"

There was a faint response from a far corner of the house.

"Come here!" Charles turned back to Bruce. "You mean she really wants them killed?"

"That's what she said."

"Did you ever kill one?"

"Sure. I choked one to death once on the farm. And another time I held a whole bag of them in the watertank until they were all drowned." Bruce grinned, showing his gapped and broken teeth, and he and Charles broke into nervous laughter and found it difficult to look at one another.

"What do you want *now?*" a plaintive voice said, and a small boy with a freckled face and freckled shoulders, wearing only a pair of bluejeans that were too big at the waist and rolled high on his shins, walked into the room. "I suppose you want——Oooo!" he said, seeing Bruce. "A guestus! You have a guestus! Oooo!" He jumped back as though in fear, made wide eyes, and held up his hands and shook them so violently his fingers made noise knocking together.

"Come on, cut it out," Charles said. "Geez." He couldn't stand it when his brother acted this way. Unless Tim was angry (and that was an uncontrollable fury that was more like madness), he was usually bashful around people, and so quiet and retreating you seldom realized he was in the room. He even seemed shy among his own family, and when expressing an opinion he spoke in a deferential voice, with his eyes lowered, as though he couldn't bear to see either smiles or disapproval. Though he was nine, he still sat in his father's lap for hours at a time, usually with an arm around his father's neck. But lately, within the last year, every time that Charles had guests Tim went into this performance, speaking in altered voices, singing, making faces, improvising strange words and languages, doing flips that landed him on the floor on the flat of his back—anything to draw attention to himself. He bowed now to Bruce and said in an innocent voice, but with crossed eyes, "I'm Tinvalin."

Bruce turned to Charles and his invisible eyebrows drew down.

"He calls himself that," Charles explained.

"No, ho," Tim said. "I'm Toonvaloon and I'm Toonva*loony.*" The tip of his tongue appeared at the corner of his mouth and his head started jerking toward his shoulder as though he had spasms.

"What's the matter with you, anyway?" Charles said. "Cut it out."

"Nat-ur-elly, Chelly."

"Listen. Bruce and I are going out for a while. You have to watch the girls."

"No, I don't. Dad told you to watch them."

"And now I'm telling you to."

"You're not my boss."

"I am when Dad's gone."

"That's not what he says."

"*I'm* saying it."

"I'll tell him you took off and left us."

"I'll tell him how you act when he's not here."

"Try it," Tim said, and began dancing and shadowboxing around the room, brushing his nose with his thumb, saying, "Snift! Snift! Snort-snort, snift!"

"Watch the girls! You hear?"

"Ahh-yahtata." One of his words for yes, said in imitation of a Chinese. He drew back his upper lip and bit over his lower one, exposing his front teeth, which were slightly bucked in an attractive way, and bowed again. "I hear."

"You better. And you better make sure they stay out of this room. If anything happens to my plane—"

"Oh! Precious. *Precious.*"

"You're damn right."

"Wow! Big he-man rips off a swear word. Scary."

"Come on," Charles said to Bruce. "I have to put on my shoes."

Bruce followed him through a living room in worse disorder than the bedroom, through a kitchen where boxes of breakfast food and dirty dishes were sitting on a table, and down a set of steps to the basement, which was damp and chilly. Charles pulled a light chain. A high double bed with a metal frame sat next to a furnace, and there was a three-hundred-gallon oil tank in a corner beyond the furnace. The cement-block walls of the basement, once painted aqua, were stained brown and yellow and dark green from seepage, and the outlines of the stains were fringed with fuzzy deposits of lime. Two mattresses, placed side by side, lay flat on the cement floor in the middle of the room. Charles sat down on one and began pulling his shoes on over bare feet.

"Is this where you sleep?" Bruce asked.

"Yes."

"On those?"

Charles looked up and saw Bruce studying the mattresses with wide eyes. "No, no, over on the bed. These are for our tag-team matches."

"Tag-team matches?"

"Sometimes we have regular matches, one against one, but most of the time we have tag-team matches."

"Oh."

"Don't you have a television?"

"No."

"It's wrestling. In a tag-team match, you each have a partner, and if you're getting trounced and need help, you tag your partner's hand and he comes in the ring and takes over for you. We have them on Thursday nights after Boy Scouts. Do you want to come sometime?"

"Sure."

"I'm pretty good. Tim and I beat the Wilson brothers last week. I'm working on a sleeper."

"Tim wrestles?"

"Yes. He's really tough for his size. About a week ago we were playing football, and Butch Crafton got mad at me—he couldn't make any headway against our defense and I tackled him real hard once—so he jumped me and started socking me in the face, and then Tim jumped him. Crafton went home with a bloody nose."

"*Butch* Crafton?" This was a wiry, powerful classmate of theirs, much feared by most everybody their age.

"Yes. When Tim gets really mad, it's like he's crazy and you can't hold him off. It's scary. He's even beat me up a few times. Let's go," Charles said, and started up the steps.

"Hey, wait," Bruce said. "What's this?"

Charles stepped down to the dark doorway where Bruce was standing, near the foot of the stairs, and turned on a light switch. Four oil-stained steps led up to a long, wide, extensive area with black walls and a black floor, and a ceiling less than five feet high.

"Holy balls," Bruce said. "What kind of a room do you call *that?*"

"This place was a gas station once. The part above this low part was a double garage before it was remodeled, and down here was the grease pit. That old grease is baked on and won't come off. We even tried muriatic acid."

"It's got a barn gutter right down the middle!"

"That's what they drained the oil and grease into, I guess. There's a big drain down at the other end that smells pretty bad."

"You'd have to be some kind of a midget or something to live in there."

"We never used it until last year. Then we made it into a shooting gallery. It's perfect."

At the far end of the room there was a cardboard backstop that reached from ceiling to floor. Two wires were strung across posts several feet in front of the backstop, and a row of paper targets, held in the jaws of clothespins, hung from each wire. Higher up, a round fruitcake can with blue target circles painted on its shiny bottom depended from a wire attached to one of the big, oil-blackened beams.

"What do you shoot with?" Bruce asked.

"A BB pistol."

"Hey, maybe we could use it on those cats, huh?"

"I doubt if it'd be powerful enough. Anyway, it's broken."

"How'd it get broke?"

"Tim got mad once and threw it on the floor. We're going to have it fixed."

"Boy," Bruce said, "you couldn't get me to go in that place for ten bucks."

"We didn't. We shot from right here."

"How'd you know if you hit anything?"

"Well, we did have to go in once and a while for a target check."

"I bet you really had to wipe your feet off afterwards, didn't you?"

Charles thought that Bruce was being very nosy and goggle-eyed, very much like a hick, with his mouth hanging open half the time, and all these questions of his were straining Charles's patience; he wanted to get at those cats.

Bruce had forgotten about the cats for the time being; he wanted to get home and tell his mother about this house.

"Let's go," Charles said, and turned off the lights. Bruce preceded Charles up the steps and as he walked into the kitchen he stopped with such suddenness that Charles bumped into him. Tim lay on his back in the middle of the floor, his head thrown back, his mouth open and the whites of his eyes visible, and his chest, along with the linoleum in his vicinity, was spattered with a thick red matter that was also trickling from his lips. The handle of a butcher knife showed above his rib cage.

"Oh, for God's sake," Charles said. "Not that again." It was about the third time Tim had used this tactic, which was instituted by Charles to frighten their sisters; the blade of the butcher knife was gripped between arm and rib cage, the red matter was ketchup. Charles walked over and prodded Tim with his toe. "Get up," he said, and Bruce, who at last realized this was another act, broke into nervous laughter.

"I thought I told you to watch the girls."

Tim lifted his head. "I can't. I'm dying. I have maybe ten seconds left." He dropped his head. "Five, four, three——"

"Get up!"

Tim jumped to his feet and tossed the knife into the sink. "Thank you," he said in a falsetto, clasping his hands together. "You've just saved my life, kind sir. How can I thank you?"

"Get over there and see what the girls are doing before I clobber you one."

"Would you care to try it?" Tim said, and began to shadowbox around. "Snift-snift, snift!" He danced to an open door, went into his fighting crouch at its edge, and began knocking the door back and forth between his fists in a noisy staccato. "The Toonvaloon rat-a-tat-tat bonecracker, folks. Practicing up. Going to use it on the he-man, the big boss, the big scary one."

Charles walked over and slapped the back of his head. "I told you to cut it out a long time ago. And I told you to get in there and watch the girls. Now *go*." Charles turned to Bruce. "Come on," he said.

As they went through the living room, Tim danced along behind them, making his snifting sound, and just as Charles reached for the door he felt a slap, half-hearted yet imperative, on his back. He swung around. Tim was dancing in front of him, revolving his fists, so furious that his face was pale and there were tears in his eyes.

"Come on," Tim cried. "Come on, you chicken! Fight!"

"Don't let the girls——"

"Come on!"

Charles gave him a long stare of impatience and disdain and walked out the door.

The old barn was overrun with cats. There must have been thirty. After a preliminary inspection, they went to the house and Mrs. Dawson, a plump, high-strung woman with coal-black hair wound in such tight curls it seemed she was wearing a wig, gave them a bowl of scraps, saying, "I haven't put out anything for them for a week or more, so they ought to go for this like it was gold cream. It'll give you a good chance to grab some. I hate to see it come to this, but they been killing robins and getting into people's garbage and gardens and causing so much general complaint there's naught I can do. When I farm them out, they're back the next day, and when other people throw out the cats they don't want, *they* congregate here, and lately they been keeping up the whole neighborhood at night with their caterwauling and making new kitties. If my John was still here, things never would have come to this pass, may the Lord bless him where he lies. Remember your Uncle John, Brucie? Sure you do. All right, you boys run along." They had started toward the barn when she cried, "Now don't kill them all! I need me a few mousers."

A rock held a side door of the barn ajar. They removed it and latched the door from the inside. Until their eyes became accustomed to the darkness of the barn, the holes in its roof and sides surrounded them like distant constellations, and Charles felt as he'd felt once in a planetarium—that the Earth had shrunk to the limits of a house and he was standing at the North Pole, gigantic, and could reach out and extinguish with a fingertip, one by one, each star. When they could see well, they searched for escape exits, Bruce carrying the bowl under one arm. The building originally must have been a horse barn; there were four stalls along one side, and the other half was open, as if for parking a carriage. There was a platform loft above the stalls and an alley in front of them for throwing down hay. In a low window, Bruce discovered a broken pane and they covered it with a piece of masonite. They placed a two-by-twelve over a gap along the bottom of a pair of rolling doors.

Bruce handed the bowl of scraps to Charles and cats began leaning into his legs, running the lengths of their bodies along him, purring and meowing, arching their backs, switching him with their tails, and pawing at his pants. Bruce went into a stall filled with gardening equipment, tools, wooden boxes of junk, buckets, part of a harness and a broken singletree, and here he found and laid out a hand scythe, a baseball bat, several window-sash weights, a ball of twine, a hammer, and a fishing knife that was badly rusted and had old fish scales glittering along its blade. He cut a couple of lengths of twine about nine feet each, and made noose snares of them. These he laid aside.

He took a gunnysack and went into each of the stalls, looking in the feedboxes and mangers, and when he came across a litter of kittens, he dropped them into the sack. Mother cats were following him around, rising on their hind legs to reach the sack, showing their teeth as they meowed at him. He tied the top of the sack with twine and started out the door.

"Hey!" Charles cried. "Where do you think you're going?"

"There's an old rain barrel out behind the barn here. I'm going to put them in there and then put this on them." He turned his butt toward Charles; there was a window-sash weight in his back pocket.

"There's about half a dozen cats following you!" Charles yelled, and was amazed at his tone; it was all out of proportion to the circumstance he was pointing out and to his place in this whole matter.

Bruce reached into his shirt pocket with his forefinger and thumb and held a baby kitten up by the scruff of its neck. "They'll follow me back," he said. His face was pale. He gave a weak smile and walked out.

More cats had gathered around Charles and they were circling and milling about his legs, rising up and leaning on him with their forepaws, pressing against him with such strength and persistence he was afraid that if he moved he'd be thrown off balance and step on one. Or fall. He heard an animal sound like a shrieking hinge (an owl?) and looked up. A row of cats had gathered along the edge of the loft and they were staring down at him with extended necks, heads moving from side to side, as though readying to spring. Bruce reentered the barn with the baby kitten between his thumb and forefinger and most of the mother cats following behind. He closed the door. "The barrel's empty," he said. "I'll just leave them outside for a while till we're done in here." He went into the stall of equipment and placed the kitten in a feedbox.

"Okay," Bruce said. "Put down the food."

"*You* put it down," Charles said, and tossed the bowl to Bruce. The cats followed its flight through the air, and by the time Bruce got it to the ground they were gathered around it like spokes around a hub. The cats in the loft began leaping to the floor, one by one, like precision divers, and bounded toward the bowl, forcing their way into the mass of milling cats already there. Fights, mostly short-lived and petty, began to break out; two cats would sit back on their haunches, teeth bared, and snarl and box at one another, then drop to their feet again and crowd toward the bowl.

"Okay," Bruce said. "Where's the biggest, ugliest one of them all?"

"Right there," Charles said, and pointed out a large tiger-striped tom, leaning back on its haunches, with an enormous flattened head, a spray of needlelike whiskers, and a badly scarred nose. One of its gold eyes was clouded a pearl-gray color, either from injury or disease. "Boy," Bruce said. "He must be the granddaddy of them all. Look at those nuts on him. We better not take any chances with him. We better use the twine. He's going to be a doozie." Bruce looped the nooses together and, when the tom was boxing at a smaller cat, slipped them both over its neck and drew them tight. The tom backed away from him, shaking its head from side to side, as if to say, No, no, no, you've made a terrible mistake.

"Watch this," Bruce said. He reeled the cat toward him until it was within a few feet, and then swung it high overhead, nearly as high as the loft, and brought it down on the floor of the stall with a wallop. Hardly stunned, still held by the twines, the cat tried to claw away from Bruce. Bruce picked up the hand scythe and hit it across the neck. It turned on Bruce, laid back its ears, and spat at him with a gasping sound.

"Get it with something!" Bruce said.

"What?"

"Anything!"

Charles picked up a window-sash weight, threw it, and in his excitement missed. Bruce swung again with the scythe and caught the cat on the tail, and it let out a loud cry of anger and challenge that sent the rest of the cats bolting toward cover. One of them leaped madly against the masonite, knocking it loose, and a stream of cats—calico, tortoiseshell, spotted, tan, gray, white—began pouring out the broken window. Bruce handed Charles the twines, ran over with the baseball bat, was nearly struck in the head by a leaping cat, knocked another down in mid-air with the bat, and got the masonite back in place.

"Geez," Charles said, as the tomcat, with its back arched and its hackles up, danced on stiff legs, fighting the leash of twine. "There has to be a better way of doing this."

"How?"

"We ought to have a rifle."

"But we don't."

"How about stringing him up?"

"We could try," Bruce said, and took the twines from Charles. "You go on up in the hayloft. I'll hand you these ends."

Charles climbed up a board ladder toward the loft, feeling his heart beat so hard at the base of his throat he felt it was knocking his air out. Cats in the loft scattered from him. He walked over until he was above Bruce, and saw that some big spikes had been hammered halfway into the facer board of the loft, perhaps for hanging harness. He lay on his stomach and reached a hand down to Bruce, who was drawing the cat toward him, trying to get enough slack in the twines to hand them up, but the cat was yowling and leaping from side to side at the end of its tether, and winning in the tug-of-war. "You bastard," Bruce said, and gave a jerk, and the cat started toward Bruce as though it meant business. Bruce got the twines to Charles, Charles reeled them quickly hand over hand, suddenly feeling at their ends a tremendous, struggling, unsteady weight, and then he stood and lifted his arms high, got the twines next to a spike, pulled them to one side, and made several turns around another spike. The cat was about five feet off the floor, kicking its hind legs, springing them as though trying to leap, and clawing at the twine with its forepaws. Its scarred and battered nose was turned upward, and its undamaged gold eye, in sharp focus, fixed on Charles. He moved back out of sight. "How long?" he asked.

"That one I choked once took quite a while."

Charles came down the ladder. The cat kicked and pawed at the twine, twisting itself in circles, making moist guttural noises, and after a prolonged minute of this, with Bruce and Charles growing more and more edgy and uncomfortable, there was still no sign that it was weakening.

"I guess it doesn't work like it does with people," Bruce said.

"Now what? If we let him down, he's going to get loose."

"No he isn't," Bruce said, and picked up a three-tined pitchfork. Charles went up to the loft and lowered the cat and Bruce maneuvered a tine on either side of its neck and drove the fork into the ground so the cat was held as in a stanchion. "OK," Bruce said. "Bring the equipment." Charles moved the weights and killing tools closer, and Bruce picked up the baseball bat and struck it across the back. Charles took the hammer and hit it over the head. It fell to its side, legs pawing, and Bruce picked up the fishing knife and stabbed its throat and the knife point skidded sideways over its tough skin without penetrating. Bruce stuck the knife in the cat's ear. "Hit it!" he said.

"*What*?"

"Hit the end of the knife here. Hury!"

"You!"

"I can't! I've got to hold him steady!"

Charles hit the knife with the hammer, driving it a ways into the cat's skull, and the cat let out such a piercing yowl of pain that Bruce jumped back, pulling loose the pitchfork, and the cat, with the knife protruding from its ear, came streaking past Charles. Charles stepped on the trailing twines, they pulled taut, and the cat went up in the air, its hind legs reversing with its head, and hit on its side. The knife dislodged. Bruce ran over with a window-sash weight, lifted it over his head, and brought it down hard on the cat's side. The cat stood, tottered, took off in the opposite direction, and did another flip around as the twine, still under Charles's shoe, pulled taut. Bruce picked up the pitchfork and stabbed with it like a gig. The center tine pierced the cat's abdomen and it began to growl and bark like a dog and claw at the fork as though it would climb it.

"Jesus God!" Bruce cried. *"Its got nine lives!"*

"Don't be stupid!"

"Why isn't it dead then?"

"We haven't got it in a vital place!"

"Where is one?"

Charles came over with the hammer and hit it twice at the base of the skull, then again. Its eyes clouded and closed, its tongue appeared, and its ears turned down toward earth. Blood ran from between its bared teeth and it lay still. Then it went into spasms. Bruce took the baseball bat and beat it until it was motionless. He carried it over to a stall, his face gray and set, and dropped it into a bucket. "Okay," he said, without looking at Charles. "Where's the next one?"

"That's it."

"What do you mean?"

"That's it," Charles said. "I'm quitting."

"You can't. We have to kill the rest."

"What for? Are you crazy about killing them or something?"

"Hell, no."

"Well, if you're so crazy about it, you keep doing it. I'm going home."

Charles walked out of the barn. The lawn in bright sunlight was alive with movement. Somehow, the kittens had escaped from the gunnysack, and they were crawling and tottering through the thick grass, heading toward the barn where Charles stood.

Cats poured out of the door behind him.

At home, Tim was standing in the front room, wearing a black suit jacket of his father's that hung to his knees and a gray wig from an old Halloween costume. He'd found something black—cigar ash, most likely—and rubbed it over his cheeks to represent stubble. "Where's Bruce?" he asked.

"Who knows?"

"Arms for the poor," Tim said, flapping a sleeve of the coat. "Arms for the poor." He seemed reluctant to go into the act he'd prepared, and his voice lacked its usual recklessness and spirit. His face was so pale it appeared white beneath the blacking, his eyes were wide and anxious, and the saddle of freckles over his nose was glittering with points of perspiration, a sign that he was greatly agitated.

"What's wrong?"

"Nothing."

"Where are the girls?"

"Over on the other side. They're coloring."

"Why aren't you there?"

"I saw you coming. Where's Bruce?"

"Busy, I guess."

Charles walked to the bedroom doorway and saw, lying on the card table, the cause of Tim's agitation. The tissue paper for his model airplane was cut into shreds the size of confetti, and somebody had piled the shreds in a neat mound. "Dammit!" he cried, turning on Tim. "What's been going on here?"

"I did it."

"*You* did it? What the hell for?"

"I don't know."

"You don't *know!*" Charles yelled, and ran over and punched Tim in the chest.

"Don't," Tim said. The corners of his mouth pulled down, his chin creased and flattened, and tears started down his cheeks. Charles put his palms on Tim's chest and gave a hard shove and Tim went stumbling backward, trying to get his balance, and struck the wall with such force his wig flew off.

"You thought if Bruce was with me, you wouldn't get it, didn't you, damn you," Charles said, and went over and slapped his head.

"Don't," Tim said. He sat passive, his hands at his sides, and cried loudly, unable to defend or protect himself; when he believed he was at fault, he was so weak and helpless with guilt it was impossible for him to move.

"Why did you *do* it?"

"I don't know! I started cutting and I couldn't stop!"

"How can you be so stupid? That's the most stupid thing I ever heard of. You're so nutty and stupid, you ought to be sent away."

"No!" Tim said, and lay on his stomach and began rocking from side to side. "*No!*"

Charles grabbed a sleeve of the suit jacket and jerked on it, rolling Tim on his back, pulled the sleeve loose, rolled Tim again, and pulled off the jacket. "And on top of it all, you've probably gone and ruined Dad's suit coat. How can you be so stupid," Charles repeated, knowing he'd struck a sensitive spot. He walked to the couch, dropped the jacket on it, and started toward the kitchen. "Now shut up," he said. "Quit crying or you'll get some more!"

He went to the other side of the house. The girls were sitting at a children's card table on small metal chairs, coloring the fashion illustrations from a newspaper ad. The oldest girl, Marie, a brunette whose long hair was stringy and oil-darkened, seldom washed or set, looked up at him; she had the placid face and the nearly circular eyes of the Neumiller family, only her eyes were enormous, owllike. "I'm going to tell Dad you and Tim been fighting again."

"We haven't been."

"Sue and I heard."

"I just gave him heck. He ruined my airplane."

"*Dee,* de, *dee,* de," Susan sang, smiling and swinging a crayon like a pendulum in front of her face. "*Dee,* de, *dee,* de. You said *I'd* break it." She gave Charles a toothy grin and stuck the crayon like a hatpin in her hair, which was flaxen and cut in a style that reminded Charles of pictures of Dutch children.

"Did he watch you two at all?"

"He was with us almost all the time you were gone," Marie said. "He told us why it was more fun to color these than color books."

"Why?"

"Because nobody else in the world colors them."

"Did you see his funny clothes!" Susan said, and began giggling.

"Yes."

"Doesn't he look dumb!"

"I guess."

"Dee, de, dee, dum. Like *that.*" She took the crayon from her hair and pointed at her coloring. The model's face was blackened out. Charles left the room. He couldn't find Tim anywhere on the other side of the house, and was about to go outside when he heard sounds of crying coming from upstairs. He went up the steps. The upstairs was still in the process of being remodeled. Two bedrooms had been partitioned off and some of the walls were partially covered with rock lath. Charles couldn't find Tim in either bedroom. Next to the steps there was a long wall that divided the main part of the house from the wing that had once been a double garage, a wall that was merely studs covered with insulation paper, and Charles went over to it and listened at a door there, and then opened the door onto blackness. There were no windows beyond the wall, not even ventilators to let in light, and Charles knew that it was a three-foot drop to the joists below; the ceiling of the wing was that much lower, and a floor had never been put down over it.

"Tim. Are you in there?"

"No!"

"Come on out."

"No!"

"Why?"

"I don't want to!"

An extension light was hanging from the doorknob. Charles turned it on and in its dim light he could discern the row of planks that led to a platform of old grain doors that had been laid down over the joists. Unpacked boxes from a previous move, old suitcases, and broken furniture were piled on the platform, and Tim was lying there on his stomach, his hands clasped over his head. Charles lowered himself onto the planks and walked out to him. "Come on," he said.

"I want to stay here!"

"Come on."

"This is the place I belong!"

Charles tried to lift him up, but Tim cried out and struggled, and his flesh felt so sensitive in Charles's hands that he let go. "It's just that—well, dammit, when I came home and—anyway, now somebody's going to have to go to Pekin or somewhere and get more of that paper. It's a special kind."

"I know! What's the *matter* with me?"

"I don't know."

"Why can't I do anything *right?*" Tim began rolling his head back and forth on the grain doors.

"Don't. You'll hurt yourself."

"I don't care!"

"I shouldn't have got so mad," Charles said, and sat beside him and put a hand on his shoulder.

"It wouldn't be so bad if——" Tim gasped for air. "If I—if I wasn't so *stupid!*"

"You're not. I just——"

"I am too! I don't even feel like you want me around! It feels worse than when you hit me!"

"I want you around. You're my brother."

Tim let out such a prolonged wail it seemed this injured him more than anything else.

"I do," Charles said. "You're great. "You're really funny sometimes. You're my greatest friend."

Tim's crying subsided and he raised up and looked at Charles with wide eyes. "Really?" he said. His face and the upper part of his body were caked with old, blackened dust from the grain doors, and the dust was streaked with perspiration, mucous from his running nose, and tears.

"Really," Charles said.

Tim sat up, put his arms around Charles, and gripped him so tightly Charles could hardly breathe. "I feel so awful all the time," Tim said. "Inside, I feel awful."

"I'm sorry I——"

"No, no, not because of you. I like you better than anybody."

"Why then?"

"I don't know!"

"You're okay," Charles said, and patted his shoulder. One day, a short while after their mother died, Charles had come home from school and found Tim marching around the front room with his teeth bared as though in fury and his eyes crossed, and as he marched he was singing in time to his step a song he'd composed, "Oh, you cross-eyed baby with the hole in your head; oh, you cross-eyed baby, don't you wish you were dead . . ." From that time, the song had become his theme. He sang it when he was angry at the girls or when he was frustrated or hyperactive. He sang it when he was too happy to express himself. And Charles had heard him singing it in bed at night when he couldn't sleep. Charles tried to think of what their mother, who never would have inflicted this unreasonable hurt on Tim, might say to Tim if she were trying to comfort him, and he remembered waking one night to total darkness, in a house kept calm and ordered by the presence of their mother, and hearing Tim, who couldn't have been more than three, screaming in his bed across the room, and then hearing the voice of their mother. "Little one, little one, what is it?"

"A tiger's after me! He's trying to eat me up!"

"There, there, you've just had a bad dream."

"No, no, it's a *real* tiger! I know it's real. The inside of his mouth is the color of a butterfly!"

And Charles had seen, like a projection upon the blackness, the white and pink and the bright red of a lion's open mouth, and he had felt as he'd felt in the darkened barn when he and Bruce, in spite of all the wounds they had inflicted, could not make the cat relinquish its hold on life—awed and mortally afraid.

"Tim," Charles said, his voice almost a whisper. "Tim, I love you."

Discussion

The duality of emotions is depicted particularly clearly in this story. The selection was chosen to illustrate love, but it is not surprising that aggression and hostility, two dimensions of love, are juxtaposed with love. In *Man Against Himself* (1938, p. 38), Karl Menninger says that "love and hate always operate simultaneously, though the proportions may vary . . . . A fundamental psychological principle is that love tends to follow hate and to neutralize it." Menninger based his work on Freud's theories, which emphasize polarities (as in the life and death instinct).

The aggressive tendencies shown in the cat killing episode in this story are in contradiction to Bruce's and Charlie's need for love and relatedness, which is the story's dominant theme. The boys show morbid enthusiasm for undertaking the project of getting rid of the cats. Clinical studies show that children whose basic needs or important goals are frustrated display unmanageable quantities of aggression parallel to Bruce's and Charlie's reactions. Woiwode provides ample evidence of the emotional impoverishment experienced by Bruce and Charles, but we sense that Bruce is the more isolated child. At school he is the brunt of vicious personal attacks by his age-mates; at home he is the victim of the personal suffocation that must exist amid the home's cleanliness and order. With a striking lack of sensitivity, Bruce is willing to go on with the grizzly job of destroying the cats.

Charles leaves, plainly affected by the episode, to return to his baby-sitting, which he dislikes but less so than the crude attempt to dispose of the cats. His aggressiveness seems to have quickened the positive, healthy feelings of love and protectiveness. The author suggests that at some time a warm mother ministered well to the needs of Charles and Tim. Although Charles is angered when he learns that Tim has cut up the tissue paper for his model airplane, he has sufficient compassion to soften the angry impulses he feels. We are relieved and assured of Charlie's emotional health when he is able to verbalize with honest feeling, "Tim, I love you."

Springboards for Inquiry

(1) The quality of love is severely tested in this story. How do you explain Charles' change of feeling toward Tim?

(2) How does Charles fill the need for relatedness to his peer group?

(3) Do you think love-oriented or power-oriented techniques have been used in disciplining Bruce? Why?

(4) The problem of the socially isolated child is serious in many classrooms. How can the adult help the isolated child to be more "lovable"?

(5) Why is satisfying experience with the emotion of love necessary for the emotional well-being of children? Describe some loving experiences you remember from your own childhood, or recall incidents of loving relationships between parents and children, between siblings, or between friends in their early years.

Jealousy

According to the classic psychoanalytic concept, the child's earliest experience with jealousy occurs during his third and fourth years of life. At this time the child "develops an intense sexualized love for the parent of the opposite sex; that love arouses jealousy, guilt, and anxiety . . ." (Lidz 1968, p. 225). The only definition of jealousy given in the English and English dictionary of psychological terms is "resentment that a beloved person shows affection to a third party" (1958, p. 281). The psychoanalytic concept of Oedipal attachment pervades the literature as the earliest experience of childhood (other than sibling jealousy, which is identifiable after the arrival of the second child) in which a social situation is the stimulus for this resentment. During this Oedipal period a boy feels emotionally attached to his mother and becomes jealous of his father, and a girl is attached to her father and is jealous of her mother. Abrahamsen, who is a psychiatrist with Freudian orientation, says, "Without this experience, there would be no personality development, no development of the superego or conscience, no emotional delineation between the sexes, no family or social situation, no identification, and above all, no mature feelings of love" (1969, p. 114).

In the case of sibling rivalry or jealousy the literature is definite. The dynamics of the development of feelings between brothers and sisters is explored by Strauss (1951); Levy's study (1943) of maternal overprotection cites instances in which children behaved violently with siblings; a searching study of the many-faceted relations between siblings may be found in the work of H. L. Koch (1960). If one discounts the enormous quantity of literature concerning the Oedipus complex, these sibling feelings of rivalry would have to be cited as the first real examples of jealousy as defined above. Age closeness between siblings seems to cause the degree of jealousy to be more marked; when a five-year spread occurs between two children, the older one may see little reason to suppose his mother is overly concerned with the younger sibling.

Jealousy, whether due to Oedipal feelings or sibling rivalry, is a normal response to the feeling that one's "place in the sun" is being usurped. It may result in both direct and indirect behavior. In *The Quiet One,** once a relationship was established between the child and a counselor, jealousy over this adult's positive responses to other children triggers direct, aggressive behavior—the child steals the counselor's cigarette lighter and runs away. In young children indirect responses to feelings of jealousy may cause regressions to infantile behavior, withdrawal from the family constellation, or the repression of those feelings of hostility and hurt.

Reference to our discussions of self-concept will verify the fact that the stronger one's trust is in himself and others, the fewer problems of jealousy one will experience. In early childhood, however, depending on the child's particular psychological orientation, no amount of ego strength achieved in the first two years will affect Oedipal feelings. Similarly, one can expect that a three-year-old presented with a newborn brother will suffer some jealous feelings. The comprehension of the adults in the child's world and their appropriate behavior can mitigate sibling jealousy. The jealous child needs to be made secure in these times of stress; thoughtful, conscious adult behavior will decrease the anxiety of the older child, and very young children need overt strengthening of the maternal bond to ease the problem.

Overambition, failure, and the desire for the material benefits of other children cause jealousy as children mature. Elementary school teachers may observe these reactions in any classroom. The amelioration of these feelings is rarely possible unless the teacher's personality responds equally to the aggressive, hostile, sad, and withdrawing youngsters and to the overt, friendly, and engaging children. Raths (1954), discussing the needs of children, maintains that the teacher's personal behavior can do much to satisfy a child's need for attention, affection, and achievement. When adults place undue stress on the accomplishments of some or the failures of others, a class reacts—in terms of joy either for all who participate or only for those who bask in the favored light of the teacher, who drowns some in approval and relegates others to social and academic limbos.

---

* McGraw-Hill Films, 1948.

"It's like a fire," she said, "in the stove." "You're lying, you don't remember!" cried the children.

All Summer in a Day

by Ray Bradbury

"READY?"

"Ready."

"Now?"

"Soon."

"Do the scientists really know? Will it happen today, will it?"

"Look, look; see for yourself!"

The children pressed to each other like so many roses, so many weeds, intermixed, peering out for a look at the hidden sun.

It rained.

It had been raining for seven years; thousands upon thousands of days compounded and filled from one end to the other with rain, with the drum and gush of water, with the sweet crystal fall of showers and the concussion of storms so heavy they were tidal waves come over the islands. A thousand forests had been crushed under the rain and grown up a thousand times to be crushed again. And this was the way life was forever on the planet Venus, and this was the schoolroom of the children of the rocket men and women who had come to a raining world to set up civilization and live out their lives.

"It's stopping, it's stopping!"

"Yes, yes!"

Margot stood apart from them, from these children who could never remember a time when there wasn't rain and rain and rain. They were all nine years old, and if there had been a day, seven years ago, when the sun came out for an hour and showed its face to the stunned world, they could not recall. Sometimes, at night, she heard them stir, in remembrance, and she knew they were dreaming and remembering gold or a yellow crayon or a coin large enough to buy the world with. She knew they thought they remembered a warmness, like a blushing in the face, in the body, in the arms and

---

legs and trembling hands. But then they always awoke to the tatting drum, the endless shaking down of clear bead necklaces upon the roof, the walk, the gardens, the forests, and their dreams were gone.

All day yesterday they had read in class about the sun. About how like a lemon it was, and how hot. And they had written small stories or essays about it:

I think the sun is a flower,
That blooms for just one hour.

That was Margot's poem, read in a quiet voice in the still classroom while the rain was falling outside.

"Aw, you didn't write that!" protested one of the boys.

"I did," said Margot. "I *did.*"

"William!" said the teacher.

But that was yesterday. Now the rain was slackening, and the children were crushed in the great thick windows.

"Where's teacher?"

"She'll be back."

"She'd better hurry, we'll miss it!"

They turned on themselves, like a feverish wheel, all tumbling spokes.

Margot stood alone. She was a very frail girl who looked as if she had been lost in the rain for years and the rain had washed out the blue from her eyes and the red from her mouth and the yellow from her hair. She was an old photograph dusted from an album, whitened away, and if she spoke at all her voice would be a ghost. Now she stood, separate, staring at the rain and the loud wet world beyond the huge glass.

"What're *you* looking at?" said William.

Margot said nothing.

"Speak when you're spoken to." He gave her a shove. But she did not move; rather she let herself be moved only by him and nothing else.

They edged away from her, they would not look at her. She felt them go away. And this was because she would play no games with them in the echoing tunnels of the underground city. If they tagged her and ran, she stood blinking after them and did not follow. When the class sang songs about happiness and life and games her lips barely moved. Only when they sang about the sun and the summer did her lips move as she watched the drenched windows.

And then, of course, the biggest crime of all was that she had come here only five years ago from Earth, and she remembered the sun and the way the sun was and the sky was when she was four in Ohio. And they, they had been on Venus all their lives, and they had been only two years old when last the sun came out and had long since forgotten the color and heat of it and the way it really was. But Margot remembered.

"It's like a penny," she said once, eyes closed.

"No it's not!" the children cried.

"It's like a fire," she said, "in the stove."

"You're lying, you don't remember!" cried the children.

But she remembered and stood quietly apart from all of them and watched the patterning windows. And once, a month ago, she had refused to shower in the school shower rooms, had clutched her hands to her ears and over her head, screaming the water mustn't touch her head. So after that, dimly, dimly, she sensed it, she was different and they knew her difference and kept away.

There was talk that her father and mother were taking her back to Earth next year; it seemed vital to her that they do so, though it would mean the loss of thousands of dollars to her family. And so, the children hated her for all these reasons of big and little consequence. They hated her pale snow face, her waiting silence, her thinness, and her possible future.

"Get away!" The boy gave her another push. "What're you waiting for?"

Then, for the first time, she turned and looked at him. And what she was waiting for was in her eyes.

"Well, don't wait around here!" cried the boy savagely. "You won't see nothing!"

Her lips moved.

"Nothing!" he cried. "It was all a joke, wasn't it?" He turned to the other children. "Nothing's happening today. *Is* it?"

They all blinked at him and then, understanding, laughed and shook their heads. "Nothing, nothing!"

"Oh, but," Margot whispered, her eyes helpless. "But this is the day, the scientists predict, they say, they *know,* the sun . . ."

"All a joke!" said the boy, and seized her roughly. "Hey, everyone, let's put her in a closet before teacher comes!"

"No," said Margot, falling back.

They surged about her, caught her up and bore her, protesting, and then pleading, and then crying, back into a tunnel, a room, a closet, where they slammed and locked the door. They stood looking at the door and saw it tremble from her beating and throwing herself against it. They heard her muffled cries. Then, smiling, they turned and went out and back down the tunnel, just as the teacher arrived.

"Ready, children?" She glanced at her watch.

"Yes!" said everyone.

"Are we all here?"

"Yes!"

The rain slackened still more.

They crowded to the huge door.

The rain stopped.

It was as if, in the midst of a film concerning an avalanche, a tornado, a hurricane, a volcanic eruption, something had, first, gone wrong with the sound apparatus, thus muffling and finally cutting off all noise, all of the blasts and repercussions and thunders, and then, second, ripped the film from the projector and inserted in its place a peaceful tropical slide which did not move or tremor. The world ground to a standstill. The silence was so immense and unbelievable that you felt your ears had been stuffed or you had lost your hearing altogether. The children put their hands to their ears. They stood apart. The door slid back and the smell of the silent, waiting world came in to them.

The sun came out.

It was the color of flaming bronze and it was very large. And the sky around it was a blazing blue tile color. And the jungle burned with sunlight as the children, released from their spell, rushed out, yelling, into the springtime.

"Now, don't go too far," called the teacher after them. "You've only two hours, you know. You wouldn't want to get caught out!"

But they were running and turning their faces up to the sky and feeling the sun on their cheeks like a warm iron; they were taking off their jackets and letting the sun burn their arms.

"Oh, it's better than the sun lamps, isn't it?"

"Much, much better!"

They stopped running and stood in the great jungle that covered Venus, that grew and never stopped growing, tumultuously, even as you watched it. It was a nest of octopi, clustering up great arms of fleshlike weed, wavering, flowering in this brief spring. It was the color of rubber and ash, this jungle, from the many years without sun. It was the color of stones and white cheeses and ink, and it was the color of the moon.

The children lay out, laughing, on the jungle mattress, and heard it sigh and squeak under them, resilient and alive. They ran among the trees, they slipped and fell, they pushed each other, they played hide-and-seek and tag, but most of all they squinted at the sun until tears ran down their faces, they put their hands up to that yellowness and that amazing blueness and they breathed of the fresh, fresh air and listened to the silence which suspended them in a blessed sea of no sound and no motion. They looked at everything and savored everything. Then, wildly, like animals escaped from their caves, they ran and ran in shouting circles. They ran for an hour and did not stop running.

And then—

In the midst of their running one of the girls wailed.

Everyone stopped.

The girl, standing in the open, held out her hand.

"Oh, look, look," she said trembling.

They came slowly to look at her opened palm.

In the center of it, cupped and huge, was a single raindrop.

She began to cry, looking at it.

They glanced quietly at the sky.

"Oh. Oh."

A few cold drops fell on their noses and their cheeks and their mouths. The sun faded behind a stir of mist. A wind blew cool around them. They turned and started to walk back toward the underground house, their hands at their sides, their smiles vanishing away.

A boom of thunder startled them and like leaves before a new hurricane, they tumbled upon each other and ran. Lightning struck ten miles away, five miles away, a mile, a half mile. The sky darkened into midnight in a flash.

They stood in the doorway of the underground for a moment until it was raining hard. Then they closed the door and heard the gigantic sound of the rain falling in tons and avalanches, everywhere and forever.

"Will it be seven more years?"

"Yes. Seven."

Then one of them gave a little cry.

"Margot!"

"What?"

"She's still in the closet where we locked her."

"Margot."

They stood as if someone had driven them, like so many stakes, into the floor. They looked at each other and then looked away. They glanced out at the world that was raining now and raining and raining steadily. They could not meet each other's glances. Their faces were solemn and pale. They looked at their hands and feet, their faces down.

"Margot."

One of the girls said, "Well . . . ?"

No one moved.

"Go on," whispered the girl.

They walked slowly down the hall in the sound of cold rain. They turned through the doorway to the room in the sound of the storm and thunder, lightning on their faces, blue and terrible. They walked over to the closet door slowly and stood by it.

Behind the closet door was only silence.

They unlocked the door, even more slowly, and let Margot out.

Discussion

This selection, although set against the science fiction atmosphere of Venus, is basically a story that explores the emotion of jealousy. Feelings of jealousy arouse many negative reactions such as hatred, anger, and self-doubt.

In this story Margot, who experienced the sun daily for several years, heightens the children's sense of deprivation. Inhabitants of Venus all their lives, their sunless existence is accentuated by Margot's presence. The children also resent the alternative of returning to earth that is open to Margot but ruled out of their future. Jealousy is known to be a sufficient motive for malicious behavior, as illustrated in this story. After the children have reacted with anger and hostility to Margot, they find that their behavior has not appeased their feelings of being less privileged than she; their existence and future is no less dismal as a result of locking Margot in the closet. The children seem remorseful when they remember what they have done to Margot and they go down the hall to release her.

Springboards for Inquiry

(1) We have the feeling at the end of this story that the children's remorse will be short-lived and will perhaps erupt again into open aggression of a more violent nature. Do you agree? What does the emotion of jealousy tell us about the frustration of goal-seeking behavior?

(2) Give other examples of how jealousy may erupt among children of school age. How can adults help children to deal with this emotion?

(3) When a child is restrained from openly expressing the negative feelings associated with jealousy he may feel for a sibling, he may use displacement and reaction formation. Give examples.

Fear

The capacity to experience fear is born into man; what to be afraid of is learned. Specific fear reactions are not instinctive, then, but are conditioned. An early researcher (Hagman 1932) found a correlation of .60+ between the things that frighten a child and those that frighten his mother. Fear is a natural way of preparing for danger and withdrawing from it. When Franklin D. Roosevelt* said, "The only thing we have to fear is fear itself," he was suggesting that the feeling of fear can also be dangerous when it generates disastrous responses, such as panic, anxiety, or immobility.

In a lecture in Watertown National Park, Alberta, Canada, an American authority on the grizzly bear indicated that when a person is confronted by a grizzly in the wilds, fear and its concomitant reactions—anxiety, aggression, hostility, and combat—will panic people into running away or attacking the bear. Both actions will assure the demise of the individual. Instead, the expert counseled control of fear through knowledge of the facts: grizzlies would rather avoid humans, and a steady walking toward the bear will cause him to retreat.

Fear not only affects behavior but it also produces physiological responses. The stability of the body may be severely disturbed in fear reactions and the resulting lack of homeostasis may produce ulcers, hyperthyroidism, and bronchial asthma (Hans Selye 1946 and 1956). Lidz (1968, pp. 537–38) reports an experiment performed by Selye in which tying rats' legs produced great fright in them and caused severe emotional trauma which resulted in adrenocortical exhaustion. In classrooms in which fear is the dominant motivating factor children

---

* Inaugural Address, March 4, 1933.

often urinate and defecate in their schoolroom seats rather than in appropriate places. In *Children Under Pressure* (Doll and Fleming 1966) we read of conditions in schools and society that have caused childhood suicide—a physiological response only in the broadest sense—to become a major problem.

We mentioned that learned responses figure greatly in the etiology of fear. In general, memories of traumatic experiences play the most significant role in the development of fear in children. Indeed, infants and young children may be said to be fearless until they have had either personal experiences: "I woke up in the dark, cried for my mother, and when she did not come I associated darkness with my wanting my mother"; or from being instructed: "My mother was always terrified of dogs and when I was a toddler and a dog came up to me my mother screamed and beat off the dog. She told me to run into the house if any dog ever came near me. Since then I have been terrified of dogs if they walk right up to me."

In the early school years, school phobia or fear of school has been identified and assessed (Leton 1962). It is usually associated with the concern for being separated from one's mother, who may be overprotective or dominant. For many children school means a separation from home, where until this time the child has been the center of attention. The condition of now being one among many children may contribute to a general sense of inadequacy. Fear of the unknown and the known ("school teachers are mean or may hit you if you don't behave") combine to affect the child's adjustment to this new situation. Many schools attempt to overcome the onset of this phobia by holding early class meetings of very small groups and gradually increasing the size of the class in the first few days of the school year. Extreme school phobia * produces marked physiological reactions in some children—gagging, nausea, crying, hysterics, stomach pains—and some psychological dependency reactions such as clinging to mother and refusing even to enter the school.

Some general findings show that fear is greater in the young child than it is in the infant or in the older child, and is thus related to the developing intelligence; the young child can realize the potential for danger in situations to which he was oblivious as a baby and to which he becomes accustomed as he grows older. There is also some evidence that the mass media influences the fears of young children (Albert 1957). As children grow older, then, fears decrease in number and severity and yield to feelings of anxiety, which in many ways are

---

* A follow-up study of 140 children who were hospitalized for school phobia shows that within five to ten years of their hospitalization, 14 of them became earnest school workers. The report says: "The overall adaptation of this group . . . was surprisingly good. With few exceptions these young people maintained a good work or school performance. . . . They had achieved an emotional independence from the primary family. They had an adequate self-identity and functioned reasonably well in adult society" (Morris Akis and Autheta Burke, "A Five to Ten Year Follow-up of Hospitalized School Phobia Children and Adolescents," *American Journal of Orthopsychiatry* 40 [1970]: 674).

more pernicious. Anxiety states lead to timidity, withdrawal from life situations, and generalized feelings of uneasiness that are difficult to cope with.

As children grow older, fear of the supernatural and of death increases, but overt indications of fear decrease. The peer group at this time pressures the child to be fearless, and children go to great lengths to avoid having their fear detected. It is not uncommon to see retreats from reality ("I don't want to go out to play") and the development of imaginary ills, both of which suggest childhood fear and anxiety that are being suppressed (a conscious act), repressed (unconscious behavior), or positively reinforced by the attention and sympathy paid to the child's emotional behavior.

Modern schools and other institutions have learned to reduce fear-producing situations.* Others accept Hebb's cognitive dissonance theory (1946), which explains that fear is produced because a child does not have a response to a new stimulus that differs too much from earlier experiences. Anxiety develops when cognitive pathways are lacking for any stimulus, so schools typically subscribe to the prevailing general child development theory and put a high premium on the role of wide and varied experiences. The therapeutic approach to the optimum development of the child suggests that while the absence of all stressful situations is unrealistic, conscious attempts to minimize climate that aggravates and incites fear are important aspects of any institutional setting.

---

* Anesthesiologists have recognized children's fears of being put to sleep (often equated with death) and so hospitals prepare children for the experience by puppet shows depicting the events or filmstrips that detail the procedures.

"You don't need to be afraid, Peter, we're here. And soon you'll have a dog of your own to sleep here with you. . . ."

The Dog

by Carol Reilley

The man said every son should have a dog. It was a part of his training, part of his growing up. The woman said she wasn't sure, after all, the furniture and all, you know. Of course, if it were a little dog . . .

"Little dog!" The man pounded his fist on the table, until the forks bounced, and the coffee splashed dangerously. "A boy needs a big dog; little dogs are for women and sissies. It takes a big dog with a big heart for a boy."

The man glared angrily, and the woman shivered back into her chair. The subject was closed. For a minute there was only the sound of knives and forks against the battered china plates. Then the man began speaking slowly of his day at work.

But the dog still lurked in the shadows. Peter toyed with his food, mixing the horrible spinach and the horrible peas together, and then carefully separating them into two sickening piles. Dogs were not good things. He had never known one very well, but he knew they were not good.

"Can you eat your peas, Peter?" the woman asked. "They're good for you. They'll make you a strong, big man."

"Yes'm," Peter said, and squashed one cruelly with his spoon. He did not dare look at her face. He knew that she wanted him to call her "Mother," but he could not. He felt sorry for her, dimly sensing the longing that lay at the bottom of her weakness. He squashed another pea. He wondered if it felt the pain. He hoped it did. He hated peas.

"Peter," the man said, "clean up your plate, and when you're finished, we'll go into the living room while Mother clears off the table, and we'll talk about the dog. Would you like that, Peter, boy?"

Peter put his spoon down on the plate. He stared at the horrible spinach and the horrible peas. He felt suddenly, softly sick.

"Sir," he mumbled. "I don't think I would care for a dog." He wiggled uneasily, sensing the man's hurt. "They're so expensive and things," he added quickly.

"Nonsense," said the man. "Now clean up your plate!"

"Oh, don't make him, Charles, if he doesn't want to, just this once——"

"Quiet!" shouted the man. "He'll eat that food before he leaves the table. He's only been here a couple of weeks and already you want to spoil him!"

The woman moved from the table and silently cleared the dishes away. Peter knew that her silence was not anger. It had something to do with the hurt in her body, and the hurt in the body of her man. Peter knew that he had put the hurt there.

He ate the spinach and peas quietly. The sickness in his stomach was not from them. There was a dark shadow in the corner by the stove. Peter moved on his chair, away from it. His eyes kept coming back in tingling horror. He was sure he saw the shapeless form of a dog, crouching there.

Bed was a terrible thing, in this new house. It was a frightening thing, there, all alone in the room, high, cold, and white.

Before, bed had always been a little cot, lined up against the wall with four other little cots. Before it had been friendly, with pillow fights, and the light of a street lamp through the window, and sleep, and the quiet breathing coming from the moonlit humps of other boys.

Here there was only loneliness. There was not even a street light. There were only shadows, blending into one frightening shadow in the darkness. Peter hated bed in the new house. He had never known his mother, never cried for her, and inside he had always felt a superiority over these boys who sobbed softly into their pillows in the nighttime. But here, in the new house, he, too, knew the sickening sobs. When he could not sleep with his fear, he lay and cried for his little cot, and the warmth of the Marshall Home.

This night he climbed into the bed and lay trembling beneath the cold sheet. He lay still while the woman bent to kiss him. He had never known such fear. Every shadow was a dog. He could not let the woman go. He clung to her.

"What's wrong, Peter, darling?" she asked softly.

He was ashamed of his fear, "Nothing, ma'am," he said.

She opened the window, and adjusted the shade. She smoothed the covers across his legs. He lay stiff, unspeaking, afraid of her leaving.

"Good night, Peter, honey," she said. She smiled down at him. She turned out the light, and stood there for a moment, her fingers lingering on the switch. "Good night," she said again, and waited for his answer.

"Good night, ma'am," Peter said. She sighed, and then he heard her slowly going down the steps.

He lay stiffly in the darkness. He did not dare to close his eyes. He watched the shadows warily, fearfully, trying to make out the crouched figure of a dog. He lay still, so it would not see him. He pressed his hands against his throat, to protect it from the tearing fangs. He waited. The shadows drew together, came closer. There was a scraping across the floor. He could not breathe. There was a roaring in his ears. A cold breath brushed his cheek. His stomach tightened. He clutched the sheets, and drew himself up. The dog shadows were all around him. All around him . . .

Peter screamed. "Mother!" he screamed. "Father!" He choked, and then screamed again, hysterically.

He could not hear the sounds they made, until they were there, and the light had blinded on, and chased the shadow dog away. He sobbed, and clung to them.

They asked him things he could not bear to answer, until the sobs inside of him had died away.

"Peter, Peter, honey!" the woman said, and her arms were close around him, and her hand was warm in his hair.

"What's wrong, son?" the man said. "Have a nightmare, or something?"

He lay quietly, sensing the new warmth in them. He did not dare to say anything about the dog. He was afraid the hurt would come back to their eyes.

They sat with him a while. The man's arm was warm across Peter's shoulders. "You don't need to be afraid, Peter, we're here. And soon you'll have a dog of your own to sleep here with you . . ."

"On the bed?" the woman started to say, and then she stopped, and smiling, brushed her cheek across the man's chest.

They left him there.

"Should I leave the light on, Peter?" the woman said.

"Yes—Mother," Peter answered carefully, "if you would."

She came over to him, and kissed him again, and held him close. Peter knew her hunger, and slipped his arm around her neck experimentally.

She let him go, and moved away. "Good night," she said, and waited.

"Good night, Mother," said Peter carefully. "Good night, Father."

He heard them laugh. He heard the man say, "You're spoiling him, darling."

The woman answered, "A boy needs a father to give him a dog, and make a man out of him, and a mother to spoil him, just a little."

Peter listened to their happy laughter. It was a new thing to him, and he knew that he had put it there.

He lay for a long time, his eyes still open, staring unseeingly at the books and toys that lined the walls of the lonely room. His mind was dulled from fear. He did not actually think of the dog. He just lay there, dumbly, until sleep came.

The next three days were slow ones. Peter tried very hard to remember to call them "Mother" and "Father." It seemed such a little thing to say, and he could sense the glow inside of them when he said it.

He still could not make himself go up into the room, and play there with all the toys and books they had brought him. He was afraid to be alone in the room, even in the daytime. The fear of that night was still with him.

Bed was sheer terror. He spent those next three days in shadow of the coming night. They left the light on for him now. The first time he asked for it again, the man was angry. Lord, he shouted, what am I raising for a son, a pantywaist. The woman had pleaded with him, clinging to his arm. No, no, he had cried.

"Please, Dad," Peter had said.

"Just for now," the woman begged.

"Dad, please," Peter whispered.

The man had turned to him, hugged him close. "I'm spoiling him, too," he had said. "For a while then, Peter, but remember, if I get you a dog, you'll have to act like a man, and not be afraid of the dark."

Peter could say nothing, only slip back among the pillows, and pray hollowly the man would forget the dog.

So the three days passed. Peter spent the afternoon of the third one in the kitchen with the woman. She was making an apple pie. He stayed close to her, following her wherever she went, not daring to be away from the warmth of her body.

"Be a good boy, Peter, darling," she laughed, "and fetch me the sugar."

"Yes, ma'am," he said, and ran across the floor to the cupboard. He liked the cold sound of his feet against the linoleum. He liked this linoleum. It was red and white and black, not the smooth dull brown of the linoleum on the floors of the Marshall Home. He brought the sugar back to her, put the can into her waiting hands. He saw a kind of pain around her eyes. He did not like it there.

"Here—Mother," he said, and smiled.

The woman laughed, and tried to lift him in her arms.

"You're heavy, Peter," she said. "O Peter, Peter, you do like it here, don't you?"

"Yes, ma'am—Mother," he said.

"We love you so," and she was not talking to him any more. "We don't want them ever to take—to, oh, Peter, honey! Miss Rodgers is coming tomorrow, maybe, or Saturday. You know who she is. She brought you here. She'll come quite often at first, once a month, maybe, until she's sure you're going to fit in here. And you will, Peter. We love you so; we'll be good to you. Sometimes, at night . . ." She stopped, and laughed, a little ashamed.

She turned back to the mixing bowl. "Your father will be home soon," she said. "This will be a good night, Peter."

He slipped to the floor, and sat contemplating the good, clean, black and white squares of linoleum. He traced his fingers around a slim red line of circle. The color was warm, but the touch was cool.

The woman moved back and forth beside him, humming and talking. Her legs brushed his back. He did not listen to her words. He began playing a game on the squares, seeing how many he could touch, with his palm pushed down, and his fingers spread out across the cold floor.

The afternoon was gone, and dusk had come. The front door rattled.

"It's your father," the woman said. "You go, Peter."

He gave his truck another shove across the soft livingroom rug, and then made himself stand up, and go to the door. He opened it slowly, and stared into the dusk.

The man was standing there, smiling. "Surprise, Peter," he said, and Peter watched dumbly, while the man pulled gently at the rope in his hand.

"It's a dog, Peter," the man said. "See, it's an Irish setter. Isn't she a beauty? Here, Peter."

Peter stared at the dog. The woman came up behind him. "It is a little big," she said doubtfully, "but it is pretty." She rested a hand on Peter's shoulder. "What's her name?"

"Well, whatever Peter wants to call her, I suppose," the man said.

Peter lost the sound of their words in a dull drone. He stared at the dog. It looked back at him, and whimpered. Peter backed up against the woman.

"Don't be afraid, son," the man said. "Here, pet her. She won't hurt you."

The man stepped inside. The dog moved toward Peter. Its cool nose brushed his hand.

Out of the depths of his mind, a cold fear arose. It came from a cold, sharp, blue place, in the back of his head. It put its fingers around his heart, and pushed into his throat. It choked his breath.

The dog pushed its eager body against him. Peter screamed, and wrenched free. He ran, not knowing where he was going. He thought he could feel the breath of the dog against his neck.

He slammed the kitchen door shut behind him, and held it, screaming hysterically. He swayed, and the linoleum reeled dizzily up to meet him.

Peter lay there, and retched weakly all over the cool black and white squares, and the swimming red circles.

The next day, Miss Rodgers came, and Peter went back with her. He clung to her, screaming, begging when she came, and the man and woman stood there together, stunned, and crying a little.

"It happens this way, sometimes," Miss Rodgers explained, "that the child doesn't adjust. Once in a while it comes suddenly like this. Other times, it comes slowly, several months, or even a year. Sometimes it is a difference in temperament not apparent at first, and sometimes, like this, it is a fear buried in the child. I'm sorry for this, but I think you'll understand."

Peter got his coat, and Miss Rodgers helped him pack some of his things in a little box. They left the bedroom, and there was no sadness inside of Peter. They went downstairs to say good-by, and he clung tightly to the familiar warmth of her plump fingers.

Miss Rodgers talked to the man and the woman a little longer, and then she told him it was time to go.

"Say good-by, Peter," she said gently.

The woman sat lost in the heavy chair, and there were tears on her cheeks. The man stood beside her.

The dog scratched on the basement door, and barked hoarsely. Peter did not even shiver. The man swore softly. Peter saw the woman's fingers tighten around his hand. He knew again that there was hurt in their bodies, he knew again that he had put it there.

"Good-by, ma'am," he said softly. "Good-by, sir."

All the way back to the Marshall Home, he sat stiffly next to Miss Rodgers in the car. It was not until they were almost there, that he began to cry, softly, and slowly. He was not sure, inside of him, the reason why.

Discussion

As this story opens we are introduced to two characters—a man who holds firmly set opinions about boys and their development of masculinity and a woman who is houseproud and who does not dispute her husband's decisions. These two adults, who have been knit together over a long period of time by their respective needs—one to dominate and the other to submit—ultimately provide an irreconcilable atmosphere for Peter.

Coming from an institutional environment, Peter is unused to the loneliness imposed by being the only child in a family setting. His early experiences lacked the fortification of warm, loving, close relationships and he is thus more vulnerable to feelings of fear in the face of the unknown. A psychological appraisal of Peter's early years would suggest that he has not progressed through the early stages of development as defined by Erikson—stages that lay the foundation for trust and success in the face of new experiences.

Peter's relationship with this childless couple lacks spontaneity and warmth. A novice in the role of son, Peter is painfully self-conscious in the performance of his duties. Peter is particularly upset by the prospect of the father bringing home a dog for him, and he feels not only fear of the dog but also guilt at his inability to share the father's enthusiasm for the dog.

Although many children have a fear of dogs based on reality, Peter's fear does not seem to stem from prior bad experiences. The physiological responses to fear that Peter experiences are clinically described. He feels a pounding heart, constriction around the neck making it difficult to breathe, a tight stomach, roaring in the ears, and a feeling of nausea leading to vomiting. Indeed, the fear of the dog acts as a catalyst to give expression to all of Peter's fears, as he projects his total discomfort in the new and tense environment into nightmare visions of attacking dogs.

Springboards for Inquiry

(1) Discuss how pathological you think Peter's fear of the dog was. What incident besides the appearance of the dog might have precipitated similar anxiety-fear reactions in Peter?

(2) Explain your view of Peter's chances of adjusting to a family relationship and the complex interrelatedness that it requires.

(3) How do parents' fears influence children?

(4) Cite some fears which are prevalent during the school years. Suggest ways in which adults may help children to handle the fears of middle childhood.

Courage

The topic of courage has rarely been the subject of specific research; that is, children who have performed courageous acts or who have behaved in courageous ways—overcoming a physical handicap, for instance—have not been subjected to rigorous study. Under the headings "Fear" and "Coping" we discussed aspects of emotional development that approached the topic of courage. Interestingly, the particular approach of this book—learning about child development from literature—seems to be the most valid way (other than the pure research-oriented method) to discover the dimensions of courage. Although we know little about the origins of courage—its etiology and transmission—from research findings, we often meet manifestations of courage in literature and in the daily press.

In children's literature examples of courage are frequent—from the story of the little boy who plugged the hole in the dike with his finger to Armstrong Sperry's *Call It Courage.** In *The Black Pearl* by Scott O'Dell† we read of a youth who dares to search for a fabulous black pearl that is guarded by a giant manta ray. In Maia Wojciechowska's *Shadow of a Bull*‡ a different kind of courage—the understanding of one's personal limitations—is portrayed. In this Newbery Award story a young boy realizes his feelings of fear and inadequacy as he tries to live up to the reputation of his dead father, once the greatest matador in the village. The boy withdraws from training as a matador

---

* See also Alice Dalgleish *The Courage of Sarah Noble* (New York: Charles Scribners Sons, 1954).

† Boston: Houghton Mifflin Co., 1967.

‡ New York: Atheneum, 1964.

even though it crushes the dreams of a city, providing an example of unusual personal courage.

Examples of children who rescue others from dangerous situations point to the ideas that courage is related to states of tension. Some people react to danger by becoming depressed; others spawn courage and are able to act beyond their capacities. Courage seems to be related to ignorance, too—that is, very young children will enter situations that older ones will not enter because the younger ones have less knowledge of the possibilities of danger. A ten-year-old we know completed climbing school in the Grand Teton Mountains of Wyoming, accomplishing at the age of ten a forty-foot free fall and a rope exercise in mountain climbing, while his father refused to start. Again, we have personal knowledge of children who undergo operations that would test the courage of an adult. In the journal *Dialogue** a story tells about a child of six dying from bone leukemia. After months of seeing him slowly waste away, his parents have already lost their courage and are unable to comprehend the meaning of life. The emaciated child, sensing that his last moments are near, asks them to take him for a ride in their station wagon to get a hamburger. As he starts to eat his final meal, his strength leaves him and he hands his mother the hamburger, saying, "Mommy, I'll finish it in heaven." Courage in the face of death, a peculiar attribute of children, is probably an admixture of simple faith and lack of knowledge.

Erikson's discussion of fear in the concluding chapter of *Childhood and Society,* 2nd ed. (1963, p. 406) offers some clues to at least one aspect of courage, particularly if we view courage as either the absence of fear or the opposite of fear. He says, "Fears are states of apprehension which focus on isolated and recognizable dangers. . . ." Thus, when there is no circuitry for knowledge, when there is no previous experience to base one's reaction on, it is not courage that is developed, but "irrational tension" (Erikson 1963, p. 407). Jersild's advice (1960) for dealing with fear or building courage is to try to explain to children the dynamics of the situation.† He also suggests that adults set examples of fearlessness and try to recondition the child so that he reacts to the stimulus in a positive way.

It would appear, then, that courage is related to tension and anxiety, and that knowledge of possible problems and dangers can contribute to the development of courage. Finally, children learn to cope with fear through rational explanation, parental example, and positive reconditioning.

---

* Carole C. Hansen, "The Death of a Son," *Dialogue* 2 (Autumn 1967): 91–96.

† Although this may not be the place to discuss what children can understand, it seems worthwhile to help children develop courage by talking directly about anxiety-producing situations. If the cognitive substance of the explanation does not "take," the mere fact of spending time will reduce tension. See Erikson's description of explaining to a four-year-old something about the reasons for the child's refusal to defecate (1963, pp. 53–55).

"About what time do you think I'm going to die?" he asked.

A Day's Wait

by Ernest Hemingway

HE CAME into the room to shut the windows while we were still in bed and I saw he looked ill. He was shivering, his face was white, and he walked slowly as though it ached to move.

"What's the matter, Schatz?"

"I've got a headache."

"You better go back to bed."

"No. I'm all right."

"You go to bed. I'll see you when I'm dressed."

But when I came downstairs he was dressed, sitting by the fire, looking a very sick and miserable boy of nine years. When I put my hand on his forehead I knew he had a fever.

"You go up to bed," I said, "you're sick."

"I'm all right," he said.

When the doctor came he took the boy's temperature.

"What is it?" I asked him.

"One hundred and two."

Downstairs, the doctor left three different medicines in different colored capsules with instructions for giving them. One was to bring down the fever, another a purgative, the third to overcome an acid condition. The germs of influenza can only exist in an acid condition, he explained. He seemed to know all about influenza and said there was nothing to worry about if the fever did not go above one hundred and four degrees. This was a light epidemic of flu and there was no danger if you avoided pneumonia.

Back in the room I wrote the boy's temperature down and made a note of the time to give the various capsules.

"Do you want me to read to you?"

"All right. If you want to," said

---

the boy. His face was very white and there were dark areas under his eyes. He lay still in the bed and seemed very detached from what was going on.

I read aloud from Howard Pyle's *Book of Pirates;* but I could see he was not following what I was reading.

"How do you feel, Schatz?" I asked him.

"Just the same, so far," he said.

I sat at the foot of the bed and read to myself while I waited for it to be time to give another capsule. It would have been natural for him to go to sleep, but when I looked up he was looking at the foot of the bed, looking very strangely.

"Why don't you try to go to sleep? I'll wake you up for the medicine."

I'd rather stay awake."

After a while he said to me, "You don't have to stay in here with me, Papa, if it bothers you.

"It doesn't bother me."

"No, I mean you don't have to stay if it's going to bother you."

I thought perhaps he was a little lightheaded and after giving him the prescribed capsules at eleven o'clock I went out for a while.

It was a bright, cold day, the ground covered with a sleet that had frozen so that it seemed as if all the bare trees, the bushes, the cut brush and all the grass and the bare ground had been varnished with ice. I took the young Irish setter for a little walk up the road and along a frozen creek; but it was difficult to stand or walk on the glassy surface and the red dog slipped and slithered and I fell twice, hard, once dropping my gun and having it slide away over the ice.

We flushed a covey of quail under a high clay bank with overhanging brush and I killed two as they went out of sight over the top of the bank. Some of the covey lit in trees, but most of them scattered into brush piles and it was necessary to jump on the ice-coated mounds of brush several times before they would flush. Coming out while you were poised unsteadily on the icy, springy brush they made difficult shooting and I killed two, missed five, and started back pleased to have found a covey close to the house and happy there were so many left to find on another day.

At the house they said the boy had refused to let anyone come into the room.

"You can't come in," he said. "You mustn't get what I have."

I went up to him and found him in exactly the position I had left him, white-faced, but with the tops of his cheeks flushed by the fever, staring still, as he had stared, at the foot of the bed.

I took his temperature.

"What is it?"

"Something like a hundred," I said. It was one hundred and two and four tenths.

"It was a hundred and two," he said.

"Who said so?"

"The doctor."

"Your temperature is all right," I said. "It's nothing to worry about."

"I don't worry," he said, "but I can't keep from thinking."

"Don't think," I said. "Just take it easy."

"I'm taking it easy," he said and looked straight ahead. He was evidently holding tight onto himself about something.

"Take this with water."

"Do you think it will do any good?"

"Of course it will."

I sat down and opened the *Pirate* book and commenced to read, but I could see he was not following, so I stopped.

"About what time do you think I'm going to die?" he asked.

"What?"

"About how long will it be before I die?"

"You aren't going to die. What's the matter with you?"

"Oh, yes, I am. I heard him say a hundred and two."

"People don't die with a fever of one hundred and two. That's a silly way to talk."

"I know they do. At school in France the boys told me you can't live with forty-four degrees. I've got a hundred and two."

He had been waiting to die all day, ever since nine o'clock in the morning.

"You poor Schatz," I said. "Poor old Schatz. It's like miles and kilometers. You aren't going to die. That's a different thermometer. On that thermometer thirty-seven is normal. On this kind it's ninety-eight."

"Are you sure?"

"Absolutely," I said. "It's like miles and kilometers. You know, like how many kilometers we make when we do seventy miles in the car?"

"Oh," he said.

But his gaze at the foot of the bed relaxed slowly. The hold over himself relaxed too, finally, and the next day it was very slack and he cried very easily at little things that were of no importance.

Discussion

Ernest Hemingway was known for his interest in man's courage in the face of danger. In his personal life and through his major characters he pursued this theme. Courage, which we usually associate with adults, is often a part of the child's everyday life. Since he has had no prior experience with many situations that arise, the child has many opportunities to mobilize courage. It takes courage to learn to ride a two-wheel bicycle, to swim, or to face the doctor's needle for necessary injections.

To "screw up your courage" implies putting down fear and making oneself face some dangerous unknown, which Schatz does when he believes he is facing imminent death. Hemingway shows him as mentally and physically tense; he cannot release mental energy to involve himself in a story or permit himself to unwind sufficiently to sleep. For a boy of nine years Schatz shows a great deal of consideration for his father—he does not wish to infect his father with the deadly flu or to inflict the pain of watching him die. In this case, concern and an overriding love for his father helps Schatz to act with courage. The last sentence of the story, on the other hand, casts Schatz back into a routine world where courage is not called for and one may cry over little things.

Springboards for Inquiry

(1) Don Dinkmeyer and Rudolf Dreikurs (1963, p. 33) remind us that courage is more than putting down fear. They say that the courageous person is characterized by "his conviction that he can work toward *finding* solutions and, what is more important, that he can cope with any predicament." How does Schatz reveal this optimism that he can cope?

(2) Think of examples in school, hospital, and home in which children reveal courage based on the above definition.

(3) What kind of child rearing is most likely to foster courage in a child?

Compassion

Although researchers have been concerned with what are known as the disintegrative emotions—fear, anxiety, jealousy, guilt, and aggression—they have spent little time studying the integrative emotions, those that produce human satisfaction and feelings of well-being. Disintegrative emotions have been studied because clinics deal with the problems caused by undue fear or hostility. Such emotions as wonder, generosity, altruism, and compassion have eluded careful research since they do not appear in clinical settings.

All children have a rich store of both integrative and disintegrative emotions, both loving and angry feelings. Freudian psychologists (see Abrahamsen 1969; Lidz 1968) would insist that these feelings exist in large measure in the first five years of life, and one or the other is reinforced during this time. The child who enters adolescence and adulthood with largely disintegrative emotions has been the product of a lifespace in which the prevailing experiences have been conducive to hostility. The physiological basis for emotional development has been related to what has been termed the visceral brain (MacLean 1955). Nonetheless, Lidz (1968, p. 35) and others recognize that "what arouses emotions, how emotions combine, and which are most readily and frequently aroused in an individual organism depend largely upon experience."

Since the neonate is largely dependent his experiences arouse few emotions of either the integrative or disintegrative variety, but as the child grows older his experiences with parents, siblings, and peers color his emotional responses. Murphy and Murphy (1960) note that children under the age of three years (toddlers) are generally unmoved when shown pictures of people with severe black and blue wounds. Landreth (1958, p. 228) reports that children were angry when a confrontation between a rabbit and a police dog was stopped by a teacher who wished to spare the children an almost certain unpleasant experience. Kindergarten children, reports Leland Jacobs,* have exhibited vociferous compassion for the bears when told the Goldilocks story. When Jacobs once recounted how Goldilocks tested each porridge pot for temperature, finally found the porridge in baby bear's pot to be just right, and ate up every bit of it, a little child, moved by Goldilocks' avarice, exclaimed, "Why, the damn dirty pig!"

In early childhood the youngster learns love in his familial background, and only in cases of severe maternal deprivation, where the environment is emotionally sterile, are compassionate emotions likely to wither (Earle and Earle 1961; Piaget 1952; Rheingold and Bayley 1959; Wolman 1970). If a child develops without affection and compassion, he becomes "self-bound" (Alexander 1951) and thus is unable to have any emotional exchange with others.

A provocative essay, "Identity and Interpersonal Competence" (Foote and Cottrell 1955), in *Human Development* (Haimowitz and Haimowitz 1966, p. 63) lists the following conditions that depress the empathic capacity:

(1) Prolonged illness increases habituation to a relationship of dependency and thus depresses empathic capacity, . . . especially in the dependent member.
(2) Empathic capacity is negatively correlated with repression of biological functions. There is a negative correlation between the degree of repression of sexual functions and empathic capacity. . .
(3) Unwanted children are lower in empathic development than children who are desired and planned for.
(4) There is a critical point beyond which closer contact with another person will no longer lead to an increase in empathy, . . . when others are too constantly present, the organism appears to develop a protective resistance to responding. . . .

In general, the scant literature says that there is a maturing factor in the development of compassion and that its growth depends on both environmental nurture and physiology. The capacity for compassion is an important function in the personal development of humans, and failure to develop compassion may prohibit meaningful adult interrelationships based on mutual exchanges of love and concern.

---

* Professor Jacobs of Columbia University recounts this story with some relish.

"If I am your little girl tonight, can pretend there isn't enough water to wash?" said Felicia.

Winter Night

by Kay Boyle

There is a time of apprehension which begins with the beginning of darkness, and to which only the speech of love can lend security. It is there, in abeyance, at the end of every day, not urgent enough to be given the name of fear but rather of concern for how the hours are to be reprieved from fear, and those who have forgotten how it was when they were children can remember nothing of this. It may begin around five o'clock on a winter afternoon when the light outside is dying in the windows. At that hour the New York apartment in which Felicia lived was filled with shadows, and the little girl would wait alone in the living room, looking out at the winter-stripped trees that stood black in the park against the isolated ovals of unclean snow. Now it was January, and the day had been a cold one; the water of the artificial lake was frozen fast, but because of the cold and the coming darkness, the skaters had ceased to move across its surface. The street that lay between the park and the apartment house was wide, and the two-way streams of cars and buses, some with their headlamps already shining, advanced and halted and poured swiftly on to the tempo of the traffic signals' altering lights. The time of apprehension had set in, and Felicia, who was seven, stood at the window in the evening and waited before she asked the question. When the signals below would change from red to green again, or when the double-decker bus would turn the corner below, she would ask it. The words of it were already there, tentative in her mouth, when the answer came from the far end of the hall.

"Your mother," said the voice among the sound of kitchen things,

---

"she telephoned up before you came in from nursery school. She won't bc back in time for supper. I was to tell you a sitter was coming in from the sitting parents' place."

Felicia turned back from the window into the obscurity of the living room, and she looked toward the open door, and into the hall beyond it where the light from the kitchen fell in a clear yellow angle across the wall and onto the strip of carpet. Her hands were cold, and she put them in her jacket pockets as she walked carefully across the living-room rug and stopped at the edge of light.

"Will she be home late?" she said.

For a moment there was the sound of water running in the kitchen, a long way away, and then the sound of the water ceased, and the high, Southern voice went on:

"She'll come home when she gets ready to come home. That's all I have to say. If she wants to spend two dollars and fifty cents and ten cents' carfare on top of that three or four nights out of the week for a sitting parent to come in here and sit, it's her own business. It certainly ain't nothing to do with you or me. She makes her money, just like the rest of us does. She works all day down there in the office, or whatever it is, just like the rest of us works, and she's entitled to spend her money like she wants to spend it. There's no law in the world against buying your own freedom, that's all we're doing. And we're not doing nobody no harm."

"Do you know who she's having supper with?" said Felicia from the edge of dark. There was one more step to take, and then she would be standing in the light that fell on the strip of carpet, but she did not take the step.

"Do I know who she's having supper with?" the voice cried out in what might have been derision, and there was the sound of dishes striking the metal ribs of the drainboard by the sink. "Maybe it's Mr. Van Johnson, or Mr. Frank Sinatra, or maybe it's just the Duke of Wincers for the evening. All I know is you're having softboiled egg and spinach and applesauce for supper, and you're going to have it quick now because the time is getting away."

The voice from the kitchen had no name. It was as variable as the faces and figures of the women who came and sat in the evenings. Month by month the voice in the kitchen altered to another voice, and the sitting parents were no more than lonely aunts of an evening or two who sometimes returned and sometimes did not to this apartment in which they had sat before. Nobody stayed anywhere very long any more, Felicia's mother told her. It was part of the time in which you lived, and part of the life of the city, but when the fathers came back, all this would be miraculously changed. Perhaps you would live in a house again, a small one, with fir trees on either side of the short brick walk, and Father would drive up every night from the station just after darkness set in. When Felicia thought of this, she stepped quickly into the clear angle of light, and she left the dark of the living room behind her and ran softly down the hall.

The drop-leaf table stood in the kitchen between the refrigerator and the sink, and Felicia sat down at the place that was set. The voice at the sink was speaking still, and while Felicia ate it did not cease to speak until the bell of the front door rang abruptly. The girl walked around the table and went down the hall, wiping her dark palms in her apron, and, from the drop-leaf table, Felicia watched her step from the angle of light into darkness and open the door.

"You put in an early appearance," the girl said, and the woman who had rung the bell came into the hall. The door closed behind her, and the girl showed her into the living room, and lit the lamp on the bookcase, and the shadows were suddenly bleached away. But when the girl turned, the woman turned from the living room too and followed her, humbly and in silence, to the threshold of the kitchen. "Sometimes they keep me standing around waiting after it's time for me to be getting on home, the sitting parents do," the girl said, and she picked up the last two dishes from the table and put them in the sink. The woman who stood in the doorway was a small woman, and when she undid the white silk scarf from around her head, Felicia saw that her hair was black. She wore it parted in the middle, and it had not been cut, but was drawn back loosely into a knot behind her head. She had very clean white gloves on, and her face was pale, and there was a look of sorrow in her soft black eyes. "Sometimes I have to stand out there in the hall with my hat and coat on, waiting for the sitting parents to turn up," the girl said, and, as she turned on the water in the sink, the contempt she had for them hung on the kitchen air. "But you're ahead of time," she said, and she held the dishes, first one and then the other, under the flow of steaming water.

The woman in the doorway wore a neat black coat, not a new-looking coat, and it had no fur on it, but it had a smooth velvet collar and velvet lapels. She did not move, or smile, and she gave no sign that she had heard the girl speaking above the sound of water at the sink. She simply stood looking at Felicia, who sat at the table with the milk in her glass not finished yet.

"Are you the child?" she said at last, and her voice was low, and the pronunciation of the words a little strange.

"Yes, this here's Felicia," the girl said, and the dark hands dried the dishes and put them away. "You drink up your milk quick now, Felicia, so's I can rinse your glass."

"I will wash the glass," said the woman. "I would like to wash the glass for her," and Felicia sat looking across the table at the face in the doorway that was filled with such unspoken grief. "I will wash the glass for her and clean off the table," the woman was saying quietly. "When the child is finished, she will show me where her night things are."

"The others, they wouldn't do anything like that," the girl said, and she hung the dishcloth over the rack. "They wouldn't put their hand to housework, the sitting parents. That's where they got the name for them," she said.

Whenever the front door closed behind the girl in the evening, it would usually be that the sitting parent who was there would take up a book of fairy stories and read aloud for a while to Felicia; or else would settle herself in the big chair in the living room and begin to tell the words of a story in drowsiness to her, while Felicia took off her clothes in the bedroom, and folded them, and put her pajamas on, and brushed her teeth, and did her hair. But this time, that was not the way it happened. Instead, the woman sat down on the other chair at the kitchen table, and she began at once to speak, not of good fairies, or bad, or of animals endowed with human speech, but to speak quietly, in spite of the eagerness behind her words, of a thing that seemed of singular importance to her.

"It is strange that I should have been sent here tonight," she said, her eyes moving slowly from feature to feature of Felicia's face, "for you look like a child that I knew once, and this is the anniversary of that child."

"Did she have hair like mine?" Felicia asked quickly, and she did not keep her eyes fixed on the unfinished glass of milk in shyness any more.

"Yes, she did. She had hair like yours," said the woman, and her glance paused for a moment on the locks which fell straight and thick on the shoulders of Felicia's dress. It may have been that she thought to stretch out her hand and touch the ends of Felicia's hair, for her fingers stirred as they lay clasped together on the table, and then they relapsed into passivity again. "But it is not the hair alone, it is the delicacy of your face, too, and your eyes the same, filled with the same spring lilac color," the woman said, pronouncing the words carefully. "She had little coats of golden fur on her arms and legs," she said, "and when we were closed up there, the lot of us in the cold, I used to make her laugh when I told her that the fur was so pretty, like a little fawn's skin on her arms, would always help to keep her warm."

"And did it keep her warm?" asked Felicia, and she gave a little jerk of laughter as she looked down at her own legs hanging under the table, with the bare calves thin and covered with a down of hair.

"It did not keep her warm enough," the woman said, and now the mask of grief had come back upon her face. "So we used to take everything we could spare from ourselves, and we would sew them into cloaks and other kinds of garments for her and for the other children. . . ."

"Was it a school?" said Felicia when the woman's voice had ceased to speak.

"No," said the woman softly, "it was not a school, but still there were a lot of children there. It was a camp—that was the name the place had; it was a camp. It was a place where they put people until they could decide what was to be done with them." She sat with her hands clasped, silent a moment, looking at Felicia. "That little dress you have on," she said, not saying the words to anybody, scarcely saying them aloud. "Oh, she would have liked that little dress, the little buttons shaped like hearts, and the white collar——"

"I have four school dresses," Felicia said. "I'll show them to you. How many dresses did she have?"

"Well, there, you see, there in the camp," said the woman, "she did not have any dresses except the little skirt and the pullover. That was all she had. She had brought just a handkerchief of her belongings with her, like everybody else—just enough for three days away from home was what they told us, so she did not have enough to last the winter. But she had her ballet slippers," the woman said, and her clasped fingers did not move. "She had brought them because she thought during her three days away from home she would have the time to practice her ballet."

"I've been to the ballet," Felicia said suddenly, and she said it so eagerly that she stuttered a little as the words came out of her mouth. She slipped quickly down from the chair and went around the table to where the woman sat. Then she took one of the woman's hands away from the other that held it fast, and she pulled her toward the door. "Come into the living room and I'll do a pirouette for you," she said, and then she stopped speaking, her eyes halted on the woman's face. "Did she—did the little girl—could she do a pirouette very well?" she said.

"Yes, she could. At first she could," said the woman, and Felicia felt uneasy now at the sound of sorrow in her words. "But after that she was hungry. She was hungry all winter," she said in a low voice. "We were all hungry, but the children were the hungriest. Even now," she said, and her voice went suddenly savage, "when I see milk like that, clean, fresh milk standing in a glass, I want to cry out loud, I want to beat my hands on the table, because it did not have to be . . ." She had drawn her fingers abruptly away from Felicia now, and Felicia stood before her, cast off, forlorn, alone again in the time of apprehension. "That was three years ago," the woman was saying, and one hand was lifted, as in weariness, to shade her face. "It was somewhere else, it was in another country," she said, and behind her hand her eyes were turned upon the substance of a world in which Felicia had played no part.

"Did—did the little girl cry when she was hungry?" Felicia asked, and the woman shook her head.

"Sometimes she cried," she said, "but not very much. She was very quiet. One night when she heard the other children crying, she said to me, 'You know, they are not crying because they want something to eat. They are crying because their mothers have gone away.' "

"Did the mothers have to go out to supper?" Felicia asked, and she watched the woman's face for the answer.

"No," said the woman. She stood up from her chair, and now that she put her hand on the little girl's shoulder, Felicia was taken into the sphere of love and intimacy again. "Shall we go into the other room, and you will do your pirouette for me?" the woman said, and they went from the kitchen and down the strip of carpet on which the clear light fell. In the front room, they paused hand in hand in the glow of the shaded lamp, and the woman looked about her, at the books, the low tables with the magazines and ash trays on them, the vase of roses on the piano, looking with dark, scarcely seeing eyes at these things that had no reality at all. It was only when she saw the little white clock on the mantelpiece that she gave any sign, and then she said quickly: "What time does your mother put you to bed?"

Felicia waited a moment, and in the interval of waiting the woman lifted onc hand and, as if in reverence, touched Felicia's hair.

"What time did the little girl you knew in the other place go to bed?" Felicia asked.

"Ah, God, I do not know, I do not remember," the woman said.

"Was she your little girl?" said Felicia softly, stubbornly.

"No," said the woman. "She was not mine. At least, at first she was not mine. She had a mother, a real mother, but the mother had to go away."

"Did she come back late?" asked Felicia.

"No, ah, no, she could not come back, she never came back," the woman said, and now she turned, her arm around Felicia's shoulders, and she sat down in the low soft chair. "Why am I saying all this to you, why am I doing it?" she cried out in grief, and she held Felicia close against her. "I had thought to speak of the anniversary to you, and that was all, and now I am saying these other things to you. Three years ago today, exactly, the little girl became my little girl because her mother went away. That is all there is to it. There is nothing more."

Felicia waited another moment, held close against the woman, and listening to the swift, strong heartbeats in the woman's breast.

"But the mother," she said then in a small, persistent voice, "did she take a taxi when she went?"

"This is the way it used to happen," said the woman, speaking in hopelessness and bitterness in the softly lighted room. "Every week they used to come into the place where we were and they would read a list of names out. Sometimes it would be the names of children they would read out, and then a little later they would have to go away. And sometimes it would be the grown people's names, the names of the mothers or big sisters, or other women's names. The men were not with us. The fathers were somewhere else, in another place."

"Yes," Felicia said. "I know."

"We had been there only a little while, maybe ten days or maybe not so long," the woman went on, holding Felicia against her still, "when they read the name of the little girl's mother out, and that afternoon they took her away."

"What did the little girl do?" Felicia said.

"She wanted to think up the best way of getting out so that she could go find her mother," said the woman, "but she could not think of anything good enough until the third or fourth day. And then she tied her ballet slippers up in the handkerchief again, and she went up to the guard standing at the door." The woman's voice was gentle, controlled now. "She asked the guard please to open the door so that she could go out. 'This is Thursday,' she said, 'and every Tuesday and Thursday I have my ballet lessons. If I miss a ballet lesson, they do not count the money off, so my mother would be just paying for nothing, and she cannot afford to pay for nothing. I missed my ballet lesson on Tuesday,' she said to the guard, 'and I must not miss it again today.' "

Felicia lifted her head from the woman's shoulder, and she shook her hair back and looked in question and wonder at the woman's face.

"And did the man let her go?" she said.

"No, he did not. He could not do that," said the woman. "He was a soldier and he had to do what he was told. So every evening after her mother went, I used to brush the little girl's hair for her," the woman went on saying. "And while I brushed it, I used to tell her the stories of the ballets. Sometimes I would begin with *Narcissus*," the woman said, and she parted Felicia's locks with her fingers, "so if you go and get your brush now, I will tell it while I brush your hair."

"Oh, yes," said Felicia, and she made two whirls as she went quickly to the bedroom. On the way back, she stopped and held on to the piano with the fingers of one hand while she went up on her toes. "Did you see me? Did you see me standing on my toes?" she called to the woman, and the woman sat smiling in love and contentment at her.

"Yes, wonderful, really wonderful," she said. "I am sure I have never seen anyone do it so well." Felicia came spinning toward her, whirling in pirouette after pirouette, and she flung herself down in the chair close to her, with her thin bones pressed against the woman's soft, wide hip. The woman took the silver-backed, monogrammed brush and the tortoise-shell comb in her hands, and now she began to brush Felicia's hair. "We did not have any soap at all and not very much water to wash in, so I never could fix her as nicely and prettily as I wanted to," she said, and the brush stroked regularly, carefully down, caressing the shape of Felicia's head.

"If there wasn't very much water, then how did she do her teeth?" Felicia said.

"She did not do her teeth," said the woman, and she drew the comb through Felicia's hair. "There were not any toothbrushes or tooth paste, or anything like that."

Felicia waited a moment, constructing the unfamiliar scene of it in silence, and then she asked the tentative question.

"Do I have to do my teeth tonight?" she said.

"No," said the woman, and she was thinking of something else, "you do not have to do your teeth."

"If I am your little girl tonight, can I pretend there isn't enough water to wash?" said Felicia.

"Yes," said the woman, "you can pretend that if you like. You do not have to wash," she said, and the comb passed lightly through Felicia's hair.

"Will you tell me the story of the ballet?" said Felicia, and the rhythm of the brushing was like the soft, slow rocking of sleep.

"Yes," said the woman. "In the first one, the place is a forest glade with little pale birches growing in it, and they have green veils over their faces and green veils drifting from their fingers, because it is the springtime. There is the music of a flute," said the woman's voice softly, softly, "and creatures of the wood are dancing——"

"But the mother," Felicia said as suddenly as if she had been awakened from sleep. "What did the little girl's mother say when she didn't do her teeth and didn't wash at night?"

"The mother was not there, you remember," said the woman, and the brush moved steadily in her hand.

"But she did send one little letter back. Sometimes the people who went away were able to do that. The mother wrote it in a train, standing up in a car that had no seats," she said, and she might have been telling the story of the ballet still, for her voice was gentle and the brush did not falter on Felicia's hair. "There were perhaps a great many other people standing up in the train with her, perhaps all trying to write their little letters on the bits of papers they had managed to hide on them, or that they had found in forgotten corners as they traveled. When they had written their letters, then they must try to slip them out through the boards of the car in which they journeyed, standing up," said the woman, "and these letters fell down on the tracks under the train, or they were blown into the fields or onto the country roads, and if it was a kind person who picked them up, he would seal them in envelopes and send them to where they were addressed to go. So a letter came back like this from the little girl's mother," the woman said, and the brush followed the comb, the comb the brush in steady pursuit through Felicia's hair. "It said good-by to the little girl, and it said please to take care of her. It said: 'Whoever reads this letter in the camp, please take good care of my little girl for me, and please have her tonsils looked at by a doctor if this is possible to do.' "

"And then," said Felicia softly, persistently, "what happened to the little girl?"

"I do not know. I cannot say," the woman said. But now the brush and comb had ceased to move, and in the silence Felicia turned her thin, small body on the chair, and she and the woman suddenly put their arms around each other. "They must all be asleep now, all of them," the woman said, and in the silence that fell on them again, they held each other closer. "They must be quietly asleep somewhere, and not crying all night because they are hungry and because they are cold. For three years I have been saying 'They must all be asleep, and the cold and the hunger and the seasons or night or day or nothing matters to them——' "

It was after midnight when Felicia's mother put her key in the lock of the front door, and pushed it open, and stepped into the hallway. She walked quickly to the living room, and just across the threshold she slipped the three blue foxskins from her shoulders and dropped them, with her little velvet bag, upon the chair. The room was quiet, so quiet that she could hear the sound of breathing in it, and no one spoke to her in greeting as she crossed toward the bedroom door. And then, as startling as a slap across her delicately tinted face, she saw the woman lying sleeping on the divan, and Felicia, in her school dress still, asleep within the woman's arms.

Discussion

Kay Boyle sets this story effectively in the late afternoon when the routine of daytime activity ceases and people seek the comfort of others to share the approaching nighttime hours. In this case, both the little girl and the sitter are in need of companionship, and their association is immediately a source of mutual satisfaction. The sitter tells a story from her own past of another little girl who was much like Felicia. The nurturing feelings of the sitter for the little girl of her story is transmitted, and Felicia is able to invest something of herself in the experience of others. Felicia's progression of questions about the little girl's feelings and activities and her desire to go to bed without washing as the little girl did suggest that Felicia is attempting to identify with the experiences of the child in her sitter's story.

We do not usually consider empathy and compassion as part of a child's repertoire of emotions; the ability to show compassion for another is generally considered a development of adulthood dependent on a backlog of experience. This story suggests, however, that a child is capable of this kind of emotional responsiveness.

Springboards for Inquiry

(1) Since compassion is an integrative and healthy function, educators and parents should attempt to discover techniques to foster growth in empathy before adulthood. Can you suggest ways for a teacher to help children in her class to be more compassionate? What can parents do to foster experiences for their children which will promote empathic feelings toward others?

(2) What may account for individual differences in the ability to be empathic or to express sympathy?

(3) How (other than verbally) may children express compassion?

(4) Using Bandura's* † work with the acquisition of aggressive behavior in children as a model, devise methods of increasing empathic behavior in children through modelling techniques.

---

* Bandura, Albert, Dorothea Ross, and Sheila Ross. "Transmission of Aggression Through Imitation of Aggressive Models." *Journal of Abnormal and Social Psychology* 63, 1961: 575–582.

† Bandura, Albert, Dorothea Ross, and Sheila Ross. "Imitation of Film Mediated Aggressive Models." *Journal of Abnormal and Social Psychology* 66, 1963: 3–11.

Anger

Anger may be simply defined as an emotion that results when one's aim or goal is blocked. The term *frustration tolerance* has been used to indicate the point at which people will respond aggressively to the thwarting of their desires.

In babyhood, anger is the most common emotion experienced. Typically, the child cries, kicks, screams, and even learns to hold his breath (Jersild 1960) in what is the beginning of temper tantrums (Kanner 1957). Undue parental attention to these negative behaviors reinforces them, and the child learns what behavior brings him the attention he wants.* It is thus possible to understand that home and school environments play important roles in determining the causation, intensity, and frequency of a child's anger (Hurlock 1964, p. 283; 1968, p. 154). For instance, if the parents give in to the child's first display of anger, the child may learn that all he needs to do is to turn red, quiver, and have his eyes well up with tears or simply to have a cyanotic† attack, and his parents are panicked into a flurry of action to meet his demands.

An only child may have less frequent temper outbursts, presumably because there are fewer "others" to contend with (Macfarlane, Allen, and Honzik 1954). Evidence indicates that the more punitive the atmosphere is at home or in school, the more occasions there are for anger to appear, possibly because

---

* This is often called instrumental learning (McCandless 1967, p. 19).

† When a child holds his breath, he will soon turn blue from lack of oxygen (cyanosis) and will begin to lose consciousness, at which point nature takes over and the breathing process is restored.

punishment reinforces the behavior punished and thus that behavior tends to be repeated. When anger is met with anger, it is certain that there will be no diminution in the anger-producing behavior.

As children grow and develop, the things that anger them and their responses to anger change. Whereas the young child becomes angry when his immediate wants or needs are not met, the child in the middle school years is angered by teasing, ridicule, criticism, or long "lectures" about his behavior. In his expanded world, he becomes angry at others—teachers, parents, and other authority figures. The older child's anger may take the form of sulking, staring stonily, or swearing.

It appears that a relationship exists between socioeconomic status (class or caste) and ways of expressing anger. For example, lower-class children tend to be more physically aggressive when angry than middle-class children, who tend to use verbal means to vent their anger because they have learned from their culture that violence is not "nice."

As people grow older they learn to control anger in a variety of ways. Outbursts * and crying persist and can be effective in controlling adult reactions, but when adults react to anger by a display of temper tantrums they are considered childish. With age and maturity people learn not to "blow up," but to use anger as a catalyst to change behavior. In moments of utter loss of control people plot revenge, and it is not uncommon for adolescents to daydream about murdering or torturing their parents. For normal children a satisfying fantasy is a healthy response to anger;† disturbed children may not stop with fantasy, and the plot can brew into violent reality.

Anger is a disintegrative emotion that is expressed in various ways as children grow and develop. Both cultural background and degree of maturity affect the ways of demonstrating anger. Another factor that has been little discussed or researched is the relationship of the individual personality structure to the expression of anger, but the uniqueness of human response to frustration and needs (conscious or unconscious) is greatly affected by the individual personality. In some people, the anger caused by frustration produces persistent behavior directed toward satisfying needs. In others there is a giving up and a giving into the feelings of anger.

Selye's description of human reaction to physical or psychological stress (1950) is useful in understanding responses to anger. His theory of the general adaptation syndrome postulates three physiological stages in the adjustment to stress: (a) an initial alarm reaction, (b) resistance, and (c) exhaustion. These physiological reactions to stress are paralleled by psychological responses to anger and frustration: (a) aggressive feelings, (b) some defense mechanism, and (c) maladjustment. The course of anger may thus be traced in both physio-

---

* Alfred Speer's new book on Nazi Germany, *Inside the Third Reich* (New York: The Macmillan Co., 1970), describes Hitler's tantrums and rug-chewing when he became so angry that he lost control of himself.

† (Hartley 1957).

logical and psychological terms. Each of these circuits adds to our understanding of this common emotion, but neither reveals the visceral nature of anger. For this we need to turn to literature.

"You dirty filthy stinkin' sow . . . wish you were fryin' in the middle of hell right this minute."

The White Circle

by John Bell Clayton

As soon as I saw Anvil squatting up in the tree like some hateful creature that belonged in trees I knew I had to take a beating and I knew the kind of beating it would be. But still I had to let it be that way because this went beyond any matter of courage or shame.

The tree was *mine*. I want no doubt about that. It was a seedling that grew out of the slaty bank beside the dry creek-mark across the road from the house, and the thirteen small apples it had borne that year were the thirteen most beautiful things on this beautiful earth.

The day I was twelve Father took me up to the barn to look at the colts—Saturn, Jupiter, Devil, and Moonkissed, the whiteface. Father took a cigar out of his vest pocket and put one foot on the bottom plank of the fence and leaned both elbows on the top of the fence and his face looked quiet and pleased and proud and I liked the way he looked because it was as if he had a little joke or surprise that would turn out nice for me.

"Tucker," Father said presently, "I am not unaware of the momentousness of this day. Now there are four of the finest colts in Augusta County; if there are four any finer anywhere in Virginia I don't know where you'd find them unless Arthur Hancock over in Albemarle would have them." Father took one elbow off the fence and looked at me. "Now do you suppose," he asked, in that fine, free, good humor, "that if I were to offer you a little token to commemorate this occasion you could make a choice?"

"Yes sir," I said.

"Which one?" Father asked. "Devil? He's wild."

"No sir," I said. "I would like to have the apple tree below the gate.

Father looked at me for at least a minute. You would have to understand his pride in his colts to understand the way he looked. But at twelve how could I express how *I* felt? My setting such store in having the tree as my own had something to do with the coloring of the apples as they hung among the green leaves; it had something also to do with their ripening, not in autumn when the world was full of apples, but in midsummer when you *wanted* them; but it had more to do with a way of life that had come down through the generations. I would have given one of the apples to Janie. I would have made of it a ceremony. While I would not have said the words, because at twelve you have no such words, I would have handed over the apple with something like this in mind: "Janie, I want to give you this apple. It came from my tree. The tree stands on my father's land. Before my father had the land it belonged to his father, and before that it belonged to my great-grandfather. It's the English family land. It's almost sacred. My possession of this tree forges of me a link in this owning ancestry that must go back clear beyond Moses and all the old Bible folks."

Father looked at me for that slow, peculiar minute in our lives. "All right, son," he said. "The tree is yours in fee simple to bargain, sell, and convey or to keep and nurture and eventually hand down to your heirs or assigns forever unto eternity. You have a touch of poetry in your soul and that fierce, proud love of the land in your heart; when you grow up I hope you don't drink too much."

I didn't know what he meant by that but the tree was mine and now there perched Anvil, callously munching one of my thirteen apples and stowing the rest inside his ragged shirt until it bulged out in ugly lumps. I knew the apples pressed cold against his hateful belly and to me the coldness was a sickening evil.

I picked a rock up out of the dust of the road and tore across the creek bed and said, "All right, Anvil—climb down!"

Anvil's milky eyes batted at me under the strangely fair eyebrows. There was not much expression on his face. "Yaannh!" he said. "You stuck-up little priss, you hit me with that rock. You just do!"

"Anvil," I said again, "climb down. They're my apples."

Anvil quit munching for a minute and grinned at me. "You want an apple? I'll give you one. Yaannh!" He suddenly cocked back his right arm and cracked me on the temple with the half-eaten apple.

I let go with the rock and it hit a limb with a dull chub sound and Anvil said, "You're fixin' to git it—you're real-ly fixin' to git it."

"I'll shake you down," I said. "I'll shake you clear down."

"Clear down?" Anvil chortled. "Where do you think I'm at? Up on top of Walker Mountain? It wouldn't hurt none if I was to fall out of this runty bush on my head."

I grabbed one of his bare feet and pulled backwards, and down Anvil came amidst a flutter of broken twigs and leaves. We both hit the ground. I hopped up and Anvil arose with a faintly vexed expression.

He hooked a leg in back of my knees and shoved a paw against my chin. I went down in the slate. He got down and pinioned my arms with his knees. I tried to kick him in the back of the head but could only flail my feet helplessly in the air.

"You might as well quit kickin' " he said.

He took one of my apples from his shirt and began eating it, almost absent-mindedly.

"You dirty filthy stinkin' sow," I said.

He snorted. "I couldn't be a sow, but you take that back."

"I wish you were fryin' in the middle of hell right this minute."

"Take back the stinkin' part," Anvil said thoughtfully. "I don't stink."

He pressed his knees down harder, pinching and squeezing the flesh of my arms.

I sobbed, "I take back the stinkin' part."

"That's better," Anvil said.

He ran a finger back into his jaw to dislodge a fragment of apple from his teeth. For a moment he examined the fragment and then wiped it on my cheek.

"I'm goin' to tell Father," I said desperately.

" 'Father,' " Anvil said with falsetto mimicry. " 'Father.' Say 'Old Man.' You think your old man is some stuff on a stick, don't you? You think he don't walk on the ground, don't you? You think you and your whole stuck-up family don't walk on the ground. Say 'Old Man.' "

"Go to hell!"

"Shut up your blubberin'. Say 'Old Man.' "

"Old Man. I wish you were dead."

"Yaannh!" Anvil said. "Stop blubberin'. Now call me 'Uncle Anvil.' Say 'Uncle Sweetie Peetie Tweetie Beg-Your-Pardon Uncle Anvil.' Say it!"

"Uncle Sweetie . . . Uncle Peetie, Tweetie Son-of-a-bitch Anvil."

He caught my hair in his hands and wallowed my head against the ground until I said every bitter word of it. Three times.

Anvil tossed away a spent, maltreated core that had been my apple. He gave my head one final thump upon the ground and said "Yaannh!" again in a satisfied way.

He released me and got up. I lay there with my face muscles twitching in outrage.

Anvil looked down at me. "Stop blubberin'," he commanded.

"I'm not cryin'," I said.

I was lying there with a towering, homicidal detestation, planning to kill Anvil—and the thought of it had a sweetness like summer fruit.

There were times when I had no desire to kill Anvil. I remember the day his father showed up at the school. He was a dirty, half-crazy, itinerant knick-knack peddler. He had a club and he told the principal he was going to beat the meanness out of Anvil or beat him to death. Anvil scudded under a desk and lay there trembling and whimpering until the principal finally drove the ragged old man away. I had no hatred for Anvil then.

But another day, just for the sheer filthy meanness of it, he crawled through a classroom window after school hours and befouled the floor. And the number of times he pushed over smaller boys, just to see them hit the packed hard earth of the schoolyard and to watch the fright on their faces as they ran away, was more than I could count.

And still another day he walked up to me as I leaned against the warmth of the schoolhack shed in the sunlight, feeling the nice warmth of the weather-beaten boards.

"They hate me," he said dismally. "They hate me because my old man's crazy."

As I looked at Anvil I felt that in the background I was seeing that demented, bitter father trudging his lonely, vicious way through the world.

"They don't hate you," I lied. "Anyway I don't hate you." That was true. At that moment I didn't hate him. "How about coming' home and stayin' all night with me?"

So after school Anvil went along with me—and threw rocks at me all the way home.

Now I had him for no soft feeling of any kind. I planned—practically—his extinction as he stood there before me commanding me to cease the blubbering out of my heart.

"Shut up now," Anvil said. "I never hurt you. Stop blubberin'."

"I'm not cryin'," I said.

"You're still mad though." He looked at me appraisingly.

"No, I'm not," I lied. "I'm not even mad. I was a little bit mad, but not now."

"Well, whattaya look so funny around the mouth and eyes for?"

"I don't know. Let's go up to the barn and play."

"Play whut?" Anvil looked at me me truculently. He didn't know whether to be suspicious or flattered. "I'm gettin' too big to play. To play much, anyway," he added undecidedly. "I might play a little bit if it ain't some sissy game."

"We'll play anything," I said eagerly.

"All right," he said. "Race you to the barn. You start."

I started running toward the wire fence and at the third step he stuck his foot between my legs and I fell forward on my face.

"Yaannh!" he croaked. "That'll learn you."

"Learn me what?" I asked as I got up. "Learn me what?" It seemed important to know that. Maybe it would make some difference in what I planned to do to Anvil. It seemed very important to know what it was that Anvil wanted to, and never could, teach me and the world.

"It'll just learn you," he said doggedly. "Go ahead, I won't trip you any more."

So we climbed the wire fence and raced across the burned field the hogs ranged in.

We squeezed through the heavy sliding doors onto the barn floor, and the first thing that caught Anvil's eye was the irregular circle that father had painted there. He wanted to know what it was and I said "Nothing" because I wasn't yet quite ready, and Anvil forgot about it for the moment and wanted to play jumping from the barn floor out to the top of the fresh rick of golden straw.

I said, "No. Who wants to do that, anyway?"

"I do," said Anvil. "Jump, you puke. Go ahead and jump!"

I didn't want to jump. The barn had been built on a hill. In front the ground came up level with the barn floor, but in back the floor was even with the top of the straw rick, with four wide, terrible yawning feet between.

I said, "Nawh, there's nothing to jumpin'."

"Oh, there ain't, hanh!" said Anvil. "Well, try it—"

He gave me a shove and I went

out into terrifying space. He leaped after and upon me and we hit the pillowy side of the straw rick and tumbled to the ground in a smothering slide.

"That's no fun," I said, getting up and brushing the chaff from my face and hair.

Anvil himself had lost interest in it by now and was idly munching another of my apples.

"I know somethin'," I said. "I know a good game. Come on, I'll show you."

Anvil stung me on the leg with the apple as I raced through the door of the cuting room. When we reached the barn floor his eyes again fell on the peculiar white circle. That's to play prisoner's base with," I said. "That's the base."

"That's a funny-lookin' base," he said suspiciously. "I never saw any base that looked like that."

I could feel my muscles tensing, but I wasn't particularly excited. I didn't trust myself to look up toward the roof where the big mechanical hayfork hung suspended from the long metal track that ran back over the steaming mows of alfalfa and red clover. The fork had vicious sharp prongs that had never descended to the floor except on one occasion Anvil knew nothing about.

I think Father had been drinking the day he bought the hayfork in Staunton. It was an unwieldly involved contraption of ropes, triggers, and pulleys which took four men to operate. A man came out to install the fork and for several days he climbed up and down ladders, bolting the track in place and arranging the various gadgets. Finally, when he said it was ready, Father had a load of hay pulled into the barn and called the men in from the fields to watch and assist in the demonstration.

I don't remember the details. I just remember that something went very badly wrong. The fork suddenly plunged down with a peculiar ripping noise and embedded itself in the back of one of the work horses. Father said very little. He simply painted the big white circle on the barn floor, had the fork hauled back up to the top, and fastened the trigger around the rung of a stationary ladder eight feet off the floor, where no one could inadvertently pull it.

Then he said quietly, "I don't ever want anyone ever to touch this trip rope or to have occasion to step inside this circle."

So that was why I didn't now look up toward the fork.

"I don't want to play no sissy prisoner's base," Anvil said. "Let's find a nest of young pigeons."

"All right," I lied. "I know where there's a nest. But one game of prisoner's base first."

"You don't know where there's any pigeon nest," Anvil said. "You wouldn't have the nerve to throw them up against the barn if you did."

"Yes, I would too," I protested. "Now let's play one game of prisoner's base. Get in the circle and shut your eyes and start countin'."

"Oh, all right," Anvil agreed wearily. "Let's get it over with and find the pigeons. Ten, ten, double ten, forty-five—"

"Right in the middle of the circle," I told him. "And count slow. How'm I goin' to hide if you count that way?"

Anvil now counted more slowly. "Five, ten, fifteen—"

I gave Anvil one last vindictive

look and sprang up the stationary ladder and swung out on the trip rope of the unpredictable hayfork with all my puny might.

The fork's whizzing descent was accompanied by that peculiar ripping noise. Anvil must have jumped instinctively. The fork missed him by several feet.

For a moment Anvil stood absolutely still. He turned around and saw the fork, still shimmering from its impact with the floor. His face became exactly the pale green of the carbide we burned in our acetylene lighting plant at the house. Then he looked at me, at the expression on my face, and his Adam's apple bobbed queerly up and down, and a little stream of water trickled down his right trouser leg and over his bare foot.

"You tried to kill me," he said thickly.

He did not come toward me. Instead, he sat down. He shook his head sickly. After a few sullen bewildered moments he reached into his shirt and began hauling out my apples one by one.

"You can have your stinkin' old apples," he said. "You'd do that for a few dried-up little apples. Your old man owns everything in sight. I ain't got nothin'. Go ahead and keep your stinkin' old apples."

He got to his feet and slowly walked out of the door.

Since swinging off the trip rope I had neither moved nor spoken. For a moment more I stood motionless and voiceless and then I ran over and grabbed up the nine apples that were left and called, "Anvil! Anvil!" He continued across the field without even pausing.

I yelled, "Anvil! Wait, I'll give them to you."

Anvil climbed the fence without looking back and set off down the road toward the store. Every few steps he kicked his wet trouser leg.

Three sparrows flew out of the door in a dusty chattering spiral. Then there was only the image of the hayfork shimmering and terrible in the great and growing and accusing silence and emptiness of the barn.

Discussion

This story contrasts the anger of Anvil, a boy who is pathologically angry all the time, with the anger of a boy who is momentarily sufficiently motivated to commit an act of violence. Anvil, the victim in this incident, is reminiscent of the case studies included in the book, *Children Who Hate* by Fritz Redl and David Wineman.* Anvil's daily behavior is a succession of angry, hostile, and destructive acts toward others, and as a result he is hated by everyone. We are not told in the story if he has a mother or siblings, but his angry behavior suggests that he is not receiving love, direction, or protection from

* (Glencoe, Ill.: Free Press, 1951).

anyone. We do know that his father is a "dirty, half-crazy, itinerant knick-knack peddler" who comes to school with a club to beat the meanness out of Anvil. Anvil sees as his model a bitter, perhaps psychotic, violent person who intermittently moves in and out of his lifespace. The cruelty, neglect, and inconstancy Anvil has suffered have left him with no control over his angry impulses. His stream of hostile acts is a smokescreen for a boy with a severely disturbed personality. An act of compassion and goodwill, as displayed by the boy in the story who invites Anvil home after school, cannot cure Anvil. The extent of Anvil's disturbance suggests the need for special methods pursued by professionals who try to make inroads into the cure of pathologically angry young people.

The boy in the story who offers help to Anvil and then becomes his victim feels angry and helpless. Anvil transgresses upon the apple tree, which is particularly precious to this boy. Anvil also initiates a fight in which he reduces his opponent to a particularly impotent position. The anger that Anvil's opponent feels is "white hot" in its intensity. Anger is frequently referred to as hot or blinding, which suggests its physical as well as its psychological implications. During this period of time Anvil's victim is out of touch with his superego, and the uninhibited emotion of anger is sufficient for him to attempt to kill Anvil. Unlike Anvil, the boy feels remorseful following the shock of the event. His normal ego and superego functions are restored and he wishes to relieve his guilt by giving the apples to Anvil. Anvil is thoroughly frightened by the experience. He has no insight into his earlier provocations. Again he finds himself the victim of hatred. He is given nothing. He is thought of as nothing. He is nothing.

Springboards for Inquiry

(1) List the ways in which anger was expressed in this story. Name other ways in which children express anger.

(2) Trace sources of anger and how they may be expressed at different developmental stages—i.e., What may anger the infant, eighteen month old, two year old, four to five year old, early school age child, and middle school age child?

(3) Discuss insightful ways of handling children's anger at any of the developmental stages mentioned above, from the varying points of view of a parent, teacher, physical therapist, nurse, and psychologist.

(4) How do individual differences affect the feeling and expression of anger?

(5) Is there a sex difference in the expression of anger?

Shame

As shame and guilt are often related in the literature of psychology, it might be well to clarify the differences between these two terms. Both are negative emotional reactions associated with behavior that meets with disapproval. Guilt implies self-deprecation and a lowered self-esteem: "Guilt may be conceptualized as a special kind of negative self-evaluation which occurs when an individual acknowledges that his behavior is at variance with a given moral value" (Ausubel 1955). "Shame," Margaret Mead (1949) says, "the agony of being found wanting and exposed to the disapproval of others," is a different kind of sanction, distinguishable from guilt yet "neither dichotomous nor mutually exclusive" (Ausubel 1955). For example, Helen Lynd (1958) quotes *Shame and Guilt* (Piers and Singer 1953, p. 22) to indicate that there is no clear-cut difference between the two terms: "Whereas guilt is generated whenever a boundary . . . is touched or transgressed, shame occurs when a goal . . . is not being reached. It thus indicates a real 'shortcoming.' Guilt anxiety accompanies transgression, shame, failure." Lynd concludes with this summation: "Experiences of shame . . . are experiences of exposure, exposure . . . of the self. The exposure may be to others but, whether others are or are not involved, it is always . . . exposure to one's own eyes" (Lynd 1958, pp. 27–28).*

---

* It is particularly gratifying to the compilers of this volume that Lynd, in order to adequately define shame, quotes from at least two dozen different novelists and playwrights. Better than 90 percent of her second chapter depends on specific examples from literature.

Psychoanalytically oriented students of these emotions see feelings of guilt and shame engendered in the early periods of the child's life. For example, during the early toilet training period when a child is learning self-control, frequent accidents occur. A mother's remarks about the child being "bad" or "dirty" may diminish his developing sense of autonomy and lead to strong feelings of doubt and shame (Lidz 1968, p. 81).

Ausubel (1955) identifies two kinds of shame: nonmoral shame and moral shame. The former may be associated with "embarrassment in committing a breach of propriety . . . and suffering a 'loss of face' resulting from exposure of ignorance or incompetency." Moral shame is a reaction to the negative moral judgments of others. Ausubel further subdivides moral shame into internalized and noninternalized. When a child is caught lying he may be ashamed, yet not accept the idea that lying is wrong. The child is ashamed and depreciates himself, but this type of shame requires that he be caught. When the value is internalized, the child really believes that lying is wrong and discovery is unnecessary. It is such shame that often provoked hari-kari in Japan and suicide in the primitive Ojibuay (Mead 1950, p. 366).

It may be concluded from this review of the literature that shame relies on external sanctions alone and guilt relies on both internal and external sanctions. Pervasive feelings of shame or guilt erode human personality and prevent it from functioning fully. Guilt feelings often serve to regulate behavior and, "if children felt no sense of accountability or moral obligation to curb their hedonistic and irresponsible impulses, to conform to acceptable social norms, or to acquire self-control, the socializing process would be slow, arduous and incomplete (Ausubel 1955). Yet, if an individual is overwhelmed by feelings of guilt or shame he may shun reality while he builds up his defense mechanisms. There is a therapeutic value in shame, however, and Lynd's concluding words (1958, p. 257) seem particularly relevant:

> "Living in terms of the confronting of shame—and allowing shame to become a revelation of one's self and of one's society—makes way for living beyond the conventions of a particular culture. It makes possible the discovery of an integrity that is peculiarly one's own. . . ."

"Filth, filth, filth, from morning to night. I know they're poor but they could wash."

A Tree Grows in Brooklyn

by Betty Smith

Francie was seven and Neeley six. Katie had held Francie back wishing both children to enter school together so that they could protect each other against the older children. On a dreadful Saturday in August, she stopped in the bedroom to speak to them before she went off to work. She awakened them and gave instructions.

"Now when you get up, wash yourselves good and when it gets to be eleven o'clock, go around the corner to the public health place, tell them to vaccinate you because you're going to school in September."

Francie began to tremble. Neeley burst into tears.

"You coming with us, Mama?" Francie pleaded.

"I've got to go to work. Who's going to do my work if I don't?" asked Katie covering up her conscience with indignation.

Francie said nothing more. Katie knew that she was letting them down. But she couldn't help it, she just couldn't help it. Yes, she should go with them to lend the comfort and authority of her presence but she knew she couldn't stand the ordeal. Yet, they had to be vaccinated. Her being with them or somewhere else couldn't take that fact away. So why shouldn't one of the three be spared? Besides, she said to her conscience, it's a hard and bitter world. They've got to live in it. Let them get hardened young to take care of themselves.

"Papa's going with us then," said Francie hopefully.

"Papa's at Headquarters waiting for a job. He won't be home all day. You're big enough to go alone. Besides, it won't hurt."

Neeley wailed on a higher key. Katie could hardly stand that. She loved the boy so much. Part of her reason for not going with them was that she couldn't bear to see the boy hurt . . . not even by a pin prick. Almost she decided to go with them. But no. If she went she'd lose half a day's work and she'd have to make it up on Sunday morning. Besides, she'd be sick afterwards. They'd manage somehow without her. She hurried off to her work.

Francie tried to console the terrified Neeley. Some older boys had told him that they cut your arm off when they got in the Health Center. To take his mind off the thing, Francie took him down into the yard and they made mud pies. They quite forgot to wash as mama had told them to.

They almost forgot about eleven o'clock, the mud pie making was so beguiling. Their hands and arms got very dirty playing in the mud. At ten to eleven, Mrs. Gaddis hung out the window and yelled down that their mother had told her to remind them when it was near eleven o'clock. Neeley finished off his last mud pie, watering it with his tears. Francie took his hand and with slow dragging steps the children walked around the corner.

They took their place on a bench. Next to them sat a Jewish mama who clutched a large six-year-old boy in her arms and wept and kissed his forehead passionately from time to time. Other mothers sat there with grim suffering furrowed on their faces. Behind the frosted glass door where the terrifying business was going on, there was a steady bawling punctuated by a shrill scream, resumption of the bawling and then a pale child would come out with a strip of pure white gauze about his left arm. His mother would rush and grab him and with a foreign curse and a shaken fist at the frosted door, hurry him out of the torture chamber.

Francie went in trembling. She had never seen a doctor or a nurse in all of her small life. The whiteness of the uniforms, the shiny cruel instruments laid out on a napkin on a tray, the smell of antiseptics, and especially the cloudy sterilizer with its bloody red cross filled her with tongue-tied fright.

The nurse pulled up her sleeve and swabbed a spot clean on her left arm. Francie saw the white doctor coming towards her with the cruelly-poised needle. He loomed larger and larger until he seemed to blend into a great needle. She closed her eyes waiting to die. Nothing happened, she felt nothing. She opened her eyes slowly, hardly daring to hope that it was all over. She found to her agony, that the doctor was still there, poised needle and all. He was staring at her arm in distaste. Francie looked too. She saw a small white area on a dirty dark brown arm. She heard the doctor talking to the nurse.

"Filth, filth, filth, from morning to night. I know they're poor but they could wash. Water is free and soap is cheap. Just look at that arm, nurse."

The nurse looked and clucked in horror. Francie stood there with the hot flamepoint of shame burning her face. The doctor was a Harvard man, interning at the neighborhood hospital. Once a week, he was obligated to put in a few hours at one of the free clinics. He was going into a smart practice in Boston when his internship was over. Adopting the phraseology of the neighborhood, he referred to his Brooklyn internship as going through Purgatory when he wrote to his socially prominent fiancée in Boston.

The nurse was a Williamsburg girl. You could tell that by her accent. The child of poor Polish immigrants, she had been ambitious, worked days in a sweatshop and gone to school at night. Somehow she had gotten her training. She hoped some day to marry a doctor. She didn't want anyone to know she had come from the slums.

After the doctor's outburst, Francie stood hanging her head. She was a dirty girl. That's what the doctor meant. He was talking more quietly now asking the nurse how that kind of people could survive; that it would be a better world if they were all sterilized and couldn't breed anymore. Did that meant he wanted her to die? Would he do something to make her die because her hands and arms were dirty from the mud pies?

She looked at the nurse. To Francie, all women were mamas like her own mother and Aunt Sissy and Aunt Evy. She thought the nurse might say something like:

"Maybe this little girl's mother works and didn't have time to wash her good this morning," or, "You know how it is, Doctor, children *will* play in dirt." But what the nurse actually said was, "I know. Isn't it terrible? I sympathize with you, Doctor. There is no excuse for these people living in filth."

A person who pulls himself up from a low environment via the bootstrap route has two choices. Having risen above his environment, he can forget it; or, he can rise above it and never forget it and keep compassion and understanding in his heart for those he has left behind him in the cruel up climb. The nurse had chosen the forgetting way. Yet, as she stood there, she knew that years later she would be haunted by the sorrow in the face of that starveling child and that she would wish bitterly that she had said a comforting word then and done something towards the saving of her immortal soul. She had the knowledge that she was small but she lacked the courage to be otherwise.

When the needle jabbed, Francie never felt it. The waves of hurt started by the doctor's words were racking her body and drove out all other feeling. While the nurse was expertly tying a strip of gauze around her arm and the doctor was putting his instrument in the sterilizer and taking out a fresh needle, Francie spoke up.

"My brother is next. His arm is just as dirty as mine so don't be surprised. And you don't have to tell him. You told me." They stared at this bit of humanity who had become so strangely articulate. Francie's voice went ragged with a sob. "You don't have to tell him. Besides it won't do no good. He's a boy and he don't care if he is dirty." She turned, stumbled a little and walked out of the room. As the door closed, she heard the doctor's surprised voice.

"I had no idea she'd understand what I was saying." She heard the nurse say, "Oh, well," on a sighing note.

Discussion

A Tree Grows in Brooklyn explores the variety of social and emotional problems that arise in the everyday life of a poor Irish family living on the East side of New York City in the early 1900s. In this selection from the novel, Francie and Neeley must use the services of the local Public Health Center. Katie, their mother, is as intimidated as the children are by the symbols of the Center—antiseptic smells, white coats, unfamiliar faces, and painful needles for shots—and leaves the children to go there alone to cope with the frightening consequences of being vaccinated.

Francie find that she is more pained by the loss of her self-esteem brought about by the intern's remarks than by the vaccination. The feeling of shame is interpreted in this selection as "waves of hurt." Children are frequently subjected to shaming techniques on the part of adults. The adult, as in this situation, is honestly unaware of his ability to hurt someone through insensitive remarks.

Hopefully, reaction to years of insensitivity to minority cultures has made significant changes in the education of professionals, who predominantly come from middle-class backgrounds. As professionals enter agencies and institutions that provide services to the public, they should be attuned to the silent and spoken language of their clientele. They should reflect on the vast number of circumstances that can prompt feelings of shame in school and agency environments. Naturally these feelings are not confined to the poor or minority child, there are latent feelings of shame in *all* children.

Springboards for Inquiry

(1) Presumed inferiority in intellectual, social, or moral realms constitutes the feeling of shame. Using your own childhood as a resource, recall instances when you felt shame and how it was provoked.

(2) Identify commonly used words or expressions that could cause a child to feel ashamed.

(3) Describe ways in which children handle feelings of shame in front of an adult. What part does the child's cultural background play in his behavioral expression of shame?

References

Abrahamsen, David. *The Emotional Care of Your Child.* New York: Trident Press, 1969.

Albert, Robert S. "The Role of Mass Media and the Effect of Aggressive Film Content upon Children's Aggressive Responses and Identification Choices." *Genetic Psychology Monographs,* No. 55 (1957): 221–85.

Alexander, Theron. "Certain Characteristics of the Self as Related to Affection." *Child Development* 22 (1951): 285–90.

Alexander, Theron. *Children and Adolescents.* New York: Atherton Press, 1969.

Ausubel, David P. "Relationships between Shame and Guilt in the Socializing Process." *Psychological Review* 62 (1955): 378–90.

Bowlby, John. "The Nature of the Child's Tie to His Mother." *Internat'l. Journal of Psycho-Analysis* 39 (1958): 350–73.

Dinkmeyer, Don, and Rudolf Dreikurs. *Encouraging Children to Learn.* Englewood Cliffs, N. J.: Prentice-Hall, 1963.

Doll, Ronald C., and Robert C. Fleming. *Children under Pressure.* Columbus: C. E. Merrill Co., 1966.

Earle, A. M., and B. V. Earle. "Early Maternal Deprivation and Later Psychiatric Illness." *American Journal of Orthopsychiatry* 31 (1961): 181–86.

English, Horace B., and Ava C. English. *A Comprehensive Dictionary of Psychological and Psychoanalytical Terms.* New York: David McKay Company, Inc., 1958.

Erikson, Erik. *Childhood and Society,* 2nd ed. New York: W. W. Norton & Co., 1963.

Eron, Leonard D., Leopold O. Walder, Romolo Toigo, and Monroe M. Lefhowitz. "Social Class, Parental Punishment for Aggression, and Child Aggression." *Child Development* 34 (1963): 849–67.

Evans, Richard I. *Dialogues with Erich Fromm.* New York: Harper & Row, Publishers, Inc., 1966.

Foote, Nelson N., and Leonard S. Cottrell, Jr. *"Identity and Interpersonal Competence"* in *Human Development* eds. Morris L. Haimowitz and Natalie R. Haimowitz. New York: Thomas Y. Crowell Co., 1966, pp. 55–70.

Fromm, Erich. *The Art of Loving.* New York: Harper & Row, Publishers, Inc., 1956.

Hagman, Elmer R. "A Study of Fears of Children of Pre-school Age." *Journal of Experimental Education* 1 (1932): 110–30.

Haimowitz, Morris L., and Natalie R. Haimowitz. *Human Development.* New York: Thomas Y. Crowell Co., 1966.

Hartley, Ruth E. "Some Safety Valves in Play." *Child Study* 34 (1957): 12–14.

Hebb, D. O. "On the Nature of Fear." *Psychological Review* 53 (1946): 259–76.

Hurlock, Elizabeth. *Child Development.* New York: McGraw-Hill Book Co., 1964.

Hurlock, Elizabeth. *Developmental Psychology,* 3rd ed. New York: McGraw-Hill Book Co., 1968.

Jersild, Arthur T. *Child Psychology.* 5th ed. Englewood Cliffs, N. J.: Prentice-Hall, 1960.

Kanner, Leo. *Child Psychiatry.* Springfield, Ill.: Charles C Thomas, 1957.

Koch, Helen Lois. "The Relation of Certain Formal Attributes of Siblings to Attitudes Held toward Each Other and toward Their Parents." *Monographs of the Society for Research in Child Development,* No. 4 (1960). Chicago: University of Chicago Press.

Landreth, Catherine. *Psychology of Early Childhood.* New York: Alfred A. Knopf, Inc., 1958.

Leton, Donald A. "Assessment of School Phobia." *Mental Hygiene* 46 (1962): 256–64.

Levy, David. *Maternal Overprotection.* New York: Columbia University Press, 1943.

Levy, David. "Primary Affect Hunger." *American Journal of Psychiatry* 94 (1937): 643–652.

Lidz, Theodore. *The Person.* New York: Basic Books, Inc., 1968.

Lynd, Helen. *On Shame and the Search for Identity.* New York: Harcourt Brace Jovanovich, Inc., 1958.

McCandless, Boyd R. *Children: Behavior and Development.* 2nd Ed. New York: Holt, Rinehart, and Winston, 1967.

Macfarlane, Jean W.; Lucile Allen, and Marjorie P. Honzik. *A Developmental Study of the Behavior Problems of Normal Children between Twenty-one Months and Fourteen Years.* Berkeley and Los Angeles: University of California Press, 1954.

MacLean, Paul D. "The Limbic System ('Visceral Brain') in Relation to Central Gray and Reticulum of the Brain Stem." *Psychosomatic Medicine* 17 (1955): 355–66.

McCord, William; Joan McCord, and Alan Howard. "Familial Correlates of Aggression in Nondelinquent Male Children."

Journal of Abnormal and Social Psychology 62 (1961): 79–93.

Mead, Margaret. "Social Change and Cultural Surrogates." In *Personality in Nature, Society, and Culture,* ed. by Clyde Kluckhohn and Henry A. Murray. New York: Alfred A. Knopf, Inc., 1949.

Mead, Margaret. "Some Anthropological Considerations Concerning Guilt," in *Feelings and Emotions,* ed. by Martin L. Reymert. New York: McGraw-Hill Book Co., 1950.

Menninger, Karl. *Man against Himself.* New York: Harcourt, Brace & Co., 1938.

Murphy, Gardner, and Lois B. Murphy. "The Child as Potential." In *The Nation's Children,* ed. by Eli Ginzberg. Vol. 2. New York: Columbia University Press, 1960.

Piaget, Jean. *The Origins of Intelligence in Children.* New York: International University Press, 1952.

Piers, Gerhart, and Milton Singer. *Shame and Guilt.* New York: Charles C Thomas, 1953.

Raths, Louis. *A Theory of Needs.* New York: Bronxville Press, 1954.

Rheingold, Harriet L., and Nancy Bayley. "The Later Effects of an Experimental Modification of Mothering." *Child Development* 30 (1959): 363–72.

Sears, Robert R. "Relation of Early Socialization Experience to Aggression in Middle Childhood." *Journal of Abnormal and Social Psychology* 63 (1961): 466–92.

Selye, Hans. "The General Adaptation Syndrome and the Diseases of Adaptation." *Journal of Clinical Endocrinology* 6 (1946): 117–230.

Selye, Hans. *The Physiology and Pathology of Exposure to Stress.* Montreal: Acta, Inc., 1950.

Selye, Hans. *The Stress of Life.* New York: McGraw-Hill Book Co., 1956.

Strauss, Bernard V. "The Dynamics of Ordinal Position Effects." *Quarterly Journal of Child Behavior* 3 (1951): 133–45.

Wolman, Benjamin B. *Children without Childhood.* New York: Grune & Stratton, 1970.

Intellectual Development

No aspect of child development is more embroiled in the nature–nurture controversy than intellectual development. It is safe to say that no reputable child development specialist discounts heredity as a factor in intellectual development.* † However, since it is impossible to determine the true extent of the contribution of heredity to intellectual potential, most specialists believe that we should view each individual as capable of developing to an unknowable upper limit if he is given optimum environmental conditions.

Challenge and motivation, particularly in the home and school environments, loom large as stimulators in the development of the intellect. Russian research on infants postulates that things to push, wiggle, and shake will stimulate responses even in the first few months of life. The verbal influence of the mother in direct, frequent interaction with very young children is even more important than educational toys and gadgets. (Levenstein 1970). This research is reinforced by long-standing knowledge that there is a lasting depressive effect on the intellectual development of children who are reared in institutional settings. Presumably, the lack of a consistent mother-figure to emulate and to encourage curiousity significantly lowers the intellectual level of these children. Krech, Rosenzweig, and Bennett have contributed evidence that the freedom

---

* The student will want to become acquainted with the views of Arthur R. Jensen ("How Much Can We Boost IQ and Scholastic Achievement?" *Harvard Educational Review* 39 [Winter 1969]: 1–123) and the responses to his conclusions by seven other specialists ("Discussion," *Harvard Educational Review* 39 [Spring 1969]: 273–356; "Reducing the Heredity–Environment Uncertainty: A Reply," *Harvard Educational Review* 39 [Summer 1969]: 449–83).

† Also see Richard Herrnstein "IQ." *The Atlantic*. Vol. 228 No. 3 (September 1971): pp. 43–64.

to experience and the experiences themselves have a positive (and probably chemical) effect on cognitive development.* We need to know more about how and at what ages humans may be optimally stimulated by the manipulation of their environments.

Discussion of intellectual development must take into consideration the limited concept of intelligence defined by standardized IQ tests, which are used to make comparative measurements of intellectual functioning. Intelligence test items measure a narrow spectrum of thinking; they tend to measure what one has learned from his environment. In addition, there is incontrovertible evidence that a middle-class bias exists in the standard tests of intelligence (we discuss this point again in the introduction to the section on the influences of society on the growing child). Many psychologists believe that there are as many as one hundred twenty subaspects of intelligence (Guilford 1967), most of them never tested by conventional tests. Torrance reveals that creative children, who tend to think divergently, are penalized when tested for intelligence levels because they do not make the responses required to achieve full credit.

Research in intellectual functioning is increasingly placing emphasis on language and concept formation as they relate to mental ability. Jean Piaget, who has investigated many aspects of the growing child's world, has also made important contributions to our understanding of the language and thought of the child. According to Piaget, the very young child's first learning reflects knowledge of the specific things in his environment. Intellectual growth is marked by the child's increasing ability to conceptualize and to use reason and logic. The most advanced stage of intellectual ability is reached when the child can reason deductively without having to experience concretely the event he is thinking about. Piaget is responsible for emphasizing that children's thinking is essentially unlike that of adults.

---

* Their contribution has been to focus the attention of educators and psychologists on the need for early environmental stimulation to promote the cognitive development of children. For the original work see David Krech, Mark Rosenzweig, and Edward Bennett. "Effects of Environmental Complexity and Training on Brain Chemistry." *Journal of Comparative Physiological Psychology* 53, 1960, pp. 509–519.

Growth of Language

The learning of language has been called an "adaptive technique that is uniquely human" (Lidz 1968, p. 169). Research concerned with the communication patterns of porpoises may one day explode the theory that language is a human achievement only, but to this date language, as a system by which meanings are communicated through appropriate noises or symbols, is still considered an accomplishment limited to man.

Research findings agree that the child's development of language is a learning task (MacGinitie 1969). Since language categorizes a large part of the environment, the ability to master the environment depends on how much and from whom the child learns to talk. Lidz (1968, p. 169) puts it this way: "Learning to use language . . . involves the acquisition of an existing complex system of sounds, meanings, and syntax through interaction with tutors, primarily the family members." Skinner (1957) believes that language behavior cannot be viewed differently from learning any other type of behavior. Chomsky (1965) insists that the human infant is particularly endowed with learning mechanisms especially designed for the learning of language. Piaget's sensorimotor schemata (1959) are often used to explain how this language develops in a creature helpless and dependent on adult reactions.

Perhaps the most useful summary and description of earlier theories of language development is found in Dorothea McCarthy's work (1954), which is characterized by scientifically primitive studies of the growth of vocabulary, parts of speech, and measures of sentence length and complexity. Since that exhaustive list of early research, attention has been focused on the transformational grammar of Chomsky (1965), who has used modern technology to discover and place in sequence the components the child assimilates when he learns language. A major development is in the field of language automation, in which language samples are fed into computers that analyze their content and structure (MacGinitie 1969).

Research into the function of language shows that the referential function of language is central to other functions. Lidz' (1968) description of the word *mama* illustrates this principle. When a child is about a year old he learns to associate *mama* with an object he drops from his crib because his mother comes and picks up his toy. The word thus develops a diffuse meaning—that is, *mama* does not stand for *mother* as we know it but for the act of retrieving. Piaget tells us that his son said "mummy" at fourteen months when his mother was swinging her body; at fifteen months he said it when he wanted something; at sixteen months he said it when he wanted his *father* to light a lamp. Experience contracts meanings and enlarges vocabulary, and the child's diffuse referents become specific. Piaget (1951) tells of how "bow-wow" meant a dog seen from her balcony to his thirteen-month-old. Then "bow-wow" for a time meant anything seen from the balcony. Not until some time later was "bow-wow" reserved for dogs only.

When the child puts several words together he becomes involved with syntax. The mother's interpretations of the child's two-word and three-word utterances, which she may repeat in a context of more words, become the models for the child to imitate.* Technical data about the emergence of grammatical structure after one-word and two-word sentences may be found in the work of Martin Braine (1959) and Wick Miller and Susan Ervin (1964). For the student particularly interested in the way children discover the rules of language, the research of Jean Berko (1958) is suggested. The work of Walter Loban (1963; 1966) and Ruth Strickland (1962) are particularly important for following the language development of school-age children. Vocabulary studies, particularly on the comprehension of words and the difficulty of certain words, may be found in MacGinitie's article (1969).

Many students of language feel that the acquisition of language is less significant than learning to understand the affective meaning systems, that is, how words mean and why they mean what they do, because language is closely related to the functioning of human beings.† How words come to have meaning for the individual and precisely what they mean to him was explored by DiVesta (1966), using children in grades two through seven.

---

* John B. Carroll describes this process in the third edition of the *Encyclopedia of Educational Research* and there is no new data to refute his observations.

† The works of semanticists such as Alfred Korzybski (*Science and Sanity* [Lakeville, Conn. International Non-Aristotelian Library Pub. Co., 1948]), Charles K. Ogden and I. A. Richards (*The Meaning of Meaning* [New York: Harcourt Brace Jovanovich, Inc., 1923]), and S. I. Hayakawa (*Language in Thought and Action* [New York: Harcourt Brace Jovanovich, Inc., 1939]), are startling in their implications for students of language.

It is generally agreed that the home is the most significant environmental influence on language development. Since schooling is a highly verbal learning experience, it is important to view school achievement as not entirely a matter of native intelligence† but as a reflection of the opportunities for linguistic interaction in the home. Awareness of this problem led to the introduction of Head Start programs by the federal government and educational television program "Sesame Street," both of which are intended to enrich the linguistic storehouses of children who were born into deprived homes. Both Loban (1963; 1966) and William Labov (1965) comment on the serious effects on learning that can result from discrepancies between the language patterns learned from one's race and social class and the patterns in traditional middle-class schools.

---

* The controversy over the intelligence of Negroes as compared with the intelligence of Caucasians has been raised again by Arthur R. Jensen, whose work was cited in the essay on Intellectual Development. ("How Much Can We Boost IQ and Scholastic Achievement?") *Harvard Educational Review* 39 (Winter 1969): 1–123. This research is still provoking heated arguments.

'An akkerpeetie, man—and he had a toople too.'

Spring Song *by Joyce Cary*

SPRING in the park with an east wind and a sky as blue as winter milk, an obvious duty day for children to be given the first sunshine of the year. A tall girl in spectacles is in charge of a small brother and sister. Her nose is magenta; her mouth and forehead, the stoop of her neck, express a resignation not so much virtuous as necessary. She stops for the third time in five minutes to let her charges catch up. 'Oh, do come on, Mag.'

The little girl in the blue cap is pushing a doll's perambulator which has lost a wheel. She balances and propels it with immense muscular effort and, at the same time, pours out a long story in successive bursts.

'And when he went into the castle, he called out three times, "Tooboody, tooboody, tooboody," but of course he was an akkerpeetie man.'

'What say?' with a patience that grieves for itself.

'He was an akkerpeetie man.'

'That's nothing, Maggie.'

'Yes, it is.' The little girl with an adroit unexpected twist drives the perambulator over the iron edging of the path, on to the worn grass. Tall daffodils, florists' daffodils, wave in the fenced-off beds; but the grass is still wintry. Empty cigarette-cartons lie about the children's feet.

'It's the akkerpeetie,' the little girl pants in a loud voice. 'The akkerpeetie man—he was made of fishbones.'

'Oh well, go on if you won't talk sense.'

'And the tooboody came skinking along the collidor.'

'Corridor, you mean.'

'No I don't, it wasn't a corridor. It was a collidor, with a round top—and the akkerpeetie man let down his beard to the ground and said, "I'm not afraid of *anybody*." He had a toople too.' And with the rising note that goes with rising inspiration, she chants, 'He had a toople too—with bla-ck whiskers—on a sil-ver chain. And it was shaved all down the back—once every Friday.'

'Oh, a poodle, like your Uncle John's.'

'No, a toople—because it had such a long face.'

'A dog, then.'

'It wasn't a dog—it was a singum—because—because—it came from Baffrica where all the dogs are scats.'

'Oh well, go on,' with a sigh from the very heart of overburdened teen-age.

The little girl is silent. There is a pause.

'Go on, what's next?'

'But you never believe nothing I say.' Suddenly she lets go the perambulator, which at once falls over, spilling a large rag doll on the brittle grass, and rushes at the brother walking on the other flank of the party. This brother, aged about five, is wearing a pair of blue corduroy shorts which obviously give him great pleasure. He carries both hands in his pockets, and doubling his fists pushes them out sideways forming two large bumps over his hips. As he walks he looks down at the effect and throws out his legs in a swaggering gait. He is studying swagger in all its details, including the proper way to hold the hands in the pockets. When Margaret suddenly appears before him, he stops and looks at her with a totally blank expression, as if he has never seen anything like her before.

'Tom, Tom, did you be-lieve my story?'

'Yes, I did.'

'Oh Tommy, how can you?' says the tall sister. 'You weren't even listening.'

'Yes, I was, it was a very nice story.'

'What's it about then?'

'I don't know.'

'There you are!'

'But I liked it,' Tom says. 'I liked it *very* much.' And he looks down again at his hands, pushes them still further apart and kicks out his right leg in a kind of embryo goose-step. Margaret has, meanwhile, circled twice round Tom in a series of skips, performed sideways so that her face is always directed to him as a centre. She is examining him with the greatest interest and a growing pleasure. Now, stopping right in front of him, she pushes her face close to his, and says, 'A toople.' Suddenly she bumps into him and shouts, 'A toople—a toople—is a singum.' She utters a loud triumphant laugh.

The boy gazes at her in amazement. She begins to explain, between shouts of laughter. 'Glad said, "What's an akkerpeetie man?" and I said, "He had a toople too." So Glad said, "What's a toople?" and I said, "A toople is a singum,"—I said, "He had a toople too." '

Tom bursts into shouts of laughter. The tall girl, surprised and irritated by this senseless explosion, calls out, 'That's enough.'

'A toople—a toople—he had a toople too.' And the children reel about as if they are drunk; running into each other, bumping each other.

They are crowing with delight. 'An akkerpeetie man—and he had a toople too.'

Two soldiers in battle-dress, strolling by, look around at the children and grin. One of them lifts his forage-cap back from his forehead as if to say, 'Yes, it's almost warm—it's really spring.' But the tall girl is furious. She turns crimson and rushes at the children. 'Stop that, you hear. I won't have it.' Her voice quivers; one would have said that she is frightened.

The children dodge her—'An akkerpeetie man—and he had—he had,' they choke with laughter, 'a toople too.'

She springs upon them and tears them apart. 'You want slapping, that's what you do.' The little girl, jerked and shaken, turns also red. She says in a high offended voice, 'But I didn't do nothing.'

The boy has already forgotten the episode. With his hands once more in his pockets, he glances downwards to adjust the bumps at the correct angle. Margaret turns down her lips, as if about to cry, but thinks better of it. She rights the perambulator, stoops for the doll, and in the same movement, with an acrobatic whisk of her whole body, catches the perambulator, before it can fall over again, on her left buttock.

'Oh, do come on, Maggie—you make me tired.' Gladys is indeed tired. Her whole form droops; her voice mourns to Heaven a cruel injustice, a neglected fate. The little girl frowns. Then she puts the doll into the perambulator and says in a low determined voice, 'Lie down, Vera, or I'll give you such a smack on your poly.'

Discussion

This story is particularly appropriate to illustrate the language play of the preschool age child. At this time, according to Piaget (1959), the child has entered the preoperational period of language development, the hallmark of which is the child's ready use of words to stand for physical objects and actions. During this period a great deal of the young child's speech is egocentric in nature; the child talks and says out loud what he is thinking, just for the pleasure of talking. This is the kind of monologue in which Maggie is engaged when she talks about the "akkerpeetie man." Obviously Maggie is not going to take well to Gladys' suggestions and corrections.

Maggie is comfortable with her younger brother, who can laughingly tumble with her from one verbal invention into another. For them the world of fantasy and imagination are as comfortable as reality. Children are entertained by imaginative verbal play; they respond not just with pleasure but with rapture to language based on rhythm and rhyming.

Springboards for Inquiry

(1) Explain why Margaret's verbal inventions are so much fun for her.

(2) There is still controversy about whether language is innate or learned. Present arguments for both points of view. How would you describe the acquisition of language in terms of learning theory?

(3) What language experiences would you plan to include in a preschool program?

(4) Late development of speech may serve as a signal to parents that their child's progress is not evolving as it should. What are some of the possible causes of delayed speech?

"Why—it's just the sun. When it comes up, you know. It rises every morning. Sun . . . rising . . . that's the sunrise."

The Sunrise

by W. E. Fishbaugh

THEY WERE at breakfast and his father, looming big at the head of the table, was buttering a slice of bread with enthusiasm. The house was still chilly. The fire had not "come up" yet, they both had said, and he was thickly wrapped in his woolens with even blankets swathed around his feet for warmth. His mother was reaching around in front of him busily tucking in a napkin and drawing up his dish of oatmeal and beneath the table, seeming at a great distance, he rubbed one foot against the other contentedly.

She sugared his oatmeal and gave him a spoon to eat it with.

"A wonderful sunrise this morning!" his father remarked loudly and warmly from the table end.

With a chuckle of remembrance he reached for the coffeepot, swooped it toward him and tipped it up above his cup.

"Was it?" his mother murmured. "I didn't notice."

The coffee poured glittering dark amber. He watched it.

She took the pitcher of milk and refilled his oatmeal dish. He looked down in front of him and saw it swim over the warm, gray porridge.

"Rose and gold!" his father said, with a tremor of worship. "Rose and gold!"

He clumped the pot heavily back on its pad and then began spooning coffee into his mouth noisily.

"I didn't notice," his mother murmured.

She lifted small spoonfuls to her mouth, humbly.

He only played at eating his oatmeal. Usually he much enjoyed it. Also his warm feet. But he was waylaid now by the strange talk.

What was a sunrise? he wondered, stirring with his spoon.

"Wouldn't have missed it for the world," his father commented between gulps.

He ate his bread butter side to the tongue, always with great gestures, and he leaned his shoulders over and dominated his place at the table as though he would take the whole thing in, tablecloth and all.

"Great sight! Something to miss, I can tell you!"

He sat then, with a stilled spoon watching his father's heavy, swooping gestures fascinatedly, and a little mistrustfully. He was almost too much for him. His great activity was bewildering, disturbing. His voice boomed and he handled everything with great hearty movements of his arms and shoulders.

When his father had finally gone away from the table to work he finished his oatmeal very quickly. He pushed the empty dish away from him, not thinking about it.

"What's a sunrise?" he asked his mother.

She took his napkin off and wiped his mouth with it.

"Why, you know what the sun is, don't you, Paul?"

"Yes, but what's a sunrise?"

"Why—it's just the sun. When it comes up, you know. It rises every morning. Sun . . . rising . . . that's the sunrise."

"Well—but what's it like?"

"Oh, it's—always different. . . . It's before you *see* the sun, really . . . and the sky gets colored."

She looked off trying to think how to explain it to him.

"Why! Like a sun*set*!" she exclaimed, suddenly realizing. "Like a sun*set*, only it's *behind* our house instead of in front of it! And it's in the morning, of course."

"Like a *sunset*?" he asked doubtfully.

He had seen *them*. *They* weren't strange, like his father seemed to make out sunrises were. The birds got silent then, and other things began to make a noise (crickets they told him). That was what happened at sunset. There wasn't any of that strangeness any more. But he couldn't make his mother understand what he meant. He didn't have the words.

"Yes. That's what it's like. Just like a sunset," she told him, starting to clear the table. "Only it's turned around, you see."

But he knew it couldn't be. His father had never acted like that about sunsets. Nothing at all like that.

"Rose and gold!" his father had said. And the tone of the voice and its trembling had struck deep down in his mind.

What were they really like? he wanted to know. What could a sunrise be that it did that to his father? He would like to feel that way.

One night at supper his father, before the rest of the family had sat down to the table, looked at him in a queer way and said, "Your mother tells me you want to know what a sunrise is."

And then his feeling of strangeness about his father was gone, suddenly. He swallowed and looked up at him and said eagerly, "Yes. What is it?"

His father paused a moment, and then said, still looking queerly, "Well, it can't be told very well. You'll have to see one yourself, first."

And of course he realized he couldn't do that and he began to feel bad.

But they kept on looking at each

other. "Sometime," his father said, "when I see one at the proper time, maybe I'll wake you up and show it to you. Shall I?"

"Yes," he said, squirming forward. "I want to!"

"All right," his father said, picking up the carving knife, "sometime soon."

"What's this? What's this?" the others who had now come to the table were asking.

"Tend to your plates," his father told them. "It's between Paul and me. Tend to your plates, now!"

Then his mother came and set the platter of meat on the table.

"It's rather fat beef," she said. "You'd better not give them too much at first . . ."

Each night after that he lay in his bed in the dimming light listening to the sparrows chirping monotonously in the eaves outside his window, and hearing the clatter of the dishes being washed downstairs and he would wonder if the next morning would be the one. Moving sleepily beneath the warm covers he would wonder drowsily how it would be.

At the proper time, his father had said, and rose and gold. And you hear the milkman then, one of his brothers had told him. He would like looking out the window at the fading light, seeing the branches of the maples becoming less and less distinct against the sky, and sometimes hearing people walking by on the sidewalk below, and sometimes horses' hoofs and with them the grind of wheels, or far off he would hear shouts, or laughter. And sometimes he would hear the older neighbor kids playing Stillwaters. Then after a while everything would become too warm and comfortable for listening and it would all get hazy and soft and he would forget it all and lie there and sink down far away, with the room darkening.

When it did happen the bed was shaking and everything was dark. Everything was shaking and someone big and dark was there, leaning over him and the shaking bed and saying over and over, "Are you awake? . . . Are you awake?"

And then he suddenly knew he was awake. But he was too frightened to think of answering and then the bed stopped shaking.

"Come on now," his father said then, "there's a fine one this morning."

And then the air was cold as the covers suddenly went back off of him and he was lying there in the center of the bed with no covers, shivering in the cold, and he couldn't think at first, or do anything. But his father helped him. He lifted him up then, and wrapped a blanket around him and held him up against his shoulder and carried him off through his dark unfamiliar room and down the dim, cold hall and he saw that the wallpaper was a color he had never seen it before and the light all looked different and as he passed them he saw all the doors to the others' bedrooms were closed yet, and there was the side gas jet glinting with the new light on one wall and there wasn't any sound at all except what they made themselves.

His father's footsteps were just thumps along the hall because he didn't have shoes on and he was carried along like a baby, swaying with the lilt of his stride out into the East storeroom where it was cold and all the trunks were.

He saw they had the same strange

light on them and then he was swung around and his eyes hurt from the many windows the light was coming in, and his stomach turned over from the swinging, but then suddenly there it was, all over the sky. And his father said, gently, "There it is. Right up there in the East. Do you see it? It's always there in the East!"

And it was. It was there. He saw it.

There were things that from the shape of them ought to be clouds, but he had never seen clouds a color like they were, and there were bars, or something, going up from behind the furthest houses, but he couldn't look at them long; they hurt his eyes when he tried to. He saw it all, though. He saw everything. And the *East* his father called it. The *East*. So the *East* was the *sunrise* to him, then.

He stared silently at it a long time, and his father looked down at him and chuckled inside. Then he shifted him in his arms. His eyes were strange and flashing.

"Well, now you've seen one," he said. "You've seen your first one."

He pulled the blanket up closer around him, but he couldn't speak yet. He could just keep looking.

"What do you think of it?" his father asked him, chuckling. "There's your sunrise—what do you think of it? Hm-m-m?"

And he looked up quickly into his father's eyes and then back at the sky.

"Has it come up to your expectations?" his father asked. "Hm-m-m? Has it?"

But he couldn't really say anything. He just kept pulling at the blanket and looking out at the sky, and somehow he couldn't release himself from it. He didn't have any words to say anything with and he hardly had any thoughts. The sunrise had him. Something about it had him. While he looked he didn't matter any more. He was gone from himself. And he looked at it for such a long time without speaking that his father began to get tired. He would have looked at it a lot longer, but his father finally said, "Come on, I've got to start the fire and you'd better get back to bed."

So they went back thumping along the hall and he got into his cold bed again and his father went on downstairs.

Then he lay there in the cold bed, thinking, and listening to the noises his father made down in the kitchen. He had seen a sunrise! He didn't know whether it was rose and gold for he didn't know colors. He only knew it had been there, and he had seen it. He had seen a sunrise. It was in the *East* that it came. In the *East*. *Sunrise*. He thought about it a long time and even though the bed got warm again he did not fall asleep.

Then, later, downstairs at breakfast, he sat again in his special chair at the table and watched his father and mother.

He had a different feeling inside him now.

His mother tucked in his napkin and drew up his oatmeal dish. Then she reached down and felt of his feet. They were cold, and so she got his usual blanket and wrapped them in it. She gave him a spoon to eat with and then she turned away and prepared her own dish.

His father was gulping his coffee and reaching for things the way he always did at breakfast, and soon his mother was lifting her small spoonfuls, humbly.

He ate erratically this morning, in spurts. He would take four spoonfuls of oatmeal in quick succession, and then he would sit still, watching his father, wonderingly. Now and then he glanced at his mother. He wondered why his father didn't speak about it.

After a while he saw his father looking at him.

And then he realized that his father meant there was something new between them.

So they both stopped eating and looked at each other a while.

His mother noticed the stillness and looked up.

She looked over at his father but he was looking down at him. So then she turned and then they both were looking down at him. His mother's look was questioning. His father chuckled and reached for another slice of bread.

"He was up pretty early this morning," he said.

His mother smiled at him, still questioningly. "Was he?" she asked.

"He saw a sunrise this morning," his father told her.

"Did you, Paul?" his mother asked him.

She smiled and wiped his mouth clean with his napkin.

"He didn't have much to say about it though," his father said. "Lost his tongue there for a minute."

His knife flashed in the buttering.

"*Did* you lose your tongue, Paul?" she asked him, smiling.

She poured more milk on his oatmeal.

He began eating it again.

"So now you *know* what a sunrise is!" she said a little later. "And we don't have to tell you. What *is* a sunrise, Paul? Maybe you can tell *us*, now. . . ."

And he let his spoon rest in the dish and sat back, thinking. Could he?

He remembered it all right. The hallway, the cold storeroom, the new light, the tremendous sky, the cold, the *East*.

"Yes . . ." he began unsurely. "Yes . . . it's like—it's like. . . ." And then he felt very moved.

"But it's *not* like you said," he told her, shaking his head anxiously. "It's not! It's not like a sunset . . . It's like . . . it's . . . it's a . . . why, it's a *sunrise*!"

And he laughed then.

"It's a *sunrise!*" he went on jubilantly. And suddenly he looked wildly, wide-eyed with the new understanding, at his father.

"It *is*!" he said.

And his father nodded, laughing.

"Yes, it *is*!" he said.

Then he sat back thoughtfully in his chair.

Somehow, it didn't sound quite right, said that way. Something seemed missing. And yet, it was really very clear to him, now he had seen one. . . . The Sunrise. . . .

Discussion

The school-age child is learning to use language to suit his growing capacity for comprehending abstractions, although his level of comprehension may still surpass his facility for expressing subtleties of meaning. In this story the boy seems to comprehend the depth of his father's emotion about the sunrise. Children not only learn language from significant adults in their environment, they also absorb the unspoken emotion that accompanies the words. The tone of his father's voice and its trembling had "struck deep down in his mind." Both parents try to fill the gap between "empathizing and knowing," but attempts to verbalize this intense experience are pointless because the boy does not have the background to fully comprehend this aesthetic happening.

At the end of the story we learn that intense experience cannot always be put into words that adequately convey the individual's intention. That is why poets, novelists, and writers of short stories are admired—they can phrase human experience in unique and satisfying ways.

The good relationship the boy has with his father should be emphasized. The father wishes to share significant events with his children, and personalizes them by including each child individually in experiences with him. In an environment as open and empathic as this household seems to be the transmission of knowledge should proceed exceedingly well.

Springboards for Inquiry

(1) We know that individuals form unique meanings and associations for concepts. What unique associations will this little boy have regarding the concept of "sunrise"?

(2) In what ways does this family make it easier for their children to learn new concepts?

(3) Can you recall from your own childhood either words that had a unique meaning to you and your family or an incident which revealed that you held a misconception? (We sometimes remember the development of a misconception, which nevertheless gives clues to the development of all concepts.)

"Lady, that isn't all he said. . . About talked my ear off. Told me you said his Uncle Archie wears a girdle."

The Day We Lost Max

by Lael Littke

We probably wouldn't even have noticed that Max had fallen out of the truck if Randolph hadn't seen him go. That's the way Max was. He could sit right next to you for hours, sucking his thumb and sometimes humming a little to himself, and you wouldn't even know he was there, and when you finally noticed he wasn't, you wouldn't be able to remember just when it was he left. He was Aunt Veona's youngest, the last of eleven robust children, and Aunt Veona herself said she sometimes had a hard time remembering he was around since in all his five years he had made hardly any more noise than the soft slurping as he sucked his thumb, and the occasional humming.

Aunt Veona, Mama, three of our kids, and six of Aunt Veona's were on our way to visit Aunt Blanche up Pigeon Creek when Max fell out. It was crowded in the back of the pickup truck, what with nine of us kids trying to cling somewhere so we wouldn't bounce out. Randolph said Max stood up, probably to shift his position, and just then the truck hit a bump in the rutted dirt road. Max went over the side without a sound.

"Max fell out," said Randolph in a hoarse, scared voice.

We didn't hear him over the roar of the old truck's engine, so Randolph began pointing frantically back down the road. There, beside a clump of weeds into which he had fallen, Max stood watching us retreat, a thumb still in his mouth.

"Mama!" screamed Utahna, banging on the driver's cab. "Mama, Max fell out!"

"Stop that banging!" bellowed Aunt Veona.

Reprinted by permission of Larry Sternig Literary Agency. First printed in October 1969 issue of *Ladies' Home Journal*.

My brother Orvid pounded on Mama's side. "Max fell out!" he yelled.

Mama called something, but we couldn't hear it above the engine's noise.

We all looked at one another, our eyes enormous. "Mama!" we wailed collectively. "Stop!"

Alas! Too often had we cried "Wolf" in the past. Too often we had played tricks on Mama and Aunt Veona. If they heard us at all they discounted our cries as just another prank.

What could we do? Leonard volunteered to crawl out of the truck bed onto the running board, but Aunt Veona saw him in the mirror and in turning around to tell him to get back in, made the truck zigzag across the road.

Through the window of the cab we could see Mama and Aunt Veona talking together, so engrossed in their conversation that they probably wouldn't have noticed if all of us had fallen out. They always discussed Life when they were driving along like that, and any child lucky enough to ride up front could learn some pretty interesting things since they were apt to forget you were there, especially if you sat still and pretended to be asleep.

I had an idea they were talking about how Opal Calder had run off with a linoleum salesman three months ago, and had just come home; and how everyone told Orville he shouldn't take her back. But he said he was tired of feeding the chickens and getting his own meals, and Opal was a good worker and a fine cook even though she did crave a little excitement now and then.

By the time Aunt Veona stopped the truck in Aunt Blanche's yard we were all in a state of shock and just sat there trying to find our voices.

Aunt Blanche and several of her children came running out to welcome us.

"My stars," she said looking into the back of the truck where we sat, "the kids are all carsick. All pale and bug-eyed."

Aunt Veona climbed down from the cab and looked at us. "What's the matter?" she asked.

"Max fell out," whispered Utahna.

"Max?" said Aunt Veona.

"Fell out," whispered Randolph.

Mama got down from the running board where she was standing, and she and Aunt Veona stirred through all of us children as if they expected to uncover Max somewhere in our midst.

"Max isn't here," Aunt Veona said.

"He fell out," said Maudie.

"In some weeds," said Arthur. "He ain't hurt bad."

"Unless his head was cracked," suggested Utahna.

Aunt Veona grabbed the nearest child, who happened to be Arthur, and shook him hard. "Why didn't you tell me?" she demanded.

"They banged on the top of the cab," recalled Mama. "I thought they were playing."

"We'd better hurry back and get him," said Aunt Blanche. She, Mama, and Aunt Veona climbed into the cab, and five of her kids got in back with us.

Max was nowhere in sight when we got to the place where he had fallen out.

"He's gone," Aunt Veona said weakly after we had searched all the clumps of bushes nearby.

"Maybe he's dead," whispered Utahna.

"Hush," said Mama. "If he were dead he'd still be here, wouldn't he?"

We stared at each other silently.

"Remember, how he used to not cry when he fell and hurt himself?" said Maudie, sniffing back her tears. "How he'd just suck his thumb all the harder?"

"Remember how he used to just sit and listen when all of us were talking around the stove at night?" Randolph said. "And how once he fell asleep by the woodbox and we forgot he was there and left him all night?"

Georgie broke into loud wails. Violet, one of Aunt Blanche's kids, joined him. "I can't remember which one was Max," she wept.

Aunt Veona was close to tears herself. "He was the best little boy," she sniffed. "Made me a little birthday card last week all by himself."

"No, Mama," said Leonard. "That was me."

"Well," said Aunt Blanche briskly, "let's not stand here talking about him as if we'd never see him again. Let's all get back in and drive down the road. Maybe somebody picked him up and is looking for us."

"Maybe he's kidnapped," whispered Utahna, creating another crisis. Faced with thirteen blubbering children, Aunt Veona shoved us all in the truck and we drove back down the road, peering all along the way for a small boy who sucked his thumb.

"If Max was here," said Randolph as we bounced along, "I would ask him if he was hurt and I'd tell everybody to shut up long enough to hear what he said."

"Look," cried Utahna, who was standing up so she could see better, "here comes the sheriff."

We cowered down in the truck bed, since we were all a little afraid of the tall law man with his big hat and vast stomach.

As the sheriff's car drew alongside us, we saw Max sitting beside Sheriff Smith.

"Maybe it's against the law to fall out," whispered Utahna.

Sheriff Smith hailed Aunt Veona, who stopped the truck with a jerk. "Max," she shrieked, tumbling from the cab and almost strangling Max as she hugged him through the open window of the sheriff's car. After a short spell of weeping, she lifted him out, and felt his head for possible injuries.

"Feller picked him up and brought him to town," said Sheriff Smith.

Max looked at the ground, sucked his thumb, and said nothing.

"I didn't know whose kid he was," continued the sheriff. "Said his name was Macth, but didn't know if he had another name. Said he fell out of a big truck full of more people than he could count." Sheriff Smith looked us over and nodded, "Had to be you."

"He *said* all that?" exclaimed Aunt Veona.

"Lady, that isn't all he said," Sheriff Smith told her. "About talked my ear off. Told me you said his Uncle Archie wears a girdle. Said your kids smoked a pack of cigarettes out in the willows yesterday."

We wilted under his gaze.

"Let's see now. He said he didn't think you'd notice he was gone because his Uncle Ellis said you're kind of careless and it runs in the family and that's why you've got so many kids."

"That's enough," snapped Mama. She nodded toward all of us kids who were listening with our mouths ajar.

Aunt Veona's mouth was ajar, too. "Max said all that?"

The sheriff nodded. "And more. Talked like he'd never get another chance."

Our gazes shifted to Max, who stood tracing a furrow in the dust with his toe while he sucked his thumb and hummed softly.

"Max," said Aunt Veona. "Are you all right? How do you feel?"

Max looked at her. His eyes shifted to the vast crowd of us children who looked at him quietly and expectantly. It was probably the first time he'd ever seen us all silent.

Suddenly he removed his thumb from his mouth and shoved his hand into his pocket. A grin split his face.

"Thwell," he said.

Discussion

This story presents a caricature of a large family. On a serious level, however, it reveals how a young child can lose his identity in a large family that is insensitive to individual differences and needs. Max, who is the youngest, regresses to thumb-sucking and humming because no one person among the many is available to listen to him. Although Max is five years old, he does not communicate verbally. Older brothers and sisters undoubtedly anticipate his important needs and respond to his gestures and manner. One less voice asking for something, arguing, and adding to the noise level in the home is probably a relief to a mother of eleven.

Barring a physical or emotional dysfunction there is no reason why Max should not have developed speech when there were examples available for him to imitate. Therefore, it is no great surprise when we learn at the end of the story that Max has an adequate vocabulary and facility with language. The story is exaggerated for effect, but we now know enough about the growth of language in young children to realize that putting ideas into words is necessary for intellectual growth. Selectively withheld speech usually has more dire intellectual or emotional consequences or both for the child than it did for Max.

Springboards for Inquiry

(1) How might a large family aid or retard the language development of its youngest member?

(2) Why do you think Max "sucked his thumb" and hummed instead of communicating verbally to others?

(3) What language experiences are needed in the first few years of life to help children be successful in their school years?

(4) Give examples to show that Max has not only learned to communicate verbally but that he has also assimilated the system of meanings that exist in his cultural environment.

Development of Concepts

Through the process of building concepts, children learn about the world they live in. From these concepts they develop meanings and values. Since language is used to order this world, a concept is "a bit of meaning which is at least partially organized into a recognizable and meaningful idea" (Woodruff 1962, p. 64). According to Gilbert Sax (1969), "No simple consensus of the meaning of concept exists." We use Asahel Woodruff's definition because it is simple and eclectic. Woodruff also says (1962, p. 64), "When through experience we get a mental picture in our minds of one of the objects or forces which make up our world, we have a concept, which . . . becomes our "set" for . . . further perception of that same thing." *

One might assume from the foregoing definition that the development of concept is modeled after the early behaviorists' stimulus-response bond. Woodruff and Piaget use an expanded stimulus-response model in order to be more precise by including the individual. The S-O-R (stimulus-organism-response)

---

* Other definitions, perhaps more psychological in nature, may be found in *Analysis of Concept Learning*, ed. by Herbert J. Klausmeier and Chester W. Harris (New York: Academic Press, 1966). In this volume E. James Archer ("The Psychological Nature of Concepts," pp. 37–49) defines concept as "the label of a set of things that have something in common." Earlier definitions of concept that generally agree can be found in D. E. Berlyne, *Structure and Direction in Thinking* (New York: John Wiley and Sons, 1965); in Howard H. Kendler, "The Concept of the Concept," in *Categories of Human Learning*, edited by A. W. Melton (New York: Academic Press, 1964); and in John B. Carroll, "Words, Meanings, and Concepts" (*Harvard Educational Review* 34 [1964]: 178–202).

model makes clear that each individual mediates every stimulus and then responds in his own fashion.

Concepts are not simply "categories or classifications, abstractions that apply to a class or group of objects or activities that have certain qualities in common" (Michaelis, Grossman, and Scott 1967). Woodruff's figure (1961, p. 64) diagrams the composite nature of a concept:

MEANING (understanding)	FEELING (preference)	SYMBOLS (language)
	CONCEPT	

In Piaget's thinking, as viewed by Herbert Ginsburg and Sylvia Opper (1969), "symbols or words do not refer to things, but instead stand for one's knowledge of things." They suggest that whereas one child uses the term *bicycle* to mean two wheels, a seat, handlebars, and something that goes very fast, another may see the same object as something that made him fall many times and that he therefore feels is dangerous. According to Piaget, each child has assimilated the word (symbol) *bicycle* into a different set of schemes. The child's personal mental symbol for the word *bicycle* does not refer solely to the physical thing but also to his understanding of it. The child incorporates features of external reality (bicycle) into his own psychological structure, or mental schemes. What the symbol refers to is always personal, although there is enough agreement about words to allow communication. Theoretically, the more experience a person has the more he brings to his thinking; this is why a young child first calls any man "Daddy" and finally formulates his concept of the referent. A concept, then, involves personal contact through sensory organs, and thinking about the referent based on personal experiences. It is fair to equate intellectual growth with conceptual growth.

A consideration of the conceptual growth of the child must include a discussion of Piaget's four major periods: infancy (birth to 18–24 months), the sensorimotor stage; the toddler years (18 months to the preschool years), the preoperational stage; the early school years (7 to 11 years), the stage of concrete operations; and early adolescence (11 or 12 years to 14 or 15 years), the stage of formal operations (because this volume does not consider adolescence the years of formal operation will not be discussed).

Piaget indicates two surprising things about the period of infancy: the infant is capable of more complex behavior than had been imagined, and there are developmental areas in which the infant is surprisingly deficient. Piaget's observations show the newborn as an active initiator of behavior, but up to the age of two years the infant operates in an essentially nonverbal atmosphere. According to Kagan (1966), the primary duties of infancy are the acquisition of schema*

* The best definition we can find, even though Kagan apologizes for being unable to adequately define the term any better than Piaget, is that schema is an organized pattern of behavior (1966). Thumb-sucking is *not* considered by Piaget to be a habit but rather a learned activity.

and orientation to the external world. Even the seemingly natural search for his mother's nipple is an accommodation. The finding of the nipple seems to depend on chance, but it is, in effect, the result of a fairly systematic method of searching. It is interesting to note that Kagan believes *sensory* ought to be omitted from the term *sensorimotor* and the emphasis placed on *motor.*

The second period of growth is noteworthy for the development of expressive language and thought. The growth of a labeling vocabulary allows the toddler to express himself beyond the data of his experience. Kagan postulates that there are four fundamental conceptual dimensions the preschool child uses to organize his world: big–small, adult–child, male–female, and good–bad.

Although the growth of labeling behavior continues in the early school years, it is now secondary to cognitive development about rules and the habit of evaluation. Kagan labels two types of children: (a) the reflectives, who brood over answers, labels, and ideas; and (b) the fast evaluators, who are impulsive. During this time sex-role identification with models and evaluative concepts about regression, instrumental dependence, anxiety, lying, aggression, and destruction are developing.

We summarize Piaget's schema for conceptual growth and conclude by citing the heart of the conflict between his cognitive theories and those held by American psychologists. Kagan (1966) lists four principles that epitomize Piaget's approach to conceptual growth: (a) Intelligence is defined as the possession of operations or rules of transformation; (b) Development is associated with passage from one stage of operations to another; (c) Passage from one stage to another is a function of both experience and maturation; (d) The operations that define intelligence and which change with age are logical structures that are neither dependent on nor derivative from language. This last statement confounds American scholars, who see language as the heart of reasoning. It does appear, however, that conceptual growth is characterized by identifiable stages; that is individual, orderly, and continuous; and that it is characterized further by a marked shift between infancy and toddlerhood, from sensorimotor schema to reflective schema that continually undergo refinement as the child advances in age.

"How do you go to heaven? I mean, if your bones are in the coffin, and you haven't got any eyes. . . ."

Jonathan and the Tooth Fairy

by Ann Plaat Stone

I've got a kid brother named Jonathan (not to mention two baby sisters) and naturally it is my lot in life to sleep above that kid in a double bunk bed.

Well, last night in the small hours, Jonathan got out his flashlight and was very busy prowling around the house. I pretended to be asleep because naturally, if he'd known I was awake, I'd have gotten involved with that kid and ended up answering some fool question like is the sun shining in Kansas City now? That's because he has some fool thing about *The Wizard of Oz.* Anyway, I went back to sleep before I knew what he was up to.

But this morning I was rudely awakened when he climbed up and sat on my stomach and dripped his crummy tears all over me saying, "She didn't come. She didn't come. My tooth fell out last night, and I got an envelope and put my tooth in it like I always do, and she didn't come." With one hand he socked my pitching arm and waved the lousy envelope with the other.

"Look, kid," I said, "maybe she'd made the rounds before your tooth fell out. She'll probably come by tonight."

"But you said the tooth fairy always knows when a kid's got a tooth under his pillow. You said she always comes. You said that."

"Yeh, Ok," I said. "Maybe she's on vacation. You know, like we went to River Ranch last summer and Dad didn't go to the office. Ok?"

He looked me straight in the eye and acted like I was stupid. "You know Daddy got somebody at the office to do his job. Like at school we get a substitute when Mrs. Fitzgerald is sick," he said. "The tooth fairy would have a substitute too. I just

---

"Jonathan and the Tooth Fairy," by Ann Plaat Stone (unpublished story, 1971).

know she would. The tooth fairy's an angel you know."

"Well maybe she got sick all of a sudden, Jonny," I said.

But then, after the angel bit, he stopped crying and started on another track. "I was thinking, Steve, after I put my tooth under my pillow, what I'd do with the dollar the tooth fairy would leave me. I was thinking about getting one of those underwater swimming masks."

A dollar! Boy is that kid spoiled. I used to get a dime. And even with inflation Jonny used to get only a quarter. But then one day he told Mom and Dad that his friend Mary Lou next door got a dollar for her tooth. So you know what? The next time he lost a tooth he got out the blackboard Uncle Joe gave him for Christmas two years ago, and he made me print: "I don't think it's fair that you should leave a dollar next door and only a quarter at our house. I don't think Abraham Lincoln would like that." Yeh, just like that. And I'll be darned if he didn't get a dollar from then on.

I didn't know what to say next, but anyway the small fry came in then.

Pamela asked, "What day is this day?"

"Saturday," I answered, not too cheerfully.

"Oh, goody. You baby-sit us today."

Ellen, who was madly working on pulling off the bottom half of her sleepers, echoed, "Goody, goody, goody." And added, "I got wee-wee's."

Boy, I tell you, what did I do to deserve two baby sisters? You'd think Jonathan would be enough trouble for any guy. And besides I did have to take care of those stupes today. But it was a last resort, let me tell you. I mean, I tried to get a job mowing lawns, delivering papers, and even being a ball boy down at the tennis courts. But a million other guys had the same idea, and I was out, just out. So when Mom suggested I baby-sit on Saturdays for fifty cents an hour, I was a drowning man holding on to the last hunk of wood. You see, there's this absolutely neat tent Bob Saunders and I are saving up for to go camping in this summer, not to mention the junk we're gonna need for the layout. So here I am.

Pamela was singing, "Ellen is a wee-wee. I'm dry. I'm not a baby." Not much, sister!

"Go on, Ellen, tell Mom." I got Jonny off my stomach, grabbed my jeans and made for the bathroom.

I got into the kitchen just in time to hear Jonathan telling his tale of woe to Dad, who was biding his time and looking at me for a signal. So we went through the whole business again.

Meals at our house are absolutely enough to give a guy indigestion. I mean you'd think Mom was running a restaurant. When Mom came in with the girls, Ellen started in, "I want Rice Koopies."

"Can I have a peanut butter sandwich?" Pamela wanted to know.

"Didn't you make any corn muffins?" Jonathan asked.

Mom started to explain, "We're out of milk because Ellen had three bottles last night. There's scrambled eggs and toast."

"Gosh, no corn muffins," Jonathan said. "This just isn't my day." He looked like he was going to bawl again.

"I'll make some tomorrow," Mom promised. Boy is that kid spoiled.

"I want Ricc Koopics," Ellen repeated. That one never gives up either.

"You'll have to eat them dry, dear," Mom said, handing her a bowl of cereal.

Ellen started wailing, "I want mi-ilk."

Mom began to explain again. But I guess she figured what was the use and started fixing eggs. Since I am the only sensible offspring in this house, I started the toast. Pamela was still pursuing the subject of peanut butter sandwiches. Dad began reading the newspaper.

"Those swimming masks are really keen, Mommy," Jonathan was saying.

"What?" she asked. "What's keen?"

"You never listen to me," Johnny complained. "What's the use?"

"I'll listen, dear. Now start again."

And so for the third time that morning I had to hear about that tooth. "If the tooth fairy had come last night," Jonathan was saying, "I could have bought one of those underwater swimming masks. You know, they wear them on "Deep Sea" on TV. I need that mask very badly. I really do need one. I bet I could find all sorts of stuff in the swimming pool if I had one of those masks."

"I see," Mom said. Jonny is always needing things very badly. On the top shelf of our closet are dozens of things he has needed very badly in the last couple of years . . . things like a lock and key, which he was going to use to lock up everything he didn't want Pam and Ellen to touch; a crazy Mickey Mouse hat he used to wear when he was watching TV; a toy flute he once played eight hours a day for three weeks in a row to a record of "Peter and the Wolf" (what torture!), and other junk like that.

"If the tooth fairy had come, I would of bought that mask, all right."

Dad looked up from his paper. "Suppose we lend you the money, Jonny, and tomorrow you can pay us back after the tooth fairy comes."

Jonathan lit up. "Suppose she leaves me more than a dollar. I mean, she might leave more because she was sorry she forgot me the first time. Suppose she leaves me two dollars?"

I could see Dad thinking over that one.

"I don't think the tooth fairy could afford to leave you that much money," he said. And then, I guess not wanting to be too wise on the subject, he added, "If she did leave you more than a dollar, why then, of course, you could keep the extra money." But I guess he didn't think it fair to build up Jonathan's hopes, so he said, "I wouldn't count on it if I were you."

Dad left for the office, and Jonny turned to me. "Can we go to the store this morning, Steve? If I could buy the mask this morning I could use it in the pool this afternoon."

What could I do? I mean, it was Saturday. On Saturdays I was paid to be accommodating. "Get dressed and we'll go over to the Toy Plaza."

"Oh goody," Pamela clapped her hands. "Can me and Ellen get something?"

Ellen clapped too. I looked at Mom, who naturally nodded. See what I mean? They're all spoiled.

There were no other customers in the Toy Plaza, and the kids were set to have a ball.

"Don't touch the dolly, El."

"I'm not touching," was her answer as she cradled the doll in her arms.

"Look Steve. Dinosaurs; a Tyrannosaurus rex, Pteranodon, Triceratops, Stegosaurus and Diplodocus," Jonny recited for the clerk's benefit.

"How about the swimming mask?" I asked, wanting to get the heck out of there as soon as possible.

"Gosh, can't I look around for awhile?" he pleaded.

"For a minute," I said, trying to keep track of Pamela and Ellen who were now on their way toward a jungle gym. We've got one in the backyard creaky from disuse, but Pamela and Ellen got on the glider as though it was the first one they'd ever seen.

"That's for display, girls," I said trying to pull them off. I wasn't successful, and feeling like a helpless idiot I looked to the clerk for help.

"That's all right," she said. "It's a floor sample and we don't mind."

So I relaxed, and walked over to the baseball stuff. I was just trying on a mitt for size when Jonathan called me.

"Hey, Steve, what's this say?" I dropped the mitt and went over to take a look.

"It says, 'The Visible Man.' "

"What's *visible*?"

"It means you can see it."

"That's nutty. Of course you can see it. It's just an old stickembottom."

He carefully examined the skeleton. "Is it a real skeleton? I mean do they use real bones to make it?"

"No," I said. "It's plastic, I think."

"Is it a skeleton of a person?"

"It's a model," I told him. "You can see where everything is."

"Where's the soul?" he asked.

"The soul?" I repeated. I didn't know Jonathan had any information on souls. "Who told you about souls?"

"Mrs. Fitzgerald told me. She said people have souls but dinosaurs don't. That's why, she said, I won't get to see any dinosaurs in heaven."

"Oh," I said. "Gosh, well, I guess 'The Visible Man' has an invisible soul. Let's get your swimming mask."

We spent ten hours choosing the right mask, and then Pamela and Ellen finally found something that met both their approval. As we left the store, Jonathan's last comment was "I could sure use that stickembottom. I could learn a lot if I had that."

After lunch Mom put the girls down for their nap, and Jonathan (mask and all) and I got on the bus to go to his swimming lesson.

The lesson started late because naturally Jonathan had to pass his darn mask around to everybody in the class. Then the teacher made him give me the mask to hold while she taught them something that looked like they were floating on their backs holding a pillow under their head with one hand, and practicing morse code with the other while their legs were doing a "cha cha." All the kids were trying to catch their mothers' eyes to make sure their efforts were being appreciated. Jonny waved to me at least fifty times. I smiled encouragingly. Gosh what you don't have to do for fifty cents an hour.

When the teacher announced "free

play," Jonny got his mask back. "Watch me, Steve. I'm going to stay down for ten minutes. Maybe I'll find some money or something."

He did find a bobby pin and a Band-Aid, which he stuck in my pants pocket for safekeeping. He held my hand on the way back to the bus. "I love you, Steve. You're a stickembottom and you eat grass." He laughed uproariously. I squeezed his hand. He wasn't a bad kid, really.

On the way home Jonny sang something from "The Mikado." He conducted with his swimming mask, holding it by one limp band and swinging it in time to "Here's a How-De-Do!" Presently he sang, "Here's a how-de-do, a stickembottom too." I looked out the window and pretended I didn't know him. Yet I thought maybe if I had any money left, I'd buy that stupid stickembottom and put it away until his birthday.

Later, Mom went to the store to do her grocery shopping. Pamela and Ellen were blowing soap bubbles on the patio (they naturally picked something messy at the store). While I was looking in the refrigerator for something to hold me over until dinner, Jonathan sat down at the kitchen table. "Can I have a carrot, Steve?"

"All right," I said. "But eat it here. If you go outside with it, Pam and El will want one too, and I don't feel like fixing two more."

For a moment he sat, crunching, and then he asked, "When people get buried in coffins . . . I mean, when you put them in there, are their hands at their sides?"

What had gotten him started on that, I wondered. I answered "Yes," and waited for the inevitable next question.

"If you opened the coffin in a hundred years, would their hands still be that same way?"

"Only the bones," I said.

"What happens to their hands?"

"They decay."

"What's *decay*?"

"Well, after a long time, everything except the bones just kind of wastes away," I explained.

"Even the eyes? What happens to the eyes?"

"They decay too."

"Oh." Jonny swallowed the last of the carrot.

"How do you go to heaven? I mean, if your bones are in the coffin, and you haven't got any eyes . . ." He couldn't seem to finish.

"Just your soul goes to heaven."

"You mean just your soul gets to be an angel?"

"Jonny, be a good kid and go watch your cartoons."

He wasn't listening to me anymore, though. And his next words were not directed to me, but were more a kind of thinking out loud.

"If angels are souls, how can they get sick? Angels can't get sick. That's nutty."

He sat for a moment, his tongue exploring the space left by the lost tooth. Finally he started for the front room. "Nutty, nutty," I heard him repeating. He came back into the kitchen.

"But I *know* I'm going to get corn muffins for breakfast tomorrow."

That kid. I mean we hadn't even had dinner yet, and he was thinking about breakfast tomorrow.

I was about to say something when I saw that Jonny was trying his best not to cry. So I looked at him for a long time. Finally, I got the picture.

"Well," I said, "Wizard, welcome to the human race." I stuck out my hand.

After we shook on it, I fished around in my pocket. There was that bobby pin and Band-Aid. I put them on the kitchen table and handed Jonny a dime.

"Look partner," I said, "How about watching the girls til Mom comes home? Ok?"

"Ok!" he said, Ok!" he grabbed the Band-Aid and bobby pin and tossed them into the garbage bag under the sink. Then he dashed off, his mouth one stupid toothless grin.

Me—I went off to pitch a few before dinner.

Discussion

This story provides the exact line of reasoning Jonathan pursues to bring him to the logical conclusion that the tooth fairy is an adult hoax. With the demise of the tooth fairy goes the collapse of Jonathan's belief in the existence of angels. This is a turning point for Jonathan, and even he realizes that there is a little sadness in growing up.

The emergence of Jonathan into a new period in his life, characterized in part by great curiosity about abstract causes and conditions, suggests that he is probably seven years old. This is an age that can be considered transitional in several respects. Physically, Jonathan has a gap-toothed smile, and he probably is losing the cherub or babylike appearance that has made him so easily lovable and forgivable in adults' eyes. He is trying very hard to rise to meet new expectations. He may feel like crying over small hurts, such as not having corn muffins for breakfast, but the tears are either short-lived or concealed behind brimming eyes. Jonathan tries to impress others with high-sounding bits of knowledge, such as his feat of rattling off the correct terms for members of the prehistoric dinosaur family.

Jonathan, like other seven-year-olds, enjoys being active and being silly, but he is also inclined to spend more time alone thinking than in the past. We expect children of this age, who ponder abstract concepts like God and death or a cultural myth such as the tooth fairy, to draw rather realistic conclusions about them. Their insight into concepts of space, measurement, and time will lead them to find inconsistencies in imaginative views that had previously suited them. It may be that despite Jonathan's new knowledge about the tooth fairy, the monetary reward for "believing" will keep him from disavowing her existence to anyone but his big brother.

Springboards for Inquiry

(1) Diagram Jonathan's line of reasoning from "believing" to realizing that the tooth fairy cannot possibly exist.

(2) Why do American scholars believe that language development is necessary for growth in reasoning ability?

(3) Piaget believed that children's thinking was qualitatively different from adults. Name the principal periods in the development of the intellect of children as outlined by Piaget.* If you can repeat some of Piaget's experiments in teaching the principle of conservation of mass, weight, and volume† with children of the same ages as Piaget's subjects report what you find.

(4) According to Piaget, can the child's development of intellect be accelerated?‡

(5) Are individual differences in understanding concepts a function of experience or heredity?

---

* Jean Piaget *Origins of Intellect in Children*, N.Y.: International Universities Press, 1952.

† For additional descriptions of Piaget's experiments which will be helpful see David Elkind, "Childrens' Discovery of Conservation of Mass, Weight & Volume*. Piaget's Replication Study II" *J. of Genetic Psychology* 98, 1961, 219–227. John L. Phillips, *The Origins of Intellect—Piaget's Theory*. San Francisco: W. H. Freeman & Co. 1969.

‡ See Hans G. Furth. *Piaget for Teachers*. Englewood Cliffs, New Jersey: Prentice-Hall, Inc. 1970 for many ideas for thinking tasks for children.

Understanding Birth and Death

Research into children's understanding of the birth process seems usually to be linked to the study of sex education. The many books about sex education that have been published in the last few years have the following consensus: children are concerned about their origins, and parents facing the initial question of "Where did I come from?" are frequently at a loss for an answer, often because the question seems to come at an inopportune time.

Helene Arnstein (1967) believes that it is important to the preschool child's conceptual framework that he reasonably understand where he came from. Although children often prefer a science-fiction version of birth, sex education specialists agree that it is important to allow a child to verbalize his questions and theories and to give him, on demand, as much scientific information as he can comprehend. Arnstein quotes the delightful story of six-year-old Sheila who, when informed by her friends about the father's role in the conception process, went to her parents in great alarm to ask for clarification about the making of babies. The parents, adhering to modern child development theory, told her the truth. Completely desolate, Sheila ran back to her companions, one of whom consoled her: "Don't worry, Sheila. When we grow up, we'll find a better way."

Although children need to be given accurate information in response to their questions about birth, simplicity should be the watchword. In general, children ought to hear only what they want to know. A complete, literal explanation of the entire birth process is not usually appropriate. One of the authors recalls when his own child asked him a question of this nature. When told that he should consult his mother he replied, "I can't ask Mom because she always tells me more than I really want to know."

As stated in the discussion of the development of concepts, whenever possible the parent should make explanations understandable by relating his words to real things (referents); the concept will be better grounded than if the child were simply to hear explanations of birth in abstract terms. Although explanations of birth should not be overtechnical, when they become mere verbalisms children may seek concrete information from their peers, who will probably give them a combination of misguided information and reality. Birth should be considered by parents to be a natural process and one that is easily explained to a child. Many books have simple diagrams that make clear the basic functions of the uterus, the vagina, and the birth canal, and at times in children's preschool years, these books may be helpful. It goes without saying that evasions such as "You came from the hospital" are not in keeping with present thinking.

Whereas research in the field of children's concepts of birth is limited, the literature concerning children's concepts of death is extensive. The primary concerns of child development specialists are the course of the child's development of the concept of death and how he can be helped to develop a "mature" concept of death when he needs it. The first point was discussed in the section on the development of concepts. The second point presumes that a "mature" concept exists. Robert Kastenbaum (1967, pp. 91–92) says that "it will be doubted that we have attained even a close approximation to a perfected conception of death." He states further that whereas children are often very open about death,* the adult world full of "uncertainties, anxieties, perplexities . . . may complicate rather than facilitate the child's quest for understanding."

A brief, specific review of the development of the concept of death in children shows that in general "death is regarded by children as a deprivation" (Mitchell 1966, p. 157). There seems to be reasonable agreement that in the first two years of life there is no understanding of death (Gesell and Ilg 1946; Anthony 1940). Piaget (1954) reports that genuine conceptual operations occur near puberty, yet during the third year of life children think more about death and even deny that death is a final event (Nagy 1948). Corroboration of this idea comes from the unusual works of Chukovsky (1963, pp. 46–47), the tireless student of the language development of Russian children: "Optimism is as essential to the child as the air he breathes. . . . No sooner . . . is the child convinced of the inevitability of death for all living creatures than he hastens to assure himself that he will eternally remain immortal." He cites the case of a four-year-old boy who looked out a bus window at a funeral procession and said, "Everyone will die, but I'll remain."

There is general agreement that the child begins with a matter-of-fact orientation—a belief that death is accidental and, barring this unfortunate event, the child himself will not die (Nagy 1948; Gesell and Ilg 1946; Anthony 1940; Schilder and Wechsler 1934). With the advent of television and its graphic portrayals of events, we can expect that death will become more vivid and evident, but that these findings will remain viable. After the age of approximately

---

* In *From Two to Five* (Berkeley and Los Angeles: University of California Press, 1963) Korner Chukovsky frequently indicates that Russian children are utterly frank about death and boundlessly optimistic.

five years* the child seems to gradually accommodate the idea that death is "final, inevitable, universal, and personal," according to Kastenbaum (Grollman 1967, p. 101).† There seems to be no satisfactory way of providing realistic conceptions of death for children at an earlier age. Not until children make clear distinctions between the living and the nonliving is death not viewed as separation, the most dreaded experience of childhood.

All that has been said is subject to modifications that religious‡ and cultural influences have on children. Even the remarkable prophecy of Selye that medical science will one day progress to the point where death will be unknown except for accidents will not automatically protect children from their misconceptions. Fears of death are natural, and children cannot be and should not be protected from seeing death as an inevitable part of life.

---

* Despite much work, both old and new, that uses chronology as the means of dividing cognitive changes in children, the reader needs to remember that ages are always approximate, lest unnecessary concern over the "proper" development ensue.

† Chukovsky reports the conversation of five-year-old Misha when he heard about the death of a family acquaintance: "To die—that's very bad. It's forever" (1963, p. 50).

‡ Mitchell (1966) doubts that any religious philosophy has made children more comfortable about death.

For weeks I went around wishing that I were a girl and could have an engine and buffers instead of an old starting handle like Father.

The Genius *by Frank O'Connor*

Some kids are sissies by nature; I was a sissy by conviction. I was an intelligent, rational child and could see for myself that not only was fighting sinful; it was exceedingly dangerous.

My way, when someone wanted to fight with me and I couldn't get away, was to climb on the nearest wall and argue like hell in a very loud voice in hopes of being overheard by the neighbors. I argued about Jesus and good manners and it usually worked, for the other fellow, after staring up at me for a couple of minutes in disgust and incredulity, wondering whether he'd have time to hammer my head on the pavement before I succeeded in gathering a crowd, usually muttered something about "blooming sissies" and went away. I didn't mind being called a sissy; I could forget all about that in two minutes, but a hammering left consequences that upset my powers of concentration for much longer than that.

I toyed with games for a while and enjoyed kicking a football about the road by myself, but when I discovered that the moment anyone joined me he started to get violent and push and kick, I took a dislike to that as well. Little girls didn't generally fight, so I preferred them to little boys, but on the whole they were rather silly and preferred little boys who played football and fought, so I had few playmates. I didn't miss them. The only people I really liked were grown girls of about thirty, and I had a real passion for the girl next door, who let me help her with the garden.

But she only gardened when she was home from the office, and my favorite amusement was getting on my tricycle and going for long voy-

---

ages of discovery. Our bungalow was in an estate between two main roads, one terraced high above the other with glimpses of the bay below, and without crossing any main road I could leave our house, follow the upper road for over a mile, then turn left down a connecting road to the sea front and finally reach home almost without leaving the pavement. Another voyage of discovery ran in the opposite direction, and as time went on I extended them both and when I came home wrote my adventures down in a book called *Voyages of Discovery by Johnson Martin 3/6 net*. Johnson Martin was my writing name. When I grew up I intended to be famous and have a statue put up to me.

Some instinct told me that the best way to set about it was to find out the reason for everything, but Father couldn't see this at all. When I asked him questions he was always quite forthcoming, but afterward Mother would take me aside and tell me that Father was only joking again. It used to make me mad with rage because I never knew when he was joking. She and Father were always rowing about me. "But, Mick," I heard her say once, "the child must learn." "I like a child to be natural," growled Father. Either Mother didn't like children to be natural or she thought I was natural enough already, for she nearly always tried to explain anything I wanted to know.

Now, one of the things I particularly wanted to know was where babies came from; I wanted to know if I had ever been a baby myself—which struck me as highly improbable anyhow—and if so, how I had arrived. It seemed to me a fairly simple, intelligent question, but I was damned if I could get a reply to it. Mother talked about flowers and bees and birds till she made me sick. I asked Father and he said they dropped them out of airplanes and if you caught one he was yours. "By parachute?" I asked, and he looked surprised and said, "Oh, no, nothing sissy like that." After that Mother took me aside and explained that Father was only joking again. Father was like that and we must try and sympathize with him. I didn't see anything to be sympathetic with. I went quite dotty with fury and told Mother that one of these days Father would go too far with his joking and regret it.

Finally Mother seemed to decide that I must be told. It was a heavy responsibility and she didn't welcome it, but she was a woman of principle. She took an awful long time about it, but at last I gathered that mummies had an engine in their tummies and fathers had a starting handle that caused the engine to work and the engine laid an egg and the egg broke and a baby came out. This explained lots of things I hadn't understood until then, for instance, the fact that Mother had buffers on her chest while Father hadn't, and, above all, the reason for the existence of fathers. For weeks I went around wishing that I were a girl and could have an engine and buffers instead of an old starting handle like Father.

Then I went to school for the first time. It was one of the most alarming experiences in my life. There were about twenty of us in the little school, four of us juniors ("babies," they called us) all in one room, and it went on endlessly for a full three hours. Those who could read the clock were not so badly off, but I could only read Arabic numerals and I was completely lost. During all this time we were supposed to sit still and listen to information, which I found intolerable because the information that the teacher addressed to us juniors was beneath contempt and I could concentrate only on what the seniors were doing. I kept on firing questions at the woman about their work, and she kept on saying, "Hush, Bobby!" to me, which made me flaming mad, because if there was one thing I could not stand it was people saying "hush!" to me. Father was always at it.

During playtime a tall girl in the seniors came up to me.

"What's your other name, Bobby?" she asked.

"MacCarthy," I said.

"And do you like school?"

"No, I said. "I hate it. The woman talks too much."

Then I began to talk for a change and it was a real pleasure to me. It seemed to be a pleasure to the girl too. Her name was Una Dwyer. She listened very attentively while I told her about my adventures on my tricycle, the numbers of buses and the times of trains from all the principal stations as well as the book I was writing.

Una had to stay in till three, so I didn't see her again till next day, and then she came and took my hand and we walked about the playground together. This time she told me about herself. She had two other sisters, and a brother nearly as old as herself at the school. Her younger brother had been killed the year before by a car. She asked me to come and play at their house on Saturday.

When I told Mother this she was delighted. She agreed at once to my going to the Dwyers' to play. She had already told me that I'd make friends at the school and I had. Poor soul! Little did she know the sort of friend I was making!

Next day when I came out to play one of the seniors said, "Bobby, your girl isn't out yet." Another senior put on a serious air and asked, "Has Bobby a girl?" and the first replied, "Oh, yes, Una Dwyer is Bobby's girl. He goes out with Una. Don't you, Bobby?"

Now, to tell the truth, since it was my first time I had not realized that Una was my girl. I hadn't realized even that I was in love. Thinking it over, I saw that the girls were right. It seems to me still that they were right, for it has always happened like that. All a woman has to do to make me fall head and ears in love with her is to shut up and listen to me. But at the time it made me thoughtful and rather nervous. I was not quite certain if I should like being in love or if, like football, it was one of those games that two people couldn't play at without getting violent. For the first time I didn't tell Mother. Up to this I had always assumed that she was my girl and that I should marry her when I grew up; it had always been understood between us and I felt certain she would be disappointed. I even wondered whether I couldn't have one girl for a mother and another for a wife, but decided that it was probably not allowed since otherwise somebody would have been bound to think of it. I was sorry for Mother and cried quite a bit thinking of her desolate state, but I was sufficiently prudent to keep the secret, at least until I saw what Una's house was like and whether I really preferred it to our own. For my age I was really temperate and long-sighted.

When I saw the house my mind was made up. It was a far nicer place than ours, not so big or so cold or so surrounded by other houses. In fact it was a little lodge inside a gate with great fields behind, a big house at the end of the avenue and cows, poultry and rabbits. All the Dwyer children and their parents gathered in the little kitchen. Mrs. Dwyer, who was a dressmaker, struck me as a really well-informed person. At first it was disturbing to hear so many people talking at once. I was used to planning discussions so that they went on for a very long time, but here when I began one it was immediately interrupted by someone's asking a question and I found it hard to remember where I had left off. Besides, all the children, even Una, shouted, and this alarmed me until I realized that they didn't mean any harm and only shouted to draw attention to themselves. When I saw that no one would get hurt I was quite pleased and even shouted and jumped over chairs myself. Una kept on encouraging me.

When night was falling she took me home. Outside the gate she stopped and said, "This is where little Joe was killed." It was just a gate like any other gate, with trees overhanging it, and I saw no prospect of acquiring much useful information.

"Was it a Ford or a Morris?" I asked, out of politeness more than anything else.

"I don't know," she said with a look of surprise. "It was Donegan's old car. They couldn't look where they were going. He was only three."

"Jesus probably wanted him," I said in the same tone.

"I suppose so," she said with the same look, and it occurred to me that she doubted my view of the matter. "He was my pet."

"You should get your mummy to make you another," I said.

"What's that?" she asked, and this time I could see she was quite astonished. So I explained to her how babies came, and she listened to me with a funny smile. I found myself wondering whether I hadn't got some detail wrong in connection with the engine or the buffers. I was very fond of engines but I didn't know a whole lot about them.

"Who told you that?" she asked incredulously.

"Mummy," I said. "Didn't your mummy tell you?"

"That's not what she tells us," she said in the same slightly superior, half-laughing way.

"What does she tell you?"

"Oh, just that you buy babies."

"But where?"

"From the nurse, of course."

"I wouldn't really believe that," I said confidently, but in fact I was much less confident than I sounded. Una had succeeded in filling me with doubts again. I began at once to see the flaws in Mother's story and wondered at myself for having accepted it so readily, so childishly, in fact. This, it seemed to me, was the principal drawback in childhood; you took everything uncritically. I had even been prepared to accept Father's story that babies were dropped out of airplanes until Mother warned me against it. Now it seemed that I must distrust her as well. There was no knowing where really accurate information was to be obtained about anything, and it made me terribly depressed. At the same time I could not see why she had told me such a highly improbable story in the first place.

I said nothing to her. I no longer trusted anything she told me on the subject. Instead I made discreet inquiries from the other children at school. I heard some astonishing stories. One boy admitted to having arrived on a snowflake, dressed in a blue shirt, but as his mother (to his own great disgust) had given the shirt away to a poor child it was impossible to verify. I felt almost as bitter as he did about this wanton destruction of evidence. But the one thing no one had ever heard of, even as a joke, was of girls having engines in their tummies. That theory might have been fashionable when Mother was a girl but it was definitely out now.

It left me really disappointed in Mother. Whether it was just ignorance on her part or—as I sometimes suspected—false shame that prevented her admitting that she had merely bought me in the same way as you buy any other pet, it made me more critical of her. That is another thing I was discovering about love: that you never really are in love with a girl until you start being ashamed of your mother. I looked at Mrs. Dwyer, loud-voiced, brisk and cheerful, and realized that she would have no compunction about telling her children the truth, even if it wasn't as romantic as Mother's story.

I did not quite know what to do about being in love. I was concerned about the disparity, not in age, which didn't worry me at all (as I say, I preferred women of thirty), but in information. I didn't think Una would like to have a lover who was only in first book, so I nagged the life out of Mother until I succeeded in getting a complete set of books for the fifth class, and set myself to studying fifth-class work in the evenings. Being the only pupil in my own class, I treated myself with great severity, not even allowing myself to speak. At the same time I thought it might be as well to ask Mother's advice, hoping that she would not notice the direction my feelings had taken.

"If a gentleman asks a lady to marry him, what does he say?" I asked one night when she was tucking me up.

"Oh, different things," she said lightly. "It depends on the gentleman quite a lot. Some gentlemen have a great deal to say for themselves. Why?"

"If a gentleman said, 'Excuse me, will you marry me?' would that be enough?"

"Well, it's the custom for him to tell her first how fond of her he is."

"Why?"

"Well, if the lady didn't think he was really fond of her she mightn't want to marry him at all."

"Oh!" I said with a sigh. This was a fresh complication. I decided to put off the proposal until after Christmas. I had saved a good deal of money and was determined to give Una a present that would leave her in no doubt at all of how fond of her I was.

All that autumn I saw her almost

every day and some weekends as well. Usually it was at the Dwyers' house. Mother wanted me to bring the Dwyer children more frequently to our house and I did so once or twice, but each time it proved too much of a strain. I felt that they must always be making damaging comparisons between their own house and ours, and particularly between their mother and mine. I was on tenterhooks the whole time, wondering what Mother was going to say next. A woman who could say a thing like that about people having engines in their tummies was capable of saying anything, and every time the subject of babies was mentioned I flew into a panic and began to talk wildly about buses and trains. For myself, I didn't really mind. She could believe what she liked, say what she liked. I knew it wasn't altogether her fault that she was old-fashioned and stuffy, but I couldn't bear to think of how the Dwyers would giggle over it, of how they would return home and, sitting together over the fire, tell Mrs. Dwyer the ridiculous things that Mother had said. I broke into a cold sweat when I thought of it.

At Christmas I bought Una a beautiful book on railways; a book I badly wanted for myself, as a matter of fact, and my only consolation in parting from it was the thought that when we were married I should have plenty of opportunity to study it. Una sent me a Teddy bear, which I felt rather sore about. It did not strike me as a suitable present from a lady to a gentleman she was about to marry, and it left me somewhat doubtful of her intentions.

In January we returned to school. I found another little boy in my class who was new to the school, and the teacher asked me to look after him. When he wanted to go out I took him by the hand and buttoned him up after. I rather enjoyed this, but I soon found that Jimmy tagged onto me almost as though he owned me and talked to me all the time in class so that I could get no work done.

It was the same at playtime. I wanted to walk around the playground with Una, but he followed me, asking me to play with him. He didn't want to play with Una; he wanted to play with me and he was a terribly persistent child.

"Run away now, Jimmy!" I kept saying.

But he skipped after me on one leg, with a curling pin in his fair hair just like a baby, shouting, "Will you play now, Bobby? Will you play?"

"I can't play," I said severely. "Don't you see I'm engaged?"

"Ah, Bobby, why won't you play?" he shrieked.

"Ah, play with him!" Una said, laughing. "He's only a baby."

So the two of us played with him, and she didn't seem to mind his perpetual shouting and childishness. He talked about railways but he didn't even know the terminus of the Great Southern Railway. After two days of this I gave him a fountain pen and he promised to let Una and me alone during playtime, but he was so childish that he didn't even understand the nature of a promise and within five minutes of playtime's beginning he was running after me shouting, "Will you play, Bobby? Will you play?"

On the third morning Father was

cycling in to school with me in a seat on the handle bars. Long before he did I saw the Dwyer children strung out on their own way to school. I saw something else, which made my heart turn over. I saw Jimmy skipping along beside them. Father waved to them, and they to Father, and I heard Una call, "Hullo, Bobby!" but I didn't look round; I didn't reply. I sat staring straight ahead at the tree-covered, dripping, gloomy slope of the road before me.

"Didn't you see Una waving to you?" asked Father in surprise.

"No," I replied coldly, trying to keep from tears. It was my first experience of real jealousy and it was awful. I didn't know it was jealousy any more than I had known it was love, but at playtime I kept far away from the corner where Una was playing with Jimmy, the only place in the world I wanted to be. I stared at them gloomily, at Jimmy with his sissy curling pins, skipping and screaming like a mad creature, and Una's long face all lit up, and I wondered what she saw in him. No doubt, I thought, he knew where babies came from. He had a mother who didn't conceal the facts of life from him, while I had nobody.

At night I lay awake brooding on it and wondering whether I could survive the blow. I thought of giving Una back her Teddy bear and asking for my own beautiful book on railways, but this seemed to reveal a small and ungenerous spirit that had nothing in common with the passion that racked me. What frightened me most was the violence it roused in me. As I say, I had always been a pacifist by conviction, but now when I thought of Jimmy it was of challenging him to a fight and killing him with a heavy blow. It was an awful temptation, for I knew I had no practice in killing people and it was just possible that Jimmy would kill me instead. Besides, it was wrong. I knew it was wrong, yet every time I had persuaded myself again of the truth of this I found myself jumping on Jimmy and battering his head on the pavement, tripping Jimmy and kicking him in the stomach, dancing on Jimmy's face—ideas that were all highly unsafe and all contrary to my dearest principles. And this was something I could not ask Mother about. How could I ask her what a gentleman did when a lady took his present and then went with another gentleman without revealing that I was the gentleman wronged?

Then one day I was in the schoolyard watching Una and Jimmy play when he turned and laughed at me. Suddenly a peculiar idea took hold of me that he was laughing at me because I didn't know where babies came from. Emotion overcame me. I went across the playground and hit him deliberately. I had intended to hit him on the chest but I wasn't a good boxer and I hit him on the arm instead. It can't have been much of a blow either, for Jimmy was surprised and pleased. He began to dance round me and cry, "Will you play now, Bobby? Will you play?" I knew then he hadn't really been laughing at me but I had gone too far to turn back. My honor was now at stake. Next time I took more careful aim and this time I managed to hit him, but as a blow this too was a complete washout for he didn't even seem to be aware of it. He just looked at me with his blue, uncomprehending eyes. But Una saw what my real feelings were.

"What are you hitting that child for, Bobby MacCarthy?" she asked in an angry, grown-up voice, grabbing me roughly by the arm.

"You let me alone!" I said in a low voice. "I don't want you. Go away!"

"You let little Jimmy alone, then!" she shouted.

"Go away or I'll kick you," I said savagely and drew back my foot. She dropped my arm and turned away with a contemptuous look over her shoulder.

"Dirty, mean, jealous thing!" she said.

I managed to reach the toilet before I broke down. I didn't cry for long really. I felt relieved and very interested in the peculiar light it threw upon things. I saw that love, like football, was one of those games that two people could never play at without getting violent. It was no suitable occupation for a child who had decided that his life should be governed by reason.

Discussion

In this story, as in "My Oedipus Complex," Frank O'Connor writes with humor about a painful childhood experience. Bobby is taking his first adventurous steps out of the home and into the world of school. At five or six years of age he is bright and full of questions about himself and the world about him. He is attempting to assimilate huge quantities of information in order to make sense out of his relationship to the people and things in his environment. As a natural extension of his data gathering he attempts through questioning to learn about his own babyhood, which is a state he can barely imagine ever existed. He also wants to know where babies come from and how they arrive.

Children often ask these two questions before they are of school age, but no matter when they are asked, these questions head the list in the area of sex education. A birds and bees kind of response will not satisfy a child, because the child cannot perceive the relationship between that response and his question. Much to his disgust, Bobby's mother, to cover her discomfort, launches into a birds and bees explanation in response to his questions. When Bobby turns to his father for the answers to his questions, his father attempts to assuage his curiosity with the tall tale of babies dropped from airplanes. Bobby, who is perfectly serious in his quest for the information, accepts the response as true. His mother is appalled by the father's tall tale and she attempts to correct the father's story with a response that is more plausible but not true either.

Why do parents want children to remain "natural," as Bobby's father puts it? Perhaps adults need to romanticize childhood as a state of innocence and bliss. Undoubtedly a residue of guilt feelings about adult sexuality keeps parents from being totally straightforward and truthful about human reproduction. Bobby finds that he cannot verify his mother's story about engines and starters with his friends at school. This episode teaches Bobby two negative lessons: he cannot rely on his parents to answer questions in a straightforword manner, and he infers that he has asked for information that makes adults uncomfortable. Matters of sex education will be colored by this early deceit.

Similar situations are probably repeated in many households. Parents can gain their young children's trust, however, by giving accurate sex information when it is requested. Furthermore, each time a child asks a question about sex and receives a truthful, consistent response, he assimilates more information and comes closer to a complete understanding of the reproduction process. We know that children of Bobby's age are assuming a defined sex identification. Discussion of how babies are conceived, born, and cared for as infants offers a good opportunity to emphasize the differences and likenesses in sex roles, with emphasis on the importance of each in its respective functions.

Springboards for Inquiry

(1) Who do you think should have the primary responsibility for teaching family life education to children?

(2) What do you think of sex education in public schools?

(3) How much information is requested when a preschooler asks where babies come from? When a seven-year-old asks? When a ten-year-old asks?

(4) How do parents' attitudes toward their own sexuality affect the child's view of sexual relationships?

"Son, your father went to sleep last night and he's never going to wake up again."

Wanderer *by Sterling Hayden*

My father was dead before I knew he was dying.

It was a Friday morning in February, and I was nine years old. I came downstairs to find the house full of people. I thought a celebration was going on because Uncle Mont was there, and my grandmother, who looked like a pussycat with one shoulder lower than the other, and all kinds of people.

My heart plunged when I saw my mother. She had been crying, and I knew my father was dead. He had been ill all winter—since around Thanksgiving. And what else could cause such a fuss? Uncle Mont and Mother took me out to the sun porch. The sun was bright and it was cozy and warm in spite of the snow outside. There was suet in the pine tree in the front yard: before I died I would have to find out what suet was made from.

I sat on my mother's lap, and she started to speak but all she could do was gasp. Uncle Mont leaned toward me with his fine tan face and said: "Son, your father went to sleep last night and he's never going to wake up again." I nodded and tried not to cry. I thought of what had happened just before Thanksgiving, and I wanted to ask if it was my fault.

When they had gone, I stood by the goldfish bowl. The fish swam in and out of the castle on the sand. It was a pretty fair castle, with levels and windows, and just because a fish went in one floor was no guarantee he wouldn't come out on another.

People were going and coming, and all I wanted was to get away so I wouldn't have to avoid looking at anybody and no one would have to avoid looking at me. I put on my galoshes and jacket and took my

---

mittens from their place by the stove. Then I started down to the cellar, and suddenly it came to me—from now on, who would tend the furnace?

I stopped by the laundry room and turned on the light and looked in, and I could almost see him as he had been the day it happened. This frightened me so I went out the cellar entrance and slipped away without being seen and across to the field where the trouble had started. The snow was fairly deep but I could see the outline of leaves humped up where the little fort used to be.

It was the first store-bought slingshot I had had: the price had been 29 cents. My friend Bobby Gies had one, too. We built an outpost in honor of the occasion. It was just before Thanksgiving, and we had two types of ammunition, acorns and staples. Acorns were for people and staples for cars and crows.

Tires were our principal target. Mostly we missed—you could be sure of that because a staple hitting the side of a car makes quite a noise.

A Maxwell roadster with isinglass curtains cruised toward us, its windshield wipers going. Bobby took the rear wheel, and I the front. I fixed a staple in the leather sling and pulled back. But it slipped, and there came the worst scream I had ever heard and a screech of brakes. Bobby flew across the field through the dead goldenrod and over the bodies of long-gone Indians.

A tall man in a long black slicker came toward me, and I dropped the sling and sprinted for home. But he was very fast and he caught me alongside Uncle Jack's garage. He grabbed me by the ear and twisted it, and when he spoke his voice was breathless and thin. "Is this your—house?"

I shook my head.

"Is—that—your house?" indicating Virginia's house.

Again I shook my head. Then I pointed toward our back door and he half carried me by the ear to the kitchen. At that moment my mother rounded the driveway with my father erect and sad in the seat next to her.

The rest is vague. We returned to the scene of the trouble. I found the slingshot and surrendered it. The wife of the man had a gash along her cheek, and there were apologies and an exchange of names and numbers.

One naked bulb hung over the laundry tubs. He rolled up his sleeves slowly; there was something new in his face. He took the stick and began to soak it in one of the tubs. I started to cry. Then he sat on the fireless cooker and I lay across his legs. I screamed as loud as I could, but he was carried away with anger. I remember my mother stamped on the kitchen floor; he only yelled something. Then suddenly his body froze and the stick slipped out of his hand.

He was fighting for breath and calling my mother's name. I stood to one side when she rushed down; then I ran and called some neighbors, who carried him up to his room.

That night the doctor came. And every week all winter long he came back, but it never occurred to me that my father was sick enough to die.

They kept me away from the funeral and afterwards it was understood that we would never mention my father. I began to go for long walks up and down the place where the brook ran under its dome of ice and snow. The brook led along one side of the cemetery, and I wondered where he was buried—and where the rest of him had gone. I didn't believe in heaven, but now it seemed you had to go some place.

Suddenly he seemed the most sensitive man I'd ever known, far more so than Colonel MacNair, who was a blustery sort of a man, when you came right down to it, or Uncle Mont, who smiled too much and was always anxious to please.

I sat on the sun-warmed face of a boulder and held my knees in my arms. I wondered again where in the cemetery he was buried. I had a place picked out where great old trees stood with arms interlocked above cool marble vaults. That was best. Next to that I hoped he was in the rolling part, where there were shrubs all around and the grass was pretty and green.

One day I scaled the fence and walked back and forth among the graves searching for his tombstone. It hadn't occurred to me that he might not have a stone, or that he might not be in the attractive part of the cemetery. But he was: the gardener showed me a mound with some dried-up wreaths and a jar of dead flowers. Out on Valley Road the snout-nosed buses rattled past and I pictured him lying beneath my feet looking up with that wide-nostrilled thoroughbred look. His life hadn't amounted to much and this wasn't much of a place to be buried . . . Boys don't cry very often, because it's so important to be tough. But sometimes their heart just starts aching; then they hide somewhere and let it all pour out, which helps—unless they're really frightened.

Discussion

This chapter about a nine-year-old boy who faces the death of his father is taken from Sterling Hayden's account of his early years. We know that no one is ever fully prepared for the death of a loved one, but this boy seems particularly unprepared for the event. Since his father was ill for several months, his mother had obviously missed opportunities to discuss the nature of his father's illness and the possibility of his death. At the moment of tragedy she is not in sufficient control of her emotions to communicate with the boy in a supportive way about their shared grief. The boy's ability to assimilate this important event is greatly impaired by the awkward handling of the situation.

The questions, emotions, and fantasies about death that occur to a nine-year-old should be explained and answered as honestly as possible. We know, for instance, that children frequently feel responsible for the death of a loved one because the child may have had occasion to cause displeasure to an adult with whom he has had a close association. In this selection there is a particularly obvious link between the boy's spanking and the father's illness and subsequent death. The guilt that can be associated with death is particularly onerous for a child and should not be permitted to smolder.

To dispel guilt feelings a child may harbor, communication about the deceased needs to be encouraged. It may even be necessary for the adult to verbalize the child's fantasies for him. By closing off communication, as this family does, the boy is denied that relief from his guilt feelings. The boy needs to have factual, reasonable, and reassuring explanations of his father's illness. The absence of communication also denies the boy an opportunity to renew past experiences with his father that would help to put the memory of their relationship in a positive prospective.

It is unfortunate that the family considers the boy too young to participate in the home and church rituals associated with the burial of his father. These prescribed ceremonies give an appropriate setting and opportunity for family members to express grief through tears. They also give friends, neighbors, and relatives an opportunity to express their sympathy to the bereaved family, thus easing future contacts. Denied inclusion in the burial ceremony, the boy finds that others are uncomfortable when they see him, and he, too, avoids seeing the mourners. Left alone without the comfort of ritual or human contact, the boy is sure to feel even more uneasy about the concept of death.

The boy no doubt is absorbed in trying to understand the meaning of death. He wants to know what happens to the body after death, and he will probably fantasize about the possibility of life after death. Attending the funeral and burial would have been a comforting experience, providing opportunities for him to learn his family's cultural and religious beliefs about death and the hereafter.

This boy will soon realize that all his prayers and wishes will not bring back his father. Since he is at the age when children begin to test their capabilities and powers, his inability to change a crucial aspect of his life may make him feel especially impotent and abandoned. The transition from boy to man of the house will be more difficult for him because he has been denied appropriate expression of feelings regarding his loss.

Springboards for Inquiry

(1) Beginning with the first incident in this story, illustrate by roles playing how you would have handled this boy with compassion and concern for his emotional health during this critical period in his life.

(2) Arnold Gesell and Frances Ilg (1946) trace the child's developing understanding of death. Describe this changing understanding.

(3) Discuss whether you think the predominant American culture keeps children from exposure to death. Are there religious differences within our culture, however, which account for the fact that some children are included in rituals concerning death?

Reality versus Make-Believe

The ultimate task of each individual is to become a self-directed being (Maslow 1954; Lidz 1968, p. 240). Freud's contribution in this area is of supreme importance. He has given us the terms, *id, ego,* and *superego* to represent those abstracts or influences that enable the individual to leave his parents and regulate his own behavior. The growth and development of the child is essentially the behaviors he learns as he comes to terms with reality. In effect, then, as children mature they are continually in the process of comparing immature concepts of reality with the "real world" (Bernard 1970, p. 268). The psychiatric term for this process of assessing experience is *reality-testing.**

Piaget† recognizes that exploration and sensory experience combine to develop the child's view of reality. Frequently these beginning concepts are inaccurate; the limited number of words and names a child knows combined with very limited experience makes an accurate perception of reality impossible. In other words, the child's world of make-believe is a personal construction based

---

* For further amplification see Leland Hansie and Robert J. Campbell, *Psychiatric Dictionary*, New York: Oxford University Press (1960), p. 632.

† In original translated form, Piaget's work is extremely difficult even for advanced students. Nevertheless, reading *The Child's Conception of Physical Causality* translated by Marjorie Worden, New York: Harcourt Brace Jovanovich, Inc., (1932) and *The Child's Conception of the World* translated by Joan and Andrew Tomlinsen, New York: Harcourt Brace Jovanovich, Inc., (1930) will shed light on this attempt to reduce Piaget's complicated syntax and methodology to its simplest form. The paperback volume by Herbert Ginsberg and Sylvia Opper is especially valuable.

on little information. As the child's experience widens, his ego—that part of personality that makes decisions and is concerned with "language, memory, knowledge, reason, etc." (Lidz 1968, p. 241)*—gains experience with the objective world and begins to organize the child's subjective world so that the disparities between the two become fewer. Alexander *Children and Adolescents: A Biocultural Approach to Psychological Development* (1969) provides a typically inaccurate view of reality held by a child:

Donald: Daddy, there is a wolf in those woods down there.
Father: A wolf lives in those woods?
Donald: Yes, there is a wolf down there because Glen told me there was.
Father: I don't think that a wolf lives in there. There are very few wolves left in the whole country.
Donald: There *is* a wolf in there! Glen told me there is and I *know* there is one there.
Father: Since Glen told you that there is a wolf in there, you *think* there is.
Donald: Yes, there is!
Donald and his father continued their walk in the yard and after some time had passed Donald again brought up the subject of the wolf: "Daddy, you know, I don't really think there is a wolf in those woods. I think that Glen just told me that."

The normal process of growth in a child is an "erratic, continuous, and individual" development of percepts that approximate reality (Landau 1967, p. 11). Yet in perfectly healthy children the make-believe world plays a significant part in his cognition of reality. Jersild (1960) cites numerous studies that indicate that a child's imagining reflects his emotional state. Thus, imaginary companions and extravagant happenings may be acceptable temporary responses to trauma or anxiety.† Often, personal problems too difficult to face force children (and adults) into make-believe worlds where fear, anxiety, and threats may be handled more easily than they would be by facing up to reality and the prospect of failure. In many cases the quip "We have faced the enemy and he is us" defines the problem.

Maturation, experience, and instruction combine to aid the construction of reality. Of the three, instruction is probably the most frequently used means of helping children to face reality. Those who work with children do much "telling." The National Council of Teachers of English estimates that teachers talk nearly

---

* The term *ego* should not be confused with the popular use of the word meaning the total self or with the meaning that has the negative connotation of pride.

† Much in children's literature reflects the significance of make-believe in the emotional life of the child. For example, "Binker" in *Now We Are Six* by A. A. Milne clearly details some reasons for the child's need to imagine (New York: E. P. Dutton & Co., 1927, p. 15). The award-winning *Where the Wild Things Are* by Maurice Sendak (New York: Harper & Row, Publishers, Inc., 1963), graphically details how children temporarily drop out of the objective world because it hurts too much. A vivid account of the genesis of this book is in an interview with Mr. Sendak by Nat Hentoff (*The New Yorker*, 22 January 1966).

70 percent of the time. Marie Hughes (1959), elaborating further, concludes on the basis of minute verbal interaction patterns of teachers and children that much of what is told children is negative and not conducive to constructive responses. In other words, the perception of reality depends on maturation, experience, and instruction, and it is likely that none of these alone would develop accurate concepts of reality.

Adults' desires to bring children to their own "state of supreme perfection" (Hazard 1960, p. 3) have too often caused them to neglect to furnish the relevant experiences that match the vocabulary used in instruction. Adults do not understand that the child gives all his experiences about "the same weight—fairy tales or fictional experiences on television cannot be distinguished from actual experiences" (Alexander 1969, p. 80). With the gradual accrual of experiences and the maturation of mind and body unhindered by either emotional or physical deprivation, the growing child accurately learns to distinguish between make-believe and reality.

" 'Mr. Owl', Roger Skunk said, 'all the other little animals run away from me because I smell so bad.' . . ."

Should Wizard Hit Mommy?

by John Updike

In the evenings and for Saturday naps like today's, Jack told his daughter Jo a story out of his head. This custom, begun when she was two, was itself now nearly two years old, and his head felt empty. Each new story was a slight variation of a basic tale: a small creature, usually named Roger (Roger Fish, Roger Squirrel, Roger Chipmunk), had some problem and went with it to the wise old owl. The owl told him to go to the wizard, and the wizard performed a magic spell that solved the problem, demanding in payment a number of pennies greater than the number Roger Creature had but in the same breath directing the animal to a place where the extra pennies could be found. Then Roger was so happy he played many games with other creatures, and went home to his mother just in time to hear the train whistle that brought his daddy home from Boston. Jack described their supper, and the story was over. Working his way through this scheme was especially fatiguing on Saturday, because Jo never fell asleep in naps any more, and knowing this made the rite seem futile.

The little girl (not so little any more; the bumps her feet made under the covers were halfway down the bed, their big double bed that they let her be in for naps and when she was sick) had at last arranged herself, and from the way her fat face deep in the pillow shone in the sunlight sifting through the drawn shades, it did not seem fantastic that something magic would occur, and she would take her nap like an infant of two. Her brother, Bobby, was two, and already asleep with his bottle. Jack asked, "Who shall the story be about today?"

"Roger . . ." Jo squeezed her eyes shut and smiled to be thinking she was thinking. Her eyes opened, her mother's blue. "Skunk," she said firmly.

A new animal; they must talk about skunks at nursery school. Having a fresh hero momentarily stirred Jack to creative enthusiasm. "All right," he said. "Once upon a time, in the deep dark woods, there was a tiny little creature name of Roger Skunk. And he smelled very bad—"

"Yes," Jo said.

"He smelled so bad none of the other little woodland creatures would play with him." Jo looked at him solemnly; she hadn't foreseen this. "Whenever he would go out to play," Jack continued with zest, remembering certain humiliations of his own childhood, "all of the other tiny animals would cry, 'Uh-oh, here comes Roger Stinky Skunk,' and they would run away, and Roger Skunk would stand there all alone, and two little round tears would fall from his eyes." The corners of Jo's mouth drooped down and her lower lip bent forward as he traced with a forefinger along the side of her nose the course of one of Roger Skunk's tears.

"Won't he see the owl?" she asked in a high and faintly roughened voice.

Sitting on the bed beside her, Jack felt the covers tug as her legs switched tensely. He was pleased with this moment—he was telling her something true, something she must know—and had no wish to hurry on. But downstairs a chair scraped, and he realized he must get down to help Clare paint the living-room woodwork.

"Well, he walked along very sadly and came to a very big tree, and in the tiptop of the tree was an enormous wise old owl."

"Good."

" 'Mr. Owl,' Roger Skunk said, 'all the other little animals run away from me because I smell so bad.' 'So you do,' the owl said. 'Very, very bad.' 'What can I do?' Roger Skunk said, and he cried very hard."

"The wizard, the wizard," Jo shouted, and sat right up, and a little Golden Book spilled from the bed.

"Now, Jo. Daddy's telling the story. Do you want to tell Daddy the story?"

"No. You tell me."

"Then lie down and be sleepy."

Her head relapsed onto the pillow and she said, "Out of your head."

"Well. The owl thought and thought. At last he said, 'Why don't you go see the wizard?' "

"Daddy?"

"What?"

"Are magic spells *real*?" This was a new phase, just this last month, a reality phase. When he told her spiders eat bugs, she turned to her mother and asked, "Do they *really*?" and when Clare told her God was in the sky and all around them, she turned to her father and insisted, with a sly yet eager smile, "Is He *really*?"

"They're real in stories," Jack answered curtly. She had made him miss a beat in the narrative. "The owl said, 'Go through the dark woods, under the apple trees, into the swamp, over the crick—' "

"What's a crick?"

"A little river. 'Over the crick, and there will be the wizard's house.' And that's the way Roger Skunk went, and pretty soon he came to a little white house, and he rapped on the door." Jack rapped on the window sill, and under the covers Jo's tall figure clenched in an infantile thrill. "And then a tiny little old man came out, with a long white beard and a pointed blue hat, and said, 'Eh? Whatzis? Whatcher want? You smell awful.' " The wizard's voice was one of Jack's own favorite effects; he did it by scrunching up his face and somehow whining through his eyes, which felt for the interval rheumy. He felt being an old man suited him.

" 'I know it,' Roger Skunk said, 'and all the little animals run away from me. The enormous wise owl said you could help me.'

"Eh? Well, maybe. Come on in. Don't git too close.' Now, inside, Jo, there were all these magic things, all jumbled together in a big dusty heap, because the wizard did not have any cleaning lady."

"Why?"

"Why? Because he was a wizard, and a very old man."

"Will he die?"

"No. Wizards don't die. Well, he rummaged around and found an old stick called a magic wand and asked Roger Skunk what he wanted to smell like. Roger thought and thought and said, 'Roses.' "

"Yes. Good," Jo said smugly.

Jack fixed her with a trancelike gaze and chanted in the wizard's elderly irritable voice:

"Abracadabry, hocus-poo,
Roger Skunk, how do you do,
Roses, boses, pull and ear,
Roger Skunk, you never fear:
Bingo!"

He paused as a rapt expression widened out from his daughter's nostrils, forcing her eyebrows up and her lower lip down in a wide noiseless grin, an expression in which Jack was startled to recognize his wife feigning pleasure at cocktail parties. "And all of a sudden," he whispered, "the whole inside of the wizard's house was full of the smell of—*roses*! 'Roses!' Roger Fish cried. And the wizard said, very cranky, 'That'll be seven pennies.' "

"Daddy."

"What?"

"Roger *Skunk*. You said Roger Fish."

"Yes. Skunk."

"You said Roger *Fish*. Wasn't that silly?"

"Very silly of your stupid old daddy. Where was I? Well, you know about the pennies."

"Say it."

"O.K. Roger Skunk said, 'But all I have is four pennies,' and he began to cry." Jo made the crying face again, but this time without a trace of sincerity. This annoyed Jack. Downstairs some more furniture rumbled. Clare shouldn't move heavy things; she was six months pregnant. It would be their third.

"So the wizard said, 'Oh, very well. Go to the end of the lane and turn around three times and look down the magic well and there you will find three pennies. Hurry up.' So Roger Skunk went to the end of the lane and turned around three times and there in the magic well were *three pennies!* So he took them back to the wizard and was very happy and ran out into the woods and all the other little animals gathered around him because he smelled so good. And they played tag, baseball, football, basketball, lacrosse, hockey, soccer, and pick-up-sticks."

"What's pick-up-sticks?"

"It's a game you play with sticks."

"Like the wizard's magic wand?"

"Kind of. And they played games and laughed all afternoon and then it began to get dark and they all ran home to their mommies."

Jo was starting to fuss with her hands and look out of the window, at the crack of day that showed under the shade. She thought the story was all over. Jack didn't like women when they took anything for granted; he liked them apprehensive, hanging on his words. "Now, Jo, are you listening?"

"Yes."

"Because this is very interesting. Roger Skunk's mommy said. 'What's that awful smell?' "

"Wha-at?"

"And Roger Skunk said, 'It's me, Mommy. I smell like roses.' And she said, 'Who made you smell like that?' And he said, 'The wizard,' and she said, 'Well, of all the nerve. You come with me and we're going right back to that very awful wizard.' "

Jo sat up, her hands dabbling in the air with genuine fright. "But Daddy, then he said about the other little animals run *away*!" Her hands skittered off, into the underbrush.

"All right. He said, 'But Mommy, all the other little animals run away,' and she said, 'I don't care. You smelled the way a little skunk should have and I'm going to take you right back to that wizard,' and she took an umbrella and went back with Roger Skunk and hit that wizard right over the head."

"No," Jo said, and put her hand out to touch his lips, yet even in her agitation did not quite dare to stop the source of truth. Inspiration came to her. "Then the wizard hit *her* on the head and did not change that little skunk back."

"No," he said. "The wizard said 'O.K.' and Roger Skunk did not smell of roses any more. He smelled very bad again."

"But the other little amum—*oh*!—amum—"

"Joanne. It's Daddy's story. Shall Daddy not tell you any more stories?" Her broad face looked at him through sifted light, astounded. "This is what happened, then. Roger Skunk and his mommy went home and they heard *Woo-oo, woooo-oo* and it was the choo-choo train bringing Daddy Skunk home from Boston. And they had lima beans, pork chops, celery, liver, mashed potatoes, and Pie-Oh-My for dessert. And when Roger Skunk was in bed Mommy Skunk came up and hugged him and said he smelled like her little baby skunk again and she loved him very much. And that's the end of the story."

"But Daddy."

"What?"

"Then did the other little ani-mals run away?"

"No, because eventually they got used to the way he was and did not mind it at all."

"What's evenshiladee?"

"In a little while."

"That was a stupid mommy."

"It was *not*," he said with rare emphasis, and believed, from her expression, that she realized he was defending his own mother to her, or something as odd. "Now I want you to put your big heavy head in the pillow and have a good long nap." He adjusted the shade so not even a crack of day showed, and tiptoed to the door, in the pretense that she was already asleep. But when he turned, she was crouching on top of the covers and staring at him. "Hey. Get under the covers and fall faaast asleep. Bobby's asleep."

She stood up and bounced gingerly on the springs. "Daddy."

"What?"

"Tomorrow, I want you to tell me the story that that wizard took that magic wand and hit that mommy"—her plump arms chopped fiercely—"right over the head."

"No. That's not the story. The point is that the little skunk loved his mommy more than he loved aaalll the other animals and she knew what was right."

"No. Tomorrow you say he hit that mommy. Do it." She kicked her legs up and sat down on the bed with a great heave and complaint of springs, as she had done hundreds of times before, except that this time she did not laugh. "Say it, Daddy."

"Well, we'll see. Now at least have a rest. Stay on the bed. You're a good girl."

He closed the door and went downstairs. Clare had spread the newspapers and opened the paint can and, wearing an old shirt of his on top of her maternity smock, was stroking the chair rail with a dipped brush. Above him footsteps vibrated and he called, *"Joanne.* Shall I come up there and spank you?" The footsteps hesitated.

"That was a long story," Clare said.

"The poor kid," he answered, and with utter weariness watched his wife labor. The woodwork, a cage of moldings and rails and baseboards all around them, was half old tan and half new ivory and he felt caught in an ugly middle position, and though he as well felt his wife's presence in the cage with him, he did not want to speak with her, work with her, touch her, anything.

Discussion

There is always something special about having a father's attention all to oneself. The little girl in this story is lucky because her father not only devotes time to her but he is a good storyteller as well. He has worked out a story formula with all the ingredients to keep a preschooler happy. He uses animal characters and includes enough magic to satisfy his daughter's delight in make-believe. He recognizes that Jo, at four years of age, is going through a reality phase, and he is not surprised when she attempts to verify her concept of what is real and what is unreal. Previously the boundary between fact and fantasy was not particularly important to Jo, since in her own mind there was no clear distinction between them. Her present interest in reality prompts her question about the old wizard. In this case, her question reflects an admixture of both worlds; the wizard is make-believe, but if he is old, that must mean that he will die.

Why is Jo so agitated by the ending of the story? For one thing, the story reached a satisfactory conclusion for her when Roger Skunk finds the extra pennies and was again accepted by his animal friends. Young children become very attached to ritual, and characteristically the finding of the additional pennies marked the successful completion of the animal's central problem in each story. Furthermore, since Roger Skunk's problem was solved, Jo was confused and agitated when her father introduced the problem of Roger's mother's acceptance. Jo's father is clearly expecting too much when he expects Jo to shift gears and empathize with a new problem. Jo's way of showing displeasure with the new concern is to strike back with the idea that the wizard should overrule the mother in the story.

Springboards for Inquiry

(1) Some specialists in the field of early childhood education feel that fairy tales have no place in the nursery school curriculum. What child development theories underlie this contention? State and support your own view on this issue.

(2) How can one relate early childhood fears to the young child's imprecise distinction between real and make-believe?

(3) What is the young child's understanding of such phenomena as television and dreams?

(4) Distinguish between fantasy, humor, and lying on the part of a preschooler.

(5) Daydreaming is not uncommon throughout childhood. How can we distinguish between normal, healthy daydreaming and that which is symptomatic of psychological problems?

References

Alexander, Theron. *Children and Adolescents*. New York: Atherton Press, 1969.

Anthony, Sylvia. The Child's Discovery of Death. New York: Harcourt Brace Jovanovich, Inc., 1940.

Arnstein, Helene S. *Your Growing Child and Sex.* New York: Bobbs-Merrill Co., 1967.

Berko, Jean. "The Child's Learning of English Morphology." *Word* 14 (1958): 150–77.

Bernard, Harold Wright. *Human Development in Western Culture.* 3rd. ed. Boston: Allyn & Bacon, 1970.

Braine, Martin. "Ontogeny of Certain Logical Operations: Piaget's Formulation Examined by Non-Verbal Methods, vol. 73, no. 5, *Psychological Monographs* (1959): 1–43.

Chomsky, Noam. *Aspects of the Theory of Syntax.* Cambridge, Mass.: Massachusetts Institute of Technology Press, 1965.

Chukovsky, Kornei. *From Two to Five.* Berkeley and Los Angeles: University of California Press, 1963.

DiVesta, Francis J. "A Developmental Study of the Semantic Structures of Children." *Journal of Verbal Learning and Verbal Behavior* 5 (1966): 249–59.

Gesell, Arnold, and Frances L. Ilg. *The Child from Five to Ten.* New York: Harper & Row, 1946.

Ginsburg, Herbert, and Sylvia Opper. *Piaget's Theory of Intellectual Development.* Englewood Cliffs, N. J.: Prentice-Hall, 1969.

Grollman, Earl A., ed. *Explaining Death to Children.* Boston: Beacon Press, 1967.

Guilford, Joy Paul. *The Nature of Human Intelligence.* New York: McGraw-Hill Book Co., 1967.

Hazard, Paul. *Books, Children, and Men.* Translated by *Marguerite Mitchell.* Boston: Horn Book, 1960.

Hughes, Marie. *Development of the Means for the Assessment of the Quality of Teaching in Elementary Schools.* Salt Lake City, Utah: University of Utah Press, 1959.

Jenkins, James A. "Meaningfulness and Concepts; Concepts and Meaningfulness." In *Analyses of Concept Learning,* eds. Herbert J. Klausmeier and Chester W. Harris. New York: Academic Press, 1966.

Jersild, Arthur T. *Child Psychology.* 5th ed. Englewood Cliffs, N. J.: Prentice-Hall, 1960.

Kagan, Jerome M. "Approach to Conceptual Growth." In *Analyses of Concept Learning,* eds. H. J. Klausmeier and C. W. Harris, New York: Academic Press, 1966.

Kastenbaum, Robert. "The Child's Understanding about Death: How Does It Develop?" In *Explaining Death to Children,* edited by Earl A. Grollman. Boston: Beacon Press, 1967.

Labov, William. "Linguistic Research on the Nonstandard English of Negro Children." Paper read at Society for the Experimental Study of Education, 1965, New York.

Landau, Elliott D. *You and Your Child's World.* Salt Lake City, Utah: Deseret Book Co., 1967.

Levenstein, Phyllis. "Cognitive Growth in Preschoolers through Verbal Interaction with Mothers." *American Journal of Orthopsychiatry* 40 (April 1970): 426–432.

Lidz, Theodore. *The Person.* New York: Basic Books, 1968.

Loban, Walter. *The Language of Elementary School Children.* Champaign, Ill.: National Council of Teachers of English. Research Report no. 1. 1963.

Loban, Walter. *Problems in Oral Language.* National Council of Teachers of English Research Report no. 5. 1966.

McCarthy, Dorothea. "Language Development in Children." In *Manual of Child Psychology,* edited by Leonard Carmichael, 2d ed. New York: John Wiley and Sons, 1954, pp. 492–630.

MacGinitie, Walter. "Language Development." In *Encyclopedia of Educational Research,* edited by Robert L. Ebel, 4th ed. New York and London: Macmillan Co., 1969, pp. 686–99.

Maslow, Abraham H. *Motivation and Personality.* New York: Harper & Row, Publishers, 1954.

Michaelis, John U.; Ruth E. Grossman, and Lloyd F. Scott, *New Designs for the Elementary School Curriculum.* New York: McGraw-Hill Book Co., 1967.

Miller, Wick, and Susan Ervin. "The Development of Grammar in Child Language." In "The Acquisition of Language," eds. Ursula Bellugi and Roger Brown. *Monographs of the Society for Research in Child Development*, vol. 29, no. 1, 1964, pp. 9–34.

Mitchell, Marjorie E. *The Child's Attitude to Death.* London: Barrie Books, 1966.

Nagy, Maria. "The Child's View of Death." *Journal of Genetics and Psychology* 73 (1948): 3–27.

Piaget, Jean. *The Construction of Reality in the Child,* translated by Margaret Cook, New York: Basic Books, 1954.

Piaget, Jean. *The Language and Thought of the Child*, translated by Marjorie S. Gabain, New York: Humanities Press, 1959.

Piaget, Jean. *Play, Dreams, and Imitation in Childhood,* translated by Gattegno and F. M. Hodgson, New York: W. W. Norton & Co., 1951.

Sax, Gilbert. "Concept Formation." In *Encyclopedia of Educational Research,* ed. Robert L. Ebel, 4th ed. (pp. 196–205) New York and London: Macmillan & Co. Ltd. 1969.

Schilder, Paul, and Wechsler, David. "The Attitude of Children towards Death." *Journal of Genetics and Psychology* 45 (1934): 406–51.

Skinner, B. F. *Verbal Behavior.* Appleton-Century-Crofts, 1957.

Strickland, Ruth. *The Language of Elementary School Children.* School of Education Bulletin No. 38. Bloomington, Ind.: Indiana University Press, 1962.

Taylor, Calvin W. "Identifying the Creative Individual," in *Creativity: Second Minnesota Conference on Gifted Children,* ed. by E. Paul Torrance. Minneapolis: Center for Continuation Study, Univ. of Minn., 1960.

Torrance, E. Paul. *Guiding Creative Talent.* Englewood Cliffs, N.J.: Prentice-Hall, Inc. 1962.

Woodruff, Asahel D. *Basic Concepts of Teaching.* San Francisco: Chandler Publishing Co., 1962.

Communication

Communication modifies and regulates the interaction between the developing child and the members of his family. As the child grows older, it becomes increasingly important that verbal and nonverbal communication verify the reliability of those who speak to him. The rapid acquisition by the child of a very complex system of symbolic habits (language) is coupled with the equally complex problem of mastering this system to adequately communicate thought and feeling.

We communicate many facts to children. We warn them of danger, we suggest the course to take if they wish to avoid unpleasantness, and we classify things for them—in short, we use language in the cognitive domain rather well. However, the semanticist warns of common pitfalls in attempts to communicate, and other experts indicate that a discernible "silent language" pervades our attempts to make our ideas understood. When parents clutch their children's shoulders and insist that they "say good night and thank you," the child learns that he has not behaved satisfactorily or with the proper degree of propriety, yet in front of company the criticism is not verbalized.

Recent discussion of the art of language emphasizes the importance of communicating understanding, insight, empathy, and comprehension in contrast to ancient attempts, which simply stressed language precision. Many authorities believe that the ultimate goal should be to refine communication skills so that one person is able to know what happens "in" another human being. Intellectual training in language at home and at school inhibits the process of feeling *with* and *in* things. Children are often taught to observe facts and events in cold, sober ways. Indeed, feelings about things are often regarded as inferior to intellectual consideration. "Understanding," says Joost Meerloo

(1967), "is pausing momentarily, stepping outside the continual stream of occurrences to observe the passing scene." Too often preoccupation with the precision of communication interferes with this "stepping outside" and using the heritage of language to step into the interior lives of those with whom we interact.

The developing child's major task is to learn to trust the world around him so that ultimately he may learn to trust himself. The child's trust in the verbal communications he receives depends on the consistency between the words and the behavior of the speaker. The nonverbal behavior that accompanies verbal communication is often inconsistent with what is said. More than one parent has experienced the necessity of using soothing words while simultaneously holding the child rigidly, indicating the chasm between the spoken word and the unspoken feelings.

Family relations may be disrupted by communications that never say what they mean and never mean what they say. Children depend on the verbal world to put their world in order. The extent to which the symbol truthfully stands for the territory it purports to describe determines the degree of trust the child learns to place in the adult world. What he trusts he loves; what he loves he trusts. The problems of childhood are in many ways related to the confusion a child may learn from the communications he receives from the world that surrounds him.

Discipline

Discipline in the classroom is the preeminent problem reported by teachers. As soon as children (and adults) are placed in groups,* for whatever reason, those responsible for their welfare face discipline problems. It might be well to attempt a set of operational definitions for the term *discipline,* so that we understand the multiplicity of possible meanings. Fritz Redl (1966, pp. 260–61) assigns three meanings to discipline. His first meaning correlates discipline with the "degree of order we have established in a group." For example, when we say that Nurse A has no discipline in her ward we are referring to the quality of organization that seems to be lacking. Redl's second meaning refers to discipline as a means of establishing order. When we ask a mother how she achieves such wonderful discipline in the home we are really inquiring about the strategies she uses to maintain order. Finally, the term *discipline* is equated with punishment.

B. O. Smith (1969) makes no such careful distinction but says, "The procedures, including rules, by which order is maintained [Redl's first meaning] in a school are referred to as discipline." Smith characterizes Western discipline as having evolved from the concept of force to persuasion, and as increasingly moving in the direction of self-control.

Rogers (1969) sees discipline as either love-oriented or power-oriented. In love-oriented discipline reasoning becomes an integral part of what Redl calls the "therapeutic milieu" (1959). In power-oriented discipline the parent simply

---

* In this sense *groups* does not refer specifically to either homogeneity or heterogeneity for the purposes of instruction. Instead we mean "where more than one are gathered together."

lays down the law, expects to be obeyed, and punishes if he is not. Needless to say, research deals more frequently with the effects of power-oriented discipline. It is difficult to read James Hymes (1955) and not be convinced that love-oriented discipline, which stresses discussion, interpretation, and explanation, is superior to aversive control. Experimental research is still not definitive enough to state that punishment and threats of punishment are necessarily harmful or that positive reinforcement of good behavior and ignoring of negative behavior is the absolute answer. Bandura and Walters (1963) feel that the effect of the method of discipline depends on the complexities of each situation—the punisher, the personality of the recipient, and the nature of the unacceptable behavior.

However, if we view discipline as moving in the direction of self-control, or internalized obedience, the works of Glasser (1965; 1969) are especially convincing. Glasser maintains that neither the nonauthoritarian nor the punitive approach to discipline produces change; the development of conscience comes from making it clear to children that they are individually responsible for their behavior and that neither early childhood nor parents nor teachers are responsible for their bad behavior. Comparing children in the USSR and the United States, Urie Bronfenbrenner (1970) discusses at length the Soviet concern for developing *distsiplinirovannost* (self-discipline) in what has ordinarily been conceived of as a highly authoritarian society. Apparently the evolution of the philosophy of discipline in the Western world from force to persuasion to internalized obedience has had its parallel in Eastern Europe. The Soviet concept of discipline, while ultimately seeking self-discipline, seems to depend first on firm obedience from which, in some completely mysterious way, evolves internalized behavior.

It is important to understand that in the American home and school neither aversive teacher or parent behavior nor reality therapy techniques nor therapeutic milieus have been the major means of achieving discipline. The typical American way of inducing children to obey their parents and teachers is to threaten the withdrawal of love.* Obviously, the more gratifying the relationship between mother and child prior to the threat of withdrawal or de facto withdrawal ("Go away, you've hurt me" or "You are a great disappointment to me" or, worse yet, "Is this the way you repay my love?") the more effective this mode of discipline. The iatrogenic efforts of such "love-oriented" techniques leave much to be desired.

In the normal growth and development of children some discipline provides security. Research data more than suggests that restrictive discipline develops overdependent behavior and rebelliousness, but the absence of discipline (in

---

* Those who wish to follow this line of thought further should read Urie Bronfenbrenner, "The Changing American Child" (*Journal of Social Issues* 17, no. 1 [1961]: 9).

the sense of order) produces chaos. Menninger (1968; 1963) and Ausubel (1968) sum up research data: *

(a) Children learn only those attitudes and behaviors that gain some measure of reinforcement.

(b) Persuasion and example are more effective than demands for obedience and conformity.

(c) There is a difference between authoritarian authority and authoritative authority—the difference between rule as rule and rule as reason.

(d) The views of authority and discipline that adults hold are as much a function of their personality and their orientation to children as they are a function of knowledge and experience.

The attention-getting power of the method of discipline is important to some children because it becomes one of the few methods they have of engaging their parents and teachers. Discipline, however defined, is a powerful factor in establishing relationships between people; it defines and clarifies boundaries and makes possible sensible, humane interaction.

---

* After Harold W. Bernard's summation in *Human Development in Western Culture,* 3rd ed., Boston: Allyn & Bacon, Inc. (1962), p. 227.

Aren't you ashamed, the mother yelled at her. Aren't you ashamed to act like that in front of the doctor?

The Use of Force

by William Carlos Williams

They were new patients to me, all I had was the name, Olson. Please come down as soon as you can, my daughter's very sick.

When I arrived I was met by the mother, a big startled looking woman, very clean and apologetic who merely said, Is this the doctor? and let me in. In the back, she added, You must excuse us, doctor, we have her in the kitchen where it is warm. It is very damp here sometimes.

The child was fully dressed and sitting on her father's lap near the kitchen table. He tried to get up, but I motioned for him not to bother, took off my overcoat and started to look things over. I could see that they were all very nervous, eyeing me up and down distrustfully. As often, in such cases, they weren't telling me more than they had to, it was up to me to tell them; that's why they were spending three dollars on me.

The child was fairly eating me up with her cold, steady eyes, and no expression to her face whatever. She did not move and seemed, inwardly, quiet; an unusually attractive little thing, and as strong as a heifer in appearance. But her face was flushed, she was breathing rapidly, and I realized that she had a high fever. She had magnificent blonde hair, in profusion. One of those picture children often reproduced in advertising leaflets and the photogravure sections of the Sunday papers.

She's had a fever for three days, began the father and we don't know what it comes from. My wife has given her things, you know, like people do, but it don't do no good. And there's been a lot of sickness around. So we tho't you'd better look her

---

over and tell us what is the matter.

As doctors often do I took a trial shot at it as a point of departure. Has she had a sore throat?

Both parents answered me together, No . . . No, she says her throat don't hurt her.

Does your throat hurt you? added the mother to the child. But the little girl's expression didn't change nor did she move her eyes from my face.

Have you looked?

I tried to, said the mother, but I couldn't see.

As it happens we had been having a number of cases of diphtheria in the school to which this child went during that month and we were all, quite apparently, thinking of that, though no one had as yet spoken of the thing.

Well, I said, suppose we take a look at the throat first. I smiled in my best professional manner and asking for the child's first name I said, come on, Mathilda, open your mouth and let's take a look at your throat.

Nothing doing.

Aw, come on, I coaxed, just open your mouth wide and let me take a look. Look, I said opening both hands wide, I haven't anything in my hands. Just open up and let me see.

Such a nice man, put in the mother. Look how kind he is to you. Come on, do what he tells you to. He won't hurt you.

At that I ground my teeth in disgust. If only they wouldn't use the word "hurt" I might be able to get somewhere. But I did not allow myself to be hurried or disturbed but speaking quietly and slowly I approached the child again.

As I moved my chair a little nearer suddenly with one catlike movement both her hands clawed instinctively for my eyes and she almost reached them too. In fact she knocked my glasses flying and they fell, though unbroken, several feet away from me on the kitchen floor.

Both the mother and father almost turned themselves inside out in embarrassment and apology. You bad girl, said the mother, taking her and shaking her by one arm. Look what you've done. The nice man . . .

For heaven's sake, I broke in. Don't call me a nice man to her. I'm here to look at her throat on the chance that she might have diphtheria and possibly die of it. But that's nothing to her. Look here, I said to the child, we're going to look at your throat. You're old enough to understand what I'm saying. Will you open it now by yourself or shall we have to open it for you?

Not a move. Even her expression hadn't changed. Her breaths however were coming faster and faster. Then the battle began. I had to do it. I had to have a throat culture for her own protection. But first I told the parents that it was entirely up to them. I explained the danger but said that I would not insist on a throat examination so long as they would take the responsibility.

If you don't do what the doctor says you'll have to go to the hospital, the mother admonished her severely.

Oh yeah? I had to smile to myself. After all, I had already fallen in love with the savage brat, the parents were contemptible to me. In the ensuing struggle they grew more and more abject, crushed, exhausted while she surely rose to magnificent heights of insane fury of effort bred of her terror of me.

The father tried his best, and he was a big man but the fact that she was his daughter, his shame at her behavior and his dread of hurting her made him release her just at the critical moment several times when I had almost achieved success, till I wanted to kill him. But his dread also that she might have diphtheria made him tell me to go on, go on though he himself was almost fainting, while the mother moved back and forth behind us raising and lowering her hands in an agony of apprehension.

Put her in front of you on your lap, I ordered, and hold both her wrists.

But as soon as he did the child let out a scream. Don't, you're hurting me. Let go of my hands. Let them go I tell you. Then she shrieked terrifyingly, hysterically. Stop it! Stop it! You're killing me!

Do you think she can stand it, doctor! said the mother.

You get out, said the husband to his wife. Do you want her to die of diphtheria?

Come on now, hold her, I said.

Then I grasped the child's head with my left hand and tried to get the wooden tongue depressor between her teeth. She fought, with clenched teeth, desperately! But now I also had grown furious—at a child. I tried to hold myself down but I couldn't. I know how to expose a throat for inspection. And I did my best. When finally I got the wooden spatula behind the last teeth and just the point of it into the mouth cavity, she opened up for an instant but before I could see anything she came down again and gripping the wooden blade between her molars she reduced it to splinters before I could get it out again.

Aren't you ashamed, the mother yelled at her. Aren't you ashamed to act like that in front of the doctor?

Get me a smooth-handled spoon of some sort, I told the mother. We're going through with this. The child's mouth was already bleeding. Her tongue was cut and she was screaming in wild hysterical shrieks. Perhaps I should have desisted and come back in an hour or more. No doubt it would have been better. But I have seen at least two children lying dead in bed of neglect in such cases, and feeling that I must get a diagnosis now or never I went at it again. But the worst of it was that I too had got beyond reason. I could have torn the child apart in my own fury and enjoyed it. It was a pleasure to attack her. My face was burning with it.

The damned little brat must be protected against her own idiocy, one says to one's self at such times. Others must be protected against her. It is social necessity. And all these things are true. But a blind fury, a feeling of adult shame, bred of a longing for muscular release are the operatives. One goes on to the end.

In a final unreasoning assault I overpowered the child's neck and jaws. I forced the heavy silver spoon back of her teeth and down her throat till she gagged. And there it was—both tonsils covered with membrane. She had fought valiantly to keep me from knowing her secret. She had been hiding that sore throat for three days at least and lying to her parents in order to escape just such an outcome as this.

Now truly she *was* furious. She had been on the defensive before but now she attacked. Tried to get off her father's lap and fly at me while tears of defeat blinded her eyes.

Discussion

The doctor enters the Olson home at a disadvantage. The little girl made up her mind before his arrival not to cooperate, and the parents do not know how to exercise discipline in this tense situation. The parents' appeals to elicit Mathilda's compliance with the doctor's instructions run a standard course. Their first ploy to encourage her to cooperate is to plead, assuring her that the doctor is a nice man who will not hurt her. The doctor is furious with this approach, since the suggestion that he will not hurt implies that there is a possibility of being hurt. Their next approach is to shame Mathilda into cooperating by calling her "you bad girl." Shaming is a particularly unproductive route for parents who wish to achieve discipline with their child. By putting the child down in front of a stranger, the parents have further alienated the child by deflating her self-esteem. They have added fuel to the child's feelings of indignation and anger at the coercive parents. The parents' last resort is to threaten: "If you don't do what the doctor says you'll have to go to the hospital." Threats are often an invitation to continue the desired behavior because they also put the child in the position of needing to save face before the parents.

Throughout this encounter the little girl can justifiably feel that none of the adults really cares about her feelings. The confrontation reaches such a fevered pitch that neither the adults nor Mathilda are behaving rationally. The little girl is frightened by the adults' persistence at any price. She is also frightened by the amount of anger she has provoked.

How could this situation have been handled better? Admittedly, the doctor walked into a household that seemed to have a long-standing history of poor communication between parents and child. We do not suggest that this strange adult could have improved the relationship by properly handling this one incident, but it may be that he could have reached his limited aim, which was to look at her throat. He did not need a throat culture nor was any instrument needed to accomplish his examination successfully. It is possible, therefore, that he could have reached his goal by getting her to open her mouth entirely by herself. He could have let the little girl know that he recognized how she was feeling. He might have been resourceful enough to bring diversionary games, dolls, or trinkets to establish trust and willingness to cooperate. He then may have been able to work out with the little girl a system of rewards for opening her mouth. Some small sweet might have been more rewarding to the little girl than her defiant stance. Of course, this is all in the realm of conjecture. It may be that defiance of her parents was the primary goal for her or that her fear of revealing the sore throat was overwhelming.

Springboards for Inquiry

(1) Through role playing the parts of the parents, the doctor, and Mathilda produce a scene that is opposite to the one in the story. Analyze the new behavior of each of the characters.

(2) What do you think of a reward approach to discipline?

(3) What is the difference between self-discipline and external discipline? How can significant adults in the child's life help the child to attain a standard for self-discipline?

(4) What is meant by the statement "Discipline should not be viewed as an end in itself"?

(5) Give examples of changes in behavior that might occur as a result of setting reasoned limits. Show how the same situations might be altered by the imposition of force alone.

(6) Cite studies that reveal the effect of socioeconomic status on modes of discipline used in the home. Comment on these studies.

"Not *my* child," the little man was saying. "I do not permit anyone to lay a finger on *my* child! I do the disciplining!"
"Do it then! Your kid comes up the ladder behind my kid and pushes him, a big push—"

Apple Seed and Apple Thorn

by Elizabeth Enright

October sunshine bathed the park with such a melting light that it had the dimmed, impressive look of a landscape by an old master. Leaves, one, two at a time, sidled down through the windless air. High up the treetops were perfectly still, but down below, on the walks and grass plots, all was a Saturday turmoil of barking dogs and ringing bells and shrieking children.

Barbara and Dickie, still new to the park, entered the playground tentatively. Everyone looked so well established, as if they needed no new friends. On the sunniest benches the mothers sat in a row surrounded by their possessions: baby carriages, toys, sand pails, market bags. They smoked, laughed, talked, yelled admonishment, paused to kiss the wounded. Here and there, since it was Saturday morning, a male parent wandered self-consciously beside a small child or sat and sunned his bald spot as he waited.

"What would you like to do, dear, swing?" suggested Barbara to her son. But Dickie did not hear. Used to country quiet, he stood amazed, pail in one hand, shovel in the other, staring at the scene before him. The place was a hive of activity. The sand pit seethed with infant life, the seesaws cawed and clanked, the swings flew.

The boys on tricycles made Barbara think of little centaurs, mechanized baby centaurs. There was something so lordly about their progress and their pauses. Magnificent in cowboy hats, heavily armed with gemmed weapons, they would suddenly convene in a group for as much as a minute at a time, boasting and vying, still in the saddle, and then

---

at a signal or an impulse off they all wheeled together, their fat legs jigging above the pedals and their cap pistols snapping like popcorn. Yes, lordly; Dickie found them so. He stood beside her, quietly staring, too young to use pride as a mask or to know that it was ever used for this. He seemed very still and humble at her side.

"Maybe Dickie will get a bike too," Barbara suddenly said, although he had not asked for one.

"Maybe?" he said, and turned his face up to look at her, smiling his slow, perfect smile.

She put her hand under his chin. That's how it begins, she thought. Mothers begin it. What they've got you shall have too, they say; you're just as good as they are, honey, and I'll teach you to compete first thing.

Dickie gave one little jump, both feet together. "Maybe I get a bike?" he cried. "A really *bike*?"

"Probably not till Christmastime, my darling."

But Christmas was not a date to Dickie, it was a condition in which he would find the world one morning on awaking. There would be a pine tree smell and all things would have come true. Who knew when it would happen? It might be tomorrow.

"I'm going to have a bike too!" he shouted to a passing centaur, who responded with a stony glance and continued on his way.

"Watch out, sonny," warned a man of four, narrowly missing Dickie's toes as he rode by. Dickie shouted the news about the bike to his departing back.

"*Now* I swing," he said jubilantly, and thrust the pail and shovel into Barbara's hands.

At the swings she stood in front of him to push so that she could watch his face as it flew away and then came blooming toward her, alert and joyful. The reiterative motion, the occupation, brought to her mind an old count-out chant that she had not thought of in thirty years, and as she pushed her son she said it aloud, making it fit the rhythm of the swing.

Intery, mintery, cutery, corn,
Apple seed and apple thorn;
Wire, briar, limber-lock,
Three geese in a flock.
One flew East and one flew West,
And one flew over the cuckoo's nest.

The rhyme pleased Dickie, and Barbara sang it to him several times, making up a tune to match it. She felt contented, deeply satisfied, without a worry. The past and the future lay asleep like beasts in cages . . .

A voice beside them burst the spell. "You *dumb,* whaddaya wanna *do,* break open your head?" Barbara turned to see the child who had tried to stand up in the next swing being slapped into place by the raw, red hand of his mother. "My God, whadda I do? Turn my head, just, and here you are half outa the damn swing; you coulda broke your head open!" The scolding went on and on, loud and angry, and during it the rough hand continued to push the swing steadily, reached up to adjust a cap string, reached down to twitch a trouser cuff, busily caring for the baby as the voice railed. The baby sat impassive, staring at his mother, clad from top to toe in woolen garments although the day was mild. Under the ribbed edge of his cap his eyes, dark, Italian, were trimmed with lashes one inch long.

His olive cheeks were smooth and fat, his lips red; he seemed well nourished on his diet of love and fury.

Roused from her trance, Barbara turned to look at the neighbors on her left: a woman and a little girl.

"Higher," the child was saying. "*Higher*. I said higher!" Her face was expressionless, without color, her hair hung limp into her collar. It was strange that anyone so young and pale could give such an impression of desperation.

Her mother was smiling determinedly and speaking through the smile.

"No, you don't need to go any higher. My arms are tired. It's time to go home anyway."

"I said higher," repeated the little girl tonelessly. "Damn you, I *told* you."

"So that's the way you're going to talk, is it?" said her mother with a sort of pleasure, as though some goal had been reached. "Very well then, swing yourself." She turned and started from the enclosure. Her child, watching her, gave a high, wild scream.

"Yes, scream," agreed her mother in a low, trembling voice, turning back for an instant. "Go on and scream." Then she walked away, out past the slides and past the railings, red in the face but still smiling, toward the other mothers on the benches.

"But I can't get down by myself!" shrieked the little girl. To and fro in lessening arcs she swung and screamed. Tears flashed dazzling from her cheeks.

"I'll help you down," Barbara offered.

"No, no. I want my mommy to."

"I guess she wants her mamma to," the mother of the wool-clad baby translated helpfully.

The little girl's swing came to a stop. She sat in it, a captive, her feet in black strapped slippers dangling, her face expressionless again, with tear tracks drying on her cheeks. She sat there for a long time.

"Would you like a push?" Barbara offered at last.

"No," said the child remotely.

The mother returned.

"Now are you ready to go home?"

"No. You push me. Push me high."

"Oh, Estelle! Please let's go *home*."

"You push me."

"Just once more then, understand? This time I mean it."

It was plain to see who was the victor, if such an outcome could be called a victory. The mother, her face sad and raddled with resentment, regarded her daughter without joy, and the child stared back, expressionless: a pair of enemies faced one another.

Barbara stopped Dickie in midair to press a kiss on his warm cheek. Life is so dangerous, she thought, people are so dangerous for each other, and love's so spotty.

Everywhere were signs of rage. In the swarming sand pit they were constantly on view: often as not a shovel was brought down upon a head; often as not a dimpled hand reached out to slap, and sand, a loose and handy weapon, was forever flying forth to sting the foe.

Now, as though her thoughts had been a prelude, she became aware of a commotion near the slides and turned to see two adults, two fathers, engaging in an argument. Their voices were suddenly rising, transcending the prosaic bounds of ordinary conversation.

One man she recognized, a European, small and dark and decent; the other she had never seen before, tall and heavy-set, with his wife beside him and two scared children clinging to his coat.

"Not *my* child," the little man was saying. "I do not permit anyone to lay a finger on *my* child! I do the disciplining!"

"Do it, then! Your kid comes up the ladder behind my kid and pushes him, a big push—"

"It was an accident, I tell you, he did not mean it."

"Accident, hell, he done it on purpose! I seen him, my wife seen him, and no kid's going to get away with that with my kid."

"Nevertheless they are children only. You had no right to slap my son!"

"I'd do it again—"

"You would have me to contend with, or the police!"

The little man was crimson with anger, the big one chalky-pale for the same reason; they seemed to tremble toward each other, closer and closer.

"You don't know what the hell you're talkin' about."

"On the contrary, I know *exactly . . .*"

The Italian woman at Barbara's right left her lump of wool and, smiling broadly, walked over to the rail of the enclosure and rested her arms on it, openly drinking in the sight. The woman at the left stopped arguing to listen. As for Barbara, though she frowned in distress, was it distress she felt or was it really pleasure? And she was listening as eagerly as any.

Then suddenly it was over. The big man, muttering, was stalking from the playground, his family hurrying beside him. The little foreigner, no longer crimson, seated himself on a bench and opened a newspaper, which quivered in his hands. Outrage had fatigued him; but for the onlookers the air had been mysteriously cleared.

"I thought the little fella was gonna hit the big fella," the Italian woman said to Barbara, happy and hearty. "Gee, I thought sure he was gonna knock'm down. Come on, Joe, we gotta go home and eat." Loving, maternal, she unloaded her baby from the swing, while at the left the little girl made no further objection when her mother lifted the bar; also refreshed, it seemed, she slipped down and skipped from the enclosure.

Now, as people departed and noise diminished, a stuttering sound of machinery came from across the park.

"Look, Dickie," said Barbara, stopping the swing. "I see a steam roller way over there."

"A steam roller!" Dickie was down in an instant and on his way, his red overalls flashing, and his mother jogtrotted in his wake along the concrete pathways to the far side of the park.

The roller, a squat orange machine, backed and bunted fussily on its carpet of wet tar. In its saddle sat the driver, lordly as any tricycle rider and lordly in exactly the same way. An audience admired him.

Nearby on the grass a bench had been constructed with a board and two sawhorses. Some workmen sat there with their lunch pails, a yellow-leafed bush spread out beyond them like a fan. One was drinking wine from a bottle wrapped in newspaper, one was slicing an onion onto some bread; the one on the end, finished with his meal, sat idle, his hands clasped loosely between his knees. He had stuck a pink paper carnation in his cap. The shoes, clothes, caps of all of them were dim and work-colored; their faces seemed related and blank. In their short hour of repose they might have been the laborers of any century; Breughel had painted many like them.

The one with the carnation turned his head and looked at Dickie standing near. He held out his big shovel of a hand. Dickie inspected it warily and backed away, his own hands clasped behind him.

The man laughed and glanced at Barbara. He had white teeth and two broad, disarming dimples. His eyes seemed more mobile than other people's eyes, they rolled in his face like beautiful dark marbles: his expression was simple and benevolent and gay. Presently he turned away and spoke to his companions.

Dickie waited a moment or two and began cautiously to advance, paused, and, seeing that nobody was going to coax him, climbed up on the end of the board bench and perched beside the man. Sudden pleasure and triumph were in the laborer's face; his great hand pulled Dickie close and then traveled up to stroke the little boy's cheek with a finger tough as kindling wood. From where she stood Barbara could hear the deep, masculine tones of his voice, then Dickie's piping treble in reply. She liked what she saw: the Breughel men, the golden bush, the paper flower, the friendship formed without a bond. After a while it was with reluctance that she approached.

"Come, Dickie, it's time for lunch."

"No," he frowned at her. "I like it here."

"But I'm afraid we must go."

"No. I don't want to."

The shovel hand pressed Dickie's shoulder and released it.

"Yes, yes," said the man. "You gotta do like Mamma says. Gotta go home, gotta eat, get strong to fighta da big guys, see? Gotta *fight,* see?" And he bowed out his elbows and made his mighty hands into two fists, with a smile as warm as sunshine.

Dickie accepted his advice and slipped down, walking backward to his mother, still watching his new friend with admiration. Halfway across the park he continued to turn and wave farewell.

But the sun was suddenly gone. Gray clouds had taken up the sky and a few large, separated drops of rain drove the last of the loiterers out of the playgrounds. All at once the park seemed darkened and desolate; the falling leaves as sad as rags.

Impervious to the weather, a fat old man in a billowing overcoat approached. He looked like a broken-down sofa with sagging springs and ripped upholstery covered all over with the keepsakes of past meals. In one hand he carried a paper bag; with the other he sowed the earth with scraps of bread, and down from the air above him came the pigeons. They covered the pavement around him in a piebald, mussy crowd. Here were the symbols of peace, waddling and gobbling in the dirt.

Where was that for which they stood, Barbara wondered? Where could she ever find it? Not in herself, alas, not in anyone she knew or had ever known. Perhaps it did not exist except in the imagination.

Yet even if only in the imagination . . .

"Go! Go! Fly!" cried Dickie, suddenly wild, galloping forward amongst the flock of pigeons and clapping his hands. The sound of their alarmed flight, heavy and cluttered, was like the flapping pages of telephone books. A few feathers fell, a few crumbs, and the old man in the overcoat glared down at Dickie.

"Now whatcha wanna go and do that for?"

"Come, Dickie," said Barbara, taking his hand in hers. "It's late and cold and raining. Wc must hurry home."

Discussion

This story describes a number of the ways adults communicate with children. When Barbara sees the other little boys on bicycles, the deeply rooted drive to compete surfaces and Barbara reacts by offering Dickie a bicycle too, but she is immediately aware of the competitive note she conveys to her son.

In two brief episodes at the swing the story provides examples of hostile kinds of communicating in the context of discipline. One mother smothers her child with love, which ensures dependence and emotional immaturity. The boy is overdressed and overly handled, even as the mother roundly scolds him. The resentful mother and unfulfilled little girl at the swing exemplify a parent–child communication that is too often angry. The parent, in her inability to define and keep limits, actually gives tacit approval for the child to overstep. The parent then feels resentful and angry at the transgression. The child appears to be the winner in this encounter, but no one really wins because an angry relationship in which neither feels comfortable is perpetuated between mother and child.

The argument between the fathers at the slide seems to vicariously appease both the parents' and the children's aggressive instincts in the overcrowded play space. Finally, the spontaneous warm feelings between Dickie and the workman also become laced with aggression. The workman's message delivered with love to his little friend is *you have to fight to survive in this world.*

Springboards for Inquiry

(1) Give examples of typical situations which arise between mothers and five year old boys at home, on the playground, and at the homes of relatives and friends. Role play how Barbara would handle each of these situations.

(2) List some of the ways parents discipline children. Which of these ways were prevalent in your own background? Which methods do you think you will use in your own parenting?

(3) Discuss some of the conflicts which might arise between a mother and father concerning the disciplining of their children. How might a child react if he is aware that his parents differ in the area of his discipline?

(4) Do you think all children within a family should receive the same discipline? How would you answer a child who states, "It isn't fair" when he believes he is being treated differently from a brother or a sister?

Building Trust

"Trust is a conditioning kind of experience that brings about social responsiveness and social spontaneity" (Alexander 1969). Inherent in this statement is the idea that throughout the growth and development of a child, all his experiences with his environment condition the development of trust. The literature, while frequently not using the word *trust,* is replete with references to certain qualities of parent–child interactions that either diminish or enhance the development of trust. Parents who are hostile or rejecting, who criticize too much, who demand too much discipline, or who in other ways coerce and dominate their children excessively, contribute to a diminution of trust on the part of the child.

Lois Hoffman, Sidney Rosen, and Ronald Lippitt (1960) report that parental coerciveness, which could be related to a lack of trust on the part of the parents, arouses hostility and the need to be self-assertive in boys. Although engendered by coerciveness, hostility leads to a high degree of autonomy (the extent to which the child is free to act without immediate adult supervision). In fact, these researchers report that children who come from highly coercive families perform well in school, assume leadership well, and are significantly more friendly than similar children who do not come from highly coercive families. Observation of children from highly rejecting mothers (Brody 1969) shows that there is a conditioning away from consulting the mother; children are more independent (autonomous). The many conditions of parent–child closeness that need to be present for the best communication patterns to exist are not found where parents are highly authoritarian or rejecting. Grace Brody (1969) says, "the children of high-rejecting mothers engaged in significantly *less attentive* observation of the mother, . . . were *less seeking* of information from the mother, . . . and had a *lower* rate of compliance with the mother's requests . . ." than children from accepting mothers.

Richard Brodie and Marian Winterbottom (1967) studied the communication patterns of parents who handled situations by resorting to secrecy, deception, distortion of reality, or similar devices of communication, and they report that "the withholding of information, . . . the blatant denial of the existence of information which is patently apparent to the child arouses a conflict in the child between his trust in his mother as the principal interpreter of reality and the evidence of his own perceptions . . . ." Trust cannot develop under these circumstances, and these authors allege further that secrecy and derogation, among other negative childhood experiences, "can lead the child to renounce his ability to learn and to view himself as lacking the capacity to master his environment."

Trust has both psychological and physical components, and where communication is either poor, lacking, or negative (as in the case of derogation) psychological trust cannot develop. There is data to support the contention that children need to be physically trusted enough to allow for the exploration of their physical surroundings. Elizabeth Bing's study (1963) bears out the assumption that where mothers do not trust their children to explore their environments and even try to impress their children with the dangers lurking in the environment, the children are anxious, insecure, and dependent, and are thus less capable of dealing with cognitive tasks.

Haim Ginott (1965) uses the term *respect* to refer to the monologue-type conversations that go on between parent and child. The tragedy of such "communication" lies not in the lack of love but in the lack of respect, not in the lack of intelligence but in the lack of skill on the part of the parents. He says that one must trust (respect) children enough to hear them out in order for real communication to exist. In *Between Parent and Child* (1965, p. 21) Ginott says, "The new code of communication with children is based on respect and on skill. It requires (a) that messages preserve the child's as well as the parent's self-respect; (b) that statements of understanding precede statements of advice or instruction."

Trust develops in children if in infancy and in early childhood they have a close, giving relationship with a mothering person. It is strengthened by living with people who respect them enough to trust them to assume responsibility and to explore their environments. Children learn to communicate with people who trust them enough to listen openly, who give them access to information, and who let them participate in the search for answers. Finally, they develop trust when they are not rejected, overly disciplined, or subjected to derogation. Ralph Waldo Emerson once said, "Trust men and they will be true to you, treat them greatly and they will show themselves great."

"Father, you must lend me five cents for the skipping-rope. If you will lend me five cents for the skipping-rope, I'll give you *forty* cents back . . ."

My Little Boy

by Carl Ewald

My little boy and I have had an exceedingly interesting walk in the Frederiksberg Park.

There was a mouse, which was irresistible. There were two chaffinches, husband and wife, which built their nest right before our eyes, and a snail, which had no secrets for us. And there were flowers, yellow and white, and there were green leaves, which told us the oddest adventures: in fact, as much as we can find room for in our little head.

Now we are sitting on a bench and digesting our impressions.

Suddenly the air is shaken by a tremendous roar:

"What was that?" asks my little boy.

"That was the lion in the Zoological Gardens," I reply.

No sooner have I said this than I curse my own stupidity.

I might have said that it was a gunshot announcing the birth of a prince; or an earthquake; or a china dish falling from the sky and breaking into pieces: anything whatever, rather than the truth.

For now my little boy wants to know what sort of thing the Zoological Gardens is.

I tell him.

The Zoological Gardens is a horrid place, where they lock up wild beasts who have done no wrong and who are accustomed to walk about freely in the distant foreign countries where they come from. The lion is there, whom we have just heard roaring. He is so strong that he can kill a policeman with one blow of his paw; he has great, haughty eyes and awfully sharp teeth. He lives in Africa and, at

---

My Little Boy by Charles Ewald, translated by Alexander Teizeria DeMattos (Copyright 1906 Charles Scribner's Sons) is reprinted with the permission of Charles Scribner's Sons.

night, when he roars, all the other beasts tremble in their holes for fear. He is called the king of beasts. They caught him one day in a cunning trap and bound him and dragged him here and locked him up in a cage with iron bars to it. The cage is no more than half as big as Petrine's room. And there the king walks up and down, up and down, and gnashes his teeth with sorrow and rage and roars so that you can hear him ever so far away. Outside his cage stand cowardly people and laugh at him, because he can't get out and eat them up, and poke their sticks through the rails and tease him.

My little boy stands in front of me and looks at me with wide-open eyes:

"Would he eat them up, if he got out?" he asks.

"In a moment."

"But he can't get out, can he?"

"No. That's awfully sad. He can't get out."

"Father, let us go and look at the lion."

I pretend not to hear and go on to tell him of the strange birds there: great eagles, which used to fly over every church-steeple and over the highest trees and mountains and swoop down upon lambs and hares and carry them up to their young in the nest. Now they are sitting in cages, on a perch, like canaries, with clipped wings and blind eyes. I tell him of gulls, which used to fly all day long over the stormy sea: now they splash about in a puddle of water, screaming pitifully. I tell him of wonderful blue and red birds, which, in their youth, used to live among wonderful blue and red flowers, in balmy forests a thousand times bigger than the Frederiksberg Park, where it was as dark as night under the trees with the brightest sun shining down upon the tree-tops: now they sit there in very small cages and hang their beaks while they stare at tiresome boys in dark-blue suits and black stockings and waterproof boots and sailor-hats.

"Are those birds really blue?" asks my little boy.

"Sky-blue," I answer. "And utterly broken-hearted."

"Father, can't we go and look at the birds?"

I take my little boy's hands in mine:

"I don't think we will," I say. "Why should still more silly boys do so? You can't imagine how it goes to one's heart to look at those poor captive beasts."

"Father, I should so much like to go."

"Take my advice and don't. The animals there are not the real animals, you see. They are ill and ugly and angry because of their captivity and their longing and their pain."

"I should so much like to see them."

"Now let me tell you something. To go to the Zoological Gardens costs five cents for you and ten cents for me. That makes fifteen cents altogether, which is an awful lot of money. We won't go there now, but we'll buy the biggest money-box we can find: one of those money-boxes shaped like a pig. Then we'll put fifteen cents in it. And every Thursday we'll put fifteen cents in the pig. By-and-by, that will grow into quite a fortune: it will make such a lot of money, that, when you are grown up, you can take a trip to Africa and go to the desert and hear the wild, the real lion roaring and tremble just like the people tremble down there. And you can go to the great, dark forests and see the real blue birds flying proud and free among the flowers. You can't think how glad you will be, how beautiful they will look and how they will sing to you. . . ."

"Father, I would rather go to the Zoological Gardens now."

My little boy does not understand a word of what I say. And I am at my wit's end.

"Shall we go and have some cakes at Josty's?" I ask.

"I would rather go to the Zoological Gardens."

I can read in his eyes that he is thinking of the captive lion. Ugly human instincts are waking up in his soul. The mouse is forgotten and the snail; and the chaffinches have built their nest to no purpose.

At last I get up and say, bluntly, without any further explanation:

"You are not going to the Zoological Gardens. Now we'll go home."

And home we go. But we are not in a good temper.

Of course, I get over it and I buy an enormous money-box pig. Also we put the money into it and he thinks that most interesting.

But, later in the afternoon, I find him in the bed-room engaged in a piteous game.

He has built a cage, in which he has imprisoned the pig. He is teasing it and hitting it with his whip, while he keeps shouting to it:

"You can't get out and bite me, you stupid pig! You can't get out!" . . .

. . . It has been decreed in the privy council that my little boy shall have a weekly income of one cent. Every Sunday morning, that sum shall be paid to him, free of income-tax, out of the treasury and he has leave to dispose of it entirely at his own pleasure.

He receives this announcement with composure and sits apart for a while and ponders on it.

"Every Sunday?" he asks.

"Every Sunday."

"All the time till the summer holidays?"

"All the time till the summer holidays."

In the summer holidays, he is to go to the country, to stay with his godmother, in whose house he was pleased to allow himself to be born. The summer holidays are, consequently, the limits of his calculation of time: beyond them lies, for the moment, his Nirvana.

And we employ this restricted horizon of ours to further our true happiness.

That is to say, we calculate, with the aid of the almanac, that, if everything goes as heretofore, there will be fifteen Sundays before the summer holidays. We arrange a drawer with fifteen compartments and in each compartment we put one cent. Thus we know exactly what we have and are able at any time to survey our financial status.

And, when he sees that great lot of cents lying there, my little boy's breast is filled with mad delight. He feels endlessly rich, safe for a long time. The courtyard rings with his bragging, with all that he is going to do with his money. His special favorites are invited to come up and view his treasure.

The first Sunday passes in a normal fashion, as was to be expected.

He takes his cent and turns it straightway into a stick of chocolate of the best sort, with almonds on it and sugar, in short, an ideal stick in every way. The whole performance is over in five minutes: by that time, the stick of chocolate is gone, with the sole exception of a remnant in the corners of our mouth, which our ruthless mother wipes away, and a stain on our collar, which annoys us.

He sits by me, with a vacant little face, and swings his legs. I open the drawer and look at the empty space and at the fourteen others:

"So *that's* gone," I say.

My accent betrays a certain melancholy, which finds an echo in his breast. But he does not deliver himself of it at once.

"Father . . . is it long till next Sunday?"

"Very long, my boy; ever so many days."

We sit a little, steeped in our own thoughts. Then I say, pensively:

"Now, if you had bought a top, you would perhaps have had more pleasure out of it. I know a place where there is a lovely top: red, with a green ring around it. It is just over the way, in the toyshop. I saw it yesterday. I should be greatly mistaken if the toyman was not willing to sell it for a cent. And you've got a whip, you know."

We go over the way and look at the top in the shop-window. It is really a splendid top.

"The shop's shut," says my little boy, despondently.

I look at him with surprise:

"Yes, but what does that matter to us? Anyway, we can't buy the top before next Sunday. You see, you've spent your cent on chocolate. Give me your handkerchief: there's still a bit on your cheek."

There is no more to be said. Crestfallen and pensively, we go home. We sit a long time at the dining-room window, from which we can see the window of the shop.

During the course of the week, we look at the top daily, for its does not do to let one's love grow cold. One might so easily forget it. And the top shines always more seductively. We go in and make sure that the price is really in keeping with our means. We make the shopkeeper take a solemn oath to keep the top for us till Sunday morning, even if boys should come and bid him much higher sums for it.

On Sunday morning, we are on the spot before nine o'clock and acquire our treasure with trembling hands. And we play with it all day and sleep with it at night, until, on Wednesday morning, it disappears without a trace, after the nasty manner which tops have.

When the turn comes of the next cent, something remarkable happens.

There is a boy in the courtyard who has a skipping-rope and my little boy, therefore, wants to have a skipping-rope too. But this is a difficult matter. Careful enquiries establish the fact that a skipping-rope of the sort used by the upper classes is nowhere to be obtained for less than five cents.

The business is discussed as early as Saturday:

"It's the simplest thing in the world," I say. "You must not spend your cent tomorrow. Next Sunday you must do the same and the next and the next. On the Sunday after that, you will have saved your five cents and can buy your skipping rope at once."

"When shall I get my skipping-rope then?"

"In five Sundays from now."

He says nothing, but I can see that he does not think my idea very brilliant. In the course of the day, he derives, from sources unknown to me, an acquaintance with financial circumstances which he serves up to me on Sunday morning in the following words:

"Father, you must lend me five cents for the skipping-rope. If you will lend me five cents for the skipping-rope, I'll give you *forty* cents back. . . ."

He stands close to me, very red in the face and quite confused. I perceive that he is ripe for falling into the claws of the usurers:

"I don't do that sort of business, my boy," I say. "It wouldn't do you any good either. And you're not even in a position to do it, for you have only thirteen cents, as you know."

He collapses like one whose last hope is gone.

"Let us just see," I say.

And we go to our drawer and stare at it long and deeply.

"We might perhaps manage it this way, that I give you five cents now. And then I should have your cent and the next four cents . . ."

He interrupts me with a loud shout. I take out my purse, give him five cents and take one cent out of the drawer:

"That won't be pleasant next Sunday," I say, "and the next and the next and the next . . ."

But the thoughtless youth is gone.

Of course, the instalments of his debt are paid off with great ceremony. He is always on the spot himself when the drawer is opened and sees how the requisite cent is removed and finds its way into my pocket instead of his.

The first time, all goes well. It is simply an amusing thing that I should have the cent; and the skipping-rope is still fresh in his memory, because of the pangs which he underwent before its purchase. Next Sunday, already the thing is not *quite* so pleasant and, when the fourth instalment falls due, my little boy's face looks very gloomy:

"Is there anything the matter?" I ask.

"I should so much like a stick of chocolate," he says, without looking at me.

"Is that all? You can get one in a fortnight. By that time, you will have paid for the skipping-rope and the cent will be your own again."

"I should so much like to have a stick of chocolate now."

Of course I am full of the sincerest compassion, but I can't help it. What's gone is gone. We saw it with our own eyes and we know exactly where it has gone to. And, that Sunday morning, we part in a dejected mood.

Later in the day, however, I find him standing over the drawer with raised eyebrows and a pursed-up mouth. I sit down quietly and wait. And I do not have to wait long before I learn that his development as an economist is taking quite its normal course.

"Father, suppose we moved the cent now from here into this Sunday's place and I took it and bought the chocolate-stick . . ."

"Why, then you won't have your cent for the other Sunday."

"I don't mind that, Father . . ."

We talk about it, and then we do it. And, with that, as a matter of course, we enter upon the most reckless peculations.

The very next Sunday, he is clever enough to take the furthest cent, which lies just before the summer holidays. He pursues the path of vice without a scruple, until, at last, the blow falls and five long Sundays come in a row without the least chance of a cent.

Where should they come from? They were there. We know that. They are gone. We have spent them ourselves.

But, during those drab days of poverty, we sit every morning over the empty drawer and talk long and profoundly about that painful phenomenon, which is so simple and so easy to understand and which one must needs make the best of.

And we hope and trust that our experience will do us good, when, after our trip, we start a new set of cents.

Discussion

The pace of this selection by Carl Ewald, the Danish writer, reveals a life style common to a European culture in the early 1900s. Yet despite its turn-of-the-century background the elements of the father–son relationship remain valid, illustrating a two-way communication that contains within it the positive basis for building trust. In this relationship the father is companion, teacher, and storyteller. He spends a great deal of unhurried time with his son and attempts to teach him some concepts difficult for a little boy to comprehend. The father is not discouraged by the boy's faltering grasp of the concepts of time and money. He is a very human father who feels exasperated and gets out of humor at times, but he recovers his perspective and with persistence goes on with his labor of love—the instruction of his small son in moral, ethical, and financial matters.

The father seems to have a clear idea of the values he wishes to transmit to his son, and he therefore has little difficulty in being consistent. He may be able to empathize with his son when he must go for several Sundays without an allowance, but he does not destroy the lesson on thrift by permitting his emotions to take over and by relieving the boy of his financial obligations. Furthermore, the father is willing to involve himself in any commitment he considers valuable to the boy's development. Time to spend with his son holds high priority for the father. Because of this particularly supportive relationship the boy is able to achieve levels of understanding not ordinarily expected of children of his age.

Springboards for Inquiry

(1) Discuss your views of this father's role with his son. Does he seem old fashioned and overly rigid in his expectations for his little boy in comparison with the contemporary American life style?

(2) It is said that only a proportion of what we communicate is reported through words. What are other sources of communication between this father and son?

(3) A child's self-concept is fashioned in part through his communications with the important adults in his environment. What messages about himself are communicated to the boy through this father?

"You'll learn how real he is!" shouted his father after him. "If you can't learn it at one end, you shall learn it at the other. I'll have your breeches down."

Thus I Refute Beelzy

by John Collier

"THERE GOES the tea bell," said Mrs. Carter. "I hope Simon hears it."

They looked out from the window of the drawing room. The long garden, agreeably neglected, ended in a waste plot. Here a little summerhouse was passing close by beauty on its way to complete decay. This was Simon's retreat. It was almost completely screened by the tangled branches of the apple tree and the pear tree, planted too close together, as they always are in the suburbs. They caught a glimpse of him now and then, as he strutted up and down, mouthing and gesticulating, performing all the solemn mumbo-jumbo of small boys who spend long afternoons at the forgotten ends of long gardens.

"There he is, bless him!" said Betty.

"Playing his game," said Mrs. Carter. "He won't play with the other children any more. And if I go down there—the temper! And comes in tired out!"

"He doesn't have his sleep in the afternoons?" asked Betty.

"You know what Big Simon's ideas are," said Mrs. Carter. "'Let him choose for himself,' he says. That's what he chooses, and he comes in as white as a sheet."

"Look! He's heard the bell," said Betty. The expression was justified, though the bell had ceased ringing a full minute ago. Small Simon stopped in his parade exactly as if its tinny dingle had at that moment reached his ear. They watched him perform certain ritual sweeps and scratchings with his little stick, and come lagging over the hot and flaggy grass toward the house.

Mrs. Carter led the way down to the playroom, or garden room, which was also the tea room for hot days. It had been the huge scullery of this tall Georgian house. Now the walls

---

were cream-washed, there was coarse blue net in the windows, canvas-covered arm chairs on the stone floor, and a reproduction of Van Gogh's "Sunflowers" over the mantelpiece.

Small Simon came drifting in, and accorded Betty a perfunctory greeting. His face was an almost perfect triangle, pointed at the chin, and he was paler than he should have been. "The little elf-child!" cried Betty.

Simon looked at her. "No," said he.

At that moment the door opened, and Mr. Carter came in, rubbing his hands. He was a dentist, and washed them before and after everything he did. "You!" said his wife. "Home already!"

"Not unwelcome, I hope," said Mr. Carter, nodding to Betty. "Two people canceled their appointments; I decided to come home. I said, I hope I am not unwelcome."

"Silly!" said his wife. "Of course not."

"Small Simon seems doubtful," continued Mr. Carter. "Small Simon, are you sorry to see me at tea with you?"

"No, Daddy."

"No, what?"

"No, Big Simon."

"That's right. Big Simon and Small Simon. That sounds more like friends, doesn't it? At one time little boys had to call their father 'sir.' If they forgot—a good spanking. On the bottom, Small Simon! On the bottom!" said Mr. Carter, washing his hands once more with his invisible soap and water.

The little boy turned crimson with shame or rage.

"But now, you see," said Betty, to help, "you can call your father whatever you like."

"And what," asked Mr. Carter, "has Small Simon been doing this afternoon? While Big Simon has been at work."

"Nothing," muttered his son.

"Then you have been bored," said Mr. Carter. "Learn from experience, Small Simon. Tomorrow, do something amusing, and you will not be bored. I want him to learn from experience, Betty. That is my way, the new way."

"I have learned," said the boy, speaking like an old, tired man, as little boys so often do.

"It would hardly seem so," said Mr. Carter, "if you sit on your behind all the afternoon, doing nothing. Had *my* father caught me doing nothing, I should not have sat very comfortably."

"He played," said Mrs. Carter.

"A bit," said the boy, shifting on his chair.

"Too much," said Mrs. Carter. "He comes in all nervy and dazed. He ought to have his rest."

"He is six," said her husband. "He is a reasonable being. He must choose for himself. But what game is this, Small Simon, that is worth getting nervy and dazed over? There are very few games as good as all that."

"It's nothing," said the boy.

"Oh, come," said his father. "We are friends, are we not? You can tell me. I was a Small Simon once, just like you, and played the same games you play. Of course there were no airplanes in those days. With whom do you play this fine game? Come on, we must all answer civil questions, or the world would never go round. With whom do you play?"

"Mr. Beelzy," said the boy, unable to resist.

"Mr. Beelzy?" said his father raising his eyebrows inquiringly at his wife.

"It's a game he makes up," said she.

"Not makes up!" cried the boy. "Fool!"

"That is telling stories," said his mother. "And rude as well. We had better talk of something different."

"No wonder he is rude," said Mr. Carter, "if you say he tells lies, and then insist on changing the subject. He tells you his fantasy: you implant a guilt feeling. What can you expect? A defense mechanism. Then you get a real lie."

"Like in *These Three*," said Betty. "Only different, of course. *She* was an unblushing little liar."

"I would have made her blush," said Mr. Carter, "in the proper part of her anatomy. But Small Simon is in the fantasy stage. Are you not, Small Simon? You just make things up."

"No, I don't," said the boy.

"You do," said his father. "And because you do, it is not too late to reason with you. There is no harm in a fantasy, old chap. There is no harm in a bit of make-believe. Only you have to know the difference between daydreams and real things, or your brain will never grow. It will never be the brain of a Big Simon. So come on. Let us hear about this Mr. Beelzy of yours. Come on. What is he like?"

"He isn't like anything," said the boy.

"Like nothing on earth?" said his father. "That's a terrible fellow."

"I'm not frightened of him," said the child, smiling. "Not a bit."

"I should hope not," said his father. "If you were, you would be frightening yourself. I am always telling people, older people than you are, that they are just frightening themselves. Is he a funny man? Is he a giant?"

"Sometimes he is," said the little boy.

"Sometimes one thing, sometimes another," said his father. "Sounds pretty vague. Why can't you tell us just what he's like?"

"I love him," said the small boy. "He loves me."

"That's a big word," said Mr. Carter. "That might be better kept for real things, like Big Simon and Small Simon."

"He is real," said the boy, passionately. "He's not a fool. He's real."

"Listen," said his father. "When you go down the garden there's nobody there. Is there?"

"No," said the boy.

"Then you think of him, inside your head, and he comes."

"No," said Small Simon. "I have to make marks. On the ground. With my stick."

"That doesn't matter."

"Yes, it does."

"Small Simon, you are being obstinate," said Mr. Carter. "I am trying to explain something to you. I have been longer in the world than you have, so naturally I am older and wiser. I am explaining that Mr. Beelzy is a fantasy of yours. Do you hear? Do you understand?"

"Yes, Daddy."

"He is a game. He is a let's-pretend."

The little boy looked down at his plate, smiling resignedly.

"I hope you are listening to me," said his father. "All you have to do is to say, 'I have been playing a game of let's-pretend. With someone I make up, called Mr. Beelzy.' Then no one will say you tell lies, and you will know the difference between dreams and reality. Mr. Beelzy is a daydream."

The little boy still stared at his plate.

"He is sometimes there and sometimes not there," pursued Mr. Carter. "Sometimes he's like one thing, sometimes another. You can't really see him. Not as you see me. I am real. You can't touch him. You can touch me. I can touch you." Mr. Carter stretched out his big, white, dentist's hand, and took his little son by the nape of the neck. He stopped speaking for a moment and tightened his hand. The little boy sank his head still lower.

"Now you know the difference," said Mr. Carter, "between a pretend and a real thing. You and I are one thing; he is another. Which is the pretend? Come on. Answer me. What is the pretend?"

"Big Simon and Small Simon," said the little boy.

"Don't!" cried Betty, and at once put her hand over her mouth, for why should a visitor cry "Don't!" when a father is explaining things in a scientific and modern way? Besides, it annoys the father.

"Well, my boy," said Mr. Carter, "I have said you must be allowed to learn from experience. Go upstairs. Right up to your room. You shall learn whether it is better to reason, or to be perverse and obstinate. Go up. I shall follow you."

"You are not going to beat the child?" cried Mrs. Carter.

"No," said the little boy. "Mr. Beelzy won't let him."

"Go on up with you!" shouted his father.

Small Simon stopped at the door. "He said he wouldn't let anyone hurt me," he whimpered. "He said he'd come like a lion, with wings on, and eat them up."

"You'll learn how real he is!" shouted his father after him. "If you can't learn it at one end, you shall learn it at the other. I'll have your breeches down. I shall finish my cup of tea first, however," said he to the two women.

Neither of them spoke. Mr. Carter finished his tea, and unhurriedly left the room, washing his hands with his invisible soap and water.

Mrs. Carter said nothing. Betty could think of nothing to say. She wanted to be talking for she was afraid of what they might hear.

Suddenly it came. It seemed to tear the air apart. "Good God!" she cried. "What was that? He's hurt him." She sprang out of her chair, her silly eyes flashing behind her glasses. 'I'm going up there!" she cried, trembling.

"Yes, let us go up," said Mrs. Carter. "Let us go up. That was not Small Simon."

It was on the second-floor landing that they found the shoe, with the man's foot still in it, like that last morsel of a mouse which sometimes falls unnoticed from the side of the jaws of the cat.

Discussion

The interaction between Big Simon and Small Simon reminds the reader of a game of cat and mouse. Big Simon seems like a large, overbearing, dangerous cat who keeps the mouse, Small Simon, on the run, scurrying this way and that, trying to read his opponent's messages in order to find an area of safety. The cat–mouse image is completed at the end of the fantasy when the author allows the reader to believe that the tables have turned, and Big Simon is the victim in his cat–mouse game with Mr. Beelzy.

This story may be fantasy, but it has much to say about real communication between parents and children. The selection reveals a parent whose language and behavior are full of inconsistencies. Big Simon wants to appear modern and in tune with the latest psychological theories of child raising, but his authoritarian, punitive behavior indicates that his verbal communications cannot be trusted. Big Simon acknowledges that Small Simon is in the fantasy stage, but he demands that Small Simon malign his fantasy by acknowledging that Mr. Beelzy is only make-believe. Small Simon, faced with an oppressively insensitive and self-righteous parent, has created a fantasy friend in order to cope with his unmanageable life situation. Mr. Beelzy protects Small Simon from the unreasonable and inconsistent demands of Big Simon. Mr. Beelzy is a dependable and trustworthy presence in Small Simon's life because he can be funny or loving or anything that Small Simon wishes him to be. It is suggested that Small Simon has given up playing with his usual playmates in favor of turning inward to his imaginary companion. This is not a desirable preference for a young child, but frequently children will adopt unhealthy methods of coping when an unhealthy parent–child relationship exists.

Springboards for Inquiry

(1) Project the dialogue between Big Simon and Little Simon if each were to reveal his real thoughts and feelings about the other.

(2) What kind of role does the mother play in this family?

(3) Cite some discrepancies between Big Simon's avowed theories of child rearing and the demands he makes on Little Simon.

(4) How does Big Simon's attitude toward his son affect Little Simon's self concept?

(5) Support or refute the idea that Little Simon's fabrication of Mr. Beelzy is an unhealthy sign.

"Mother?"
"Yes"
"Mother?"
"Go back to bed, Arnold," she called sharply. But he waited. "Go back! Is night when you get afraid?"

The Stone Boy

by Gina Berriault

Arnold drew his overalls and raveling gray sweater over his naked body. In the other narrow bed his brother Eugene went on sleeping, undisturbed by the alarm clock's rusty ring. Arnold, watching his brother sleeping, felt a peculiar dismay; he was nine, six years younger than Eugie, and in their waking hours it was hc who was subordinate. To dispel emphatically his uneasy advantage over his sleeping brother, he threw himself on the hump of Eugie's body.

"Get up! Get up!" he cried.

Arnold felt his brother twist away and saw the blankets lifted in a great wing, and, all in an instant, he was lying on his back under the covers with only his face showing, like a baby, and Eugie was sprawled on top of him.

"Whassa matter with you?" asked Eugie in sleepy anger, his face hanging close.

"Get up," Arnold repeated. "You said you'd pick peas with me."

Stupidly, Eugie gazed around the room as if to see if morning had come into it yet. Arnold began to laugh derisively, making soft, snorting noises, and was thrown off the bed. He got up from the floor and went down the stairs, the laughter continuing, like hiccups, against his will. But when he opened the staircase door and entered the parlor, he hunched up his shoulders and was quiet because his parents slept in the bedroom downstairs.

Arnold lifted his .22-caliber rifle from the rack on the kitchen wall. It was an old lever-action Winchester that his father had given him because nobody else used it any more. On their way down to the garden he and Eugie would go by the lake, and if there were any ducks on it

---

he'd take a shot at them. Standing on the stool before the cupboard, he searched on the top shelf in the confusion of medicines and ointments for man and beast and found a small yellow box of .22 cartridges. Then he sat down on the stool and began to load his gun.

It was cold in the kitchen so early, but later in the day, when his mother canned the peas, the heat from the wood stove would be almost unbearable. Yesterday she had finished preserving the huckleberries that the family had picked along the mountain, and before that she had canned all the cherries his father had brought from the warehouse in Corinth. Sometimes, on these summer days, Arnold would deliberately come out from the shade where he was playing and make himself as uncomfortable as his mother was in the kitchen by standing in the sun until the sweat ran down his body.

Eugie came clomping down the stairs and into the kitchen, his head drooping with sleepiness. From his perch on the stool Arnold watched Eugie slip on his green knit cap. Eugie didn't really need a cap; he hadn't had a haircut in a long time and his brown curls grew thick and matted, close around his ears and down his neck, tapering there to a small whorl. Eugie passed his left hand through his hair before he set his cap down with his right. The very way he slipped his cap on was an announcement of his status; almost everything he did was a reminder that he was eldest—first he, then Nora, then Arnold—and called attention to how tall he was (almost as tall as his father), how long his legs were, how small he was in the hips, and what a neat dip above his buttocks his thick-soled logger's boots gave him. Arnold never tired of watching Eugie offer silent praise unto himself. He wondered, as he sat enthralled, if when he got to be Eugie's age he would still be undersized and his hair still straight.

Eugie eyed the gun. "Don't you know this ain't duck season?" he asked gruffly, as if he were the sheriff.

"No, I don't know," Arnold said with a snigger.

Eugie picked up the tin washtub for the peas, unbolted the door with his free hand and kicked it open. Then, lifting the tub to his head, he went clomping down the back steps. Arnold followed, closing the door behind him.

The sky was faintly gray, almost white. The mountains behind the farm made the sun climb a long way to show itself. Several miles to the south, where the range opened up, hung an orange mist, but the valley in which the farm lay was still cold and colorless.

Eugie opened the gate to the yard and the boys passed between the barn and the row of chicken houses, their feet stirring up the carpet of brown feathers dropped by the molting chickens. They paused before going down the slope to the lake. A fluky morning wind ran among the shocks of wheat that covered the slope. It sent a shimmer northward across the lake, gently moving the rushes that formed an island in the center. Killdeer, their white markings flashing, skimmed the water, crying their shrill, sweet cry. And there at the south end of the lake were four wild ducks, swimming out from the willows into open water.

Arnold followed Eugie down the

slope, stealing, as his brother did, from one shock of wheat to another. Eugie paused before climbing through the wire fence that divided the wheatfield from the marshy pasture around the lake. They were screened from the ducks by the willows along the lake's edge.

"If you hit your duck, you want me to go in after it?" Eugie said.

"If you want," Arnold said.

Eugie lowered his eyelids, leaving slits of mocking blue. "You'd drown 'fore you got to it, them legs of yours are so puny," he said.

He shoved the tub under the fence and, pressing down the center wire, climbed through into the pasture.

Arnold pressed down the bottom wire, thrust a leg through and leaned forward to bring the other leg after. His rifle caught on the wire and he jerked at it. The air was rocked by the sound of the shot. Feeling foolish, he lifted his face, baring it to an expected shower of derision from his brother. But Eugie did not turn around. Instead, from his crouching position, he fell to his knees and then pitched forward onto his face. The ducks rose up crying from the lake, cleared the mountain background and beat away northward across the pale sky.

Arnold squatted beside his brother. Eugie seemed to be climbing the earth, as if the earth ran up and down, and when he found he couldn't scale it he lay still.

"Eugie?"

Then Arnold saw it, under the tendril of hair at the nape of the neck—a slow rising of bright blood. It had an obnoxious movement, like that of a parasite.

"Hey, Eugie," he said again. He was feeling the same discomfort he had felt when he had watched Eugie sleeping; his brother didn't know that he was lying face down in the pasture.

Again he said, "Hey, Eugie," an anxious nudge in his voice. But Eugie was as still as the morning about them.

Arnold set his rifle on the ground and stood up. He picked up the tub and, dragging it behind him, walking along by the willows to the garden fence and climbed through. He went down on his knees among the tangled vines. The pods were cold with the night, but his hands were strange to him, and not until some time had passed did he realize that the pods were numbing his fingers. He picked from the top of the vine first, then lifted the vine to look underneath for pods and then moved on to the next.

It was a warmth on his back, like a large hand laid firmly there, that made him raise his head. Way up on the slope the gray farmhouse was struck by the sun. While his head had been bent the land had grown bright around him.

When he got up his legs were so stiff that he had to go down on his knees again to ease the pain. Then, walking sideways, he dragged the tub, half full of peas, up the slope.

The kitchen was warm now; a fire was roaring in the stove with a closed-up, rushing sound. His mother was spooning eggs from a pot of boiling water and putting them into a bowl. Her short brown hair was uncombed and fell forward across her eyes as she bent her head. Nora was lifting a frying pan full of trout from the stove, holding the handle with a dish towel. His father had just come in from bringing the cows from the north pasture to the barn, and was sitting on the stool, unbuttoning his red plaid Mackinaw.

"Did you boys fill the tub?" his mother asked.

"They ought of by now," his father said. "They went out of the house an hour ago. Eugie woke me up comin' downstairs. I heard you shootin'—did you get a duck?"

"No," Arnold said. They would want to know why Eugie wasn't coming in for breakfast, he thought. "Eugie's dead," he told them.

They stared at him. The pitch crackled in the stove.

"You kids playin' a joke?" his father asked.

"Where's Eugene?" his mother asked scoldingly. She wanted, Arnold knew, to see his eyes, and when he had glanced at her she put the bowl and spoon down on the stove and walked past him. His father stood up and went out the door after her. Nora followed them with little skipping steps, as if afraid to be left alone.

Arnold went into the barn, down along the foddering passage past the cows waiting to be milked, and climbed into the loft. After a few minutes he heard a terrifying sound coming toward the house. His parents and Nora were returning from the willows, and sounds sharp as knives were rising from his mother's breast and carrying over the sloping fields. In a short while he heard his father go down the back steps, slam the car door and drive away.

Arnold lay still as a fugitive, listening to the cows eating close by. If his parents never called him, he thought, he would stay up in the loft forever, out of the way. In the night he would sneak down for a drink of water from the faucet over the trough and for whatever food they left for him by the barn.

The rattle of his father's car as it turned down the lane recalled him to the present. He heard voices of his Uncle Andy and Aunt Alice as they and his father went past the barn to the lake. He could feel the morning growing heavier with sun. Someone, probably Nora, had let the chickens out of their coops and they were cackling in the yard.

After a while another car turned down the road off the highway. The car drew to a stop and he heard the voices of strange men. The men also went past the barn and down to the lake. The undertakers, whom his father must have phoned from Uncle Andy's house, had arrived from Corinth. Then he heard everybody come back and heard the car turn around and leave.

"Arnold!" It was his father calling from the yard.

He climbed down the ladder and went out into the sun, picking wisps of hay from his overalls.

Corinth, nine miles away, was the county seat. Arnold sat in the front seat of the old Ford between his father, who was driving, and Uncle Andy; no one spoke. Uncle Andy was his mother's brother, and he had been fond of Eugie because Eugie had resembled him. Andy had taken Eugie hunting and had given him a knife and a lot of things, and now Andy, his eyes narrowed, sat tall and stiff beside Arnold.

Arnold's father parked the car before the courthouse. It was a two-story brick building with a lamp on each side of the bottom step. They went up the wide stone steps, Arnold and his father going first, and entered the darkly paneled hallway. The shirt-sleeved man in the sheriff's office said that the sheriff was at Carlson's Parlor examining the Curwing boy.

Andy went off to get the sheriff while Arnold and his father waited on a bench in the corridor. Arnold felt his father watching him, and he lifted his eyes with painful casualness to the announcement, on the opposite wall, of the Corinth County Annual Rodeo, and then to the clock with its loudly clucking pendulum. After he had come down from the loft his father and Uncle Andy had stood in the yard with him and asked him to tell them everything, and he had explained to them how the gun had caught on the wire. But when they had asked him why he hadn't run back to the house to tell his parents, he had had no answer—all he could say was that he had gone down into the garden to pick the peas. His father had stared at him in a pale, puzzled way, and it was then that he had felt his father and the others set their cold, turbulent silence against him. Arnold shifted on the bench, his only feeling a small one of compunction imposed by his father's eyes.

At a quarter past nine, Andy and the sheriff came in. They all went into the sheriff's private office, and Arnold was sent forward to sit in the chair by the sheriff's desk; his father and Andy sat down on the bench against the wall.

The sheriff lumped down into his swivel chair and swung toward Arnold. He was an old man with white hair like wheat stubble. His restless green eyes made him seem not to be in his office but to be hurrying and bobbing around somewhere else.

"What did you say your name was?" the sheriff asked.

"Arnold," he replied, but he could not remember telling the sheriff his name before.

"Curwing?"

"Yes."

"What were you doing with a .22, Arnold?"

"It's mine," he said.

"Okay. What were you going to shoot?"

"Some ducks," he replied.

"Out of season?"

He nodded.

"That's bad," said the sheriff. "Were you and your brother good friends?"

What did he mean—good friends? Eugie was his brother. That was different from a friend, Arnold thought. A best friend was your own age, but Eugie was almost a man. Eugie had had a way of looking at him, slyly and mockingly and yet confidentially, that had summed up how they both felt about being brothers. Arnold had wanted to be with Eugie more than with anybody else but he couldn't say they had been good friends.

"Did they ever quarrel?" the sheriff asked his father.

"Not that I know," his father replied. "It seemed to me that Arnold cared a lot for Eugie."

"Did you?" the sheriff asked Arnold.

If it seemed so to his father, then it was so. Arnold nodded.

"Were you mad at him this morning?"

"No."

"How did you happen to shoot him?"

"We was crawlin' through the fence."

"Yes?"

"An' the gun got caught on the wire."

"Seems the hammer must of caught," his father put in.

"All right, that's what happened," said the sheriff. "But what I want you to tell me is this. Why didn't you go back to the house and tell your father right away? Why did you go and pick peas for an hour?"

Arnold gazed over his shoulder at his father, expecting his father to have an answer for this also. But his father's eyes, larger and even lighter blue than usual, were fixed upon him curiously. Arnold picked at a callus in his right palm. It seemed odd now that he had not run back to the house and wakened his father, but he could not remember why he had not. They were all waiting for him to answer.

"I come down to pick peas," he said.

"Didn't you think," asked the sheriff, stepping carefully from word to word, "that it was more important for you to go tell your parents what had happened?"

"The sun was gonna come up," Arnold said.

"What's that got to do with it?"

"It's better to pick peas while they're cool."

The sheriff swung away from him, laid both hands flat on his desk. "Well, all I can say is," he said across to Arnold's father and Uncle Andy, "he's either a moron or he's so reasonable that he's way ahead of us." He gave a challenging snort. "It's come to my notice that the most reasonable guys are mean ones. They don't feel nothing."

For a moment the three men sat still. Then the sheriff lifted his hand like a man taking an oath. "Take him home," he said.

Andy uncrossed his legs. "You don't want him?"

"Not now," replied the sheriff. "Maybe in a few years."

Arnold's father stood up. He held his hat against his chest. "The gun ain't his no more," he said wanly.

Arnold went first through the hallway, hearing behind him the heels of his father and Uncle Andy striking the floor boards. He went down the steps ahead of them and climbed into the back seat of the car. Andy paused as he was getting into the front seat and gazed back at Arnold, and Arnold saw that his uncle's eyes had absorbed the knowingness from the sheriff's eyes. Andy and his father and the sheriff had discovered what made him go down into the garden. It was because he was cruel, the sheriff had said, and didn't care about his brother. Was that the reason? Arnold lowered his eyelids meekly against his uncle's stare.

The rest of the day he did his tasks around the farm, keeping apart from the family. At evening, when he saw his father stomp tiredly into the house, Arnold did not put down his hammer and leave the chicken coop he was repairing. He was afraid that they did not want him to eat supper with them. But in a few minutes another fear that they would go to the trouble of calling him and that he would be made conspicuous by his tardiness made him follow his father into the house. As he went through the kitchen he saw the jars of peas standing in rows on the workbench, a reproach to him.

No one spoke at supper, and his mother, who sat next to him, leaned her head in her hand all through the meal, curving her fingers over her eyes so as not to see him. They were finishing their small, silent supper when the visitors began to arrive, knocking hard on the back door. The men were coming from their farms now that it was growing dark and they could not work any more.

Old Man Matthews, gray and stocky, came first, with his two sons, Orion, the elder, and Clint, who was Eugie's age. As the callers entered the parlor, where the family ate, Arnold sat down in a rocking chair. Even as he had been undecided before supper whether to remain outside or take his place at the table, he now thought that he should go upstairs, and yet he stayed to avoid being conspicuous by his absence. If he stayed, he thought, as he always stayed and listened when visitors came, they would see that he was only Arnold and not the person the sheriff thought he was. He sat with his arms crossed and his hands tucked into his armpits and did not lift his eyes.

The Matthews men had hardly settled down around the table, after Arnold's mother and Nora had cleared away the dishes, when another car rattled down the road and someone else rapped on the back door. This time it was Sullivan, a spare and sandy man, so nimble of gesture and expression that Arnold had never been able to catch more than a few of his meanings. Sullivan, in dusty jeans, sat down in the other rocker, shot out his skinny legs and began to talk in his fast way, recalling everything that Eugene had ever said to him. The other men interrupted to tell of occasions they remembered, and after a time Clint's young voice, hoarse like Eugene's had been, broke in to tell about the time Eugene had beat him in a wrestling match.

Out in the kitchen the voices of Orion's wife and of Mrs. Sullivan mingled with Nora's voice but not, Arnold noticed, his mother's. Then dry little Mr. Cram came, leaving large Mrs. Cram in the kitchen, and there was no chair left for Mr. Cram to sit in. No one asked Arnold to get up and he was unable to rise. He knew that the story had got around to them during the day about how he had gone and picked peas after he had shot his brother, and he knew that although they were talking only about Eugie they were thinking about him and if he got up, if he moved even his foot, they would all be alerted. Then Uncle Andy arrived and leaned his tall, lanky body against the doorjamb and there were two men standing.

Presently Arnold was aware that the talk had stopped. He knew without looking up that the men were watching him.

"Not a tear in his eye," said Andy, and Arnold knew that it was his uncle who had gestured the men to attention.

"He don't give a hoot, is that how it goes?" asked Sullivan, trippingly.

"He's a reasonable fellow," Andy explained. "That's what the sheriff said. It's us who ain't reasonable. If we'd of shot our brother, we'd of come runnin' back to the house, cryin' like a baby. Well, we'd of been unreasonable. What would of been the use of actin' like that? If your brother is shot dead, he's shot dead. What's the use of gettin' emotional about it? The thing to do is go down to the garden and pick peas. Am I right?"

The men around the room shifted their heavy, satisfying weight of unreasonableness.

Matthews' son Orion said: "If I'd of done what he done, Pa would've hung my pelt by the side of that big coyote's in the barn."

Arnold sat in the rocker until the last man had filed out. While his family was out in the kitchen bidding the callers good night and the cars were driving away down the dirt lane to the highway, he picked up one of the kerosene lamps and slipped quickly up the stairs. In his room he undressed by lamplight, although he and Eugie had always undressed in the dark, and not until he was lying in his bed did he blow out the flame. He felt nothing, not any grief. There was only the same immense silence and crawling inside of him; it was the way the house and fields felt under a merciless sun.

He awoke suddenly. He knew that his father was out in the yard, closing the doors of the chicken houses so that the chickens could not roam out too early and fall prey to the coyotes that came down from the mountains at daybreak. The sound that had wakened him was the step of his father as he got up from the rocker and went down the back steps. And he knew that his mother was awake in her bed.

Throwing off the covers, he rose swiftly, went down the stairs and across the dark parlor to his parents' room. He rapped on the door.

"Mother?"

From the closed room her voice rose to him, a seeking and retreating voice. "Yes?"

"Mother?" he asked insistently. He had expected her to realize that he wanted to go down on his knees by her bed and tell her that Eugie was dead. She did not know it yet, nobody knew it, and yet she was sitting up in bed, waiting to be told, waiting for him to confirm her dread. He had expected her to tell him to come in, to allow him to dig his head into her blankets and tell her about the terror he had felt when he had knelt beside Eugie. He had come to clasp her in his arms and, in his terror, to pommel her breasts with his head. He put his hand upon the knob.

"Go back to bed, Arnold," she called sharply.

But he waited.

"Go back! Is night when you get afraid?"

At first he did not understand. Then, silently, he left the door and for a stricken moment stood by the rocker. Outside everything was still. The fences, the shocks of wheat seen through the window before him were so still it was as if they moved and breathed in the daytime and had fallen silent with the lateness of the hour. It was a silence that seemed to observe his father, a figure moving alone around the yard, his lantern casting a circle of light by his feet. In a few minutes his father would enter the dark house, the lantern still lighting his way.

Arnold was suddenly aware that he was naked. He had thrown off his blankets and come down the stairs to tell his mother how he felt about Eugie, but she had refused to listen to him and his nakedness had become unpardonable. At once he went back up the stairs, fleeing from his father's lantern.

At breakfast he kept his eyelids lowered as if to deny the humiliating night. Nora, sitting at his left, did not pass the pitcher of milk to him and he did not ask for it. He would never again, he vowed, ask them for anything, and he ate his fried eggs and potatoes only because everybody ate meals—the cattle ate, and the cats; it was customary for everybody to eat.

"Nora, you gonna keep that pitcher for yourself?" his father asked.

Nora lowered her head unsurely.

"Pass it on to Arnold," his father said.

Nora put her hands in her lap.

His father picked up the metal pitcher and set it down at Arnold's plate.

Arnold, pretending to be deaf to the discord, did not glance up, but relief rained over his shoulders at the thought that his parents recognized him again. They must have lain awake after his father had come in from the yard: had they realized together why he had come down the stairs and knocked at their door?

"Bessie's missin' this morning," his father called out to his mother, who had gone into the kitchen. "She went up the mountain last night and had her calf, most likely. Somebody's got to go up and find her 'fore the coyotes get the calf."

That had been Eugie's job, Arnold thought. Eugie would climb the cattle trails in search of a newborn calf and come down the mountain carrying the calf across his back, with the cow running down along behind him, mooing in alarm.

Arnold ate the few more forkfuls of his breakfast, put his hands on the edge of the table and pushed back his chair. If he went for the calf he'd be away from the farm all morning. He could switch the cow down the mountain slowly, and the calf would run along at its mother's side.

When he passed through the kitchen his mother was setting a kettle of water on the stove. "Where you going?" she asked awkwardly.

"Up to get the calf," he replied, averting his face.

"Arnold?"

At the door he paused reluctantly, his back to her, knowing that she was seeking him out, as his father was doing, and he called upon his pride to protect him from them.

"Was you knocking at my door last night?"

He looked over his shoulder at her, his eyes narrow and dry.

"What'd you want?" she asked humbly.

"I didn't want nothing," he said flatly.

Then he went out the door and down the back steps, his legs trembling from the fright his answer gave him.

Discussion

It is possible that shock and terror at the enormity of Eugene's accidental death could have numbed nine-year-old Arnold into substituting silence for the accustomed emotional response to death. However, we feel that a strong basis for his silence is the pattern of lack of communication or emotion in this family, particularly among the men. With little experience in a verbal interchange of feeling, it may be that Arnold has experienced a detachment from his own feeling. The Puritan ethic requires a certain stoicism, particularly in men, and only women may at times give way to emotion. In this story only the mother openly weeps when she hears of Eugene's death. When Arnold finally needs to confess his terror he goes to his mother, who is the person in the household who accepts emotion and permits herself emotional responsiveness.

The punitive nature of silence is powerfully conveyed when Arnold is ignored. Yet at the end of the story, when the opportunity arises for Arnold to reopen verbal communication, we appreciate how impossible it is for Arnold to summon the trust it requires to reveal himself, even to those close and well-meaning. The risk of revealing innermost thoughts is more threatening than the terrible prospect of silence. Assumption of silence seems to be Arnold's only option in the light of his background.

We have the feeling that the family will in time resume its accustomed pattern of relating. The everyday silence will be broken but the communication of emotion will remain unchanged, leaving basically alienated people. This is not an unfamiliar situation. Many young people today are seeking encounter groups in order to increase their sensitivity to others and to help facilitate their communication of feeling. They are in search of rich and satisfying human relationships, which require a basis of mutual trust in order to unfold and grow.

Springboards for Inquiry

(1) What do you think is the meaning of Arnold's silence and behavior following the accidental shooting?

(2) What has happened to Arnold's mother's sense of trust in her younger son?

(3) Interpret the meaning of the last sentence in this story.

(4) Cite the causes of diminished affective communication within a family.

(5) Could you enter into a dialogue that is not really communication with another class member? What would the characteristics of your conversation be?

(6) Verbal communication at an encounter group session is frequently called "risk taking." Explain this phrase.

References

Alexander, Theron. *Children and Adolescents.* New York: Atherton Press, 1969.

Ausubel, David P. *Educational Psychology: A Cognitive View.* New York: Holt, Rinehart, and Winston, 1968.

Bandura, Albert, and Walters, Richard H. *Social Learning and Personality Development.* New York: Holt, Rinehart, & Winston, 1963.

Bing, Elizabeth. "Effect of Child-Rearing Practices on Development of Differential Cognitive Abilities." *Child Development* 34 (1963): 631–48.

Brody, Grace F. "Maternal Child-Rearing Attitudes and Child Behavior." *Developmental Psychology* 1 (1969): 66.

Brodie, Richard D., and Winterbottom, Marian R. "Failure in Elementary School Boys as a Function of Traumata, Secrecy, and Derogation." *Child Development* 38 No. 1 (1967): 701–11.

Bronfenbrenner, Urie. *Two Worlds of Childhood.* New York: Russell Sage Foundation, 1970.

Glasser, William. *Reality Therapy.* New York: Harper & Row, 1965.

Glasser, William. *Schools without Failure.* New York: Harper & Row, 1969.

Ginott, Haim. *Between Parent and Child.* New York: Macmillan Co., 1965.

Hoffman, Lois W.; Rosen, Sidney; and Lippitt, Ronald. "Parental Coerciveness, Child Autonomy, and Child's Role at School." *Sociometry* 23 (1960): 15–22.

Hymes, James L. *Behavior and Misbehavior.* Englewood Cliffs, N. J.: Prentice-Hall, 1955.

Meerloo, Joost A. M. "Conversation and Communication." In *The Human Dialogue,* edited by Floyd W. Matson and M. F. Ashley-Montagu. New York: Free Press, 1967.

Menninger, Karl. "The Crime of Punishment." *Saturday Review,* 7 September 1968, pp. 21–25.

Menninger, Karl. *The Vital Balance,* written with Martin Mayman and Paul Pruyser. New York: Viking Press, 1963.

Redl, Fritz. "The Concept of a 'Therapeutic Milieu.' " *American Journal of Orthopsychiatry* 29 (October 1959): 721–36.

Redl, Fritz. *When We Deal with Children.* New York: Free Press, 1966.

Rogers, Dorothy. *Child Psychology.* Belmont, Calif.: Brooks/Cole Publishing Co., 1969.

Smith, B. Othanel. "Discipline." In *Encyclopedia of Educational Research*, ed. Robert L. Eble. 4th ed. pp. 292–96. London: Macmillan & Co. Ltd., 1969.

The Meaning of Play

It is said that play is the child's work. An examination of the young child's day-long occupation indicates that his play reflects necessary and helpful stages in his development. Play is far more purposive and orderly in its progression than the term ordinarily connotes. The child is nourished mentally and physically through play. Jean Piaget (1951) identifies several stages of play and relates them to sensorimotor and intellectual development. According to Piaget, the child's play reflects the organism's inherent need to develop in the physical and psychological spheres.

Activity is the toddler's main occupation—opening, closing, shoving, pulling, squeezing, pounding—as he investigates the limited world around him. The activities at first represent intelligent investigations of the environment and become play when they are repeated for the sheer delight of the activity itself. The beginning of dramatic play is associated with the ability of the child to imagine or conceptualize without needing the concrete representation of his thought. When a few blocks can represent an airport the child is ready for make-believe. This fantasy world can be an opportunity for the child to repeat the familiar or it may be used to test the unknown. Fears, wishes, and aggressive impulses may be acted out through imaginative play. Some researchers feel that children who can play-act their aggressive impulses may be less likely to act them out in real life.

Dramatic play also provides an opportunity for children to try on adult roles. The popularity of the playhouse corner in nursery school and kindergarten reveals the young child's interest in recreating themes of domestic life in play. Boys as well as girls enjoy imitating mother's work. Adults are often surprised by the child's sharp eye for detail and keen perception of nuances of feeling that are reflected in his reenactment of the scolding parent or angry teacher. This may be instructive to the adult, but more importantly, it provides the child with an opportunity to try out adult power in a situation that is safe. It is healthy for children to model adult roles because this modeling suggests identification with grown-ups and is supportive of growth toward adulthood.

Children's play can be a significant source of data for those studying child growth and development. In the child's play we see his "world" mirrored. The way he perceives the adults in his world, the way he wishes the world to be are all reflected in the child's play.

Making Friends

As the child leaves infancy and enters toddlerhood, he begins to develop special relationships with other children. While his relationship with the entire peer group is important, his social development also requires the singling out of an individual outside the family circle with whom he can form an emotional attachment. Society calls this attachment friendship.

Marian Breckenridge and Lee Vincent (1965, p. 363) identify three types of friendship: (a) involvement with people on a superficial social level; (b) the maintenance of smooth relationships with people whether or not there is a mutual liking; and (c) the intimate harmonizings of persons who have sincere feelings for each other. Friendships in early childhood are not likely to be of either the first or second types, but while they remain generally nonerotic, childhood relationships are nevertheless intimate. By the time a child is three or four he will likely have made at least one close friend (Jersild 1960).

In early childhood friendships are much less intense than during adolescence but they do serve important needs. Personal confidences that might be buried in the unconscious are brought to the surface and aired in the normal course of friendship. Conflicts, doubts, and wonderings are shared by friends, so that the mutual exploration of ideas broadens the experiences of both parties. Lonely children frequently gain ego support from one particularly close friend. Despite the fact that friendship does not stop quarreling (indeed, an early study by Elise Green (1933) indicates that friends quarrel more than casual acquaintances), the bond that develops between children is strong and it often persists throughout a lifetime.

Factors such as personal compatibility account for the development of friendships. Natalie Reader and Horace English (1947) report that there is a high degree of similarity between the scores of female adolescent friends on tests of dominance, self-confidence, security, and social adjustment. We suspect that similar data would emerge from studies of younger friends. Children also select their friends on the basis of race and social status (Elkins 1958). Stories about children being color-blind are not supported by research data (McCandless and Hoyt 1961). One of the most potent factors in the development of all friendships is situation. Adults tend to become friendlier with those who live close than with those who are inaccessible, and the child, too, may choose a friend because he lives next door, goes to the same nursery school, or is in the same car pool. The rearrangement of children's sleeping quarters and the like can affect the choice of friends and catalyze the development of friendships (Campbell and Yarrow 1958).

It seems safe to conclude that as children grow older they begin to prefer playmates of their own sex. By the time they are in the middle elementary grades (fourth through sixth grades) physiology has started to dictate more interest in heterosexual friendships but with no clear-cut preference for this type of friendship. The patterns of friendship developed through the child's growing years are important to the quality of his life during those years. Friendships are also part of the early socializing experience that prepares the ground for fruitful interpersonal relationships later in life.

'Tom, you naughty boy, is this the way you entertain your guests? Poor little Jenny, all by herself under the table.'

A Special Occasion

by Joyce Cary

The nursery door opened and Nurse's voice said in the sugary tone which she used to little girl guests, 'Here you are, darling, and Tommy will show you all his toys.' A little brown-haired girl, in a silk party frock sticking out all round her legs like a lampshade, came in at the door, stopped, and stared at her host. Tom, a dark little boy, aged five, also in a party suit, blue linen knickers, and a silk shirt, stared back at the girl. Nurse had gone into the night nursery, next door, on her private affairs.

Tom, having stared at the girl for a long time as one would study a curiosity, rare and valuable, but extremely surprising, put his feet together, made three jumps forward and said, 'Hullo.'

The little girl turned her head over one shoulder and slowly revolved on one heel, as if trying to examine the back of her own frock. She then stooped suddenly, brushed the hem with her hand, and said, 'Hullo.'

Tom made another jump, turned round, pointed out of the window, and said in a loud voice something like 'twanky tweedle.' Both knew that neither the gesture nor the phrase was meant to convey a meaning. They simply expressed the fact that for Tom this was an important and exciting, a very special occasion.

The little girl took a step forward, caught her frock in both hands as if about to make a curtsy, rose upon her toes, and said in a prim voice, 'I beg your pardon.'

They both gazed at each other for some minutes with sparkling eyes. Neither smiled, but it seemed that both were about to smile.

Tom then gave another incompre-

---

hensible shout, ran round the table, sat down on the floor and began to play with a clockwork engine on a circular track. The little girl climbed on a tricycle and pedalled round the floor. 'I can ride your bike,' she said.

Tom paid no attention. He was trying how fast the engine could go without falling off the track.

The little girl took a picture book, sat down under the table with her back to Tom, and slowly, carefully, examined each page. 'It's got a crooked wheel,' Tom said, 'that's what it is.' The little girl made no answer. She was staring at the book with round eyes and a small pursed mouth—the expression of a nervous child at the zoo when the lions are just going to roar. Slowly and carefully she turned the next page. As it opened, her eyes became larger, her mouth more tightly pursed, as if she expected some creature to jump out at her.

'Tom.' Nurse, having completed her private business, came bustling in with the air of one restored to life after a dangerous illness. 'Tom, you naughty boy, is this the way you entertain your guests? Poor little Jenny, all by herself under the table.' The nurse was plump and middle-aged; an old-fashioned nanny.

'She's not by herself,' Tom said.

'Oh Tom, that really is naughty of you. Where are all your nice manners? Get up, my dear, and play with her like a good boy.'

'I am playing with her,' Tom said, in a surly tone, and he gave Nurse a sidelong glance of anger.

'Now Tom, if you go on telling such stories, I shall know you are trying to be naughty. Get up now when I ask you.' She stooped, took Tom by the arm, and lifted him up. 'Come now, you must be polite, after you've asked her yourself and pestered for her all the week.'

At this public disclosure, Tom instantly lost his temper and yelled, 'I didn't—I didn't—I won't—I won't.'

'Then I'll have to take poor little Jenny downstairs again to her mummy.'

'No—no—no.'

'Will you play with her, then?'

'No, I hate her—I never wanted her.'

At this the little girl rose and said, in precise indignant tones, 'He *is* naughty, isn't he?'

Tom flew at her, and seized her by the hair; the little girl at once uttered a loud scream, kicked him on the leg, and bit his arm. She was carried screaming to the door by Nurse, who, from there, issued sentence on Tom, 'I'm going straight to your father, as soon as he comes in.' Then she went out, banging the door.

Tom ran at the door and kicked it, rushed at the engine, picked it up and flung it against the wall. Then he howled at the top of his voice for five minutes. He intended to howl all day. He was suffering from a large and complicated grievance.

All at once the door opened and the little girl walked in. She had an air of immense self-satisfaction as if she had just done something very clever. She said in a tone demanding congratulation, 'I've come back.'

Tom gazed at her through his tears and gave a loud sob. Then he picked up the engine, sat down by the track. But the engine fell off at the first push. He gave another sob, looked at the wheels, and bent one of them straight.

The little girl lifted her party

frock behind in order not to crush it, sat down under the table, and drew the book on to her knee.

Tom tried the engine at high speed. His face was still set in the form of anger and bitterness, but he forgot to sob. He exclaimed with surprise and pleased excitement, 'It's the lines too—where I trod on 'em.'

The little girl did not reply. Slowly, carefully, she opened the book in the middle and gazed at an elephant. Her eyes became immense, her lips minute. But suddenly, and, as it were, accidentally, she gave an enormous sigh of relief, of very special happiness.

Discussion

Children have individual ways of relating to new people, depending on their age and temperament. Tom and Jenny are five years old, and for their age they behave appropriately. Developmentally they should be ready to engage in cooperative play, but under the stress of this initial encounter they retreat to parallel play, a former stage in their development. During parallel play children play side by side in different individual activities, but they enjoy being in the same play space. Tom and Jenny are aware of the other's presence but use individual activity to provide comfortable social distance to observe and become familiar with each other.

The children's ways are wise and the nurse's expectation is inappropriate. The nurse is also insensitive to Tom's feelings. She shames Tom in Jenny's presence by revealing that he had asked repeatedly if Jenny could be invited to visit. In order to save face at Tom's denial of this accusation, Jenny puts on a display of indignation. When the adults leave the scene the children's natural harmony is restored and Tom and Jenny can once again resume their developmentally appropriate, friendly behavior.

Springboards for Inquiry

(1) What are the elements of friendship evident between Tom and Jenny in this story?

(2) Trace the pattern of friendship that children establish in early school age through the middle years with regard to sex preference and choice of games. What are some of the particular problems that arise at each period?

(3) What should the adult's role be in facilitating play or friendships at each of these age levels?

(4) Some children find it extremely difficult to make friends. What observable behavior patterns might be associated with the child who cannot make friends?

(5) What are some of the characteristics of the child who is popular with his peers in the middle school years?

Creativity

A review of the research concerned with creativity reveals a veritable academic jungle of notions about what creativity is, if it "is" anything, how it can be nurtured (Getzels 1969; Nash 1970), and to what other factors it is related. There is general agreement that creativity is a prime goal of education and that it is probably multifactorial, thus elusive for the purposes of simple definition.

Discussions by educators regarding the characteristics of creativity revolve around the idea of novelty—originality both in the product of creative minds and as the process by which some invention is produced. (Ghiselin 1952).* Maslow (1963), in a burst of latter-day transcendentalism, uses the Emersonian term *flash of insight* to indicate a brilliant and intuitive—hence "creative"—response to a problem. While many researchers focus on the response of creative people to problems ("Name all the things you can do with a brick"), Jacob Getzels (Getzels and Csikszentmihalyi 1964, p. 202), sees the fruitful question as being most significant. Getzels (1964, p. 267) himself uses the criteria described by Newall et al. (1962): creative thinking is unconventional, is intense, formulates problems out of vague and disorganized information, and leads to a novel product that has value to the culture.

The work of J. Paul Guilford (1959) also merits attention, since his theoretical model focuses on thought processes. He contributed the terms *convergent* and *divergent* thinking processes to the literature. Convergent thinking results in

---

* Brewster Ghiselin, author of *The Creative Process* and a colleague at the University of Utah, suggests that a certain dynamic quality in the psychic life of an individual leads to invention (not necessarily to be construed as being a product).

making the greatest use of what is known; divergent thinking refers to new data that is devised from a minimum of human information. Divergent thinking is highly correlated with creativity.

McCandless (1967, p. 332) concludes that a description of creative individuals would include such words as "original, imaginative, curious, enthusiastic, impulsive, less contented and conventional, assertive and authoritative, gloomy, loud, unstable, bitter, cool, dissatisfied, emotional, nonneurotic, reflective, etc." No one seems to take issue with these often mutually exclusive terms or questions the logic involved in the contradictions (for instance, reflective versus impulsive and cool versus emotional).

It would seem productive to examine relationships between facets of everyday existence and creativity. In 1950 Guilford predicted that the relation between creativity and intelligence would be low. Calvin Taylor (1959) accounts for the discrepancy by the fact that Western culture stresses the speed at which unimportant problems are solved with a minimum of error. Guilford (1950) maintains further that IQ tests are not creative, and besides, a creative response is difficult to measure. To date, the most exhaustive study (Wallach and Kogan 1965) of the relationships between creativity and intelligence concludes that intelligence does not guarantee creativeness. Furthermore, although creativity is probably limited by low intelligence, a correlation with high intelligence appears doubtful as measured by IQ tests.

The literature generally agrees that in school the creative child is stifled (Torrance 1962); creative people tend to be "self-actualizing" (Maslow 1954); mothers of creative children worry less about dangers in the world, are less vigilant about the child's school performance, and restrict the child's independence less than the mothers of high IQ children (Getzels and Jackson 1962, p. 293); creative people are able to take risks in their perceptions of the world and are nonconforming (McClelland 1963); creative children see that their parents consider them responsible and expectations are not enforced by authoritarian controls (Datta and Parloff 1967); and there are some positive results when children are "trained" to react creatively or think divergently (Cartledge and Krauser 1963).

Creativity, like many other psychological concepts, has varied definitions. Educators are influenced by the impact of this concept and are adjusting their curriculums and assignments to accommodate and encourage creativity, however it may ultimately be defined.

"What's the point about the brown suit, old man?" It was Caroline who explained, "It's got a holster pocket at the back where he can carry his pretend pistol."

The Rainy Day, The Good Mother, and The Brown Suit

by Dorothy Canfield

And yet she had done exactly what the books on child training assured mothers would ward off trouble on a stormy day. She had copied off the list of raw material recommended by the author of "The Happy Child Is the Active Child": colored paper, blunt scissors, paste, pencils, crayons, plasticine—she had bought them all, well ahead of time, and had brought them out this morning after breakfast, when the rain settled down with that all-day pour. But, unlike the children in the books, Caroline and Freddy and little Priscilla had not received these treasures open-mouthed with pleasure, nor had they quietly and happily exercised their creative instinct, leaving their mother free to get on with her work. Perhaps her children hadn't as much of that instinct as other people's. At least, after a little listless fingering of colored paper Freddy turned away. "Say, Mother, I want to put on my brown suit," he said. Little did she dream then what the brown suit was to cost her. She answered casually, piling up the breakfast dishes, "I washed that suit yesterday, Freddy, and the rain came, So it's not dry yet."

He trotted back and forth after her as she stepped to and fro with the slightly nervous haste of a competent woman who has planned a busy morning. "But, Mother," he persisted, "I *want* to put it on. I *want* to." He raised his voice. "Mother, I want to put my brown suit on."

From the pantry where she had just discovered that the cream she had planned to use for the dessert was soured, she answered him with some asperity, "I told you it isn't dry yet!" But she reminded herself of the excellent rule, "Always make

---

From *Fables for Parents* by Dorothy Canfield, copyright, 1937, by Harcourt Brace Jovanovich, Inc., renewed, 1965, by Sarah Fisher Scott. Reprinted by permission of the publisher.

children understand the reasons for your refusals," and added, "It's hanging on the line on the side porch. Look out there, dear. You can see for yourself how wet it is."

He did as she bade him, and stood staring out, leaning his forehead on the glass.

Yet a little later as she stood before the telephone, grocery list in hand, he tugged at her skirt and as Central asked, "What number, please?" he said with plaintive obstinacy, "Mother, I *do* want to put on my brown suit."

She said with considerable warmth, "Somerset three six one. For heaven's sake, Freddy, that suit is WET. Is this Perkins and Larsen? How *could* you put it on! What price are your grapefruit today? Freddy, let go of my skirt. Grapefruit, I said. No, no—G for glory, r for run—"

But when she turned away from her struggle with the clerk, Freddy plucked at her hand and whimpered in the nasal fretting tone she had sworn (before she had children) no child of hers should ever use, "Mother I waa-a-nt to pu-u-t my brown—"

"Don't whine," she told him with a ferocity so swift and savage that he recoiled and was silent. She thought remorsefully, "Oh, dear, to scold is just as bad as to whine."

Going back into the pantry she recalled with resentment that the psychologists of family life say the moods of children are but the reflections of moods of the mother. She did not believe a word of it. "Did *I* start this?" she asked herself unanswerably, and, "How can anybody help being irritated when they're so perfectly unreasonable!"

But she was really a very good mother. She remembered that the basis of child-rearing is to understand each child at all times, and went resolutely back into the other room, determined to understand Freddy, if it were her last act. Disconcertingly, it was not Freddy, but Priscilla who ran to take her hand, who said pleadingly, timidly, as if appealing from the cruel decree of a tyrant, "Mummy, Fred *does* so want to have you let him wear his brown suit this morning!" The mother contained herself, collected the children—three-year-old Priscilla, five-year-old Fred, six-and-half-year-old Caroline—led them to the window and said, "Now, just look at that suit! How can I let Freddy wear anything that's as wet as sop?"

At least that was what she thought she said. What the children distinctly heard was, "You're in the wrong, wrong, wrong. And I am right, right, right, as I always am. There's no use your trying to get around that!"

They stared gloomily out at this idea rather than at the wet clothes. Their mother went on, "What in the world does Fred want to wear his brown suit for, anyhow? What's the matter with the suit he's got on?"

What the children heard was, "No matter what Freddy said his reason was, I'd soon show you it was all foolishness."

They attempted no answer, shaken as they were by wave after invisible wave of her impatience to be done with them and at something else. Indeed she was impatient. Why not, with her morning work all waiting to be done. She held her children for a moment with the bullying eye of a drill-sergeant, and then said, challengingly, "Well-?" She meant, and they knew she meant, "I hope you realize that I have you beaten."

Something in Fred— it was something rather fine—exploded with a crash. His round face grew grim and black. He looked savagely at his mother, thrust out his lower jaw and, keeping his eyes ragingly on hers, kicked a footstool, viciously, as if he were kicking her.

"Fred-*dy*" she said in a voice meant to cow him. But he was not cowed. He kicked again with all his might, looking at his mother and hating her.

And then—he was only a little boy —he broke. His hard defiant face crumbled up into despair. He crooked his arm to hide his suffering from his mother—from his mother! —and turned away to lean against the wall in the silent, dry, inexplicable misery which often ended what his mother called "Fred's tantrums." Little Priscilla began whimpering. Caroline put her hands up to her face and hung her head.

Their mother thought, her nerves taut with exasperation, "I'd just like to see one of those child-specialists manage *my* children on a rainy day! They'd find out a thing or two!" But she loved her children. She loved them dearly. With her next breath she was ashamed of being angry with them. The tears came to her eyes and an aching lump into her throat. Bewildered, dismayed, she asked herself, in the purest surprise, "Why, how did we get into this dreadful state? What can the trouble be?"

She went back into the pantry, took a long breath, took a drink of water, tried to relax her muscles, cast her mind back to the book about what to do on a rainy day. But she could recall nothing else in it but that appeal to the creative instinct. She had tried that, and it had failed.

She heard the front door open. The voice of a young cousin—no special favorite of hers—cried, "Ye gods and little fishes, what weather!" He slammed the door behind him. Although he was nineteen, he still slammed doors as if he were twelve. He had come as he sometimes did when it rained, to wait in the living room for the bus that took him to college. One of its stopping places was their corner.

Priscilla, the literal, asked, "What does 'gods and little fishes' mean?"

"Mean?" said the freshman, laughing and flinging his books and his rain-coat down on the floor. "What do you mean, mean? You mean too much Prissy. What does this mean?" As she began to wash the dishes the mother could see that he had flung his heels in the air and was walking on his hands. "He's too old for such foolishness," she thought severely. And sure enough, out of the pockets of his adult suit of clothes, now upside down, little-boy junk rattled down around his hands. The children squealed and made a rush toward the bits of string, dirty handkerchiefs, knives, fishhooks, nails, pieces of cork, screws and pencils. "No you don't!" said he, returning his feet to the floor with a bang. "Everything there is a part of an important enterprise."

"What's a 'portant enter—" began Priscilla.

"Whatever I do," he told her coolly, "were it only to make a mousetrap. If *I* made mousetraps there'd be a four-strip concrete road to my door in a week's time, you bet. No mousetrap of mine would ever have let out Uncle Peter's mouse, believe me."

"What? Who? What's Uncle Peter's mouse?" clamored the children.

"Oh, surely you know that story. No child of our family gets brung up without hearing that one. No? Well, one morning when Uncle Peter and Aunt Molly came down to breakfast —Priscilla, do *not* ask who they were and where they lived, it's no matter— they found a mouse in their trap. It was the kind of trap that catches the mouse alive, so they got the cat, and they all went out on the porch to open the trap and let the cat catch the mouse. Priscilla, do *not* say this was horrid of them, it was, and I can't help it, but that was the way it happened, and it was so long ago probably they didn't know any better. So there they all were"—he illustrated how tensely they stood, stooping over an imaginary trap—"the two children and Uncle Peter and Aunt Molly. And the cat. She was scrooched right close in front of the cage"—he quivered and crouched with such vivacity of acting that the children began to laugh—"while Uncle Peter s-l-o-w-l-y, s-l-o-w-l-y lifted the door of the trap till it was open enough for the mouse to get out." He drew a long breath and made a dramatic pause. The children gazed at him, mouths open, eyes unwinking. "And then—!" he sprang into the air, "the cat jumped!" He clutched at Fred. "Uncle Peter hollered!" He ran to Caroline and seized her arm. "The children yelled bloody murder!" He flung the children to right and left. "Aunt Molly shrieked!" He sank back on the floor. "But the mouse was gone!"

He gazed with enormous solemnity at his spellbound listeners. "The cat was prowling around, sniffing and lashing her tail"—he sniffed the air and getting up on his hands and knees lashed an imaginary tail—"But-there-was-no-mouse."

He sat cross-legged and earnest and went on, "Well, Aunt Molly was terribly afraid of mice, and she always had the idea that all a mouse wanted to do was to run up folks' clothes, so she was sure the mouse had done that to one of them. So she took one child and then the other, shook them till their teeth nearly dropped out"—he shot out a long arm and seized Priscilla, Caroline, and Freddy one after the other, shaking them hard and setting them into giggling fits—"and put first one and then the other inside the house and shut the door, quick! Then she shook herself hard. And she went into the house and shut the door. Then Uncle Peter shook *himself* hard. And went in quick and shut the door. And then they all had breakfast, wondering all the while about where that mouse could have gone to. And after they'd finished breakfast, Uncle Peter stood up to go to the office and took hold of the lower edge of his vest to pull it down"—he seized the lower edge of an imaginary vest vigorously and stood appalled, a frantic expression of horror on his face—*"and there was the mouse!"* The children shrieked. "It had been right under the edge of his vest and when he grabbed the vest he put his hand right around it, and when he took his hand away the mouse was in it, squirming." He showed them how it squirmed, and then, speeding up to express-train speed, finished the story all in one breath. "And he was so rattled he flung it right away without looking to see where, and it went sprang into Aunt Molly's face and she fainted dead away—and the mouse beat it so quick they never did see it again."

He grinned down at the children, literally rolling on the floor, as pleased with the story as they. "Say, kids, what-d'you-say we act it out? Let's. Who'll be what? I'll be Uncle Peter. Priscilla, you be one of the children. Caroline, you be Aunt Molly—that's a swell part! You must yell your head off when I throw the mouse in your face. Fred you be—"

"I'll be the cat," said Fred, scrambling to his feet.

So they acted out the little drama, throwing themselves passionately into their roles, Caroline so magnificent with her scream and faint at the end that Priscilla said, "Oh, *I* want to be Aunt Molly."

"I'd kind o'like to be Uncle Peter," said Fred.

"Okay by me," said the student. "I'll be the cat."

By the time they had finished it again they were out of breath, what with screaming and running and laughing and acting, and sank down together on the floor. Little by little their laughter subsided to a peaceful silence. Freddy sprawled half over the knobby knees of the tall boy, Priscilla was tucked away under his arm, Caroline leaned against him. From the pantry where, unheeded, the mother washed the dishes, she thought jealously, "What do they see in him? That story is nothing but nonsense." And then—she was really an intelligent person—it came over her, "Why, that is just what they like in it."

Out of the silence, almost as though she were thinking aloud, little Priscilla murmured, "Freddy was bad this morning." There was compassion in her tone.

"What was eating him?" asked the student, not particularly interested.

"He wanted to wear his brown suit. And it was wet, and he couldn't. So he kicked the footstool and was bad."

"What's the point about the brown suit, old man?"

The question was put in a matter-of-fact tone of comradely interest. But even so Fred hesitated, opened his mouth, shut it, said nothing.

It was Caroline who explained, "It's got a holster pocket at the back where he can carry his pretend pistol."

The mother in the pantry, astounded, remorseful, reproachful, cried out to herself, "Oh, why didn't he tell *me* that!" But she knew very well why he had not. She had plenty of brains.

"Oh, I see," said the student. "But why don't you sew a holster pocket on the pants you've got on, boy? On all your pants. It's nothing to sew on pockets. You girls, too. You might as well have holster pockets. When I was your age I had sewed on dozens of pockets." He took a long breath, and began to rattle off nonsense with an intensely serious face and machine-gun speed. "My goodness, by the time I was fourteen I had sewed on five hundred and thirty-four pockets, and one small watch-pocket but I don't count that one. Didn't you ever hear how I put myself through college sewing on pockets? And when I was graduated, the President of Pocket Sewing Union of America sent for me, and—"

"But you've only just got in to

college," Priscilla reminded him earnestly.

(In the pantry, her mother thought, with a stab of self-knowledge, "Why, is that *me*? Was I being literal, like that, about rainy-day occupations?")

"Priscilla," said the college student, sternly, "don't you know what happens to children who say 'go-up-bald-head' to their elders—oh, but—." He clutched his tousled hair, and said, imitating Priscilla's serious little voice, "Oh, but I'm not bald yet, am I?"

A horn sounded in the street. He sprang up, tumbling the children roughly from him, snatched his books. "There's my bus." The door slammed.

The children came running to find their mother. "Oh, Mother, Mother, can we have some cloth to make pockets out of?"

She was ready for them. "I've got lots of it that'll be just right," she said, telling herself wryly, "I can get an idea all right if somebody'll push it half way down my throat."

But for the rest of the morning, as the children sat happily exercising their creative instinct by sewing on queer pockets in queer places on their clothes, she was thinking with sorrow, "It's not fair. That great lout of a boy without a care in the world takes their fancy with his nonsense, and they turn their backs on me entirely. I represent only food and care—and refusals. I work my head off for them—and the first stranger appeals to them more."

Yet after lunch they put their three heads together and whispered and giggled, and "had a secret." Then, Caroline at their head, they trotted over to the sofa where their mother had dropped down to rest. "Mother," said Caroline in her little-girl bird-voice, "wouldn't you like to play Uncle-Peter-and-Aunt-Molly-and-the-mouse? You didn't have a single chance to this morning—not once—you were working so." They looked at her with fond shining eyes of sympathy. "Come on, Mother! You'll love it!" they encouraged her.

A lump came into her throat again—a good lump this time. She swallowed. "Oh, thanks, children. I know I'd like to. What part are you going to have me take?"

The secret came out then. They let Freddy tell her, for it had been his inspiration. He looked proudly at his mother and offered her his best. "Ye gods and little fishes! We're going to let you be the *mouse!*"

She clasped her hands. "Oh, children!" she cried.

From their pride in having pleased her, a gust of love-madness blew across them, setting them to fall upon their mother like soft-pawed kittens wild with play, pushing her back on the pillows, hugging her, worrying her, rumpling her hair, kissing her ears, her nose, whatever they could reach.

But Priscilla was not sure they had been clear. She drew away. "You don't have to get caught, you know," she reassured her mother earnestly. "The mouse wasn't caught—never!"

Discussion

The mother in this story did all the conventionally correct things to provide her young children with the proper equipment to spend a rainy day in creative pursuits. For the mother, scissors, crayons, paste, and colored paper are, because of their link with art, synonymous with creativity. Her line of reasoning is a failure, however, and the children are disinterested in the tools she has provided. Instead, they are cranky and they make unreasonable requests such as asking for the brown suit, which is hanging, soaking wet, on the line. When the young cousin arrives, he is immediately successful in lifting the children's spirits and motivating them toward satisfying activity.

For what reasons was he successful? For one thing, he does not deliver a double message; he is totally available to the children. The mother had indicated that she was available to her children on this rainy day when, in fact, she was not; her housework and grocery list took priority over the children's interests. The cousin is also imaginative and spontaneous. He tells a tall story that he uses to create a new form of play. Beginning with an idea that contains within it the catalyst for expansion is often the basis for creative interaction in play. In his approach to the children the cousin also leaves room for them to bring their own individuality to the activity. Creating possibilities for imaginative play is a challenge to the parent as well as to the professional who has responsibility for children.

Springboards for Inquiry

(1) Name some imaginative games and toys on the market. What common qualities earn some games, toys, and apparatus the label creative? Describe some differences in American toys and games from those of other countries.

(2) Try inventing an imaginative game. Designate the age group you think would be receptive to your game.

(3) What qualities of child rearing are likely to promote creativity in children? Describe child rearing in terms of communication, discipline, achievement expectation, and sex typing.

(4) Do you think the dramatic play of boys is more creative than the dramatic play of girls? Is it less creative? Is there a basis for claiming a qualitative difference in creativity based on sex?

Fantasy

Children develop imagination and the ability to create fantasy images at an early age. The term *fantasy* is equivalent to *daydreaming.* Jung (1928) defines fantasy thus: "Those phantasies which are forms of imaginative activity are either products of daydreaming or reverie or else they are perceived by intuition as a sort of vision or inspiration." The retreat to a fantasy world is common among those who cannot control their environment.* What cannot be gained in reality is readily obtainable in fantasy. Between the ages of three and five nearly every child starts to daydream (Abrahamsen 1969). When the child retreats into his world of fantasy, this ego-defense mechanism makes frustrations bearable. It is thought by some that the consolation of daydreaming often prevents violent acts (Rogers 1969).

Selma Fraiberg (1959, p. 141) explains that the young child may use fantasy as a way to preserve self-esteem. She points out that a child may invent an imaginary friend when he cannot accept his own selfishness or naughtiness. In this way he casts out any negative attributes by ascribing them to a mythical friend. Thus, a little boy who has broken his mother's best china cup can still maintain a good self-concept as well as parental approval by stoutly maintaining that Stevie, his imaginary companion, has done the terrible deed.

---

* A vivid example of how daydreams can serve as an outlet for completely subdued individuals is found in a reprint of a letter by George Jackson, the Soledad brother incarcerated in the California youth authority facility, Paso Robles. In "Soledad Brother: Two Prison Letters from George Jackson" (*The New York Times Review of Books*, 8 October 1970, pp. 27–36), Jackson writes: " I read Jack London's . . . military novels and dreamed of smashing my enemies entirely, overwhelming, vanquishing, crushing them completely, sinking my fangs into the hunter's neck and never, never letting go."

Sometimes fantasies are unfulfilled wishes. Children may even lie as part of their fantasy attempt to get what they want. In this instance, lack of knowledge of right and wrong permits children to lie. In a sense, the fantasy world that he can control is a precursor to the real world he will at least partially control. Therefore fantasizing, when it does not interfere with adaptation, is preparation for living. Fanciful stories for children do not hurt them, fantasizing becomes a necessary stepping-stone to coping with real situations. Indeed, Lidz (1968, p. 289) indicates that those parents who repress fantasies in their children and always insist on reality discourage divergent thinking. He concludes that "fantasy is a precursor of creativity."

Fantasy plays a role in the Oedipal stage of development. A boy who becomes preoccupied with his mother and wishes to eliminate his father may have a fantasy of winning his mother from his father. Although he models his behavior after his father, he feels hostile toward him. Eventually his hostility subsides, especially if the parents do not get upset when their four-year-old son waves good-bye to his father saying, "You don't have to come back; I'll take care of Mommy" (Abrahamsen 1969, p. 127).

Finally, fantasy compensates for feelings of inadequacy. Fantasy can energize a child's desire to achieve on a level beyond his present possibility. William Steig's cartoons (Lidz 1968, p. 293) entitled "Dreams of Glory" represent how fantasies of being the hero of the game can compensate for pubescent feelings of inadequacy.

It is important for man to be able to "suspend temporarily disbelief," and fantasize in order to control an uncontrollable world. He is thus able to siphon off violent behavior, to maintain self esteem, to fulfill impossible wishes, and to prepare himself to cope with later realities.

Suddenly the corpse scrambled out of the box. The parson threw down the paper and shouted in disgust, "Oh, what's the good."

A Glory of the Moon

by Joyce Cary

The children were playing funerals. A small dark boy of about six was lying in an orange box at the edge of the leaf pit. His eyes were closed; his hands crossed on his breast. The box was too short for him and he had to draw up his knees, but he held them sideways in the effort to make himself as flat and dead as possible.

A square-shouldered girl of about ten, with a very round brown face, was holding one end of a skipping rope which was passed under the box. The other end was in the hand of the parson, a thin fair boy, the same height as the girl, with a singularly long thin nose and large gray eyes which seemed to bulge with impatience. A maid's apron, pinned to the shoulders of his jersey, made a surplice. He was holding a piece of folded newspaper from which he was pretending to read, using such striking phrases as he had picked up in church or from broadcasts. He intoned these words in High Church style with a peculiar quivering intensity, excited both by their quality and his own success as a parson. "We are like the grass. It is green in the morning but in the evening it is cut and withered—and worms will eat our body."

The little boy in the orange box fluttered his long lashes and blinked. A smaller, very fair little girl, standing beside the box as mourner, did not look at him but stared with round fascinated eyes at the speaker. Her lips moved now and then as she tried to repeat the words after him.

The parson, after a moment's pause for recollection, shrilled with the same dramatic emphasis: "The last enemy is death for he puts everything under his feet—come on, Mag."

This was to the brown-faced girl,

---

who had been attending with a nervous frown and kept her eyes fixed anxiously on the boy in the coffin.

"Come on, Mag," the parson repeated sharply, jerking his end of the rope. "Wake up."

The girl started and pulled on the rope. The head of the box was lifted slightly and together they dragged it down the ramp of the pit until it was resting among the dead leaves and yellowed grass cuttings, withered flowers and bracken which filled the hole.

The brown girl said to the little boy, "You all right, David?" whereupon the parson turned upon her and exclaimed angrily, "Do shut up, Mag."

"But I only—"

"He's dead—he's dead, I tell you—how can he talk to you? And he's absolutely all right if you'd only let him alone. He doesn't mind a bit."

At this David pressed his lips together more tightly. The parson said loudly: "In the midst of life we are in death."

Suddenly the corpse scrambled out of the box. The parson threw down the paper and shouted in disgust, "Oh, what's the good."

The little boy was climbing up the ramp. He thrust out his lower lip and glanced sideways at his elders with that look which, in small children, means "Kill me if you like—but I'm through."

"He's frightened," Mag said. "I said he would be."

"Oh, well, let's chuck it—I thought you wanted to do the thing properly. But, of course, if you're going to go fussing about the kids—"

"I'm not fussing about the kids. I only said that David—"

"All right, I've chucked it. It's chucked," and he threw his newspaper on the ground in all the rage of a frustrated artist. Mag, indignant, turned to the small girl. "Kate wouldn't mind, would you, Kate?" Kate answered in a high, dreamy voice as if her ideas were far away: "No, I wouldn't mind."

"Oh, let's chuck it, it's no good."

"You always say that." Mag was still indignant. "Here, I'll bury her myself if you don't. Get in Kate." The little girl at once lay down in the box, which she just fitted, crossed her hands on her breast and shut her eyes. Mag dived for the newspaper but the parson got it first. "All right, Kate—only don't forget you're dead. Absolutely dead."

The little girl's lips moved. She was accepting this condition, but in a whisper appropriate to someone in another state of existence.

The service continued. "Man that is born of woman has but a short time to live. He goes like a shadow—he is cut down like a flower . . ."

Kate silently repeated after him and her cheeks turned slowly pink.

The parson picked up a handful of leaves and scattered them over her. One dead aspen leaf, with its long stem attached, fell on her neck, but she lay like stone. "Dust to dust—ashes to ashes." He paused to examine the excellent corpse—then, in a triumph of realization, and more and more excited by the sound of his own voice, broke into full song. "There is a glo-ory of the sun, and a glo-ory of the stars, and a glo-o-ory of the moon."

The child's lips moved again to follow the words. Suddenly her face crinkled and shortened. She gave a sob. A line of moisture glistened between her closed lids.

The parson stopped and said furiously: "Dash it all, what's wrong now?"

"N-nothing."

"Oh, get up, for goodness' sake. I said you kids would ruin everything."

"But I don't want to get up. I like it."

"Then what are you crying for?"

The little girl looked wondering from the box. The withered leaves shook on the breast of her frock while she tried to catch her sobs.

"I don't know."

Discussion

Dramatic play is a vehicle that can unite children of varying ages in an enjoyable activity. Children act out any adult activities with which they are familiar. Because our culture tends to shield young children from the knowledge of death, they are much less likely to reenact the funeral ceremony than the wedding ceremony, which the young child is encouraged to understand.

The boy who plays the parson is the eldest child in the group. He seems to have had some experience with a funeral since he is able to capture the phrases and even the voice quality of a parson during a funeral service. He is proud of his performance and he enjoys the authenticity he is able to bring to the role. For him the play-acting is satisfying. He is immersed in his role, which does not evoke threatening images of death. His play-acting casts him in the part of an adult with power and knowledge.

The other children are obviously less pleased with their roles. David, who is about six, grows weary of lying still in the box. His attention span is short and he cannot sustain a fantasy that does not give him an active imaginative role to play. Spacemen and cowboys and Indians would be fantasy play appealing to him. Kate, who is about David's age, is willing to take his place as the corpse, but she soon begins to cry. She is unable to encompass the abstraction of death, but she does perceive the serious quality of the play and this frightens her.

Springboards for Inquiry

(1) Why do you think the children in this story recreated the ritual of the funeral?

(2) What kinds of adult roles do children like to recreate in fantasy play at pre-school level, during early school years, and in the middle school years?

(3) Is there a relationship between the amount of aggressiveness shown by children in real day-to-day situations and the amount of aggressiveness they display in fantasy play? *

* Robert R. Sears, "Relation of Fantasy Aggression to Interpersonal Aggression" *Child Development* 21, 1950, pp. 5–6.

(4) A high percentage of children have imaginery companions of some type. What are some of the possible needs an imaginary companion may fill? How should the adult deal with a child who involves an imaginery companion into conversations, meals, and other family functions?

References

Abrahamsen, David. *The Emotional Care of Your Child.* New York: Trident Press, 1969.

Breckenridge, Marian E., and Lee E. Vincent. *Child Development.* Philadelphia: W. B. Saunders Co., 1965.

Campbell, John D., and Marian Yarrow Radke. "Personal and Situational Variables in Adaptation to Change." *Journal of Social Issues* 14, no. 1 (1958): 29–46.

Cartledge, Connie J., and Edwin L. Krauser. "Training First-Grade Children in Creative Thinking under Quantitative and Qualitative Motivation." *Journal of Educational Psychology* 54 (1963): 295–99.

Datta, Lois, and Morris B. Parloff. "On the Relevance of Anatomy: Parent–Child Relationships and Early Scientific Creativity." *Proceedings of the 75th Annual Convention of the American Psychological Association* 2 (1967): 149–50.

Elkins, Deborah. "Some Factors Related to the Choice Status of Ninety Eighth-Grade Children in a School Society." *Genetic Psychology Monographs*, no. 58 (1958), pp. 207–72.

Fraiberg, Selma H. *The Magic Tears.* New York: Charles Scribner's Sons, 1959.

Getzels, Jacob W. "Creativity." *The Encyclopedia of Educational Research,* edited by Robert L. Ebel. 4th ed. London: Macmillan & Co., Ltd., 1969.

Getzels, Jacob W., and Mihaly Csikszentmihalyi. *Creative Thinking in Art Students: An Exploratory Study.* Cooperative Research Project no. E008. Chicago: University of Chicago Press, 1964.

Getzels, Jacob W., and Phillip W. Jackson. *Creativity and Intelligence: Explorations with Gifted Students.* New York: John Wiley and Sons, 1962.

Ghiselin, Brewster. *The Creative Process.* Berkeley, Calif.: University of California Press, 1952.

Green, Elise H. "Friendships and Quarrels among Preschool Children." *Child Development* 4 (1933): 237–52.

Guilford, J. Paul. "Creativity." *American Psychologist* 5 (1950): 444–45.

Guilford, J. Paul. "Traits of Creativity." In *Creativity and Its Cultivation: Interdisciplinary Symposium on Creativity,* edited by Harold H. Anderson. New York: Harper, 1959.

Jersild, Arthur T. *Child Psychology.* 5th ed. Englewood Cliffs, N. J.: Prentice-Hall, 1960.

Jung, Carl G. *Contributions to Analytical Psychology.* Translated by H. G. and Cary F. Baynes, London: Routledge & Kegan Paul Ltd. 1948, 1928.

Lidz, Theodore. *The Person.* New York: Basic Books, 1968.

McCandless, Boyd R. *Children: Behavior and Development.* 2d ed. New York: Holt, Rinehart, and Winston, 1967.

McCandless, Boyd R., and June M. Hoyt. "Sex, Ethnicity, and Play Preferences of Preschool Children." *Journal of Abnormal and Social Psychology* 62 (1961): 683–85.

McClelland, David C. "The Calculated Risk: An Aspect of Scientific Performance." In *Scientific Creativity: Its Recognition and Development,* edited by Calvin W. Taylor and Frank Barron. New York: John Wiley and Sons, 1963.

Maslow, Abraham H. "The Creative Attitude." *The Structurist* 3 (1963): 4–10.

Maslow, Abraham H. *Motivation and Personality.* New York: Harper & Row, 1954.

Nash, John. *Developmental Psychology.*

Englewood Cliffs, N. J.: Prentice-Hall, Inc., 1970.

Newell, Allen, J. C. Shaw, and Herbert A. Simon. "The Process of Creative Thinking." In *Contemporary Approaches to Creative Thinking*, eds. Howard E. Gruber, Glenn Terrell, Michael Wertheimer. New York: Atherton Press, 1962.

Piaget, Jean. *Play, Dreams, and Imitations in Childhood,* translated by C. Gattegno and F. M. Hodgson. New York: W. W. Norton & Co., 1951.

Reader, Natalie and Horace B. English, "Personality Factors in Adolescent Female Friendships." *Journal of Consulting Psychology* 11 (1947): 212–20.

Rogers, Dorothy. *Child Psychology.* Belmont, Calif.: Brooks/Cole Publishing Co., 1969.

Taylor, Calvin W. "The Identification of Creative Scientific Talent." *American Psychologist* 14 (1959): 100–102.

Torrance, Ellis P. *Guiding Creative Talent.* Englewood Cliffs, N. J.: Prentice-Hall, 1962.

Wallach, Michael A., and Nathan Kogan. *Modes of Thinking in Young Children: A Study of the Creativity–Intelligence Distinction.* New York: Holt, Rinehart, and Winston, 1965.

The Handicapped Child

All children need attention, understanding, and patience, but handicapped children need more of it more often. Whatever the handicap, the child must develop adequacy in stages comparable to those of the normal child. In his attempts to meet each step of development successfully, the handicapped child must make adjustments beyond those of the normal child. It is therefore not surprising to find that the stress he undergoes may make him more moody, irritable, and demanding than other children. This combination of normal needs and abnormal frustration explains the comment frequently made by parents and teachers of handicapped children: "He is like any other child, only more so."

The advent of a handicapped child into any family constellation draws the entire family into a relationship of heightened intrafamily dynamics. The child has trouble building a good self-concept because he questions his ability to function with competence and independence. The child's concern with adequacy extends to his parents. Parents typically experience grief and conflict regarding the etiology of the child's problem. In the case of sensory deficits or physical impairment or both, the early milestones of development such as sitting up, walking, and talking are delayed, detracting from the usual pride and delight parents enjoy. The delays further escalate early doubts and premonitions about the child's normalcy, and this anxiety is often protracted throughout the early years of childhood.

Siblings are also drawn into the circle of concern for the handicapped child. Frequently they feel ambivalent toward their handicapped brother or sister. They may feel delight in each small gain made by the disabled child, but the additional burdens of responsibility imposed by the handicapped child often lead to resentment.

The community and its view of handicapped persons is another dimension impinging upon the handicapped child and his family. Myths and stereotypes about the capacities and traits of handicapped people are difficult to dispel. The ability to predict the potential of any individual is immensely difficult, and predicting the potential of the handicapped child is even more complex. An enlightened community will provide open-ended educational and recreational experiences for all children. Given the opportunity, handicapped persons can sometimes perform on levels not usually considered appropriate for them—for example, swimming competitions are held for the blind, and national Olympic games are held for the retarded and for persons in wheelchairs.

The ability to come to terms with one's disability does not accompany the problem. This ability develops—in the affected child, in his parents, and in his brothers and sisters—when support and encouragement is provided. Once optimism is interjected into the atmosphere of the handicapped child, his response may encourage his family and peers to continue to have positive feelings toward him. We are all familiar with cases of exceptional individuals whose successful adjustment has permitted them to make outstanding contributions to society. For each of these notables there are other, less conspicuous individuals who have been able to face the difficult task of accepting themselves as they are and who have refused to be bound by their handicaps.

Physical Handicaps

The child who has a physical handicap is faced with two problems of adjustment, problems that normally occur in the development of any child and those that arise from his particular physical handicap. Two kinds of reactions to a child's physical handicap are evident. Roger Barker (1948) says: "By virtue of the fact of being different and requiring an unusual amount of help and attention he is inevitably a person of unusual importance." Parental reaction to children thus handicapped can result in either rejection of the child because of parental guilt or recompense to the child for his unfortunate condition. In either case, feelings of guilt and resentment may develop in parent and child.

Both repressed and expressed hostility and guilt may be the constellation of factors that trigger behavioral and personality problems. Charles Wenar (1962) reports that when comparing the integration ability* of three groups of children —nonhandicapped, moderately handicapped, and severely handicapped—there are significant differences between nonhandicapped children and handicapped children, with a corresponding decrease in integration ability as the severity of the handicap increases. Since the behavior of physically handicapped children is at variance with the integrative behavior of nonhandicapped children, it may be concluded that something in the experience of the handicapped retards his ability to handle the complexities of life. Inasmuch as all humans seek to minimize insecurity and anxiety, it appears likely that the decrease in integration

* In this case *integration ability* means the degree of conscious choice, planning, reasoning, and conceptualization a child brings to an unstructured task.

ability "represents a defensive maneuver to protect the child from anxiety" (Wenar 1962).

At Illinois Children's Hospital in Chicago, Rudolf Dreikurs (1948) reports that nearly half of a sample of 40 severely crippled children deliberately used their disabilities to appear inferior and more helpless than they really were. Case studies of these children indicate a poor self-concept in nearly all cases. Dreikurs points out that what is important in the life development of the child is not his hereditary and environmental endowment but what he does with what he has.

Handicapped children are partially isolated from their physical environment —that is, their interaction with the world around them is limited by the degree of their handicap. Particular types of handicaps also exert an influence on the quality and extent of the child's isolation from his environment. Bernard Friedlander (1971, p. 249) says, "Specialists in different disciplines may quibble as to which disability is more catastrophic for a child to endure. But there can be no question that any inhibition in the growth of language strikes very close to the central path of mental development. . . . It is difficult to overestimate the seriousness of the barriers to language learning when a child cannot effectively hear and organize the sounds of speech." The particular deprivation imposed by deafness was commented upon by Helen Keller (1929, pp. 81–82) who said that she felt "the impediment of deafness far more keenly than that of blindness."

Hilton McAndrew (1948) studied the variability and adaptability of blind and deaf children to tasks that required the child to adjust his level of aspiration after he became aware of his level of performance. (The ability to adapt is referred to as one's degree of rigidity.) The study concludes that blind and deaf children "develop less differentiated and more rigid personalities" than normal children.

William M. Cruikshank (1948) says: "Study after study reports greater personal maladjustment among handicapped groups of children than among other groups." It is evident that both cognitive and affective knowledge of this fact are indispensable to the role of the professional who works with children. The physically handicapped child is different. Until he is viewed as a unique individual with problems peculiar to his lifespace, it is likely that he will be blurred by the generalized picture even professionals have of the handicapped.*

---

* Spencer F. Brown's article "General Semantics and Physical Disability" (*Journal of Social Issues 4* [Fall 1948]: (pp. 95–100) neatly describes how even professional clinicians may not realize the importance of seeing patients for each one's particular problem and not attempting to place all disabled people under the rubric, "physically handicapped."

"Get out of here, you cripple!" This was a word never uttered in our household, except by my sister, who used it in passion to flog herself.

Castle in the Sand

by Irene Orgel

We always went to Ramsgate in the summer. The sea air did Eric ever so much good, brought the color into his cheeks and really made him look a healthy little boy. There is no place on earth like the southeast corner of Kent which juts out into the ocean showing its gaunt white cliffs like the bones of a skeleton picked clean. The east wind blows diagonally across the cliffs and blows the cornfields so that they are always writhing and in motion. It is the only part of England where the sky is swept clear and blue many days in the year; only a few shreds of cloud are visible like blown cobwebs in the sky, and they very soon scurry off the scene. Below the cliff is the shadowy harbor full of old ships which toss beside the cobblestoned quays. Eric loved the boats.

We used to stay at Mrs. Banbury's boardinghouse, which was called "Sea-View." Our perennial joke was that the only way to see the sea from "Sea-View" was to fall out of the best bedroom window, although this would have been extremely difficult, for a great mahogany dressing table was placed, in the fashion of the times, directly in front of the window, and it was a massive piece of furniture to move for a glimpse of the sea. There were nine of us children, as well as several grownups including two nannies. I ought to explain that though I am poor Eric's aunt, there is only five years' difference in age between us. I grew up like a weed during my early teens and outgrew my strength, so that the doctor forbade me violent exercise, and I was more often with Eric than with the other children at their games. I can honestly claim that I knew Eric at this period bet-

---

Reprinted from *Odd Tales of Irene Orgel*. New York: The Eakins Press, 1967, by permission of the author.

ter than anybody else in the world. Of course he was an amazing child, and he used to read a great deal, but how much I did not know until I read the recent biographies of him.

My sister, Eric's mother, was a proud beauty and extremely vain. There was nothing trivial or laughable about her vanity; it was an integral part of her character, an extension of her aesthetic sense. She was passionately fond of all beauty, including her own, and she was unhappy in the presence of anything imperfectly formed. She hated Eric deeply, and this hatred was really anger against herself for producing such a misformed child. She tried hard to forget his existence, and Eric, in the manner of so many children ignored by their parents, craved the love of that parent all the more. He actually worshipped her as something to be seen from afar, unapproachable and very precious. Sometimes when she was out, he would enter her bedroom and approach her dressing table as if it were an altar, hoist himself up on her quilted stool, and examine himself in the triptych of mirrors. Then he would unstopper the crystal jars of perfume and raise each reverently to his nostrils, and take her swansdown powder puffs and feel their softness against his cheeks.

Once when I entered the room with my sister we found him sitting in full guilt before the mirror. With rouge on his lips and cheeks, he looked like some freshly painted cherub in a picture of the Italian school. My sister flew upon him with a shriek:

"What are you doing here, you naughty, dirty, crooked little boy?"

Eric made haste to scramble down from off the stool. He was, at that time, wearing heavy braces on his legs, and he tore the yellow taffeta of my sister's upholstered furniture.

"Get out of here, you cripple!" This was a word never uttered in our household, except by my sister, who used it in passion to flog herself. Beneath her watchful eye, Eric crossed the room, his steps ploughing deeply into the white pile of the bearskin rug on the floor.

"And pick your feet up!" groaned my sister as if she were about to expire.

I quickly took Eric by the hand and led him upstairs to his own cold little room, where I poured some water from a golden-lipped ewer into a china bowl which had violets painted on the inside. I plunged his hands into the cold water, and with a soapy brush I began to scrub at his small rosy-tipped fingers with their black-lined nails. After this I sternly commanded him to wash his face, which he accomplished with a great deal of giggling and spluttering and blowing of soap bubbles. He seemed to regard the whole episode as a joke, and he kept looking at me mischievously from behind the towel and going off into gales of laughter.

Meanwhile my sister was lying prostrate across her bed, with a bottle of smelling salts pressed to her nostrils, sobbing about "the cross she had to bear." I am reminded of this incident particularly because you have made a point of asking me, for the purpose of the biography which you are writing, whether Eric displayed as a child any of his famous temper. I must report, on the contrary, that he had a remarkably unruffled good nature. I can only recall seeing him lose his temper on one occasion, and that occasion I will recount to you as faithfully as I can remember.

We were staying at Ramsgate the summer when Eric was nine years old. He followed us down the steep cobblestoned path from the cliff to the beach. The grownups seated themselves in the striped deck chairs, and the children played at their feet on the sand until they were all completely bored and, it being a sufficient time after breakfast, a nurse took them off to the bathing machine to undress and go into the sea. I was feeling completely grown up that morning, as my father had actually paid for a deck chair for me. When the man who collected the money for the chairs came round, I was ready to slip off my seat and join the children who were sitting in the sand. But my father took out twopence and paid for me, so I remained among the adults feeling very grown up although my hair was not up, and knitting quite sedately after the noisy children had been taken to the bathing machines.

Eric sat on the sand, somewhat apart from our family group, building a wonderful castle. He had staggered several times to the water's edge to bring water in pails to fill in the deep moat he had dug around his castle. With his spade he had dug a channel to the sea so that the tide fed his moat, floating in with white foam and seaweed. He had constructed his castle with flying buttresses which he had read about in Ruskin's *Seven Lamps of Architecture.* He made battlements, pinching the sand into little squares with his fingers. He wetted his hand in the pail and patted the sand to a hard, condensed consistency. Then he sprinkled silver sand on the gravel of the courtyard. He had gathered shells which he arranged elaborately in a mosaic of design. He was rapt, intent, completely at peace. He was a craftsman working at his work, like one of the great anonymous builders of a medieval cathedral.

A shadow fell across his work in the sunny sand. A young man and his girl, taking a stroll along the beach, had paused to look at Eric's work. Eric's nurse had dressed him that day in a sailor suit and had placed on his curls a little round hat which had the words "H.M.S. INDOMITABLE" embroidered on it in gold. He had taken off his sailor hat and thrown it on the ground beside him together with his crutch. The young man wore a straw boater, and the lady was dressed in white organdy. The sun filtered through her lace hat and speckled her fair face. The bottom of her dress scratched the sand and left a queer little pattern on the bank of Eric's moat. When she moved Eric saw that she had little white kid boots on her feet.

Eric, pleased with the attention he was receiving, worked all the harder, bending over his work with a flushed, contented face. The lady called the attention of her friend to the cunning little battlements which Eric had built round the top of his castle. She pointed to them with the end of her white lace parasol, and one of the little squares of sand fell down. Contrite, she stooped to pinch the sand together and put it right again. She smelt of lavender, and Eric considered her the most beautiful lady he had ever seen. When she apologized, he assured her that it did not matter. Blushing, he repaired the ruined parapet.

"What a fine castle!" said the lady in her beautiful voice. "And aren't you sorry that the tide will soon come in and wash it all away?"

Eric looked down one moment at the sand, and he remembered a line of poetry. After judging the faces of his audience, he said shyly:

One day I wrote her name upon the strand,
But came the waves and washed it all away:
Again I wrote it with a second hand,
But came the tide, and made my pains his prey.

"Spenser, by Jove!" exclaimed the young man, eager to put his cap on the quotation. "Would you believe it, Clarissa? He's quoting from the 'Amoretti.' "

Clarissa looked in admiration first at her young man and then at the child on the sand.

"How old are you, little boy?"

"Nine'm."

"You're very advanced in school, no doubt?"

"I don't go to school."

"What a shame!" whispered the lady, looking up at her young man, her face radiant with pity.

Eric dug ferociously with his spade and looked sullen. He resolved then finally and irrevocably never to say poetry out loud to anybody again. The same thing always happened. First they asked how old you were, then what class you were in at school. Then they said what a pity.

He looked up and saw that other people had stopped beside the young couple. He had quite an audience, so he set to work harder than ever before. He was the artist performing before his public. He was the creator, and everybody watched him thunderstruck. He made a rock garden of shells on one of the banks of the moat, and he etched carefully with a matchstick a coat of arms above one of the entrances. He trailed some seaweed like ivy up the walls of the twin turrets. Whenever he looked up, he saw interested faces looking down upon him. He unconsciously began to act a little, parting his mouth with his tongue out, as if the work were causing him a great deal of exertion. Beside him on the sand were his spade and other tools, and a little further off was his crutch. His round sailor hat was upside down on the sand.

Cautiously he tinkered with the top battlements and gave a final pat with his hands to the stout walls of the castle. Then, after surveying his audience with a pause for suspense, he finally reached into his pocket, like a conjurer pulling out a white rabbit, and produced a small Union Jack. This he suddenly hoisted on the roof of his edifice, and looked up happily for the applause of his audience.

There was quite a bit of clapping and some cries of "Bravo!" Then suddenly there came a rain of pennies falling into his upturned hat. For a moment Eric looked up, not understanding. Then it suddenly occurred to him that instead of seeing him as a creator, a toiler after beauty, they saw him as a beggar with a crutch and a begging hat. Impatiently he snatched his hat, spilling the coins on the sand; then savagely he began to destroy his castle, the proud creation of his hands. When the crowd murmured against this wanton destruction, he took up handfuls of sand and began throwing it into their faces, screaming. Then he collapsed on top of his ruined battlements, convulsed with sobs and howling piteously.

Eric's nurse was only a short way off. She was sitting heavily in a sagging deck chair, crocheting a tray cloth. When she heard his screams she raised herself laboriously out of her chair and bustled along the beach. Elbowing her way through the crowd, she dragged the hysterical red-faced child to his feet, while a chorus of voices denounced him.

"Eric, say you're sorry!" said the nurse briskly. "Say you're sorry, this very minute!"

I picked up his bucket and spade and some of the shells I knew he wanted to save, and I shook the sand out of his hat marked "H.M.S. INDOMITABLE." Eric was in disgrace that afternoon, and in the whole family I was his only friend. I stayed indoors in Mrs. Banbury's boardinghouse that afternoon with Eric, who was feeling out of sorts. We had a long conversation about the people who lived on the moon, and whether the Martians were going to conquer the earth. By tea time he was feeling quite all right again, and he spread jam thickly on his cake and ate it.

Discussion

It is usual for a parent of a handicapped child to experience guilt as well as pain as a result of bringing a less-than-perfect child into the world. Mothers especially often blame themselves for the child's handicapping condition, viewing the child as a reflection of imperfection in themselves. These feelings are usually strongest immediately after the child's birth or in his earliest years. If the parents' adjustment to a child's disability is a healthy one, however, guilt and anxieties will be replaced by a growing interest in the child's progress, and the parents will take delight in each advance the child makes to overcome his handicap.

Eric's mother, whose vanity is an integral part of her character, has never made the step toward a mature acceptance of and adjustment to her child's orthopedic problem. Instead, self-pity and impatience with her child has marked her life. She uses the word *cripple* to hurt and shame herself and Eric. Despite the poor relationship between Eric and his mother, Eric appears to be a talented, buoyant, and imaginative personality. The story provides examples of several of Eric's talents.

Eric evidently does not attend ordinary school because of his handicap. He is probably individually tutored and appears to be a very bright and creative student. His personality is outgoing and he enjoys attention for his accomplishments. However, he does harbor great sensitivity to his handicap and is readily provoked. He is always prepared for the reaction of pity when grown-ups ask him the standard questions put to children—how old are you and what school do you go to? Responding to these associated questions is always a painful experience for Eric and one he prefers to avoid if possible.

The incident at the beach catches Eric with his defenses down. He is enjoying his creation and reveling in the attention he is receiving from the crowd. He is caught by surprise and is humiliated and defeated, therefore, when the crowd that has gathered responds to him as a cripple rather than as a creator and artist.

Springboards for Inquiry

(1) The psychological implications of an obvious physical handicap can be more devastating than the handicap itself. What are the pros and cons of special school placement or private tutoring as opposed to regular classroom participation for a child like Eric? Which is more psychologically wounding?

(2) Why are some normal children disturbed by the sight of a handicapped child, particularly one who is wearing a brace, using a crutch, or sitting in a wheelchair?

(3) What subject areas should organizations for parents of handicapped children emphasize? What are some of the obvious pitfalls for leaders of these groups?

(4) If you have been friendly with a physically handicapped person, try to analyze to what extent, if any, the handicap entered the relationship.

Mental Retardation

Mental retardation is a difficult term to define because the etiology and the pathological processes of retardation are many and varied. Generally, "mental retardation refers to subaverage general intellectual functioning which originates during the developmental period and is associated with impairment in adaptive behavior" (Flanigan, Baker, La Follette 1970).

Three categories are generally used to describe mental retardation (Dybwad 1964): persons who are mildly retarded or educable, those who are moderately retarded or trainable, and those who are severely retarded or who require custodial care. In educational terms the three categories refer to designations that are made on the basis of an individually administered intelligence test such as the Stanford-Binet or the Wechsler Intelligence Scale for Children. The mildly retarded individual will achieve an IQ score of 50 to 75. The child in this category usually has enough potential to acquire skills in basic school subjects. It is estimated that 75 percent of the retarded are in the mildly retarded category. The moderately retarded child will achieve an IQ score of 30 to 50. Children in this category have the capacity to communicate verbally and to develop habits of self-care. They can become economically productive in a sheltered workshop but cannot become literate or enter the competitive job market. The severely mentally retarded person will achieve an IQ score below 30, is unable to acquire self-help skills, and therefore needs permanent care.

In the discussion of intellectual development we pointed out the difficulty of determining the relative importance of heredity and environmental factors (personal, social, and cultural factors) on the development of intellect. Obviously the concept of mental deficiency is enmeshed in the same controversy. Specialists in the field of mental retardation are particularly alert to the possibility of pseudo-retardation, a term applied to the constellation of symptoms that resembles mild mental retardation when, in fact, children are showing the results of cultural deprivation or deviance, emotional disturbance, or a neurological disorder (Doll 1966). Researchers are seeking refined methods to more accurately diagnose mental subnormality in order to distinguish those cases in which early cultural deprivation, lack of sensory stimulation, neurological factors, or other phenomena cause children to simulate the behavior and intellectual capacity of the retarded.

The classification *mild mental retardation* used in schools and clinics provokes dissatisfaction because the category is frequently used as a catchall. Too often a child receives this label, which indicates functional inadequacy, when in reality the evaluative instrument or the educational system or both are at fault. The Stanford-Binet Intelligence Scale, the instrument primarily used for screening children for retardation, is a test that was standardized using white children who came from homes of slightly higher socioeconomic status than the general population.* The built-in bias makes it an undesirable test for use with children from homes of low socioeconomic status, children of Mexican-American or Afro-American heritage, or with any group whose language or customs vary greatly from the population used for test standardization.

Joseph Wortis and some colleagues (1970, p. 6) castigate the educational system when educational inflexibility contributes to retardation in children. They state: "The vast majority of these educationally backward children are capable of normal development if provided with appropriate educational experience. . . . The frequent failure of such children in conventional programs should be interpreted less in terms of their own inadequacy and more often in terms of the inadequacy of the school experience."

Antenatal or genetically determined factors frequently contribute to the development of severe mental retardation. One result of worldwide research to investigate and ameliorate conditions of genetic origin is a new vaccine to prevent German measles, a prenatal infection that may cause damage to the fetus. Advances in techniques to detect defects caused by blood group incompatibilities or hereditary biochemical defects such as phenylketonuria† have now been routinely adopted as part of the examination of newborns. Genetic counseling is also available to couples who may suspect that their genetic make-up could increase the possibility of having a child with mental deficiency.

In all cases of mental retardation early diagnosis and amelioration of the handicap are the goals. In order to facilitate these goals community diagnostic and counseling centers are being established to perform services that were formerly available only in large state institutions for the retarded and emotionally disturbed, which were usually located in outlying areas. The community center

---

* Lewis M. Terman and Maud A. Merrill, *Stanford Binet Intelligence Scale Manual for the Third Revision Form L-M* (Boston: Houghton Mifflin Co., 1960), p. 9.

† Phenylketonuria is an inherited defect in the metabolism of the amino acid phenylalanine that can cause severe mental deficiency if not treated soon after birth.

employs a multidisciplinary approach to the problem of mental retardation and is staffed by a team of specialists. A pediatrician examines the child physically, a social worker gathers data on his early developmental history and present home environment, a psychologist examines the child's intellectual and adaptive functioning, a psychiatrist evaluates his emotional status, a neurologist examines the central and peripheral nervous system, specialists in the field of speech and hearing examine these systems, and a representative from the field of education discusses appropriate school placement.*

The problems of mental retardation hold challenges for the many specialists concerned with its effects. In the coming years early diagnosis of mental retardation will be particularly important in the light of biomedical and behavioral science discoveries that make some conditions preventable.

---

* This team approach is described in relation to the development of a traveling clinic in Southern California in Richard Koch's "Diagnosis in Infancy and Early Childhood," in *Prevention and Treatment of Mental Retardation*, ed. Irving Phillips (New York: Basic Books, Inc., 1966).

Mrs. Whipple almost screamed out at the neighbor. "He does know what He's doing! He's as able as any other child! Come down out of there, you!"

He *by Katherine Anne Porter*

Life was very hard for the Whipples. It was hard to feed all the hungry mouths, it was hard to keep the children in flannels during the winter, short as it was: "God knows what would become of us if we lived north," they would say: keeping them decently clean was hard. "It looks like our luck won't never let up on us," said Mr. Whipple, but Mrs. Whipple was all for taking what was sent and calling it good, anyhow when the neighbors were in earshot. "Don't ever let a soul hear us complain," she kept saying to her husband. She couldn't stand to be pitied. "No, not if it comes to it that we have to live in a wagon and pick cotton around the country," she said, "nobody's going to get a chance to look down on us."

Mrs. Whipple loved her second son, the simple-minded one, better than she loved the other two children put together. She was forever saying so, and when she talked with certain of her neighbors, she would even throw in her husband and her mother for good measure.

"You needn't keep on saying it around," said Mr. Whipple, "you'll make people think nobody else has any feelings about Him but you."

"It's natural for a mother," Mrs. Whipple would remind him. "You know yourself it's more natural for a mother to be that way. People don't expect so much of fathers, some way."

This didn't keep the neighbors from talking plainly among themselves. "A Lord's pure mercy if He should die," they said. "It's the sins of the fathers," they agreed among themselves. "There's bad blood and bad doings somewhere, you can bet on that." This behind the Whipples'

---

backs. To their faces everybody said, "He's not so bad off. He'll be all right yet. Look how He grows!"

Mrs. Whipple hated to talk about it, she tried to keep her mind off it, but every time anybody set foot in the house, the subject always came up, and she had to talk about Him first, before she could get on to anything else. It seemed to ease her mind. "I wouldn't have anything happen to Him for all the world, but it just looks like I can't keep Him out of mischief. He's so strong and active, He's always into everything; He was like that since He could walk. It's actually funny sometimes, the way He can do anything; it's laughable to see Him up to His tricks. Emly has more accidents; I'm forever tying up her bruises, and Adna can't fall a foot without cracking a bone. But He can do anything and not get a scratch. The preacher said such a nice thing once when he was here. He said, and I'll remember it to my dying day, 'The innocent walk with God—that's why He don't get hurt.' " Whenever Mrs. Whipple repeated these words, she always felt a warm pool spread in her breast, and the tears would fill her eyes, and then she could talk about something else.

He did grow and He never got hurt. A plank blew off the chicken house and struck Him on the head and He never seemed to know it. He had learned a few words, and after this He forgot them. He didn't whine for food as the other children did, but waited until it was given Him; He ate squatting in the corner, smacking and mumbling. Rolls of fat covered Him like an overcoat, and He could carry twice as much wood and water as Adna. Emly had a cold in the head most of the time—"she takes that after me," said Mrs. Whipple—so in bad weather they gave her the extra blanket off His cot. He never seemed to mind the cold.

Just the same, Mrs. Whipple's life was a torment for fear something might happen to Him. He climbed the peach trees much better than Adna and went skittering along the branches like a monkey, just a regular monkey. "Oh, Mrs. Whipple, you hadn't ought to let Him do that. He'll lose His balance sometime. He can't rightly know what He's doing."

Mrs. Whipple almost screamed out at the neighbor. "He does know what He's doing! He's as able as any other child! Come down out of there, you!" When He finally reached the ground she could hardly keep her hands off Him for acting like that before people, a grin all over His face and her worried sick about Him all the time.

"It's the neighbors," said Mrs. Whipple to her husband. "Oh, I do mortally wish they would keep out of our business. I can't afford to let Him do anything for fear they'll come nosing around about it. Look at the bees, now. Adna can't handle them, they sting him up so; I haven't got time to do everything, and now I don't dare let Him. But if He gets a sting He don't really mind."

"It's just because He ain't got sense enough to be scared of anything," said Mr. Whipple.

"You ought to be ashamed of yourself," said Mrs. Whipple, "talking that way about your own child. Who's to take up for Him if we don't, I'd like to know? He sees a lot that goes on, He listens to things all the time. And anything I tell Him to do He does it. Don't never let anybody hear you say such things. They'd think you favored the other children over Him."

"Well, now I don't, and you know it, and what's the use of getting all worked up about it? You always think the worst of everything. Just let Him alone, He'll get along somehow. He gets plenty to eat and wear, don't He?" Mr. Whipple suddenly felt tired out. "Anyhow, it can't be helped now."

Mrs. Whipple felt tired too, she complained in a tired voice. "What's done can't never be undone, I know that good as anybody; but He's my child, and I'm not going to have people say anything. I get sick of people coming around saying things all the time."

In the early fall Mrs. Whipple got a letter from her brother saying he and his wife and two children were coming over for a little visit next Sunday week. "Put the big pot in the little one," he wrote at the end. Mrs. Whipple read this part out loud twice, she was so pleased. Her brother was a great one for saying funny things. "We'll just show him that's no joke," she said, "we'll just butcher one of the suckling pigs."

"It's a waste and I don't hold with waste the way we are now," said Mr. Whipple. "That pig'll be worth money by Christmas."

"It's a shame and a pity we can't have a decent meal's vittles once in a while when my own family comes to see us," said Mr. Whipple. "I'd hate for his wife to go back and say there wasn't a thing in the house to eat. My God, it's better than buying up a great chance of meat in town. There's where you'd spend the money!"

"All right, do it yourself then," said Mr. Whipple. "Christamighty, no wonder we can't get ahead!"

The question was how to get the little pig away from his ma, a great fighter, worse than a Jersey cow. Adna wouldn't try it: "That sow'd rip my insides out all over the pen." "All right, old fraidy," said Mrs. Whipple, *"He's* not scared. Watch *Him* do it." And she laughed as though it was all a good joke and gave Him a little push towards the pen. He sneaked up and snatched the pig right away from the teat and galloped back and was over the fence with the sow raging at His heels. The little black squirming thing was screeching like a baby in a tantrum, stiffening its back and stretching its mouth to the ears. Mrs. Whipple took the pig with her face stiff and sliced its throat with one stroke. When He saw the blood He gave a great jolting breath and ran away. "But He'll forget and eat plenty, just the same," thought Mrs. Whipple. Whenever she was thinking, her lips moved making words. "He'd eat it all if I didn't stop Him. He'd eat up every mouthful from the other two if I'd let Him."

She felt badly about it. He was ten years old now and a third again as large as Adna, who was going on fourteen. "It's a shame, a shame," she kept saying under her breath, "and Adna with so much brains!"

She kept on feeling badly about all sorts of things. In the first place it was the man's work to butcher; the sight of the pig scraped pink and naked made her sick. He was too fat and soft and pitiful-looking. It was simply a shame the way things had to happen. By the time she had finished it up, she almost wished her brother would stay at home.

Early Sunday morning Mrs. Whipple dropped everything to get Him all cleaned up. In an hour He was dirty again, with crawling under fences after a possum, and straddling along the rafters of the barn looking for eggs in the hayloft. "My Lord, look at you now after all my trying! And here's Adna and Emly staying so quiet. I get tired trying to keep you decent. Get off that shirt and put on another, people will say I don't half dress you!" And she boxed Him on the ears, hard. He blinked and blinked and rubbed His head, and His face hurt Mrs. Whipple's feelings. Her knees began to tremble, she had to sit down while she buttoned His shirt. "I'm just all gone before the day starts."

The brother came with his plump healthy wife and two great roaring hungry boys. They had a grand dinner, with the pig roasted to a crackling in the middle of the table, full of dressing, a pickled peach in his mouth and plenty of gravy for the sweet potatoes.

"This looks like prosperity all right," said the brother; "you're going to have to roll me home like I was a barrel when I'm done."

Everybody laughed out loud; it was fine to hear them laughing all at once around the table. Mrs. Whipple felt warm and good about it. "Oh, we've got six more of these; I say it's as little as we can do when you come to see us so seldom."

He wouldn't come into the dining room, and Mrs. Whipple passed it off very well. "He's timider than my other two," she said, "He'll just have to get used to you. There isn't everybody He'll make up with, you know how it is with some children, even cousins." Nobody said anything out of the way.

"Just like my Alfy here," said the brother's wife. "I sometimes got to lick him to make him shake hands with his own grand-mammy."

So that was over, and Mrs. Whipple loaded up a big plate for Him first, before everybody. "I always say He ain't to be slighted, no matter who else goes without," she said, and carried it to Him herself.

"He can chin Himself on the top of the door," said Emly, helping along.

"That's fine, He's getting along fine," said the brother.

They went away after supper. Mrs. Whipple rounded up the dishes, and sent the children to bed and sat down and unlaced her shoes. "You see?" she said to Mr. Whipple. "That's the way my whole family is. Nice and considerate about everything. No out-of-the-way remarks—they *have* got refinement. I get awfully sick of people's remarks. Wasn't that pig good?"

Mr. Whipple said, "Yes, we're out three hundred pounds of pork, that's all. It's easy to be polite when you come to eat. Who knows what they had in their minds all along?"

"Yes, that's like you," said Mrs. Whipple. "I don't expect anything else from you. You'll be telling me next that my own brother will be saying around that we made Him eat in the kitchen! Oh, my God!" She rocked her head in her hands, a hard pain started in the very middle of her forehead. "Now it's all spoiled, and everything was so nice and easy. All right, you don't like them and you never did—all right, they'll not come here again soon, never you mind! But they *can't* say He wasn't dressed every lick as good as Adna—oh, honest, sometimes I wish I was dead!"

"I wish you'd let up," said Mr. Whipple. "It's bad enough as it is."

It was a hard winter. It seemed to Mrs. Whipple that they hadn't ever known anything but hard times, and now to cap it all a winter like this. The crops were about half of what they had a right to expect; after the cotton was in it didn't do much more than cover the grocery bill. They swapped off one of the plow horses, and got cheated, for the new one died of the heaves. Mrs. Whipple kept thinking all the time it was terrible to have a man you couldn't depend on not to get cheated. They cut down on everything, but Mrs. Whipple kept saying there are things you can't cut down on, and they cost money. It took a lot of warm clothes for Adna and Emly, who walked four miles to school during the three-months session. "He sets around the fires a lot, He won't need so much," said Mr. Whipple. "That's so," said Mrs. Whipple, "and when He does the outdoor chores He can wear your tarpaullion coat. I can't do no better, that's all."

In February He was taken sick, and lay curled up under His blanket looking very blue in the face and acting as if He would choke. Mr. and Mrs. Whipple did everything they could for Him for two days, and then they were scared and sent for the doctor. The doctor told them they must keep Him warm and give Him plenty of milk and eggs. "He isn't as stout as He looks, I'm afraid," said the doctor. "You've got to watch them when they're like that. You must put more cover onto Him, too."

"I just took off His big blanket to wash," said Mrs. Whipple, ashamed. "I can't stand dirt."

"Well, you'd better put it back on the minute it's dry," said the doctor, "or He'll have pneumonia."

Mr. and Mrs. Whipple took a blanket off their own bed and put His cot in by the fire. "They can't say we didn't do everything for Him," she said, "even to sleeping cold ourselves on His account."

When the winter broke he seemed to be well again, but He walked as if His feet hurt Him. He was able to run a cotton planter during the season.

"I got it all fixed up with Jim Ferguson about breeding the cow next time," said Mr. Whipple. "I'll pasture the bull this summer and give Jim some fodder in the fall. That's better than paying out money when you haven't got it."

"I hope you didn't say such a thing before Jim Ferguson," said Mrs. Whipple. "You oughtn't to let him know we're so down as all that."

"Godamighty, that ain't saying we're down. A man is got to look ahead sometimes. *He* can lead the bull over today. I need Adna on the place."

At first Mrs. Whipple felt easy in her mind about sending Him for the bull. Adna was too jumpy and couldn't be trusted. You've got to be steady around animals. After He was gone she started thinking, and after a while she could hardly bear it any longer. She stood in the lane and watched for Him. It was nearly three miles to go and a hot day, but He oughtn't to be so long about it. She shaded her eyes and stared until colored bubbles floated in her eyeballs. It was just like everything else in life, she must always worry and never know a moment's peace about anything. After a long time she saw Him turn into the side lane, limping. He came on very slowly, leading the big hulk of an animal by a ring in the nose, twirling a little stick in His hand, never looking back or sideways, but coming on like a sleepwalker with His eyes half shut.

Mrs. Whipple was scared sick of bulls; she had heard awful stories about how they followed on quietly enough, and then suddenly pitched on with a bellow and pawed and gored a body to pieces. Any second now that black monster would come down on Him, my God, He'd never have sense enough to run.

She mustn't make a sound nor a move; she mustn't get the bull started. The bull heaved his head aside and horned the air at a fly. Her voice burst out of her in a shriek, and she screamed at Him to come on, for God's sake. He didn't seem to hear her clamor, but kept on twirling His switch and limping on, and the bull lumbered along behind him as gently as a calf. Mrs. Whipple stopped calling and ran towards the house, praying under her breath: "Lord don't let anything happen to Him. Lord, you *know* people will say we oughtn't to have sent Him. You *know* they'll say we didn't take care of Him. Oh, get Him home, safe home, safe home, and I'll look out for Him better! Amen."

She watched from the window while He led the beast in, and tied him up in the barn. It was no use trying to keep up, Mrs. Whipple couldn't bear another thing. She sat down and rocked and cried with her apron over her head.

From year to year the Whipples were growing poorer and poorer. The place just seemed to run down of itself, no matter how hard they worked. "We're losing our hold," said Mrs. Whipple. "Why can't we do like other people and watch for our best chances? They'll be calling us poor white trash next."

"When I get to be sixteen I'm going to leave," said Adna. "I'm going to get a job in Powell's grocery store. There's money in that. No more farm for me."

"I'm going to be a schoolteacher," said Emly. "But I've got to finish the eighth grade, anyhow. Then I can live in town. I don't see any chances here."

"Emly takes after my family," said Mrs. Whipple. "Ambitious every last one of them, and they don't take second place for anybody."

When fall came Emly got a chance to wait on table in the railroad eating-house in the town near by, and it seemed such a shame not to take it when the wages were good and she could get her food too, that Mrs. Whipple decided to let her take it, and not bother with school until the next session. "You've got plenty of time," she said. "You're young and smart as a whip."

With Adna gone too, Mr. Whipple tried to run the farm with just Him to help. He seemed to get along fine, doing His work and part of Adna's without noticing it. They did well enough until Christmas time, when one morning He slipped on the ice coming up from the barn. Instead of getting up He thrashed round and round, and when Mr. Whipple got to Him, He was having some sort of fit.

They brought Him inside and tried to make Him sit up, but He blubbered and rolled, so they put Him to bed and Mr. Whipple rode to town for the doctor. All the way there and back he worried about where the money was to come from: it sure did look like he had about all the troubles he could carry.

From then on He stayed in bed. His legs swelled up double their size, and the fits kept coming back. After four months, the doctor said, "It's no use, I think you'd better put Him in the County Home for treatment right away. I'll see about it for you. He'll have good care there and be off your hands."

"We don't begrudge Him any care, and I won't let Him out of my sight," said Mrs. Whipple. "I won't have it said I sent my sick child off among strangers."

"I know how you feel," said the doctor. "You can't tell me anything about that, Mrs. Whipple. I've got a boy of my own. But you'd better listen to me. I can't do anything more for Him, that's the truth."

Mr. and Mrs. Whipple talked it over a long time that night after they went to bed. "It's just charity," said Mrs. Whipple, "that's what we've come to, charity! I certainly never looked for this."

"We pay taxes to help support the place just like everybody else," said Mr. Whipple, "and I don't call that taking charity. I think it would be fine to have Him where He'd get the best of everything . . . and besides, I can't keep up with these doctor bills any longer."

"Maybe that's why the doctor wants us to send Him—he's scared he won't get his money," said Mrs. Whipple.

"Don't talk like that," said Mr. Whipple, feeling pretty sick, "or we won't be able to send Him."

"Oh, but we won't keep Him there long," said Mrs. Whipple. "Soon's he's better, we'll bring Him right back home."

"The doctor has told you and told you time and again He can't ever get better, and you might as well stop talking," said Mr. Whipple.

"Doctors don't know everything," said Mrs. Whipple, feeling almost happy. "But anyhow, in the summer Emly can come home for a vacation, and Adna can get down for Sundays: we'll all work together and get on our feet again, and the children will feel they've got a place to come to."

All at once she saw it full summer again, with the garden going fine, and new white roller shades up all over the house, and Adna and Emly home, so full of life, all of them happy together. Oh, it could happen, things would ease up on them.

They didn't talk before Him much, but they never knew just how much He understood. Finally the doctor set the day and a neighbor who owned a double-seated carryall offered to drive them over. The hospital would have sent an ambulance, but Mrs. Whipple couldn't stand to see Him going away looking so sick as all that. They wrapped Him in blankets, and the neighbor and Mr. Whipple lifted Him into the back seat of the carryall beside Mrs. Whipple, who had on her black shirtwaist. She couldn't stand to go looking like charity.

"You'll be all right, I guess I'll stay behind," said Mr. Whipple. "It don't look like everybody ought to leave the place at once."

"Besides, it ain't as if He was going to stay forever," said Mrs. Whipple to the neighbor. "This is only for a little while."

They started away, Mrs. Whipple holding to the edges of the blankets to keep Him from sagging sideways. He sat there blinking and blinking. He worked His hands out and began rubbing His nose with His knuckles, and then with the end of the blanket. Mrs. Whipple couldn't believe what she saw; He was scrubbing away big tears that rolled out of the corners of His eyes. He sniveled and made a gulping noise. Mrs. Whipple kept saying, "Oh, honey, you don't feel so bad, do you? You don't feel so bad, do you?" for He seemed to be accusing her of something. Maybe He remembered that time she boxed His ears, maybe He had been scared that day with the bull, maybe He had slept cold and couldn't tell her about it; maybe He knew they were sending Him away for good and all because they were too poor to keep Him. Whatever it was, Mrs. Whipple couldn't bear to think of it. She began to cry, frightfully, and wrapped her arms tight around Him. His head rolled on her shoulder: she had loved Him as much as she possibly could, there were Adna and Emly who had to be thought of too, there was nothing she could do to make up to Him for His life. Oh, what a mortal pity He was ever born.

They came in sight of the hospital, with the neighbor driving very fast, not daring to look behind him.

Discussion

The Whipples are a family with so many problems that the addition of a mentally retarded child seems more than they can handle. The author, Katherine Ann Porter, accentuates the anguish the boy's presence causes by not assigning a name to him. The boy is always referred to as "He," thereby emphasizing the magnitude of concern he poses. The overriding problem in this family is probably Mrs. Whipple's guilt regarding this boy. Her own anxiety, augmented by the anxiety she experiences concerning other people's view of her, almost immobilizes her. Mrs. Whipple's anxiety also creates unnecessary problems between Mr. Whipple and herself. The Whipples' lives are bleak and marginal, and Mrs. Whipple exacerbates their problems with self-pity because of their retarded son.

This story illustrates many of the specific concerns that arise in families with retarded children. Even affluent and educated families find it difficult to manage these concerns without help and support. Counseling for families of retarded children is now available in many regional centers. Certainly Mrs. Whipple would profit from some type of counseling. Even attending a mothers' group to discuss the everyday problems the mentally retarded present can help a mother like Mrs. Whipple to feel less alone with her problems and to eliminate some of her guilt.

A proper diagnostic evaluation of the Whipples' boy would have given the family more information about his mental retardation and would have helped them to adjust to and plan for the boy's future. From the amount of information given in this story, the boy seems to be in the range of the trainable retarded. His limited speech and emotion suggest that his functioning is not at a level appropriate for formal academic learning. Although He is able to carry out simple tasks and is a source of help around the farm, Mrs. Whipple is sure she is exploiting him. A professional evaluation could have done much to ease Mrs. Whipple's mind.

Mrs. Whipple also needs assistance in such a practical matter as planning a good diet for the boy. In this case there may be a physical malfunctioning that accounts for the boy's overweight condition, or if Mrs. Whipple is overindulging the boy or the boy is overeating out of boredom, a counselor could advise corrective measures.

The boy's illness at the end of the story and his need for treatment in an institution at that time allow the reader to understand Mrs. Whipple's feelings, which are so encumbered with guilt and rejection that one can only wonder how she has managed to cope at all. The kind of misfortune the Whipples have suffered can be greatly mitigated through community services that provide professional diagnosis and counseling in the area of retardation.

Springboards for Inquiry

(1) What are some of "His" attributes that might justifiably be a source of pleasure for Mrs. Whipple?

(2) Identify the incidents that point to Mrs. Whipple's extreme defensiveness and self-pity because of her retarded son.

(3) What do you learn from this story about the stereotyped ideas people have concerning the mentally retarded?

(4) To what extent would apartment life in a city, as opposed to farm life, influence a boy of "His" limitations?

Every time that some boy yelled "Hey — here comes Screwloose Saunders!" my stomach clenched as tight as my fists. I must have been the only boy in town who actually looked forward to the end of summer vacations.

Destroying Angel

by Eric Cameron

Sometimes I wonder if memories of an event tend to change, or if it is that people change over the years? It might even be that the memories themselves change people a little. Like the memory of what happened to my brother, Ernest.

It had been bad enough having an older brother, but to have one I forever had to protect from the bullying of other boys was a humiliating burden. Ernest was three years older and so much bigger, yet he followed me everywhere. My mother explained that while his sturdy body had developed normally, Ernest's mind had lagged. Anguish and remorse accentuated the lines in her face, as if she blamed herself for his condition.

"What'll happen to Ernie when he gets big like Dad?" I asked when I was twelve years old. "Won't he ever learn to read and write?"

Mother shook her head and sighed.

"Will I always have to mind Ernie when he's grown up?" I asked anxiously.

"You'll have to decide that for yourself when the time comes, Paul."

There were so many occasions when I felt ashamed of being seen with Ernest; sometimes he embarrassed me so much I could have struck him dead. He did things impulsively, without thinking, and it was sheer waste of time and words to scold him. As words scattered around him like pebbles, Ernest would smile vaguely and give a helpless little shrug.

One day, I overheard a woman visitor say to mother: "Ernest is such a handsome boy. It's a pity that Paul couldn't have had the looks instead."

After that, whenever I looked in the mirror the acid of envy etched

---

her words deeper. I suspected that when people made comparisons between me and my older brother, they concluded that my weak face should have been matched with Ernest's weak mind.

The easiest way to exact obedience from my older brother was to promise to read to him. Ernest would listen as raptly to a problem from my arithmetic book as to any boy's adventure story. If it was a problem about the five juicy apples that a boy named Harry wanted to divide equally with two of his friends, Ernest would lick his lips as if he could taste the apples. One evening, I read him a new problem about a boy who rode his bicycle for one mile due west, three-quarters of a mile north, six hundred yards east, and one-third of a mile southeast. The boy's name happened to be Ernest, and you had to work out how many feet he traveled on the bicycle. It became Ernest's favorite story and I had to read it so often I began to detest it. The fact that I was utterly incapable of calculating the precise distance the boy had traveled might also have influenced my attitude.

The story was what aroused Ernest's interest in bicycles, an interest that became a passion. So much so that he took possession of any bicycle he saw without a rider and tried to wheel it away.

Finally, after a number of embarrassments, my father decided that the best solution would be to let Ernest have a secondhand bicycle. My mother feared the worst, as she was convinced that Ernest would kill himself if he ever mastered the art of riding a bicycle. I had been secretly hoping for a bicycle for my birthday, and my parents had hinted at one. But they talked to me about Ernest and asked me to be patient for another year. There was no point in trying to raise objections once my father had made up his mind about something, and I knew that because the mill was on part time he couldn't afford two bicycles. They reasoned that if they gave *me* the bicycle Ernest would be always trying to take it. I accepted with a casual shrug that camouflaged a cancer of jealousy which began from that moment to gnaw at me. There was one consolation in the prospect. If Ernest was on a bicycle they couldn't expect me to be his constant shepherd.

"How will Paul be able to keep track of Ernest if he's on a bicycle?" my mother asked, destroying my blooming hope of liberation.

"I've got that problem figured out," my father answered with a smile. "We'll just take off the chain, then lower the seat so he can touch the ground with his feet and push himself around."

"Like a kiddy-car," I observed with bitter satisfaction.

"Well, more or less," he said, avoiding mother's stricken look.

I have excruciating memories of that summer when there was no classroom to free me from the dawn-to-dark humiliation of minding my good-looking, good-for-nothing brother. Every time that some boy yelled "Hey—here comes Screwloose Saunders!" my stomach clenched as tight as my fists. I must have been the only boy in town who actually looked forward to the end of summer vacations.

As time went on, I noted with

mounting apprehension that Ernest seemed to be growing more headstrong; it was as if the bicycle had given him a certain freedom he had not been aware of before. I was apprehensive because it meant that instead of obeying my grumpy commands, he might one day suddenly challenge my authority and refuse to do what I had ordered. He was so much stronger that if he ever lost his fear of me he would become his own master. But not quite. He might become stubborn but he would never be able to decide things for himself, never be able to avoid getting into trouble. And so my burden would only grow heavier, for his welfare was my responsibility. Mother steadfastly refused to have Ernest "put away" somewhere.

The thought was a chilling one for me when I heard my father suggest it to her one sultry evening as they sat on the porch swing, holding hands, her head on his shoulder and his heavily muscled arm around her shoulders. The expression "put away" brought to mind the death chamber behind the police station, which consisted of a large packing box with a length of hose that policemen slipped over the exhaust pipe of a car whenever they had to "put away" a stray dog or cat. I wasn't surprised when mother objected that under no circumstances was Ernest to be "put away."

I had crept around in the dark from the garden, stalking a firefly that Ernest had begged me to capture and put in a Mason jar. Seeing my parents sitting on the swing like the Wilson girl next door and her bank clerk boy friend was a surprise. When my father leaned down and brushed his lips on the top of my mother's head, my throat tightened and through wet eyelids I saw the blurry light of the firefly go flickering across the lawn. Giving a loud, warning cough, I raced in pursuit. When I carried the jar to our bedroom, Ernie stayed awake half the night watching the firefly and I regretted my generous impulse.

It was the bicycle that exasperated me most, and I began to wish that somebody would steal it; but it was too old, too battered, too rusty for anyone to bother with. One day Ernest discovered a hill. As the bicycle picked up speed, he laughed helplessly the way he did when we wrestled and I tickled him to break his hold on me. The hill provided a temporary respite for me. I stretched out in the shade of a tree and watched the wind sculpture the massed cloud banks into ever-changing shapes as they drifted majestically across the sky. Ernest would swoop happily down the hill and I could follow his course without looking, because the bicycle squeaked in spite of frequent oilings. Then he would trudge slowly up to the top and repeat the descent again and again.

One afternoon I was fascinated by a squirrel stalking a bird's nest when the screech of tortured tires was followed by a clang of metal against metal. As goose pimples crawled over me. I strained to hear, but was afraid to look because I was overwhelmed by a surge of guilt and remorse. In that moment I had been aware of a feeling of secret relief, as if something had parted the chain binding me to Ernest.

But my brother had not been killed. Apart from a slight cut on the forehead and a grazed elbow he was unscathed. The bicycle, however, was jammed under the front of the coal truck it had rammed. When the truck driver pronounced it mangled beyond repair I had to restrain my enthusiasm because Ernest wept bitterly.

After trying in vain for a week to get the wreck to go again, Ernest in a frenzy of rage and despair picked up the bicycle and hurled it over the back fence. It narrowly missed Mrs. Dawson who was bent over weeding her vegetable patches.

Minutes later, the bicycyle sailed back impelled by Mr. Dawson, a huge, beetle-browed railroad brakeman with tobacco-stained teeth and a carpet of red hair on his barrel chest. Hair curled from his ears and nose like tangled rusty wire and even his broad back was liberally forested. He bellowed a warning that Ernest would be torn limb from limb if he ever tried any more crazy stunts. The twisted skeleton of the bicycle rusted all summer until the energetic weeds concealed it from view. There were times when I was tempted to heave the wreck back into the Dawson's yard just to see if the ferocious man might carry out his threat. In a book of children's stories there was an illustration for the Jack the Giant Killer tale, of a scowling, snaggletoothed giant with red hair that Ernest called Mr. Dawson. He avoided looking at it and I could paralyze him with dread simply by chanting in a deep voice: "Fe, fo, fi, fum . . . Mr. Dawson's going to come!"

The winter I remember most vividly had suddenly collapsed into spring, and mild weather bearded the eaves of every roof with icicles. On a Saturday afternoon when the school rink was too soft for hockey, I decided to walk out of town along the tracks to the railroad bridge. It spanned the river where it narrowed to a steep gorge and plunged down in a series of almost vertical steps. The ice formations would be striking to see, particularly if any of them thawed enough to break free and thundered down on the rocks. Ernest, as usual, was as inseparable as my shadow.

It was a brilliant, windless day; everything seemed to be standing still in anticipation of spring's arrival. I balanced on one of the rails, pretending I was a performer on the circus high wire, working without a safety net, concentrating on keeping my footing and holding my arms out. Every time I lost my balance I could imagine the gasp of horror from the spectators who breathed as one, and I saw the white mass of tilted faces whirling up to meet me as I tumbled down to the sawdust ring.

When we came to a short tunnel through a hill, Ernest wanted to detour around it. He was frightened of the unseen terrors in its gloomy, dripping depths. It had a sooty, cindery smell that made you feel you wanted to sneeze.

"Stop being such a big baby." I snapped impatiently.

Clutching my hand, Ernest stumbled after me into the dark and I half-hoped a train would catch us in the tunnel and really give him something to fear. The prospect of yet another summer as his daily keeper made me cranky and morose. I gave a shout and echoes boomed along the tunnel.

A vague, black form suddenly

hovered before us and then disappeared. Ernest whimpered in fear as we hurried on through the tunnel toward the patch of light that was the other end. The shape rose before us once more and huge wings seemed to stretch right across the tunnel, yet there was no sound but of our breathing and crunching footsteps. I remembered a book at my grandmother's that contained an illustration of an angel with fiery sword, hovering over some cowering people. She had called him "The Destroying Angel." Whatever it was had been much too big to be a bat; in any case, I knew that bats hibernated during the cold weather.

"Was it a ghost?" Ernest quavered, blinking in the sun when we left the coffin-like confines of the tunnel.

"Don't be stupid," I snapped, angry with myself for having succumbed to fear.

As we walked on down the tracks, Ernest kept glancing anxiously behind as if he thought something might be following us. He made me so nervous I thought there *was* something flitting among the trees lining the right of way. Ernest tripped over a switchplate and went sprawling, but quickly jumped up with an apologetic laugh. Then he froze, his eyes widening as he stared beyond me. He pointed to a fat birch tree about fifty feet distant. On a branch close to the trunk was the biggest bird I had ever seen. The snow owl's great wings unfolded like sails and made lazy, silent sweeps. After a hundred yards, the effortless movement of the six-foot wings seemed to falter. The owl staggered, then alighted as gently as a huge snowflake on a drift. When we drew near it again took flight. There was something uncanny about the utter silence of its movements, and I realized that the bird was what had frightened us in the tunnel.

The owl made shorter flights, as if its strength was ebbing. When it rested on a fence post, I noticed that one wing dropped and the pinions were streaked with dried blood. Someone had crippled it with a gunshot. Unless the wing mended very soon the bird would die of hunger or be finished off by some other predator. I began to visualize Ernest and myself walking through town holding the great owl by its wingtips, drawing curious looks and comments. The Weekly Clarion might even publish a picture!

Ernest shivered with excitement as we stalked the owl to the top of the steep, forested river bank. The owl's expressionless, unblinking black eyes never strayed from us and the fierce scimitar of beak suggested caution. Just when I had gathered myself for a sudden rush and capture, the owl's wings rose and fell and it went sailing down through the trees, ghosting in and out of the shadows like a wraith of smoke.

Amid the boulders along the river's edge, weathered branches and roots of felled trees thrust up through the snow like the bones of decayed prehistoric monsters. The owl alighted on a branch about three feet above the snow and we scrambled as quietly as we could down the bank. From downstream came the muted roar of the falls and a cloud of vapor hung in the sky like the breath of a snoring giant.

Under the lee of a boulder I found two stones the size of tennis balls. I wanted to stun the owl and capture it before it decided to escape across the river, where we could not follow because the sun had rotted the river ice and in places it sagged ominously, forming glistening pools.

My second throw struck the bird's breast. Wings flailing helplessly, it tumbled backward off its perch. We dashed forward, slipping and falling on the ice-coated rocks and driftwood. The owl scuttled out on the river ice, sculling on the clear, windswept surface with its broad wings. It no longer seemed able to support itself in the air. A twisted ankle and bruised elbow had dampened my enthusiasm, but Ernest's had reached fever-pitch. Snatching up a length of driftwood, he ran out on the ice in pursuit of the fleeing bird, slipping and slithering, blind to the dangers.

Ernest hurled the club. By some fluke it struck the bird's uninjured wing and knocked it over. As he threw himself upon the fluttering mass of plumage, I felt a pang of jealousy that Ernest had succeeded where I had failed. The glory of the triumphant march through town would be his.

Suddenly Ernest screamed . . . a long-drawn howl of pain and terror that rooted me to the rock I was perched on. Lurching to his feet, he began to stagger around drunkenly on the water-slicked ice, trying vainly to free himself from the hooked talons sunk into his face. The fluttering wings resembled the headdress of a tribal medicine man engaged in some weird ritual dance of supplication to the gods.

"Paul! Paul!" was the only word my brother screamed, the word that had always summoned help when he had needed it.

But I was bound to the shore by a knot of fear that tightened as Ernest bobbed and turned in the grotesque ballet.

With a slushy groan, the ice under Ernest sagged lower and lower. Unable to scramble up the saucerlike incline, he sprawled on his knees in the rapidly rising water, tearing at the owl. When the ice parted like the jaws of a whale, Ernest was sucked down into the greedy, swirling black water with a faint, despairing cry. The owl's wings flailed the surface, then vanished. Only the water gurgled with an evil, chuckling sound.

The moment began to fill with a sense of sadness and departure and a frightened melancholy bloomed inside me. And then, as I turned away from the ominous hole in the ice, I was suddenly swept with a great feeling of freedom and liberation, as if a dark fungus growth compounded of accumulated shame, resentment and jealousy had been excised from my mind.

But the rapture of release was short-lived. As I climbed the river bank, the bare branches of the somber trees ticked softly in a slight wind that had sprung up, like the whispering voices of those who might ask what I had done to try and save my brother. I had a chilling vision of Ernest and the snow owl, locked in their everlasting embrace, being swept over the boiling falls to the jagged rocks below. I began to run.

By the time I reached the railroad tunnel, the sun had gone and soft snowflakes sifted from the leaden sky. When I was a few yards from the tunnel entrance, a snow owl suddenly swept out from its throat and sailed over me without a sound, so low that I could have reached up and touched it. As it melted into the gloomy woods, I wondered, trembling, if it had been an apparition.

Somehow, the memory of Ernest's tragedy became associated in my mind with the picture of "The Destroying Angel." In time, I believed that perhaps the strange bird had performed an act of mercy, savage though it was. For after all, what would life have been like for Ernest if he had grown up? I never saw another snow owl in our region, and when I told people what had happened I began to sense that they thought I was imagining that part of the incident. They knew that Ernest had not been "all there" so naturally they came to certain conclusions, one being that what ran in the family ran in the family. Years later I was relieved to have a wildlife expert suggest that the owls probably had been a pair driven south by a shortage of food.

My parents never held me responsible for what had happened. In fact, my mother maintained that it wouldn't have happened if Ernest had heeded my warning about the dangerous state of the ice. When I awake in the still of the night and lie there in the dark, remembering that moment in every detail, I recall having warned him about the ice. At first I didn't remember, but as time went on the memory became clearer. In the excitement, I suppose I wasn't aware of having tried to restrain Ernest from venturing after the owl. They say it's the same with car accidents; the witnesses don't always recall precisely what happened until someone jogs their memory. And if my mother believed that I had tried to stop Ernest, then I must have. It makes me feel a little better to remember it that way.

Discussion

Whenever a family member has a substantial handicap, it is expected that all members of the family will need to share the responsibility for his welfare. This story emphasizes the problems of the normal sibling living with a retarded brother. In this case Paul is asked to assume more than his fair share of the care of Ernie. The sacrifice of all his free time during the summer months, when he would have preferred the companionship of his age-mates, was an inordinate burden of responsibility.

It can be expected that the retarded child within the family will assume the position of the youngest child no matter what the actual order of birth. Although parents may be able to understand this situation, it is particularly difficult for chronologically younger siblings to accept. Ernie is older and bigger than Paul, yet Paul must shelter and protect him from the derision of other children. Paul also has to stand by while Ernie is accorded the privileges usually reserved for the youngest in the family. Paul can understand intellectually the urgency of catering to Ernie's needs, but resentment and jealousy are inevitable when he must forfeit his own pleasures.

In addition to resentment and jealousy Paul suffers the guilt of knowing that he would prefer to have Ernie "put away." Paul is concerned about the present burden Ernie presents, but he is equally concerned about the future responsibility he must assume for him. The hurt and concern other family members live with in cases of a severely handicapped child are well documented by the incidents in this story. We can empathize with Paul when Ernie disappears under the ice and Paul "was suddenly swept with a great feeling of freedom and liberation."

Community awareness of the many complex problems that mentally retarded children and their families face can be of great assistance in working toward imaginative and practical solutions. Many parent organizations for the retarded are interested in establishing halfway houses or residential centers that can be run by retardates with professional assistance. Such centers can provide real work for the adult retardate and can also provide an alternative to home supervision for younger retardates. A family can benefit from a respite from the continuing responsibility of care and supervision of their retarded child.

Springboards for Inquiry

(1) Describe the conflict of emotion Paul felt about his brother's handicap. Which incidents document your impressions?

(2) Investigate the services for the retarded in your community. What diagnostic facilities, sheltered workshops, halfway houses, residential care centers are available? Do you consider them adequate for the needs in your community?

(3) Have you ever known a family with a retarded member? If so, what positive or negative impressions were you left with?

Emotional Disturbances

The term *emotionally disturbed* has been used as a classification in child development only within the last fifty years. Louise Despert (1965) says: "Children affected with what we would describe today as neurotic or psychotic illness were variously labeled through the ages as 'possessed,' 'wicked,' 'guilty,' 'insubordinate,' 'incorrigible,' 'maladjusted,' and 'problem children.' " Although we know that the behavior of emotionally disturbed children still causes reactions of fear and discomfort in a wide segment of the population, the use of the term *emotionally disturbed* indicates that there is also considerable compassion for the emotionally ill child.

The psychiatric literature indicates that different kinds of emotional disturbance make their appearances at different ages. We know that emotional problems can be attributed to events the baby experiences during his first year of life. Margaret Ribble (1943) discusses the infant's physical and emotional needs during that crucial period. She relates cuddling, fondling, and all body contact given to the infant as necessary to establish a loving and secure relationship between mother and child. Ribble also relates handling of the newborn to the respiratory needs of the infant—handling of the baby provides the stimulation to promote steady, deep respiration: "The importance of mothering in helping the child to breathe . . . can hardly be overstressed (Ribble, 1943, p. 19). David Levy (1937) further supports the idea of the relationship between the physical and the emotional needs of earliest infancy. He describes the sucking reflex in infancy, which he considers a source of nourishment, pleasure, and security for the child. René Spitz (1945; 1950) and Bowlby (1952) have documented the serious negative effects on the emotional health of children who are deprived of their mothers in the first year of life.

In the first months of life emotional disturbances are expressed biologically, since ego development does not begin until the latter part of the first year. Motor indicators of possible emotional distress within the first year are head banging, rocking, motor restlessness, or listlessness. Breath holding is an example of a disturbance that involves the respiratory tract. Emotional disturbance that affects the gastrointestinal tract often results in either diarrhea or constipation.

Following the first year the child's symptoms of emotional disturbance may continue to manifest themselves in biological dysfunctions, but problems are also indicated by inappropriate social adjustments. The important warning symptoms in the preschool years are language problems, behavior that is overly passive or dependent, and extremely aggressive behavior or impulsivity or both. In their early years children may naturally fear strange people and places; however, overwhelming fear of these experiences may be indicative of poor emotional adjustment. In the school years difficulty with school work, anger without cause, compulsive lying or stealing, and psychosomatic illness may be signals of emotional maladjustment.

In any discussion of the less severe emotional disturbances of childhood it is necessary to stress that the point at which normal behavior can be classified as pathological may be obscure. There is wide variation in behavioral characteristics of children as they meet developmental tasks. At certain crucial stages the child may develop transient symptoms that appear like pathology; however, the severity and persistence of the problem behavior constitutes the distinction between normal and abnormal.

The two most serious disturbances in childhood are autism and schizophrenia. Some authors classify autism as a variant of childhood schizophrenia, while others differentiate the two according to the period of onset of the disturbance (Kessler 1966). Leo Kanner (1943) first identified and described early infantile autism. Since then autistic children have been the subject of considerable interest and research because of their baffling behavioral patterns. These children appear normal and often have normal or superior motor coordination, but they avoid eye contact and any evidence of responsiveness to the people in their environment. Their behavior is typified by ritualistic, repetitive acts. Another significant defect is the frequent failure to acquire speech. In some cases language is acquired but it is used to echo parts of phrases the child hears in others' speech, not for communication or an interchange between listener and speaker.

There are two main schools of thought regarding the etiology of autism. One school sees autism as a failure of interpersonal relations to develop as a result of severe emotional frustrations. Many students of autism cite the lack of an affective relationship between mother and child in the earliest days of infancy. Another school of thought sees autism as a result of "genetically rooted inferior intellect or of cerebral lesions dating from the earliest stages of development or of pathologic metabolic processes" (Bosch 1970, p. 130).

Although childhood schizophrenia* bears a resemblance to autism in its symptomotology, it is an illness that tends to develop gradually over a number of years. The diagnosis is usually made around school age, when the child's schizophrenic behavior causes increased social problems. In some cases the facial expression of the schizophrenic child betrays detachment from the everyday world around him. Some schizophrenic children, however, have agitated expressions and stare intently at objects in the environment that attract their attention, and others smile and grimace in bizarre ways. The schizophrenic child often has language disturbances and his speech may be filled with bizarre words and newly coined phrases that hold meaning for him alone. Because of the severity and inevitability of its outcome, early recognition of childhood schizophrenia is urgent.

Many researchers have attempted to devise preventive mental health programs. Eli Bower (1969), recognizing the school as an ideal setting for identifying and helping the child with an emotional handicap, has devised a screening procedure to be used in the classroom by teachers and students. There are five tasks that result in a profile incorporating a teacher rating, peer rating, and self-rating. The work of Erich Lindeman, Warren Vaughan, and Manon McGinnis (1955) represents an attempt to identify family crisis situations in strategic moments of the family's life cycle out of which the child may develop maladaptive behavior patterns.

Often the family physician, pediatrician, clergyman, family social caseworker, or teacher is in a position to observe the first symptoms of emotional stress in children. In order to help these professionals meet the mental health needs of their clients, a vigorous new specialty has developed—community mental health consultant (Haylett and Rapaport 1964). The community mental health consultant is a trained professional in the field of mental health e.g., a psychiatrist, psychologist, or psychiatric social worker. He functions as a resource person to such community workers as the pediatrician, teacher, or clergyman by helping them to understand mental health needs. The community mental health consultant assists in evaluating possible solutions to clients' emotional problems and helps in initiating the chosen course of action. This new procedure provides wide coverage of mental health needs, education for community workers about mental health services, and intervention early enough in the child's life to make a significant difference in his development.

---

* The following description is adapted from Arthur H. Chapman, *Management of Emotional Problems of Children and Adolescents* (Philadelphia: J. B. Lippincott Co., 1965).

She looked evil the way she stood there, Nils thought, beautiful and evil, she was like the evil queen.

The Blue Parakeets

by H. C. Branner

Nils was afraid of Katrine. When he was playing in the road, she often came up and teased him, sometimes she hit him, even though he hadn't done anything to her. She came up dead serious and slapped the flat of her hand right in his face so that he saw stars, behind the stars was her white, three-cornered face with two large eyes in the center. Nils never quite dared to hit back, because her face with its two cold eyes didn't change, it only became a shade more white and cold if he hit back. She didn't defend herself, she only looked at him.

Once she put a stick in his bicycle wheel so that it got all bent, and when he came home with it his dad gave him a thrashing. It was a furious, unfair thrashing, but that didn't make Nils defiant, he wasn't the type of boy that gets defiant. He wrapped both arms around his dad's knees, he sobbed and asked forgiveness. That wasn't a very good method, his dad only got more furious and gave him another thrashing, but at last the voices of the grown-ups calmed down enough to allow Nils to tell how it had happened. Then his dad put on his hat and wanted to go and complain to Katrine's father. But Nils ran after him down the garden path and clung to his trouser-legs: "Oh no! No, dad! No, dad!"

His dad continued a few steps with Nils hanging on to his legs, then he stopped: "Why not, son? Why not, I'd like to know!" Nils couldn't explain it. "Have you lied to me?" No, Nils couldn't explain. But there had to be some explanation and in a solemn room of subdued voices and Nils' brothers and sisters eavesdropping behind the door, it finally

---

came out that he had told a lie, it wasn't Katrine. But when he saw the expression on his father's face he got scared and took it back. No, he really hadn't told a lie, it was Katrine. But, of course, in either case he had told a lie, he was sent to bed and stayed there till the next morning. He wasn't at all rebellious, all the time he lay as quiet as a mouse, and at bedtime he hugged his mother and dad around their necks and wept and promised. He'd rather have all that than have to meet Katrine's white cat face after his dad had been to see her dad.

Katrine's dad was an assistant professor at the government school. She had also had a mother once, but now she didn't any more, and that had come about in a strange way. One day suddenly Katrine had been fetched by her uncle, he came in his car and took her to his home in the countryside. She was only five then, but she remembered it because it had been so sudden, and when after a long time she came back home, her mother was gone. Her dad took her on his lap and explained that her mother was on a trip, but maybe she'd soon come back. She didn't understand a thing of it, but everything was so new at home, and she forgot again. But the next day she asked again, and her dad said the same thing about a trip and maybe. He said that each time she asked, but at last she knew it wasn't true: her parents were divorced and her mother was living with another man. She didn't know from whom she got it or if she had got it from anyone at all, but she knew it and from that time on she stopped asking.

Now Katrine was nine, she went to school every morning and came home again some time in the afternoon. Sometimes way late in the afternoon. Her face was as dead serious when she left as when she came back, she always stared straight ahead, she walked awkwardly, and when there was a puddle she didn't step around it. She didn't see it, she looked straight ahead, her nose pointed in the air. Her bookbag hung by a strap over her shoulder and slapped against her hip as she walked, sometimes she let it down and dragged it behind her like a little brown dog. If there was a puddle, she didn't pick up the bag, she dragged it through the puddle, very serious.

On her way down town something often happened. Sometimes the greengrocer had a box of apples standing outside his shop, Katrine's hand might dart out and snatch one in passing. Her face was still serious, and she didn't look at the apple, she looked straight ahead. It wasn't for the sake of the apple, anyhow, she didn't eat it after all, when she came to Skolevej she let it drop and gave it a kick so that it bounced down the side walk in three, four pieces. Then the others flocked around the clear-eyed thief, Katrine, and sometimes they sang in a chorus: "Shame on Katrine, ha-ha-ha-ha-ha!"

Katrine looked straight ahead and let them shout. As she got closer to school she hunched her shoulders more and more and walked flat-footed, and her face became more and more stiff and arrogant. But if they kept up with their "ha-ha-ha," she drew back her upper lip a bit so you could see two prominent eye-teeth.

"Shut up!" she said, and her eyes were two sick slits.

And that was enough to make them quiet. They never told on her either, even though they knew a lot about her. She told lies and stole and cheated, she pinched the other's homework from their desks and copied it, she had also forged her dad's name on notes to school. But she remained dead serious through it all, and the others were afraid of that seriousness. When she had done something awful they'd whisper at a distance and look at her with frightened eyes, but they never said anything.

"Well, let's hear about Turkey," the geography teacher said and looked down the two rows of desks where some were eager to be heard, and others hung back and turned away their eyes. Katrine did neither, she sat as if it all didn't concern her. "Katrine—get up—what's the capital of Turkey?"

Katrine stood and looked straight ahead as if it were a matter of course that she didn't know. As if she had nothing to do with Turkey.

"What is it, Nils!"

"Constantinople."

"Thank you, stay in your seat, I want to ask Katrine. Katrine, how many inhabitants does Constantinople have?"

The whole class was groaning with eagerness to get the question, the figure was whispered from desk to desk. Katrine stood bright-eyed and said nothing.

"You don't want to tell me that you've read this over, do you?"

"Yes?"

"When?"

"Yesterday."

"Then why don't you know it?"

"I don't know."

"But you knew it yesterday?"

"I don't know."

"But you've read it?"

"Yes."

The questioning dragged on with difficulty while the class sat in breathless suspense. It ended with the teacher's picking up Katrine's geography book—it was frayed and used and was missing a page here and there. The page about Turkey was missing. Katrine didn't know where it had gone to, she knew nothing, she stood with her hands on her back and her weight resting on one foot. The whole thing didn't concern her, she looked past it all and far out the window. The teacher's face was red and his glasses vibrated ominously. He banged the book on his desk.

"Go back to your seat. You can stay after school then and learn it."

But when he peeked into the detention hall after school was over, Katrine wasn't there. She was long since on her way home through the puddles, her nose pointing in the air and her bookbag dangling from her hip.

Katrine knew very well where the missing pages were: her two parakeets had eaten them. Or they hadn't eaten them but pecked them into shreds and used them to line the nesting box. She had fallen into thinking about it when she had been standing in front of the teacher's desk, and while she was being bawled out she stood looking out the window wondering if there might be any eggs in the nesting coop. It was silly to be so excited about it, but the rest of the day in school she sat and was excited and let the questions and answers go past her, and now on her way home her thoughts were again with the parakeets. It was spring that day. Although it was only March it was spring just the same, with glistening sunshine and soggy ground, all around there was water glittering and an arch of finely spun twigs and sailing blues and whites moved across Katrine's serious bright eyes. The breasts of the parakeets were like the mirroring blue, they were blue parakeets. Katrine felt a wild joy well up toward them even though there was such serious dignity in her flat-footed trot.

Her dad had given them to her on her birthday, and at first she wasn't interested in them. If for a moment her eyes had lit up when she saw them, her expression quickly got stiff and arrogant again. Her dad explained that they couldn't be without each other, and if one died the other would die also—Katrine stood and smiled at that with her eyeteeth. The parakeets were put in the window nook in her room, but it didn't occur to her to change the sand under them and give them bird seeds and fresh water—she wasn't interested in them and didn't take care of them.

But in the afternoon the sun shone in that window nook, and the parakeets were blue: whenever they as much as bobbed their tails, a blue flash crossed Katrine's eyes. At last it was impossible not to notice them, one day her white cat face came up without a sound and stood in front of the cage.

"Hush!" she said, when she had been standing there a while, and put in a ruler so the birds fluttered in confusion.

Then she laughed. The next day her eyes came close up to the cage again, but she didn't put in the ruler and frighten them, she just made faces at them. They sat there so stupidly and squeezed close together, maybe it was true that if one died, the other would die also. She knew, of course, that her dad had only said it out of *love,* and that that, also, was why she had got the parakeets—ugh, *love,* they must all be so good to one another. People and birds and puppies. Still, maybe it was true. You could try letting one out the window and see what would happen to the other one. She put a hand in and got hold of one of them, she took it out of the cage and sat with both hands folded around it so that only the head and the long blue tail poked out. It was very frightened and fought in little desperate jerks, she could feel how delicate and warm it was under the feathers and how hard its heart was beating. She laughed savagely and looked up at the window, and yet she didn't let the bird out after all, she stayed sitting with it. At last it wasn't so frightened any more, it lay calmly between her hands and didn't fight. She carefully took away her upper hand, but the bird didn't fly, it lay quiet. She stiffened inwardly, her heart stopped beating: a blue bird was lying there right before her eyes, shining blue as if molded in glass, with a long, smooth tail and black pearl eyes. It was pulsating with life, but it didn't fly away. She held her breath, her tongue stood still in her mouth, her hand with the bird crept with infinite caution toward the cage and in through the chicken wire. Not until it was in there did it get off her hand and jump up to its perch, it behaved as usual, it sat preening itself. Phew, the silly bird, the stupid, silly love bird. But she was strangely out of breath and her cheeks were burning, there was a restlessness about her. At twilight she went out and drew a hopscotch on the sidewalk a short distance away from her house. She drew it with a piece of chalk that she had snitched in school. It was still light enough for the chalk lines to stand out, and for her blue marble. She was jumping and singing in the twilight. The silly birds, the stupid, silly love birds.

But after a while she was able to put her hand in the cage without frightening the birds, one of them might come and sit on her index finger. She took her hand out again with the bird sitting on her finger. She brought it close to her face, she opened her mouth as if to gobble up the blue bird, but it just looked at her with its blinking black eyes.

"You silly bird!" she said.

Her hand would also cup itself into a soft hollow, and the blue bird lay there very calmly in the sunshine, a film sliding across its bright black eyes. That way they sat for a long time without moving. The sunshine made small dimples in Katrine's white face, her hand was so shining and tender, there were little scabs on it, it smelled faintly of moss and warm earth. She also had names for the blue birds and could say many things to them, wise things and nonsensical things, she'd jump up and down and sing to them whatever occurred to her. She could safely do this, for nobody knew about her and them. She definitely counted on nobody's knowing anything. When somebody came in, the blue blue birds were in their cage, and Katrine never glanced in their direction.

But today it was spring, and there were eggs in the nesting coop. She couldn't see the eggs, but she knew it already at the door, because the female was lying with her head poking out of the round hole and letting herself be fed by the male. As a matter of fact, she had known it all along on her way home as the sun shone on rich dirt and the puddles glittered: now it was ripe, what she had been waiting for for many days. The female had looked as wretched as if it were going to die, and every bit of straw and scraps of paper that she offered them they had unravelled and used to line the nest. She hadn't told anybody that they were building a nest, nor did she tell anybody that there were eggs now, she didn't rush out slamming the doors and shouting the news. Nor was there any change in her expression, but she sneaked about strangely quiet and didn't dare to come up close to the cage, it made her lose her breath if she came close. So she sat down in the opposite corner and drew up her legs beneath her. It was nothing to be concerned about, she thought, the silly birds! But she was full of a wild joy. From within her a strong gleam came into her eyes, it covered them like a black moist film. In that film the objects around were mirrored clear to the point of bursting, when the male jumped in the cage there was a blue flash. The male flew to and fro, the female lay with her head outside the round hole of the nest, Katrine sat in the farthest corner watching it.

She sat with her legs pulled up under her and her chin on her knees, and in that position she stayed without moving so long that she didn't know herself for how long.

Late that afternoon she called into her dad's room. It was a Spartan room, rather dark and with many books, the lights hadn't been turned on yet, although it was getting dark. Katrine's dad sat dark against the window correcting papers in the last remnant of the daylight. He didn't say anything at once when she came in, but finished the paper he was working on. Katrine had stopped just inside the door, she stood with her hands on her back and her weight resting on one foot.

"Come here, Katrine, and sit down."

She came up without a sound and dropped a curtsey as she sat down on the very edge of a chair.

"There've been complaints from school again. The principal has called. She doesn't know what to do with you. You tear the pages out of your books, and you don't know what you're supposed to, and when you've been told to stay after school, you just quietly scamper off. Well, what do you think we should do with you, Katrine?"

"I don't know," Katrine said.

"You must admit that I've been patient. I've put up with it for a long time. But it can't go on like this, you must realize that. I shall have to punish you this time, and I shall have to punish you in such a way that you'll feel it. So now I'm going to take your birds away from you and I'm going to give them to someone else."

"All right," Katrine said.

He turned heavily in his chair and looked straight at her. Her face was white in the twilight, her legs were long and thin in a pair of light grey socks. But all she said was "all right," she didn't cry, she didn't even show the slightest shock. So he knew that he had already suffered a defeat. He only wished that he hadn't come up with that threat, for he couldn't take the birds away from her, anyhow. He got up and took a step or two.

"Why won't you be sensible, Katrine? You know, don't you, that we want nothing but your own good. Why do you act this way to us?"

"I don't know," Katrine said.

She would have liked to say something else, but she really didn't know what. She sat there tense like a strange animal in a strange forest. She wished he'd sing out, beat her and scold her, something harsh and decisive. But she knew he wouldn't do that, she knew it was coming now. He was already standing before her, strangely large and soft. She could smell his clothes.

"Is it really the same to you if I take the birds away from you? Don't you care one bit for those birds?

"I don't know. . . ."

"But I know. I know you're fond of those birds. I haven't wanted to say anything, but I've been happy about it. I've seen you with them. Yes, you don't know it, but I've often seen you with them."

"Seen me with them!" Katrine said in a smooth and grown-up voice. "What do you mean? I don't understand. . . ."

He smiled. "Yes, yes, you can deny it if you want to. I won't interfere with your birds. I saw it quite by chance from my window. We won't tell anybody about it, all right. But we know what we know, you and I. And now that the young are coming. . . ."

"The young?"

"Ah, so you don't know that either? Well, well, then we don't know it." He smiled in despair and talked himself deeper into defeat. He wished he hadn't got started on this about the birds, and yet he kept talking about them, he couldn't let be. "Well, then, there'll be no young. I only meant that if there were to be a brood some day, it might be a good idea to have a larger cage, a real aviary. I've had my eye on a cage of that kind. But maybe that isn't anything either?"

She didn't answer, he hurried to sit down and take her on his lap. He pulled her to him, strangely awkward.

"Yes, yes, you don't need to say anything, Katrine, I know how you feel. I understand you better than you think. It isn't always easy to be a child, either. We'll leave you and your birds alone, I don't want to take them away from you. Not if you'll promise me that there'll be a change. Come here, put your cheek close to mine, and let's promise each other that we won't have any more complaints from school, all right?"

"No," Katrine said.

"No, look at me. Let me see your eyes."

She looked at him.

"Here, give me a kiss."

She gave him a kiss.

"Now run along. No, come, give me your hand. I know how you feel, Katrine, I want you to know that. We understand each other, you and I. . . ."

The next day after school, Nils was spinning his top on the sidewalk. It was a fine top he had, a flying top, and when he saw Katrine come out of the gate, he hurriedly gathered it up, for he wouldn't take the chance of letting her snatch it and dart off with it. And then he wouldn't get it back unless his mother went to fetch it. And then he'd rather do without it.

But Katrine just stood still. Her face glimmered white in the sunshine, there was a dimple in one of her cheeks. Nils got the courage to start the top up again, he put himself to great trouble and let it fly. Katrine followed it with her eyes and laughed aloud, it became all red when it went spinning and flew. But then it came down in a depression in the road and toppled over.

"It reels like a drunkard," Katrine said and laughed again.

When the top was still you could see that it wasn't only red, it was blue also. Nils had painted it himself. Katrine asked if she could look at it, and Nils handed it over hesitantly, he stood holding his breath, for you never knew. But the top lost nothing from being turned between Katrine's fingers, it was even more red and blue than he had seen before.

"Do you want to see my birds?" Katrine asked suddenly.

Nils didn't quite know what to say. He didn't know that she had birds in the first place, and maybe she was just being tricky. He scraped the ground a bit with his shoe. "Your birds?" he said.

"Yes my parakeets," Katrine said. "Come!"

She went through the gate first, and Nils followed behind. It was so strange to come into Katrine's yard, he hadn't been there before. And it was stranger still to come into Katrine's house and all the way into Katrine's room, he had often wondered what it looked like in there. Now he was suddenly there. He was ill at ease and suddenly saw things he'd always remember. Fortunately there were no grown-ups. Nils was a nice quiet boy, his hair looked strange and chalk-white in the sunshine in Katrine's room, it was combed down smooth over his forehead and made his head look like an egg. He stopped in front of the cage with the two parakeets and stayed there, since it was to see them that he had come.

"Hey," Nils said, for it was true about the birds, he had never before seen such lovely, blue parakeets. The female was lying in the nesting coop with her head out of the round hole, the male sat preening himself in the sun. Nils dared to come forward with a bent finger and touch the cage lightly.

"Is she sitting on her eggs?" he asked. "Are they going to have young."

"I don't know," Katrine said, "maybe they are."

She walked around loose-jointed and didn't look at the birds at all herself. Nils didn't understand her answer, she ought to know. The nesting coop was outside the cage, and the cover could be taken off, Nils opened it a little and peeked in.

"Oh yes," he said, "she's got eggs. I'll say she's got eggs. Come here yourself and look."

"All right," Katrine said, but she didn't come. She was sitting over at the table with Nils' top. It was a long pointed top, it needed speed to get started, it wouldn't work on a table. But she had often watched the boys playing with tops, she'd love to own a top like that instead of playing that silly hopscotch.

"Are you out of your mind!" Nils said hotly from over by the cage, he had forgotten that he was a stranger and afraid. "You're getting young ones, Katrine, I think you're going to get a lot of them. And then what, when *they* get young in turn! . . ."

Katrine sat with the top, she scratched it a little with her nail, smoothing it.

"Hey," she said, "want to swap? I get the top, and you get the cage with birds and all?"

"Ha!" Nils said, "sure, we'll swap! The top for the cage and the birds, that's something, eh!"

He kept laughing at it, it was so crazy. But why didn't she say anything? Why was she sitting there so serious with the top?

"It's up to you," she said at last. "If you don't want to, someone else will. But I'd rather have your top."

"Oh, go on," Nils said. "You must be crazy, Katrine!" And so a while passed without a word from either. Nils stood toying with the cage with a bent finger. Of course she must be fooling. But you never knew with her, she was often so strange. Finally he did ask, however, if she really was serious.

"Why, of course," Katrine said. "You'll get them, if you'll take them along now, right away."

Ha, then she didn't really mean it after all, it was as he thought: she was just fooling. But she sat there dead serious and meant it, she didn't care about the birds, they were silly and stupid. Nils stood by the birds and chatted with them between these exchanges; they seemed bluer and bigger and more glorious to him, they were priceless with all their sounds and movements and their shining black eyes. Nils was hot and irresolute beneath his smooth white hair, they couldn't do it just like that, could they? Wouldn't she have to ask her dad first? And he ought to ask his dad. No, Katrine said, she wasn't going to ask anybody. The birds were hers. And he should take them now at once, or else it wasn't a deal. It only was a deal right now.

And so, in the end, they took the cage between them and carried it over to Nils's place. They walked with it in silence and very serious, the birds fluttered around inside, and the female left her eggs and flapped wildly. Nils walked praying to God that this was all true, and that none of the grown-ups would see them. They parted by Nils' kitchen door, there Katrine suddenly let go of the cage and went away, she walked where her nose was pointing and never turned around once. And Nils didn't know any longer if she was there or not, he dragged the cage to safety through the kitchen and got it in onto the table in the living room, it was getting frightfully big and heavy. Oh God, oh God! And the birds, the blue, blue birds. A wave welled up within him, he couldn't be alone about it any more, he dashed through the house slamming the doors: "Mum! mum, mum, guess what! . . ."

It turned into a frantic afternoon, filled with joy and anguish and angry voices and bitter tears and behind the tears a remnant of hope. Nils's mother didn't dare to say yes or no, she wanted to talk to Nils's dad first. And Nils's dad came home and got angry and didn't want to hear of it. And Nils cried and had his brothers and sisters on his side, and Nils's mother and dad had a talk in private with Nils and his brothers and sisters anxiously eavesdropping behind the door, and finally his dad agreed to go over and talk with Katrine's dad. And after another, miserable period of waiting he came back again and gave his consent at last: Katrine's father had said that the birds were hers, and if she wanted to present them to somebody, that was up to her. Nils' mother and dad looked at each other and shook their heads. And Nils got a pat on the cheek and nodded that he was happy, but there was no real conviction in his joy any more, he was deadly pale with agitation and wobbly at the knees. There was still another reason why he couldn't be completely happy, he didn't himself know why, but there it was. And the blue birds were already causing concern: the female wouldn't go in to sit on the eggs, she sat all the way up in a corner of the cage and was afraid. Nils tried chatting with her and coaxing her, and Nils's mother took her out of the cage and put her down in the nesting coop from the outside, but she came right out of the round hole again. She wouldn't brood. Perhaps it was the new surroundings and all the turmoil that were responsible for this, they tried putting a cover over the cage and staying away, but each time they sneaked up and peeked under the hood, the female was still in her corner. Maybe the eggs were already cold and couldn't be hatched. Nils's brother spoke of making a hole in them with a pin and blowing them out and giving them to the collection in school, and Nils got mad, and again there were tears.

Only with the evening darkness did quiet come to the house. It was just before bedtime, Nils was sitting alone by the birds, but he didn't dare to turn on the light and peek under the cover, for if she wasn't on the eggs now, there'd be nothing else for them to do but to blow them out. And he was almost sure that she wasn't sitting on the eggs. He pulled up a chair below the window and put himself on his knees in order to peek out through the curtains. There was a lamp outside that shone yellow and calm between the spring trees and the bushy dark of the hedge.

And as he sat there, Katrine came out through her gate strangely slow and without a sound, and went to stand right under the lamp, she leaned her back against it and her white arrogant face was in the center of the light. She looked evil the way she stood there, Nils thought, beautiful and evil, she was like the evil queen. But if he was a prince, he wanted to love the evil queen and not the princess. He was drawn to her, even though he never understood the things she did, she hit him right in the face when he hadn't done anything and presented him with a cage with blue birds. Maybe there was this about her that people call sin, maybe the birds were birds of sin? The whole thing made him feel queer, suddenly he fervently wished that it was still the afternoon, and they were standing in the sun by her window and the female was brooding. He jumped down from the chair, he wanted to go out and tell her that she could have the birds back if she was sorry now, or that she could come and watch them at his house as much as she wanted, they could have the birds together, she and he. He took a big orange from the glass bowl on the table, in case she liked oranges.

But out by the gate he hid the orange behind his back after all, and he began to drag his feet, for there she was looking at him. She didn't move from the spot, and her face didn't change, it only looked a shade more white and cold as she watched him. His legs began to wobble, he slouched and scraped with the toe of his shoe, he only wished he hadn't come out.

"Hey, Katrine," he said, "if you're sorry about the birds, you . . . I mean, you sure can have them back."

To this Katrine didn't even answer. Her white nose pointed in the air a little more, but she didn't say a thing. He stood with the orange behind his back, he shifted it from one hand to the other and let it come into view for an instant. Rather indifferently.

"It's just an orange," he said. "I thought maybe. Do you care for oranges?"

"Give it," Katrine said.

She didn't let him hand it to her himself, her hand darted out and snatched it. It was a queer way. But, anyway, she took it.

"Hey," he said, "you can come in and look at them as much as you want to. We could say they are ours together, couldn't we?"

Katrine's eyes narrowed to two sick slits. "Shut up!" she said. "Beat it! Beat it, you nice little mama's boy, you little pet! Beat it to your darling mama and fall around her neck and kiss her from me!"

He stood there stunned and watched her walk toward her gate flatfooted and with hunched shoulders. A short distance away she turned around and let the orange drop, her long grey leg swung and gave it a kick. She struck it very hard and accurately, it flew in a reddish shining arc up past the lamp and plopped down heavily to the ground somewhere in the dark.

Discussion

Katrine is obviously a child whose behavior pattern reveals a serious disruption in the normal flow of relationships with other children and with adults. Katrine does not display the range of emotions we expect in children. Her face is expressionless and continues to be so even when she is obviously provoked or provoking. Her gait, posture, and general body carriage reflect her troubled emotional state. She walks mechanically and without discrimination, readily walking into a puddle if it is directly in front of her. She has no attachment even to her belongings, dragging her sack of books behind with little concern. Her behavior in any situation is unpredictable. She may lie or take something from a classmate's desk without asking. Her behavior is without appropriate motivation and appropriate emotion.

The children are aware that Katrine is different. They consider her strange, and although they are afraid of her, they try to shield her from adult criticism because they seem to understand that she is not responsible for her actions. Surprisingly, the adults do not seem to wish to recognize the extent of Katrine's problem. The principal and teacher expect better performance and call the father to demand some change in the level of her cooperation. Katrine's father, a man more comfortable with work and study than with emotional problems, sees his role as trying to find a strong enough punishment to stop the objectionable school behavior. He says it is hard to be a child and is verbally sympathetic, but he does not probe further into his daughter's disturbance. Parents frequently do not wish to recognize symptoms of emotional disorder. Rarely would a child whose physical illness was as severe as Katrine's emotional illness go untreated. In this case, even the school is not more specific regarding its concerns about Katrine's behavior. Hesitation on the part of school personnel to suggest emotional malfunctioning is understandable, since there is a wide range of normal behavior, particularly in children, who go through many stages that evoke emotional distress in the process of growing up. However, Katrine's behavior seems to be well outside the bounds of normalcy.

We are not given sufficient information about Katrine's earliest years nor about the relationship between Katrine and her mother or between Katrine's parents to be able to estimate the reasons for her severe behavior disorder. We can conjecture that the onset was associated with the traumatic separation from her mother. The loss of hope for her return may have precipitated Katrine's depressed state. With neither recognition nor help for her extreme distress over this sudden loss of probably the most important figure in her life, Katrine may have adopted a seriously distorted behavior pattern.

At this point Katrine seems unable to relate in nine-year-old fashion either to her father or to others. When she finally has a possession she enjoys (the parakeets) she gives them away, as if to punish herself and her father, who is also deriving satisfaction from her attachment to the birds. Her last remark to Nils seems to suggest the overwhelming anger that seethes beneath her expressionless pose to the outside world. Her remark is a particular reference to his relationship with his mother, perhaps the author's way of suggesting the severity of Katrine's distress in relationship to her own mother.

Springboards for Inquiry

(1) What is your interpretation of Katrine's emotional problem?

(2) Describe some of the warning signals of emotional disturbance that should alert significant adults in a child's environment, specifically a parent of a seven-year-old, a nursery school teacher, a pediatrics nurse, an educational aide in a middle school grade.

(3) How can the school help children who are experiencing emotional distress?

(4) What family crisis situations may trigger emotional upheaval for any of the family members?

(5) The following are well known procedures for the treatment of the emotionally disturbed child: (a) play therapy, (b) group psychotherapy, (c) art therapy, (d) child psychoanalysis, (e) behavior therapy. Discuss the underlying theory, some individuals whose names are associated with the treatment, and give your impressions of each treatment procedure.

References

Barker, Roger G. "The Social Psychology of Physical Disability." *Journal of Social Issues* 4, No. 4 (Fall 1948): 28–38.

Bosch, Gerhard. *Infantile Autism.* Berlin: Springer-Verlag, 1970.

Bowlby, E. J. *Maternal Care and Mental Health.* World Health Organization, Monograph Series No. 2. Geneva: World Health Organization, 1952.

Bower, Eli. *Early Identification of Emotionally Handicapped Children in School.* Springfield, Ill.: Charles C Thomas, 1969.

Cruikshank, William M. "The Impact of Physical Disability on Social Adjustment." *Journal of Social Issues* 4, No. 4 (Fall 1948): 78–83.

Despert, Louise J. *The Emotionally Disturbed Child: Then and Now.* New York: Vintage Press, 1965.

Doll, Edgar A. "Recognition of Mental Retardation in the School-Age Child." In *Prevention and Treatment of Mental Re-*

tardation, edited by Irving Phillips. New York: Basic Books, 1966.

Dreikurs, Rudolf. "The Socio-psychological Dynamics of Physical Disability: A Review of the Adlerian Concept" *Journal of Social Issues* 4, No. 4 (Fall 1948): 39–54.

Dybwad, Gunnar. "Mental Retardation: Readings and Resources." In *Mental Retardation*, edited by Jerome Rothstein. New York: Holt, Rinehart, & Winston, 1964.

Flanigan, Patrick J., George R. Baker, and Lynn G. LaFollette. *An Orientation to Mental Retardation.* Springfield, Ill.: Charles C Thomas Publisher, 1970.

Friedlander, Bernard Z. "Listening, Language and the Auditory Environment." in *Exceptional Infant Vol. II Studies in Abnormalities,* ed. by Jerome Hellmuth. New York: Brunner-Mazel, Inc. 1971.

Haylett, Clarice, and Lydia Rapaport. "Mental Health Consultation." In *Handbook of Community Psychiatry and Community Mental Health*, edited by Leopold Bellak. New York: Grune & Stratton, 1964.

Kanner, Leo. "Autistic Disturbances of Affective Contact." *The Nervous Child* 2 (1943): 217–250.

Keller, Helen. *Midstream. My Later Life.* Garden City: Doubleday Doran, 1929.

Kessler, Jane W. *Psychopathology of Childhood.* Englewood Cliffs, N. J.: Prentice-Hall, Inc., 1966.

Levy, David. "Primary Affect Hunger." *American Journal of Psychiatry* 94 (1937): 643–652.

Lindemann, Erich; Warren T. Vaughan, and Manon McGinnis. "Prevention Intervention in a Four-Year-Old Child Whose Father Committed Suicide." In *Emotional Problems of Early Childhood*, edited by Gerald Caplan. New York: Basic Books, 1955.

McAndrew, Hilton. "Rigidity in the Deaf and the Blind." *Journal of Social Issues* 4, no. 4 (Fall 1948): 72–77.

Ribble, Margaret A. *The Rights of Infants.* New York: Columbia University Press, 1943.

Spitz, René. "Hospitalism: An Inquiry into the Genesis of Psychiatric Conditions in Early Childhood." In *The Psychoanalytic Study of the Child.* Vol. 1. New York: International University Press, 1945.

——— "Anxiety in Infancy: A Study of Its Manifestations in the First Year of Life." *International Journal of Psychoanalysis* 31 (1950): 138–143.

Wenar, Charles. "The Effects of a Motor Handicap on Personality, 2: The Effects on Integrative Ability." In *Readings on the Exceptional Child,* eds. E. Philip Trapp and Philip Himelstein. New York: Appleton-Century-Crofts, 1962.

Wortis, Joseph, ed. *Mental Retardation: An Annual Review.* New York: Grune & Stratton, 1970.

Home Influences

Although some sociologists call for a reexamination of the family, the present nuclear organization of the American family (mother, father, and children living together) is still considered an effective way of life. Each family produces its own style of life, and since people tend to learn what they live, they imitate the patterns of living learned at home. There is general agreement that the most significant single influence on the development of the child is the home.

Chief among the components of the home influence is the specific relationship between the child and his parents. Erikson maintains that whether a child learns trust depends on the nature of his early experiences with his parents. The role of the mother in the development of the child probably receives the most attention. She has been termed the expressive-affectional leader of the family, the specialist in child rearing. The father is traditionally the protector and provider, but the trend seems to be for the father to share more responsibility for affective responses to the children. The literature agrees that a coalition of mutual support between the parents lends unity and direction to the development of the family.

Second only to the influence of the parents on the developing child is the influence of his relationships with his brothers and sisters. Sibling relationships frequently determine the child's future attitudes toward himself, his peers, and his own family. Positive relationships between siblings are often overlooked in the abundance of literature describing conflicts and rivalry between siblings, which can create turmoil and affect human relationships for a lifetime.

The trauma of separation resulting from death or divorce sems to be real, although the effects of death are more clearly documented than the effects of divorce. Trauma is suffered in divorce but studies indicate that divorce causes few long-term adverse effects on children (Burchinal 1964; Goode 1956).

The home, then, is a microcosm. Its values and its patterns of human relationships are the prime factors in the development of the child.

Parent-Child Relationships

A central problem of research into parent-child relationships is the unreliability of studies. Marian Radke Yarrow (1963) asserts that "even most charitably, research in parent-child relations cannot be viewed as a field in which methodology is exemplary and in which evidence is firm and consistent" (1963). Yarrow's objection to the methodology revolves around the fact that the major technique has been interrogation of the mother. Her second objection is that a standard repertoire of child-rearing dimensions has been studied—namely, infant feeding, weaning, toilet training, the mother's handling of aggression, the depending needs of the child, achievement goals, and sex-role typing. For the past quarter of a century and more few other variables have been included in the intensive interviews of mothers. Yarrow evinces disappointment in the "emergence of clearly discernible relations between parental variables and child outcomes," citing correlations of .21 and significance at the .05 percent level of confidence as "barely holding out indications that something is there." In the same article Yarrow asks for research that: (a) deals with the *actual* behavior of mother and child; (b) considers additional variables; (c) concerns itself with genotypic (hereditary) differences and similarities; (d) deals with interactions; and (e) permits more defensible causative inferences. Since this article's publication, although no clear reversal in research methodology is evident, there has been evidence of more stress on (a) and (d).

The two variables most frequently analyzed are the dimensions of dependence–independence and acceptance–rejection. When the home encourages the child's confidence in himself, he tends to become independent. When the parent-child relationship encourages abject dependence, a child grows up unable to cope with experiences unless he is supported by the family. Related to these variables is the definition of parents as high or low authoritarian people. Whiting and

Child (1953) identify three kinds of discipline: (a) love-oriented, (b) denial of love, and (c) threats of ostracism. Research indicates that authoritarian parents (Hart 1957) tend to use the denial of love as a means of discipline, thus encouraging dependence on the parents for direction.

It is generally agreed that acceptance, or nurturance, encourages healthy growth and development. Much research has studied maternal rejection of children. For example, Donald Kinstler (1961), studying the open and covert rejection by mothers of male stutterers, indicates that mothers of "normal" children accept their children more than they reject them. Despite its specialized nature, this study supports the contention that rejection, especially by the mother (Slater 1962), results in overdependency (and sometimes overindependency) and hostility (Stagner 1961).

An interesting area of study is the relationship of the parent's view of himself to either acceptance or rejection of children. Fromm (1939), Horney (1950), Rogers (1951), and others maintain that self-love and love of others go hand in hand, that without self-love no other love can follow, and that acceptance of self eventually allows the acceptance of others. Gene Medinnus and Curtis (1963) studied 56 mothers in a cooperative nursery school and, using the Bills Index of Adjustment and Values, concluded that there is "a significant positive relation between maternal self-acceptance and child acceptance."

Even this cursory review of the literature suggests that neither the authoritarian nor the permissive parent–child relationship is best for the developing personality of the child. A middle ground, which we shall call the authoritative relationship, seems to be the most efficacious description of the ideal parent–child relationship. It is a relationship in which the maximum of child choice and freedom is allowed, with full recognition of the authority role of the parent at the proper time and in the proper place.

The boy was looking down at his gun, trying not to hear them quarrel, but he knew what his mother's face would be like—hurt and a little flushed, her chin trembling into stubbornness.

Butcher Bird

by Wallace Stegner

That summer the boy was alone on the farm except for his parents. His brother was working at Orullian's Grocery in town, and there was no one to run the trap line with or swim with in the dark, weed-smelling reservoir where garter snakes made straight rapid lines in the water and the skaters rowed close to shore. So every excursion was an adventure, even if it was only a trip across the three miles of prairie to Larsen's to get mail or groceries. He was excited at the visit to Garfield's as he was excited by everything unusual. The hot midsummer afternoon was still and breathless, the air harder to breathe than usual. He knew there was a change in weather coming because the gingersnaps in their tall cardboard box were soft and bendable when he snitched two to stick in his pocket. He could tell too by his father's grumpiness accumulated through two weeks of drought, his habit of looking off into the southwest, from which either rain or hot winds might come, that something was brewing. If it was rain everything would be fine, his father would hum under his breath getting breakfast, maybe let him drive the stoneboat or ride the mare down to Larsen's for mail. If it was hot wind they'd have to walk soft and speak softer, and it wouldn't be any fun.

They didn't know the Garfields, who had moved in only the fall before; but people said they had a good big house and a bigger barn and that Mr. Garfield was an Englishman and a little funny talking about scientific farming and making the desert blossom like the rose. The boy's father hadn't wanted to go, but his mother thought it was unneigh-

---

borly not to call at least once in a whole year when people lived only four miles away. She was, the boy knew, as anxious for a change, as eager to get out of that atmosphere of waiting to see what the weather would do—that tense and teeth gritting expectancy—as he was.

He found more than he looked for at Garfield's. Mr. Garfield was tall and bald with a big nose, and talked very softly and politely. The boy's father was determined not to like him right from the start.

When Mr. Garfield said, "Dear, I think we might have a glass of lemonade, don't you?" the boy saw his parents look at each other, saw the beginning of a contemptuous smile on his father's face, saw his mother purse her lips and shake her head ever so little. And when Mrs. Garfield, prim and spectacled, with a habit of tucking her head back and to one side while she listened to anyone talk, brought in the lemonade, the boy saw his father taste his and make a little face behind the glass. He hated any summer drink without ice in it, and had spent two whole weeks digging a dugout icehouse just so that he could have ice water and cold beer when the hot weather came.

But Mr. and Mrs. Garfield were nice people. They sat down in their new parlor and showed the boy's mother the rug and the gramophone. When the boy came up curiously to inspect the little box with the petunia-shaped horn and the little china dog with "His Master's Voice" on it, and the Garfields found that he had never seen or heard a gramophone, they put on a cylinder like a big spool of tightly wound black thread and lowered a needle on it, and out came a man's voice singing in Scotch brogue, and his mother smiled and nodded and said, "My land, Harry Lauder! I heard him once a long time ago. Isn't it wonderful, Sonny?"

It was wonderful all right. He inspected it, reached out his fingers to touch things, wiggled the big horn to see if it was loose or screwed in. His father warned him sharply to keep his hands off, but then Mr. Garfield smiled and said, "Oh, he can't hurt it. Let's play something else," and found a record about the saucy little bird on Nelly's hat that had them all laughing. They let him wind the machine and play the record over again, all by himself, and he was very careful. It was a fine machine. He wished he had one.

About the time he had finished playing his sixth or seventh record, and George M. Cohan was singing "She's a grand old rag, she's a high-flying flag, and forever in peace may she wave," he glanced at his father and discovered that he was grouchy about something. He wasn't taking any part in the conversation but was sitting with his chin in his hand staring out of the window. Mr. Garfield was looking at him a little helplessly. His eyes met the boy's and he motioned him over.

"What do you find to do all summer? Only child, are you?"

"No, sir. My brother's in Whitemud. He's twelve. He's got a job."

"So you come out on the farm to help," said Mr. Garfield. He had his hand on the boy's shoulder and his voice was so kind that the boy lost his shyness and felt no embarrassment at all in being out there in the middle of the parlor with all of them watching.

"I don't help much," he said. "I'm too little to do anything but drive the stoneboat, Pa says. When I'm twelve he's going to get me a gun and then I can go hunting."

"Hunting?" Mr. Garfield said. "What do you hunt?"

"Oh, gophers and weasels. I got a pet weasel. His name's Lucifer."

"Well," said Mr. Garfield. "You seem to be a pretty manly little chap. What do you feed your weasel?"

"Gophers." The boy thought it best not to say that the gophers were live ones he threw into the weasel's cage. He thought probably Mr. Garfield would be a little shocked at that.

Mr. Garfield straightened up and looked round at the grown folks. "Isn't it a shame," he said, "that there are so many predatory animals and pests in this country that we have to spend our time destroying them? I hate killing things."

"I hate weasels," the boy said. "I'm just saving this one till he turns into an ermine, and then I'm going to skin him. Once I speared a weasel with the pitchfork in the chicken coop and he dropped right off the tine and ran up my leg and bit me after he was speared clean through."

He finished breathlessly, and his mother smiled at him, motioning him not to talk so much. But Mr. Garfield was still looking at him kindly. "So you want to make war on the cruel things, the weasels and the hawks," he said.

"Yes, sir," the boy said. He looked at his mother and it was all right. He hadn't spoiled anything by telling about the weasels.

"Now that reminds me," Mr. Garfield said, rising. "Maybe I've got something you'd find useful."

He went into another room and came back with a .22 in his hand. "Could you use this?"

"I . . . yes, *sir!*" the boy said. He had almost, in his excitement, said "I hope to whisk in your piskers," because that was what his father always said when he meant anything real hard.

"If your parents want you to have it," Mr. Garfield said and raised his eyebrows at the boy's mother. He didn't look at the father, but the boy did.

"Can I, Pa?"

"I guess so," his father said. "Sure."

"Thank Mr. Garfield nicely," said his mother.

"Gee," the boy breathed. "Thanks, Mr. Garfield, ever so much."

"There's a promise goes with it," Mr. Garfield said. "I'd like you to promise never to shoot anything with it but the bloodthirsty animals—the cruel ones like weasels and hawks. Never anything like birds or prairie dogs."

"How about butcher birds?"

"Butcher birds?" Mr. Garfield said.

"Shrikes," said the boy's mother. "We've got some over by our place. They kill all sorts of things, snakes and gophers and other birds. They're worse than the hawks because they just kill for the fun of it."

"By all means," said Mr. Garfield. "Shoot all the shrikes you see. A thing that kills for the fun of it . . ." He shook his head and his voice got solemn, almost like the voice of Mr. McGregor, the Sunday School Superintendent in town, when he was asking the benediction. "There's something about the way the war drags on, or maybe just this country," he said, "that makes me hate killing. I just can't bear to shoot anything any more, even a weasel."

The boy's father turned cold eyes away from Mr. Garfield and looked out of the window. One big brown hand, a little dirty from the wheel of the car, rubbed against the day-old bristles on his jaws. Then he stood up and stretched. "Well, we got to be going," he said.

"Oh, stay a little while," Mr. Garfield said. "You just came. I wanted to show you my trees."

The boy's mother stared at him. "Trees?"

He smiled. "Sounds a bit odd out here, doesn't it? But I think trees will grow. I've made some plantings down below."

"I'd love to see them," she said. "Sometimes I'd give almost anything to get into a good deep shady woods. Just to smell it, and feel how cool . . ."

"There's a little story connected with these," Mr. Garfield said. He spoke to the mother alone, warmly. "When we first decided to come out here I said to Martha that if trees wouldn't grow we shouldn't stick it. That's just what I said, 'If trees won't grow we shan't stick it.' Trees are almost the breath of life to me."

The boy's father was shaken by a sudden spell of coughing, and the mother shot a quick look at him and looked back at Mr. Garfield with a light flush on her cheekbones. "I'd love to see them," she said. "I was raised in Minnesota, and I never will get used to a place as barren as this."

"When I think of the beeches back home in England," Mr. Garfield said, and shook his head with a puckering smile round his eyes.

The father lifted himself heavily out of his chair and followed the rest of them out to the coulee edge. Below them willows grew profusely along the almost-dry creek, and farther back from the water there was a grove of perhaps twenty trees about a dozen feet high.

"I'm trying cottonwoods first because they can stand dry weather," Mr. Garfield said.

The mother was looking down with all her longings suddenly plain and naked in her eyes. "It's wonderful," she said. "I'd give almost anything to have some on our place."

"I found the willows close by here," said Mr. Garfield. "Just at the south end of the hills they call Old-Man-on-His-Back, where the stream comes down."

"Stream?" the boy's father said. "You mean that trickle?"

"It's not much of a stream," Mr. Garfield said apologetically. "But . . ."

"Are there any more there?" the mother said.

"Oh, yes. You could get some. Cut them diagonally and push them into any damp ground. They'll grow."

"They'll grow about six feet high," the father said.

"Yes," said Mr. Garfield. "They're not, properly speaking, trees. Still . . ."

"It's getting pretty smothery," the father said rather loudly. "We better be getting on."

This time Mr. Garfield didn't object, and they went back to the car exchanging promises of visits. The father jerked the crank and climbed into the Ford, where the boy was sighting along his gun. "Put that down," his father said. "Don't you know any better than to point a gun around people?"

"It isn't loaded."

"They never are," his father said. "Put it down now."

The Garfields were standing with their arms round each other's waists, waiting to wave good-bye. Mr. Garfield reached over and picked something from his wife's dress.

"What was it, Alfred?" she said peering.

"Nothing. Just a bit of fluff."

The boy's father coughed violently and the car started with a jerk. With his head down almost to the wheel, still coughing, he waved, and the mother and the boy waved as they went down along the badly set cedar posts of the pasture fence. They were almost a quarter of a mile away before the boy, with a last wave of the gun, turned round again and saw that his father was purple with laughter. He rocked the car with his joy, and when his wife said, "Oh, Harry, you big fool," he pointed helplessly to his shoulder. "Would you mind," he said. "Would you mind brushing that bit o' fluff off me showldah?" He roared again, pounding the wheel. "I shawn't stick it," he said. "I bloody well shawn't stick it, you knaow!"

"It isn't fair to laugh at him," she said. "He can't help being English."

"He can't help being a sanctimonious old mudhen either, braying about his luv-ly luv-ly trees. They'll freeze out the first winter."

"How do you know? Maybe it's like he says—if they get a start they'll grow here as well as anywhere."

"Maybe there's a gold mine in our back yard too, but I'm not gonna dig to see. I couldn't stick it."

"Oh, you're just being stubborn," she said. "Just because you didn't like Mr. Garfield . . ."

He turned on her in heavy amazement. "Well, my God! Did you?"

"I thought he was very nice," she said, and sat straighter in the back seat, speaking loudly above the creak of the springs and cough of the motor. "They're trying to make a home, not just a wheat crop. I liked them."

"Uh, huh." He was not laughing any more now. Sitting beside him, the boy could see that his face had hardened and the cold look had come into his eye again. "So I should start talking like I had a mouthful of bran, and planting trees around the house that'll look like clothesline poles in two months."

"I didn't say that."

"You thought it though." He looked irritably at the sky, misted with the same delusive film of cloud that had fooled him for three days, and spat at the roadside. "You thought it all the time we were there. 'Why aren't you more like Mr. Garfield, he's such a nice man.' " With mincing savagery he swung round and mocked her. "Shall I make it a walnut grove? Or a big maple sugar bush? Or maybe you'd like an orange orchard."

The boy was looking down at his gun, trying not to hear them quarrel, but he knew what his mother's face would be like—hurt and a little flushed, her chin trembling into stubbornness. "I don't suppose you could bear to have a rug on the floor, or a gramophone?" she said.

He smacked the wheel hard. "Of course I could bear it if we could afford it. But I sure as hell would rather do without than be like that old sandhill crane."

"I don't suppose you'd like to take

me over to the Old-Man-on-His-Back some day to get some willow slips either."

"What for?"

"To plant down in the coulee, by the dam."

"That dam dries up every August. Your willows wouldn't live till snow flies."

"Well, would it do any harm to try?"

"Oh, shut up!" he said. "Just thinking about that guy and his fluff and his trees gives me the pleefer."

The topless Ford lurched, one wheel at a time, through the deep burnout by their pasture corner, and the boy clambered out with his gun in his hand to slip the loop from the three-strand gate. It was then that he saw the snake, a striped limp ribbon, dangling on the fence, and a moment later the sparrow, neatly butchered and hung by the throat from the barbed wire. He pointed the gun at them. "Lookit!" he said. "Lookit what the butcher bird's been doing."

His father's violent hand waved at him from the seat. "Come on! Get the wire out of the way!"

The boy dragged the gate through the dust, and the Ford went through and up behind the house, perched on the bare edge of the coulee in the midst of its baked yard and framed by the dark fireguard overgrown with Russian thistle. Walking across that yard a few minutes later, the boy felt its hard heat under his sneakers. There was hardly a spear of grass within the fireguard. It was one of his father's prides that the dooryard should be like cement. "Pour your wash water out long enough," he said, "and you'll have a surface so hard it won't even make mud." Religiously he threw his water out three times a day, carrying it sometimes a dozen steps to dump it on a dusty or grassy spot.

The mother had objected at first, asking why they had to live in the middle of an alkali flat, and why they couldn't let grass grow up to the door. But he snorted her down. Everything round the house ought to be bare as a bone. Get a good prairie fire going and it'd jump that guard like nothing, and if they had grass to the door where'd they be? She said why not plow a wider fireguard then, one a fire couldn't jump, but he said he had other things to do besides plowing fifty-foot fireguards.

They were arguing inside when the boy came up on the step to sit down and aim his empty .22 at a fence post. Apparently his mother had been persistent, and persistence when he was not in a mood for it angered the father worse than anything else. Their talk came vaguely through his concentration, but he shut his ears on it. If that spot on the fence post was a coyote now, and he held the sight steady, right on it, and pulled the trigger, that old coyote would jump about eighty feet in the air and come down dead as a mackerel, and he could tack his hide on the barn the way Mr. Larsen had one, only the dogs had jumped and torn the tail and hind legs off Mr. Larsen's pelt, and he wouldn't get more than the three-dollar bounty out of it. But then Mr. Larsen had shot his with a shotgun anyway, and the hide wasn't worth much even before the dogs tore it. . . .

"I can't for the life of me see why not," his mother said inside. "We could do it now. We're not doing anything else."

"I tell you they wouldn't grow!"

said his father with emphasis on every word. "Why should we run our tongues out doing everything that mealy-mouthed fool does?"

"I don't want anything but the willows. They're easy."

He made his special sound of contempt, half snort, half grunt. After a silence she tried again. "They might even have pussies on them in the spring. Mr. Garfield thinks they'd grow, and he used to work in a greenhouse, his wife told me."

"This isn't a greenhouse, for Chrissake."

"Oh, let it go," she said. "I've stood it this long without any green things around. I guess I can stand it some more."

The boy, aiming now toward the gate where the butcher bird, coming back to his prey, would in just a minute fly right into Dead-eye's unerring bullet, heard his father stand up suddenly.

"Abused, aren't you?" he said.

The mother's voice rose. "No, I'm not abused! Only I can't see why it would be so awful to get some willows. Just because Mr. Garfield gave me the idea, and you didn't like him. . . ."

"You're right I didn't like Mr. Garfield," the father said. "He gave me a pain right under the crupper."

"Because," the mother's voice said bitterly, "he calls his wife 'dear' and puts his arm around her and likes trees. It wouldn't occur to you to put your arm around your wife, would it?"

The boy aimed and held his breath. His mother ought to keep still, because if she didn't she'd get him real mad and then they'd both have to tiptoe around the rest of the day. He heard his father's breath whistle through his teeth, and his voice, mincing, nasty. "Would you like me to kiss you now, *dear?*"

"I wouldn't let you touch me with a ten-foot pole," his mother said. She sounded just as mad as he did, and it wasn't often she let herself get that way. The boy squirmed over when he heard the quick hard steps come up behind him and pause. Then his father's big hand, brown and meaty and felted with fine black hair, reached down over his shoulder and took the .22.

"Let's see this cannon old Scissorbill gave you," he said.

It was a single-shot, bolt-action Savage, a little rusty on the barrel, the bolt sticky with hardened grease when the father removed it. Sighting up through the barrel, he grunted. "Takes care of a gun like he takes care of his farm. Probably used it to cultivate his luv-ly trees."

He went out into the sleeping porch, and after a minute came back with a rag and a can of machine oil. Hunching the boy over on the step, he sat down and began rubbing the bolt with the oil-soaked rag.

"I just can't bear to shoot anything any more," he said, and laughed suddenly. "I just cawn't stick it, little man." He leered at the boy, who grinned back uncertainly. Squinting through the barrel again, the father breathed through his nose and clamped his lips together, shaking his head.

The sun lay heavy on the baked yard. Out over the corner of the pasture a soaring hawk caught wind and sun at the same time, so that his light breast feathers flashed as he banked and rose. Just wait, the boy thought. Wait till I get my gun working and I'll fix you, you hen-robber. He thought of the three chicks a hawk had struck earlier in the summer, the three balls of yellow with the barred mature plumage just coming through. Two of them dead when he got there and chased the hawk away, the other gasping with its crop slashed wide open and the wheat spilling from it on the ground. His mother had sewed up the crop, and the chicken had lived, but it always looked droopy, like a plant in drought time, and sometimes it would stand and work its bill as if it were choking.

By golly, he thought, I'll shoot every hawk and butcher bird in twenty miles. I'll . . .

"Rustle around and find me a piece of baling wire," his father said. "This barrel looks like a henroost."

Behind the house he found a piece of rusty wire, brought it back and watched his father straighten it, wind a bit of rag round the end, ram it up and down through the barrel, and peer through again. "He's leaded her so you can hardly see the grooves," he said. "But maybe she'll shoot. We'll fill her with vinegar and cork her up tonight."

The mother was behind them, leaning against the jamb and watching. She reached down and rumpled the father's black hair. "The minute you get a gun in your hand you start feeling better," she said. "It's just a shame you weren't born fifty years sooner."

"A gun's a good tool," he said. "It hadn't ought to be misused. Gun like this is enough to make a guy cry."

"Well, you've got to admit it was nice of Mr. Garfield to give it to Sonny," she said. It was the wrong thing to say. The boy had a feeling somehow that she knew it was the wrong thing to say, that she said it just to have one tiny triumph over him. He knew it would make him boiling mad again, even before he heard his father's answer.

"Oh, sure, Mr. Garfield's a fine man. He can preach a better sermon than any homesteader in Saskatchewan. God Almighty! everything he does is better than what I do. All right. All right, *all right!* Why the hell don't you move over there if you like it so well?"

"If you weren't so blind . . . !"

He rose with the .22 in his hand and pushed past her into the house. "I'm not so blind," he said heavily in passing. "You've been throwing that bastard up to me for two hours. It don't take very good eyes to see what that means."

His mother started to say, "All because I want a few little . . ." but the boy cut in on her, anxious to help the situation somehow. "Will it shoot now?" he said.

His father said nothing. His mother looked down at him, shrugged, sighed, smiled bleakly with a tight mouth. She moved aside when the father came back with a box of cartridges in his hand. He ignored his wife, speaking to the boy alone in the particular half-jocular tone he always used with him or the dog when he wasn't mad or exasperated.

"Thought I had these around," he said. "Now we'll see what this smokepole will do."

He slipped a cartridge in and locked the bolt, looking round for something to shoot at. Behind him the mother's feet moved on the floor, and her voice came purposefully. "I can't see why you have to act this way," she said. "I'm going over and get some slips myself."

There was a long silence. The angled shade lay sharp as a knife across the baked front yard. The father's cheek was pressed against the stock of the gun, his arms and hands as steady as stone.

"How'll you get there?" he said, whispering down the barrel.

"I'll walk."

"Five miles and back."

"Yes, five miles and back. Or fifty miles and back. If there was any earthly reason why you should mind . . ."

"I don't mind," he said, and his voice was soft as silk. "Go ahead."

Close to his mother's long skirts in the doorway, the boy felt her stiffen as if she had been slapped. He squirmed anxiously, but his desperation could find only the question he had asked before. His voice squeaked on it: "Will it shoot now?"

"See that sparrow out there?" his father said, still whispering. "Right out by that cactus?"

"Harry!" the mother said. "If you shoot that harmless little bird!"

Fascinated, the boy watched his father's dark face against the rifle stock, the locked, immovable left arm, the thick finger crooked inside the trigger guard almost too small to hold it. He saw the sparrow, gray, white-breasted, hopping obliviously in search of bugs, fifty feet out on the gray earth. "I just . . . can't . . . bear . . . to . . . shoot . . . anything," the father said, his face like dark stone, his lips hardly moving. "I just . . . can't . . . stick it!"

"Harry!" his wife screamed.

The boy's mouth opened, a dark wash of terror shadowed his vision of the baked yard cut by its sharp angle of shade.

"Don't, Pa!"

The rocklike figure of his father never moved. The thick finger squeezed slowly down on the trigger, there was a thin, sharp report, and the sparrow jerked and collapsed into a shapeless wad on the ground. It was as if, in the instant of the shot, all its clean outlines vanished. Head, feet, the white breast, the perceptible outlines of the folded wings, disappeared all at once, were crumpled together and lost, and the boy sat beside his father on the step with the echo of the shot still in his ears.

He did not look at either of his parents. He looked only at the crumpled sparrow. Step by step, unable to keep away, he went to it, stooped, and picked it up. Blood stained his fingers, and he held the bird by the tail while he wiped the smeared hand on his overalls. He heard the click as the bolt was shot and the empty cartridge ejected, and he saw his mother come swiftly out of the house past his father, who sat still on the step. Her hands were clenched, and she walked with her head down, as if fighting tears.

"Ma!" the boy said dully. "Ma, what'll I do with it?"

She stopped and turned, and for a moment they faced each other. He saw the dead pallor of her face, the burning eyes, the not-quite-controllable quiver of her lips. But her words, when they came, were flat and level, almost casual.

"Leave it right there," she said. "After a while your father will want to hang it on the barbed wire."

Discussion

In a parent–child relationship the language of the parent, whether spoken or unspoken, is explicit to the child. Children know how to interpret correctly a parent's half-smile, raised eyebrow, or reflective pipe smoking. In this story the boy infers from studying the father's facial expression that his father is uncomfortable visiting with the Garfields. The boy is also aware that the visit will bring the long-harbored unspoken dissension between his parents into open conflict. This knowledge makes the boy uncomfortable because he feels strong loyalty to both parents. He knows his father's taciturn ways, but he knows and admires his father's good qualities; his dad is someone a boy can depend on to fix a gun, he has thorough knowledge of the terrain in that part of the country, and he knows what to expect from the weather and the land.

Yet in the home the boy and the mother are conspirators in reading the father's moods, always alert to indications that he is cross. The mother is the peacemaker and the compromiser in the family; she is careful never to get quite as angry as her husband. She, too, respects his knowledge of the land, and she respects and is dependent on his breadwinning capacity in an environment that is often harsh and brutal to the farmer. However, the mother is filled with resentment. The visit exposes her need for affection and her frustrated longings and desires.

The boy tries to ward off the oncoming exposure of his parents' long-standing differences. He tries to divert the inflaming line of conversation between the parents. Yet when dissension is brought into the open, as happens in this story, it is better for all concerned. Even in an ideal home conflict cannot be avoided; differences in personality, interests, likes, and dislikes are bound to cause some dissatisfaction among family members. Children are particularly uneasy about conflict between parents, and their distress is often attributable to the concern that they somehow are responsible for the conflict. In this story the boy knows he has angered his father by accepting the gun and by obviously enjoying the warmth and hospitality shown by their neighbors. There is a very special quality to the parent–child relationship that is not repeated between the parents, because no parent can experience the other parent in exactly the same way the child does. The child views each parent from his own perspective. The boy undoubtedly would like to see his mother pleased with the planting of trees on their property but no more so than he would like to keep his father in good spirits.

Although these parents express their anger, we are concerned about their ability to seek accord. The father is not used to exposing his emotions and probably views such exposure as a sign of weakness in a man. The mother has not really accepted her husband's unemotional style, which is different from her own. Both parents need to make their wants more readily known instead of permitting them to go unheeded for such a long period of time that an explosive scene becomes inevitable. The boy, in turn, is not learning the best way of communicating openly and honestly in a close relationship.

Springboards for Inquiry

(1) What is the influence of hostility between parents on children?

(2) The boy in this story finds himself a victim of the anger between both parents. How permanent may be the damage of an experience like this?

(3) How do you think the bitterness between the parents will be resolved?

(4) Do you think the parents are aware of the boy's distress? What does your response imply about these adults' attitudes regarding children and their place in the family?

(5) If you were to counsel this family, what would be some of your objectives?

(6) To which agencies should we turn for better provisions for marital counseling?

She was stroking his back, down inside the neck of his shirt. What do you want to follow me for?"

The Houses of the City

by Gina Berriault

On some days he longed to be with his mother before the hour of her return to their rooms. In the afternoon he would seek her out at whatever house she was cleaning that day, even though the place was halfway across the city, up in the heights where the big houses stood apart like rich merchants' wives watching their husbands' ships entering the bay below. In his small body was the quality of the pointer dog. He walked slightly stooped, pushing forward, his feet going down in a plodding way.

It was late in his ninth year when he began this practice. Something drew him to her. He would be in the midst of a scuffle after school, along a sidewalk somewhere, and suddenly he would think of her and at that moment offer nothing further to the struggle. This silent urgency was more effective in breaking his opponent's grip than was his fierce, animal strength. Always in the morning she told him where she would be that day, so that if anything happened to him at school his teacher could call her right away. He felt that it was impossible for anything to happen to him. The only way that harm could befall him was by its befalling her.

She was alarmed the first time she opened a door to him. He was not sick, he assured her. But he had no other reason to give for his coming. Of his fear of her dying he could not tell, because to give words to this fear was like pronouncing sentence upon her. If he kept it to himself, the fear might prove groundless. After the first time they said nothing on his arrival. He made no demands upon her, and complyingly sat in the chair she designated, his hands folded

---

obviously away from the lure of knick-knacks and magazines. He listened to the sounds of her cleaning in other rooms, and was not restless.

Certain women were fascinated by him, as if, in his silent clinging to one chair, he were a large moth, its wings of exquisite design but its intentions unknown. Once, as he sat in a glass-enclosed sunporch, a large-leafed plant growing from a blue, glazed bowl on the carpet fingered his cheek, touched his elbow each time he fidgeted, but he did not move to another chair, hypnotized by the plant and its curiosity as if it were the lady of the house. Then one afternoon he was sitting in the hallway of an upstairs apartment, facing in a dutiful way the opposite wall and taking a small liberty in examining minutely the oval piece of wood that hung on the wall, a yellow horse painted on it, the long, white tail of the horse touching the green grass sprouting up. Aside from the sounds of his mother at her tasks, he heard another person astir in the bedroom beyond the oval picture. He heard the sluggish movement of a person turning under blankets, then the sound of slippers scraped along the floor. He heard a man talking to himself with the voice that is acquired while the body is lying down: a voice pocketed deep in the throat, granular, caressing, complaining.

From the half-open bedroom door came a young man, not much older than a high-school boy. His hair was red and stood up in curls, as if startled in advance, and he paused there in the doorway, staring in exaggerated surprise at the boy in the hallway chair. He was tying the tasseled belt of his bathrobe, which was a jewel-green silk, and one end of the belt he held in surprise across the palm of his right hand.

"Fran!" he called. "Who is this you let in?" His voice was cajoling and demanding; he listened to his own voice like a violin pupil listens to the music he makes. "Do you want to see me?" he asked, dropping his head in a pointing way. "If you have any business with me, speak up! If it's a debt I owe, let me congratulate you on getting past the door. Most of my creditors sit on the steps outside. Well, how much do I owe you? Whatever it is, I can't pay it."

Now he placed his hands on the arms of the chair, leaning over the boy, and the boy turned his face away, embarrassed, from the corners of his eyes meeting the young man's eyes.

"I can't pay you for this reason," explained the young man. "Do you see this house, how clean it is? Well, you should have seen it before that woman took a mop and vacuum to it." His close face was extremely square, and his hair, so near, was something to be puzzled out, something with an answer to it, its curls were so many and entwined. "If anyone is going to be paid," he said, "it's her, and you'll have to wait your turn. She works like a dog and stands for a lot of abuse from her employers, and she's constantly worrying all the time about that son of hers. She's got to keep him decently clothed, you know, and fed." Their eyes met, forced by the young man's eyes to a mutual comprehension of her plight. "But I'll tell you," he said, laying his hand on the boy's shoulder. "Come into the kitchen with me and settle for a cup of chocolate."

Under the spell the boy slid off the chair so abruptly that his head hit the young man in the chest. With the nape of his neck in his host's hand, the boy was marched down the narrow hallway. In the kitchen his mother was seated on a high stool, polishing silverware at the sink, a silk scarf of many faded colors wrapped around her head. She glanced over her shoulder at them, an absentness in her eyes as if she watched a dog or a cat, a household pet, saunter into the kitchen. Afraid suddenly that his presence jeopardized her job and that she was not going to recognize him, he stumbled as the young man pressed him down into a chair. For a moment he did not know who he should be, her son or the bill collector.

From the refrigerator, the host drew out a bottle of milk, poured some into a pan. Then he stirred in several teaspoons of cocoa and several of sugar, in this process spilling some of both on the waxed linoleum, and his leather slippers made a sticky, rasping sound as, uncaring, unhearing, he walked about.

"He don't need no chocolate," she said.

Up went the young man's spoon in a gesture of amazement and chagrin. The young man was startled out of his wits by this rudeness. "Is that the way to talk to a guest of mine?" he cried.

The boy laughed out loud because he was sure now of who he was, and he shifted in his chair, granted a freedom of movement in the chairs of this house.

"For that," said the young man to her, "you can't have any. She can't, can she?" he asked, but he asked it of her, leaning his face close to hers, delicately close, the two profiles, presented to the boy in the chair, reminding him of the approach, the courtship of butterflies, touching and yet not touching in an ascending spiral of understanding. At once he was left out of the game. He had thought the game was for him and he learned that it was played only to accentuate some knowledge between his mother and the young man. And the boy was caught in the midst of his laughter, his elbows lifted eccentrically behind him like wings going up.

They had hot chocolate together, the young man and he, the host sitting with his legs crossed, his robe falling away from his bare thighs, not at all embarrassed that a woman could see so much of his body. The young man drank in a hungry, nervous way, bobbing his head down impatiently to meet the cup on its way up. It was when he was lifting his head, swallowing elaborately in his haste to continue what he was saying, that he spoke the boy's name: "Matt," he said, "you've got catch-all ears. Listen to this," and went on with his story. But the boy glanced up at his mother, unbelievingly. She had told his name to the young man, but of the young man the boy had been told not a thing.

When the host said, "Well, come along," Matt followed him up the hallway and into the bedroom. The curtains were closed, and the young man switched on the lamp by the bed, got down on his knee, and rummaged through a pile of magazines that lay under the bed. This room hadn't been cleaned yet. It smelled of cigarette smoke, of night perspiration, and upon the lamp's table were strewn a number of little things: magenta theater tickets, manicure scissors, a red glass ashtray, a man's green-edged handkerchief, a life-saver candy, a dime and four pennies. Was the young man an actor? he wondered, for he had heard that actors slept all day. There was something dramatic in the young man's bowed back, covered with the slick green robe, and in the leg stretched out behind the bent knee with its white knot of calf and its quivering heel. Rising, the young man placed in the boy's hand a thick magazine, a photograph of a Dalmatian dog on its cover, and gently prodded him to turn around; and the boy, lifting his head so that he could find his way out through the dimness beyond the lamp, saw his mother's black coat thrown over the back of a rocker, and on the seat of the rocker lay her small brown hat.

Again he sat in the hallway, turning the pages of the sports magazine, while in the bedroom the young man poked about, getting dressed. The magazine had pictures of men in hip boots, fishing, of dogs carrying ducks from reedy water, of horses; and the smell of the paper was clean, strong as lacquer, the pages satin smooth and weighted in his hands. He turned up the palm of his right hand to see if it were dirty and would soil the white luster. Usually, he thought, she left her coat and hat in the kitchen. Once, in another house, when it was time for them to go, she had brought her coat from the back porch, where a late afternoon rain had flicked it through the screen; it was too shabby, she had said, to hang in the hall closet, because, if a guest came, he would not want to hang his coat next to hers. But in this house her coat was lying on a chair in a bedroom. His right hand was again on the magazine, but he still could not say whether his hands were clean or grimy. Lifting his hand again, he decided that it was not clean enough, and he closed the magazine, placing it on the floor beside his chair.

Closely he listened to the sound of her in the kitchen, his hands clasped in his lap. By such devout observance of her presence he was proving to her that he was a more loving son than the young man could ever be, no matter how hard the other tried.

They would ride home together in the evening, boarding a trolley or a cable car, depending upon which neighborhood she was working in, and something in the waning day and in sitting beside her on the yellow, wooden seat, watching the tall, narrow houses slip by like boards in one long fence, caused him to become tired of premonition. With the onset of evening's soft glamour, she would become for him quite alive and everlasting. On their journey home that evening, he sat beside her in the trolley, clasping between his knees her black cloth shopping bag filled with garments the young man had given her for mending, and each time she laid her hand upon his knee the love and shame of the betrayed wrinkled across his face. If he were unduly frightened by the way her hands were turning translucent, by the way her veins were rising along her forearms, if she was, after all, not going to die, there was, he thought, another way she could be lost. When they climbed down from the trolley and walked along the street to their rooming house, he swung the shopping bag in his left hand so that the bag separated her and himself. But when the bag, light as it was, scraped against her ankle, his heart contracted with remorse as if he had deliberately hit her.

When she unlocked the door, he slipped in before her, lay directly down upon the couch. Since their kitchen had no window, she switched on its ceiling light, and gradually as the street grew darker, as the sunlight, shining eastward down the street, withdrew its flame from the lamp at the corner, leaving a dark gray smudge in the globe, the panes of the bow window in which he lay became black mirrors and he saw in the one that was near to his face the reflection of the kitchen doorway and his mother by the stove. The picture was miniature, unreal, and when she spoke to him he answered her by speaking to the reflection, but this disturbed him and he turned his face inward to the rooms.

She came from the kitchen carrying plates, but instead of placing them on the table she continued to hold them in her hands while she faced him, pressing her hip against the edge of the table. Her face and down the front of her were obscured by the darkness of the room, but the sides of her thin body and some outer strands of her short, colorless hair were lit by the light from the kitchen behind her. She laughed a bit, in a dry, unanimated way that did not change the set of her head. "What do you want to follow me for?" she said.

It was like an accusation of a crime he had been concealing. He put his hands over his ears.

When she had set the table, she came and stood above him, her arms hanging awkwardly at her sides. Into this room whose cold was not yet dispelled by the warm air from the kitchen, she brought in her body the heat from the stove and on her skin the steam from the kettle.

"Well?" she asked, and receiving no answer from him, said, "Come, sit down and eat."

Obediently he sat up, but as he got to his feet she put her hands against his chest, pushing him down again. Before he knew it, she was lying beside him and they were holding each other so closely that to breathe he had to turn his face upward.

She was stroking his back, down inside the neck of his shirt. "What do you want to follow me for?"

With his arms around her he found himself listening to her body and heard her listening to his, and it was comical, almost, like two persons staring at each other through the same keyhole. In that moment he changed his reason for following her. It was not the possibility of her dying that troubled him, but something else that he had picked up just an hour ago, and it was this they were both listening to. The young man was pretending to be her son, and she did not object. This disloyalty of hers became so loud in their bodies that she had to let go of him and sit up, unable, he knew, to bear him any more against her.

But he lay on his stomach, his face in the damp plush. "How did he know my name?" he asked.

"I told him," she said. "Can't I talk about my own son?"

"But you never told me you told him my name."

"Do I have to tell you about everybody I tell about my son?"

Was it something he had exaggerated all along, he wondered, their alliance against the persons she worked for? Although she came home bringing stories about them, describing them and their visitors jabbingly, vindictively, had he believed mistakenly that with these stories she bound herself and him together?"

"Come now," she said. "Get up and eat."

But he made no effort to rise. He saw her standing away from him, weary of her own guilt. But he knew that she was as uncertain as he of which side she was on, his or the young man's with the crudely bared legs.

Discussion

The bond between Matt and his mother presages an unhealthy emotional development for Matt. At a time when Matt's peers should be holding increasing interest for him, Matt is reaching out for more closeness and dependency on his mother. He harbors a morbid fear that she may die, which suddenly intrudes itself upon him when he is engaged in the usual after-school tussles with his schoolmates. Matt will then leave the group to seek out his mother at any of the various homes at which she does domestic work. He is content to spend the remainder of the afternoon sitting quietly, waiting for her to finish so that they may go home together. Matt's fear of losing his mother is reminiscent of the very early and primitive fear in children of being abandoned. Usually children work through this fear between the ages of four and five. It is usual in the next stage of development for the child to strike out more assertively in an attempt to define his own sense of self and to move toward a maturing sense of independence.

Other elements in Matt's home life do not offer solace to his fear of being abandoned. Matt has no siblings with whom to share experiences. The fact that there is no father in the family picture also makes Matt vulnerable to his fears, but this does not explain entirely his overwhelming need to maintain so exclusive a relationship with his mother. When Matt visits his mother at the young man's home, he suddenly faces the specter of losing her in still another way—to another person. This knowledge stirs deep feelings of disquiet and jealousy. Matt is angry at his mother for her intimacy with another person, but he is unable to express this anger for fear of jeopardizing his relationship with her. Matt is the victim of his obsession. His fear can draw an ever tighter knot around his range of emotional expression because of his vulnerability, and ultimately his functioning can be severely limited.

Springboards for Inquiry

(1) We arc uncomfortable for Matt, who at nine years of age is overly enmeshed in a dependency relationship with his mother. What situation might precipitate the mother's recognition of the full extent of her son's problem and the need for intervention?

(2) Who needs help most, Matt or his mother? Should both receive help?

(3) What kind of mental health intervention would you envision for Matt or his mother or both?

(4) Learn about the resources your community offers for families who need mental health services.

Sibling Relationships

As far back as literature goes, one of the most complicated subjects is the area of sibling relationships. In the Old Testament we become aware of such problems as the relationship between Cain and Abel and the cheating of Esau by Jacob. Inevitably the sharing of the family's nurturance by more than one child causes problems. The two most frequently researched areas of sibling relationships are sibling rivalry and jealousy.

When a new baby arrives, older children may feel a degree of jealousy precipitated by the sudden forced sharing of time, affection, and lifespace. The arrival of a baby in the family is usually not too traumatic for a very young child, who does not necessarily equate a change with the arrival of the new baby (Lasko 1954). How that new baby feels about his older siblings depends largely on how they treat him; if they view him positively he will like them, otherwise he can be conditioned to fear and dislike them (Bossard and Boll 1960).

The three-year-old is perhaps the most vulnerable to the arrival of a new baby. Although he looks forward to the arrival of the baby as a playmate, his new brother or sister cannot even do things with him.* As he grows older the new arrival may become jealous of the prerogatives accorded the older child. This reciprocal envy–jealousy relationship has been known to persist well into adulthood.†

---

* For further amplification consult Lidz 1968.

† In *You and Your Child's World* (Landau 1967) the comparison of the growth of two brothers all through childhood is noted as causing alienation from the parents and lifelong jealousy between the brothers.

Lidz (1968) is the only source who discusses the positive relationship between siblings. Parents tend to pay attention to fights and disagreements, and siblings can fight with a ferocity that will distract parents from whatever task is occupying their attention. Thus siblings may be building a bond while they appear to be brewing hostilities. Indeed, because they often share (in their own individual ways) the same superego influences of the parents, siblings often have a deep and abiding feeling for one another unmatched in tone by any other human relationship.

A review of the literature indicates a wide variety of effects of siblings on one another. Rosenberg (1965) reports that being born a male in a family after a succession of girls tends to raise the boy's self-image. In one of the largest studies yet done of siblings' attitudes toward each other and their parents, Koch (1960) indicates that firstborn children like their brothers and sisters although they often find them a nuisance. Siblings reported in the main that they either quarrel very much (28.4 percent) or occasionally (38 percent). Nearly 40 percent of the siblings want to change places with their other siblings. In an earlier study Koch (1956) found a positive correlation between the influence of the parents and the age span between their children. Specialized studies of siblings are also reported in many areas of child development. Siblings in schizophrenic families (Meissner 1970) is one study that illustrates the range of research.

There is no overwhelming body of information about siblings, but it is generally agreed that although life may be bad with siblings, it is often worse without them. Perhaps Lidz (1968, p. 224) makes the most appropriate psychological summation: "The opportunity to share intimately in childhood, to know how someone close feels in various situations, to become familiar with the ways of the opposite sex, to assume responsibility for a brother or sister, to have a sibling show pride and happiness over what one accomplishes are among the many benefits of having siblings."

"Eat the spider."
"No."
"Yes. Eat the spider."
"Please."

Boys and Girls Together

by William Goldman

His life, or at least the early years of it, should have been pleasant. Deprivations were few, mothers were warm, fathers omnipotent but *in absentia* more than not. Yet his early years were filled with an almost perennial fear.

Arnold.

"Hey, Ugly." (They were four and seven and Walt had just eaten his first meal without spilling, an event that caused parental disbelief, then joy. Walt lay in his dark bedroom, ready for sleep.) "Hey, funny-looking, I'm talking to you."

"What is it, Arnold?"

"You're gonna cry, Ugly. You know that? Every day till you're dead."

"I am not."

"Y'are too." Arnold's fingers began pinching him.

"Stop it, Arnold."

"Make me."

The fingers dug at the flesh on his ribs. He tried to struggle but Arnold was strong. "Stop it, Arnold."

"Shut up. If you ever tell them, I'll make you cry twicc as bad."

"Arnold, you're hurting."

"Cry."

Walt bit his lip but it hurt. It really hurt. Disobeying his orders, the tears came. But Arnold continued to pinch. That was the thing about Arnold: he enjoyed it.

"Hey, funny-looking." (A summer noon and he had his first real suit, fresh from the store all the way in St. Louis.)

"What?"

"C'mere and help me a sec."

"Why?" Already wary.

"Just c'mere and hold the hose. I gotta spray the garden."

"You gonna get me wet?"

"How can I get you wet? The water's not turned on."

That was true. Walt took the hose from his brother. "Now what?"

"Just hold it. Whatsa matter, doncha trust me?"

"No."

"Well, just hold it." Arnold walked toward the house. "That's a nice suit, Walt. I really like that suit."

"You do?"

"Yeah. You really look good in it. No kidding."

"It comes all the way from St. Louis."

"It does?"

"Mama helped me buy it. She drove me in the car."

"No kidding?"

"You really like it?"

"I'll say I do. I wish I had a suit like that. Hey, Walt, is there something stuck in the end of the hose?"

"I don't see—" The water gushed from the nozzle, drenching his body, turning the blue suit a darker blue.

Walt fled toward the house but Arnold grabbed him. "Don't you tell them or you'll really get it."

Walt broke free and continued his run, Arnold's laughter keeping him company.

"Hey, Goofy." (It was Walt's birthday, and he was in his room, getting ready for a boat ride on the Mississippi with his mother.)

"What'd you close the door for?"

Arnold leaned against the door. "No special reason."

"What do you have behind your back?"

"Nothing."

"Then let me see your hands."

"Sure." Arnold brought one hand out, opened it, put it behind his back, then brought out the other hand. "See? Nothing."

"Both at the same time, I meant."

Arnold crossed to the bed, keeping his hands behind his back. "That boat ride sure oughta be fun."

Walt continued getting dressed, keeping an eye on his brother.

"Ice cream and cake. All you can eat. That's what I heard Mother tell P.T."

"You did?"

"That's right. All the chocolate cake you can eat. Hey, Walt. Guess what I found today?"

"I give up."

"Oh, go on, guess."

"I'm late, Arnold."

"Guess."

"What have you got behind your back, Arnold?"

"Jar."

"What's in it?"

"Guess."

"Cut it out, Arnold."

"You know what I got."

"Don't."

"Doncha know?"

"Spider!" Walt said and he bolted for the door but Arnold blocked him. Walt retreated.

Arnold waved the jar at him. "Baby. It can't hurt you. Not while it's in the jar. I wonder what would happen if it got out?" He twisted the cap and then the spider was crawling crazily on the rug.

"Arnold—"

"If they hear you, you're dead, you know that."

"Please, Arnold."

"Eat the spider."

"No."

"Yes. Eat the spider."

"Please."

Arnold scooped it up and ran for Walt, grabbing him, forcing him down, pushing the twisted black mass toward Walt's face. Walt screamed and got sick on the rug.

"Hey, four eyes." (It was suppertime and Maudie was feeding them at the kitchen table while she and the other servants served cocktails to company in the living room far away.)

Walt silently finished his mashed potatoes.

"You better answer me, Egbert. You know what'll happen if you don't."

Maudie came in, big and black, and took their plates, depositing them in the sink. She crossed to the icebox door and brought out two large bowls of chocolate pudding. "Surprise," she said as she set the bowls in front of them.

"Oh boy," Walt said. "Oh boy." Maudie turned and left the room. Walt picked up his spoon.

"Wait!" Arnold said.

Walt looked over at him, spoon poised.

"Don't touch that. There's something wrong with it."

"Oh, you don't fool me, Arnold. Not this time, you don't."

"I'm not trying to fool you."

"You just want my pudding, I know. Well, you can't have it."

"I don't want your pudding, Berty. I don't even want mine." He pushed his plate a few inches away.

"Why don't you?"

"Because there's something wrong with it." He sniffed his pudding. "It's spoiled or something. Smell it yourself if you don't believe me."

Walt stuck his nose close to the pudding and that was when Arnold pushed his face down, right into the bowl. The pudding splattered all over and Walt's glasses were caked with chocolate so he could hardly see.

"All right now, what's the fuss?" Maudie, big and black, stood by the table.

"Walt had an accident," Arnold hollered. "He thought the pudding smelled funny and then he had an accident."

"I do believe you're right," Maudie said, picking up Walt's bowl, sniffing it. "I must have used spoiled cream. It sure does smell funny."

"It does?" Arnold said, and he sniffed at his bowl of pudding until the great black hand slammed down, shoving his face into the chocolate. Arnold kicked but the hand held firm, forcing his nose flat against the bottom of the plate. Arnold flailed his arms but the great black hand did not move. It pushed and pushed and only when Arnold began coughing convulsively did it raise up.

Arnold ran sobbing from the room, crying, "P.T., P.T." over and over.

"He's going to tell them," Walt murmured. "He's running right to them."

Then Maudie had him, shaking him hard. "You! You are so gullible I want to cry. You know what that means? Gullible? It means sucker and you stop being one!"

Then Arnold was back in the kitchen, screaming, "You're gonna get it now, you're gonna get it now!" and then P.T. strode in, followed by Emily.

P.T. pointed to his eldest son.

"You do that, Maudie?"

"Bet yo' ass!"

P.T. hesitated, staring at the folded black arms. "Oh," he said finally. "Well, you probably had a good reason."

"That's my feeling."

"Just checking," P.T. said, and he returned to his guests.

Emily approached Maudie. "Maudie," she whispered, "you must try to watch your language in front of the children."

"You're absolutely right, Emily. I gotta do that."

"Yes," Emily said, and she followed her husband. Arnold just stood there, staring around.

Walt looked at him. "Chicken!" he said. "Yellow chicken!"

Arnold began to shake. Then he (1) stamped his foot in anger; (2) burst into tears; (3) fled.

"He's yellow," Walt said. "I never told them. Never even once."

"Shut up and eat your pudding," Maudie said.

Walt ate his pudding. And didn't it taste good!

Discussion

Many of the stories in this anthology touch on the interplay between siblings, but no relationship is as vividly hostile and destructive as the relationship between Arnold and Walt. The family relationship, which in part explains their enormous ill will for each other, is described earlier in the novel *Boys and Girls Together,* from which this selection was taken. Arnold and Walt are the offspring of a marriage between P. T. Kirkaby, a self-made, ruthless social climber, and Emily Harding, a wealthy socialite. Early in the marriage a pattern of infidelity and angry, punitive behavior is established. The boys, living in this home environment that is serene to outsiders only, receive little parental attention and are cared for primarily by their mother's maid, Maudie. In their relationship, the boys mirror the lines of power drawn in their parents' relationship. Arnold, like his father, takes the role of the ruthless omnipotent; Walt and his mother are always the victims. The setup is vicious and pathological, and the victims are as unhealthy as their tormentors.

Some of the teasing between the boys, like the pinching or the prank with the water hose, is like normal sibling horseplay. Unlike healthy sibling infighting, in which threats are jokingly set aside after the preliminary ruse, Arnold acts out his practical jokes to their painful conclusion. Walt's experiences with Arnold have taught him both to fear and to hate Arnold. These emotions are not unusual feelings between siblings, but hate or fear or both are usually short-lived in sibling relationships and are relieved by instances of fun, sharing, warmth, protectiveness, and general goodwill. This healthy, resilient side of a sibling relationship is never displayed between Walt and Arnold. They have not learned to be gentle and loving from their adult models, their parents. Unconsciously each boy has modeled his life style on the behavior of one of the parents. Walt vents his suffering and anger at Arnold only indirectly by playing at shooting Arnold with hundreds of bullets.

In a section of the novel preceding this selection we learn that Walt has always been compared unfavorably with his older brother. The author writes of Walt: "God, how he loathes his brother, his three-years-older, and twice as big brother, his handsome, picky, graceful, strong, sniveling, popular, Walt, why can't you be more like Arnold? brother." Evidently a poorly coordinated little boy Walt could not manage a meal without spilling, Walt's concept of himself does not help him to rise above his victim role. As for Arnold, it is suggested that he enjoys extracting complete submission from his brother. If this is so, his pleasures depend on being on the winning side of a power struggle. Early sibling relationships are significant because people frequently repeat in adult lives the pattern of relationships learned in childhood.

Springboards for Inquiry

(1) How pathological do you consider the relationship between Walt and Arnold?

(2) According to the research literature what are some of the effects of siblings on each other?

(3) What are some of the possible effects of being an identical twin?

(4) Describe the traits the "only" child in the family might have?

(5) What do research findings indicate about the influence of ordinal position in the family?

Divorce

It has been quipped that one out of every four marriages in the United States ends in divorce (LeMasters 1970) and the other three marriages are unhappy. This survey of the literature documents the above assertion and adds the term *emotional divorce* to the familiar liturgy on divorce. It is important to consider divorce as an event that involves not only husbands and wives but also literally thousands of children. In 1940 Kingsley Davis (quoted in Goode 1966) reported that up to 200,000 children were affected by divorce each year. The 1960 census* indicates that over 460,000 children were affected and the 1970 census, not yet released, will undoubtedly show a marked increase.

It is the impact of divorce on the lives of children with which we are most concerned. Goode's classic volume, *After Divorce* (1956), devotes a major section to the children of divorce. Goode maintains that most people agree that the divorce experience is damaging to children, but he goes on to ask: Are the damaging effects of divorce on the child greater than those of continued home conflict? Even if there is a divorce and we measure some of its effects, which is more important, the divorce itself and its aftermath or the conflict leading to the divorce? and What kinds of divorce or marital conflict have what kinds, or degrees, of effect on the child? Goode reports: "We should not be surprised that in spite of . . . initial doubts and worries, almost all . . . mothers thought the children were no worse off after the divorce than before" (1956, p. 318).

---

* The 1960 U.S. census reports that 3,152,320 people claim to be divorced. In *Children of Divorced Couples*, (U.S. Department of Health, Education and Welfare, February 1970), Fig. 1, p. 1 indicates a 1965 figure of nearly 650,000 children involved in over 470,000 decrees.

Some of Goode's conclusions are: if the divorce was traumatic for the wife, then the children were more likely to have at some time shown behavioral problems; nearly half the mothers who did not have custody felt their children missed them very much; and in almost all the cases the mothers believed that their children had better lives as divorced children than they would have had as children in marital conflict. The most questionable aspect of the study is that Goode based his data on interviews with mothers, who might not wish to appear to have erred in their decision to divorce and would be inclined to minimize ill effects on the children. Furthermore, it is doubtful that mothers are reliable judges of how good their children's lives are. All mothers, not just divorced ones, may lack the necessary objectivity to evaluate their own children.

Nearly all the reports substantiate Despert's assertion that emotional divorce is especially difficult on children. Nye (1957) found that children from broken homes show less psychosomatic illness, less delinquent behavior, and better adjustment to parents than those from unhappy, unbroken homes. Even more striking was Burchinal's finding (1964) that there are no adverse effects on children due to divorce, separation, or remarriage. Recent statistics from the state of Utah* further refute the traditional idea that divorce may lead to delinquent children: of 6,937 children referred for delinquency in 1969, 61 percent (4,214) lived with their natural parents and 67 percent (4,627) of 6,884 cases lived in a home where the parents were living together.†

There is no definitive empirical evidence about the effect of divorce on developing children. The effects of divorce on children range from severe trauma to positive effects, but if anything, the evidence probably shows that divorce has ultimate salutary effects on the life adjustment of the children.

---

* *Annual Report of the Juvenile Court for the State of Utah* (1969).

† These figures, while noticeably higher than those from other areas, nonetheless support the statement that there is a low correlation between divorce and delinquency. The 1968 *Annual Report: Juvenile and Domestic Relations Court* for Montgomery County, Ohio (Dayton), shows that only 30 percent of the children referred to the court came from divorced homes, whereas 41 percent came from homes in which the parents were married and living together. The 1968 *Annual Report of the Court of Common Pleas: Juvenile Division* for Hamilton County, Ohio (Cincinnati), indicates that of 6,552 cases, 16 percent of the children were from divorced homes and 43 percent came from homes in which the parents were married and living together.

"Let me speak to your father," she said.
"He's gone to get a peach."
"One peach?"
"One with people."
"You haven't been with your father for two days and already you sound like him."

Gaston *by William Saroyan*

THEY WERE to eat peaches, as planned, after her nap, and now she sat across from the man who would have been a total stranger except that he was in fact her father. They had been together again (although she couldn't quite remember when they had been together before) for almost a hundred years now, or was it only since day before yesterday? Anyhow, they were together again, and he was kind of funny. First, he had the biggest mustache she had ever seen, although to her it was not a mustache at all; it was a lot of red and brown hair under his nose and around the ends of his mouth. Second, he wore a blue-and-white striped jersey instead of a shirt and tie, and no coat. His arms were covered with the same hair, only it was a little lighter and thinner. He wore blue slacks, but no shoes and socks. He was barefoot, and so was she, of course.

He was at home. She was with him in his home in Paris, if you could call it a home. He was very old, especially for a young man—thirty-six, he had told her; and she was six, just up from sleep on a very hot afternoon in August.

That morning, on a little walk in the neighborhood, she had seen peaches in a box outside a small store and she had stopped to look at them, so he had bought a kilo.

Now the peaches were on a large plate on the card table at which they sat. There were seven of them, but one of them was flawed. It looked as good as the others, almost the size of a tennis ball, nice red fading to light green, but where the stem had been there was now a break that went straight down into the heart of the seed.

He placed the biggest and best-

---

looking peach on the small plate in front of the girl, and then took the flawed peach and began to remove the skin. When he had half the skin off the peach he ate that side, neither of them talking, both of them just being there, and not being excited or anything—no plans, that is.

The man held the half-eaten peach and looked down into the cavity, into the open seed. The girl looked, too.

While they were looking, two feelers poked out from the cavity. They were attached to a kind of brown knob-head, which followed the feelers, and then two large legs took a strong grip on the edge of the cavity and hoisted some of the rest of whatever it was out of the seed, and stopped there a moment, as if to look around.

The man studied the seed dweller, and so, of course, did the girl.

The creature paused only a fraction of a second, and then continued to come out of the seed, to walk down the eaten side of the peach to wherever it was going.

The girl had never seen anything like it—a whole big thing made out of brown color, a knob-head, feelers, and a great many legs. It was very active, too. Almost businesslike, you might say. The man placed the peach back on the plate. The creature moved off the peach onto the surface of the white plate. There it came to a thoughtful stop.

"Who is it?" the girl said.

"Gaston."

"Where does he live?"

"Well, he used to live in this peach seed, but now that the peach has been harvested and sold, and I have eaten half of it, it looks as if he's out of house and home."

"Aren't you going to squash him?"

"No, of course not, why should I?"

"He's a bug. He's ugh."

"Not at all. He's Gaston, the grand *boulevardier*."

"Everybody hollers when a bug comes out of an apple, but you don't holler or anything."

"Of course not. How would we like it if somebody hollered every time we came out of our house?"

"Why should they?"

"Precisely. So why should we holler at Gaston?"

"He's not the same as us."

"Well, not exactly, but he's the same as a lot of other occupants of peach seeds. Now, the poor fellow hasn't got a home, and there he is with all that pure design and handsome form, and nowhere to go."

"Handsome?"

"Gaston is just about the handsomest of his kind I've ever seen."

"What's he saying?"

"Well, he's a little confused. Now, inside that house of his he had everything in order. Bed here, porch there, etc."

"Show me."

The man picked up the peach, leaving Gaston entirely alone on the white plate. He removed the peeling and ate the rest of the peach.

"Nobody else I know would do that," the girl said. "They'd throw it away."

"I can't imagine why. It's a perfectly good peach." He opened the seed and placed the two sides not far from Gaston. The girl studied the open halves.

"Is that where he lives?"

"It's where he used to live. Gaston

is out in the world and on his own now. You can see for yourself how comfortable he was in there. He had everything."

"Now what has he got?"

"Not very much, I'm afraid."

"What's he going to do?"

"What are we going to do?"

"Well, we're not going to squash him, that's one thing we're not going to do," the girl said.

"What are we going to do, then?"

"Put him back?"

"Oh, that house is finished."

"Well, he can't live in our house, can he?"

"Not happily."

"Can he live in our house at all?"

"Well, he could try, I suppose. Don't you want a peach?"

"Only if it's a peach with somebody in the seed."

"Well, see if you can find a peach that has an opening at the top, because if you can, that'll be a peach in which you're likeliest to find somebody."

The girl examined each of the peaches on the big plate.

"They're all shut," she said.

"Well, eat one, then."

"No. I want the same kind that you ate, with somebody in the seed."

"Well, to tell you the truth, the peach I ate would be considered a bad peach, so of course stores don't like to sell them. I was sold that one by mistake, most likely. And so now Gaston is without a home, and we've got six perfect peaches to eat."

"I don't want a perfect peach. I want one with people."

"Well, I'll go out and see if I can find one."

"Where will I go?"

"You'll go with me, unless you'd rather stay I'll only be five minutes."

"If the phone rings, what shall I say?"

"I don't think it'll ring, but if it does, say hello and see who it is."

"If it's my mother, what shall I say?"

"Tell her I've gone to get you a bad peach, and anything else you want to tell her."

"If she wants me to go back, what shall I say?"

"Say yes if you want to go back?"

"Do you want me to?"

"Of course not, but the important thing is what *you* want, not what I want."

"Why is that the important thing?"

"Because I want you to be where you want to be."

"I want to be here."

"I'll be right back."

He put on socks and shoes, and a jacket, and went out.

She watched Gaston trying to find out what to do next. Gaston wandered around the plate, but everything seemed wrong and he didn't know what to do or where to go.

The telephone rang and her mother said she was sending the chauffeur to pick her up because there was a little party for somebody's daughter who was also six, and then tomorrow they would fly back to New York.

"Let me speak to your father," she said.

"He's gone to get a peach."

"One peach?"

"One with people."

"You haven't been with your father two days and already you sound like him."

"There are peaches with people in them. I know. I saw one of them come out."

"A bug?"

"Not a bug. Gaston."

"Who?"

"Gaston the grand something."

"Somebody else gets a peach with a bug in it, and throws it away, but not him. He makes up a lot of foolishness about it."

"It's not foolishness."

"All right, all right, don't get angry at me about a horrible peach bug of some kind."

"Gaston is right here, just outside his broken house, and I'm not angry at you."

"You'll have a lot of fun at the party."

"Okay."

"Are you glad you saw your father?"

"Of course I am."

"Is he funny?"

"Yes."

"Is he crazy?"

"Yes. I mean, no. He doesn't holler when he sees a bug crawling out of a peach seed or anything. He just looks at it carefully. But it *is* just a bug, isn't it really?"

"That's all it is."

"And we'll have to squash it?"

"That's right. I can't wait to see you, darling. These two days have been like two years to me. Goodbye."

The girl watched Gaston on the plate, and she actually didn't like him. He was all ugh, as he had been in the first place. He didn't have a home any more and he was wandering around on the white plate and he was silly and wrong and ridiculous and useless and all sorts of other things. She cried a little, but only inside, because long ago she had decided she didn't like crying because if you ever started to cry it seemed as if there was so much to cry about you almost couldn't stop, and she didn't like that at all. The open halves of the peach seed were wrong, too. They were ugly or something. They weren't clean.

THE MAN bought a kilo of peaches but found no flawed peaches among them, so he bought another kilo at another store, and this time there were two that were flawed. He hurried back to his flat and let himself in.

His daughter was in her room, in her best dress.

"My mother phoned," she said, "and she's sending the chauffeur for me because there's another birthday party."

"Another?"

"I mean, there's always a lot of them in New York."

"Will the chauffeur bring you back?"

"No. We're flying back to New York tomorrow."

"Oh."

"I liked being in your house."

"I liked having you here."

"Why do you live here?"

"This is my home."

"It's nice, but it's a lot different from our home."

"Yes, I suppose it is."

"It's kind of like Gaston's house."

"Where is Gaston?"

"I squashed him."

"Really? Why?"

"Everybody squashes bugs and worms."

"Oh. Well. I found you a peach."

"I don't want a peach any more."

"Okay."

He got her dressed, and he was

packing her stuff when the chauffeur arrived. He went down the three flights of stairs with his daughter and the chauffeur, and in the street he was about to hug the girl when he decided he had better not. They shook hands instead, like strangers.

He watched the huge car drive off, then he went around the corner where he took coffee every morning, feeling a little, he thought, like Gaston on the white plate.

Discussion

In "Gaston," Saroyan uses dialogue between a six-year-old girl and alternately her father and her mother to reveal the incompatibility between the parents, who respect diametrically opposed value systems. The story raises concern for the emotional health of the child, who is caught in the crosscurrent between adults in conflict. The little girl in this selection seems to be able to cope with the difference in her parents' life styles, but her mother does not accept this possibility. She does not approve of her estranged husband's way of life and seems intent on imposing her values on the little girl.

The mother is very effective in the pursuit of her ends, and in a short telephone conversation she manages to devastate her opponent, the husband, and leaves no choice for the little girl to extend her stay with her father. The one-upmanship she employs is frequently used in this kind of embittered husband–wife relationship. The mother attempts to belittle the father in the little girl's eyes. She is scornful of his ideas and labels his behaviour "crazy", thereby removing him as a credible force in their lives. The mother also arouses guilt feelings in her daughter by implying that the little girl has caused her pain by making the two-day absence seem like two years. Finally, in order to be sure the child will leave immediately, she bribes her with an invitation to a birthday party. These are all irresistible ploys to set before a young child.

When the father returns, he accepts (with a deliberate absence of emotion) the girl's announcement that she is returning to her mother. Perhaps he considers a tug-of-war between adults for a child's affection and loyalty more detrimental than the present arrangement.

Springboards for Inquiry

(1) What adjustments would this little girl have to make in order to adapt to both parents' life styles?

(2) How might the mother's attitude toward the father affect the little girl's future attitude toward men and marriage?

(3) In this story do you think the mother or the father would be the more adequate parent? Why?

(4) What does the research tell us of the influence of a father on his daughter?

"I'm going to call you Mummy because I love you best."

My First Two Women

by Nadine Gordimer

I HAVE BEEN trying to remember when and where I saw my father's second wife for the first time. I must have seen her frequently, without singling her out or being aware of her, at many of those houses, full of friends, where my father and I were guests in the summer of 1928. My father had many friends, and it seems to me (I was not more than four years old at the time) that, at week ends at least, we were made much of at a whole roster of houses, from tiny shacks, which young couples had "fixed up" for themselves, to semi-mansions, where we had two guest rooms and a bathroom all to ourselves. Whether we sat under a peach tree on painted homemade chairs at a shack, or around the swimming pool on cane chaises longues at a mansion, the atmosphere of those Saturdays and Sundays was the same: the glasses of warm beer, full of sun, into which I sometimes stuck a finger; the light and color of a Johannesburg summer, with thousands of midges, grasshoppers, and other weightless leaping atoms exploding softly over your face as you lay down on the grass; the laughter and voices of the men and women, as comforting and pleasant as the drunken buzz of the great bluebottles that fell sated from rotting fruit, or bees that hung a moment over your head, on their way to and fro between elaborate flowering rockeries. She must have been there often—one of the women who would help me into the spotted rubber Loch Ness monster that kept me afloat, or bring me a lemonade with a colored straw to drink it through—so often that I ceased to see her.

Reprinted from the author's collection of short stories titled "Six Feet of the Country" copyright 1956 by Nadine Gordimer, by permission of the Shirley Collier Agency.

During the months of that summer, I lived at one or another of those friends' houses, along with the children of the house; sometimes my father stayed there with me, and sometimes he did not. But even if he was not actually living in the same place with me, he was in and out every day, and the whole period has in my mind the blurring change and excitement of a prolonged holiday—children to play with, a series of affectionate women who arranged treats, settled fights, and gave me presents. The whereabouts of my mother were vague to me and not particularly troubling. It seems to me that I believed her not to be back yet from her visit to my grandmother in Kenya, and yet I have the recollection of once speaking to her on the telephone, as if she were in Johannesburg after all. I remember saying, "When are you coming back?" and then not waiting for her to answer but going on, "Guess what I've got in my hand?" (It was a frog, which had just been discovered to have completed its metamorphosis from a tadpole in a tin basin full of stones and water.)

The previous winter, when my mother had gone to Kenya, my father and I had lived in our house, my parents' own house, alone. This was not unusual; I am aware that I had been alone with him, in the care of servants, time and again before that. In fact, any conception I have in my mind of my mother and father and me living together as a family includes her rather as a presence—rooms that were hers, books and trinkets belonging to her, the mute testimony of her grand piano—rather than a flesh-and-blood actuality. Even if she *was* there she did little or nothing of an intimate nature for me; I do not connect her with meal or bath times. So it came about, I suppose, that I scarcely understood, that summer, that there was a real upheaval and change over my head. My father and I were never to go back to that house together. In fact, we both had left it for good; even though I, before the decision was to be made final for me, was to return for a few weeks, it was not to the *same house,* in any but the brick-and-mortar sense, and my position in it and the regrouping of its attention in relation to me were so overwhelmingly changed that they wiped out, in a blaze of self-importance and glory, the dim near babyhood that had gone before.

For, suddenly, in a beautiful autumn month (it must have been March) I found myself back in our house with my mother. The willows around the lawn were fountains spouting pale yellow leaves on the grass that was kept green all year round. I slept with my mother, in her bed. Surely I had not done so before. When I said to her, "Mummy, didn't I used to sleep in the nursery before you went to Kenya?" she said, "Darling, I really have no idea where your Daddy put you to sleep while I was away."

She had short, shiny black hair cut across her forehead in a fringe. She took me to the barber and had my hair, my black hair, cut in a fringe. (Daddy used to brush my hair back, first dipping the brush in water. "Water dries out the hair," she said.) We would get out of her car together, at the houses of friends, and she would walk with me slowly up the path toward them, hand in hand. We looked exactly alike, they all said, exactly alike; it was incredible that a small boy could look so much the image of his mother.

My mother would put me up on the long stool beside her while she played the piano; I had never been so close to a piano while it was being played, and sometimes the loud parts of the music swelled through my head frighteningly, like the feeling once when I slipped through my Loch Ness monster and went under in a swimming pool. Then I got used to the sensation and found it exciting, and I would say to her, "Play loudly, Mummy. Make it boom." Sometimes she would stop playing suddenly and whirl around and hold me tight, looking out over my head at the guests who had been listening. I would hear the last reverberation die away in the great rosewood shape behind us while silence held in the room.

My mother walked up and down a room when she talked, and she talked a great deal, to people who seemed to have no chance to answer her, but were there to listen. Once, in the bathroom, I threw a wet toy and it hit my African nanny on the mouth, and when she smacked my behind and I yelled, my mother rushed in and raged at her, yelling as loudly as I did. My mother was beautiful when she was angry, for she was one of those women who cry with anger, and her eyes glistened and her natural pallor was stained bright with rising blood.

She took me to a circus. She took me to a native mineworkers' "war" dance. She came home from town with a pile of educational toys and sat over me, watching, while I hesitated, caught her long, black, urging eye, brilliant as the eye of an animal that can see in the dark, and then, with a kind of hypnotized instinct born of the desire to please, fitted the right shape on the right peg.

There were still a few leaves, like droplets not yet shaken off, on the twigs of the willows when my clothes and toys were packed up again and my father came to fetch me away.

This time I went to the sea, with the family of three little boys and their mother, with whom I had stayed before. I had a wonderful time, and when I came back, it was to a new house that I had never seen. In it were my father and his second wife.

I was not surprised to see this woman, and, as I have said, she was not a stranger to me. I liked her, and, made gregarious by the life of the past year, asked, "How much days can Deb stay with us?"

"For always," said my father.

"Doesn't she ever have to go home?"

"This is her home, and yours, and Daddy's."

"Why?"

"Because she is married to me now, Nick. She is my wife, and husband and wives love each other and live together in the same house."

There was a pause, and when I spoke again, what I said must have been very different from what they expected. They did not know that while I was on holiday at the sea I had been taken, one rainy afternoon, along with the older children, to the cinema. There I had seen, in all the rose and crystalline blur of Technicolor, a man and woman dance out beneath the chandeliers of a ballroom. When I had asked what they were doing, I was told that this was a wedding—the man and the woman had just been married.

"Do you mean like this?" I asked my father and my stepmother, taking my father's hand, bending my knees, and shaping out my arms in a jiglike posture. I hopped around solemnly, dragging him with me.

"Dancing?" guessed my father, mystified and affectionate, appealing to his wife.

"Oh, that's wonderful!" she cried in sudden delight. "Bless his formal heart! A real wedding!"

There followed a confusion of hugging, all around. I was aware only that in some way I had pleased them.

I was now nearly five years old and due to begin going to school. My stepmother took me to town with her, and together we bought the supplies for my birthday party, and my school uniform, and a satchel with a fancy lock—soon to be stained as greasy as an old fish-and-chip wrapping with the print of successive school lunches—and the elaborate equipment of pencil sharpeners, erasers, and rulers indispensable to the child who has not yet learned to write. Deb understood what a birthday party for a five-year-old boy should be like. She had ideas of her own, and could sway a wavering torment of indecision between candleholders in the guise of soldiers or elephants, imparting to the waverer a comforting sense of the rightness of the final choice, but she also knew when to efface her own preferences entirely and let me enjoy my own choice for my own unexplained reasons. In fact, she was so good at the calm management of the practical details of my small life that I suppose I quickly assumed this stability as my right, and took it altogether for granted, as children, in their fierce unconscious instinct for personal salvation, take all those rights which, if withheld from them, they cannot consciously remark, but whose lack they exhibit and revenge with equal unconscious ferocity. Of course Deb bought neat and comfortable clothes for me, found the books I would best like to hear her read from, took me with her on visits that would be interesting to me, but left me at home to play when she was going where there would be nothing to amuse me; she always had, hadn't she, right from the first day?

The children at school wanted to know why I called my mother "Deb." When I said that she was not my mother, they insisted that she must be. "Are you my mother now, Deb?" I asked her.

"No," she said. "You know that you have your own mother."

"They say you must be, because you live with Daddy and me."

"I'm your second mother," she said, looking to see if that would do.

"Like my godmother?"

"That's right."

I dashed off to play; it was perfectly satisfactory.

There came a stage when school, the preparation for which had been so enjoyable, palled. I suppose there must have been some incident there, some small failure which embarrassed or shamed me. I do not remember. But I know that, suddenly, I didn't want to go to school. Deb was gentle but insistent. I remember my own long, sullen silence one day, after a wrangle of "Why's" from me and firm explanations from her. At last I said, "When I'm at my mother's I stay home all the time."

My stepmother was squatting on her heels in front of a low cupboard, and her eyes opened up toward me like the eyes of those sleeping dolls which girl children alternately lower and raise by inclining the doll's body, but her voice was the same as usual. "If you lived with your mother now, you would go to school just as you do here," she said.

I stood right in front of her. She looked up at me again, and I said, "No, I wouldn't" I waited. Then I said, "She lets me do what I like." I waited again. "I can even play her piano. She's got a big piano. As big as this room."

My stepmother went on slowly putting back into the cupboard the gramophone records she had been sorting and cleaning. Standing over her, I could see the top of her head, an unfamiliar aspect of a grownup. It was then, I think, that I began to see her for the first time, not as one of the succession of pretty ladies who petted and cared for me, but as Deb, as someone connected in wordless depths with my father and me, as my father and I and, yes, my mother were connected. Someone who had entered, irrevocably, the atavistic tension of that cunning battle for love and supremacy that exists between children and parents sometimes even beyond the grave, when one protagonist is dead and mourned, and lives on in the fierce dissatisfaction of the other's memory.

She was a fair woman, this Deb, this woman beloved of my father; on all faces there is some feature, some plane that catches the light in characteristic prominence of that face, and on her face, at that moment and always, it was her long golden eyebrows, shining. They were bleached from much swimming, but her dull, curly hair, always protected from sun and water by a cap, hung colorless and nowhere smooth enough to shine. The face was broad and brown across strong cheekbones, and she had a big, orange-painted mouth, the beautiful underlip of which supported the upper as calmly as a carved pediment. Her eyes, moving from record to cupboard, lowered under my presence, were green or blue, depending upon what color she wore. She was the sort of fair woman who would never be called a blonde.

Deb. I knew what it smelled like in that pink freckled neck. I knew the stiff and ugly ears that she kept hidden under that hair, and that sometimes, when she was hot and lifted her hair off her neck a moment for coolness, were suddenly discovered.

I shall never forget the feeling I had as I stood there over her. If I search my adult experience as a man to approximate it, I can only say that now it seems to me that physically it was rather like the effect of the first drink you take after a long wet day of some strenuous exercise—rowing or hunting. It was a feeling of power that came like an inflow of physical strength. I was only five years old but power is something of which I am convinced there is no innocence this side of the womb, and I knew what it was, all right; I understood, without a name for it, what I had. And with it came all the weapons—that bright, clinical set that I didn't need to have explained to me, as my father had

had to explain to me the uses of the set of carpenter's tools I had been given for my birthday. My hand would go out unfalteringly for these drills and probes, and the unremembered pain of where they had been used on me would guide me to their application.

"Deb," I said, "why didn't Daddy marry my mother?"

"He did," she said. "Once he was married to her. But they were not happy with each other. Not like Daddy and me—and you. Not happy together like us." She did not ask me if I remembered this, but her voice suggested the question, in spite of her.

Daddy. My mother. My mother was simply a word I was using at that moment. I could not see her in my head. She was a mouth moving, singing; for a second she sat at the piano, smiled at me, one of her swift, startling smiles that was like someone jumping out of concealment and saying "Boo!" Inside me, it gave me a fright. If my dog had been there, I would have pulled back his ears, hard, to hear him yelp. There was Deb, squatting in front of me. I said, "My mother's got a piano as big as this house. I want to go and stay with her."

Deb got up from the floor. "Soon," she said. "You'll go on a visit soon, I'm sure. Let's see if tea's ready." We did not take each other's hand, but walked out onto the porch side by side, with a space between us.

It was after that day that I began to be conscious of the relationship between my father and Deb. This was not the way he and those others —the pretty, helpful friends who were the mothers of my friends—had behaved toward each other. I watched with unbiased interest as I would have watched a bird bringing his mate tidbits where she balanced on our paling fence, when my father ate an apple bite-and-bite-about with this woman, or, passing her chair at breakfast, after he had kissed me good-by in the morning, paused to press his cheek silently, and with closed eyes, against hers. Sometimes, in the evenings, both she and I sat on his lap at once.

There were no images in my memory to which to match these. They were married, Deb and my father. This behavior was marriage. Deb herself had told me that marriage once had existed between my father and my mother. One day I came home from a visit to my mother and remarked, conversationally, in the bedroom Deb and my father shared, "My mother's got a bed just like yours, Deb, and that's where Daddy and she used to sleep when he lived there, didn't you, Daddy?"

It was Sunday, and my father still lay in bed, reading the paper, though Deb's place was empty and she was gathering her clothes together before she went off to the bathroom. He said, "No, son. Don't you remember? Mine was the room with the little balcony."

"Oh, yes," I said. "Of course, I know." All at once I remembered the smell of that rather dark, high room, a smell of shirts fresh from the iron, of the two leather golf bags in the corner, and some chemical with which the carpet had been cleaned. All this—the smell of my father—had disappeared under the warmer, relaxing, and polleny scents of the room he now shared with a woman, where peach-colored dust from her powder settled along his hairbrushes, and the stockings she peeled off retained the limp, collapsed semblance of her legs, like the newly shed skin of a snake I had come upon in the bush when I was on holiday at the sea.

I think there must have been something strongly attractive to me in the ease of the feminine intimacy to which my father and I found ourselves admitted with such naturalness. Yet because it was unfamiliar, the very seductiveness of its comfort seemed, against the confusion of my short life, a kind of disloyalty, to which I was party and of which I was guilty. Disloyalty—to what? Guilty—of what?

I was too young for motives; I could only let them bubble up, manifest in queer little words and actions. I know that that Sunday morning I said stoutly, as if I were explaining some special system of living, "There we each had our *own* rooms. Everybody slept in their own room."

Before the end of the first year of the marriage that power that had come to me like a set of magical weapons, the day when my stepmother knelt before me at the record cupboard, became absolute. It crushed upon my little-boy's head the vainglory and triumph of the tyrant, crown or thorn. I was to wear it as my own for the rest of my childhood.

I was cuddling Deb, secure in her arms one day, when I said, out of some gentle honey of warmth that I felt peacefully within me, "I'm going to call you Mummy because I love you best." I am sure that she knew that the statement was not quite so stunning and meaningful as it sounds now, out of the context of childhood. Quite often, she had heard me say of an animal or a new friend, "You know whom I love. I love only Eddie." (Or "Sam," or "Chris.") Sometimes the vehement preference was expressed not out of real feeling for the friend or animal in question, but out of pique toward some other child or animal. At other times it was merely an unreasonable welling up of well-being that had to find an object. But I had never before said this particular thing to her. She shook back her hair fumblingly and held her face away from mine to look at me; she was awkward with joy. I looked up into the stare of her eyes—grown-up eyes that fell before mine—and in me, like milk soured by a flash of lightning, the sweet secretion of affection became insipid in the fearful, amazed thrill of victim turned victor.

That was our story, really, for many years. My father and Deb were deeply in love and theirs was a serene marriage. The three of us lived together in amity; it was a place of warmth for a child to grow in. I visited my mother at regular, if widely spaced, intervals. I went to her for short periods at Christmas, birthdays, and during holidays. Thus along with her, with that elegant black head and those hard wrists volatile with all the wonderful bracelets she had picked up all over the world, went excitement and occasion, treats and parties, people who exclaimed over me, and the abolishment of that guillotine of joys, bedtime. Sometimes the tide of grown-up activities would pass on over my head and leave me stranded and abandoned on a corner of somebody's sofa, rubbing my eyes against the glare of forgotten lights. It did not matter; the next day, or the day after that, I was sure to be delivered back to Deb and my father and the comfort of my child's pace.

Thus it was, too, that along with home and Deb and my father went everyday life, the greater part of life, with time for boredom, for transgressions and punishments. When I visited my mother for a week end or a day, I was on my best behavior, befitting a treat or an occasion; I was never with her long enough to need chastisement. So when, at home, I was naughty and my father or Deb had to punish me, I would inflame myself against them with the firm belief that my mother would never punish me. At these times of resentment and injury, I would see her clearly and positively, flaming in the light of a Christmas tree or the fiery ring of candles on a birthday cake, my champion against a world that would not bend entirely to my own will. In the same way, for the first few days after my return from a visit to her, everything about the way she lived and the things about her were lit up by the occasion with which my visit had coincided; her flat (when I was seven or eight she moved into a luxurious penthouse in a block overlooking a country club) was like the glowing cardboard interior of the king's castle, carried away in my mind from a pantomime matinee. "There's a swimming pool right on top of the building, on the roof garden," I would tell Deb. "I swim there every morning. Once I swam at night. My mother lets me. The lift doesn't go up to the top—you have to walk the last flight of stairs from the twelfth floor." "My mother's got a car with an overhead drive. Do you know what that is, Deb? It means you don't have to change the gears with your hands." "I wish we had a swimming pool here. I don't like this old house without even a swimming pool."

Deb always answered me quietly and evenly. Never, even when I was very young, did she try to point out rival attractions at home. But in time, when I grew older and was perhaps eleven or twelve, I struggled against something that went more than quiet—went dead—in her during these one-sided conversations. I felt not that she was not listening, but that she was listless, without interest in what I said. And then I did not know at whom the resentment I suddenly felt was directed, whether at my mother—that glossy-haired kingfisher flashing in and out of my life—for having a roof-garden swimming pool and a car without gears, or at Deb, for her lack of attention and negative reaction to my relation of these wonders. This reaction of hers was all the more irking, and in some vague, apprehensive way dismaying, when one remembered the way she watched and listened to me sometimes, with that look in her eyes that wanted something from me, wondered, hesitated, hopeful—that look I had known how to conjure up ever since the first day when I suggested I would call her my mother, and that, in perverse, irresistible use of the same power, I had also known how never to allow to come to articulacy, to emotional fulfillment, between us. The business of my calling her mother, for instance; it had come up several times again, while I was small. But she, in the silence that followed, had never managed anything more than, once, an almost unintelligibly murmured "If you like." And I, once the impulsive, casually pronounced sentence had exploded and left its peculiar after-silence, had dropped my avowal as I left a toy, here or there, for someone else to pick up in house or garden. I never did call her mother; in time, I think I should have been surprised to hear that there had ever been any question that she should be anything else but "Deb."

I was strongly attached to her, and when, at twelve or thirteen, I entered adolescence and boarding school at the same time, there was in fact a calm friendship between us, unusual between a woman and a boy walking the knife edge dividing small-boy scorn of the feminine from awakening sex interest. I suppose, if she had been truly in the position of a mother, this relationship would not have been possible. Her position must have been curiously like that of the woman who, failing to secure as a lover the man with whom she has fallen in love, is offered instead his respect and his confidences.

I was fifteen when I asked the question that had taken a thousand different forms—doubts, anxieties, and revenges—all through my life but had never formulated itself directly. The truth was, I had never known what that question *was*—only felt it, in all my blood and bones, fumbled toward it under the kisses of people who loved me, asked it with my seeking of my father's hands, the warmth of Deb's lap, the approval of my form master's eye, the smiles of my friends. Now it came to me matter-of-factly, in words.

I was home from school for the week end, and there had been guests at lunch. They had discussed the divorce of a common friend and the wrangle over the custody of the children of the marriage. One of the guests was a lawyer, and he had gone into the legal niceties in some detail. After the guests had gone, my father went off for his nap and Deb and I dragged our favorite canvas chairs out onto the lawn. As I settled mine at a comfortable angle, I asked her, curiously, "Deb, how was it that my mother didn't get me? The custody of me, I mean."

She thought for a moment, and I thought she must be trying how best to present some legal technicality in a way that both she and I would understand.

"I mean, their divorce was an arranged thing, wasn't it—one of those things arranged to look like desertion that Derrick spoke about? Why didn't my mother get me?" The lawyer had explained that where parents contested the custody, unless there was some strong factor to suggest that the mother was unsuitable to rear a child, a young child was usually awarded to her care.

Then quite suddenly Deb spoke. Her face was red and she looked strange, and she spoke so fast that what she said was almost blurted. "She gave you up."

Her face and tone so astonished me that the impact of what she had said missed its mark. I stared at her, questioning.

She met my gaze stiffly, with a kind of jerky bravado, intense, looking through me.

"How do you mean?"

"Voluntarily. She gave you over to your father."

The pressure in her face died

slowly down; her hands moved, as if released, on the chair arms. "I should never have told you," she said flatly. "I'd promised myself I never should."

"You mean she didn't want me?"

"We don't know what her reasons were, Nick. We can't know them."

"Didn't try to get me?"

There was a long silence. "We made up our minds. We decided it was best. We decided we would try and make your relationship with her as normal as possible. Never say anything against her. I promised myself I wouldn't try—for myself. I often wanted to tell you—oh, lots of things. I wanted to punish you for what I withheld for your sake. I wanted to hurt you; I suppose I forgot you were a child. . . . Well, what does it matter anyway? It's all worked itself out, long ago. Only I shouldn't have told you now. It's pointless." She smiled at me, as at a friend who can be counted on to understand a confession. "It didn't even give me any pleasure."

My stepmother talked about this whole situation in which we had all lived as if it were something remembered from the past, instead of a living situation out of the continuity of which I was then, at that moment, beginning my life as a man. All worked itself out, long ago. Perhaps it had. Yes, she was right. All worked itself out, without me. Above and about me, over my head, saving me the risk and the opportunity of my own volition.

My mother? That black-haired, handsome woman become rather fleshy, who, I discovered while I sat, an awkward visitor among her admiring friends (I had inherited her love of music), sang off-key.

But it was not toward her that I felt anger, regret, and a terrible, mournful anguish of loss, which brought up from somewhere in my tall, coarse, half-man's, half-child's body what I was alarmed to recognize as the racking turmoil that precedes tears.

"We're really good friends, aren't we?" said my stepmother lovingly, with quiet conviction.

It was true: that was what we were—all we were.

I have never forgiven her for it.

Discussion

This story contrasts with Saroyan's story about divorce, in which conflict is open and acknowledged. On the surface the atmosphere in Nick's home seems much more amicable to his welfare. Deb seems to carry out all the motherly functions. The husband and wife have a compatible and satisfying relationship, and there are no other children to create competition for the parents' attention and affection. Yet there is an underlying disquiet that intrudes itself in a look, a sudden flare-up of Nick's temper, or a too quiet response to a serious question. The charismatic personality of Nick's natural mother flashes as a presence in the relationship, despite the fact that she is never physically present in their household. Nick uses his natural mother against Deb when he wishes to get his own way. He knows that any reference to her can cause Deb pain, and he is both exhilarated and frightened by his power over an adult. By the end of the story we are aware of the difficult role Deb has assumed in trying to make her relationship with Nick a natural extension of her marriage to his father. She relishes loving moments with Nick, but Nick's exciting visits with his mother keep her influence a tool which he employs at will. This story emphasizes the significance that each person in a family triangle plays in the life of a young child.

Springboards for Inquiry

(1) What were some of the unresolved (even inadmissable) feelings Nick had toward Deb during his years with her and his father?

(2) How could Nick and Deb have worked out their new relationship more honestly during his earlier years?

(3) What factors do you think should be considered in awarding children to the custody of either parent? How should the courts make the most desirable decision for the interests of children in custody cases?

Development of Moral Judgment

The literature concerning the development of moral judgment is not as yet definitive. The only agreement is that moral judgment comes from a variety of sources—the family, the peer group, and the school.

Piaget (1948) proposes three stages in the development of moral behavior: an egocentric stage, a stage of incipient cooperation, and a final stage of genuine cooperation. These stages are predicated on Piaget's definition of the essential aspect of morality—namely, the tendency to accept and follow a system of rules which . . . regulate interpersonal behavior (Ginsburg and Opper 1969, p. 100). The force that produces moral change is at first *constraint,* because the child believes himself to be inferior to the adult world and he accepts the adult value system even though he does not understand it (Lidz 1968, p. 282). After the age of ten a *morality of cooperation* develops, in which the child realizes that there are rules and that they develop out of the reasonable needs of society.

Describing the *egocentric stage,* Piaget observed two boys of four to seven years playing marbles and concluded that each child was merely playing an individual (egocentric) game and did not really need the other. This stage is highly related to egocentric speech and to parallel play; in all cases the child is centered on himself and fails to take into account another person's point of view. In children of ages seven to eleven, the stage of incipient cooperation, the game begins to acquire a definite social character. During this time the child cooperates and competes with his partner. All is not perfect, though—there are arguments, yet some consideration of an opposing view. The final stage of moral behavior, genuine cooperation, commences at age eleven or twelve and is the stage at which the child gains mastery of the rules and tries to win, based on mutual agreement about those rules.

Ginsburg and Opper (1969, p. 100), discussing the validity of using children's games to understand the development of moral concepts in children, say:

On closer inspection it would seem as if the rules governing the game of marbles fulfill all the defining conditions of a moral system. The rules control how individuals behave toward one another in terms of the actions which comprise the game; they determine individual and property rights; and they are a cultural product which has been passed down from generation to generation. The game of marbles also has a unique advantage from the point of view of child psychology. The rules have been developed largely by children, and the game is played almost exclusively by children. Therefore, the child's conception of the game and his playing of it reflect the workings of his own mind and is subject to little adult influence. Unlike rules dealing with lying or stealing, marbles is the child's game, not the adult's. If we question the child about the game, his answers do not simply parrot the teachings of adults, but give a genuine indication of his own thought. But is not the game just play, something that is not at all taken seriously, and that therefore bears no relation to morality which is a grave matter?

We may answer this criticism by pointing out that the child does take the game seriously. While a game has its "fun" aspects, if one observes children playing, one realizes that they are deeply engrossed in their activities, consider the other players' actions of some importance, and are not entirely disinterested in the outcomes.

Other research, less interested in the age and stage approach, looks at the family as the major source of moral development. Hartshorne and May (1928)* were some of the earliest researchers to predict the vital influence of the family. The studies generally conclude that parents and relatives become models for their children's behavior (Fisher 1948). Based on studies of the development of conscience, Sears (1960) and Rogers (1969), note that a strong conscience failed to develop if the parent did not meet the child's needs or point out conditions of approval. Sears (1960) found that if on performances of a disapproved act, the parent failed to withdraw approval or set limits, this too was detrimental to the development of a strong conscience.

Bruno Bettelheim and Lawrence Kohlberg examined the complexities of the moral development and education of children at a lecture series held in the spring of 1968 at the Harvard Graduate School of Education. Bettelheim (1970, p.103) pointed out that in Freud's Vienna and Piaget's Geneva the parental standard was accepted and unquestioned by the child; whereas, in contemporary American society the peer group becomes "more important and important much sooner in life."

---

* See also Paul H. Whiteman and Kenneth R. Cozier, "Development of Children's Moralistic Judgment: Age, Sex, I.Q. and Certain Experiential Variables," *Child Development* 35 (1964): 843–50; U. Bronfenbrenner, "The Role of Age, Sex, Class and Culture in Studies of Moral Development," *Religious Education: Research Supplement*, 1962; and A. Bandura and F. J. McDonald, "The Influence of Social Reinforcement and the Behavior of Models in Shaping Children's Moral Judgments," *Journal of Abnormal and Social Psychology* 63 (1961): 575–82.

Kohlberg maintained that the "bag of virtues" approach to moral education does not work. Parents and educators cannot list a group of desirable qualities or moral attributes and expect children to incorporate them as their own standard for behavior. Kohlberg (1970, p. 58) advised that "the teaching of virtue is the asking of questions and the pointing of the way, not the giving of answers." He particularly emphasized that all values are united in the concept of justice, and that education for justice is not an intellectual exercise. His message indicated that we lead our children to a concept of justice when our institutions—the family, society, and the schools—are just.

"Anna, why was the tramp a bad man?"

"You are not to talk about it."

"But he didn't do anything!"

"Oh, God," she said, reviving her sense of shock with hushed pleasure.

The Dawn of Hate

by Paul Horgan

But if I had made promises to God, He let me go to sleep in His promise to me. Even then I knew it was a stronger promise than mine. In this knowledge there was the beginning of the end of innocence. Another stage of this loss presently came along.

One day I built a boat out of a board with twigs for masts and string for railings. I took it to show Anna in the kitchen.

"Can't we go and sail it?" I asked.

"I'm busy," she said in her sing-song, dreamy voice. Anna, our old cook and laundress, lived a visionary life which she pursued above the task in hand. Dreaming awake, she would sing monotonously to herself of love (her husband had disappeared years ago), or of God (she went to Mass every morning), or of nothing at all; and when she had time she tended me as nurse. A friend to us all, she could bridle with privilege and mourn her estate in the same instant. Now and then she would seize me in her large, lumbering grasp in which she hugged fugitively the graces of a time when she was young and venturesome long ago, before living in other people's kitchens, or spending long mornings in their basement laundries whiling away the acrid steamy hours with hooted song and muffled memory. Her ardent nature expressed itself in one way through her pores, which exuded a fume of oniony sweat that for a reason I cannot quite capture always gave me the feeling of, "Poor Anna!"

"Well," I said, blurring my eyes to see my boat as great and real, "I will go and sail it by myself, then."

"You-will-not."

Chapter II from *Things As They Are*, pp. 21–34, by Paul Horgan. Reprinted by permission of Virginia Rice.

"Why not?"

"You know you're too young to go out alone."

"I'm five."

"And I'm a hundred and five, and I'm busy, and I'm tired."

She leaned aside, looking upward, a martyr, with her lonely life, her sense of sin, and this boy nagging at her.

"Please, Anna, don't you love my boat?"

"Oh, Lord, it's glorious!" she shouted, but she began to take off her apron and joyfully I knew we were going to Yates Circle, at the end of our street, where in the center an immense round bowl of polished granite enclosed a pool from which rose a forest of water spouts. It was the finest fountain in Dorchester, and it made music in air and sunshine all day long. All the children of the neighborhood, and some from across town, came there to sail their boats.

"Come on, Richard," sighed Anna, "bring your old boat."

"It's my new boat."

"Your new boat, then, God give me strength."

This was on a golden afternoon in October. My mother was upstairs sewing in the bay window of her bedroom, where thin white curtains blurred the sunlight all about her, until she seemed to me a creature of light herself.

Anna called up from the foot of the stairs that she was taking me to the Circle.

"Put on his light overcoat," replied my mother in a lifted, happy voice. "It's chilly even in the sun. Come straight home. Do you want me to watch anything in the kitchen?"

"No," said Anna, "we'll be back to start things for dinner."

While I held my boat first with one hand and then the other, she roughly hauled my overcoat on to my arms and buttoned me up.

"That boat," she said scornfully. But her voice and acts were full of love, and I was content, for I loved her as she loved me. I never thought of her grey, pock-marked, wide face, and her loose, colorless hair, and her dark tight clothes that strained across the full shapes of her old womanly arms and bosom and belly. She was to me neither young nor old, beautiful nor ugly. She belonged to me, and was therefore worthy. All persons seemed to commit their acts for my benefit, and all events were interesting only as they pleased me or met my needs.

"Come on," she said rudely, and we went out the front door.

Leaves were whispering down through the yellow air. The street was empty, or so we thought. Far ahead I could see the white crests of the water at the fountain.

"Come on, Anna, you are so slow."

"Wait till your feet kill you some day."

"Well, I know, but come *on*."

She began to sing gently one of her hooting tunes. She was holding one of my hands while with the other I cradled my ship. It was meant to be an ocean greyhound. I could not wait to learn whether it would float on an even keel.

We were not even half-way to the Circle when Anna stopped and halted me.

"What's the matter?" I asked.

"Never mind."

She was peering up the street at a

figure which came idling into view along the sidewalk on our side of the street. It was a man. He moved slowly, with little steps that hardly advanced his progress. His body was oddly in motion, almost as if he were dancing in his shoes with tiny movements. From a distance I could see that he was dressed in old grey clothes, very shabby, which were too large for him.

"Is it a tramp?" I asked, with a leap of interest and fright—for the word tramp was one to strike terror in the women of our household, who took great precautions against tramps when my father was not at home.

"I think so. Come," said Anna, "we will cross the street and go on the other walk."

She led me abruptly across and quickened her pace. Looking proud and unafraid in case the man really was a tramp, she lifted her head and began to exhibit her idea of what a grand lady was like, striding daintily yet hugely, and making angry little tosses of her head. She picked up with thumb and one finger a fold of her dress and held it athwart her hip. She seemed to say, I'll show him, that tramp, I'll dare him to ask me for a nickel for a glass of beer, he wouldn't dare try anything, me with my boy along here with me, going to sail a boat in Yates Circle, where there's often *a policeman* around to see that the children don't fall in the water and drownd theirself!

I lagged, staring at the tramp with fascination as we approached to pass each other on opposite sides of the street. Anna refused even to see him, but kept up her lofty plan to pass him by as if he did not exist.

Now I could see him clearly and intimately. He had a wide grin on his unshaven grey face with red cheeks and nose and bleached-looking places about the eyes. He blinked at us and bowed in a friendly way. Shabby, drifting, uncertain, he seemed to be reaching for us—for me, I was sure, since all life was directed toward me. There was an ingratiating gaiety about him, and when he left his sidewalk to come toward us, in his shambling little dance, I saw something else which puzzled me.

He nodded and smiled, and I thought he nodded and smiled at me. When he was halfway across the street toward us, keeping pace now with Anna's angry, ladylike advance —her eyes forward and her head up— I tugged at her and asked,

"Anna, what's he doing?"

At the sound of my voice the tramp laughed weakly in a beery little cough, and ducked his head, and smiled and smiled, hungry for response. I then saw how his clothes were disarrayed in what was later called indecent exposure.

"Anna!" I insisted.

"Never mind, come along," she said with a toss of her head as though she wore plumes.

"But he wants to show me something," I protested.

At this, she glanced aside at the tramp, who presented himself and his antic lewdness hilariously at her.

It took her only that glance to understand.

"Holy God in heaven!" she cried, and turned and in a single sweep of her heavy arm swung me all but through the air toward home, causing me to drop my boat. At a half-run she dragged me along the walk toward our house.

"My boat! My boat!" I kept crying,

but she paid no heed, only muttering and groaning the names of saints, giving forth holy ejaculations. We came breathless to the house, where she slammed and locked the front door behind us, and ran through to the kitchen door and locked that too. Hearing this, and the sound of my angry sobs at the loss of my new ship, my mother came downstairs laughing, and saying,

"Slam, slam, cry, cry—what on earth is happening? Why are you home so soon?"

"My boat!" I stormed, running against her and angrily hugging her hips and butting my head against her waist. "She made me lose it! We didn't even sail it once!"

"Anna?" called my mother through the hall.

Anna loomed in the pantry door and beckoned to my mother.

"Don't bring him," Anna said, raising her chin at me. "I must tell you."

The manly voice which Anna now used as she caught her breath conveyed to my mother an air of something ominous.

"Then, Richard," said my mother, "take your coat off and put it away, and go upstairs and wash your face. You are a fright. Wait for me in your room."

Unwillingly I took the stairs one step at a time, and as the pantry door closed after my mother, I heard in Anna's voice the words "tramp" and "crazy drunk," and then a grand, long, running line of narrative blurred away from detail by the shut door, punctuated by little screams of shock and horror from my mother.

My room was at the front of the house next to the bedroom of my father and mother. I sat in the window seat looking out, mourning for my ship, which lay broken and worthless up the street, and then I saw the tramp, of whom I still thought as my funny new friend, come idling into view along the sidewalk. Now restored to modesty, he was eating with a sad air a crust-end of a sandwich. He leaned against a tree and rubbed his back against the bark like an old dog. He nodded right and left at the afternoon in general. He was a small man, I now saw, and he seemed sleepy and lonesome. In another moment, he slid gently against the tree trunk to the ground, and fastidiously searched in his loose pockets for something, and brought it forth—it was a pint bottle, empty. He raised it to his mouth. Nothing to drink ran forth, and with a little heave, he threw the empty bottle up on the lawn of the house next door, and then he fell sideways into a deep sleep on the ground, resembling a bundle of old clothes ready for the poor.

The voices downstairs went on, now heavy and baleful, now light and firm. I heard my mother use the telephone—she was calling my father at his office. Then a long silence fell in the house, while I wondered. In a quarter of an hour I heard a thrilling sound of clanging gongs come down the street, mixed with the rattle of hooves on the pavement. I leaned to see, and sure enough, it was a police patrol wagon, all shiny black with big gold lettering on the sides of the van.

The driver slowed down before our house to let two policemen, in their long-coated blue uniforms and domed grey helmets, and carrying their gleaming clubs, jump down from the rear door. I greatly admired the police for their uniforms, their horses, and their power. Anna had threatened me with their authority many times when I misbehaved. I watched now with abstracted excitement as they went to the tree where the tramp lay asleep. They took him up and shook him awake.

With an air of courtesy, he awoke and smiled his dusty, weak-necked smile at the two policemen.

For being smiled at by a degenerate, one of the policemen struck him in the face with his immense open hand.

A look of bewilderment came into the tramp's face.

The other policeman gave an order to hold the tramp, and then ran up to our front door and jabbed at the bell. In a moment Anna was taken forth to confront the man whom she had reported as a committer of public outrage. I saw her nod when the police pointed at the tramp. She identified him, though in her agitated modesty she could only look at him over her crooked elbow.

But this was enough for the police, They told her to go, she returned to the porch, and I heard her heavy steps running for the door and then the door slam behind her.

At the street curbing, while I knelt up on the window seat to see, one policeman knocked the tramp to the ground with his club and the other kicked him in the belly to make him stand up again. He tried to become a ball like a bear asleep in the zoo against the cold of winter, but they pulled his arms away from his head and between their hands they punched his head back and forth. They knocked his knees down from protecting his loins and kicked him there until he screamed silently. Suddenly he went to the ground of his own weight. The policemen looked at each other and in silent, expert accord took him up between them and carried him to the patrol wagon, threw him in the door, climbed in after him, and the wagon got up and away from a starting trot. I watched until they were all gone. My thoughts were slow, separate, and innocent.

Why did they beat him so?

Did they arrest him just because he was a tramp?

Or because he didn't look like everybody else?

Or because he was a "crazy-drunk?"

Or for sleeping under somebody else's tree?

Or for how he had presented himself to me and Anna?

Why didn't they want him to do what he had done up the street?

Didn't they know it hurt when they kicked and beat someone else?

In any case, it was an immense event, full of excitement and mystery, and I fell asleep on the window seat from the sheer emotion of it. When I awoke it was to find the barricade of our house lifted, and my mother, pretending that nothing whatever had happened, standing by me to say that it was time for me to get ready for supper.

"Daddy will be home soon, and he will come and see you when you have your tray."

But he did not.

I heard him come in, and then I heard the famous sounds of private, grown-up discussion in the living room, with the sliding doors closed. Anna was summoned to give all over again her account of what had happened, while my father listened in silence, and my mother made little supplementary exclamations.

The mystery grew for me as all such attention was paid to it, and it became complete when my father ran upstairs at last to put me to bed. There was something stern and righteous in his air. I understood that we had all survived a dreadful danger, though of what nature I was not sure.

"Well, Doc," he said, "it was quite a day. Sit down here on my knee and listen to me for a minute."

He pretended to knock me out with a fisted blow to my chin, and he smiled and scowled at the same moment. In his dark blue eyes there was a light like that of retained tears, as he mourned for the presence of evil in the world and the tender vulnerability of innocence. Trying his best to resolve for us all the event of the afternoon, he said,

"Doc?"

"Yes, Daddy."

"Promise me something."

"Yes, Daddy."

"Promise me to forget absolutely everything that happened this afternoon, with that tramp. Will you?"

"Yes."

"We must never keep thoughts about those things"—(what things?) —"in our heads. God does not want us to. When we see something terrible that happens near us we must get away and forget it as fast as we can. Do you understand?"

"Yes."

"Good."

"You mean," I asked, "what the policeman did to the man?"

"No, no, I mean what the man did. He was crazy and he was drunk and nobody else acts that way. Don't think other men are like that. They don't go around in public that way."

"Was he a bad man?"

"Oh, yes. A very bad man. But forget him. Promise?"

"Yes."

"He can't scare you again if you forget him, you see."

"He didn't scare me. He scared Anna."

"Well, then, Doc, it is because you didn't understand." He set me down and stood up. "All right, now? We won't have a thing to do again about it?"

"No."

"Good. Then up comes the young giant and the old giant will take him to his castle for the night!"

And he swung me to his shoulders and walking hunchily and with great heavy spread steps the way giants walked he took me to my bed across the room and undressed me and put my pajamas on me and laid me down and kissed my forehead and said, "We'll leave just a crack," and went to the door and left it open just a crack so the upstairs hall light would stand like a golden lance of safety all night long between me and the dark, and went downstairs to dine with my mother. Their voices grew easier as the minutes passed and faded into sleep.

But the very first thing I thought of when I awoke was the tramp, and the more I said to myself that I had promised to forget him and all of it, the more I remembered. During the morning, when Anna was in the basement laundry, I went down to see her.

"Anna, why was the tramp a bad man?"

"You are not to talk about it."

"But he didn't do anything!"

"Oh, God," she said, reviving her sense of shock with hushed pleasure.

"He was trying to make friends with me. He was doing something funny, but—".

"Don't you know," she asked in a hoarse whisper, "what he was doing?"

"No, I don't."

She pointed to my groin.

"There, and all like that," she moaned, "and it was a terrible sin he committed, doing that, and doing it to a lady and a little boy, and Hell don't have fires enough to punish him for what he did!"

"It doesn't?"

"Not fires enough!"

I stared at her. Her tired, sad, grey bulk was alive with some glory of rage, some fullness of life, and suddenly I knew for the first time in my years what it was she and all the others in the house had been talking about. From I could not know where, the knowledge of new sins, and their power, dawned within me, and they seemed to reside just there where Anna had pointed.

I began to jig up and down.

"Anna!" I cried, "He was a bad man, my father said he was! He was bad!"

"Well," she said with the massive placidity of vested virtue, "why do you suppose I dragged you away from seeing such a thing, and why do you suppose your Máma called Pápa, and he called the police station, and they sent a patrol wagon for the man? Well, I know, and you know, now."

"The police beat him!" I cried exultantly.

"I saw," she said. "Nothing they could do to him would be too much."

How could I ever have liked the tramp, or have felt sorry for him?

"Bash!" I exclaimed, imitating the blows of the police, "Blong!"

"Run along now, and don't think any more about it, it is all over."

But my interest was at a high pitch since I knew how to think about the affair, and I ran next door to see my friend Tom Deterson, who was my age, and with whom I exchanged secrets.

"Did you hear about the tramp?" I asked out of breath.

"No," said Tom. "What tramp?"

I had the rich opportunity, then, to tell him everything—all that I had seen and heard and was supposed to forget. Tom and I were in the old carriage house at the foot of his yard. Nothing was kept there but the discards of the Deterson household. It made a fine playhouse, for it was removed, musty, dim, and private. As I told him what I knew, we sat on an old ruined sofa whose springs sagged into view below. Its cushions were awry and stained.

Tom's eyes were huge in his flushed, thin little face. He had curly hair and jangling nerves. He was never at rest. He was like a hot-nosed, insistent puppy climbing against all objects and persons and mysteries with an assumption of universal good will. At that time he was my best friend.

When I reached the most dreadful part of my story, I showed in pantomime what the tramp kept doing. Tom stared and jiggled as if he saw the actuality instead of a mockery of the scandal.

"What for?" he asked.

"I don't know. But he was crazy-drunk. They all do it. You know what?"

"No. What?"

"He was a bad man."

"He was?"

"Yes, he was. My father said so, and Anna said so, and the police took him away."

"What did they do?"

"I'll show you what they did."

I seized an old split cushion from the sofa and threw it on the floor of the carriage house and I began to kick it.

"This is what they did!" I cried in heightening excitement. I picked up the cushion and punched it and threw it to Tom. He caught it and punched it and his eyes fired with power and purpose, and he threw the cushion down and he kicked it, and I kicked it again, and then we found some old thin brass curtain rods on the floor and we took these up and with them whipped the cushion.

"I'll tell you what I would do to that tramp!" I shouted. "I would beat him and push him until all his stuffing came out, and I would hit him"—and I did—"and I would kick him"—and I did—"and I would burn him in hell with all the fire that all the fire engines can't put out!"

"I have some matches!" cried Tom.

"Get them!"

He dug them from under the upholstery at the arm of the sofa and he lit a match and touched it to the split cushion where its dismal cotton stuffing showed through. It took on a feeble flame, making heavy white smoke. Exalted, we danced about the victim, telling each other to kick him, to whip him, to burn him. Suddenly the cushion made a spurt of fire and scared us. We had more fire than we expected.

"Say!" shouted Tom in a changed voice.

"Yes, yes, put it out!" I called.

He began to stamp with his flat sandalled feet at the burning corner of the cushion, but without much effect.

"Danged old tramp!" he said, "doing that!"

The cotton stuffing made little explosions with flying sparks.

"I know what," I said, "we can put out the fire—let's both of us—" and seeing what I did, Tom did the same, and with a sense of high glee, triumph, and even carnal fulfillment, we made our water together over the cushion and quelled the flame. The fire in the cushion guttered down into little worms of crinkling coal which finally expired yielding up a few last threads of noisome smoke.

"There!" said Tom.

"Yes!" I said.

We made ourselves proper again as passion gave way to shame. We kicked the cushion against the brick wall behind the sofa and went out into the unknowing, cool, golden October morning.

This loss of innocence was not in seeing what I saw, but in hearing what I was told about it—for we are subject to what we are taught to hate.

Discussion

The book *Things as They Are,* from which this chapter is taken, begins with this statement: " 'Richard, Richard,' they said to me in my childhood, 'When will you begin to see things as they are?' But they forgot that children are artists who see and enact through simplicity what their elders have lost through experience. The loss of innocence is a lifelong process."

Chapter two, "The Dawn of Hate," is an excellent example of how the natural friendliness and trust children have for others is distorted by the hysteria and prejudice of adults. The incident is related with utmost skill as the author reveals through the detail in the story an almost textbook understanding of the principles of child development. The author is careful to substantiate the fond relationship between the little boy and Anna, the cook and laundress, thereby underscoring the importance the little boy would attach to Anna's values and opinions. At five years of age the boy's existence is still dominated by egocentricity. In the author's words, "All persons seemed to commit their acts for my benefit, and all events were interesting only as they pleased me or met my needs." He therefore could not see Anna objectively. To him she was a source of wisdom, a trusted adult who loved him and whom he loved.

The boy, having no prior experience with a drunk, sees the disheveled man as a smiling and funny man. He is neither startled nor frightened by his appearance. Anna's reaction confuses the boy. He is made aware only by the adult response to the situation that something very bad has happened. As is natural for a boy of five his only concern is for his broken boat. The event takes on mysterious connotations and becomes emotionally provocative as he witnesses the police beating the man. The admonition to forget the incident, of course, serves to reinforce its significance, and we are not surprised at the boy's renewed desire on awakening to understand the events of the day before.

He goes to Anna, his adult source of truth. Feelings of love and trust in a relationship are the basis on which children incorporate the teachings of the adults closest to them. It is from Anna that the boy learns that the genitals are "bad." An aura of sin is to be associated with this area, thereby distorting any pleasure the boy has experienced. (By the age of five little boys have already had pleasurable experiences associated with handling their genitals.)

The retelling of the incident to a friend seems the appropriate next step for the little boy. Reenacting the scene of the policemen beating the tramp, the boys become increasingly violent as they continue to beat the pillows, and overtones of concomitant sexual arousal are evident. They proceed to set the pillows on fire and then to put out their fire with a stream of urine. This scene is an excellent literary example of the fire-setting phenomenon described in the psychoanalytic literature.

Freud (1953) first discussed fire as a symbol of sexual arousal and urination to put out the fire as an attempt to dampen the sexual excitement in his case study of Dora. Studies of children involved in setting fires indicate that by this behavior they may be acting out hostile and destructive urges. Therefore, we see in this episode of moral teaching a distortion of good mental health practices. In the name of morality the adult demonstrates confused feelings of anger, hate, and fear in relation to a rather pathetic incident of a harmless vagrant behaving foolishly. From this perversion of moral teaching the boys learn to link violence and guilt with sexual arousal. They substitute fear and punishment for compassion and hysteria for reason.

Springboards for Inquiry

(1) How would more enlightened parents and "baby sitter" have handled a situation similar to the one that occurred in this story?

(2) Explain why parents are considered the most effective transmitters of moral standards in children by both Freudians and social-learning theorists?

(3) According to Piaget, the little boy in this story is at an age when "moral realism" governs his reasoning. By referring to Piaget's work in the moral development of children,* † explain the term "moral realism." Perhaps you can repeat some of Piaget's work with children at this stage by asking children in your acquaintance, who are the same age as Piaget's Swiss subjects, some of the same and similar questions about moral wrong doing and its punishment. What did you learn?

(4) Discuss whether there are sex differences in conscience development.

---

* Piaget, Jean. *The Moral Judgment of the Child.* Chicago: The Free Press of Glencoe, 1948.

† Inhelder, B. and Jean Piaget. *The Early Growth of Logic in the Child.* New York: Harper & Row, Publishers, Inc., 1964.

". . . you're a disgrace and a bum. You got no right to parade the streets with your bastard where innocent children can see you."

A Tree Grows in Brooklyn

by Betty Smith

That summer Saturday was a day that should have gone down in her diary as one of the happiest days of her life. She saw her name in print for the first time. The school got out a magazine at the end of the year in which the best story written in composition class from each grade was published. Francie's composition called "Winter Time" had been chosen as the best of the seventh grade work. The magazine cost a dime and Francie had had to wait until Saturday to get it. School closed for the summer the day before and Francie worried that she wouldn't get the magazine. But Mr. Jenson said he'd be working around on Saturday and if she brought the dime over, he'd give her a copy.

Now in the early afternoon, she stood in front of her door with the magazine opened to the page of her story. She hoped someone would come along to whom she could show it.

She had shown it to mama at lunch time but mama had to get back to work and didn't have time to read it. At least five times during lunch, Francie mentioned that she had a story published. At last mama said.

"Yes, yes. I know. I saw it all coming. There'll be more stories printed and you'll get used to it. Now don't let it go to your head. There are dishes to be washed."

Papa was at Union Headquarters. He wouldn't see the story till Sunday but Francie knew he'd be pleased. So she stood on the street with her glory tucked under her arm. She couldn't let the magazine out of her hands even for a moment. From time to time she'd glance at her name in

---

From pp. 127–130, 201–207 (Perennial Library Edition), *A Tree Grows in Brooklyn* by Betty Smith.

print and the excitement about it never grew less.

She saw a girl named Joanna come out of her house a few doors away. Joanna was taking her baby out for an airing in its carriage. A gasp came up from some houswives who had stopped to gossip on the sidewalk while going to and fro about their shopping. You see, Joanna was not married. She was a girl who had gotten into trouble. Her baby was illegitimate—bastard was the word they used in the neighborhood—and these good women felt that Joanna had no right to act like a proud mother and bring her baby out into the light of day. They felt that she should have kept it hidden in some dark place.

Francie was curious about Joanna and the baby. She had heard mama and papa talking about them. She stared at the baby when the carriage came by. It was a beautiful little thing sitting up happily in its carriage. Maybe Joanna *was* a bad girl but certainly she kept her baby sweeter and daintier than these good women kept theirs. The baby wore a pretty frilled bonnet and a clean white dress and bib. The carriage cover was spotless and showed much loving handiwork in its embroidery.

Joanna worked in a factory while her mother took care of the baby. The mother was too ashamed to take it out so the baby got an airing only on week-ends when Joanna wasn't working.

Yes, Francie decided, it was a beautiful baby. It looked just like Joanna. Francie remembered how papa had described her that day he and mamma were talking about her.

"She has skin like a magnolia petal." (Johnny had never seen a magnolia.) "Her hair is as black as a raven's wing." (He had never seen such a bird.) "And her eyes are deep and dark like forest pools." (He had never been in a forest and the only pool he knew was where each man put in a dime and guessed what the Dodgers' score would be and whoever guessed right got all the dimes.) But he had described Joanna accurately. She was a beautiful girl.

"That may be," answered Katie. "But what good is her looks? They're a curse to the girl. I heard that her mother was never married but had two children just the same. And now the mother's son is in Sing Sing and her daughter has this baby. There must be bad blood all along the line and no use getting sentimental about it. Of course," she added with a detachment of which she was astonishingly capable at times, "it's none of my business. I don't need to do anything about it one way or the other. I don't need to go out and spit on the girl because she did wrong. Neither do I have to take her in my house and adopt her because she did wrong. She suffered as much pain bringing that child into the world as though she *was* married. If she's a good girl at heart, she'll learn from the pain and the shame and she won't do it again. If she's naturally bad, it won't bother her the way people treat her. So, if I was you, Johnny, I wouldn't feel too sorry for her." Suddenly she turned to Francie and said, "Let Joanna be a lesson to *you*."

On this Saturday afternoon, Francie watched Joanna walk up and down and wondered in what way she was a lesson. Joanna acted proud about her baby. Was the lesson there? Joanna was only seventeen and friendly and she wanted everybody to be friendly with her. She smiled at the grim good women but the smile went away when she saw that they answered her with frowns. She smiled at the little children playing on the street. Some smiled back. She smiled at Francie. Francie wanted to smile back but didn't. Was the lesson that she musn't be friendly with girls like Joanna?

The good housewives, their arms filled with bags of vegetables and brown paper parcels of meat, seemed to have little to do that afternoon. They kept gathering into little knots and whispered to each other. The whispering stopped when Joanna came by and started up when she had passed.

Each time Joanna passed, her cheeks got pinker, her head went higher and her skirt flipped behind her more defiantly. She seemed to grow prettier and prouder as she walked. She stopped oftener than needed to adjust the baby's coverlet. She maddened the women by touching the baby's cheek and smiling tenderly at it. How dare she! How dare she, they thought, act as though she had a right to all that?

Many of these good women had children which they brought up by scream and cuff. Many of them hated the husbands who lay by their sides at night. There was no longer high joy for them in the act of love. They endured the love-making rigidly, praying all the while that another child would not result. This bitter submissiveness made the man ugly and brutal. To most of them the love act had become a brutality on both sides; the sooner over with, the better. They resented this girl because they felt this had not been so with her and the father of her child.

Joanna recognized their hate but wouldn't cringe before it. She would not give in and take the baby indoors. Something *had* to give. The women broke first. They couldn't endure it any longer. They had to do something about it. The next time Joanna passed, a stringy woman called out:

"Ain't you ashamed of yourself?"

"What for?" Joanna wanted to know.

This infuriated the woman. "What for, she asks," she reported to the other women. "I'll tell you what for. Because you're a disgrace and a bum. You got no right to parade the streets with your bastard where innocent children can see you."

"I guess this is a free country," said Joanna.

"Not free for the likes of you. Get off the street, get off the street."

"Try and make me!"

"Get off the street, you whore," ordered the stringy woman.

The girl's voice trembled when she answered. "Be careful what you're saying."

"We don't have to be careful what we say to no street walker," chipped in another woman.

A man passing by stopped a moment to take it in. He touched Joanna's arm. "Look, Sister, why don't you go home till these battle-axes cool off? You can't win with them."

Joanna jerked her arm away. "You mind your own business!"

"I meant it in the right way, Sister. Sorry." He walked on.

"Why don't you go with him," taunted the stringy woman. "He might be good for a quarter." The others laughed.

"You're all jealous," said Joanna evenly.

"She says we're jealous," reported the interlocutor.

"Jealous of what, you?" (She said "you" as though it were the girl's name.)

"Jealous that men like me. That's what. Lucky you're married already," she told the stringy one. "You'd never get a man otherwise. I bet your husband spits on you—afterwards. I bet that's just what he does."

"Bitch! You bitch!" screamed the stringy one hysterically. Then, acting on an instinct which was strong even in Christ's day, she picked a stone out of the gutter and threw it at Joanna.

It was the signal for the other women to start throwing stones. One, droller than the rest, threw a ball of horse manure. Some of the stones hit Joanna but a sharp pointed one missed and struck the baby's forehead. Immediately, a thin clear trickle of blood ran down the baby's face and spotted its clean bib. The baby whimpered and held out its arms for its mother to pick it up.

A few women, poised to throw the next stones, dropped them quietly back into the gutter. The baiting was all over. Suddenly the women were ashamed. They had not wanted to hurt the baby. They only wanted to drive Joanna off the street. They dispersed and went home quietly. Some children who had been standing around listening, resumed their play.

Joanna, crying now, lifted the baby from the carriage. The baby continued to whimper quietly as though it had no right to cry out loud. Joanna pressed her cheek to her baby's face and her tears mixed with its blood. The women won. Joanna carried her baby into the house not caring that the carriage stood in the middle of the sidewalk.

And Francie had seen it all; had seen it all. She had heard every word. She remembered how Joanna had smiled at her and how she had turned her head away without smiling back. Why hadn't she smiled back? Why hadn't she smiled back? Now she would suffer—she would suffer all the rest of her life every time that she remembered that she had not smiled back.

Some small boys started to play tag around the empty carriage, holding on to its sides and pulling it way over while being chased. Francie scattered them and wheeled the carriage over to Joanna's door and put the brake on. There was an unwritten law that nothing was to be molested that stood outside the door where it belonged.

She was still holding the magazine with her story in it. She stood next to the braked carriage and looked at her name once more. "Winter Time, by Frances Nolan." She wanted to do something, sacrifice something to pay for not having smiled at Joanna. She thought of her story, she was so proud of it; so eager to show papa and Aunt Evy and Sissy. She wanted to keep it always to look at and to get that nice warm feeling when she looked at it. If she gave it away, there was no means by which she could get another copy. She slipped the magazine under the baby's pillow. She left it open at the page of her story.

She saw some tiny drops of blood on the baby's snowy pillow. Again she saw the baby; the thin trickle of blood on its face; the way it held out its arms to be taken up. A wave of hurt broke over Francie and left her weak when it passed. Another wave came, broke and receded. She found her way down to the cellar of her house and sat in the darkest corner on a heap of burlap sacks and waited while the hurt waves swept over her. As each wave spent itself and a new one gathered, she trembled. Tensely she sat there waiting for them to stop. If they didn't stop, she'd have to die —she'd have to die.

After awhile they came fainter and there was a longer time between each one. She began to think. She was now getting her lesson from Joanna but it was not the kind of lesson her mother meant.

She remembered Joanna. Often at night on her way home from the library, she had passed Joanna's house and seen her and the boy standing close together in the narrow vestibule. She had seen the boy stroke Joanna's pretty hair tenderly; had seen how Joanna put up her hand to touch his cheek. And Joanna's face looked peaceful and dreamy in the light from the street lamp. Out of that beginning, then, had come the shame and the baby. Why? Why? The beginning had seemed so tender and so right. Why?

She knew that one of the women stone-throwers had had a baby only three months after her marriage. Francie had been one of the children standing at the curb watching the party leave for the church. She saw the bulge of pregnancy under the virginal veil of the bride as she stepped into the hired carriage. She saw the hand of the father closed tight on the bridegroom's arm. The groom had black shadows under his eyes and looked very sad.

Joanna had no father, no men kin. There was no one to hold her boy's arm tight on the way to the altar. That was Joanna's crime, decided Francie—not that she had been bad, but that she had not been smart enough to get the boy to the church.

Discussion

It is unusual for children to have the opportunity to reexamine their moral judgments as early in life as Francie does in this excerpt from *A Tree Grows in Brooklyn.* By the age of nine or ten, children have usually learned their parents' prejudices and judgments, without either parent or child being particularly aware that this has happened. Children learn not only their attitudes from their parent-model, but frequently children repeat verbatim the controversial things they have heard parents say about people or situations. These attitudes are usually not examined by the child until late adolescence, when, as an emerging adult, he begins to question parental values and judgments and frequently comes to independent decisions about many assumptions he had previously taken for granted.

Francie is not sure why, but she turns her head when Joanna passes with her baby. This gesture is meant as disdain and is assumed almost without volition on Francie's part. She has heard Joanna talked about at home, which in itself suggests that there must be something different, something bad about Joanna. When confronted with the reality of the situation Francie is confused. The appearance of Joanna and her baby arouses the same feelings of tenderness toward mother and child that any similar pair arouses in the romantic Francie. The baby is pretty and well kept in Francie's estimation. The jeers and name-calling seem inappropriate for a baby and its proud parent. To Francie, Joanna seems no more shameful than any other mother and child. When the baby is hurt, Francie is crushed and she is aware of pangs of conscience. She knows she has done something wrong, and this makes Francie question her earlier unquestioned judgment about Joanna. This incident helps Francie to come to an independent decision about a moral judgment at a very early age.

Springboards for Inquiry

(1) It is unusual when a child as young as Francie is able to reject the moral values of her community. Discuss whether you think young people are making independent moral judgments at an earlier age in today's society, and if so, what influences have encouraged this independence?

(2) To what extent, if any, should the school involve itself in the teaching of moral and ethical values?

(3) How will children react if home and school teach different values?

(4) What are some of the traditional moral values parents inculcate in children during the growing up years? Which of these traditional values are being challenged as "absolutes" by today's youth?

References

Bettelheim, Bruno. "Moral Education" in *Moral Education*. Cambridge, Mass.: Harvard University Press, 1970.

Bossard, James H. S., and Eleanor S. Boll. *The Sociology of Child Development*. New York: Harper & Row, Publishers, Inc., 1960.

Burchinal, Lee G. "Characteristics of Adolescents from Unbroken, Broken, and Reconstituted Families." *Journal of Marriage and Family Living* 26 (1964): 44–59.

Fisher, Sara C. "The Relationship of Attitudes, Opinions, and Values among Family Members." In *Publications in Culture and Society*. Berkeley and Los Angeles: University of California Press, 1948, pp. 29–99.

Freud, Sigmund. In *The Standard Edition of the Complete Works of Sigmund Freud*, edited by Jerome Strachey. Vol. 3. London: Hogarth Press and Institute of Psychoanalysis, 1953.

Fromm, Erich. "Selfishness and Self-Love." *Psychiatry* 2 (1939): 507–23.

Ginsburg, Herbert, and Sylvia Opper. *Piaget's Theory of Intellectual Development*. Englewood Cliffs, N. J.: Prentice-Hall, 1969.

Goode, William J. *After Divorce*. Glencoe, Ill.: Free Press, 1956.

Hart, I. "Maternal Child-Rearing Practices and Authoritarian Ideology." *Journal of Abnormal and Social Psychology* 55 (1957): 232–37.

Hartshorne, Hugh, and Mark A. May. *Studies in Service and Self-Control*. Vol. 2. *Studies in the Nature of Character*. New York: Columbia University Teachers' College, 1928.

Havighurst, Robert J. "How the Moral Life

Is Formed." *Religious Education* 57 (1962): 432–39.

Horney, Karen. *Neurosis and Human Growth.* New York: W. W. Norton & Co., 1950.

Kinstler, Donald B. "Covert and Overt Maternal Rejection in Stuttering." *Journal of Speech and Hearing Disorders* 26 (1961): 145–55.

Koch, Helen L. "The Relation of Certain Formal Attributes of Siblings to Attitudes Held toward Each Other and toward Their Parents." *Monographs of the Society for Research in Child Development*, Lafayette, Ind.: Publication of the Society for Research in Child Development. No. 4 (1960).

——— "Some Emotional Attitudes of the Young Child in Relation to Characteristics of His Siblings." *Child Development* 27 (1956): 393–426.

Kohlberg, Lawrence. "Education for Justice: A Modern Statement of the Platonic View." in *Moral Education.* Cambridge, Mass.: Harvard University Press, 1970.

Lasko, John K. "Parent Behavior toward First and Second Children." *Genetic Psychology Monographs,* Vol. 49 (1954), pp. 97–137.

LeMasters, E. E. *Parents in Modern America.* Homewood, Ill.: Dorsey Press, 1970.

Lidz, Theodore. *The Person.* New York: Basic Books, 1968.

Medinnus, Gene R., and Floyd J. Curtis. "The Relation between Maternal Self-Acceptance and Child Acceptance." *Journal of Consulting Psychology* 27 (1963): 542–64.

Meissner, W. W., S. J. "Sibling Relations in the Schizophrenic Family." *Family Process* 9 (March 1970): 1–25.

Nye, F. Ivan. "Child Adjustment in Broken and Unhappy Unbroken Homes." *Journal of Marriage and Family Living* 19 (1957): 356–61.

Piaget, Jean. *The Moral Judgment of the Child.* Trans. by Marjorie Eabain. Glencoe, Ill.: The Free Press, 1948.

Rogers, Carl R. *Client-Centered Therapy.* Boston: Houghton Mifflin Co., 1951.

Rogers, Dorothy. *Child Psychology.* Belmont, Calif.: Brooks/Cole Publishing Co., 1969.

Rosenberg, Morris. *Society and the Adolescent Self-Image.* Princeton, N. J.: Princeton University Press, 1965.

Sears, Robert R. "The Growth of Conscience." In *Personality Development in Childhood*, eds. Ira Iscoe and Harold W. Stevenson. Austin: University of Texas Press, 1960.

Slater, Philip E. "Parental Behavior and the Personality of the Child." *Journal of Genetic Psychology* 101 (1962): 53–68.

Stagner, Ross. *Psychology of Personality.* 3rd ed. New York: McGraw-Hill Book Co., 1961.

Whiting, John W. M., and Irvin L. Child. *Child Training and Personality: A Cross-Cultural Study.* New Haven, Conn.: Yale University Press, 1953.

Yarrow, Marian Radke. "Problems of Methods in Parent–Child Research." *Child Development* 34 (1963): 215–26.

School Influences

The school and the schoolroom may be conceived of as social climates to which the curriculum, the physical plant, teachers, and students contribute. The school's conception of its role will determine its total effect on the children who attend. Teachers who see themselves as part of a therapeutic environment will act differently from those who see themselves as textbooks wired for sound. The school that is designed to provide laboratory space and places to plant gardens will differ from the school that, because of its architecture, provides only the traditional seats in traditional rooms.

Teacher Influence

Of all the school forces, the teacher undoubtedly has the strongest influence over the developing child. The evidence from research is clear—the teacher's expectations can encourage the student to achieve or cause him to fail. It has been reported that students spend 70 percent of the school day either listening to the teacher or talking to the teacher. What the teacher says and does becomes the "script" for many a child's evening session of playing school. This continual interaction, both overt and tacit, between teachers and children is the means used to transmit some very clear value-laden messages. The standards of teachers, particularly such traditional middle-class, Anglo-Saxon values as cleanliness, thrift, correct English, and sexual and physical restraint, are emphasized in most American classrooms. In most schoolrooms the teacher is the voice of authority—politically, economically, and socially. In fact, the teacher is the literal controller of the schoolroom climate. Whether a classroom is a therapeutic place or an oppressive place to spend the day depends entirely on the way a teacher views his role. Whether the teacher accepts the ideas and ideals of children and their views of the universe depends largely on the teacher as a facilitator. And whether children dare to try, dare to be wrong depends on how the teacher sees himself in the social context of the classroom (Kohl 1969).

Peer Influence

In every sense the peer group is the child's only distinct society. Supervision may come from adults, but the society of playmates is a subculture of its own. From the pressures of the peer group the child learns what to think of school and what he thinks of himself. When a child begins school he tests his family's patterns and values against those of his peers. If he comes from a home in which he has developed good relations with his parents, he will have confidence in his family's standards and will be able to withstand the pressures of the peer group. Where family relations are tense or parents are themselves in conflict over standards of behavior, he is nearly certain to conform to his peer's ideals. Because it commands special authority, the peer group is the most efficient mechanism to regulate ideas, attitudes, and behavior.

In the child's world, rejection by the peer group is tantamount to Mafia-like exclusion from the brotherhood. Antagonism and aggression follow rejection. Emotional stress in childhood is often the result of being or feeling left out. The shifting cliques that characterize much of middle-class life is a result of peer group choices that change, leaving some children out at one time or another.

In every sense the school is a culture.* The experience of each school's unique culture has a profound effect on the children who are a part of that cultural fabric.

---

* Seymour Sarason's *The Culture of the School and the Problem of Change* (Boston: Allyn & Bacon, 1971) is a recent attempt to view critically the total school culture as it responds to and initiates change.

The Teacher

Twenty-five years ago American educators started to tear down the one-room schoolhouse in the belief that modern education demanded innovation not possible in ancient buildings at country crossroads. A veritable wave of architectural hysteria gripped educators, and buildings created new organizational forms. New arrangements of bricks and mortar did not go far in answering the relevant question George Counts (1936) asked in his book by the same title, "Dare the schools build a new social order?"* It took the perceptions of Redl (1966) and others to activate a reappraisal of teaching and teachers. Redl's concept of the therapeutic milieu (1959), or an environment largely created by the teacher,† has been expanded today so that the 1970 yearbook of the Association for the Supervision of Curriculum Development (ASCD) expresses in essence that the commitment to the seventies is "to nurture humaneness." The ASCD's concept of the purpose of education—"the development of humane individuals" (Hanna 1970)—indicates that innovation in media, teaching teams, television, pass-fail grades, and new configurations of class sizes cannot substitute for those qualities in the teacher that make learning possible for children.

---

* Charles Silberman's *Crisis in the Classroom* (New York: Random House, 1970) is the most recent intensive study of our nation's schools.

† Redl's earliest published works (in German) talked of the counseling function of the teacher in the homeroom—an advanced concept even today, yet spoken of by Redl in 1931 in "Erziehungsberatung in der Eigenen Klasse" (Counseling in One's Own Homeroom), *Zeitschift fur Padagogische Psychologies*, 11:425–501.

When Neil Postman and Charles Weingartner (1969) talked of teaching as a subversive activity, they referred to the qualities of the teacher that would not be tolerated in a society in which "the person with true charity, guided by deep regard for his fellowman, creative in using his abilities, is at most crucified, at least looked upon as immoral, insane, or stupid" (Grambs 1970).

Thus, the most potent force in that one-room schoolhouse, the teacher, viewed in the 1960s as merely the handmaiden of educational television and other technological "breakthroughs," has now become the prime target for educational renovation. The changes in the "structure of education" Hechinger (1965) talks about are, in reality, the changes that have to be affected in the human beings who teach. Taba and Elkins (1966, p. 265) describe the kind of teachers that are needed: "First of all, students need to see that the teacher cares, that she is a human being who is interested in them personally, . . . finds ways to make a student feel good about himself, . . . and helps students through some crisis."

Pygmalion in the Classroom (Rosenthal and Jacobson 1968) focuses on the role that the expectations of teachers play in the development of children. The subtitle, *Teacher Expectation and Pupil's Intellectual Achievement,* indicates that these researchers see the role of the teacher's expectations as a valid predictor of pupil achievement. In their study, 20 percent of the children in a given elementary school were reported to their teachers as "showing unusual potential for intellectual growth" (p. vii). In fact, these children who were predicted to be "spurters" were chosen randomly (the names were drawn out of a hat). Eight months later these children showed significantly greater gains on IQ tests than did the children who had not been brought to the attention of the teachers.* The authors document voluminously the "real-life" experiences of people in which the expectancy of "others" predicts performance.†

Recently Herbert Kohl (1967), Holt (1964; 1967), Kozol (1967), Hentoff (1966), and others have shaken the educational tree by their charges of teacher indifference, cruelty, lack of knowledge, and lack of interest in students. Silberman (1970), in his study of 250 schools, has documented evidence of teacher lassitude.

In 1970 at the Claremont Reading Conference, one of the editors of this volume asked some of Kohl's children from Berkeley Free School what an education was. A quick snap of the head and the answer came: "Herb Kohl." Writes Kohl, author of *36 Children* (1967, p. 42): "I have found that one of the most valuable qualities a teacher can have is the ability to perceive and build upon the needs of his pupils. . . . For this he needs antennae . . . attuning himself to the ambience of the classroom." His success is reflected in his students, who equate his name

---

* There are those who feel the data do not support the contentions, but these critics still applaud the data.

† Illustrative of the dozen studies cited (Rosenthal and Jacobson 1968) are "Sweeney's Miracle," which describes how James Sweeney's belief that a janitor can become a computer specialist helps Sweeney to teach him to be one, and Whyte's study of how friends' expectations can predict a bowler's score.

with education. Few children see methods and materials as decisive educational factors, and fewer adults recollect great texts, but nearly everyone remembers some great teacher.

"Cold-blooded little brats," she raged to herself. "I should know by this time it never pays to open your heart to them. I'll never be fooled into it again, never."

Death in the Fifth Grade

by Marjorie Marks

As soon as the first bell rang and the children took their places, Miss Steineck knew that they knew. Hardly any of the twenty-six looked at her as they said good morning.

The grade mother had called her up the evening before. "I've telephoned all the Fifth Grade mothers," she said. "They promised to keep it from the children tonight. We all agreed it would be better if you told them. You've had so much experience and besides, they're so fond of you. You'll do it, won't you?"

Miss Steineck had said she would. Although she dreaded the ordeal, she recognized its assignment as a tribute. It was true, the children were fond of her, even though sometimes they succumbed to the temptation of drawing caricatures of her with exaggerated pince-nez and a very long neck, which they labeled "Miss Stiffneck." Still, she nearly always got results with children, because she respected them and was honest with them. That's what she told the mothers when they asked her. But of course in every class there were some she defied anyone to reach. "The doltish dregs," she called them in her thoughts. But even these, she felt, were not unkindly disposed toward her.

She had lain awake most of the night trying to think of a way to tell them. "You know, Norma has been very ill," she planned to begin and would go on to say that if she had lived she probably would never have been able to move about or have fun again. They would understand that it was better for her to die than to be an invalid all her life. They must have felt, as she did herself, that Norma was someone

---

apart, especially marked by joy and grace.

All—even the doltish dregs—sat still as stones while, with exaggerated deliberateness, she checked the roll book. She was conscious, meanwhile, of Rosanne, synthetic sorrow on her fat face, dabbing at her eyes. Undoubtedly it was she who had told the others.

Quietly Miss Steineck shut the roll book and squared her shoulders. "You know, Norma has been very, very ill," she said. That was the way she had planned. So far, so good. The bell rang. There was a little flutter through the class. Evie and Carolyn exchanged nervous glances over Norma's empty desk. Miss Steineck wished now that she'd had the janitor take it away before school. She had debated during the night the wisdom of this and decided it would be less of a shock this way. But now, her sensibilities heightened by this situation, its emptiness accused her.

Jane, the youngest in the class, who hadn't much sense, piped up from the front row, "We all know she's dead, Miss Steineck, you don't need to tell us."

A snicker which was half a shudder passed through the group.

Rosanne mouthed sanctimoniously, lifting her eyes for approval from the teacher, "You mustn't say she's dead. She's gone to heaven to be an angel. That's what my mother says. It's true, isn't it, Miss Steineck?"

The eyes of all twenty-six implored her for an answer. But how could she answer? She had left heaven behind with high button boots for Sunday and a dime inside her glove for the collection. How could she tell them what she really believed—that Norma, the vivid, the golden-haired, the pink-cheeked, the winner of races, the gayest, the fairest in games, was not an angel fluttering about the Throne but simply had ceased to exist. She couldn't say that, but she had to say something. Without knowing she was beginning, she said, "When I was a little girl, we lived on a farm and I had a pet crow. He was my special friend. Whenever I whistled outside the house he would come and I would feed him. He'd sit on my hand or my shoulder and when I took a walk he'd flutter along beside me. His name was Timmie and I loved him very much."

She looked at the class. No one had moved except Rosanne, hitching about in her seat. Apparently she thought an animal story too babyish for the fifth grade. Miss Steineck looked at the others. They were waiting quietly, their eyes still unwaveringly upon her. She went on. "I used to talk to Timmie and he would answer me. He was my friend for a whole summer. When winter came I put crumbs out for him and left a window open in the toolshed for him to fly in when it got too cold outside. But one morning, the coldest I could remember, when I whistled for Timmie he didn't come, I whistled and whistled till my lips were sore. Finally at the end of the day, my father found him. He was lying at the edge of the woods, frozen stiff. His wings were spread out as though he'd tried to come when I called him. How I cried. For days and days I felt I'd never be happy again. I knew I'd never forget the way poor Timmie looked with his body all stiff and his eyes not seeing. I asked the minister on Sunday if there was a heaven for crows and he laughed and said he'd never heard of one. Then I felt worse than ever."

She paused and cleared her throat. Nobody said anything. For an instant she felt panicky, seeing how scornful Rosanne was looking, but she went on. "Well, for weeks and weeks I cried myself to sleep. My parents tried their best to comfort me. My father promised me a parrot, but I wouldn't let him buy one. Nothing could take Timmie's place. I kept seeing him in my dreams, all stiff and dead in the snow.

"But one night," said Miss Steineck slowly, because she was seeing it as she spoke, "a wonderful thing happened. I dreamed that it was spring and all the leaves and flowers were budding. I stood in the freshly planted garden and called Timmie. He came right away. How his feathers glistened! I'd never seen him look so handsome. He perched on my hand and cocked his head and spoke to me in his hoarse voice. 'Why don't you remember me this way?' he asked and began to fly, around and around, up and up, in wonderful patterns and circles that got bigger and bigger until finally he flew so high that I couldn't see him any more. Then I woke up. But I wasn't sad now, because even though Timmie was dead, I was happy remembering him and the way he flapped his wings and how beautiful he was."

She surveyed the class. Nobody was looking at her. Nobody registered any reaction at all except Rosanne, who muttered sullenly, "I don't see what a silly crow has to do with Norma." There was a sort of assenting growl from a few of the doltish dregs, and then silence.

"I've made a fool of myself," Miss Steineck thought desperately. "I've failed them when they needed me most. Whatever possessed me to make such an exhibition of myself?" She felt the tight clamp of her pince-nez on her nose, as she always did when she was upset, and she knew that a red spot had appeared at the base of her neck. Rosanne was staring at it. She felt old and ugly and futile—Miss Stiffneck to the life.

The bell rang. "First period, Art," said Miss Steineck in her crispest voice. There was the rattle and bang of desk lids going up, the clatter of pencils and crayons being set out. The children were making as much noise as they could, to annoy her. Well, she deserved it. She had been an idiot.

Like a drill sergeant, she snapped out her orders. "Quiet, please. We'll have free work." (She felt capable of nothing else.) "Draw anything you like, using crayons. Plan to finish by the end of the period and sign your name in full in the lower right hand corner with the date." They set to work, while she made ferocious corrections with red pencil on the arithmetic homework papers.

As she marked automatically her C's and X's, she imagined the evening ahead of her, punctuated by indignant telephone calls from the mothers. Tomorrow, she knew, she would be summoned to the principal's office and be raked over the coals as she had been once before at the time of the great mumblety-peg war. "I can't imagine what you thought you were accomplishing by such unorthodox procedure," he would say sadly. "If it should happen again—" This was the threat of dismissal. Well, she certainly wouldn't blame him for wanting to replace her with a younger person one with sensible ideas.

The bell rang. "Quietly, less noise, please," she sang out with a knife edge in her voice. Noisily they piled their drawings on her desk, noisily collected their equipment for history with Mr. MacVey in Room 103. Like hoodlums they scrambled for first place in line, brushing ruthlessly against a crayon landscape by Norma, which fluttered to the floor and was trampled on.

Carolyn said admiringly to Evie, who'd made first place, "Now that Norma isn't here, I guess you'll have a chance to win some races."

"I guess so," Evie giggled and Rosanne cried out in shocked tones, "It's awful to say such a thing." For once Miss Steineck agreed with her.

"The class may go now," she said, quietly icy. "Less noise, please." Regardless, they trampled up the corridor, William as usual making a noise like a muted saxophone.

Miss Steineck, smoothing Norma's crumpled drawing against her breast gazed after them. "Cold-blooded little brats," she raged to herself. "I should know by this time it never pays to open your heart to them. I'll never be fooled into it again, never." She laughed aloud in self-derision as she picked up the drawings to transfer them to the side table.

Then her eyes were arrested by the topmost. It was a picture of a child with bright yellow hair, skipping rope in a field of brilliant flowers. Norma had loved to skip rope. Breathing hard, she turned to the next. This was Evie's. Evie did not draw well, but it was easy to see what she meant to convey—a group of children racing and far in advance of the others one girl with bright pink cheeks and yellow hair streaming behind her.

Miss Steineck sat down and went over the pictures one by one, skipping quickly over the products of the doltish dregs (the usual pretty-ladies by the girls and airplanes and boats by the boys). Her heart hammered at her thin ribs. For all the other pictures were about Norma; each was different; each about Norma doing one of the things she liked best—climbing, swimming, throwing a ball. There were two exceptions. One was William's—he was the best in drawing. He had done a large crow with wings spread wide against a vivid sunset sky. The other was Rosanne's—a minutely elaborate wreath of purple flowers, with Sinserest Simpathy printed beneath in neat black letters. Miss Steineck took pleasure in marking it with a large red X. Sp.

She laid the papers on the table. And then, to her own amazement, she found herself with her head on her desk, crying as she had not cried since Timmie died.

Discussion

The atmosphere in the classroom is tense because the teacher and the children are uncomfortable with the finality and the emotional shock of death. Miss Steineck and the children are trying to handle their private and public responses to Norma's death. Although ten-year-olds accept the concept of death as a fact, children of this age also feel assured that death comes only much later in life. The death of a schoolmate is particularly disturbing, because it brings the possibility of death close to the children's own lives. They are seeking to put the knowledge of Norma's death into a framework that is acceptable and manageable for their imaginations. Perhaps they hope to have the vision of a pleasant heaven confirmed by the teacher, to whom they look for guidance and reassurance.

The teacher's immediate response to the exceptional emotional threat is to confine her actions to the perfunctory, such as marking the roll book, thereby gaining time and objective distance from the real matter at hand. The tension Miss Steineck feels is not unrealistic. She is under pressure to project herself as a model with values that will not be inconsistent with anyone's thinking. Her response to death must be real but sensitive, providing the children with a positive memory. And while she feels responsible to the children, she feels equally responsible to the administrator and parents who, experience has shown, are more inclined to criticize for an indiscretion than to praise for undertaking activities beyond the usual teaching requirements. The emotional relief in this story occurs when Miss Steineck gets positive feedback from the students in the form of their drawings. She then knows that stepping out of her usual role was not wrong but humane and effective.

Students who plan to enter the teaching profession might pause to think how difficult it is for the teacher to evaluate his effectiveness. Miss Steineck thought she had surely failed, and had it not been for the unplanned art lesson she would probably never have known that she had succeeded. Actually, she did not succeed totally. The gamut of pictures ranged from the usual airplanes to the funeral wreath—showing that even teaching at its best will not elicit the desired responses from everyone in the classroom. The goal of effective teaching is an elusive one.

Springboards for Inquiry

(1) Accountability is the current watchword in education; educators are under pressure to supply evaluative instruments for their programs. Suggest ways in which you could evaluate teacher effectiveness in the affective domain.

(2) What do you think of Miss Steineck's acceptance of the parents' request to explain the death of a classmate to the students?

(3) How well do you think Miss Steineck handled the explanation of Norma's death to the class? What other possible ways could have been used to deal with the situation?

(4) Teachers can be important influences on the personality growth of young children, since children respond to the attitudes and feelings of the adults in their environment. The teacher also sets the stage for important emotional learning in the child's early years. What emotional learning took place in the children of Miss Steineck's class that day?

(5) What might Miss Steineck's usual teaching style be? What are some of the daily pressures a teacher faces, other than the pressure of planning appropriate lessons for her class?

"I always stays two years in a grade, Miz Richards," he told her blandly. "I does better the second year."

See How They Run

by Mary Elizabeth Vroman

A bell rang. Jane Richards squared the sheaf of records decisively in the large Manila folder, placed it in the right-hand corner of her desk, and stood up. The chatter of young voices subsided, and forty-three small faces looked solemnly and curiously at the slight young figure before them. The bell stopped ringing.

I wonder if they're as scared of me as I am of them. She smiled brightly.

"Good morning, children, I am Miss Richards." As if they don't know—the door of the third-grade room had a neat new sign pasted above it with her name in bold black capitals; and anyway, a new teacher's name is the first thing that children find out about on the first day of school. Nevertheless, she wrote it for their benefit in large white letters on the blackboard.

"I hope we will all be happy working and playing together this year." *Now why does that sound so trite?* "As I call the roll will you please stand, so that I may get to know you as soon as possible, and if you like you may tell me something about yourselves, how old you are, where you live, what your parents do, and perhaps something about what you did during the summer."

Seated, she checked the names carefully. "Booker T. Adams."

Booker stood, gangling and stoop-shouldered; he began to recite tiredly, "My name is Booker T. Adams, I'se ten years old." *Shades of Uncle Tom!* "I live on Painter's Path." He paused, the look he gave her was tinged with something very akin to contempt. "I didn't do nothing in the summer," he said deliberately.

"Thank you, Booker." Her voice was even. "George Allen." *Must remember to correct that stoop . . . Where is Painter's Path? . . . How to go about correcting those speech defects? . . . Go easy, Jane, don't antagonize them. . . . They're clean enough, but this is the first day. . . . How can one teacher do any kind of job with a load of forty-three? . . . Thank heaven the building is modern and well built even though it is overcrowded, not like some I've seen —no potbellied stove.*

"Sarahlene Clover Babcock." *Where do these names come from? . . . Up from slavery. . . . How high is up?* Jane smothered a sudden desire to giggle. Outside she was calm and poised and smiling. Clearly she called the names, listening with interest, making a note here and there, making no corrections—not yet.

She experienced a moment of brief inward satisfaction: *I'm doing very well, this is what is expected of me* . . . Orientation to Teaching . . . Miss Murray's voice beat a distant tattoo in her memory. Miss Murray with the Junoesque figure and the moon face. . . . "The ideal teacher personality is one which, combining in itself all the most desirable qualities, expresses itself with quiet assurance in its endeavor to mold the personalities of the students in the most desirable patterns." . . . Dear dull Miss Murray.

She made mental estimates of the class. *What a cross section of my people they represent,* she thought. *Here and there signs of evident poverty, here and there children of obviously well-to-do parents.*

"My name is Rachel Veronica Smith. I am nine years old. I live at Six-oh-seven Fairview Avenue. My father is a Methodist minister. My mother is a housewife. I have two sisters and one brother. Last summer mother and daddy took us all to New York to visit my Aunt Jen. We saw lots of wonderful things. There are millions and millions of people in New York. One day we went on a ferryboat all the way up the Hudson River—that's a great big river as wide as this town, and——"

The children listened wide-eyed. Jane listened carefully. *She speaks good English. Healthy, erect, and even perhaps a little smug. Immaculately well dressed from the smoothly braided hair, with two perky bows, to the shiny brown oxford. . . . Bless you, Rachel, I'm so glad to have you.*

"—— and the buildings are all very tall, some of them nearly reach the sky."

"Haw-haw"—this from Booker, cynically.

"Well, they are too." Rachel swung around, fire in her eyes and insistence in every line of her round, compact body.

"Ain't no buildings as tall as the sky, is dere, Miz Richards?"

Crisis No. 1. Jane chose her answer carefully. *As high as the sky . . . musn't turn this into a lesson in science . . . all in due time.* "The sky is a long way out, Booker, but the buildings in New York are very tall indeed. Rachel was only trying to show you how very tall they are. In fact, the tallest building in the whole world is in New York City."

"They call it the Empire State Building," interrupted Rachel, heady with her new knowledge and Jane's corroboration.

Booker wasn't through. "You been dere, Miz Richards?"

"Yes, Booker, many times. Someday I shall tell you more about it. Maybe Rachel will help me. Is there anything you'd like to add, Rachel?"

"I would like to say that we are glad you are our new teacher, Miss Richards." Carefully she sat down, spreading her skirt with her plump hands, her smile angelic.

Now I'll bet me a quarter her reverend father told her to say that. "Thank you, Rachel."

The roll call continued. . . . Tanya, slight and pinched, with the toes showing through the very white sneakers, the darned and faded but clean blue dress, the gentle voice like a tinkling bell, and the beautiful sensitive face. . . . Boyd and Lloyd, identical in their starched overalls, and the slightly vacant look. . . . Marjorie Lee, all of twelve years old, the well-developed body moving restlessly in the childish dress, the eyes too wise, the voice too high. . . . Joe Louis, the intelligence in the brilliant black eyes gleaming above the threadbare clothes. *Lives of great men all remind us— Well, I have them all . . . Frederick Douglass, Franklin Delano, Abraham Lincoln, Booker T., Joe Louis, George Washington. . . . What a great burden you bear, little people, heirs to all your parents' stillborn dreams of greatness. I must not fail you.* The last name on the list . . . C. T. Young. Jane paused, small lines creasing her forehead. She checked the list again.

"C. T., what is your name? I only have your initials on my list."

"Dat's all my name, C. T. Young."

"No, dear, I mean what does C. T. stand for? Is it Charles or Clarence?"

"No'm, jest C. T."

"But I can't put that in my register, dear."

Abruptly Jane rose and went to the next room. Rather timidly she waited to speak to Miss Nelson, the second-grade teacher, who had the formidable record of having taught all of sixteen years. Miss Nelson was large and smiling.

"May I help you, dear?"

"Yes, please. It's about C. T. Young. I believe you had him last year."

"Yes, and the year before that. You'll have him two years too."

"Oh? Well, I was wondering what name you registered him under. All the information I have is C. T. Young."

"That's all there is, honey. Lots of these children only have initials."

"You mean . . . can't something be done about it?"

"What?" Miss Nelson was still smiling, but clearly impatient.

"I . . . well . . . thank you." Jane left quickly.

Back in Room 3 the children were growing restless. Deftly Jane passed out the rating tests and gave instructions. Then she called C. T. to her. He was as small as an eight-year-old, and hungry-looking, with enormous guileless eyes and a beautifully shaped head.

"How many years did you stay in the second grade, C. T.?"

"Two."

"And in the first?"

"Two."

"How old are you?"

" 'Leven."

"When will you be twelve?"

"Nex' month."

And they didn't care . . . nobody ever cared enough about one small boy to give him a name.

"You are a very lucky little boy, C. T. Most people have to take the name somebody gave them whether they like it or not, but you can choose your very own."

"Yeah?" The dark eyes were belligerent. "My father named me C. T. after hisself, Miz Richards, an dat's my name."

Jane felt unreasonably irritated. "How many children are there in your family, C.T.?"

" 'Leven."

"How many are there younger than you?" she asked.

"Seven."

Very gently, "Did you have your breakfast this morning, dear?"

The small figure in the too-large trousers and the too-small shirt drew itself up to full height. "Yes'm, I had fried chicken, and rice, and coffee, and rolls, and oranges too."

Oh, you poor darling. You poor proud lying darling. Is that what you'd like for breakfast?

She asked, "Do you like school, C. T.?"

"Yes'm," he told her suspiciously.

She leafed through the pile of records. "Your record says you haven't been coming to school very regularly. Why?"

"I dunno."

"Did you eat last year in the lunchroom?"

"No'm."

"Did you ever bring a lunch?"

"No'm, I eats such a big breakfast, I doan git hungry at lunchtime."

"Children need to eat lunch to help them grow tall and strong, C.T. So from now on you'll eat lunch in the lunchroom"—an afterthought: *Perhaps it's important to make him think I believe him*—"and from now on maybe you'd better not eat such a big breakfast."

Decisively she wrote his name at the top of what she knew to be an already too-large list. "Only those in absolute necessity," she had been told by Mr. Johnson, the kindly, harassed principal. "We'd like to feed them all, so many are underfed, but we just don't have the money." Well, this was absolute necessity if she ever saw it.

"What does your father do, C. T.?"

"He work at dat big factory crosstown, he make plenty money, Miz Richards." The record said "unemployed."

"Would you like to be named Charles Thomas?"

The expressive eyes darkened, but the voice was quiet. "No'm."

"Very well." Thoughtfully Jane opened the register; she wrote firmly: *C. T. Young.*

October is a witching month in the Southern United States. The richness of the golds and reds and browns of the trees forms an enchanted filigree through which the lilting voices of children at play seem to float, embodied like so many nymphs of Pan.

Jane had played a fast-and-furious game of tag with her class and now she sat quietly under the gnarled old oak, watching the tireless play, feeling the magic of the sun through the leaves warmly dappling her skin, the soft breeze on the nape of her neck like a lover's hands, and her own drowsy lethargy. *Paul, Paul my darling . . . how long for us now?* She had worshiped Paul Carlyle since they were freshmen together. On graduation day he had slipped the small circlet of diamonds on her finger. . . . "A teacher's salary is small, Jane. Maybe we'll be lucky enough to get work together, then in a year or so we can be married. Wait for me, darling, wait for me!"

But in a year or so Paul had gone to war, and Jane went out alone to teach. . . . Lansing Creek—one year . . . the leaky roof, the potbellied stove, the water from the well. . . . Maryweather Point—two years . . . the tight-lipped spinster principal with the small vicious face and the small, vicious soul. . . . Three hard, lonely years and then she had been lucky.

The superintendent had praised her. "You have done good work, Miss —ah—Jane. This year you are to be placed at Centertown High—that is, of course, if you care to accept the position."

Jane had caught her breath. Centertown was the largest and best equipped of all the schools in the county, only ten miles from home and Paul—for Paul had come home, older, quieter, but still Paul. He was teaching now more than a hundred miles away, but they went home every other week end to their families and each other. . . . "Next summer you'll be Mrs. Paul Carlyle, darling. It's hard for us to be apart so much. I guess we'll have to be for a long time till I can afford to support you. But, sweet, these little tykes need us so badly." He had held her close, rubbing the nape of the neck under the soft curls. "We have a big job, those of us who teach," he had told her, "a never-ending and often thankless job, Jane, to supply the needs of these kids who lack so much."

They wrote each other long letters, sharing plans and problems. She wrote him about C. T. "I've adopted him, darling. He's so pathetic and so determined to prove that he's not. He learns nothing at all, but I can't let myself believe that he's stupid, so I keep trying."

"Miz Richards, please, ma'am." Tanya's beautiful amber eyes sought hers timidly. Her brown curls were tangled from playing, her cheeks a bright red under the tightly-stretched olive skin. The elbows jutted awkwardly out of the sleeves of the limp cotton dress, which could not conceal the finely chiseled bones in their pitiable fleshlessness. As always when she looked at her, Jane thought, *What a beautiful child!* So unlike the dark, gaunt, morose mother, and the dumpy, pasty-faced father who had visited her that first week. A fairy's changeling. *You'll make a lovely angel to grace the throne of God, Tanya! Now what made me think of that?*

"Please, ma'am, I'se sick."

Gently Jane drew her down beside her. She felt the parchment skin, noted the unnaturally bright eyes. *Oh, dear God, she's burning up!* "Do you hurt anywhere, Tanya?"

"My head, ma'am, and I'se so tired." Without warning she began to cry.

"How far do you live, Tanya?"

"Two miles."

"You walk to school?"

"Yes'm."

"Do any of your brothers have a bicycle?"

"No'm."

"Rachel!" *Bless you for always being there when I need you.* "Hurry, dear, to the office and ask Mr. Johnson please to send a big boy with a bicycle to take Tanya home. She's sick."

Rachel ran.

"Hush now, dear, we'll get some cool water, and then you'll be home in a little while. Did you feel sick this morning?"

"Yes'm, but Mot Dear sent me to school anyway. She said I just wanted to play hooky." *Keep smiling, Jane. Poor, ambitious, well-meaning parents, made bitter at the seeming futility of dreaming dreams for this lovely child . . . willing her to rise above the drabness of your own meager existence . . . too angry with life to see that what she needs most is your love and care and right now medical attention.*

Jane bathed the child's forehead with cool water at the fountain. *Do the white schools have a clinic? I must ask Paul. Do they have a lounge or a couch where they can lay one wee sick head? Is there anywhere in this town free medical service for one small child . . . born black?*

The boy with the bicycle came. "Take care of her now, ride slowly and carefully, and take her straight home. . . . Keep the newspaper over your head, Tanya, to keep out the sun, and tell your parents to call the doctor." But she knew they wouldn't —because they couldn't!

The next day Jane went to see Tanya.

"She's sho' nuff sick, Miz Richards," the mother said. "She's always been a puny child, but this time she's took real bad, throat's all raw, talk all out of her haid las' night. I been using a poultice and some herb brew but she ain't got no better."

"Have you called a doctor, Mrs. Fulton?"

"No'm, we cain't afford it, an' Jake, he doan believe in doctors nohow."

Jane waited till the tide of high bright anger welling in her heart and beating in her brain had subsided. When she spoke, her voice was deceptively gentle. "Mrs. Fulton, Tanya is a very sick little girl. She is your only little girl. If you love her, I advise you to have a doctor to her, for if you don't . . . Tanya may die."

The wail that issued from the thin figure seemed to have no part in reality.

Jane spoke hurriedly. "Look, I'm going into town, I'll send a doctor out. Don't worry about paying him. We can see about that later." Impulsively she put her arms around the taut, motionless shoulders. "Don't you worry, honey, it's going to be all right."

There was a kindliness in the doctor's weatherbeaten face that warmed Jane's heart, but his voice was brusque. "You sick, girl? Well?"

"No, sir. I'm not sick." *What long sequence of events has caused even the best of you to look on even the best of us as menials?* "I'm a teacher at Centertown High. There's a little girl in my class who is very ill. Her parents are very poor. I came to see if you would please go to see her."

He looked at her, amused.

"Of course I'll pay the bill, doctor," she added hastily.

"In that case . . . well . . . where does she live?"

Jane told him. "I think it's diphtheria, doctor."

He raised his eyebrows. "Why?"

Jane sat erect. *Don't be afraid, Jane! You're as good a teacher as he is a doctor, and you made an A in that course in childhood diseases.* "High fever, restlessness, sore throat, headache, croupy cough, delirium.

It could, of course, be tonsillitis or scarlet fever, but that cough—well, I'm only guessing, of course," she finished lamely.

"Hmph." The doctor's face was expressionless. "Well, we'll see. Have your other children been inoculated?"

"Yes, sir. Doctor, if the parents ask, please tell them that the school is paying for your services."

This time he was wide-eyed.

The lie haunted her. She spoke to the other teachers about it the next day at recess. "She's really very sick, maybe you'd like to help?"

Mary Winters, the sixth-grade teacher, was the first to speak. "Richards, I'd like to help, but I've got three kids of my own, and so you see how it is?"

Jane saw.

"Trouble with you, Richards, is you're too emotional." This from Nelson. "When you've taught as many years as I have, my dear, you'll learn not to bang your head against a stone wall. It may sound hard-hearted to you, but one just can't worry about one child more or less when one has nearly fifty."

The pain in the back of her eyes grew more insistent. "I can," she said.

"I'll help, Jane," said Marilyn Andrews, breathless, bouncy newlywed Marilyn. "Here's two bucks. It's all I've got, but nothing's plenty for me." Her laughter pealed echoing down the hall.

"I've got a dollar, Richards"—this from mousy, severe little Miss Mitchell—"though I'm not sure I agree with you."

"Why don't you ask the high-school faculty?" said Marilyn. "Better still, take it up in teachers' meeting."

"Mr. Johnson has enough to worry about now," snapped Nelson. *Why, she's mad,* thought Jane, *mad because I'm trying to give a helpless little tyke a chance to live, and because Marilyn and Mitchell helped.*

The bell rang. Wordlessly Jane turned away. She watched the children troop in noisily, an ancient nursery rhyme running through her head:

Three blind mice, three blind mice,
See how they run, see how they run,
They all ran after the farmer's wife,
She cut off their tails with a carving knife,
Did you ever see such a sight in your life
As three blind mice?

Only this time, it was forty-three mice. Jane giggled. *Why, I'm hysterical,* she thought in surprise. *The mice thought the sweet-smelling farmer's wife might have bread and a wee bit of cheese to offer poor blind mice, but the farmer's wife didn't like poor, hungry, dirty blind mice. So she cut off their tails. Then they couldn't run anymore, only wobble. What happened then? Maybe they starved, those that didn't bleed to death. Running round in circles. Running where, little mice?*

She talked to the high-school faculty, and Mr. Johnson. Altogether she got eight dollars.

The following week she received a letter from the doctor:

Dear Miss Richards:

I am happy to inform you that Tanya is greatly improved, and with careful nursing will be well enough in about eight weeks to return to school. She is very frail, however, and will require *special care. I have made three visits to her home. In view of the peculiar circumstances, I am donating my services. The cost of the medicines, however, amounts to the sum of $15. I am referring this to you as you requested. What a beautiful child!*

Yours sincerely,
JONATHAN H. SINCLAIR, M.D.

P.S. She had diphtheria.

Bless you forever and ever, Jonathan H. Sinclair, M.D. For all your long Southern heritage, "a man's a man for a' that . . . and a' that!"

Her heart was light that night when she wrote to Paul. Later she made plans in the darkness. *You'll be well and fat by Christmas, Tanya, and you'll be a lovely angel in my pageant. . . . I must get the children to save pennies. . . . We'll send you milk and oranges and eggs, and we'll make funny little get-well cards to keep you happy.*

But by Christmas Tanya was dead!

The voice from the dark figure was quiet, even monotonous. "Jake an' me, we always work so hard, Miz Richards. We didn't neither one have no schooling much when we was married—folks never had much money, but we was happy. Jake, he tenant farm. I tuk in washing—we plan to save and buy a little house and farm of our own someday. Den the children come. Six boys, Miz Richards—all in a hurry. We both want the boys to finish school, mebbe go to college. We try not to keep them out to work the farm, but sometimes we have to. Then come Tanya. Just like a little yellow rose she was, Miz Richards, all pink and gold . . . and her voice like a silver bell. We think when she grow up an' finish school she take voice lessons—be like Marian Anderson. We think mebbe by then the boys would be old enough to help. I was kinda feared for her when she get sick, but then she start to get better. She was doing so well, Miz Richards. Den it get cold, an' the fire so hard to keep all night long, an' eben the newspapers in the cracks doan keep the win' out, an' I give her all my kivver; but one night she jest tuk to shivering an' talking all out her haid —sat right up in bed, she did. She call your name onc't or twice, Miz Richards, then she say, 'Mot Dear, does Jesus love me like Miz Richards say in Sunday school?' I say, 'Yes, honey.' She say, 'Effen I die will I see Jesus?' I say, 'Yes, honey, but you ain't gwine die.' But she did, Miz Richards . . . jest smiled an' laid down—jest smiled an' laid down."

It is terrible to see such hopeless resignation in such tearless eyes. . . . One little mouse stopped running. . . . *You'll make a lovely angel to grace the throne of God, Tanya!*

Jane did not go to the funeral. Nelson and Rogers sat in the first pew. Everyone on the faculty contributed to a beautiful wreath. Jane preferred not to think about that.

C. T. brought a lovely potted rose to her the next day. "Miz Richards, ma'am, do you think this is pretty enough to go on Tanya's grave?"

"Where did you get it, C. T.?"

"I stole it out Miz Adams' front yard, right out of that li'l' glass house she got there. The door was open, Miz Richards, she got plenty, she won't miss this li'l' one."

You queer little bundle of truth and lies. What do I do now? Seeing the tears blinking back in the anxious eyes, she said gently, "Yes, C. T., the rose is nearly as beautiful as Tanya is now. She will like it."

"You mean she will know I put it there, Miz Richards? She ain't daid at all?"

"Maybe she'll know, C. T. You see, nothing that is beautiful ever dies as long as we remember it."

So you loved Tanya, little mouse? The memory of her beauty is yours to keep now forever and always, my darling. Those things money can't buy. They've all been trying, but your tail isn't off yet, is it, brat? Not by a long shot. Suddenly she laughed aloud.

He looked at her wonderingly. "What you laughing at, Miz Richards?"

"I'm laughing because I'm happy, C. T.," and she hugged him.

Christmas with its pageantry and splendor came and went. Back from the holidays, Jane had an oral English lesson.

"We'll take this period to let you tell about your holidays, children."

On the weekends that Jane stayed in Centertown she visited different churches, and taught in the Sunday schools when she was asked. She had tried to impress on the children the reasons for giving at Christmastime. In class they had talked about things they could make for gifts, and ways they could save money to buy them. Now she stood by the window, listening attentively, reaping the fruits of her labors.

"I got a doll and a doll carriage for Christmas. Her name is Gladys, and the carriage has red wheels, and I got a tea set and——"

"I got a bicycle and a catcher's mitt."

"We all went to a party and had ice cream and cake."

"I got——"

"I got——"

"I got——"

Score one goose egg for Jane. She was suddenly very tired. "It's your turn, C. T." *Dear God, please don't let him lie too much. He tears my heart. The children never laugh. It's funny how polite they are to C. T. even when they know he's lying. Even that day when Boyd and Lloyd told how they had seen him take food out of the garbage cans in front of the restaurant, and he said he was taking it to some poor hungry children, they didn't laugh. Sometimes children have a great deal more insight than grownups.*

C. T. was talking. "I didn't get nothin' for Christmas, because mamma was sick, but I worked all that week before for Mr. Bondel what owns the store on Main Street. I ran errands an' swep' up an' he give me three dollars, and so I bought mamma a real pretty handkerchief an' a comb, an' I bought my father a tie pin, paid a big ole fifty cents for it too . . . an' I bought my sisters an' brothers some candy an' gum an' I bought me this whistle. Course I got what you give us, Miz Richards" (she had given each a small gift) "an' mamma's white lady give us a whole crate of oranges, an' Miz Smith what live nex' door give me a pair of socks. Mamma she was so happy she made a cake with eggs an' butter an' everything; an' then we ate it an' had a good time."

Rachel spoke wonderingly. "Didn't Santa Claus bring you anything at all?"

C. T. was the epitome of scorn. "Ain't no Santa Claus," he said and sat down.

Jane quelled the age-old third-grade controversy absently, for her heart was singing. *C. T. . . . C. T., son of my own heart, you are the bright new hope of a doubtful world, and the gay new song of a race unconquered. Of them all—Sarahlene, sole heir to the charming stucco home on the hill, all fitted for gracious living; George, whose father is a contractor; Rachel, the minister's daughter; Angela, who has just inherited ten thousand dollars—of all of them who got, you, my dirty little vagabond, who have never owned a coat in your life, because you say you don't get cold; you, out of your nothing, found something to give, and in the dignity of giving found that it was not so important to receive. . . . Christ Child, look down in blessing on one small child made in Your image and born black!*

Jane had problems. Sometimes it was difficult to maintain discipline with forty-two children. Busy as she kept them, there were always some not busy enough. There was the conference with Mr. Johnson.

"Miss Richards, you are doing fine work here, but sometimes your room is a little . . . well—ah—well, to say the least, noisy. You are new here, but we have always maintained a record of having fine discipline here at this school. People have said that it used to be hard to tell whether or not there were children in the building. We have always been proud of that. Now take Miss Nelson. She is an excellent disciplinarian. He smiled. "Maybe if you ask her she will give you her secret. Do not be too proud to accept help from anyone who can give it, Miss Richards."

"No, sir, thank you, sir, I'll do my best to improve, sir." *Ah, you dear, well-meaning, shortsighted, round, busy little man. Why are you not more concerned about how much the children have grown and learned in these past four months than you are about how much noise they make? I know Miss Nelson's secret. Spare not the rod and spoil not the child. Is that what you want me to do? Paralyze these kids with fear so that they will be afraid to move? afraid to question? afraid to grow? Why is it so fine for people not to know there are children in the building? Wasn't the building built for children?* In her room Jane locked the door against the sound of the playing children, put her head on the desk, and cried.

Jane acceded to tradition and administered one whipping. Booker had slapped Sarahlene's face because she had refused to give up a shiny little music box that played a gay little tune. He had taken the whipping docilely enough, as though used to it; but the sneer in his eyes that had almost gone returned to haunt them. Jane's heart misgave her. *From now on I positively refuse to impose my will on any of these poor children by reason of my greater strength.* So she had abandoned the rod in favor of any other means she could find. They did not always work.

There was a never-ending drive for funds. Jane had a passion for perfection. Plays, dances, concerts, bazaars, suppers, parties followed one on another in staggering succession.

"Look here, Richards," Nelson told her one day, "it's true that we need a new piano, and that science equipment, but, honey, these drives in a colored school are like the poor: with us always. It doesn't make too much difference if Suzy forgets her lines, or if the ice cream is a little lumpy. Cooperation is fine, but the way you tear into things you won't last long."

"For once in her life Nelson's right, Jane," Elise told her later. "I can understand how intense you are because I used to be like that; but, pet, Negro teachers have always had to work harder than any others and till recently have always got paid less, so for our own health's sake we have to let up wherever possible. Believe me, honey, if you don't learn to take it easy, you're going to get sick."

Jane did. Measles!

"Oh no," she wailed, "not in my old age!" But she was glad of the rest. Lying in her own bed at home, she realized how very tired she was.

Paul came to see her that weekend, and sat by her bed and read aloud to her the old classic poems they both loved so well. They listened to their favorite radio programs. Paul's presence was warm and comforting. Jane was reluctant to go back to work.

What to do about C. T. was a question that daily loomed larger in Jane's consciousness. Watching Joe Louis' brilliant development was a thing of joy, and Jane was hard pressed to find enough outlets for his amazing abilities. Jeanette Allen was running a close second, and even Booker, so long a problem, was beginning to grasp fundamentals, but C. T. remained static.

"I always stays two years in a grade, Miz Richards," he told her blandly. "I does better the second year."

"Do you *want* to stay in the third grade two years, C. T.?"

"I don't keer." His voice had been cheerful.

Maybe he really is slow, Jane thought. But one day something happened to make her change her mind.

C. T. was possessed of an unusually strong tendency to protect those he considered to be poor or weak. He took little Johnny Armstrong, who sat beside him in class, under his wing. Johnny was nearsighted and nondescript, his one outstanding feature being his hero-worship of C. T. Johnny was a plodder. Hard as he tried, he made slow progress at best.

The struggle with multiplication tables was a difficult one, in spite of all the little games Jane devised to make them easier for the children. On this particular day there was the uneven hum of little voices trying to memorize. Johnny and C. T. were having a whispered conversation about snakes.

Clearly Jane heard C. T.'s elaboration. "Man, my father caught a moccasin long as that blackboard, I guess, an' I held him while he was live right back of his ugly head—so."

Swiftly Jane crossed the room. "C. T. and Johnny, you are supposed to be learning your tables. The period is nearly up and you haven't even begun to study. Furthermore, in more than five months you haven't even learned the two-times table.

Now you will both stay in at the first recess to learn it, and every day after this until you do."

Maybe I should make up some problems about snakes, Jane mused, *but they'd be too ridiculous. . . . Two nests of four snakes—Oh, well, I'll see how they do at recess.* Her heart smote her at the sight of the two little figures at their desks, listening wistfully to the sound of the children at play, but she busied herself and pretended not to notice them. Then she heard C. T.'s voice:

"Lissen, man, these tables is easy if you really want to learn them. Now see here. Two times one is two. Two times two is four. Two times three is six. If you forgit, all you got to do is add two like she said."

"Sho' nuff, man?"

"Sho'. Say them with me . . . two times one——" Obediently Johnny began to recite. Five minutes later they came to her. "We's ready, Miz Richards."

"Very well. Johnny, you may begin."

"Two times one is two. Two times two is four. Two times three is. . . . Two times three is——"

"Six," prompted C. T.

In sweat and pain, Johnny managed to stumble through the two-times table with C. T.'s help.

"That's very poor, Johnny, but you may go for today. Tomorrow I shall expect you to have it letter perfect. Now it's your turn, C. T."

C. T.'s performance was a fair rival to Joe Louis's. Suspiciously she took him through in random order.

"Two times nine?"

"Eighteen."

"Two times four?"

"Eight."

"Two times seven?"

"Fourteen."

"C. T., you could have done this long ago. Why didn't you?"

"I dunno. . . . May I go to play now, Miz Richards?"

"Yes, C. T. Now learn your three-times table for me tomorrow."

But he didn't, not that day, or the day after that, or the day after that. . . . *Why doesn't he? Is it that he doesn't want to? Maybe if I were as ragged and deprived as he I wouldn't want to learn either.*

Jane took C. T. to town and bought him a shirt, a sweater, a pair of dungarees, some underwear, a pair of shoes, and a pair of socks. Then she sent him to the barber to get his hair cut. She gave him the money so he could pay for the articles himself and figure up the change. She instructed him to take a bath before putting on his new clothes, and told him not to tell anyone but his parents that she had bought them.

The next morning the class was in a dither.

"You seen C. T.?"

"Oh, boy, ain't he sharp!"

"C. T., where'd you get them new clothes?"

"Oh, man, I can wear new clothes any time I feel like it, but I can't be bothered with being a fancypants all the time like you guys."

C. T. strutted in new confidence, but his work didn't improve.

Spring came in its virginal green gladness and the children chafed for the out-of-doors. Jane took them out as much as possible on nature studies and excursions.

C. T. was growing more and more mischievous, and his influence began to spread throughout the class. Daily his droll wit became more and more edged with impudence. Jane was at her wit's end.

"You let that child get away with too much, Richards," Nelson told her. "What he needs is a good hiding."

One day Jane kept certain of the class in at the first recess to do neglected homework, C. T. among them. She left the room briefly. When she returned C. T. was gone.

"Where is C. T.?" she asked.

"He went out to play, Miz Richards. He said couldn't no ole teacher keep him in when he didn't want to stay."

Out on the playground C. T. was standing in a swing, gently swaying to and fro, surrounded by a group of admiring youngsters. He was holding forth.

"I gets tired of stayin' in all the time. She doan pick on nobody but me, an' today I put my foot down. 'From now on,' I say, 'I ain't never goin' to stay in, Miz Richards.' Then I walks out." He was enjoying himself immensely. Then he saw her.

"You will come with me, C. T." She was quite calm except for the telltale veins throbbing in her forehead.

"I ain't comin'." The sudden fright in his eyes was veiled quickly by a nonchalant belligerence. He rocked the swing gently.

She repeated, "Come with me, C. T."

The children watched breathlessly.

"I done told you I ain't comin', Miz Richards." His voice was patient, as though explaining to a child. "I ain't . . . comin' . . . a . . . damn . . . tall!"

Jane moved quickly, wrenching the small but surprisingly strong figure from the swing. Then she bore him bodily, kicking and screaming, to the building.

The children relaxed and began to giggle. "Oh, boy! Is he goin' to catch it!" they told one another.

Panting, she held him, still struggling, by the scruff of his collar before the group of teachers gathered in Marilyn's room. "All right, now *you* tell me what to do with him!" she demanded. "I've tried everything." The tears were close behind her eyes.

"What'd he do?" Nelson asked.

Briefly she told them.

"Have you talked to his parents?"

"Three times I've had conferences with them. They say to beat him."

"That, my friend, is what you ought to do. Now he never acted like that with me. If you'll let me handle him, I'll show you how to put a brat like that in his place."

"Go ahead," Jane said wearily.

Nelson left the room, and returned with a narrow but sturdy leather thong. "Now, C. T."—she was smiling, tapping the strap in her open left palm—"go to your room and do what Miss Richards told you to."

"I ain't gonna, an' you can't make me." He sat down with absurd dignity at a desk.

Still smiling, Miss Nelson stood over him. The strap descended without warning across the bony shoulders in the thin shirt. The whip became a dancing demon, a thing possessed, bearing no relation to the hand that held it. The shrieks grew louder. Jane closed her eyes against the blurred fury of a singing lash, a small boy's terror, and a smiling face.

Miss Nelson was not tired. "Well, C. T.?"

"I won't. Yer can kill me but I *won't!*"

The sounds began again. Red welts

began to show across the small arms and through the clinging sweat-drenched shirt.

"Now will you go to your room?"

Sobbing and conquered, C. T. went. The seated children stared curiously at the little procession. Jane dismissed them.

In his seat C. T. found pencil and paper.

"What's he supposed to do, Richards?"

Jane told her.

"All right, now write!"

C. T. stared at Nelson through swollen lids, a curious smile curving his lips. Jane knew suddenly that come hell or high water, C. T. would not write. *I musn't interfere. Please, God, don't let her hurt him too badly. Where have I failed so miserably? . . . Forgive us our trespasses.* The singing whip and the shrieks became a symphony from hell. Suddenly Jane hated the smiling face with an almost unbearable hatred. She spoke, her voice like cold steel.

"That's enough, Nelson."

The noise stopped.

"He's in no condition to write now anyway."

C. T. stood up. "I hate you. I hate you all. You're mean and I hate you." Then he ran. No one followed him. *Run, little mouse!* They avoided each other's eyes.

"Well, there you are," Nelson said as she walked away. Jane never found out what she meant by that.

The next day C. T. did not come to school. The day after that he brought Jane the fatal homework, neatly and painstakingly done, and a bunch of wild flowers. Before the bell rang, the children surrounded him. He was beaming.

"Did you tell yer folks you got a whipping, C. T.?"

"Naw! I'd 'a' only got another."

"Where were you yesterday?"

"Went fishin'. Caught me six cats long as your haid, Sambo."

Jane buried her face in the sweet-smelling flowers. *Oh, my brat, my wonderful resilient brat. They'll never get your tail, will they?*

It was seven weeks till the end of term when C. T. brought Jane a model wooden boat.

Jane stared at it. "Did you make this? It's beautiful, C. T."

"Oh, I make them all the time . . . an' airplanes an' houses too. I do 'em in my spare time," he finished airily.

"Where do you get the models, C. T.?" she asked.

"I copies them from pictures in the magazines."

Right under my nose . . . right there all the time, she thought wonderingly. "C. T., would you like to build things when you grow up? Real houses and ships and planes?"

"Reckon I could, Miz Richards," he said confidently.

The excitement was growing in her. "Look, C. T. You aren't going to do any lessons at all for the rest of the year. You're going to build ships and houses and airplanes and anything else you want to."

"I am, huh?" He grinned. "Well, I guess I wasn't goin' to get promoted nohow."

"Of course, if you want to build them the way they really are, you might have to do a little measuring, and maybe learn to spell the names of the parts you want to order. All the best contractors have to know things like that, you know."

"Say, I'm gonna have real fun, huh? I always said lessons wussent no good nohow. Pop say too much study eats out yer brains anyway."

The days went by. Jane ran a race with time. The instructions from the model companies arrived. Jane burned the midnight oil planning each day's work:

Learn to spell the following words: ship, sail, steamer—boat, anchor, airplane wing, fly.

Write a letter to the lumber company, ordering some lumber.

The floor of our model house is ten inches wide and fourteen inches long. Multiply the length by the width and you'll find the area of the floor in square inches.

Read the story of Columbus and his voyages.

Our plane arrives in Paris in twenty-eight hours. Paris is the capital city of a country named France across the Atlantic Ocean.

Long ago sailors told time by the sun and the stars. Now, the earth goes around the sun——

Work and pray, work and pray!

C. T. learned. Some things vicariously, some things directly. When he found that he needed muliplication to plan his models to scale, he learned to multiply. In three weeks he had mastered simple division.

Jane bought beautifully illustrated stories about ships and planes. He learned to read.

He wrote for and received his own materials.

Jane exulted.

The last day! Forty-two faces waiting anxiously for report cards. Jane spoke to them briefly, praising them collectively, and admonishing them to obey the safety rules during the holidays. Then she passed out the report cards.

As she smiled at each childish face, she thought, *I've been wrong. The long arm of circumstance, environment, and heredity is the farmer's wife that seeks to mow you down, and all of us who touch your lives are in some way responsible for how successful she is. But you aren't mice, my darlings. Mice are hated, hunted pests. You are normal, lovable children. The knife of the farmer's wife is double-edged for you because you are Negro children, born mostly in poverty. But you are wonderful children, nevertheless, for you wear the bright protective cloak of laughter, the strong shield of courage, and the intelligence of children everywhere. Some few of you may indeed become as the mice—but most of you shall find your way to stand fine and tall in the annals of men. There's a bright new tomorrow ahead. For every one of us whose job it is to help you grow that is insensitive and unworthy there are hundreds who daily work that you may grow straight and whole. If it were not so, our world could not long endure.*

She handed C. T. his card.

"Thank you, ma'am."

"Aren't you going to open it?"

He opened it dutifully. When he looked up, his eyes were wide with disbelief. "You didn't make no mistake?"

"No mistake, C. T. You're promoted. You've caught up enough to go to the fourth grade next year."

She dismissed the children. They were a swarm of bees released from a hive. " 'By, Miss Richards." . . . "Happy holidays, Miss Richards."

C. T. was the last to go.

"Well, C. T.?"

"Miz Richards, you remember what you said about a name being important?"

"Yes, C. T."

"Well, I talked to mamma, and she said if I wanted a name it would be all right, and she'd go to the courthouse about it."

"What name have you chosen, C. T.?" she asked.

"Christopher Turner Young."

"That's a nice name, Christopher," she said gravely.

"Sho' nuff, Miz Richards?"

"Sure enough, C. T."

"Miz Richards, you know what?"

"What, dear?"

"I love you."

She kissed him swiftly before he ran to catch his classmates.

She stood at the window and watched the running, skipping figures, followed by the bold mimic shadows. *I'm coming home, Paul. I'm leaving my forty-two children, and Tanya there on the hill. My work with them is finished now.* The laughter bubbled up in her throat. *But Paul, oh Paul. See how straight they run!*

Discussion

The style of this story, which intersperses the teacher's observations about herself and her students with the action of the story, provides particular insight into the role of the teacher. Miss Richards has all the qualities of an exceptionally fine teacher. She accepts her children for what they are—forty-three children of widely varying ages from a range of economic levels. She does not hold inappropriate standards for her class nor does she value those students who are scrubbed, neat, and polite above the less fortunate. In fact, Miss Richards probably leans more toward the child who is most in need.

Interestingly, it is Miss Richards' dedication and idealism that bring her into conflict with her colleagues and administrator. Her colleagues, who have taught for many years, admonish Miss Richards not to become involved with her students and their private lives. The administrator, whose main concern is to run an orderly school, frowns on the noise level she permits in her classroom. Mr. Johnson equates a well-disciplined school with a quiet school, and he does not recognize that silence may be incompatible with an environment that promotes learning and growth.

The story provides a well-rounded view of the teacher's school experiences. We see Miss Richards in tears inward and outward as she suffers frustration when her efforts are misunderstood or when her expectations have been too high for herself or for her pupils. She soon learns that teaching does not end at the close of the school day; dedicated teachers spend many after-school hours creating resourceful ways of teaching the hard-to-reach child. This story also includes a dreaded moment in a teacher's life—the head-on confrontation with a student who openly defies the adult's authority. No one gains from this experience. The adult usually finds that the verbal and physical battle leaves him spent and pained, and the child learns that adults can lose control and behave savagely, making the child even more mistrustful of them.

Miss Richards is able to identify wholly with the cultural customs and heritage of her students. She comprehends completely the hopes the parents have for their children. She is sensitive enough to realize the incongruity between the burden of the children's great given names and their background of prejudice and lack of opportunity. A teacher need not have the identical cultural heritage of his students as Miss Richards does, but a comprehensive knowledge of their culture and customs, if these are different from his own, is indispensable to working best with them.

Springboards for Inquiry

(1) What are some of Jane's qualities that make her a good teacher?

(2) The teacher is recognized as an important model in the child's life. To what extent do you think the race of the teacher can enhance or distort a child's self-image?

(3) How can teachers of different socioeconomic, racial, and cultural backgrounds from their students prepare themselves to work with children who do not share their heritage?

(4) The teacher is a source of motivation for achievement and aspiration in her pupils. There are many studies that deal with the variety of strategies that teachers use to influence behavior, such as praise, sarcasm, ignoring behavior, etc. From your own experience give examples of positive and negative strategies that teachers use, and discuss their effectiveness.

(5) The teacher helps the child to grow in a number of areas in addition to the three R's. Discuss the role of the teacher in the development of (a) attitudes toward responsibility, (b) ability to share and participate in a group, (c) attitude toward work and achievement, and (d) sportsmanship.

(6) If you were to prepare and rank goals for the school's responsibility toward children in their early years, which goals would you include and where would you place your priorities?

For a minute or two he just stood there, looking at the blankness of the concrete wall; then he found a piece of chalk in his pocket and wrote out all the dirty words he could think of, in block letters a foot high.

Doctor Jack-O'-Lantern

by Richard Yates

All Miss Price had been told about the new boy was that he'd spent most of his life in some kind of orphanage, and that the gray-haired "aunt and uncle" with whom he now lived were really foster parents, paid by the Welfare Department of the City of New York. A less dedicated or less imaginative teacher might have pressed for more details, but Miss Price was content with the rough outline. It was enough, in fact, to fill her with a sense of mission that shone from her eyes, as plain as love, from the first morning he joined the fourth grade.

He arrived early and sat in the back row—his spine very straight, his ankles crossed precisely under the desk and his hands folded on the very center of its top, as if symmetry might make him less conspicuous—and while the other children were filing in and settling down, he received a long, expressionless stare from each of them.

"We have a new classmate this morning," Miss Price said, laboring the obvious in a way that made everybody want to giggle. "His name is Vincent Sabella and he comes from New York City. I know we'll all do our best to make him feel at home."

This time they all swung around to stare at once, which caused him to duck his head slightly and shift his weight from one buttock to the other. Ordinarily, the fact of someone's coming from New York might have held a certain prestige, for to most of the children the city was an awesome, adult place that swallowed up their fathers every day, and which they themselves were permitted to visit only rarely, in their best clothes, as a treat. But anyone could see at a

---

glance that Vincent Sabella had nothing whatever to do with skyscrapers. Even if you could ignore his tangled black hair and gray skin, his clothes would have given him away: absurdly new corduroys, absurdly old sneakers and a yellow sweatshirt, much too small, with the shredded remains of a Mickey Mouse design stamped on its chest. Clearly, he was from the part of New York that you had to pass through on the train to Grand Central—the part where people hung bedding over their windowsills and leaned out on it all day in a trance of boredom, and where you got vistas of straight, deep streets, one after another, all alike in the clutter of their sidewalks and all swarming with gray boys at play in some desperate kind of ball game.

The girls decided that he wasn't very nice and turned away, but the boys lingered in their scrutiny, looking him up and down with faint smiles. This was the kind of kid they were accustomed to thinking of as "tough," the kind whose stares had made all of them uncomfortable at one time or another in unfamiliar neighborhoods; here was a unique chance for retaliation.

"What would you like us to call you, Vincent?" Miss Price inquired. "I mean, do you prefer Vincent, or Vince, or—or what?" (It was purely an academic question; even Miss Price knew that the boys would call him "Sabella" and that the girls wouldn't call him anything at all.)

"Vinny's okay," he said in a strange, croaking voice that had evidently yelled itself hoarse down the ugly streets of his home.

"I'm afraid I didn't hear you," she said, craning her pretty head forward and to one side so that a heavy lock of hair swung free of one shoulder. "Did you say 'Vince'?"

"Vinny, I said," he said again, squirming.

"Vincent, is it? All right, then, Vincent." A few of the class giggled, but nobody bothered to correct her; it would be more fun to let the mistake continue.

"I won't take time to introduce you to everyone by name, Vincent," Miss Price went on, "because I think it would be simpler just to let you learn the names as we go along, don't you? Now, we won't expect you to take any real part in the work for the first day or so; just take your time, and if there's anything you don't understand, why, don't be afraid to ask."

He made an unintelligible croak and smiled fleetingly, just enough to show that the roots of his teeth were green.

"Now then," Miss Price said, getting down to business. "This is Monday morning, and so the first thing on the program is reports. Who'd like to start off?"

Vincent Sabella was momentarily forgotten as six or seven hands went up, and Miss Price drew back in mock confusion. "Goodness, we do have a lot of reports this morning," she said. The idea of the reports—a fifteen-minute period every Monday in which the children were encouraged to relate their experiences over the weekend—was Miss Price's own, and she took a pardonable pride in it. The principal had commended her on it at a recent staff meeting, pointing out that it made a splendid bridge between the worlds of school and home, and that it was a fine way for children to learn poise and assurance. It called for intelligent supervision—the shy children had to be drawn out and the show-offs curbed—but in general, as Miss Price had assured the principal, it was fun for everyone. She particularly hoped it would be fun today, to help put Vincent Sabella at ease, and that was why she chose Nancy Parker to start off; there was nobody like Nancy for holding an audience.

The others fell silent as Nancy moved gracefully to the head of the room; even the two or three girls who secretly despised her had to feign enthrallment when she spoke (she was that popular), and every boy in the class, who at recess liked nothing better than to push her shrieking into the mud, was unable to watch her without an idiotically tremulous smile.

"Well—" she began, and then she clapped a hand over her mouth while everyone laughed.

"Oh, *Nancy,*" Miss Price said. "You *know* the rule about starting a report with 'well.' "

Nancy knew the rule; she had only broken it to get the laugh. Now she let her fit of giggles subside, ran her fragile forefingers down the side seams of her skirt, and began again in the proper way. "On Friday my whole family went for a ride in my brother's new car. My brother bought this new Pontiac last week, and he wanted to take us all for a ride—you know, to try it out and everything? So we went into White Plains and had dinner in a restaurant there, and then we all wanted to go see this movie, 'Doctor Jekyll and Mr. Hyde,' but my brother said it was too horrible and everything, and I wasn't old enough to enjoy it—oh, he made me so mad! And then, let's see. On Saturday I stayed home all day and helped my mother make my sister's wedding dress. My sister's engaged to be married, you see, and my mother's making this wedding dress for her? So we did that, and then on Sunday this friend of my brother's came over for dinner, and then they both had to get back to college that night, and I was allowed to stay up late and say goodbye to them and everything, and I guess that's all." She always had a sure instinct for keeping her performance brief—or rather, for making it seem briefer than it really was.

"Very good, Nancy," Miss Price said. "Now, who's next?"

Warren Berg was next, elaborately hitching up his pants as he made his way down the aisle. "On Saturday I went over to Bill Stringer's house for lunch," he began in his direct, man-to-man style, and Bill Stringer wriggled bashfully in the front row. Warren Berg and Bill Stringer were great friends, and their reports often overlapped. "And then after lunch we went into White Plains, on our bikes. Only we *saw* 'Doctor Jekyll and Mr. Hyde.' " Here he nodded his head in Nancy's direction and Nancy got another laugh by making a little whimper of envy. "It was real good, too," he went on, with mounting excitement. "It's all about this guy who—"

"About a *man* who," Miss Price corrected.

"About a man who mixes up this chemical, like, that he drinks? And whenever he drinks this chemical, he changes into this real monster, like? You see him drink this chemical, and then you see his hands start to get all scales all over them, like a reptile and everything, and then you see his face start to change into this real horrible-looking face—with fangs and all? Sticking out of his mouth?"

All the girls shuddered in pleasure. "Well," Miss Price said, "I think Nancy's brother was probably wise in not wanting her to see it. What did you do *after* the movie, Warren"?

There was a general *"Aw-w-w!"* of disappointment—everyone wanted to hear more about the scales and fangs—but Miss Price never liked to let the reports degenerate into accounts of movies. Warren continued without much enthusiasm: all they had done after the movie was fool around Bill Stringer's yard until suppertime. "And then on Sunday," he said, brightening again, "Bill Stringer came over to *my* house, and my dad helped us rig up this old tire on this long rope? From a tree? There's this steep hill down behind my house, you see—this ravine, like?—and we hung this tire so that what you do is, you take the tire and run a little ways and then lift your feet, and you go swinging way, way out over the ravine and back again."

"That sounds like fun," Miss Price said, glancing at her watch.

"Oh, it's *fun,* all right," Warren conceded. But then he hitched up his pants again and added, with a puckering of his forehead, " 'Course, it's pretty dangerous. You let go of that tire or anything, you'd get a bad fall. Hit a rock or anything, you'd probably break your leg, or your spine. But my dad said he trusted us both to look out for our own safety."

"Well, I'm afraid that's all we'll have time for, Warren," Miss Price said. "Now, there's just time for one more report. Who's ready? Arthur Cross?"

There was a soft groan, because Arthur Cross was the biggest dope in class and his reports were always a bore. This time it turned out to be something tedious about going to visit his uncle on Long Island. At one point he made a slip—he said "botormoat" instead of "motorboat"—and everyone laughed with the particular edge of scorn they reserved for Arthur Cross. But the laughter died abruptly when it was joined by a harsh, dry croaking from the back of the room. Vincent Sabella was laughing too, green teeth and all, and they all had to glare at him until he stopped.

When the reports were over, everyone settled down for school. It was recess time before any of the children thought much about Vincent Sabella again, and then they thought of him only to make sure he was left out of everything. He wasn't in the group of boys that clustered around the horizontal bar to take turns at skinning-the-cat, or the group that whispered in a far corner of the playground, hatching a plot to push Nancy Parker in the mud. Nor was he in the larger group, of which even Arthur Cross was a member, that chased itself in circles in a frantic variation of the game of tag. He couldn't join the girls, of course, or the boys from other classes, and so he joined nobody. He stayed on the apron of the playground, close to school, and for the first part of the recess he pretended to be very busy with the laces of his sneakers. He would squat to undo and retie them, straighten up and take a few experimental steps in a springy, athletic way, and then get down and go to work on them again. After five minutes of this he gave it up, picked up a handful of pebbles and began shying them at an invisible target several yards away. That was good for another five minutes, but then there were still five minutes left, and he could think of nothing to do but stand there, first with his hands in his pockets, then with his hands on his hips, and then with his arms folded in a manly way across his chest.

Miss Price stood watching all this from the doorway, and she spent the full recess wondering if she ought to go out and do something about it. She guessed it would be better not to.

She managed to control the same impulse at recess the next day, and every other day that week, though every day it grew more difficult. But one thing she could not control was a tendency to let her anxiety show in class. All Vincent Sabella's errors in schoolwork were publicly excused, even those having nothing to do with his newness, and all his accomplishments were singled out for special mention. Her campaign to build him up was painfully obvious, and never more so than when she tried to make it subtle; once, for instance, in explaining an arithmetic problem, she said, "Now, suppose Warren Berg and Vincent Sabella went to the store with fifteen cents each, and candy bars cost ten cents. How many candy bars would each boy have?" By the end of the week he was well on the way to becoming the worst possible kind of teacher's pet, a victim of the teacher's pity.

On Friday she decided the best thing to do would be to speak to him privately, and try to draw him out. She could say something about the pictures he had painted in art class—that would do for an opening—and she decided to do it at lunchtime.

The only trouble was that lunchtime, next to recess, was the most trying part of Vincent Sabella's day. Instead of going home for an hour as the other children did, he brought his lunch to school in a wrinkled paper bag and ate it in the classroom, which always made for a certain amount of awkwardness. The last children to leave would see him still seated apologetically at his desk, holding his paper bag, and anyone who happened to straggle back later for a forgotten hat or sweater would surprise him in the middle of his meal—perhaps shielding a hard-boiled egg from view or wiping mayonnaise from his mouth with a furtive hand. It was a situation that Miss Price did not improve by walking up to him while the room was still half full of children and sitting prettily on the edge of the desk beside his, making it clear that she was cutting her own lunch hour short in order to be with him.

"Vincent," she began, "I've been meaning to tell you how much I enjoyed those pictures of yours. They're really very good."

He mumbled something and shifted his eyes to the cluster of departing children at the door. She went right on talking and smiling, elaborating on her praise of the pictures; and finally, after the door had closed behind the last child, he was able to give her his attention. He did so tentatively at first; but the more she talked, the more he seemed to relax, until she realized she was putting him at ease. It was as simple and as gratifying as stroking a cat. She had finished with the pictures now and moved on, triumphantly, to broader fields of praise. "It's never easy," she was saying, "to come to a new school and adjust yourself to the—well, the new work, and new working methods, and I think you've done a splendid job so far. I really do. But tell me, do you think you're going to like it here?"

He looked at the floor just long enough to make his reply—"It's awright"—and then his eyes stared into hers again.

"I'm so glad. Please don't let me interfere with your lunch, Vincent. Do go ahead and eat, that is, if you don't mind my sitting here with you." But it was now abundantly clear that he didn't mind at all, and he began to unwrap a bologna sandwich with what she felt sure was the best appetite he'd had all week. It wouldn't even have mattered very much now if someone from the class had come in and watched, though it was probably just as well that no one did.

Miss Price sat back more comfortably on the desk top, crossed her legs and allowed one slim stockinged foot to slip part of the way out of its moccasin. "Of course," she went on, "it always does take a little time to sort of get your bearings in a new school. For one thing, well, it's never too easy for the new member of the class to make friends with the other members. What I mean is, you mustn't mind if the others seem a little rude to you at first. Actually, they're just as anxious to make friends as you are, but they're shy. All it takes is a little time, and a little effort on your part as well as theirs. Not too much, of course, but a little. Now for instance, these reports we have Monday mornings—they're a fine way for people to get to know one another. A person never feels he has to make a report; it's just a thing he can do if he wants to. And that's only one way of helping others to know the kind of person you are; there are lots and lots of ways. The main thing to remember is that making friends is the most natural thing in the world, and it's only a question of time until you have all the friends you want. And in the meantime, Vincent, I hope you'll consider *me* your friend, and feel free to call on me for whatever advice or anything you might need. Will you do that?"

He nodded, swallowing.

"Good." She stood up and smoothed her skirt over her long thighs. "Now I must go or I'll be late for *my* lunch. But I'm glad we had this little talk, Vincent, and I hope we'll have others."

It was probably a lucky thing that she stood up when she did, for if she'd stayed on that desk a minute longer Vincent Sabella would have thrown his arms around her and buried his face in the warm gray flannel of her lap, and that might have been enough to confuse the most dedicated and imaginative of teachers.

At report time on Monday morning, nobody was more surprised than Miss Price when Vincent Sabella's smudged hand was among the first and most eager to rise. Apprehensively she considered letting someone else start off, but then, for fear of hurting his feelings, she said, "All right, Vincent," in as matter-of-fact a way as she could manage.

There was a suggestion of muffled

titters from the class as he walked confidently to the head of the room and turned to face his audience. He looked, if anything, too confident: there were signs, in the way he held his shoulders and the way his eyes shone, of the terrible poise of panic.

"Saturday I seen that pitcha," he announced.

"Saw, Vincent," Miss Price corrected gently.

"That's what I mean," he said; "I sore that pitcha. 'Doctor Jack-o'-lantern and Mr. Hide.' "

There was a burst of wild, delighted laughter and a chorus of correction: "Doctor *Jekyll!*"

He was unable to speak over the noise. Miss Price was on her feet, furious. "It's a *perfectly natural mistake!*" she was saying. "There's no reason for any of you to be so rude. Go on, Vincent, and please excuse this very silly interruption." The laughter subsided, but the class continued to shake their heads derisively from side to side. It hadn't, of course, been a perfectly natural mistake at all; for one thing it proved that he was a hopeless dope, and for another it proved that he was lying.

"That's what I mean," he continued. " 'Doctor Jackal and Mr. Hide.' I got it a little mixed up. Anyways, I seen all about where his teet' start comin' outa his mout' and all like that, and I thought it was very good. And then on Sunday my mudda and fodda come out to see me in this car they got. This Buick. My fodda siz, 'Vinny, wanna go for a little ride?' I siz, 'Sure, where yiz goin'?' He siz, 'Anyplace ya like.' So I siz, 'Let's go out in the country a ways, get on one of them big roads and make some time.' So we go out—oh, I guess fifty, sixty miles—and we're cruisin' along this highway, when this cop starts tailin' us? My fodda siz, 'Don't worry, we'll shake him," and he steps on it, see? My mudda's gettin' pretty scared, but my fodda siz, 'Don't worry, dear.' He's tryin' to make this turn, see, so he can get off the highway and shake the cop? But just when he's makin' the turn, the cop opens up and starts shootin', see?"

By this time the few members of the class who could bear to look at him at all were doing so with heads on one side and mouths partly open, the way you look at a broken arm or a circus freak.

"We just barely made it," Vincent went on, his eyes gleaming, "and this one bullet got my fodda in the shoulder. Didn't hurt him bad—just grazed him, like—so my mudda bandaged it up for him and all, but he couldn't do no more drivin' after that, and we had to get him to a doctor, see? So my fodda siz, 'Vinny think you can drive a ways?' I siz, 'Sure, if you show me how.' So he showed me how to work the gas and the brake, and all like that, and I drove to the doctor. My mudda siz, 'I'm prouda you, Vinny, drivin' all by yourself.' So anyways, we got to the doctor, got my fodda fixed up and all, and then he drove us back home." He was breathless. After an uncertain pause he said, "And that's all." Then he walked quickly back to his desk, his stiff new corduroy pants whistling faintly with each step.

"Well, that was very—entertaining, Vincent," Miss Price said, trying to act as if nothing had happened. "Now, who's next?" But nobody raised a hand.

Recess was worse than usual for him that day; at least it was until he found a place to hide—a narrow concrete alley, blind except for several closed fire-exit doors, that cut between two sections of the school building. It was reassuringly dismal and cool in there—he could stand with his back to the wall and his eyes guarding the entrance, and the noises of recess were as remote as the sunshine. But when the bell rang he had to go back to class, and in another hour it was lunchtime.

Miss Price left him alone until her own meal was finished. Then, after standing with one hand on the doorknob for a full minute to gather courage, she went in and sat beside him for another little talk, just as he was trying to swallow the last of a pimento-cheese sandwich.

"Vincent," she began, "we all enjoyed your report this morning, but I think we would have enjoyed it more—a great deal more—if you'd told us something about your real life instead. I mean," she hurried on, "for instance, I noticed you were wearing a nice new windbreaker this morning. It *is* new, isn't it? And did your aunt buy it for you over the weekend?"

He did not deny it.

"Well then, why couldn't you have told us about going to the store with your aunt, and buying the windbreaker, and whatever you did afterwards. That would have made a perfectly good report." She paused, and for the first time looked steadily into his eyes. "You do understand what I'm trying to say, don't you, Vincent?"

He wiped crumbs of bread from his lips, looked at the floor, and nodded.

"And you'll remember next time, won't you?"

He nodded again. "Please may I be excused, Miss Price?"

"Of course you may."

He went to the boys' lavatory and vomited. Afterwards he washed his face and drank a little water, and then he returned to the classroom. Miss Price was busy at her desk now, and didn't look up. To avoid getting involved with her again, he wandered out to the cloakroom and sat on one of the long benches, where he picked up someone's discarded overshoe and turned it over and over in his hands. In a little while he heard the chatter of returning children, and to avoid being discovered there, he got up and went to the fire-exit door. Pushing it open, he found that it gave onto the alley he had hidden in that morning, and he slipped outside. For a minute or two he just stood there, looking at the blankness of the concrete wall; then he found a piece of chalk in his pocket and wrote out all the dirty words he could think of, in block letters a foot high. He had put down four words and was trying to remember a fifth when he heard a shuffling at the door behind him. Arthur Cross was there, holding the door open and reading the words with wide eyes. "Boy," he said in an awed half-whisper. "Boy, you're gonna get it. You're really gonna *get* it."

Startled, and then suddenly calm, Vincent Sabella palmed his chalk, hooked his thumbs in his belt and turned on Arthur Cross with a menacing look. "Yeah?" he inquired. "Who's gonna squeal on me?"

"Well, nobody's gonna *squeal* on you," Arthur Cross said uneasily, "but you shouldn't go around writing—"

"Arright," Vincent said, advancing a step. His shoulders were slumped, his head thrust forward and his eyes narrowed, like Edward G. Robinson. "Arright. That's all I wanna know. I don't like squealers, unnastand?"

While he was saying this, Warren Berg and Bill Stringer appeared in the doorway—just in time to hear it and to see the words on the wall before Vincent turned on them. "And that goes fa you too, unnastand?" he said. "Both a yiz."

And the remarkable thing was that both their faces fell into the same foolish, defensive smile that Arthur Cross was wearing. It wasn't until they had glanced at each other that they were able to meet his eyes with the proper degree of contempt, and by then it was too late. "Think you're pretty smart, don'tcha, Sabella?" Bill Stringer said.

"Never mind what I think," Vincent told him. "You heard what I said. Now let's get back inside."

And they could do nothing but move aside to make way for him, and follow him dumbfounded into the cloakroom.

It was Nancy Parker who squealed —although, of course, with someone like Nancy Parker you didn't think of it as squealing. She had heard everything from the cloakroom; as soon as the boys came in she peeked into the alley, saw the words and, setting her face in a prim frown, went straight to Miss Price. Miss Price was just about to call the class to order for the afternoon when Nancy came up and whispered in her ear. They both disappeared into the cloakroom—from which, after a moment, came the sound of the fire-exit door being abruptly slammed—and when they returned to class Nancy was flushed with righteousness, Miss Price very pale. No announcement was made. Classes proceeded in the ordinary way all afternoon, though it was clear that Miss Price was upset, and it wasn't until she was dismissing the children at three o'clock that she brought the thing into the open. "Will Vincent Sabella please remain seated?" She nodded at the rest of the class. "That's all."

While the room was clearing out she sat at her desk, closed her eyes and massaged the frail bridge of her nose with thumb and forefinger, sorting out half-remembered fragments of a book she had once read on the subject of seriously disturbed children. Perhaps, after all, she should never have undertaken the responsibility of Vincent Sabella's loneliness. Perhaps the whole thing called for the attention of a specialist. She took a deep breath.

"Come over here and sit beside me, Vincent," she said, and when he had settled himself, she looked at him. "I want you to tell me the truth. Did you write those words on the wall outside?"

He stared at the floor.

"Look at me," she said, and he looked at her. She had never looked prettier: her cheeks slightly flushed, her eyes shining and her sweet mouth pressed into a self-conscious frown. "First of all," she said, handing him a small enameled basin streaked with poster paint, "I want you to take this to the boys' room and fill it with hot water and soap."

He did as he was told, and when he came back, carrying the basin carefully to keep the suds from spilling, she was sorting out some old rags in the bottom drawer of her desk. "Here," she said, selecting one and shutting the drawer in a businesslike way. "This will do. Soak this up." She led him back to the fire exit and stood in the alley watching him, silently, while he washed off all the words.

When the job had been done, and the rag and basin put away, they sat down at Miss Price's desk again. "I suppose you think I'm angry with you, Vincent," she said. "Well, I'm not. I almost wish I could be angry—that would make it much easier—but instead I'm hurt. I've tried to be a good friend to you, and I thought you wanted to be my friend too. But this kind of thing—well, it's very hard to be friendly with a person who'd do a thing like that."

She saw, gratefully, that there were tears in his eyes. "Vincent, perhaps I understand some things better than you think. Perhaps I understand that sometimes, when a person does a thing like that, it isn't really because he wants to hurt anyone, but only because he's unhappy. He knows it isn't a good thing to do, and he even knows it isn't going to make him any happier afterwards, but he goes ahead and does it anyway. Then when he finds he's lost a friend, he's terribly sorry, but it's too late. The thing is done."

She allowed this somber note to reverberate in the silence of the room for a little while before she spoke again. "I won't be able to forget this, Vincent. But perhaps, just this once, we can still be friends—as long as I understand that you didn't mean to hurt me. But you must promise me that you won't forget it either. Never forget that when you do a thing like that, you're going to hurt people who want very much to like you, and in that way you're going to hurt yourself. Will you promise to remember that, dear?"

The "dear" was as involuntary as the slender hand that reached out and held the shoulder of his sweatshirt; both made his head hang lower than before.

"All right," she said. "You may go now."

He got his windbreaker out of the cloakroom and left, avoiding the tired uncertainty of her eyes. The corridors were deserted, and dead silent except for the hollow, rhythmic knocking of a janitor's pushbroom against some distant wall. His own rubber-soled tread only added to the silence; so did the lonely little noise made by the zipping-up of his windbreaker, and so did the faint mechanical sigh of the heavy front door. The silence made it all the more startling when he found, several yards down the concrete walk outside, that two boys were walking beside him: Warren Berg and Bill Stringer. They were both smiling at him in an eager, almost friendly way.

"What'd she do to ya, anyway?" Bill Stringer asked.

Caught off guard, Vincent barely managed to put on his Edward G. Robinson face in time. "Nunnya business," he said, and walked faster.

"No, listen—wait up, hey," Warren Berg said, as they trotted to keep up with him. "What'd she do, anyway? She bawl ya out, or what? Wait up, hey, Vinny."

The name made him tremble all over. He had to jam his hands in his windbreaker pockets and force himself to keep on walking; he had to force his voice to be steady when he said "Nunnya *business,* I told ya. Lea' me alone."

But they were right in step with him now. "Boy, she must of given you the works," Warren Berg persisted. "What'd she say, anyway? C'mon, tell us, Vinny."

This time the name was too much for him. It overwhelmed his resistance and made his softening knees slow down to a slack, conversational stroll. "She din say nothin' " he said at last; and then after a dramatic pause he added, "She let the ruler do her talkin' for her."

"The *ruler?* Ya mean she used a *ruler* on ya?" Their faces were stunned, either with disbelief or admiration, and it began to look more and more like admiration as they listened.

"On the knuckles," Vincent said through tightening lips. "Five times on each hand. She siz, 'Make a fist. Lay it out here on the desk.' Then she takes the ruler and *Whop! Whop! Whop!* Five times. Ya think that don't hurt, you're crazy."

Miss Price, buttoning her polo coat as the front door whispered shut behind her, could scarcely believe her eyes. This couldn't be Vincent Sabella—this perfectly normal, perfectly happy boy on the sidewalk ahead of her, flanked by attentive friends. But it was, and the scene made her want to laugh aloud with pleasure and relief. He was going to be all right, after all. For all her well-intentioned groping in the shadows she could never have predicted a scene like this, and certainly could never have caused it to happen. But it was happening, and it just proved, once again, that she would never understand the ways of children.

She quickened her graceful stride and overtook them, turning to smile down at them as she passed. "Goodnight, boys," she called, intending it as a kind of cheerful benediction; and then, embarrassed by their three startled faces, she smiled even wider and said, "Goodness, it *is* getting colder, isn't it? That windbreaker of yours looks nice and warm, Vincent. I envy you." Finally they nodded bashfully at her; she called goodnight again, turned, and continued on her way to the bus stop.

She left a profound silence in her wake. Staring after her, Warren Berg and Bill Stringer waited until she had disappeared around the corner before they turned on Vincent Sabella.

"Ruler, my eye!" Bill Stringer said. "Ruler, my eye!" He gave Vincent a disgusted shove that sent him stumbling against Warren Berg, who shoved him back.

"Jeez, you lie about *everything,* don'tcha, Sabella? You lie about *everything!*"

Jostled off balance, keeping his hands tight in the windbreaker pockets, Vincent tried in vain to retain his dignity. "Think *I* care if yiz believe me?" he said, and then because he couldn't think of anything else to say, he said it again. "Think *I* care if yiz believe me?"

But he was walking alone. Warren Berg and Bill Stringer were drifting away across the street, walking backwards in order to look back on him with furious contempt. "Just like the lies you told about the policeman shooting your father," Bill Stringer called.

"Even *movies* he lies about," Warren Berg put in; and suddenly doubling up with artificial laughter he cupped both hands to his mouth and yelled, "Hey, Doctor Jack-o'-lantern!"

It wasn't a very good nickname, but it had an authentic ring to it—the kind of a name that might spread around, catch on quickly, and stick. Nudging each other, they both took up the cry:

"What's the matter, Doctor Jack-o'-lantern?"

"Why don'tcha run on home with Miss Price, Doctor Jack-o'-lantern?"

"So long, Doctor Jack-o'-lantern!"

Vincent Sabella went on walking, ignoring them, waiting until they were out of sight. Then he turned and retraced his steps all the way back to the school, around through the playground and back to the alley, where the wall was still dark in spots from the circular scrubbing of his wet rag.

Choosing a dry place, he got out his chalk and began to draw a head with great care, in profile, making the hair long and rich and taking his time over the face, erasing it with moist fingers and reworking it until it was the most beautiful face he had ever drawn: a delicate nose, slightly parted lips, an eye with lashes that curved as gracefully as a bird's wing. He paused to admire it with a lover's solemnity; then from the lips he drew a line that connected with a big speech balloon, and in the balloon he wrote, so angrily that the chalk kept breaking in his fingers, every one of the words he had written that noon. Returning to the head, he gave it a slender neck and gently sloping shoulders, and then, with bold strikes, he gave it the body of a naked woman: great breasts with hard little nipples, a trim waist, a dot for a navel, wide hips and thighs that flared around a triangle of fiercely scribbled pubic hair. Beneath the picture he printed its title: "Miss Price."

He stood there looking at it for a little while, breathing hard, and then he went home.

Discussion

The arrival of a new boy who is obviously very different from the other children in the class poses a particularly difficult challenge to a well-meaning teacher. The children in this story are from an upper middle-class suburban background —a background that usually teaches little about other stratas of society. Furthermore, the children are nine and ten years old, an age when conformity is a way of life and children hold prejudices against anyone who is different, even when home values would frown on overt discrimination. A new boy or girl entering a school at this age would need an outstanding redeeming feature such as skill at athletics or good looks to compensate for his newness and to earn him a place in the group.

No such good fortune accompanies Vincent Sabella. Miss Price tries the well-known devices to make Vincent seem acceptable. His accomplishments are lavishly praised and his errors minimized. How can Miss Price improve his image with the group and help him gain acceptance? With Vincent's negative self-image and the variety of obvious negative features he possesses, the possibilities for success are slim. Miss Price is not trained to deal with the enormity of the peer group problem Vince's case represents. Even though she may provide some comfort to him in their one-to-one relationship, her sincere efforts further isolate Vincent from the group. Gaining acceptance by the teacher, moreover, is not Vincent's appropriate developmental task.

The final incident is very realistic. This kind of impossible peer group situation will frequently provoke an extremely hostile and unacceptable incident on the part of the isolated child, thereby creating a crisis that requires a change in setting. As a result of Vincent's lewd drawing, it may be determined that he needs placement in a special class or school for emotionally disturbed children. Another alternative may be to remove him from his present foster home to one in a more appropriate socioeconomic setting.

This incident, which so heavily penalizes a vulnerable child, underscores the need to help children in their earliest years to be more understanding and accepting of others. Only a very skilled teacher could make successful inroads into this almost intractable situation. Group problem-solving to discuss Vincent's problem in gaining acceptance might lead to good results, but considerable experience is needed to effect successful communication with nine-year-olds and ten-year-olds. The working out of a reasonably comfortable relationship between Vincent and other members of the class would take time, and a main objective of the teacher should be to avoid a major incident until steps have been taken toward a solution to the problem.

Springboards for Inquiry

(1) How would you describe Miss Price's behavior as a teacher? To what extent does her style contribute to the classroom environment and the class's acceptance of the new boy?

(2) What is another way Miss Price could have handled Vincent's report?

(3) Describe Vincent Sabella's feelings throughout the incidents in this story, beginning with his introduction to the class.

(4) In the story "See How They Run" the children seem to understand and make allowances for the failures of their classmate C. T., which leads the author, Margaret Vroman, to say, "Sometimes children have a great deal more insight than grownups." Under what conditions will children protect the obvious faults of a classmate? What are some of the reasons that the children in Miss Price's class did not?

The Peer Group

Bronfenbrenner contends that "children used to be brought up by their parents" (1970, p. 5). American culture has changed since the proverbial "good old days" when fathers worked in the fields, mothers worked in the home, and all was "right with the world." Today, more than one-third of the mothers of American children are gainfully employed outside the home, and fathers are jetting their lives away, so that, in effect, American parents are not raising their own children.* In answer to the question, Who is?, Bronfenbrenner cites his study of 766 sixth-grade children (1958), which reports that during the weekend these children spent an average of two to three hours a day with their parents. The rest of the time was spent with their peers. In fact, twice as much time was spent with peers as with parents.

As childhood advances, the child spends increasingly less time with his parents and more time with his peer group. Understandably the peer group exerts an increasingly stronger influence on his attitudes, interests, and values. Indeed, the logical explanation for the "generation gap" is that parents' values diminish in importance as children grow older (Bowerman and Kinch 1959), until in the middle adolescent years the peer group gains nearly total control of the individual. When a child's problems emanate from his struggles with reality, he depends on

---

* Bronfenbrenner (1958) concludes that the time parents spend with children has decreased over a twenty-five-year period. Research further documents the situation when Americans are compared with parents of other countries (Edward C. Devereaux, Urie Bronfenbrenner, and George J. Suci, "Patterns of Parent Behavior in America and West Germany: A Cross-Cultural Comparison," *International Social Science Journal* 14, no. 3 [1962]:488–506).

his parents for help, and when he is pondering questions that are not directly related to his own family life—pollution and drugs, for instance—his peers are his source of advice (Brittain 1963; Withey 1962).

When children become peer-oriented, both teacher and therapists need to observe special cautions. Apparently the feelings a teacher has for a particular student are transmitted to the peer group (Glidewell, Cantor, Smith, and Stringer 1966). Thus, when a child is perceived favorably by a teacher, the children in the class pick up this tone of feeling and adopt it. Furthermore, children work best when they are interacting in groups they enjoy. Sociometric techniques can identify the constellations of children who will form effective peer groups, thus allowing for the teacher's continuing reappraisal of the social focus at work in his class.*

Redl (1966) maintains that there are a number of problems inherent in the peer group culture among children who are being clinically treated in an institutional environment. First, when the therapist rates behavior as "improved," the peer group scale, "which has a strong natural power in the children's lives" (p. 112), may rate the child as a pawn in the adult world, a "teacher's pet," "giving in" to the adult world. Second, as the child improves his relationship with himself, his tastes change, and thus he may become hostile to those in the milieu who have not kept pace with his improvement. On the other hand, it is entirely possible for the improved child to yearn for the simpler and wilder life of his peers. Finally, the child who is making progress in therapy is not likely to be easily released by his peer group, who will subject him to loyalty tests. His personal progress thus comes into sharp conflict with the group's norms.

Perhaps the most significant influence of peers is in the socializing process (Longstreth 1968). Whereas most children are influenced by only one set of parents, they are exposed to a number of peers, all of whom may express different points of view about the world. The leavening influence of the peer group has been termed the normalizing influence (Johnson and Medinnus 1965). Interaction with peers counterbalances parental idiosyncracies. The child's references to "my friends have one" or "Jane's dad says it's OK" are checks that apprise parents of other norms. In general, peer group interaction prevents deviances; the opportunity to interact with others contributes to one's "normalcy."†

---

* Harold Bernard outlines a technique for using sociometric grouping in *Psychology of Learning and Teaching*, 2d ed. (New York: McGraw-Hill Book Co., 1965).

† "Only" children contribute disproportionate numbers to the ranks of the deviant (Longstreth 1968, p. 504). Group therapy seems to influence children more than individual therapy because of the opportunity to model behavior after members of the peer group. Even the study of monkeys by Harry F. Harlow and Margaret K. Harlow ("Social Deprivation in Monkeys," *Scientific American* 207: Nov., 1962:136–46) indicates that peer interaction prevents social and sexual deviancy.

Ernest Gaskin, he shouted in the schoolyard, *what* are you *chewing?* Raw elephant meat, said Ernest Gaskin. Jim Davy, what are *you* chewing?

The First Day of School

by William Saroyan

He was a little boy named Jim, the first and only child of Dr. Louis Davy, 717 Mattei Building, and it was his first day at school. His father was French, a small heavy-set man of forty whose boyhood had been full of poverty and unhappiness and ambition. His mother was dead: she died when Jim was born, and the only woman he knew intimately was Amy, the Swedish housekeeper.

It was Amy who dressed him in his Sunday clothes and took him to school. Jim liked Amy, but he didn't like her for taking him to school. He told her so. All the way to school he told her so.

I don't like you, he said.

I don't like you any more.

I like *you,* the housekeeper said.

Then why are you taking me to school? he said.

He had taken walks with Amy before, once all the way to the Court House Park for the Sunday afternoon band concert, but this walk to school was different.

What for? he said.

Everybody must go to school, the housekeeper said.

Did you go to school? he said.

No, said Amy.

Then why do I have to go? he said.

You will like it, said the housekeeper.

He walked on with her in silence, holding her hand. I don't like you, he said. I don't like you any more.

I like you, said Amy.

Then why are you taking me to school? he said again.

Why?

The housekeeper knew how frightened a little boy could be about going to school.

You will like it, she said. I think you will sing songs and play games.

I don't want to, he said.

I will come and get you every afternoon, she said.

I don't like you, he told her again.

She felt very unhappy about the little boy going to school, but she knew that he would have to go.

The school building was very ugly to her and to the boy. She didn't like the way it made her feel, and going up the steps with him she wished he didn't have to go to school. The halls and rooms scared her, and him, and the smell of the place too. And he didn't like Mr. Barber, the principal.

Amy despised Mr. Barber.

What is the name of your son? Mr. Barber said.

This is Dr. Louis Davy's son, said Amy. His name is Jim. I am Dr. Davy's housekeeper.

James? said Mr. Barber.

Not James, said Amy, just Jim.

All right, said Mr. Barber. Any middle name?

No, said Amy. He is too small for a middle name. Just Jim Davy.

All right, said Mr. Barber. We'll try him out in the first grade. If he doesn't get along all right we'll try him out in kindergarten.

Dr. Davy said to start him in the first grade, said Amy. Not kindergarten.

All right, said Mr. Barber.

The housekeeper knew how frightened the little boy was, sitting on the chair, and she tried to let him know how much she loved him and how sorry she was about everything. She wanted to say something fine to him about everything, but she couldn't say anything, and she was very proud of the nice way he got down from the chair and stood beside Mr. Barber, waiting to go with him to a classroom.

On the way home she was so proud of him she began to cry.

Miss Binney, the teacher of the first grade, was an old lady who was all dried out. The room was full of little boys and girls. School smelled strange and sad. He sat at a desk and listened carefully.

He heard some of the names: *Charles, Ernest, Alvin, Norman, Betty, Hannah, Juliet, Viola, Polly.*

He listened carefully and heard Miss Binney say, Hannah Winter, what *are* you chewing? And he saw Hannah Winter blush. He liked Hannah Winter right from the beginning.

Gum, said Hannah.

Put it in the waste-basket, said Miss Binney.

He saw the little girl walk to the front of the class, take the gum from her mouth, and drop it into the waste-basket.

And he heard Miss Binney say, Ernest Gaskin, what are *you* chewing?

Gum, said Ernest.

And he liked Ernest Gaskin too.

They met in the schoolyard, and Ernest taught him a few jokes.

Amy was in the hall when school ended. She was sullen and angry at everybody until she saw the little boy. She was amazed that he wasn't changed, that he wasn't hurt, or perhaps utterly unalive, murdered. The school and everything about it frightened her very much. She took his hand and walked out of the building with him, feeling angry and proud.

Jim said, What comes after twenty-nine?

Thirty, said Amy.

Your face is dirty, he said.

His father was very quiet at the supper table.

What comes after twenty-nine? the boy said.

Thirty, said his father.

Your face is dirty, he said.

In the morning he asked his father for a nickel.

What do you want a nickel for? his father said.

Gum, he said.

His father gave him a nickel and on the way to school he stopped at Mrs. Riley's store and bought a package of Spearmint.

Do you want a piece? he asked Amy.

Do you want to give me a piece? the housekeeper said.

Jim thought about it a moment, and then he said, Yes.

Do you like me? said the housekeeper.

I like you, said Jim, Do you like me?

Yes, said the housekeeper.

Do you like school?

Jim didn't know for sure, but he knew he liked the part about gum. And Hannah Winter. And Ernest Gaskin.

I don't know, he said.

Do you sing? asked the housekeeper.

No, we don't sing, he said.

Do you play games? she said.

Not in the school, he said. In the yard we do. He liked the part about gum very much.

Miss Binney said, Jim Davy, what are you *chewing*?

Ha ha ha, he thought.

Gum, he said.

He walked to the waste-paper basket and back to his seat, and Hannah Winter saw him, and Ernest Gaskin too. That was the best part of school.

It began to grow too.

Ernest Gaskin, he shouted in the schoolyard, *what* are you *chewing*?

Raw elephant meat, said Ernest Gaskin. Jim Davy, what are *you* chewing?

Jim tried to think of something very funny to be chewing, but he couldn't.

Gum, he said, and Ernest Gaskin laughed louder than Jim laughed when Ernest Gaskin said raw elephant meat.

It was funny no matter what you said.

Going back to the classroom Jim saw Hannah Winter in the hall.

Hannah Winter, he said, *what in the world* are you *chewing*?

The little girl was startled. She wanted to say something nice that would honestly show how nice she felt about having Jim say her name and ask her the funny question, making fun of school, but she couldn't think of anything that nice to say because they were almost in the room and there wasn't time enough.

Tutti-frutti, she said with desperate haste.

It seemed to Jim he had never before heard such a glorious word, and he kept repeating the word to himself all day.

Tutti-frutti, he said to Amy on the way home.

Amy Larson, he said, *what, are, you, chewing?*

He told his father all about it at the supper table.

He said, Once there was a hill. On the hill there was a mill. Under the mill there was a walk. Under the walk there was a key. What is it?

I don't know, his father said. What is it?

Milwaukee, said the boy.

The housekeeper was delighted.

Mill. Walk. Key, Jim said.

Tutti-frutti.

What's that? said his father.

Gum, he said. The kind Hannah Winter chews.

Who's Hannah Winter? said his father.

She's in my room, he said.

Oh, said his father.

After supper he sat on the floor with the small red and blue and yellow top that hummed while it spinned. It was all right, he guessed. It was still very sad, but the gum part of it was very funny and the Hannah Winter part very nice. Raw elephant meat, he thought with great inward delight.

Raw elephant meat, he said aloud to his father who was reading the evening paper. His father folded the paper and sat on the floor beside him. The housekeeper saw them together on the floor and for some reason tears came to her eyes.

Discussion

Usually the author who retells a child's first experience at school emphasizes the conflict he encounters with his peer group. In this story Jim finds his classmates a delightful source of satisfaction. The only child of an almost middle-aged physician, he seems to be a little boy who has had little experience with children of his own age. He now finds their company, jokes, and riddles a new world of excitement and fun. Why is it that Jim is not made a scapegoat as the new boy in the first grade? In part, at ages five and six there is less ritual and tradition for entry into the peer group. Jim also immediately aligns himself with the mischief-makers, and they recognize him as a conspirator with them in provoking the teacher, Jim's future as a well-liked boy among his schoolmates seems assured, but we think there may be less satisfaction in his home life unless his father becomes more interested in Jim's world of childhood. This is not to imply that parents should attempt to compete with the peer group for a child's interest and loyalty. However, while the child alternately enjoys and chafes at the conformity the peer group demands, interested parents can take an extremely supportive and sympathetic role without being judgmental.

Springboards for Inquiry

(1) Using Amy as an example, discuss some of the conflicts the adult experiences as he brings the child to school for the first time. How does the adult's reaction effect the child?

(2) What characteristics of Davy's home life will make his peer group relationships especially meaningful for him?

(3) What characteristics of this school would make the children value their peer group relationship above all else so early in their school careers?

(4) What are some of the chants, rituals and games that children enjoy in their beginning school years?

(5) What characteristics does Davy have that will make him popular with his peers?

The new boy felt that his name was the most disgraceful thing which had ever been attached to a human being.

The Fight*

by Stephen Crane

I

The child life of the neighborhood was sometimes moved in its deeps at the sight of wagonloads of furniture arriving in front of some house which, with closed blinds and barred doors, had been for a time a mystery, or even a fear. The boys often expressed this fear by stamping bravely and noisily on the porch of the house, and then suddenly darting away with screams of nervous laughter, as if they expected to be pursued by something uncanny. There was a group who held that the cellar of a vacant house was certainly the abode of robbers, smugglers, assassins, mysterious masked men in council about the dim rays of a candle, and possessing skulls, emblematic bloody daggers, and owls. Then, near the first of April, would come along a wagonload of furniture, and children would assemble on the walk by the gate and make serious examination of everything that passed into the house, and taking no thought whatever of masked men.

One day it was announced in the neighborhood that a family was actually moving into the Hannigan house, next door to Dr. Trescott's. Jimmie was one of the first to be informed, and by the time some of his friends came dashing up he was versed in much.

"Any boys?" they demanded, eagerly.

"Yes," answered Jimmie, proudly. "One's a little feller, and one's most as big as me. I saw 'em, I did."

"Where are they?" asked Willie Dalzel, as if under the circumstances he could not take Jimmie's word, but must have the evidence of his senses.

"Oh, they're in there," said Jimmie, carelessly. It was evident he

---

* Whilomville Stories.

From *Harper's Magazine*, Vol. 101 (June 1900): 56–63. Reprinted with permission.

owned these new boys.

Willie Dalzel resented Jimmie's proprietary way. "Ho!" he cried, scornfully. "Why don't they come out, then? Why don't they come out?"

"How d' I know?" said Jimmie.

"Well," retorted Willie Dalzel, "you seemed to know so thundering much about 'em."

At the moment a boy came strolling down the gravel walk which led from the front door to the gate. He was about the height and age of Jimmie Trescott, but he was thick through the chest and had fat legs. His face was round and rosy and plump, but his hair was curly black, and his brows were naturally darkling, so that he resembled both a pudding and a young bull.

He approached slowly the group of older inhabitants, and they had grown profoundly silent. They looked him over; he looked them over. They might have been savages observing the first white man, or white men observing the first savage. The silence held steady.

As he neared the gate the strange boy wandered off to the left in a definite way, which proved his instinct to make a circular voyage when in doubt. The motionless group stared at him. In time this unsmiling scrutiny worked upon him somewhat, and he leaned against the fence and fastidiously examined one shoe.

In the end Willie Dalzel authoritatively broke the stillness. "What's your name?" said he, gruffly.

"Johnnie Hedge 'tis," answered the new boy. Then came another great silence while Whilomville pondered this intelligence.

Again came the voice of authority —"Where'd you live b'fore?"

"Jersey City."

These two sentences completed the first section of the formal code. The second section concerned itself with the establishment of the newcomer's exact position in the neighborhood.

"I kin lick you," announced Willie Dalzel, and awaited the answer.

The Hedge boy had stared at Willie Dalzel, but he stared at him again. After a pause he said, "I know you kin."

"Well," demanded Willie, "kin *he* lick you?" And he indicated Jimmie Trescott with a sweep which announced plainly that Jimmie was the next in prowess.

Whereupon the new boy looked at Jimmie respectfully but carefully, and at length said, "I dun'no."

This was the signal for an outburst of shrill screaming, and everybody pushed Jimmie forward. He knew what he had to say, and, as befitted the occasion, he said it fiercely: "Kin you lick me?"

The new boy also understood what he had to say, and, despite his unhappy and lonely state, he said it bravely: "Yes."

"Well," retorted Jimmie, bluntly, "come out and do it, then! Jest come out and do it!" And these words were greeted with cheers. These little rascals yelled that there should be a fight at once. They were in bliss over the prospect. "Go on, Jim! Make 'im come out. He said he could lick you. Aw-aw-aw! He said he could lick you!" There probably never was a fight among this class in Whilomville which was not the result of the goading and guying of two proud lads by a populace of urchins who simply wished to see a show.

Willie Dalzel was very busy. He turned first to the one and then to the other. "You said you could lick him. Well, why don't you come out and do it, then? You said you could lick him, didn't you?"

"Yes," answered the new boy, dogged and dubious.

Willie tried to drag Jimmie by the arm. "Aw, go on, Jimmie! You ain't afraid, are you?"

"No," said Jimmie.

The two victims opened wide eyes at each other. The fence separated them, and so it was impossible for them to immediately engage; but they seemed to understand that they were ultimately to be sacrificed to the ferocious aspirations of the other boys, and each scanned the other to learn something of his spirit. They were not angry at all. They were merely two little gladiators who were being clamorously told to hurt each other. Each displayed hesitation and doubt without displaying fear. They did not exactly understand what were their feelings, and they moodily kicked the ground and made low and sullen answers to Willie Dalzel, who worked like a circus manager.

"Aw, go on, Jim! What's the matter with you? You ain't afraid, are you? Well, then, say something." This sentiment received more cheering from the abandoned little wretches who wished to be entertained, and in this cheering there could be heard notes of derision of Jimmie Trescott. The latter had a position to sustain; he was well known; he often bragged of his willingness and ability to thrash other boys; well, then, here was a boy of his size who said that he could not thrash him. What was he going to do about it? The crowd made these arguments very clear, and repeated them again and again.

Finally Jimmie, driven to aggression, walked close to the fence and said to the new boy, "The first time I catch you out of your own yard I'll lam the head off'n you!" This was received with wild plaudits by the Whilomville urchins.

But the new boy stepped back from the fence. He was awed by Jimmie's formidable mien. But he managed to get out a semi-defiant sentence. "Maybe you will, and maybe you won't," said he.

However, his short retreat was taken as a practical victory for Jimmie, and the boys hooted him bitterly. He remained inside the fence, swinging one foot and scowling, while Jimmie was escorted off down the street amid acclamations. The new boy turned and walked back toward the house, his face gloomy, lined deep with discouragement, as if he felt that the new environment's antagonism and palpable cruelty were sure to prove too much for him.

II

The mother of Johnnie Hedge was a widow, and the chief theory of her life was that her boy should be in school on the greatest possible number of days. He himself had no sympathy with this ambition, but she detected the truth of his diseases with an unerring eye, and he was required to be really ill before he could win the right to disregard the first bell, morning and noon. The chicken pox and the mumps had given him vacations—vacations of misery, wherein he nearly died between pain and nursing. But bad colds in the head did nothing for him, and he was not able to invent a satisfactory hacking cough. His mother was not consistently a Tartar. In most things he swayed her to his will. He was allowed to have more jam, pickles, and pie than most boys; she respected his profound loathing of Sunday school; on summer evenings he could remain out-of-doors until 8:30; but in this matter of school she was inexorable. This single point in her character was of steel.

The Hedges arrived in Whilomville on a Saturday, and on the following Monday Johnnie wended his way to school with a note to the principal and his Jersey City school books. He knew perfectly well that he would be told to buy new and different books, but in those days mothers always had an idea that old books would "do," and they invariably sent boys off to a new school with books which would not meet the selected and unchangeable views of the new administration. The old books never would "do." Then the boys brought them home to annoyed mothers and asked for ninety cents or sixty cents or eighty-five cents or some number of cents for another outfit. In the garret of every house holding a large family there was a collection of effete school books, with mother rebellious because James could not inherit his books from Paul, who should properly be Peter's heir, while Peter should be a beneficiary under Henry's will.

But the matter of the books was not the measure of Johnnie Hedge's unhappiness. This whole business of changing schools was a complete torture. Alone he had to go among a new people, a new tribe, and he apprehended his serious time. There were only two fates for him. One meant victory. One meant a kind of serfdom in which he would subscribe to every word of some superior boy and support his every word. It was not anything like an English system of fagging, because boys invariably drifted into the figurative service of other boys whom they devotedly admired, and if they were obliged to subscribe to everything, it is true that they would have done so freely in any case. One means to suggest that Johnnie Hedge had to find his place. Willie Dalzel was a type of the little chieftain, and Willie was a master, but he was not a bully in a special physical sense. He did not drag little boys by the ears until they cried, nor make them tearfully fetch and carry for him. They fetched and carried, but it was because of their worship of his prowess and genius. And so all through the strata of boy life were chieftains and sub-chieftains and assistant sub-chieftains. There was no question of little Hedge being towed about by the nose; it was, as one has said, that he had to find his place in a new school. And this in itself was a problem which awed his boyish heart. He was a stranger cast away upon the moon. None knew him, understood him, felt for him. He would be surrounded for this initiative time by a horde of jackal creatures who might turn out in the end to be little boys like himself, but this last point his philosophy could not understand in its fulness.

He came to a white meeting house sort of place, in the squat tower of which a great bell was clanging impressively. He passed through an iron gate into a playground worn bare as the bed of a mountain brook by the endless runnings and scufflings of little children. There was still a half-hour before the final clangor in the squat tower, but the playground held a number of frolicsome imps. A loitering boy espied Johnnie Hedge, and he howled: "Oh! oh! Here's a new feller! Here's a new feller!" He advanced upon the strange arrival. "What's your name?" he demanded, belligerently, like a particularly offensive customhouse officer.

"Johnnie Hedge," responded the newcomer shyly.

This name struck the other boy as being very comic. All new names strike boys as being comic. He laughed noisily.

"Oh, fellers, he says his name is Johnnie Hedge! Haw! haw! haw!"

The new boy felt that his name was the most disgraceful thing which had ever been attached to a human being.

"Johnnie Hedge! Haw! haw! What room you in?" said the other lad.

"I dun'no," said Johnnie. In the meantime a small flock of interested vultures had gathered about him. The main thing was his absolute strangeness. He even would have welcomed the sight of his tormentors of Saturday; he had seen them before at least. These creatures were only so many incomprehensible problems. He diffidently began to make his way toward the main door of the school, and the other boys followed him. They demanded information.

"Are you through subtraction yet? We study jogerfre—did you, ever? You live here now? You goin' to school here now?"

To many questions he made answer as well as the clamor would permit, and at length he reached the main door and went quaking unto his new kings. As befitted them, the rabble stopped at the door. A teacher strolling along a corridor found a small boy holding in his hand a note. The boy palpably did not know what to do with the note, but the teacher knew, and took it. Thereafter this little boy was in harness.

A splendid lady in gorgeous robes gave him a seat at a double desk, at the end of which sat a hoodlum with grimy fingernails, who eyed the inauguration with an extreme and personal curiosity. The other desks were gradually occupied by children, who first were told of the new boy, and then turned upon him a speculative and somewhat derisive eye. The school opened; little classes went forward to a position in front of the teacher's platform and tried to explain that they knew something. The new boy was not requisitioned a great deal; he was allowed to lie dormant until he became used to the scenes and until the teacher found, approximately, his mental position. In the meantime he suffered a shower of stares and whispers and giggles, as if he were a man-ape, whereas he was precisely like other children. From time to time he made funny and pathetic little overtures to other boys, but these overtures could not yet be received; he was not known; he was a foreigner. The village school was like a nation. It was tight. Its amiability or friendship must be won in certain ways.

At recess he hovered in the schoolroom around the weak lights of society and around the teacher, in the hope that somebody might be good to him, but none considered him save as some sort of specimen. The teacher of course had a secondary interest in the fact that he was an additional one to a class of sixty-three.

At twelve o'clock, when the ordered files of boys and girls marched toward the door, he exhibited—to no eye—the tremblings of a coward in a charge. He exaggerated the lawlessness of the playground and the street.

But the reality was hard enough. A shout greeted him: "Oh, here's the new feller! Here's the new feller!"

Small and utterly obscure boys teased him. He had a hard time of it to get to the gate. There never was any actual hurt, but everything was competent to smite the lad with shame. It was a curious, groundless shame, but nevertheless it was shame. He was a newcomer, and he definitely felt the disgrace of the fact.

In the street he was seen and recognized by some lads who had formed part of the group of Saturday. They shouted: "Oh, Jimmie! Jimmie! Here he is! Here's that new feller!"

Jimmie Trescott was going virtuously toward his luncheon when he heard these cries behind him. He pretended not to hear, and in this deception he was assisted by the fact that he was engaged at the time in a furious argument with a friend over the relative merits of two *Uncle Tom's Cabin* companies. It appeared that one company had only two bloodhounds, while the other had ten. On the other hand, the first company had two Topsys and two Uncle Toms, while the second had only one Topsy and one Uncle Tom.

But the shouting little boys were hard after him. Finally they were even pulling at his arms. "Jimmie—"

"What?" he demanded, turning with a snarl. "What d'you want? Leggo my arm!"

"Here he is! Here's the new feller! Here's the new feller! Now!"

"I don't care if he is," said Jimmie, with grand impatience. He tilted his chin. "I don't care if he is."

Then they reviled him. "Thought you was goin' to lick him first time you caught him! Yah! You're a 'fraid-cat!" They began to sing: " 'Fraid-cat! 'Fraid-cat! 'Fraid-cat!" He expostulated hotly, turning from one to another, but they would not listen. In the meantime the Hedge boy slunk on his way, looking with deep anxiety upon this attempt to send Jimmie against him. But Jimmie would have none of the plan.

III

When the children met again on the playground, Jimmie was openly challenged with cowardice. He had made a big threat in the hearing of comrades, and when invited by them to take advantage of an opportunity, he had refused. They had been fairly sure of their amusement, and they were indignant. Jimmie was finally driven to declare that as soon as school was out for the day, he would thrash the Hedge boy. When finally the children came rushing out of the iron gate, filled with the delights of freedom, a hundred boys surrounded Jimmie in high spirits, for he had said that he was determined. They waited for the lone lad from Jersey City. When he appeared, Jimmie wasted no time. He walked straight to him and said, "Did you say you kin lick me?"

Johnnie Hedge was cowed, shrinking, affrighted, and the roars of a hundred boys thundered in his ears, but again he knew what he had to say. "Yes," he gasped, in anguish.

"Then," said Jimmie, resolutely, "you've got to fight." There was a joyous clamor by the mob. The beleaguered lad looked this way and that way for succor, as Willie Dalzel and other officious youngsters policed an irregular circle in the crowd. He saw Jimmie facing him; there was no help for it; he dropped his books—the old books which would not "do."

Now it was the fashion among tiny Whilomville belligerents to fight much in the manner of little bear cubs. Two boys would rush upon each other, immediately grapple, and—the best boy having probably succeeded in getting the coveted "under hold"—there would presently be a crash to earth of the inferior boy, and he would probably be mopped around in the dust, or the mud, or the snow, or whatever the material happened to be, until the engagement was over. Whatever havoc was dealt out to him was ordinarily the result of his wild endeavors to throw off his opponent and arise. Both infants wept during the fight, as a common thing, and if they wept very hard, the fight was a harder fight. The result was never very bloody, but the complete dishevelment of both victor and vanquished was extraordinary. As for the spectacle, it more resembled a collision of boys in a fog than it did the manly art of hammering another human being into speechless inability.

The fight began when Jimmie made a mad, bear-cub rush at the new boy, amid savage cries of encouragement. Willie Dalzel, for instance, almost howled his head off. Very timid boys on the outskirts of the throng felt their hearts leap to their throats. It was a time when certain natures were impressed that only man is vile.

But it appeared that bear-cub rushing was no part of the instruction received by boys in Jersey City. Boys in Jersey City were apparently schooled curiously. Upon the onslaught of Jimmie, the stranger had gone wild with rage—boylike. Some spark had touched his fighting blood, and in a moment he was a cornered, desperate, fire-eyed little man. He began to swing his arms, to revolve them so swiftly that one might have considered him a small working model of an extra-fine patented windmill which was caught in a gale. For a moment this defense surprised Jimmie more than it damaged him, but two moments later a small, knotty fist caught him squarely in the eye, and with a shriek he went down in defeat. He lay on the ground so stunned that he could not even cry; but if he had been able to cry, he would have cried over his prestige—or something—not over his eye.

There was a dreadful tumult. The boys cast glances of amazement and terror upon the victor, and thronged upon the beaten Jimmie Trescott. It was a moment of excitement so intense that one cannot say what happened. Never before had Whilomville seen such a thing—not the little tots. They were aghast, dumbfounded, and they glanced often over their shoulders at the new boy, who stood alone, his clenched fists at his side, his face crimson, his lips still working with the fury of battle.

But there was another surprise for Whilomville. It might have been seen that the little victor was silently debating against an impulse.

But the impulse won, for the lone lad from Jersey City suddenly wheeled, sprang like a demon, and struck another boy.

A curtain should be drawn before this deed. A knowledge of it is really too much for the heart to bear. The other boy was Willie Dalzel. The lone lad from Jersey City had smitten him full sore.

There is little to say of it. It must have been that a feeling worked gradually to the top of the little stranger's wrath that Jimmie Trescott had been a mere tool, that the front and center of his persecutors had been Willie Dalzel; and, being rendered temporarily lawless by his fighting blood, he raised his hand and smote for revenge.

Willie Dalzel had been in the middle of a vandal's cry, which screeched out over the voices of everybody. The new boy's fist cut it in half, so to say. And then arose the howl of an amazed and terrorized walrus.

One wishes to draw a second curtain. Without discussion or inquiry or brief retort, Willie Dalzel ran away. He ran like a hare straight for home, this redoubtable chieftain. Following him at a heavy and slow pace ran the impassioned new boy. The scene was long remembered.

Willie Dalzel was no coward; he had been panic-stricken into running away from a new thing. He ran as a man might run from the sudden appearance of a vampire or a ghoul or a gorilla. This was no time for academics—he ran.

Jimmie slowly gathered himself and came to his feet. "Where's Willie?" said he, first of all. The crowd sniggered. "Where's Willie?" said Jimmie again.

"Why, he licked him *too*!" answered a boy suddenly.

"He did?" said Jimmie. He sat weakly down on the roadway. "He did?" After allowing a moment for the fact to sink into him, he looked up at the crowd with his one good eye and his one bunged eye, and smiled cheerfully.

Discussion

Peer group culture and ethic in the middle school years shares many attributes of tribal customs and rituals. The middle-school-age child is under great pressure to conform to the customs and rituals of his age-mates in order to be accepted by them. Although the peer group organization may be unstable during this period, the acknowledged leader, while he holds power, is an important decision-maker about the in-group code.

Johnnie Hedge, who has moved to a new neighborhood during the critical middle school years, is faced with a number of painful adjustments to his new school and home environment. His need to meet new academic standards is formidable, but acceptance by his peers in school and in the neighborhood is by far the most challenging of his tasks. He needs to summon all his resources to withstand the penalties inflicted by his age-mates for being new and therefore strange. At an age when chants, riddles, and tongue twisters hold special magical powers, it is expected that he, his name, or anything unusual about him will be a particularly appealing target for chants, name-calling, and singsong derision.

As is frequently the case with boys of this age, the ultimate path to acceptance by the group is proof of physical prowess. In his misery and uncertainty, Johnnie is willing to acknowledge that he cannot beat the group leader, Willie Dalzel. Johnnie does not lose face by acknowledging Willie's superior strength; in fact, this acknowledgment undoubtedly pleases Willie. However, according to the power structure Johnnie cannot refuse to fight with Jimmie Trescott. Both Johnnie and Jimmie are victims of the peer group custom. Their personal wishes are submerged in the expectation of the onlookers, who experience vicarious excitement from the encounter. Defeat by an age-mate, as in Jimmie Trescott's case, never wounds the child's person as much as it wounds his pride.

Although this story documents a boy's initiation into the peer group, a girl of this age trying to win entry into her peer group would find parallel challenges of equal severity. Boys and girls maintain separate cultures at this age, but the organization structure is equally prescribed in both groups.

Although this story was written in 1900, it seems contemporary because there has been little change in the system of peer group relations at the middle school age. In the suburbs the number of children of the same age who live in close proximity has diminished, probably affecting group acceptance in the neighborhood. However, school still presents the same hurdles to the new boy or girl.

Springboards for Inquiry

(1) Using your own childhood as a resource, discuss the group standards for acceptance by age-mates at that time. What were the criteria for being a "good sport"?

(2) Conflict and cooperation alternate within the usual peer group relations. Which situations tend to promote conflict? Which situations tend to promote cooperation?

(3) Aggressiveness among children in our society is considered both normal and desirable, particularly on the part of boys. What are some of the conflicting child-rearing theories about aggressiveness?

(4) How important is competition in the school-age group?

(5) What are the characteristics of the peer group leader?

References

Bowerman, Charles E., and John W. Kinch. "Changes in Family and Peer Orientation in Children between the Fourth and Tenth Grades." *Social Forces* 37 (1959): 206–11.

Brittain, Clay V. "Adolescent Choices and Parent–Peer Cross-Pressures." *American Sociological Review* 28 (1963): 385–91.

Bronfenbrenner, Urie. "Socialization and Social Class through Time and Space." *In Readings in Social Psychology*, eds. Eleanor E. Maccoby, Theodore M. Newcomb, and Eugene L. Hartley. New York: Holt, Rinehart, and Winston, 1958.

Bronfenbrenner, Urie. *Two Worlds of Childhood.* New York: Russell Sage Foundation, 1970.

Condry, John C., Jr.; Michael L. Simon; and Urie Bronfenbrenner. "Characteristics of Peer and Adult-Oriented Children." Unpublished manuscript. Ithaca, N. Y.: Department of Child Development, Cornell University, 1968.

Counts, George S. *Dare the Schools Build a New Social Order?* New York: John Day Co., 1936.

Glidewell, John C., Mildred B. Cantor, Louis M. Smith, and Lorene A. Stringer. "Socialization and Social Structure in the Classroom." In *Review of Child Development Research*, eds. Martin L. Hoffman and Lois W. Hoffman. Vol. 2. New York: Russell Sage Foundation, 1964.

Grambs, Jean D. "Forces Affecting American Education." In *To Nurture Humaneness: Commitment for the '70s.* 1970 Yearbook Washington, D. C.: Association for the Supervision of Curriculum Development, 1970.

Hanna, Lavonne. "An Education Imperative: Commitment to Change." In *To Nurture Humaneness: Commitment for the '70s.* 1970 Yearbook Washington, D. C.: Association for the Supervision of Curriculum Development, 1970.

Hechinger, Fred M. "Head Start to Where?" *Saturday Review,* 18 December 1965, pp. 58–59.

Hentoff, Nat. *Our Children Are Dying.* New York: Viking Press, 1966.

Holt, John. *How Children Fail.* New York: Pitman Publishing Co., 1964.

———. *How Children Learn.* New York: Pitman Publishing Co., 1967.

Johnson, Ronald C., and Medinnus, Gene R. *Child Psychology.* New York: John Wiley and Sons, 1965.

Kohl, Herbert. *The Open Classroom.* New York: Random House, 1969.

———. *36 Children.* New York: New American Library, 1967.

Kozol, Jonathan. *Death at an Early Age.* Boston: Houghton Mifflin Company, 1967.

Longstreth, Langdon. *Psychological Development of the Child.* New York: Ronald Press, 1968.

Postman, Neil, and Charles Weingartner. *Teaching as a Subversive Activity.* New York: Delacorte Press, 1969.

Redl, Fritz. "The Concept of a 'Therapeutic Milieu.' " *American Journal of Orthopsychiatry* 29 (October 1959): 721–736.

———. *When We Deal with Children.* New York: Free Press, 1966.

Rosenthal, Robert and Lenore Jacobson. *Pygmalion in the Classroom.* New York: Holt, Rinehart, and Winston, 1968.

Silberman, Charles E. *Crisis in the Classroom.* New York: Random House, 1970.

Taba, Hilda, and Deborah Elkins. *Teaching Strategies for the Culturally Disadvantaged.* Chicago: Rand McNally & Co., 1966.

Withey, Stephen B. "The Influence of the Peer Group on the Values of Youth." *Religious Education* 57 (1962): 34–44 (supplement).

Societal Influences

Human beings are born with a dual heritage—a biological inheritance transmitted through the genes and a cultural heritage into which they grow and which they must assimilate in order to become functioning persons. Culture is the customary ways of a people—their language, thoughts, perceptions, values, morals, and technology. It has been said that you can take a child away from his culture but that you cannot take the culture away from the child. The power of society is so pervasive that the child's personality is often referred to as the subjective side of culture. Ruth Benedict says that most people are shaped to the form of their culture because of the enormous malleability of their original endowment.*

Americans are now more than ever before aware that being black in America means economic and cultural deprivation that has eroded the self-concept of blacks. Only recently have blacks learned to substitute "black is beautiful" for "black is back." The black society has been forced to adopt a different concept of family. Since the early days of slavery, when black families were split up with little regard for the emotional consequences, the black family has been essentially a matriarchy. Until recently the black society has transmitted a curious admixture of values to its members—a desire to emulate the white middle-class society and its symbols, yet a reluctance to let go of a rich African heritage.

There is abundant evidence that the socioeconomic status of the family is one of the most important cultural influences on the family. Alfred Binet, who developed the widely used scale for measuring intelligence, once said that he would never again develop standard-

---

* Ruth Benedict. *Patterns of Culture*. New York: Mentor Books, 1948, p. 235.

ized measure that was not adjusted for the factor of socioeconomic status. Socioeconomic status has little to do with potential intelligence, but tests do not measure potential; they measure the experiences of the individual. In other words, a distinct social class bias is built into the typical IQ test, which discriminates in favor of those whose experience most nearly match the items included on the IQ test. Research substantiates the fact that most of these items reflect the values of white middle-class society.

The role of the father, the value system, the occupational and educational aspirations of the family members are determined by the home's socioeconomic status. The size of the family, the role of the mother, the attitudes towards child rearing, sexual practices, and husband–wife relationships are all tied closely to the economic status of the home, too.

In many ways the societies of the Chicano and the Puerto Rican have learned from the problems of blacks. The problem of how to build pride in a rich cultural tradition while one is an invisible man in American society is baffling. The Anti-Defamation League reports that the Chicano population in America has now taken the place blacks once occupied—here in this nation, yet unseen and unrecognized.

The multifaceted threads that entwine each developing child as he interacts in his society is appropriately called the tapestry of culture. It is this culture which teaches us what to expect from life, how to raise our children, and which values in society we must cherish or reject. The influence of the society which rears us casts an encompassing shadow over every facet of our lives. Without the pervasive influence of the society into which we are born it may indeed be said that life is without meaning.

Race

Although there are a wide variety of races in America, any discussion of race in this century focuses primarily on the black segment of America. The black child is almost always born into the lower social class and caste.* In 1968 28.8 percent of white males were in occupations designated as professional, technical, or managerial, whereas only 10.2 percent of nonwhite males were so classified (Corson 1970, p. 52). Rogers (1969, p. 410) says: "Black families, which constitute one in eleven within the country, generally conform to the classic picture of disorganization, inadequacy, and poverty." More than 60 percent of black children are born in slums, in cities, and to families where existence is in many ways marginal. It might be well at this juncture to heed the indictment of Alvin F. Poussaint,† associate dean and professor of psychiatry at Harvard University, that too often white textbooks obscure the definition of blacks because although the descriptions of blacks are in negative terms, they are disguised in academic jargon. Identification of the basic differences in the lifespace of white and black children needs to be made so that the student of child development will comprehend the unique social

---

* Class refers to socioeconomic status; caste refers to one's social status and mobility.

† In "Why Blacks Kill Blacks" (*Ebony*, October 1970, p. 143) Alvin F. Poussaint identifies what is probably the most potent debilitating force on the personality of the developing black child: "Black people don't *imagine* they are being persecuted by whites, they *are* being persecuted by whites."

milieu in which the black child develops and not confuse it with biological differences.*

From the rationale for the current emphasis on the development of black studies programs† one discovers that the black child does not develop an adequate black self-concept. Even at the age of four he knows he is racially different and he associates that difference with the black cultural stereotype.‡ In a racist society even the young black child understands the anti-Negro attitudes of the world around him. A child ashamed of his origins learns to fold his world around him and peek out very little. His progress as a human being is impeded even more by the tokenism of school systems, which erect pretty buildings and then put all the blacks together in an inferior academic atmosphere.¶ William Corson (1970) cites as an example an eighteen-year-old black who was valedictorian of his all-black, rural high school graduating class, yet he scored in the lowest 10th percentile on the equivalent of the Scholastic Aptitude Test and was shocked to learn that his segregated education had, in effect, not given him the academic skills of his white peers.

The black child is a part of the fabric of what has been termed a "relative deprivation theory" (Pettigrew 1964). Indeed, Pettigrew says: "The past three decades of Negro American history constitute an almost classic case for relative deprivation theory" (1969). The theory maintains that as the dominant group advances subordinate groups do too, but at a level and pace not only slower than that of the dominant group but also too slow for the aspirational level of the subordinate group. That is: (a) although the past few decades have seen accelerated gains in Negro opportunity, gains have not kept pace with the gains of white America; (b) Negro aspirations have risen, especially since 1954; (c) educated Negro youths have gained a status inconsistent with their education because their employment status level is below their educational level; and (d) in a country known as the richest in the world, the Negro has a rather formidable referent against which to judge his status. To all of this add an unpopular war, and the racial crisis of the sixties is

---

* Arthur Jensen's critique of Negro intelligence, ("How Much Can We Boost I.Q. and Scholastic Achievement?" *Harvard Educational Review* 39, No. 1 [Winter 1969], pp. 1–123) is nearly the only such piece in recent scientific literature. In the Spring 1969 (pp. 273–347) issue of the *Harvard Educational Review* Carl Bereiter, Lee Cronbach, Lester Crow, David Elkind, and J. McIver Hunt discuss "Jensenism" and in the Summer 1969 issue Jensen replies to the discussion. William R. Corson attacks Jensen in a blistering footnote on page 44 of *Promise or Peril* New York: W. W. Norton & Company, Inc. (1970).

† A summary of progress and problems in this area of study is found in Clemmont E. Vontress' article, "Black Studies—Boon or Bane?" (*Journal of Negro Education* 39, No. 3 [Summer 1970], pp. 192–201).

‡ Eugene D. Genovese's "Black Studies: Trouble Ahead" (*The Atlantic*, June 1969, pp. 37–41) documents this fact.

¶ William Corson, a teacher at Howard University, claims that black schools are "about on the level of Romper Room."

not difficult to comprehend. The Negro child has since the slavocracy of his forebearers been reared in an atmosphere of disillusionment. So disillusioning has been the relative deprivation in an era of calls for integration that the American Negro has given up any hope of integration and now calls for "separatist goals" (Pettigrew 1969).

The mother and family have been called the "hidden curriculum" of all children. Because the Negro mother passes onto her child her own feelings of futility (a sense of powerlessness), he must cope with this additional negative factor. There is little correlation between this feeling of futility and the educational achievements of Negro children in the early elementary school years, but Diana Slaughter's study (1970) indicates that futility feelings become a significant deterrent to the continuing of academic achievement.

A review of recent literature concerning the problem of growing up black in white America leaves one with the feeling that growing up despised and hated is the usual lot for the vast majority of black children. Most horrendous are the data that indicate that black youth adopt white negative, deprecatory stereotypes about blacks (Bayton et al. 1965; Calnek 1970). It is shattering to realize that Negro youth are "educated" by white mass media to "see other blacks as having less productivity and less energy and vitality than whites, as being less serious minded, more happy-go-lucky and as having less restraint" (Calnek 1970). The effects of self-fulfilling prophecy are awesome. The Communist technique of brainwashing is reviled by Americans, yet the black race in America is subjected to similar techniques throughout their entire lives.

"They b-beat m-me," I gasped. "They t-t-took the m-money."

"You just stay right where you are," she said in a deadly tone. "I'm going to teach you this night to stand up and fight for yourself."

Black Boy

by Richard Wright

Hunger stole upon me so slowly that at first I was not aware of what hunger really meant. Hunger had always been more or less at my elbow when I played, but now I began to wake up at night to find hunger standing at my bedside, staring at me gauntly. The hunger I had known before this had been no grim, hostile stranger; it had been a normal hunger that had made me beg constantly for bread, and when I ate a crust or two I was satisfied. But this new hunger baffled me, scared me, made me angry and insistent. Whenever I begged for food now my mother would pour me a cup of tea which would still the clamor in my stomach for a moment or two; but a little later I would feel hunger nudging my ribs, twisting my empty guts until they ached. I would grow dizzy and my vision would dim. I became less active in my play, and for the first time in my life I had to pause and think of what was happening to me.

"Mama, I'm hungry," I complained one afternoon. "Jump up and catch a kungry," she said, trying to make me laugh and forget.

"What's a kungry?"

"It's what little boys eat when they get hungry," she said.

"What does it taste like?"

"I don't know."

"Then why do you tell me to catch one?"

"Because you said that you were hungry," she said, smiling.

I sensed that she was teasing me and it made me angry.

"But I'm hungry. I want to eat."

"You'll have to wait."

"But I want to eat now."

"But there's nothing to eat," she told me.

"Why?"

"Just because there's none," she explained.

"But I want to eat," I said, beginning to cry.

"You'll just have to wait," she said again.

"But why?"

"For God to send some food."

"When is He going to send it?"

"I don't know."

"But I'm hungry!"

She was ironing and she paused and looked at me with tears in her eyes.

"Where's your father?" she asked me.

I stared in bewilderment. Yes, it was true that my father had not come home to sleep for many days now and I could make as much noise as I wanted. Though I had not known why he was absent, I had been glad that he was not there to shout his restrictions at me. But it had never occurred to me that his absence would mean that there would be no food.

"I don't know," I said.

"Who brings food into the house?" my mother asked me.

"Papa," I said, "he always brought food."

"Well, your father isn't here now," she said.

"Where is he?"

"I don't know," she said.

"But I'm hungry," I whimpered, stomping my feet.

"You'll have to wait until I get a job and buy food," she said.

As the days slid past the image of my father became associated with my pangs of hunger, and whenever I felt hunger I thought of him with a deep biological bitterness.

My mother finally went to work as a cook and left me and my brother alone in the flat each day with a loaf of bread and a pot of tea. When she returned at evening she would be tired and dispirited and would cry a lot. Sometimes, when she was in despair, she would call us to her and talk to us for hours, telling us that now we had no father, that our lives would be different from those of other children, that we must learn as soon as possible to take care of ourselves, to dress ourselves, to prepare our own food; that we must take upon ourselves the responsibility of the flat while she worked. Half frightened, we would promise solemnly. We did not understand what had happened between our father and our mother and the most that these long talks did to us was to make us feel a vague dread. Whenever we asked why father had left, she would tell us that we were too young to know.

One evening my mother told me that thereafter I would have to do the shopping for food. She took me to the corner store to show me the way. I was proud; I felt like a grownup. The next afternoon I looped the basket over my arm and went down the pavement toward the store. When I reached the corner, a gang of boys grabbed me, knocked me down, snatched the basket, took the money, and sent me running home in panic. That evening I told my mother what had happened, but she made no comment; she sat down at once, wrote another note, gave me more money, and sent me out to the grocery again. I crept down the steps and saw the same gang of boys playing down the street. I ran back into the house.

"What's the matter?" my mother asked.

"It's those same boys," I said. "They'll beat me."

"You've got to get over that," she said. "Now, go on."

"I'm scared," I said.

"Go on and don't pay any attention to them," she said.

I went out of the door and walked briskly down the sidewalk, praying that the gang would not molest me. But when I came abreast of them someone shouted.

"There he is!"

They came toward me and I broke into a wild run toward home. They overtook me and flung me to the pavement. I yelled, pleaded, kicked, but they wrenched the money out of my hand. They yanked me to my feet, gave me a few slaps, and sent me home sobbing. My mother met me at the door.

"They b-beat m-me," I gasped. "They t-t-took the m-money."

I started up the steps, seeking the shelter of the house.

"Don't you come in here," my mother warned me.

I froze in my tracks and stared at her.

"But they're coming after me," I said.

"You just stay right where you are," she said in a deadly tone. "I'm going to teach you this night to stand up and fight for yourself."

She went into the house and I waited, terrified, wondering what she was about. Presently she returned with more money and another note; she also had a long heavy stick.

"Take this money, this note, and this stick," she said. "Go to the store and buy those groceries. If those boys bother you, then fight.

I was baffled. My mother was telling me to fight, a thing that she had never done before.

"But I'm scared," I said.

"Don't you come into this house until you've gotten those groceries," she said.

"They'll beat me; they'll beat me," I said.

"Then stay in the streets; don't come back here!"

I ran up the steps and tried to force my way past her into the house. A stinging slap came on my jaw. I stood on the sidewalk, crying.

"Please, let me wait until tomorrow," I begged.

"No," she said. "Go now! If you come back into this house without those groceries, I'll whip you!"

She slammed the door and I heard the key turn in the lock. I shook with fright. I was alone upon the dark, hostile streets and gangs were after me. I had the choice of being beaten at home or away from home. I clutched the stick, crying, trying to reason. If I were beaten at home, there was absolutely nothing that I could do about it; but if I were beaten in the streets, I had a chance to fight and defend myself. I walked slowly down the sidewalk, coming closer to the gang of boys, holding the stick tightly. I was so full of fear that I could scarcely breathe. I was almost upon them now.

"There he is again!" the cry went up.

They surrounded me quickly and began to grab for my hand.

"I'll kill you!" I threatened.

They closed in. In blind fear I let the stick fly, feeling it crack against a boy's skull. I swung again, lamming another skull, then another. Realizing that they would retaliate if I let up for but a second, I fought to lay them low, to knock them cold, to kill them so that they could not strike back at me. I flayed with tears in my eyes, teeth clenched, stark fear making me throw every ounce of my strength behind each blow. I hit again and again, dropping the money and the grocery list. The boys scattered, yelling, nursing their heads, staring at me in utter disbelief. They had never seen such frenzy. I stood panting, egging them on, taunting them to come on and fight. When they refused, I ran after them and they tore out for their homes, screaming. The parents of the boys rushed into the streets and threatened me, and for the first time in my life, I shouted at grown-ups, telling them that I would give them the same if they bothered me. I finally found my grocery list and the money and went to the store. On my way back I kept my stick poised for instant use, but there was not a single boy in sight. That night I won the right to the streets of Memphis.

Discussion

This incident was taken from Richard Wright's autobiographical novel, *Black Boy,* which was one of the first of the searing works of black authors to confront white America with an indictment of racism practiced north and south, overtly and by "gentleman's agreement." Many experiences unique to the black child in an urban ghetto are reflected in this selection. Many emotions are depicted—love, despair, anger, and the pain of hunger—but the emotion of fear seems to be the most pervasive. The ghetto child has the very real fear of the streets, which threaten danger and sometimes violence, the generalized psychological fear of defeat and failure, which keeps the child in a perpetual state of anxiety.

Among the many depressing aspects of growing up in a ghetto is the almost complete lack of any kind of cushion to soften the blows of deprivation. Richard must subsist on the small amount of energy his mother has left for him after she is finished with her work. Matriarchy is a way of life in many black families. William Grier and Price Cobbs discuss the black mother's role in their book *Black Rage* (1968). They say that the black mother must perform two tasks—the usual child-rearing tasks as well as the interpretation of society—so that she can help shape her children's characters so they can meet the world as she knows it. In this latter context she must teach the message, "the white world is dangerous . . . if he (the child) does not understand its rules it may kill him" (p.51). The boy's mother is a sharply contradictory person to her children. She is permissive and loving, yet punitive and rigid. Her harshness is understandable in the context of the black ghetto.

Springboards for Inquiry

(1) What does this mother reveal to her children besides harshness?

(2) If you were the boy in this selection and able to articulate your feelings, how would you describe them throughout this episode?

(3) What kind of personality characteristics do you think this boy will exhibit as a result of his environmental experiences?

(4) Suggest another way that this mother could have dealt with the situation and project the consequences.

(5) What qualities are needed to deal with the kind of peer aggression that is found in overcrowded ghetto communities?

(6) Although the editors of this volume chose *Black Boy* to illustrate the problem of race, choose three other categories to which *Black Boy* would be relevant and justify your choices.

"Damn, if niggers ain't getting smarter."

The Boy Who Painted Christ Black

by John Henrik Clarke

He was the smartest boy in the Muskogee County School—for colored children. Everybody even remotely connected with the school knew this. The teacher always pronounced his name with profound gusto as she pointed him out as the ideal student. Once I heard her say: "If he were white he might, some day, become President." Only Aaron Crawford wasn't white; quite the contrary. His skin was so solid black that it glowed, reflecting an inner virtue that was strange, and beyond my comprehension.

In many ways he looked like something that was awkwardly put together. Both his nose and his lips seemed a trifle too large for his face. To say he was ugly would be unjust and to say he was handsome would be gross exaggeration. Truthfully, I could never make up my mind about him. Sometimes he looked like something out of a book of ancient history . . . looked as if he was left over from that magnificent era before the machine age came and marred the earth's natural beauty.

His great variety of talent often startled the teachers. This caused his classmates to look upon him with a mixed feeling of awe and envy.

Before Thanksgiving, he always drew turkeys and pumpkins on the blackboard. On George Washington's birthday, he drew large American flags surrounded by little hatchets. It was these small masterpieces that made him the most talked-about colored boy in Columbus, Georgia. The Negro principal of the Muskogee County School said he would some day be a great painter, like Henry O. Tanner.

For the teacher's birthday, which fell on a day about a week before

---

commencement, Aaron Crawford painted the picture that caused an uproar, and a turning point, at the Muskogee County School. The moment he entered the room that morning, all eyes fell on him. Besides his torn book holder, he was carrying a large-framed concern wrapped in old newspapers. As he went to his seat, the teacher's eyes followed his every motion, a curious wonderment mirrored in them conflicting with the half-smile that wreathed her face.

Aaron put his books down, then smiling broadly, advanced toward the teacher's desk. His alert eyes were so bright with joy that they were almost frightening. The children were leaning forward in their seats, staring greedily at him; a restless anticipation was rampant within every breast.

Already the teacher sensed that Aaron had a present for her. Still smiling, he placed it on her desk and began to help her unwrap it. As the last piece of paper fell from the large frame, the teacher jerked her hand away from it suddenly, her eyes flickering unbelievingly. Amidst the rigid tension, her heavy breathing was distinct and frightening. Temporarily, there was no other sound in the room.

Aaron stared questioningly at her and she moved her hand back to the present cautiously, as if it were a living thing with vicious characteristics. I am sure it was the one thing she least expected.

With a quick, involuntary movement I rose up from my desk. A series of submerged murmurs spread through the room, rising to a distinct monotone. The teacher turned toward the children, staring reproachfully. They did not move their eyes from the present that Aaron had brought her. . . . It was a large picture of Christ—painted black!

Aaron Crawford went back to his seat, a feeling of triumph reflecting in his every movement.

The teacher faced us. Her curious half-smile had blurred into a mild bewilderment. She searched the bright faces before her and started to smile again, occasionally stealing quick glances at the large picture propped on her desk, as though doing so were forbidden amusement.

"Aaron," she spoke at last, a slight tinge of uncertainty in her tone, "this is a most welcome present. Thanks. I will treasure it." She paused, then went on speaking, a trifle more coherent than before. "Looks like you are going to be quite an artist. . . . Suppose you come forward and tell the class how you came to paint this remarkable picture."

When he rose to speak, to explain about the picture, a hush fell tightly over the room, and the children gave him all of their attention . . . something they rarely did for the teacher. He did not speak at first; he just stood there in front of the room, toying absently with his hands, observing his audience carefully, like a great concert artist.

"It was like this," he said, placing full emphasis on every word. "You see, my uncle who lives in New York teaches classes in Negro History at the Y.M.C.A. When he visited us last year he was telling me about the many great black folks who have made history. He said black folks were once the most powerful people on earth. When I asked him about Christ, he said no one ever proved whether he was black or white. Somehow a feeling came over me that he was a black man, 'cause he was so kind and forgiving, kinder than I have ever seen white people be. So, when I painted his picture I couldn't help but paint it as I thought it was."

After this, the little artist sat down, smiling broadly, as if he had gained entrance to a great storehouse of knowledge that ordinary people could neither acquire nor comprehend.

The teacher, knowing nothing else to do under prevailing circumstances, invited the children to rise from their seats and come forward so they could get a complete view of Aaron's unique piece of art.

When I came close to the picture, I noticed it was painted with the kind of paint you get in the five and ten cent stores. Its shape was blurred slightly, as if someone had jarred the frame before the paint had time to dry. The eyes of Christ were deep-set and sad, very much like those of Aaron's father, who was a deacon in the local Baptist Church. This picture of Christ looked much different from the one I saw hanging on the wall when I was in Sunday School. It looked more like a helpless Negro, pleading silently for mercy.

For the next few days, there was much talk about Aaron's picture.

The school term ended the following week and Aaron's picture, along with the best handwork done by the students that year, was on display in the assembly room. Naturally, Aaron's picture graced the place of honor.

There was no book work to be done on commencement day and joy was rampant among the children. The girls in their brightly colored dresses gave the school the delightful air of Spring awakening.

In the middle of the day all the children were gathered in the small assembly. On this day we were always favored with a visit from a man whom all the teachers spoke of with mixed esteem and fear. Professor Danual, they called him, and they always pronounced his name with reverence. He was supervisor of all the city schools, including those small and poorly equipped ones set aside for colored children.

The great man arrived almost at the end of our commencement exercises. On seeing him enter the hall, the children rose, bowed courteously, and sat down again, their eyes examining him as if he were a circus freak.

He was a tall white man with solid gray hair that made his lean face seem paler than it actually was. His eyes were the clearest blue I have ever seen. They were the only life-like things about him.

As he made his way to the front of the room the Negro principal, George Du Vaul, was walking ahead of him, cautiously preventing anything from getting in his way. As he passed me, I heard the teachers, frightened, sucking in their breath, felt the tension tightening.

A large chair was in the center of the rostrum. It had been daintily polished and the janitor had laboriously recushioned its bottom. The supervisor went straight to it without being guided, knowing that this pretty splendor was reserved for him.

Presently the Negro principal introduced the distinguished guest and he favored us with a short speech. It wasn't a very important speech. Almost at the end of it, I remember him saying something about he wouldn't be surprised if one of us boys grew up to be a great colored man, like Booker T. Washington.

After he sat down, the school chorus sang two spirituals and the girls in the fourth grade did an Indian folk dance. This brought the commencement program to an end.

After this the supervisor came down from the rostrum, his eyes tinged with curiosity, and began to view the array of handwork on display in front of the chapel.

Suddenly his face underwent a strange rejuvenation. His clear blue eyes flickered in astonishment. He was looking at Aaron Crawford's picture of Christ. Mechanically he moved his stooped form closer to the picture and stood gazing fixedly at it, curious and undecided, as though it were a dangerous animal that would rise any moment and spread destruction.

We waited tensely for his next movement. The silence was almost suffocating. At last he twisted himself around and began to search the grim faces before him. The fiery glitter of his eyes abated slightly as they rested on the Negro principal, protestingly.

"Who painted this sacrilegious nonsense?" he demanded sharply.

"I painted it, sir." These were Aaron's words, spoken hesitantly. He wetted his lips timidly and looked up at the supervisor, his eyes voicing a sad plea for understanding.

He spoke again, this time more coherently. "Th' principal said a colored person have jes as much right paintin' Jesus black as a white person have paintin' him white. And he says. . . ." At this point he halted abruptly, as if to search for his next words. A strong tinge of bewilderment dimmed the glow of his solid black face. He stammered out a few more words, then stopped again.

The supervisor strode a few steps toward him. At last color had swelled some of the lifelessness out of his lean face.

"Well, go on!" he said, enragedly, ". . . I'm still listening."

Aaron moved his lips pathetically but no words passed them. His eyes wandered around the room, resting finally, with an air of hope, on the face of the Negro principal. After a moment, he jerked his face in another direction, regretfully, as if something he had said had betrayed an understanding between him and the principal.

Presently the principal stepped forward to defend the school's prize student.

"I encouraged the boy in painting that picture," he said firmly. "And it was with my permission that he brought the picture into this school. I don't think the boy is so far wrong in painting Christ black. The artists of all other races have painted whatsoever God they worship to resemble themselves. I see no reason why we should be immune from that privilege. After all, Christ was born in that part of the world that had always been predominantly populated by colored people. There is a strong possibility that he could have been a Negro."

But for the monotonous lull of heavy breathing, I would have sworn that his words had frozen everyone in the hall. I had never heard the little principal speak so boldly to anyone, black or white.

The supervisor swallowed dumbfoundedly. His face was aglow in silent rage.

"Have you been teaching these children things like that?" he asked the Negro principal, sternly.

"I have been teaching them that their race has produced great kings and queens as well as slaves and serfs," the principal said. "The time is long overdue when we should let the world know that we erected and enjoyed the benefits of a splendid civilization long before the people of Europe had a written language."

The supervisor coughed. His eyes bulged menacingly as he spoke. "You are not being paid to teach such things in this school, and I am demanding your resignation for overstepping your limit as principal."

George Du Vaul did not speak. A strong quiver swept over his sullen face. He revolved himself slowly and walked out of the room towards his office.

The supervisor's eyes followed him until he was out of focus. Then he murmured under his breath: "There'll be a lot of fuss in this world if you start people thinking that Christ was a nigger."

Some of the teachers followed the principal out of the chapel, leaving the crestfallen children restless and in a quandary about what to do next. Finally we started back to our rooms. The supervisor was behind me. I heard him murmur to himself: "Damn, if niggers ain't getting smarter."

A few days later I heard that the principal had accepted a summer job as art instructor of a small high school somewhere in south Georgia and had gotten permission from Aaron's parents to take him along so he could continue to encourage him in his painting.

I was on my way home when I saw him leaving his office. He was carrying a large briefcase and some books tucked under his arm. He had already said good-by to all the teachers. And strangely, he did not look brokenhearted. As he headed for the large front door, he readjusted his horn-rimmed glasses, but did not look back. An air of triumph gave more dignity to his soldierly stride. He had the appearance of a man who had done a great thing, something greater than any ordinary man would do.

Aaron Crawford was waiting outside for him. They walked down the street together. He put his arms around Aaron's shoulder affectionately. He was talking sincerely to Aaron about something, and Aaron was listening, deeply earnest.

I watched them until they were so far down the street that their forms had begun to blur. Even from this distance I could see they were still walking in brisk, dignified strides, like two people who had won some sort of victory.

Discussion

The moral victory of the principal and his prize student is significant for each child and teacher in Muskogee County School. They unfortunately are losing a leader of courage and character, but George Du Vaul leaves behind an outstanding example of allegiance and pride in his heritage.

We know that children interpret experience cognitively (with the intellect) as well as affectively (with the emotions). Religious learning in particular encompasses an emotional dimension. We can say that Aaron's "knowing" of Christ reflects the feeling dimension of himself. Therefore, his inclination to paint Christ black attests to Aaron's good feelings about himself. In a predominantly white, separatist society the tendency to associate white with positive attributes is prevalent even among the Negro population. No doubt the support and encouragement of the principal has helped Aaron to build self-esteem.

Self-esteem is the forerunner of self-confidence, an attribute that will help Aaron actualize his gifts as he grows into adulthood. A secure and confident adult can act with courage and moral integrity, thus making a contribution to the security and happiness of others. We feel that Aaron is on his way to contributing to racial pride and to society.

Springboards for Inquiry

(1) What is the nature of Aaron Crawford's self concept that gives him the courage to defend his right to paint Christ Black?

(2) How can we create the climate in the agencies where we work that will help members of a minority group develop a positive self image?

(3) Sociologists and psychologists replied to Arthur Jensen's research study * that suggested a hereditary factor to account for lowered IQ's among black children. Refer to some of the critiques of Jensen's work and summarize some of their counter-arguments.

(4) How segregated is your community in regard to real estate patterns? How do real estate patterns result in school boundaries and consequently effect children in school?

(5) James S. Coleman was the senior author of a report † which dealt in part with programs for the disadvantages and their long term effects. What are some of the observations regarding school integration and achievement that were made in this report?

---

* Jensen, Arthur. "How Much Can We Boost IQ and Scholastic Achievement?" Harvard Educational Review Vol. 29, No. 1. Winter 1969.

† Coleman, James S. *et al.*, *Equality of Educational Opportunity*, Washington, D.C.: U.S. Gov't Printing Office, 1966.

Socioeconomic Status

In egalitarian America it is unfashionable, even undemocratic to suggest that society is in any sense stratified. Yet, expressions such as "the better part of town" and "snob hill" indicate that there are differences in American society that are characterized by the ways people learn to dress, talk, and spend leisure time in the respective socioeconomic groups in which they are reared. Allison Davis says that "in spite of certain universal similarities (in moral sanctions, language, familial structure, dress, and technical adaptations) which appear in our society, the social conditions under which persons have access to fundamental biological and social goals are differentiated in many respects by a system of privilege" (1961, p. 4). Others see the concept of social class (used interchangeably with socioeconomic status) as a device to summarize "the real differences between people in income, occupation, education, and related characteristics" (Gans 1962, p. 242).

Inherent in these definitions are the ideas that we are a stratified society; that socioeconomic status accords privilege; and that income, occupation, and education are highly related to social class status. Gans (1962, p. 243) rejects in part the criteria of income, occupation, and education as being merely "easily researchable indices" and substitutes the word *subcultures* for *stratified society.* Warner et al. (1949) identify six social classes in America and Gans identifies four subcultures. The four subcultures identified by Gans are the working class, the lower class, the middle class, and the professional upper middle class.

The literature that describes the variegated social systems associated with socioeconomic status is voluminous. In the last two decades the significant variable of social class status has been considered in relation to every facet of human existence. Indeed, the student of sociology, child development, and education is likely to be deceived about the children with whom he works because of this labeling attempt. Robert Fisher (1961) warns: "The argument here is not so much with the use of social class constructs in helping teachers to accept relevant differences. The real trouble comes with the realization that some teachers are swallowing whole the categories describing social class differences. This may well be doing more to place barriers in the way of better human relations than it does to overcome misconceptions."

We have identified the reality of social class in America and have indicated that membership in a social class is characterized by behavior such as speech and the way leisure time is spent, but there is great danger in assuming that one can predict the behavior of any given individual according to his social status. The San Francisco experiment* substantiates the idea that children live up to the expectations others have for them.

Studies do show that there are many identifiable correlates between social class and human behavior. In 1946 Allison Davis and Havighurst reported that more lower-class and middle-class babies are breast fed than upper-class babies; that demand feeding is more prevalent in the lower class; that lower-class children are weaned and toilet trained later; and that lower-class children stay up later, stay in the streets later, and go to the movies more often.** Mary Egan (1969) goes back even further than infancy and asserts that the fetuses and infants of mothers from lower-class backgrounds are smaller and less viable than those from the higher classes.

Gans (1962, pp. 244–45) states that "perhaps the most important—or at least the most visible—difference between the classes is one of family structure." He maintains that the way of life of lower-class people is one that revolves around relatives because outside the family circle the world is hostile.† The failure of western education with the lower social classes may be related to their rejection of the idea that schooling should be used to separate one from his familial constellation while emphasizing personal growth. The lower-class family tends to be people-oriented whereas the middle-class culture is object-oriented. Gans speculates that low-cost housing, public libraries, the community center movement, and public and adult education programs fail to "enrich" culturally deprived persons because these things hold little attraction for lower-class people who are people-oriented. Lower-class children value toughness, aggression, and excitement more than middle-class children do (McCreary 1966). A common complaint from middle-class teachers is that lower-class children have less regard for property

---

* This refers to the work of Robert Rosenthal and Lenore Jacobson cited in the section on School Influences—The Teacher. Their study is *Pygmalion in the Classroom*. New York: Holt, Rinehart, and Winston, 1968.

** There is evidence, too, that lower-class children watch more television.

† Gans' volume *The Urban Villagers* is a study of group and class in the life of Italian-Americans. Extrapolation from this group to other groups who are defined as lower social class may be valid and should be considered.

rights (school vandalism is rampant in slum areas), police and school authority, and community responsibility (Strom 1965).*

Joseph Kahl (1967) discusses social class in relation to values and says that one way of thinking about value orientations is to realize that they represent a well-set response to the kind of historical situation in which a group finds itself. In other words, values are shared by an entire social class group because a great deal of common experience has tested the appropriateness of those values. Kahl in fact assigns a specific life-value orientation to each of five identifiable social class groups. His implication is that those within the group share goals and, of course, transmit them to their children. Kahl's designations in the social stratification of America are instructive, disheartening, and probably quite valid.

Kahl calls the upper class those who value gracious living. Their wealth and power are hereditary and they value tradition, lineage, conservatism, and the skills of gracious living. The upper-middle class values a career. Their way of life, their feelings of accomplishment and respectability hinge on the success of a career. The lower-middle class, because they will never make a big career and because their jobs go nowhere, tend to emphasize the respectability of their way of life. They are careful about their homes and furniture and in general they value things very much. The working class, on the other hand, have as their basic orientation "getting by." Once the semiskilled worker realizes he is at the end of his occupational road (and this happens in his late teens) he leaves the world for television and fishing and is content to get by. Lastly, there are the lower-class people, who feel a genuine sense of futility and hopelessness. Kahl attaches the term *apathy* to their value orientation. They are often out of work, unskilled, and unloved. Life is grim, joyless. While nearly everyone else seems to go up, these people are always down.

The children who come to schools, hospitals, and other public agencies represent these five subcultures. They come to these agencies with the values of their culture tagging behind them.

---

* The following works are indispensable reading on this complex problem: William Lloyd Warner, Robert J. Havighurst, and Martin B. Loeb, *Who Shall Be Educated?* (New York: Harper & Row, Publishers, Inc., 1944); August B. Hollingshead, *Elmtown's Youth* (New York: John Wiley and Sons, Inc., 1949); Robert S. Lynd and Helen M. Lynd, *Middletown* (New York: Harcourt Brace Jovanovich, Inc., 1929) and *Middletown in Transition* (New York: Harcourt Brace Jovanovich, Inc., 1937).

"Nancy eats good, don't she, Mom?" Darlene said.

"I never had catsup before, said Fiona. "My, it certainly is delicious, isn't it?"

Nancy *by Elizabeth Enright*

Fiona Farmer was seven years old. Her mother was forty-six, her father was fifty-five, her nurse was sixty-one, and her grandmother and grandfather, with whom they were all spending the summer, had reached such altitudes of age that no one remembered what they were. From these great heights Fiona was loved and directed.

She wore her hair as her mother had worn it in 1914, braided tight and tied back in pretzel loops with big stiff ribbons. In winter she was the only girl at school to wear a flannel petticoat and underwear with sleeves. Her mother read her all the books she had loved in her childhood; *Rebecca of Sunnybrook Farm,* and *The Five Little Peppers,* and *Under the Lilacs*. Her grandmother read her the books *she* had loved as a child: Mace's *Fairy Tales,* and *Grimm's Fairy Tales,* and *The Princess and Curdie*. On this mixed diet of decorum and brutality Fiona was rapidly turning into a "quaint little creature." She was a pensive child with large attentive eyes and rather elderly manners; all her play was quiet, accompanied at times by nothing noisier than a low continuous murmuring, so it was strange that the ranks of dolls on her nursery shelves were scalped, and eyeless, like the victims of a Sioux massacre.

"What on earth does she do to them?" her mother said to Nana, the nurse. "Why, when I was little my dollies were really like babies to me. I took such *care* of them, I *loved* them so. . . ."

"I honestly don't know, Mrs. Farmer," Nana said. "She'll be as quiet as a mouse in here for hours at a time, and then I'll come in and

---

find all this—this destruction! It seems so unlike her!"

Fiona's grandmother reproached her quietly. "How would you like it if your dear mother pulled all your hair out of your head and broke your arms and legs? Your dolls are your little responsibilities, your *children* in a way. . . ."

Her admonishments though frequent were always mild. When Fiona scratched her head, or picked her nose, she would say: "That's not very pretty, dear, is it? We don't do those things, do we?" . . . She was a lofty, dignified, conventional lady, and she smelled like an old dictionary among whose pages many flowers have been dried and pressed. She taught Fiona how to make a sachet and a pomander ball and play parcheesi.

Fiona liked her grandfather the best. He was a man of wonderful patience and politeness; deaf as a post. Every morning she followed him out to the vegetable garden where, in his old loose button-down-the-front sweater and his white canvas golf hat that sagged in a ruffle around his head, he worked along the rows of beets and cabbages with his hoe and rake. Fiona followed at his heels, speaking ceaselessly; it did not matter to her that he never heard a word she said, she told him everything. Now and then he would stop, resting on his hoe handle, and look down at her appreciatively. "Well," he would say. "You're a pleasant little companion, aren't you?" Then he would reach out his old parched hand (he was so old that he never sweated any more) and give her a brittle tap or two on the shoulder or head, and he and Fiona would smile at each other out of a mutual feeling of benevolence.

Sooner or later, though, Nana's voice would begin to caw: "Fee-ona! Fee-ona!" and she would have to go back to the house to pick up her toys or change her dress or eat a meal, or some other dull thing.

Her grandparents' house was big and cool inside. All the rooms were full of greenish light reflected from the maple trees outdoors; the floors were dark and gleaming, the carpets had been taken up for the summer and the furniture had linen dresses on. There was no dust anywhere, not even in the corners of the empty fireplaces, for Cora and Mary, the maids who had been there for thirty years, spent their lives seeing that there was not.

Cora had arthritis, and on Sundays when Fiona had noon dinner with the whole family she marveled at the extreme slowness with which the maid moved about the table, like a running-down toy. Her face looked very still and concentrated then, relaxing only when she served Fiona, whispering: "Eat it all up now, dear, every bit, so I can tell Mary."

Oh food! People were always speaking of food to Fiona; the Sunday dinners were a trial to toil through. "Eat it all up, dear," and "Clean your plate" were phrases that were ugly in her ears.

After Sunday dinner everyone went to sleep for a while and the house droned with different pitches of snoring. Wearing nothing but a pink wrapper Fiona would lie on the big white bed while Nana sat in an armchair by the window rattling the Sunday paper. Out of doors the cicadas sounded hot as drills; the lazy air coming in the window brought a smell of grass, and Fiona wished that Nana would fall asleep so that she could get up and find something to play with, but Nana would not fall asleep.

But once she did.

Once on Sunday after the usual slow massive dinner, as Fiona lay in the extremity of boredom counting mosquito bites and listening to herself yawn, she heard another sound; a new one that might promise much. Quietly she raised herself to her elbows, hardly daring to believe, and saw that the impossible had happened at last. Nana lay in the armchair, abandoned, with her head thrown back and her hair coming down and her mouth wide open like that of a fish; a faint guttural sound came out of it each time she breathed.

A great light seemed to flood the room, and a voice from on high addressed Fiona: "Get up and dress, but do not put on your shoes. Carry them in your hand till you get outside, and close the front door quietly behind you."

Fiona got up at once, dressed with the silence and speed of light, and departed. The upstairs hall hummed and trumpeted with the noises of sleeping, no one heard her running down the stairs.

Out of doors it was bright and hot; she sat on the front step and put on her sandals with her heart galloping in her chest. Though old, the members of her family were tall, their legs were long as ladders, and if they came after her they would surely catch her. Leaving the sandal straps unbuckled Fiona ran out of the gate and down the street, terrified and exhilarated. She ran till she was giddy and breathless, but when at last she stopped and looked behind her the street on which she found herself was still and empty; steeped in Sunday.

She walked for a long time. Her heart stopped racing and her breathing became comfortable again. Her fear, too, gave way to pleasure and pride. It was a beautiful afternoon. The street was very high with elms. The light that came through their roof of leaves was green and trembling like light through water. Fiona became a little crab crawling among the roots of seaweed. The parked cars were fishes which would eat her up, danger was everywhere. . . . She walked sideways, made claws out of her thumbs, hid behind trees, and felt that her eyes grew out on stems. But not for long. Suddenly, as sometimes happened, the fancy collapsed, betrayed her completely. There was no danger; the cars were cars only. Nothing was any better than real; in the end somebody would catch her and take her home or she would return of her own accord, driven by hunger or conscience, and everything would be as it had always been.

The houses sat back from their green laps of lawn, silent and substantial, regarding her like people wearing glasses. There was a smell of privet and hot asphalt in the still air; a boring smell. . . . Intolerable boredom amounting to anguish drove Fiona to turn abruptly and kick the iron palings of a fence that she was passing; a kick that hurt right through her shoe.

The big street came to an end finally at a small Civil War monument and branched out beyond it in three roads. She chose the right-hand one because there was a dog asleep on the sidewalk there, but when she got to him she saw the flies strolling up and down his face and he looked up at her balefully with a low ripple of sound in his throat and she hurried on.

This street had few trees; it was broader, and the houses, while farther apart, were shabbier. The afternoon sun was in her eyes, drawing her along the gilded road. The wind had sprung up, too, warm and lively, blowing from the west.

On the outskirts of the town she came upon her destination, though at first she did not realize it. For some time the wind had been bringing her great blasts of radio music; and she saw now that these had their source in a gray frame house that fairly trembled with melody. Though not small, this was the seediest of all the houses. It stood in the middle of a yard as full of tall grass as a field. There were paths through the field and bald patches where people had stamped and trampled, and many souvenirs abandoned and half grown over: a rusted little wagon with no wheels, somebody's shoe, an old tire . . .

The house had a queer shape, fancy, but with everything coming off or breaking. Some of the shutters hung by one hinge only; the cupola on top was crooked and so was the porch from which half the palings were gone. The fence, too, had lost many of its pickets and stood propped against the tangle like a large comb with teeth missing; but it had kept its gate and hanging onto this and swinging slowly back and forth were three little girls. Fiona walked more slowly.

One of the girls had a bandanna tied tightly around her head but the other two regarded her from under untrimmed dusty bangs, like animals peering out from under ferns. The gate gave a long snarl of sound as they pushed it forward.

"Where are you going?" said the tallest one.

Fiona could not be sure of the tone of this question: was it a friendly or a hostile challenge? She moved still more slowly touching each picket with her forefinger.

"No place," she said guardedly.

"What's your name?" demanded the girl with the bandanna. She smelled of kerosene.

"Fiona Farmer," said Fiona.

"That's a funny name. My name's Darlene, and hers is Pearl, and *hers* is Merle. Nancy is a nice name."

Fiona saw that all of them were wearing red nail polish and asked a question of her own.

"Are you all three sisters?"

"Yes, and there's more of us. *Them*," said Pearl, the tallest girl, jerking her head. "In the swing."

Beyond the house Fiona now saw for the first time an old double rocker swing full of boys.

"There's Norman and Stanley and Earl," Darlene said. "And in the house we got a baby sister named Marilyn, and down to the picture theater we got a big sister named Deanna. Come on in."

"Will they let me swing in the swing?" said Fiona.

"Sure they will. *What* did you say your name was?"

"Fiona," she admitted. "Fiona Farmer."

"Gee," said Pearl.

"We'll call her Nancy," said Darlene, who, though younger, seemed to be a leader in her way. "Come on, Nancy, you wanna swing on the gate? Get off, Merle."

Merle got off obediently, sucking her thumb.

"I would like to swing in the *swing*," Fiona said.

She came into the yard gazing up at the tipsy cupola. "Can you get up there into that kind of little tower?"

"Sure," said Darlene. "Come on up and we'll show you."

Fiona followed them through the interesting grass in which she now saw a broken doll, somebody's garter, somebody's hat, and many weathered corncobs and beer cans.

On the porch which swayed when they walked on it there were a tough-looking baby buggy, two sleds, a bent tricycle, a lot of chairs and boxes and bushel baskets and peck baskets and a baby pen and a wagon wheel and some kindling wood. The screen door was full of holes and instead of a doorknob there was a wooden thread spool to turn.

The noise of music was stunning as they went indoors; it kept the Mason jars ringing on the shelves. They walked right into it, into the thrilling heart of noise which was the kitchen, where a woman was sitting nursing a baby and shouting random conversation at an old, old woman with a beak nose.

The music ceased with a flourish and the radio announcer's tremendous tones replaced it, but this did not stop the shouted discourse of the woman with the baby. As the girls crossed the kitchen she turned for a moment to look at them, saw Fiona and said, "Who's she?"

"She's Nancy," called Darlene, against the radio.

"Who?"

"Nancy! She dropped in."

"That's Mom," Pearl said.

Fiona went over to the lady to shake her hand. She made her usual curtsy and said, "How do you do?"

Mom's hand felt limp and rather damp and startled. She was a big woman with a wide face and tired blue eyes.

"The old one's Gramma," Darlene said, so Fiona curtsied to the old lady too, and shook her hand which felt like a few twigs in a glove.

"And that's my father," Darlene added, a few seconds later when they had gone up the loud bare stairs to the next floor; Fiona peeked in the doorway of the dim strong-smelling room but all she saw of *him* was the soles of his socks and she heard him snoring.

"Just like at home," she said. 'Sunday afternoon they all sleep."

"Heck, he sleeps all *day* on Sundays," Darlene said, and Fiona felt a little humiliated for her own father.

"This is Gramma's room." Pearl threw open the door. "She likes flowers."

The room was a jungle steeped in musky twilight. A vine of some kind had crawled all over the window and parts of the wall, and on the sill, the sash, the floor below, were pots and jars and coffee tins in which stout lusty plants were growing and flowering.

"How does she open the window at night?" Fiona wondered.

"*She* don't open no windows day or night," Darlene said. "Heck, she's *old*, she's gotta stay *warm*."

They went up another flight of stairs, narrow steep ones, crowded with magazines and articles of clothing and decayed toys. "Up here's where we sleep," Darlene said. "Us girls, all of us except Marilyn. Pearl and me and Merle sleep in the big bed and Deanna she sleeps in the cot. This is the attic like."

The big bed was made of iron with the post knobs missing. It dipped in the middle like a hammock and there, Fiona knew, the little girls would lie at night, dumped together in a tangle, quarreling or giggling in whispers.

"Look at all the comic books!" she cried, and indeed they lay everywhere in tattered profusion, a drift of stained, disordered leaves.

"We got about a hundred or a thousand of 'em, I guess," Pearl said. "You want some?"

"Could I really, Pearl? Could you spare them?"

"*Atom Annie's* a good one," Pearl said. "We got a lot about her, and here's one called *Hellray* that's real good, real scarey. Take these."

Fiona looked at them longingly. "I don't know if my mother—she doesn't like for me to have comics."

"Heck, why not?"

"Well, maybe this time she won't mind," Fiona said, taking the books, determined that everything would be all right for once. "Thank you very, very much, Darlene and Pearl."

"Here's the stairs to the lookout," Darlene said. "Get out of the way, Merle, you wait till last."

They climbed the ladder steps in the middle of the room, Pearl pushed open the trap door, and one by one they ascended into the tiny chamber.

It was a tipped little cubicle like a ship's cabin in stiff weather, and stiflingly hot. It seemed remote, high, cozy, and its four soiled windows showed four different views of the town faded and reduced as pictures in an old book. Flies buzzed and butted at the hot glass. Fiona felt disappointed when she saw the steeple of the church that stood across the street from her grandfather's house. She had not thought it was so near.

"Jump!" cried Darlene. They all began to jump, and the cupola jarred and trembled under the pounding.

"Won't it break?" cried Fiona, pounding with the rest. "Won't it fall off?"

"Naw, it won't break," Darlene called back. "It never did yet."

"But it might some day, though," shouted Pearl encouragingly.

It was fun to jump riotously and yell, as the tiny tower rocked and resounded.

There was an interruption from below.

"Get out of there!" bawled Mom up the stairs. "How many times I told you kids to stay down out of there! You want to get your backs broke? You want to get killed? You scram down!"

"Get out of the way, Merle, let Nancy go first," Pearl said.

Mom stood at the foot of the steps wearing the baby around her neck. Anxiety had made her furious. "That place ain't safe, you know that!" she cried. "How many times have I told you?" She gave Pearl a slap on the cheek and would have given one to Darlene, too, if Darlene had not bent her neck adroitly.

"You let me catch you up there one more time and I'll get your father to lick you good!"

"Aw, climb a tree," said Darlene.

Fiona was aghast. What would happen now?

But nothing happened. Merle still

quietly sucked her thumb, Darlene and Pearl seemed cool and jaunty, and as they descended through the house Mom's anger dried up like dew.

"You kids want a snack?" she said. "You didn't eat since breakfast."

"Can Nancy stay?"

"Why sure, I guess. Why not?"

"Oh, thank you very, very much. . . ."

The kitchen, like the rest of the house, had a rich bold musty smell. It smelled of constant usage and memories of usage. It was crowded and crusted with objects: pots, pans, kettles, boxes, jars, cans, buckets, dippers. There were two alarm clocks, one lying on its side, and each asserting a different hour, and four big Coca-Cola calendars on the wall, none for the current year. The radio was still thundering music, and close beside it warming herself at the noise sat Gramma, dark as a crow, chewing and chewing on her empty gums.

The stove was named Ebony Gem, and behind it in a cardboard box there was something alive; something moved. . . .

"It's kittens," said Merle, removing her thumb from her mouth and speaking for the first time. "Our cat had kittens."

"Oh, let me see!" Fiona knelt by the box. There inside it lay a bland and happy group: mother cat with her yellow eyes half closed and her paws splayed out in pleasure; kittens lined up all along her, sucking.

Merle put out her little forefinger with its chipped red nail polish, stroking first one infant, then the next. "The black one's name is Blackie and the white one's name is Whitey and we call *this* one Butch because he's so . . ."

"My father usually drowns them, all but one," Darlene interrupted. She bent her kerchiefed head close to Fiona's so that there was a blinding smell of kerosene. "Tomorrow probly," she whispered. "We don't tell Merle, it makes her feel so bad." Then she raised her voice. "She knows it's going to happen but she don't know when, huh, Merle?"

"You could take one, Nancy," Merle said, still gazing at the kittens. "You could keep it and be good to it."

"Do you mean honestly and truly?" Fiona's joy was suffocating.

"Any one? Any one at all?"

"Except Butch," Darlene said. "We're going to keep him to help with the rats."

"Could I have Blackie? Really for keeps?"

Merle plucked the dark little thing from the mother as if she were plucking off a burr and gave it to Fiona.

"I can feel its little tiny heart," Fiona said. "I'll give it milk all the time and brush its fur and it can sleep in the doll cradle. Oh look at its ears, oh Merle, oh thank you!"

Shamed by gratitude Merle put her thumb back in her mouth and looked away.

"You kids get out from under my feet," Mom said. "Sit up to the table now, it's all ready. Come on Mama, come on *boys*!" She opened the screen door and put her head out, shouting so hard that great cords stood out on her neck.

They sat around the big table with its oilcloth cover, everything in easy reach: cereal in paper boxes, sugar, catsup. . . . They had cornflakes and milk, Swiss cheese sandwiches with catsup, cream soda in bottles, and little cakes out of a box with pink and green beads on them. Fiona ate everything.

"Nancy eats good, don't she, Mom?" Darlene said.

"I never had catsup before," said Fiona. "My, it certainly is delicious, isn't it?"

The table was a family battlefield. Fiona had never seen anything like it in her life. Stanley and Norman threw pieces of sandwich at each other, Earl took one of Merle's cakes and Merle cried and Mom slapped Earl; Darlene stole big swigs from Pearl's soda bottle, was loudly accused and loudly defended herself.

"You kids shut up," Mom said, eating over Marilyn's head and giving her occasional bits of cake dipped in tea. Gramma was the only quiet one; she sat bent over, all wrapped and absorbed in her old age, gazing into her cup as she drank from it with a long purring sound. Blackie was quiet too, asleep in Fiona's lap. She kept one hand on his little velvet back.

Mom pointed at Fiona with her spoon. "Looks like Margaret O'Brien used to, don't she? The ribbons and all."

"Margaret who?" said Fiona.

"O'Brien, *you* know, the kid in the movies," Darlene said.

"Oh, I never go to movies," said Fiona. "I'm not allowed."

"Not allowed!" cried Darlene incredulously. "Heck, we go all the time, don't we, Mom? Even Deanna goes. We could take Nancy with us sometimes, couldn't we, Mom?"

"Maybe, if her folks say yes."

"Oh if I went with *you* it would be all right, I'm sure," cried Fiona joyously. Drunk with noise, strange flavors, gifts, and new friendship, she really believed this.

Afterward, still with catsup on their upper lips, they went out doors to play hide-and-seek.

"You be her partner, Stanley," ordered Darlene, who was "it." "You kind of look after her, she don't know our places to hide."

Then she hid her eyes with her arm, cast herself against a tree like a girl in grief, and began to count out loud.

"The cellar," hissed Stanley, grabbing Fiona's hand. He was a big eight-year-old boy, and still clutching the kitten Fiona ran with him willingly, hesitating only for a second at sight of the dark abyss. On the steps were many cans and beer crates, but Stanley led her safely down among these and into the black deep tunnel beyond. Fiona could feel that there were solid things all around them; probably more boxes, more beer crates, but she could see nothing. Stanley's hand was warm and firm, it just fitted hers, and she liked having him lead her.

"We can stop now," he said, "but keep quiet."

Darlene could still be heard, faintly. Her counting voice sounded deserted and defiant: "*Ninety*-five, *ninety*-six, *ninety*-seven" . . . The blackness throbbed and shimmered and the air had a dense aged smell.

"Coming, ready or not!" called the faraway defiant voice.

"We're safe here anyways," Stanley said. "She won't come down *here*, she's scared to." He laughed silently and gave Fiona's hand a squeeze. "There's rats down here."

"Oh no, oh no! Oh, Stanley, let's go up again," cried Fiona, tears of panic in her voice.

But Stanley held onto her hand. "You going to be a sissy too?" he demanded. "We got the *cat*, ain't we?"

Fiona strained the tiny kitten to her chest. Her heart was banging terribly and she wanted to cry but she would not. All around the rats were closing in, large as dogs and smiling strangely; smiling like people. She almost sobbed when Stanley said, "Now we can go, hurry up, and keep still!"

They were the first ones back.

For a long time they played and Stanley always was her partner. He knew the best places to hide: up in the boughs of a pear tree, under the porch steps, and flat on their stomachs under the folded-back cellar door. Darlene was "it" till she caught Merle and Merle was "it" for hours. Fiona got spiderwebs in her mouth and gnats up her nose, tore her dress, scraped her knee, lost one hair ribbon, and gave the other to Merle, who had admired it.

When they were through with hide-and-seek they all got into the rocker swing and played gangsters. The swing leapt to and fro, to and fro, screaming wildly at the joints; surely it would break, and soon! That was the thrilling thing about this place: so many features of it—the tower, the swing, the porch—trembled at the edge of ruin, hung by a thread above the fatal plunge.

Earl and Stanley and Norman leaned over the back of one of the seats firing at the enemy. "Step on it, you guys," yelled Stanley, "they got a gat!"

"They got a rod!" yelled Norman. "They got a lotta rods!"

"What's a rod?" cried Fiona. "What's a gat?"

"Guns he means," Darlene told her. "Rods and gats is guns."

"Shoot 'em, Stanley," yelled Fiona. "With your gat, shoot the eyes out of 'em!"

Clutching the clawing kitten to her collarbone, her hair in her open mouth, she bawled encouragement to them. The swing accelerated ever more wildly: soon it would take off entirely, depart from its hinges, fly through the air, burn a hole through the sky! . . .

"Fee-ona Farmer!"

The cry was loud enough to be heard above all sounds of war and wind and radio music.

Beside the swing stood Nana, so tall, so highly charged with hurry and emotion, that the children stopped their play at once.

"Who's she?" Stanley asked.

"She's my nurse," Fiona murmured.

"Your nurse! What's the matter, are you sick?"

"No . . . she just—takes care of me."

"Takes *care* of you!"

"You get out of that swing and come this in-stant!"

Having struck the bottom of disgrace, Fiona stepped down and slowly went to Nana. From the swing the others watched as still as children posing for a photograph.

"Put down that cat and come at once."

"Oh no!" Fiona said. "It's mine, they gave it to me."

"Put. Down. That. Cat."

Darlene came to stand beside Fiona. "But we did give it to her, we want for her to have it."

Nana struck the kitten from Fiona's arms. "You will not take that creature home! It's filthy, it has fleas!"

"Oh my kitty!" shrieked Fiona, diving after Blackie, but Nana caught her wrist.

"You come!"

Fiona pulled, struggled, cast a glare of anguish at all the rapt photograph-faces in the swing.

"You should be punished. You should be whipped. Whipped!" Nana whistled the cruel words; Nana, who was never cruel! Her fingers on Fiona's wrist were hard.

"Let me say good-by to them, Nana, let me say good-by to their *mother*! You said I should *always* say good-by to the mother!"

"Not this time, this time it doesn't matter," Nana said. "You're going straight home and into the tub. Heavens knows what you will have caught!" Upon Fiona's friends she turned a single brilliant glance like one cold flash from a lighthouse.

There was nothing to commend Fiona's departure; dragged by the hand, whimpering, she looked back at her friends in desperation. "Oh, Darlene!"

But it was easy to see that Darlene had detached herself. "Good-by, Nancy," she said, not without a certain pride. She did not smile or say anything else, but her attitude showed Fiona and Nana that she had no need for either of them, could not be hurt by them, and would not think of them again. As they went out the gate she turned her back and skipped away, and Fiona heard the rocker swing resume its screaming tempo.

Halfway home Nana's recriminations began to modify, gadually becoming reproaches: "How could you have, Fiona, run away like that, why it's only by the grace of God I ever found you at all! And all the time I was half sick with worry I never said a word to your father and mother! I didn't want *them* to worry!"

Somewhere deep inside her Fiona understood exactly why Nana had said nothing to her parents, but she just kept on saying: "I want my kitty, I want my kitty."

Finally Nana said: "If you're a good girl maybe we'll get you another kitten."

"I don't want another, I want that one."

"Oh for pity's sakes, it had fleas; or worse. Anything belonging to the Fadgins would be bound to have."

"Do *you* know them?"

"I know *about* them, everybody does. They're the dirtiest, the shiftlessest, the most down-at-the-heel tribe in this whole town!"

"They are not, they're nice, I love them!"

Nana relented a little. "Maybe it's hard not to be shiftless when you're that poor."

"*They* aren't poor. You should see all the things they've got! More than Grandmother's got in her whole house!"

"All right now, dearie, all right. We'll forget about it, shall we? It will be our secret and we'll never tell anyone because we don't want them to worry, do we? But you must promise me never, never to do such a thing again, hear?"

"I want my kitty," droned Fiona.

Her grandparents' house smelled cool and sweetish. There was a bowl of white and pink stock on the hall table and her grandmother's green linen parasol leaned in a corner among the pearly company of her grandfather's canes.

In the shaded living room Fiona saw her mother knitting and her grandmother at the piano playing the same kind of music she always played, with the loose rings clicking on her fingers.

"Is that my baby?" called her mother—but Nana answered hastily,

"I'm getting her right into her bath, Mrs. Farmer. She's sim-ply fil-thy."

Upstairs Nana went in to run the water in the tub. Fiona kicked off one sandal, then the other. A terrible pain took hold of her; it began in her mind and spread down to her stomach. She had never been homesick before and did not know what ailed her: she knew only that she wanted to sleep at night in a big twanging bed full of children and to eat meals at a crowded table where people threw bread at each other and drank pop. She wanted Stanley's hand to guide her and Darlene's voice to teach her and Blackie's purr to throb against her chest. . . .

Beyond the window she saw her grandfather's wilted golf hat bobbing among the cornstalks and escaped again, running on bare feet down the back stairs and out of doors across the billowing lawn which seemed to be colliding with the trees and sky and shadows, all flooded and dazzled with tears. Blindly she flung open the garden gate and pushed her way through the green-paper corn forest to her grandfather who dropped his hoe and held out his arms when he saw her face.

"Come here now," he said in his gentle deaf voice. "Well, well, this won't do, no it won't, not at all. Come sit here with Grandpa, sit here in the arbor. Did you hurt yourself?"

He led her to the seat under the green grape trellis where he sometimes rested from the hot sun. He put his arm around her shoulders, offering himself as a support for grief, and Fiona howled against his waistcoat till the wet tweed chapped her cheek and there was not a tear left in her. He did not interrupt or ask questions but kept patting her shoulder in a sort of sympathetic accompaniment to her sobs, which he could not hear but which he felt. What's the cause of it all, he wondered. A broken toy? A scolding? Children's tragedies, he thought, children's little tragedies: there are bigger ones in store for you, Fiona, a world of them. The thought did not move him deeply; everyone must suffer, but for an instant he was not sorry to be old.

Fiona leaned against him and after a while between the hiccups left from sobbing she could hear the ancient heart inside his chest tick-tocking steadily, as tranquil and unhurried as he was himself. All the wild performance of her sorrow had not quickened its tempo by a single beat, and this for some reason was a comfort.

The sound of her grandmother's music, sugary and elegant, came sparkling from the house, and upstairs in the bedroom or the hall Nana began to call. "Fee-ona?" she cried. "Oh, *Fee-ona?*" There was a hint of panic in her voice, now, but no response came from under the green trellis: Feona's grandfather could not hear the calling, and Fiona, for the time being, did not choose to answer.

Discussion

The emphasis in this selection is on the comparison between the life styles of the Fadgins and the Farmers. Fiona is obviously not thriving on the "gracious living" her family can afford. She is bored, frustrated, and dissatisfied. Her pent-up anger at her parents, grandparents, and nurse, who overprotect and overstructure her daily existence, is vented through the mutilation of her dolls. Pulling out the eyes, hair, arms, and legs of dolls is a safe discharge of aggressive energy, but it suggests that Fiona harbors a reservoir of unexpressed emotion. With continued pressure for performance based on outmoded and inappropriate standards, more of that energy might be turned inward, as suggested by Fiona's habits of scratching her head and picking her nose.

The family seems to have little insight into the source of Fiona's nervous habits or destructiveness toward her dolls. The Farmer's way of life involves certain unquestionable values. They believe that cleanliness is next to godliness and that people like themselves always do the "nice" thing. This Victorian attitude leaves little room for honest expression of feeling or any relaxation of their impeccable manners, and the atmosphere the Farmers create is crushing the spirit of this little girl.

The shift to the life style of the Fadgins is dramatic, since the Fadgins represent the other end of the spectrum in terms of living standards. Naturally, not all households whose socioeconomic status is low are as relaxed as the Fadgins, but we do know that the birth rate tends to be higher and that customs and expectations for the children will be different in lower socioeconomic groups. At seven years of age, Fiona has not yet adopted her parents' standards and value judgments about people and proper decorum. She is able to enjoy thoroughly the haphazard but generous and lively life style of the Fadgins. Their hair, which is washed in kerosene (and tied in a bandana in order to destroy the lice), goes completely unnoticed by Fiona, except for the odor. The litter in the yard and disorder in the house is curious and interesting to Fiona rather than dirty and unsanitary as her nurse and family would see it. Obviously, Fiona has a great capacity to enjoy people and experiences. The responsiveness of the children and the kittens particularly please her. This story reminds us that children are exposed to a very narrow spectrum of people and experiences where neighborhood patterns perpetuate single racial, ethnic, or socioeconomic groupings.

Springboards for Inquiry

(1) How do you think one of the Fadgins would react if the tables were reversed and he were to spend a day with the Farmers?

(2) To what extent does the average college student have the opportunity to investigate life styles in a variety of socioeconomic settings? Relate the question to your own experience.

(3) How does socioeconomic status affect infant mortality, incidence of mental retardation, and giftedness?

(4) Joseph Stone and Joseph Church (1968, p. 199) state that "perhaps the single most important principle of human development is what Ralph Linton calls the self-fulfilling prophecy, which says simply that our children become what we expect them to become whether our expectations be phrased as hopes or fears, left implicit or made explicit." How does this theory apply to child-rearing practices in each of the identifiable socioeconomic levels in American society?

Culture

Culture has been defined as the sum total of customary ways of the people who surround us—their language, thoughts, perceptions, values, morals, and technology.* Culture influences physiological functioning. What people enjoy eating, what inhibits the appetite depends on culture more than physiology. Anger and fright are innate emotional states, but what angers and frightens people varies greatly and is prescribed by cultural endowment. For example, a teacher once berated a Puerto Rican child for coming to school in a rainstorm without overshoes. She said, "Is that the way your mother sent you to school?" Instead of the expected dejected head-hanging which ordinarily would have followed were this a middle-class school, the teacher was met by eyes reflecting hostility and anger. From somewhere in the recesses of the Puerto Rican child's larynx came the growl, "You cursed my mother." . . .

---

* Other definitions are: "Culture or civilization . . . is that complex whole which includes knowledge, belief, art, morals, law, custom, . . . and other . . . habits acquired by man as a member of society" (Edward B. Tyler, *Primitive Culture*, Vol. I, p. 1 [London: John Murray, 1871]); "Culture embraces all the manifestations of social habits of a community, the reactions of the individual as affected by the habits of the group in which he lives" (Frank Boss, "Anthropology," in *Encyclopedia of the Social Sciences*, eds. Edwin R. A. Seligman and Alvin Johnson [New York: The Macmillan Co., 1954, p. 79]); "A man is always born into the environment of culture and place, even before actual birth, into the accustomed relationships of the local civilization" (Ruth Landes, *Culture in American Education* [New York: John Wiley and Sons, Inc., 1965], p. 37).

Culture affects the way people react to life situations. Hopi Indians believe that the acts of thinking and concentrating bring about certain phenomena or cause events to happen. Lidz (1968) reports that tears are forbidden at a Hopi funeral, lest relatives think the tearful one is a witch who could be crying only if he had purchased his own life at the expense of the life of the deceased. In America, boys usually propose to girls. In old China, a father decides that the daughter of another man is appropriate for his son and he seeks an intermediary to approach the girl's father. In an Australian bush tribe, boy meets girl but the relationship is kept secret because the adult members of the tribe would pronounce a sentence of death if love were suspected.

As cultures differ, so do the personalities locked in those cultures. In general, American children of all races and social classes tend to be egocentric, realistic, concerned about independence and rights, more anxious to help themselves than to help others. Japanese children are trained to be family-oriented, and they consequently develop a personality pattern characterized by loyalty, cooperation, self-sacrifice, and often an unrealistic self-concept. That which is assimilated from the surrounding culture is called the result of enculturation. Although the brains of men are physiologically alike, what the brain stores and recollects depends entirely on the cultural forces that have programmed the brain.

On November 17, 1970, newspapers reported the case of a thirteen-year-old girl brought up in isolation. The disastrous effects of no enculturation were: she could not speak, was not toilet trained, was malnourished and malformed.*

---

* *The Salt Lake City Tribune* (November 17, 1970, p. 2, col. 3) reports the case as follows: THERE'S HOPE FOR GIRL IN BIZARRE CHILD ABUSE CASE—Arcadia, California (AP). A 13-year-old girl kept in virtual isolation from society all her life may have normal learning capacity although she now has the mind of an infant, officials said Tuesday. "The hospital thinks the whole problem was environment," said sheriff's Sgt. Frank Linley of Susan Wiley, kept in diapers all her life and never taught to talk. Susan is now undergoing special treatment at Children's Hospital by speech therapists and other experts. Authorities meanwhile were moving to officially take her from the custody of her parents, who are charged in warrants with child abuse. CAN'T TALK—"She can't talk at all—she just never learned," said Linley, a Los Angeles County juvenile officer. She can utter noises, but can understand some words and directions, Linley said. Susan is "frightened" but doesn't cry, looking about with wide eyes, Linley added. "The doctors say she is just beginning to realize that there are other people in the world." SCHOOLS UNAWARE—Officials said the girl has the mind of an infant because she was imprisoned in virtual isolation. She spent nearly all her life inside her parents' modest two-bedroom home in this Los Angeles suburb, deputies said. Once in a while she played in the yard or sat on the porch, deputies said, but neighbors who glimpsed her infrequently said she looked like a ghost and they thought she must be mentally retarded. She apparently never came to the attention of school authorities. She walks with a stooped shuffle and her fingers are long and turned up at the ends, as a result of malnutrition and lack of exercise, officials said.

Adults who are concerned with children in social institutions must have a clear understanding of the effects of culture because children do not drop their culture at the schoolroom door as the day begins. The child brings to the classroom the enculturated patterns of his home. Unfortunately the typical middle-class oriented teacher can only assume stereotypes about other cultural groups and give them superficial, if not meaningless, labels such as "poor whites," "Negroes," or "the disadvantaged." These are convenient labels but they do not help people to understand the values of children from different cultures. Also, "teachers act according to their own cultural patterns . . ." (Landes 1965, p. 48). The current conflict in the public schools about integration and busing is more a clash of cultural values than of color alone. One should not view another school or family culture as merely being alien; it is urgent that the culture of others be understood, not only intellectually but as viscerally as possible.*

George Spindler (1968) suggests that the ways of other cultures can be "coherently synthesized" with the prevailing culture. Teachers who face the problem of transmitting their culture to children who hold different value systems should strive to empathize rather than overcompensate and should not feel threatened by children from a different subculture. The report of Landes' work at Claremont College (1965) should be studied along with the New York City Board of Education's Higher Horizons Program report, *Toward Greater Opportunity* (1960). The culture gap, although not as highly publicized as the generation gap, is nonetheless a very real chasm that needs to be bridged.

---

* Urie Bronfenbrenner's *Two Worlds of Childhood: U.S. and U.S.S.R.* (New York: Russell Sage Foundation, 1970) is an attempt to have us "know" this other culture rather than to simply despise it.

"Chavez, what is this? Your new hand, ain't he going to eat with the rest of the men?"

. . . And Now Miguel

by Joseph Krumgold

By the end of the day, when the sun was going down, half the flock was all finished being sheared.

"Better than a year ago." My father was tying up the last fleece. "Isn't that so, Johnny? We didn't get anywhere near this much done the first day last year."

"Only one reason for that." Johnny hit me with his thumb again. "Got some new men around here who know how to work."

They both laughed, and I laughed too. I walked with them and the others back to the house, everyone making jokes. I wished I could remember some jokes to tell but I never can. So I just laughed with the others. On the veranda my mother laid out basins and pails of water so we could all get cleaned up for supper. I got washed up with the rest. But I couldn't comb my hair like they did because my hair is short, just stubby, like a field that's been grazed over.

It wasn't only in the shearing sheds that it was busy all day. In the house, too, they worked hard, my mother and Tomasita and Leocadia. It had to be the best supper. Because the shearers ate at many farms. And at each farm they are supposed to say, "Mama mia, this is the best, the absolute best yet!" So if you don't give them a chance to say this by serving the best supper, that's a disgrace. That's why she and my sisters, they prepare as if everyone's birthday had come together on the same day.

When we got into the kitchen, the table was laid out with only our best plates, and the knives and forks we only get to see on Christmas or Easter. It looked fine. And on the stove there wasn't even one small

---

part that wasn't covered by some kind of food cooking, a crowd of pots and pans smelling the place up good.

The big table in our kitchen is not so big for as many people as this. My mother and sisters they wait to eat until after the men finish, and so do the children, Faustina and Pedro. I waited, too. But I didn't go away. It's good to stand around and hear what the shearers have to tell, because that way you get to hear things you can't find out about any other way. I stood at the door along with Faustina and Pedro, while the men sat down and rubbed their hands together the way they always do when they're going to eat, and Tomasita and Leocadia started to bring the food from the stove where my mother was piling it on dishes.

Then what happened, if it wasn't a miracle, was something just as good.

Mr. Juan Marquez stopped from reaching across the table for a biscuit, and he turned to where I was standing.

"Ai Miguel, what're you doing there?"

"Me? Just standing. Waiting."

"Aren't you hungry?"

"It's not a question of being hungry. It's a question of everybody getting squeezed."

"Who's squeezed? What's squeezed?" He moved over his chair until there was a space of three, four inches. "Look, plenty of room. C'mon."

"It's not only squeezed. There's also the question of my father."

"What? Your father?" At that moment, my father, who sat next to Johnny, was talking to Melchior across the table. Johnny punched him in the shoulder. "Chavez, what is this? Your new hand, ain't he going to eat with the rest of the men?"

"Who, Miguel?" My father turned. "Why not? Of course. Get a stool, Mickey. Get in here."

So my father shifted over his chair, too. And I got a stool. There was just enough room at the table. I put down the stool and sat down on it right at the table. Leocadia reached across with a plate and a knife and fork of my own. I didn't believe what was going on.

Because this was the first time. It had never happened before at any other shearing. No, never before at any time when there were a lot of men who had to eat first did I ever get to sit down along with them to eat first, too.

"Wake up!" The way Johnny pushed me I almost fell off the stool. "With these wolves, you better get something quick or you'll starve sure."

"There's enough." My mother laughed. "Enough for a dozen Miguels."

I had a good time. I was hungry, and there were so many good things to eat I hardly had time to listen. But there was so many good stories to hear, about all the sheepherders up and down the Rio Grande Valley, I didn't hardly want to waste time eating. I got along as best I could doing both, eating and listening, and feeling good.

Each one tried to tell a better story than the other. My father told about one time in Penãsco and when everyone stopped laughing, Johnny said "That reminds me of one time in Bernalillo." And when he told what happened and everyone stopped laughing at that, Salvador said, "That reminds me of one time in Silver City." And after they finished laughing at his story, Melchior said, "That reminds me of one time in Questa," and this was some kind of story about a garter that was purple and pink which made my sister Leocadia laugh so hard she had to leave the kitchen.

Then I remembered a joke that Juby told me, and before I knew it, I said, "That reminds me of one time in the school at Los Cordovas." And everyone stopped quiet and looked at me. I was surprised how quiet. I didn't feel very much like going on. But, what else could I do?

I swallowed what was in my mouth, and I said it as fast as I could. "There was this fellow in Los Cordovas who told this other fellow on the way to the school, 'Last night in the middle of the night it rained cats and dogs,' and this other fellow said, 'How do you know it rained cats and dogs?' and this first fellow said, 'This morning when I came out of my house, in front of the house I found a poodle.' That's all."

Well, you never heard anything like it. How they laughed! They all understood the way I said it, and it turned out to be the best story of all. My brother Blasito across the way, he laughed so much he fell off his chair, and that made everybody laugh even more. When Gabriel helped him back into his seat Blasito was still laughing, and what's more, hiccuping. So everybody just kept on laughing. I never felt so good.

I guess it was the best supper I ever had.

Discussion

The culture of the Southwest depicted in *And Now Miguel* is influenced as much by the Spanish origins of the inhabitants as it is by sheepherding, the main occupation of the area. For Miguel and his family the year is punctuated by the arrival of holidays and feast days and by the raising of the sheep from the time the lambs are born to shearing time. The author says, "Everything comes and goes. Except one thing. The sheep."

A theme running through the book is Miguel's one great wish—to join the men in the sheep camp in the Sangre de Cristo Mountains during the three-month grazing period. Miguel has his bag packed in readiness, but he must prove that he is ready to join the men. Miguel suffers in his position as the middle son. The youngest is content with what he has; the eldest is content because as the eldest he shares the privileges of the men. Only Miguel is in-between, ready to be recognized as crossing from childhood into manhood. In this culture the way of life is prescribed, with roles and expectations well delineated. The men have their work, the women have their area of responsibility, and the children have theirs. When Miguel is finally invited to share at the table following the sheepshearing, he knows that he may now partake of the privileges of manhood.

Springboards for Inquiry

(1) If this family could no longer subsist on sheepherding and they moved to the city to find work, what kind of adjustment problems would you anticipate for Miguel?

(2) Describe another culture whose year-round activities are as well demarcated as Miguel's in the area of religious or cultural rites and festivals. How does this prescribed way of life affect the children?

(3) What do you think is the psychological significance for the individual when the line between childhood and manhood is as clearly defined for him as it is in this story?

(4) What would be the self-concept and expectations of a female child in this culture?

References

Bayton, James, Lettie J. Austin, and Kay R. Burke. "Negro Perception of Negro and White Personality Traits." *Journal of Personality and Social Psychology* 1 (1965): 250–253.

Benedict, Ruth. *Patterns of Culture*. New York: Mentor Books, 1948.

Calnek, Maynard. "Racial Factors in the Countertransference: The Black Therapist and the Black Client." *American Journal of Orthopsychiatry* 40 (January 1970): 39–46.

Corson, William R. *Promise or Peril*. New York: W. W. Norton & Co., 1970.

Davis, Allison. *Social Class Influences upon Learning*. Cambridge, Mass.: Harvard University Press, 1961.

Davis, Allison, and Robert J. Havighurst. "Social-Class and Color Differences in Child-Rearing." *American Sociological Review* 11 (1946): 698–710.

Egan, Mary C. "Combating Malnutrition through Maternal and Child Health Programs." *Children* 16, No. 2 (March-April 1969): 67–71.

Fisher, Robert. "Who Is This Lower-Class Child?" *Journal of Educational Sociology* 34, No. 7 (March 1961): 209–311.

Gans, Herbert J. *The Urban Villagers*. New York: The Free Press of Glencoe, 1962.

Grier, William, and Price Cobbs. *Black Rage*. New York: Basic Books, Inc., 1968.

Kahl, Joseph A. *The American Class Structure*. New York: Holt, Rinehart and Winston, 1967.

Landes, Ruth. *Culture in American Education*. New York: John Wiley and Sons, 1965.

Lidz, Theodore. *The Person*. New York: Basic Books, 1968.

McCreary, Eugene. "Some Positive Characteristics of Disadvantaged Learners and Their Implications for Education." In *The Disadvantaged Learner*, ed. by Stanton W. Webster. San Francisco: Chandler Publishing Co., 1966.

(New York City) Board of Education. *Toward Greater Opportunity*. New York: City of New York, 1960.

Pettigrew, Thomas F. *A Profile of the Negro American*. Princeton, N. J.: Van Nostrand, 1964.

Pettigrew, T. F. "Racially Separate or Together?" *Journal of Social Issues* 25, No. 1 (January 1969): 43–69.

Rogers, Dorothy. *Child Psychology*. Belmont, Calif.: Brooks/Cole Publishing Co., 1969.

Slaughter, Diana T. "Parental Potency and the Achievements of Inner-City Black Children." *American Journal of Orthopsychiatry* 40, No. 3 (April 1970): 433–440.

Spindler, George. "The Acculturation of the School Teacher." In *Readings in the Socio-Cultural Foundations of Education*, eds. John H. Chilcott, Norman C. Greenberg, and Herbert Wilson. Belmont, Calif.: Wadsworth Publishing Co., 1968.

Stone, L. Joseph, and Joseph Church. *Childhood and Adolescence*. 2d ed. New York: Random House, 1968.

Strom, Robert D. *Teaching in the Slum School*. Columbus, Ohio: Charles E. Merrill, 1965.

Warner, W. Lloyd, Marchia Meeker, and Kenneth Eells. *Social Class in America*. Chicago: Science Research Association, 1949.

Appendix Two

Topic-Story Correlation

3. **Coping**

Luke Baldwin's Vow—Morley Callaghan
Thus I Refute Beelzey—John Collier
A Start In Life—Ruth Suckow
The Web and the Rock—Thomas Wolfe
A Day's Wait—Ernest Hemingway
The Dog—Carol Reilley
Doctor Jack-O-Lantern—Richard Yates
The Stone Boy—Gina Berriault
A Tree Grows In Brooklyn (see Shame)—Betty Smith

4. **Concept of Self**

The Web and the Rock—Thomas Wolfe
The Boy Who Painted Christ Black—John Henrik Clarke

III Emotional Development

1. **Love**

Don't You Wish You Were Dead—L. Woiwode
My Little Boy—Carl Ewald
The Door of Life—Enid Bagnold
He—Katherine Ann Porter
The Houses of the City—Gina Berriault
Gaston—William Saroyan

2. **Jealousy**

All Summer in a Day—Ray Bradbury
The Houses of the City—Gina Berriault
Boys and Girls Together—William Goldman
Destroying Angel—Eric Cameron

3. **Fear**

The Dog—Carol Reilley
A Day's Wait—Ernest Hemingway
Black Boy—Richard Wright
The White Circle—John Bell Clayton
The Use of Force—William Carlos Williams

4. **Courage**

A Day's Wait—Ernest Hemingway
Luke Baldwin's Vow—Morley Callaghan

A Tree Grows In Brooklyn (see Shame)—Betty Smith
The Fight—Stephen Crane
Black Boy—Richard Wright

5. **Compassion**
Winter Night—Kay Boyle
Don't You Wish You Were Dead—L. Woiwode
A Tree Grows In Brooklyn (see Development of Moral Judgment) —Betty Smith

6. **Anger**
The White Circle—John Bell Clayton
Destroying Angel—Eric Cameron
Black Boy—Richard Wright
Thus I Refute Beelzy—John Collier
Nancy—Elizabeth Enright
Should Wizard Hit Mommy?—John Updike
Boys and Girls Together—William Goldman
The Blue Parakeets—H. C. Branner

7. **Shame**
A Tree Grows In Brooklyn—Betty Smith
The Dawn of Hate—Paul Horgan
Doctor Jack-O-Lantern—Richard Yates
Castle in the Sand—Irene Orgel

IV INTELLECTUAL DEVELOPMENT

1. **Growth of Language**
Spring Song—Joyce Cary
The Sunrise—W. F. Fishbaugh
The Day We Lost Max—Lael Littke

2. **Development of Concepts**
Jonathan and the Tooth Fairy—Ann Plaat Stone
Death in the Fifth Grade—Marjorie Marks
Brave New World—Aldous Huxley
The Dawn of Hate—Paul Horgan
The Sunrise—W. F. Fishbaugh

3. **Understanding Birth and Death**
The Sissy—Frank O'Connor
Wanderer—Sterling Hayden

Jonathan and the Tooth Fairy—Ann Plaat Stone
Death in the Fifth Grade—Marjorie Marks
A Glory of the Moon—Joyce Cary

4. **Reality vs. Make-Believe**

Should Wizard Hit Mommy?—John Updike
Thus I Refute Beelzy—John Collier
Jonathan and the Tooth Fairy—Ann Plaat Stone
A Glory of the Moon—Joyce Cary

V Communication

1. **Discipline**

The Use of Force—William Carlos Williams
Apple Seed and Apple Thorn—Elizabeth Enright
Thus I Refute Beelzy—John Collier
A Start In Life—Ruth Suckow
Black Boy—Richard Wright
Nancy—Elizabeth Enright

2. **Building Trust**

My Little Boy—Carl Ewald
Thus I Refute Beelzy—John Collier
The Stone Boy—Gina Berriault
The Door of Life—Enid Bagnold
Doctor Jack-O-Lantern—Richard Yates
Winter Night—Kay Boyle

VI The Meaning of Play

1. **Making Friends**

A Special Occasion—Joyce Cary
Nancy—Elizabeth Enright
The Fight—Stephen Crane
The First Day of School—William Saroyan

2. **Creativity**

The Rainy Day, the Good Mother, and the Brown Suit—Dorothy Canfield
A Glory of the Moon—Joyce Cary

3. **Fantasy**

A Glory of the Moon—Joyce Cary
Should Wizard Hit Mommy?—John Updike
Thus I Refute Beelzy—John Collier
Jonathan and the Tooth Fairy—Ann Plaat Stone

VII The Handicapped Child

1. **Physical Handicaps**

Castle in the Sand—Irene Orgel

2. **Mental Retardation**

He—Katherine Ann Porter
Destroying Angel—Eric Cameron

3. **Emotional Disturbance**

The Blue Parakeets—H. C. Branner

VIII Home Influences

1. **Parent-Child Relationships**

Butcher Bird—Wallace Stegner
The Houses of the City—Gina Berriault
The Dawn of Hate—Paul Horgan
Nancy—Elizabeth Enright
Black Boy—Richard Wright
The Stone Boy—Gina Berriault

2. **Sibling Relationships**

Boys and Girls Together—William Goldman
Destroying Angel—Eric Cameron
Don't You Wish You Were Dead—L. Woiwode

3. **Divorce**

Gaston—William Saroyan
My First Two Women—Nadine Gordimer

4. **Development of Moral Judgment**

The Dawn of Hate—Paul Horgan
A Tree Grows in Brooklyn—Betty Smith
Brave New World—Aldous Huxley
Should Wizard Hit Mommy?—John Updike

The Stone Boy—Gina Berriault
Butcher Bird—Wallace Stegner

IX School Influences

1. The Teacher

Death in the Fifth Grade—Marjorie Marks
See How They Run—Margaret Elizabeth Vroman
Doctor Jack-O-Lantern—Richard Yates

2. The Peer Group

The First Day of School—William Saroyan
The Fight—Stephen Crane
All Summer in a Day—Ray Bradbury
Doctor Jack-O-Lantern—Richard Yates
See How They Run—Margaret Elizabeth Vroman

X Societal Influences

1. Race

Black Boy—Richard Wright
The Boy Who Painted Christ Black—John Henrik Clarke
See How They Run—Margaret Elizabeth Vroman

2. Socio Economic Status

Nancy—Elizabeth Enright
A Tree Grows In Brooklyn (see Shame)—Betty Smith
Doctor Jack-O-Lantern—Richard Yates
Black Boy—Richard Wright
A Start In Life—Ruth Suckow

3. Culture

And Now Miguel—Joseph Krumgold
Black Boy—Richard Wright
Nancy—Elizabeth Enright